THE ELGAR COMPANION TO HEALTH ECONOMICS

The Elgar Companion to Health Economics

Edited by

Andrew M. Jones

Director of the Graduate Programme in Health Economics, Department of Economics and Related Studies, University of York, UK

Edward Elgar
Cheltenham, UK • Northampton, MA, USA

Published by
Edward Elgar Publishing Limited
Glensanda House
Montpellier Parade
Cheltenham
Glos GL50 1UA
UK

Edward Elgar Publishing, Inc.
136 West Street
Suite 202
Northampton
Massachusetts 01060
USA

A catalogue record for this book
is available from the British Library

ISBN-13: 978 1 84542 003 1 (cased)
ISBN-10: 1 84542 003 9 (cased)

Printed and bound in Great Britain by MPG Books Ltd, Bodmin, Cornwall

Contents

POPULATION HEALTH AND HEALTH CARE SYSTEMS

Part I   Population health

Part II   Health care finance, expenditure and use

Part IX   Economic evaluation and decision making

Figures

Tables

Contributors

Taghreed Adam	World Health Organization, Geneva, Switzerland
M. Christopher Auld	Department of Economics, University of Calgary, Canada
Pedro Pita Barros	Faculty of Economics, Universidade Nova de Lisboa, Portugal
Anirban Basu	Department of Medicine, University of Chicago, USA
Stephen Birch	Centre for Health Economics and Policy Analysis, McMaster University, Canada
David Bishai	Department of Population and Family Health Sciences, Johns Hopkins University, USA
Han Bleichrodt	Department of Economics & iMTA/iBMG, Erasmus University, the Netherlands
W. David Bradford	Center for Health Economic and Policy Studies, Medical University of South Carolina, USA
John Brazier	ScHARR, University of Sheffield, UK
Friedrich Breyer	Department of Economics, University of Konstanz, Germany
Andrew Briggs	Section of Public Health and Health Policy, University of Glasgow
James F. Burgess, Jr	Department of Health Services, School of Public Health, Boston University, USA & Management Science Group, US Department of Veterans Affairs, USA
Leonie Burgess	Department of Mathematical Sciences and Centre for the Study of Choice, University of Technology, Sydney, Australia
Martin Chalkley	Department of Economic Studies, University of Dundee, UK
Dan Chisholm	Department of Health System Financing, World Health Organization, Switzerland
Karl Claxton	Department of Economics and Related Studies & CHE, University of York, UK
Paul Contoyannis	Department of Economics, McMaster University, Canada
Richard Cookson	School of Medicine, Health Policy and Practice, University of East Anglia, UK
Gillian Currie	Department of Paediatrics and Community Health Sciences, University of Calgary, Canada
Diane Dawson	Centre for Health Economics, University of York, UK
Partha Deb	Department of Economics, Hunter College, City University of New York, USA

Paul Dolan	ScHARR, University of Sheffield, UK
Cam Donaldson	School of Population and Health Sciences & Business School, University of Newcastle upon Tyne, UK
Bryan Dowd	Division of Health Services Research and Policy, University of Minnesota, USA
Michael Drummond	Centre for Health Economics, University of York, UK
Tessa Tan-Torres Edejer	Department of Health System Financing, World Health Organization, Switzerland
Tim Ensor	Oxford Policy Management, UK
Susan L. Ettner	Schools of Medicine and Public Health, University of California Los Angeles, USA
David B. Evans	Department of Health System Financing, World Health Organization, Switzerland
David Feeny	Departments of Economics and Public Health Sciences, University of Alberta, Canada
Roger Feldman	Division of Health Services Research and Policy, University of Minnesota, USA
Elisabeth Fenwick	Department of Economics and Related Studies & CHE, University of York, UK
Amiram Gafni	Centre for Health Economics and Policy Analysis, McMaster University, Canada
Pierre-Yves Geoffard	Paris–Jourdan Sciences Economiques (PSE), Paris, France & IEMS, University of Lausanne, Switzerland
Karen Gerard	School of Nursing and Midwifery, University of Southampton, UK
Jacob Glazer	Department of Economics, Boston University, USA & Faculty of Management, Tel Aviv University, Israel
David C. Grabowski	Department of Health Care Policy, Harvard University, USA
Hugh Gravelle	National Primary Care Research and Development Centre, Centre for Health Economics, University of York, UK
Paul Grootendorst	Faculty of Pharmacy, University of Toronto, Canada
Tor Iversen	Department of Health Management and Health Economics, University of Oslo, Norway
Andrew M. Jones	Department of Economics and Related Studies, University of York, UK
Don Kenkel	Department of Policy Analysis and Management, Cornell University, USA
Andrew N. Kleit	Center for Health Care Policy, Penn State University, USA
Darius Lakdawalla	RAND Corporation, USA
Maarten Lindeboom	Department of Economics of the Free University of Amsterdam, Tinbergen Institute, IZA, HEB, Netspar

Jordan Louviere	School of Marketing and Centre for the Study of Choice, University of Technology, Sydney, Australia
Hilde Lurås	Department of Health Management and Health Economics, University of Oslo, Norway
Alistair McGuire	LSE Health and Social Care, London School of Economics, UK
Thomas G. McGuire	Department of Health Care Policy, Harvard Medical School, USA
Willard Manning	Harris School of Public Policy Studies, University of Chicago, USA
Xavier Martinez-Giralt	Department of Economics, Universitat Autonoma de Barcelona, Spain
Helen Mason	School of Population and Health Sciences & Business School, University of Newcastle upon Tyne, UK
David Meltzer	Department of Medicine, University of Chicago, USA
Anne Mills	Health Economics and Financing Programme, London School of Hygiene and Tropical Medicine, UK
Stephen Morris	Tanaka Business School, Imperial College, UK
John Mullahy	Department of Population Health Sciences, University of Wisconsin–Madison, USA
Edward C. Norton	University of North Carolina at Chapel Hill, USA
John A. Nyman	Division of Health Services Research and Policy, University of Minnesota, USA
Owen O'Donnell	Department of Balkan, Slavic and Oriental Studies, University of Macedonia, Greece
Todd A. Olmstead	School of Public Health, Yale University, USA
Natasha Palmer	Health Economics and Financing Programme, London School of Hygiene and Tropical Medicine, UK
Tomas J. Philipson	Harris School of Public Policy Studies, University of Chicago, USA
Jose Luis Pinto	Department of Economics, Pompeu Fabra University, Spain
Daniel Polsky	Division of General Internal Medicine, University of Pennyslvania, USA
Carol Propper	Department of Economics and CMPO, University of Bristol, UK
Maria Raikou	LSE Health and Social Care, London School of Economics, UK
Ravindra Rannan-Eliya	Institute for Health Policy, Sri Lanka
Nigel Rice	Centre for Health Economics, University of York, UK
Thomas Rice	School of Public Health, UCLA, USA
Jennifer Roberts	Department of Economics & ScHARR, University of Sheffield, UK
Christopher J. Ruhm	Department of Economics, University of North Carolina at Greensboro, USA

Mandy Ryan	Health Economics Research Unit, University of Aberdeen, UK
Michael Schoenbaum	RAND Corporation, USA
Mark J. Sculpher	Centre for Health Economics, University of York, UK
Phil Shackley	School of Population and Health Sciences, University of Newcastle upon Tyne, UK
Jody L. Sindelar	School of Public Health, Yale University, USA
Peter C. Smith	Centre for Health Economics, University of York, UK
Richard Smith	Health Economics Group, University of East Anglia, UK
Aparnaa Somanathan	Institute for Health Policy, Sri Lanka
Andrew Street	Centre for Health Economics, University of York, UK
Deborah J. Street	Department of Mathematical Sciences & Centre for the Study of Choice, University of Technology, Sydney, Australia
Matt Sutton	Health Economics Research Unit, University of Aberdeen, UK
Robin Thompson	Swiss Tropical Institute, Switzerland, and University of York, UK
Pravin K. Trivedi	Department of Economics, Indiana University, USA
Aki Tsuchiya	School of Health and Related Research, and Department of Economics, University of Sheffield, UK
Eddy van Doorslaer	Department of Health Policy and Management, Erasmus University, the Netherlands
David J. Vanness	Department of Population Health Sciences, University of Wisconsin–Madison, USA
Rosalie Viney	Centre for Health Economics Research and Evaluation, University of Technology, Sydney, Australia
Adam Wagstaff	Development Research Group and Human Development Unit, World Bank, USA
Milton C. Weinstein	Department of Health Policy and Management, Harvard University School of Public Health, USA
Deborah Wilson	CMPO, University of Bristol, UK
Peter Zweifel	Socioeconomic Institute, University of Zurich, Switzerland, pzweifel@soi.unizh.ch

Introduction
Andrew M. Jones

The aim of the *Elgar Companion to Health Economics* is to take an audience of advanced undergraduates, postgraduates and researchers to the frontier of research in health economics, by providing short and readable introductions to key topics. The volume brings together 50 chapters written by more than 90 contributors from around the world. Contributions to the Companion are concise and focus on specific concepts, methods and key evidence.

The Companion is intended to provide a comprehensive and authoritative reference covering theoretical and empirical issues in health economics; with a balanced range of material on equity and efficiency in health care systems, health technology assessment and issues of concern for low and middle income countries. It is organized into two broad sections. The first deals with the economics of population health and of health care systems, analysed with both equity and efficiency goals in mind. The second covers the conceptual and practical issues that arise in the evaluation of health care technologies, most often applied to pharmaceuticals but also relevant for other interventions.

Many of the contributions address topical and policy-relevant issues: the economic causes of the growth of obesity in the West, the link between illicit drug use and crime, the consequences of leaving people uninsured against the costs of health care, the impact of globalization on the international trade in health care services, the role of informal payments in many health care systems, what 'equal treatment for equal needs' means in practice, whether direct to consumer advertising of pharmaceuticals is desirable, and how economic evidence is influencing the way that new technologies are made available to patients. Other chapters stress the research done by health economists to develop theoretical models and empirical methods that illuminate the workings of health care systems.

The boundaries of health economics stretch beyond the 'economics of health care' to encompass the broader social determinants of health and the interactions between health, labour markets and other aspects of economic activity. Economists have made contributions to the analysis of public health interventions and primary prevention, along with the analysis of healthy and unhealthy behaviours, including diet and drug-use. Health economics is deeply rooted in applied microeconomics but contributions to the Companion show that the macro-economy has consequences for population health and that health services have an impact on the macro-economy and international trade.

The desire for a long and healthy life creates a demand for health care and, as the incidence of health problems is uncertain, a demand for insurance against these risks. People value insurance as a protection from risk and for the expanded range of opportunities it brings. But insurance markets bring with them the problems described by the economics of information, which helps to understand the mix of public and private financing of health care. Economists can draw on sophisticated empirical methods to model the choices that consumers make about their payments for health care and their use of health services.

Economics traditionally focuses on the efficiency of resource allocation, but health policy-makers often place a heavy emphasis on equity goals and distributional issues. In response, health economists have shown how notions of equity in health and health care can be put into practice – making value judgements explicit – and used to perform broad international comparisons of the empirical evidence.

The organization of health care systems balances the – often competing – goals of those who provide medical care and those who pay for it. Interactions between health care providers and payers can involve elements of choice-driven competition, direct negotiation and bargaining between the parties, and explicit contracting. Doctors play a special role in health care systems due to the principal–agent relationship that exists between doctor and patient. Economists are well placed to assess the implications of the menu of options available for the reimbursement of health care providers, and to assess the best way to use available data in designing such systems. In doing so it is important to assess the impact on (hard-to-measure) aspects of the quality of care, as well as on the volume of activity. Measuring the performance of health care systems at local, national and international levels has become a major focus for policy-makers around the world. But the design of these measures should be handled with care and needs to recognize that those being measured are not passive participants in the process.

Evaluation of health care technologies and policies requires an assessment of costs and benefits. Health economists have helped to pioneer the development of stated preference methods to measure benefits, developing the theoretical foundations of these methods and testing their robustness in practical applications. These developments fall into the two broad camps of health-related quality of life (HRQoL) and of willingness to pay (WTP) with, more recently, discrete choice experiments (DCE). Recent years have seen substantial progress in the understanding and use of statistical methods – both classical and Bayesian – in economic evaluation. The challenge is to provide information in a way that informs better decision-making, taking into account the special features and sources of variation in statistical data on costs and outcomes, and the differing objectives of health care policy. Health economists are actively debating how the principles of economic evaluation of health care technologies, in particular cost-effectiveness analysis, can be translated into decision rules, setting priorities for future research and for medical practice at different levels of responsibility – from the clinical to the national or international.

The authors of chapters in this Companion have had to follow a demanding brief and a tight schedule. I am very grateful to them for their contributions and for taking the time to provide constructive comments on each other's chapters. Also I should like to thank Teresa Bago d'Uva, Silvia Balia, Adriana Castelli, Cristina Hernández-Quevedo, Dolores Jiménez Rubio, Andrea Manca, Nigel Rice and Luigi Siciliani for their valuable comments on individual chapters. Thanks also to Alex Minton and Kate Emmins for their advice and assistance in preparing the Companion for publication.

POPULATION HEALTH AND HEALTH CARE SYSTEMS

PART I

POPULATION HEALTH

1 Macroeconomic conditions, health and mortality
Christopher J. Ruhm

1. Macroeconomic conditions, health and mortality

Although health is conventionally believed to deteriorate during macroeconomic downturns, the empirical evidence supporting this view is quite weak and comes from studies containing methodological shortcomings that are difficult to remedy. Recent research that better controls for many sources of omitted variables bias instead suggests that mortality *decreases* and physical health *improves* when the economy temporarily weakens. This partially reflects reductions in external sources of death, such as traffic fatalities and other accidents, but changes in lifestyles and health behaviour are also likely to play a role. This chapter summarizes our current understanding of how health is affected by macroeconomic fluctuations and describes potential mechanisms for the effects.

2. Time series analyses for single locations

There has been extensive research examining how the macroeconomy affects health and mortality using time series data aggregated over a single geographic location, such as the United States. Most influential have been a series of studies by Brenner (1971, 1973, 1975, 1979, 1987) arguing that recessions and other sources of economic instability increase overall mortality, infant deaths, and fatalities from cardiovascular disease, cirrhosis, suicide and homicide as well as morbidities, alcoholism and admissions to mental hospitals.

These findings are controversial. Many researchers (Kasl, 1979; Gravelle et al., 1981; Stern, 1983; Gravelle, 1984; Wagstaff, 1985; Cook and Zarkin, 1986) point out serious flaws in Brenner's analysis and studies correcting the problems (Forbes and McGregor, 1984; McAvinchey, 1988; Joyce and Mocan, 1993) fail to replicate his findings.[1] The results instead are sensitive to the choice of countries, time periods and proxies for health. With the exception of Brenner's research, most time series evidence suggests that the contemporaneous effect of economic downturns is to improve health and reduce mortality. Indeed, analyses undertaken as early as the 1920s by Ogburn and Thomas (1922) and Thomas (1927) identify a positive correlation between macroeconomic activity and total mortality as well as deaths from several specific causes (with the exception of suicides). Eyer (1977) obtains a similar finding using US data from 1870–1975. These correlations hint at a *pro-cylical* variation in mortality, although they are not conclusive since other determinants of health are not controlled for.

Recent time series analyses correct for some problems inherent in earlier studies. McAvinchey (1988), for instance, uses statistical rather than ad hoc methods to choose the lag length and order of the polynomial lag; Joyce and Mocan (1993) and Laporte (2004) correct for non-stationarity in the time series data; Tapia Granados (2004a) implements spectral analysis and local regression techniques; and Gerdtham and Johannesson (2005) use multiple business cycle indicators with data on individual, rather than aggregate, mortality risk. Despite these innovations, the results remain ambiguous. Most of this research continues to suggest that mortality is pro-cyclical (Laporte, 2004; Tapia Granados, 2004a, forthcoming) but some finds counter-cyclical effects (Gerdtham and Johannesson, 2005), no impact (Joyce and Mocan, 1993) or variation across countries (McAvinchey, 1988).

Such a lack of robustness should not be surprising since any lengthy time series may yield biased estimates due to omitted variables that are spuriously correlated with economic conditions and affect health.[2] This problem has long been recognized by at least some researchers. A solution proposed by Kasl (1979, p. 787) is to conduct 'a more refined ecological analysis . . . taking advantage of local and regional variations in the business cycle as well as in disease rates.' Stern (1983, p. 69) similarly points to the promise of using differencing techniques with panel data.[3] Research using these strategies has become increasingly common in the last five years and is the focus of the remainder of this chapter.

3.   Estimates using pooled data with location-specific fixed effects

A number of recent studies address the omitted variables bias issue by estimating models using panel data for multiple geographic locations at several points in time. Some analyses (including most examining mortality outcomes) use geographically aggregated variables; others (such as those focusing on morbidities or lifestyles) typically utilize individual level information but with the key macroeconomic determinants measured over larger areas.

Studies based on aggregate data usually estimate some variant of:

$$Y_{jt} = \alpha_j + X_{jt}\beta + E_{jt}\gamma + \lambda_t + \varepsilon_{jt}, \tag{1.1}$$

where Y_{jt} is a health outcome or input in location j at time t, E measures macroeconomic conditions, X is a vector of covariates, α is a location-specific fixed effect, λ a general time effect, and ε is the regression error term. The corresponding equation with microdata is:

$$Y_{ijt} = \alpha_j + X_{ijt}\beta + E_{jt}\gamma + \lambda_t + \varepsilon_{ijt}, \tag{1.2}$$

where i indexes the individual, with the macroeconomic and fixed effects referring to the geographic area.

Unemployment rates are the most common primary proxy for macroeconomic conditions but other variables (for example the employment-to-population ratio or growth in real GDP) are sometimes used. Interpretation of the results in models that also control for incomes is more complicated since, as discussed below, permanent growth may improve health but transitory increases need not. Moreover, since incomes fall during temporary downturns, their inclusion is likely to absorb and possibly explain a portion of the macroeconomic effect. Supplementary regressors vary but often include measures of age, education and race/ethnicity. Some analyses add lags of the macroeconomic variables or use other methods to capture dynamics of the adjustment process.

To illustrate the econometric strategy, consider annual mortality rates for a panel of states estimated using equation (1.1). The year effects (λ_t) hold constant determinants of death that vary uniformly across states over time, the fixed-effects (α_j) account for those that differ across locations but are time-invariant, and the impact of the macroeconomy is identified from within-state variations relative to the changes in other states. The state and year effects control for a wide variety of determinants of health – such as lifestyle differences between residents of Nevada and Utah or advances in widely used medical technologies. The model does *not* account for factors varying within states over time, but including a vector of state-specific time trends can often substantially rectify this.[4]

Unemployment rates are often used to *proxy* macroeconomic conditions but the effects need not be restricted to or concentrated among those changing employment status. For instance, the stress of job loss could have a negative impact on health that is more than offset by improvements for workers whose hours or job-related pressures are reduced.[5]

Adult mortality
Death rates are the most common dependent variables in research using the methods just described. Mortality is useful to study because it represents the most severe negative health outcome, is objective and well measured, and diagnosis generally does not depend on access to the medical system (in contrast to many morbidities).[6] Table 1.1 documents widespread evidence of a pro-cyclical fluctuation in total mortality and some specific sources of death, which is obtained despite substantial differences in samples and time periods, and some variation in model specifications.

A one-percentage point increase in the unemployment rate is typically associated with a 0.3 to 0.5 per cent reduction in total mortality, corresponding to an elasticity of -0.02 to -0.05 (Ruhm, 2000, 2004a; Johansson, 2003; Gerdtham and Ruhm, 2004; Tapia Granados, 2004b). Using German data, Neumayer (2004) estimates a significantly larger 1.1 per cent decrease.[7] Some reasons why mortality falls are obvious. Individuals drive fewer miles and so motor vehicle fatalities decrease – a one-point increase in unemployment is predicted to reduce traffic deaths by between one and three per cent (Ruhm, 2000; Neumayer; 2004; Gerdtham and Ruhm, 2004; Tapia Granados, 2004b). Other sources of accidental deaths probably decrease as well.

The results are more mixed for deaths from specific medical conditions. Cardiovascular fatalities are pro-cyclical, with variations of similar or larger magnitude (in percentage terms) than for total mortality (Ruhm, 2000; Neumayer, 2004; Gerdtham and Ruhm 2004). Particularly strong fluctuations are observed for deaths due to ischemic heart disease and especially acute myocardial infarction (Ruhm, 2004a), that are likely to be responsive to short-term changes in modifiable health behaviours and environmental risk factors. A pro-cyclical variation in influenza/pneumonia fatalities is also generally obtained. Conversely, cancer mortality is not related to the macroeconomy, which makes sense since a short-run impact of even substantial changes in behaviour seems unlikely for this cause of death. Fatalities from most other sources may increase when the economy improves but with less consistency across studies. For instance, a pro-cyclical variation in fatalities from liver disease is obtained by Ruhm (2000) and Gerdtham and Ruhm (2004) but not Neumayer (2004).

Diverse findings are obtained for suicides. Ruhm (2000) uncovers a strong counter-cyclical variation, but with weaker effects by Gerdtham and Ruhm (2004) or Tapia Granados (2004b), and a strong pro-cyclical pattern by Neumayer (2004). There is a similar variation for homicides, pointing to possible differences in the macroeconomic

Table 1.1 Macroeconomic effects on mortality estimated using pooled data with location-specific fixed effects

Study	Sample	Major Findings	Comments
Ruhm (2000)	50 states and District of Columbia, 1972–91	*Significant Unemployment Effects* ALL: −0.5% [−0.04]; 20–44 year olds: −2.0% [−0.14]; 65+ year olds: −0.3% [−0.02]; CVD: −0.5% [−0.03]; FLU: −0.7% [−0.05]; VEHICLE: −3.0% [−0.21]; EXTERNAL: −1.7% [−0.11]; suicide: 1.3% [0.09]; homicide: −1.9% [−0.13]; INFANT: −0.6% [−0.04]; NEONATAL: −0.6% [−0.04]. *Insignificant Effects* 45–64 year olds: 0.0%; CANCER: 0.0%; LIVER: −0.4%. Dynamic models generally yield largest effects in medium-run. Mixed and inconsistent income effects.	All models control for per cent of state population in specified age, race/ethnicity, education, and marital status groups. Similar results obtained using EP ratio or change in payroll employment as alternative macroeconomic proxies, or when including state-specific time trends.
Johansson (2003)	23 OECD countries, 1960–97	*Significant Unemployment Effects* ALL: −0.4%; −0.3% for observations with information on work hours. Total mortality is negatively associated with per capita incomes and work hours.	Same sample and specification as Gerdtham and Ruhm (2004), except for the addition of work hours in some models.
Neumayer (2004)	16 German states, 1980–2000	*Significant Unemployment Effects* ALL: −1.1%; females: −1.3%; males: −0.9%; 20–45 year olds: −1.1%; 65+ year olds: −1.2%, CVD: −1.8%; FLU: −3.1%; VEHICLE: −1.3%; suicide: −1.4%. *Insignificant Effects* 45–64 year olds: −0.5%; CANCER: −0.1%; LIVER: 0.4%; homicide: 0.3%; EXTERNAL: 1.7%; INFANT: 0.2%; NEONATAL: −1.9%. Dynamic models generally yield larger effects in long-run than initially. Income effects are mixed and inconsistent.	Most specifications correspond to Ruhm (2000). Standard errors corrected for heteroscedasticity and autocorrelation. Models control for personal income, age and percent foreign. Similar results using real GDP growth as macroeconomic proxy.
Economou et al., (2004)	13 EU countries, 1977–96	*Significant Unemployment Effects* ALL: 0.3% [0.02]; 45–54 year olds: 0.5% [0.04]; 55–64 year olds: 0.5% [0.05]; ISCHEMIC: 0.8% [0.07]; CANCER: 0.2% (0.02); suicide: 0.9% [0.08]; homicide: 1.5% [0.14]. *Insignificant Effects* Males: 0.2%; females: 0.2%; 25–34 year olds:	Results difficult to interpret because models control for covariates (smoking, drinking, caloric intake, hospitalization and sometimes pollution levels) that are determined by macroeconomic conditions.

Study	Coverage	Results	Notes
		−0.4%; 35–44 year olds: 0.3%; 65–74 year olds: 0.1%; 75–84 year olds: −0.1%; VEHICLE: 3.0%.	
Gerdtham and Ruhm (2004)	23 OECD countries, 1960–97	*Significant Unemployment Effects* ALL: −0.4% [−0.02]; CVD: −0.4% [−0.02]; LIVER: −1.8% [−0.10]; VEHICLE: −2.1%[−0.12]; EXTERNAL: −0.8% [−0.04]. *Insignificant Effects* CANCER: 0.1%; FLU: −1.1% [−0.05]; suicide: 0.4%; homicide: 1.1%; INFANT: −0.2%. Dynamic models yield larger long-run than initial effects for some outcomes and smaller impacts for others.	Models control for age structure, per cent male and include country-specific time trends. Stronger effects are obtained for large countries, nations with weak social safety nets and in more recent years.
Ruhm (2004b)	20 largest states, 1978–1997	*Significant Unemployment Effects* ISCHEMIC: −0.8% [−0.05]; 20–44 year olds: −1.7% [−0.11]; 45–54 year olds: −1.0 [0.07]; 65+ year olds: −0.7% [−0.05]. AMI:−1.5% [−0.10] 20–44 year olds: −2.3% [−0.15]; 45–54: −1.2 [0.08]; 65+ year olds:−1.6% [−0.10].	Macroeconomic effects similar across sex and race. Mixed effects for income, work hours and long-run versus short-run.
Tapia Granados (2004b)	50 Spanish provinces, 1980–97	*Significant Unemployment Effects* All −0.3% [−0.05]; females: −0.2% [−0.04]; males: −0.2% [−0.05]; EXTERNAL (includes VEHICLE): −0.7% [−0.13]; VEHICLE: −1.9% [−0.37]. *Insignificant Effects* CVD: −0.1%; CANCER: −0.1%; respiratory disease: 0.0%; infectious disease: −0.6%; suicide: 0.5%; homicide: −0.3%	Models control for age structure and per capita GDP. Similar results obtained using EP ratio as macroeconomic proxy. Inclusion of state specific trends attenuates effects.

Notes:
Abbreviations: ALL – total mortality; CVD – cardiovascular disease; ISCHEMIC – ischemic heart disease; AMI – acute myocardial infarction; CANCER – malignant neoplasms; FLU – pneumonia and influenza; LIVER – chronic liver disease; VEHICLE – motor vehicle; EXTERNAL – external causes/accidents other than from motor vehicles; INFANT – infant deaths (in first year); NEONATAL – neonatal deaths (in first 28 days); EP ratio – employment-to-population ratio.
Unemployment effects indicate impact of a one percentage point increase; elasticities are in brackets. All models control for location-specific effects and general time effects. Significant effects refer to rejection of the null hypothesis at 0.05 level.

determinants across countries or institutional arrangements. This is particularly salient given evidence by Gerdtham and Ruhm (2004) showing relatively weak pro-cyclical fluctuations in mortality for countries with strong social safety nets.

Infant mortality in the United States also declines when the economy weakens. Ruhm (2000) estimates that a one-point rise in unemployment decreases infant and neonatal death rates by 0.6 per cent, while Dehejia and Lleras-Muney (2004) predict 0.5, 0.3 and 0.9 per cent reductions in infant, neonatal and post-neonatal mortality. Conversely, no relationship is obtained for Germany by Neumayer (2004) or OECD countries by Gerdtham and Ruhm (2004), again suggesting variation across institutional environments.

Due to severe data restrictions, few analyses examine how macroeconomic conditions affect morbidity. One that does is Ruhm (2003). He estimates that a one-point increase in unemployment reduces the fraction of adults (30 and over) with one or more medical conditions by 1.5 per cent, which largely reflects a 3.9 per cent decrease in the prevalence of acute problems. The probability of restricted-activity and bed-days (during a two-week period) similarly falls 1.2 and 1.6 per cent. Finally, 4.3 and 8.7 per cent reductions in the predicted prevalence of ischemic heart disease and intervertebral disk problems contrast with a 7.2 per cent increase in non-psychotic mental disorders.

Health behaviours and medical care
One reason individuals become healthier during economic downturns is because of changes in behaviours and lifestyles. Alcohol use has been most widely studied. Drinking and alcohol-involved vehicle mortality vary pro-cyclically (O'Neill, 1984; Evans and Graham, 1988; Wagenaar and Streff, 1989; Ruhm, 1995; Freeman, 1999), with evidence from individual level data suggesting that the reductions during bad times are dominated by a decline in heavy use (Ruhm and Black, 2002) rather than in light drinking, which is sometimes linked to health benefits (for example Gaziano et al., 1993; Thun et al., 1997).[8]

The healthier lifestyles are not restricted to decreases in problem drinking. Ruhm (2005) finds that severe obesity, smoking and physical inactivity decline, with larger (percentage) reductions in multiple risk factors.[9] Ruhm (2000) shows that the consumption of dietary fat falls while the intake of fruits and vegetables rises. Dehejia and Lleras-Muney (2004) indicate that pregnant mothers consume less alcohol, with mixed effects for smoking. Dustmann and Windmeijer (2004) find that temporary wage reductions in Germany are associated with increases in physical exercise. However, Böckerman et al. (2004) sometimes obtain a *counter-cyclical* variation in obesity for Finnish adults (with no relationship in other models).

The improvements in health occur despite reductions in the use of medical care: the frequency of routine check-ups, screening tests, doctor visits and hospital episodes all fall during downturns (Ruhm, 2000; 2003). However, other research indicates a negative relationship between employment and the utilization of medical care (Mwabu, 1988; Vistnes and Hamilton, 1995) and pregnant women obtain earlier and more extensive prenatal care during times of high unemployment (Dehejia and Lleras-Muney, 2004).

Income effects and dynamics
Worse health during *temporary* expansions need not imply negative effects of *permanent* economic progress. Transitory increases in output usually require more intensive use of

labour and health inputs with existing technologies. Permanent growth, conversely, results from technological innovations or expansions in the capital stock that potentially ameliorate any costs to health. Individuals are also more likely to defer health investments in response to a temporary rather than lasting rise in work hours.[10]

This distinction is not hypothetical, as there is evidence of sharp differences in the effects of temporary and permanent income changes. Graham et al. (1992) find that permanent increases are associated with reduced mortality in the US, whereas temporary growth correlates with increased fatalities. Dustmann and Windmeijer (2004) show that higher wealth profiles in Germany predict improved health, whereas status worsens when wages temporarily rise.

Mixed and inconsistent results are obtained when income is included as an additional covariate in the research using the specifications focused on in this chapter. In these studies, income is sometimes positively and other times negatively correlated with mortality (see Table 1.1), while a fairly uniform protective effect is obtained for morbidities and functional limitations (Ruhm, 2003). These are accompanied by reductions in risky behaviours such as smoking and physical inactivity (Ruhm, 2005) but with increases in obesity, alcohol use and heavy drinking (Freeman, 1999; Ruhm, 2000; Ruhm, 2005).

A number of the studies examine the dynamics of the adjustment to fluctuations in the macroeconomy. The results, while not completely consistent, generally suggest that the impact of sustained changes accumulates for a period of time – at least one or two years – with subsequent attenuation observed in some studies (for example, Ruhm, 2000) but not others (for example, Neumayer, 2004; Gerdtham and Ruhm, 2004). These findings are generally in accord with Grossman's (1972) health capital model, where investment flows gradually affect the stock of health, leading to effects that increase over time. Additional research is needed, however, to identify the period before a lasting improvement in economic conditions yields health benefits (assuming this eventually occurs), since this will help to clarify the distinction between effects of temporary and permanent changes which is central to the discussion in this chapter

4.   Why does health worsen when the economy temporarily improves?

As mentioned, health could be counter-cyclical because it is an input into short-run increases in the production of goods and services. Moreover, hazardous working conditions, the physical exertion of employment and job-related stress could have negative effects, particularly when job hours are extended during economic expansions (Baker, 1985; Karasek and Theorell, 1990; Sokejima and Kagamimori, 1998; Kivimäki et al., 2002, Liu et al., 2002). Extra work hours also lead to reductions in sleep (Biddle and Hamermesh, 1990) which is linked to increased stress, decreased alertness and greater injury risk, and higher rates of obesity and physiological or psychological symptoms (Maruyama et al., 1995; Sparks and Cooper, 1997; Gangwisch and Heymsfield, 2004). Cyclically sensitive sectors, such as construction and manufacturing, have high accident rates, which may be exacerbated when the economy temporarily improves by increased hiring of inexperienced workers and speed-ups in production (Catalano, 1979; Robinson, 1988; Brooker et al., 1997).

Some joint products of economic activity, such as pollution, miles driven and traffic congestion, also present health risks (Clancy et al., 2002; Chay and Greenstone, 2003;

Peters et al., 2004). These negative consequences may be particularly pronounced for vulnerable sectors of the population – such as infants or senior citizens – who do not participate in the labour force. Economic expansions also induce migration, which could lead to increased social isolation and loss of community support, particularly among the old and young (Eyer, 1977; Tapia Granados, 2004a).

Decreases in non-market 'leisure' time make it more costly for individuals to undertake health-producing activities such as exercise and cooking meals at home. Moreover, if health is time-intensive, the demand for both health and the inputs producing it are likely to rise when time prices fall (Grossman, 1972). Evidence that higher time prices correlate with increased obesity has been provided for adults by Chou et al. (2004) and among children by Anderson et al. (2003) and Ruhm (2004b). That said, the direct evidence linking work hours to health outcomes is mixed (for example, Johansson, 2003; Ruhm, 2004a; Ruhm, 2005).

5.   Concluding thoughts

Recent empirical research suggests that physical health improves and mortality declines when the economy temporarily weakens. Some of this can be easily explained. For example, there is less driving, reducing the risk of traffic fatalities. However, mechanisms for decreases in morbidity and deaths from medical conditions such as cardiovascular disease are less well understood. In particular, it is not yet clear why individuals adopt healthier lifestyles (like reductions in smoking, drinking and physical inactivity). Some risky behaviours (for example drinking) decline when incomes fall but most do not. Individuals have more time to undertake health investments such as exercise, when working fewer hours, but the empirical evidence on this is mixed. Conversely, reductions in pollution have clear positive effects on health that are not limited to the working age population.

Future research is needed to confirm the patterns discussed in this chapter and better to identify underlying mechanisms for the effects. For instance, it would be useful to clarify whether macroeconomic conditions differentially affect physical and mental health, to distinguish more fully between the effects of transitory and permanent growth, and to examine the extent to which the results generalize across different institutional environments and levels of economic development. Additional study should also examine the sensitivity of the results to the use of alternative macroeconomic proxies, such as GDP based measures commonly used to identify economic cycles, and further investigate the extent and nature of the lifestyle changes that accompany macroeconomic fluctuations.

That said, evidence of a counter-cyclical variation in physical health suggests that economic progress need not be uniformly beneficial. Health is likely to improve when income permanently increases but the effects of transitory fluctuations may be quite different and, even in the long run, the uses of the higher incomes may be important (Sen, 2001). These results should obviously not be used to promote recessionary economic policies but they do imply that some previous advocates (for example, Brenner, 1984) have over enthusiastically cited an assumed pro-cyclical variation in health as an argument in favour of macroeconomic stabilization policies.

Notes

1.   Criticisms include Brenner's method of choosing lag lengths, the hypothesized pattern of lag coefficients, choice of covariates, use of inconsistent data series, poor data documentation, implausibility of results,

and use of different specifications across studies without justification or evidence of the robustness of the findings to such changes.

2. For example, the variation in unemployment occurring during the four decades (beginning in the 1930s) covered by much of Brenner's research is dominated by dramatic reductions in joblessness following the great depression. During this same period, mortality declined due to improved nutrition and increased availability of antibiotics.

3. Methods of testing for potential omitted variables bias when using time series data include examining whether the model estimates are structurally stable over time (Gravelle et al., 1981) and controlling for future values of the macroeconomic variables as an informal test of reverse causality (Joyce and Mocan, 1993).

4. The impact of national business cycles, which could differ from more localized fluctuations, is absorbed by the time effects. Discussions of 'cyclical' variations or 'macroeconomic' effects therefore refer to changes within locations rather than at the national level and terms like 'recessions' are used loosely to indicate deterioration in local conditions, rather than reflecting official technical definitions. Migration flows mitigate against finding a countercyclical variation in health if movers are relatively healthy and relocate into areas with robust economies.

5. The non-employed are in worse average health than workers (for example Morris et al., 1994; Ettner, 2000; Gerdtham and Johannesson, 2003). However, since poor health reduces employment probabilities, the direction of causation is not well understood (Bartley, 1996; Goldney, 1997; Stewart, 2001).

6. However, fatalities may not capture changes in non-life threatening conditions. Also, small negative shocks might cause frail individuals to die sooner, while having little effect on overall population health.

7. Evidence of a counter-cyclical variation in total mortality and many specific sources of death is provided by Economou et al. (2004). However, their specifications control for smoking, drinking, caloric intake, hospitalization and (sometimes) pollution levels that, as shown below, are directly affected by macroeconomic conditions and so provide potential mechanisms for the fluctuations in health. As a result, the unemployment coefficients do not capture the full macroeconomic effect and are difficult to interpret.

8. Two earlier investigations used microdata. Ettner (1997) concluded that alcohol consumption and dependence were pro-cyclical but with mixed effects of involuntary unemployment. Dee (2001) obtained the contradictory result that economic downturns reduced overall and heavy drinking but increased binge drinking.

9. DiSimone (2004) provides evidence of a counter-cyclical variation in obesity for high school aged boys (but not girls) that partly reflects changes in physical activity.

10. There is strong evidence that increases in permanent income improve health in developing countries but with a more ambiguous relationship observed for industrialized nations. Useful discussions of this voluminous literature are contained in Smith (1999), Deaton (2003), or Gerdtham and Johannesson (2004).

References

Anderson, Patricia M., Kristin F. Butcher and Phillip B. Levine (2003), 'Maternal employment and overweight children', *Journal of Health Economics*, **22**(3), 477–504.

Baker, Dean B. (1985), 'The study of stress at work', *Annual Review of Public Health*, **6**, 367–81.

Bartley, Mel. (1996), 'Unemployment and health selection', *The Lancet*, **348**(9032), 904.

Biddle, Jeff E. and Daniel S. Hamermesh (1990), 'Sleep and the allocation of time', *Journal of Political Economy*, **95**(5), 922–43.

Böckerman, Petri, Edvard Johansson, Sata Helakorpi, Ritva Prättälä, Erkki Vartiainen and Antti Uutela (2004), 'Does a slump really make you thinner? Finnish micro-level evidence 1978–2002', *Research Institute of the Finnish Economy Discussion Paper No. 928*.

Brenner, M. Harvey (1971), 'Economic changes and heart disease mortality', *American Journal of Public Health*, **61**(3), 606–11.

Brenner, M. Harvey (1973), *Mental Illness and the Economy*, Cambridge, MA: Harvard University Press.

Brenner, M. Harvey (1975), 'Trends in alcohol consumption and associated illnesses', *The American Journal of Public Health*, **656**(12), 1279–92.

Brenner, M. Harvey (1979), 'Mortality and the national economy', *The Lancet*, **314**(8142), 568–73.

Brenner, M. Harvey (1984), *Estimating the Effects of Economic Change on National Health and Social Well Being*, Washington, DC: Joint Economic Committee, US Congress, US Government Printing Office.

Brenner, M. Harvey (1987), 'Economic change, alcohol consumption and heart disease mortality in nine industrialized countries', *Social Science and Medicine*, **25**(2), 119–32.

Brooker, Ann-Sylvia, John W. Frank and Valerie S. Tarasuk (1997), 'Back pain claims and the business cycle', *Social Science and Medicine*, **45**(3), 429–39.

Catalano, Ralph C. (1979), 'Health costs of economic expansion: the case of manufacturing injuries', *American Journal of Public Health*, **69**(8), 789–94.

Chay, Kenneth and Michael Greenstone (2003), 'The impact of air pollution on infant mortality: evidence from geographic variation in pollution shocks induced by a recession', *Quarterly Journal of Economics*, **118**(3), 1121–67.

Chou, Shin-Yi, Michael Grossman and Henry Saffer (2004), 'An economic analysis of adult obesity: results from the behavioral risk factor surveillance system', *Journal of Health Economics*, **23**(3), 565–87.

Clancy, Luke, Pat Goodman, Hamish Sinclair and Douglas Dockery (2002), 'Effect of air-pollution on death rates in Dublin, Ireland: an intervention study', *The Lancet*, **360**(9341), 1210–14.

Cook, Philip J. and Gary A. Zarkin (1986), 'Homicide and economic conditions: a replication and critique of M. Harvey Brenner's new report to the US Congress', *Journal of Quantitative Criminology*, **2**(1), 69–80.

Deaton, Angus (2003), 'Health, inequality, and economic development', *Journal of Economic Literature*, **41**(1), 113–58.

Dee, Thomas S. (2001), 'Alcohol abuse and economic conditions: evidence from repeated cross-sections of individual-level data', *Health Economics*, **10**(3), 257–70.

Dehejia, Rajeev and Adriana Lleras-Muney (2004), 'Booms, busts, and babies' health', *Quarterly Journal of Economics*, **119**(3), 1091–1130.

DeSimone, Jeff (2004), 'The cyclicality of economic and bodyweight fluctuations among high school students', mimeo, University of South Florida, November.

Dustmann, Christian and Frank Windmeijer (2004), 'Wages and the demand for health – a lifecycle analysis', mimeo, University College London, May.

Economou, Athina, Agelike Nikolau, Ioannis Theodossiou (2004), 'Are recessions harmful to health after all? Evidence from the European Union', mimeo, University of Macedonia.

Ettner, Susan L. (1997), 'Measuring the human cost of a weak economy: does unemployment lead to alcohol abuse?', *Social Science and Medicine*, **44**(2), 251–60.

Ettner, Susan L. (2000), 'The relationship between labor market outcomes and physical and mental health: exogenous human capital or endogenous health production' in David S. Salkever and Alan Sorkin (eds), *Research in Human Capital and Development, Vol. 13: (The Economics of Disability)*, Stamford, CN: JAI Press, pp. 1–31.

Evans William and John D. Graham (1988), 'Traffic safety and the business cycle', *Alcohol, Drugs, and Driving*, **4**(1), 31–8.

Eyer, Joseph (1977), 'Prosperity as a cause of death', *International Journal of Health Services*, **7**(1), 125–50.

Forbes, John F. and Alan McGregor (1984), 'Unemployment and mortality in post-war Scotland', *Journal of Health Economics*, **3**(3), 239–57.

Freeman, Donald G. (1999), 'A note on "Economic Conditions and Alcohol Problems"', *Journal of Health Economics*, **18**(5), 661–70.

Gangwisch, James and Steven Heymsfield (2004), 'Lack of sleep may lead to excess weight', presented at the North American Association for the Study of Obesity Annual Meetings, 16 November.

Gaziano, J. Michael, Julie E. Buring, Jan L. Breslow, Samuel Z. Goldhaber, Bernard Rosner, Martin VanDenburgh, Walter Willett and Charles H. Hennekens (1993), 'Moderate alcohol intake, increased levels of high-density lipoprotein and its subfractions, and decreased risk of myocardial infarction', *New England Journal of Medicine* **329**(25), 1829–34.

Gerdtham, Ulf-G and Magnus Johannesson (2003), 'A note on the effect of unemployment on mortality', *Journal of Health Economics*, **22**(3), 505–18.

Gerdtham, Ulf-G and Magnus Johannesson (2004), 'Absolute income, relative income, income inequality, and mortality', *Journal of Human Resources*, **29**(1), 228–47.

Gerdtham, Ulf-G and Magnus Johannesson (2005), 'Business cycles and mortality: results from Swedish microdata', *Social Science and Medicine*, **60**(1), 205–18.

Gerdtham, Ulf-G and Christopher J. Ruhm (2004), 'Deaths rise in good economic times: evidence from the OECD', mimeo, Lund University, June.

Goldney, Robert D. (1997), 'Unemployment and health: a re-appraisal', *International Archives of Occupational and Environmental Health*, **70**(3), 145–7.

Graham, John D., Bei-Hung Chang and John S. Evans (1992), 'Poorer is riskier', *Risk Analysis*, **12**(3), 333–7.

Gravelle, H.S.E., G. Hutchinson and J. Stern (1981), 'Mortality and unemployment: a critique of brenner's time-series analysis', *The Lancet*, **318**(8248), 675–9.

Gravelle, Hugh S.E. (1984), 'Time series analysis of mortality and unemployment', *Journal of Health Economics*, **3**(3), 297–305.

Grossman, Michael (1972), 'On the concept of health capital and the demand for health', *Journal of Political Economy*, **80**(2), 223–55.

Johansson, Edvard (2003), 'A note on the impact of hours worked on mortality in the OECD', *The Research Institute of the Finnish Economy Discussion Paper No. 878*, November.

Joyce, Theodore J. and H. Naci Mocan (1993), 'Unemployment and infant health: time-series evidence from the state of Tennessee', *Journal of Human Resources*, **28**(1), 185–203.

Karasek, Robert A. and Töres Theorell (1990), *Healthy Work: Stress, Productivity, and the Reconstruction of Working Life*, New York: Basic Books.

Kasl, Stanislav V. (1979) 'Mortality and the business cycle: some questions about research strategies when utilizing macro-social and ecological data', *American Journal of Public Health*, **69**(8), 784–8.

Kivimäki Mika, Päivi Leino-Arjas, Ritva Luukkonen, Hilkka Riihimaki, Jussi Vahtera and Juhani Kirjonen (2002), 'Work stress and the risk of cardiovascular mortality: prospective cohort study of industrial employees', *British Medical Journal*, **325**(7369), 857–61.

Laporte, Audrey (2004), 'Do economic cycles have a permanent effect on population health? Revisiting the Brenner hypothesis', *Health Economics*, **13**(8), 767–79.

Liu, Y., H. Tanaka and the Fukouka Heart Study Group (2002), 'Overtime work, insufficient sleep, and the risk of non-fatal acute myocardial infarction in Japanese men', *Occupational and Environmental Medicine*, **59**(7), 447–51.

Maruyama, S., K. Kohno and K. Morimoto (1995), 'A study of preventive medicine in relation to mental health among middle management employees (Part 2) – effects of long working hours on lifestyles, perceived stress and working life satisfaction among white-collar middle management employees', *Nippon Eiseigaku Zasshi*, **50**(4), 849–60.

McAvinchey, Ian D. (1988), 'A comparison of unemployment, income and mortality interaction for five European countries', *Applied Economics*, **20**(4), 453–71.

Morris, Joan K., Derek G. Cook and A. Gerald Shaper (1994), 'Loss of employment and mortality', *British Medical Journal*, **308**(6937), 1135–9.

Mwabu, Germano M. (1988), 'Seasonality, the shadow price of time and effectiveness of tropical disease control programs', in Alejando N. Herrin and Patricia L. Rosenfield (eds) *Economics, Health, and Tropical Diseases*, Manila: University of the Philippines Press, pp. 259–70.

Neumayer, Eric (2004), 'Recessions lower (some) mortality rates', *Social Science & Medicine*, **58**(6), 1037–47.

Ogburn, William F. and Dorothy S. Thomas (1922), 'The influence of the business cycle on certain social conditions', *Journal of the American Statistical Association*, **18**(139), 324–40.

O'Neill, Brian (1984), 'Recent trends in motor vehicle crash deaths', *American Association for Automotive Medicine*, **6**, 29–32.

Peters, Annette, Stephanie von Klot, Margit Heier, Ines Trentinaglia, Allmut Hörmann, Erich Wichmann and Hannelore Löwel for the Cooperative Health Research in the Region of Augsburg Study Group (2004), 'Exposure to traffic and the onset of acute myocardial infarction', *New England Journal of Medicine*, **351**(17), 1721–30.

Robinson, James C. (1988), 'The rising long-term trend in occupational injury rates' *American Journal of Public Health*, **78**(3), 276–81.

Ruhm, Christopher J. (1995), 'Economic conditions and alcohol problems', *Journal of Health Economics*, **14**(5), 583–603.

Ruhm, Christopher J. (2000), 'Are recessions good for your health?', *Quarterly Journal of Economics*, **115**(2), 617–50.

Ruhm, Christopher J. (2003), 'Good times make you sick', *Journal of Health Economics*, **22**(4), 637–58.

Ruhm, Christopher J. (2004a), 'Macroeconomic conditions and deaths from coronary heart disease', mimeo, University of North Carolina at Greensboro, June.

Ruhm, Christopher J. (2004b), 'Maternal employment and adolescent development', *National Bureau of Economic Research Working Paper No. 10691*, August.

Ruhm, Christopher J. (2005) 'Healthy living in hard times', *Journal of Health Economics*, **24**(2), 341–63.

Ruhm, Christopher J. and William E. Black (2002), 'Does drinking really decrease in bad times?', *Journal of Health Economics*, **21**(4), 659–78.

Sen, Amartya (2001), 'Economic progress and health', in David A. Leon and Gill Walt (eds), *Poverty, Inequality and Health: An International Perspespective*, New York: Oxford University Press, pp. 333–45.

Smith, James P. (1999), 'Healthy bodies and thick wallets: the dual relationship between health and economic status', *Journal of Economic Perspectives*, **13**(2), 145–66.

Sokejima, Shigeru and Sadanobu Kagamimori (1998), 'Working hours as a risk factor for acute myocardial infarction in Japan: a case-control study', *The British Medical Journal*, **317**(7161), 775–80.

Sparks, Kate and Cary Cooper (1997), 'The effects of work hours on health: a meta-analytic review', *Journal of Occupational and Organizational Psychology*, **70**(4), 391–408.

Stern, J. (1983), 'The relationship between unemployment and morbidity and mortality in England', *Population Studies*, **37**(1), 61–74.

Stewart, Jennifer M. (2001), 'The impact of health status on the duration of unemployment spells and the implications for studies of the impact of unemployment on health status', *Journal of Health Economics*, **20**(5), 781–96.

Tapia Granados, José (2004a), 'Mortality and economic fluctuations in Sweden, 1800–1998', mimeo, University of Michigan.

Tapia Granados, José (2004b), 'Recessions and mortality in Spain: reconceptualizing and empirical relationship', mimeo, University of Michigan.

Tapia Granados, José (forthcoming), 'Increasing mortality during the expansions of the US Economy, 1900–1996', *International Journal of Epidemiology*.

Thomas, Dorothy Swaine (1927), *Social Aspects of the Business Cycle*, New York: Alfred A. Knopf.

Thun, Michael J., Richard Peto, Alan D. Lopez, Jane H. Monaco, S. Jane Henley, Clark W. Heath Jr. and Richard Doll (1997), 'Alcohol consumption and mortality among middle-aged and elderly US adults', *New England Journal of Medicine*, **337**(24), 1705–14.

Vistnes, Jessica P. and Vivian Hamilton (1995), 'The time and monetary costs of outpatient care for children', *American Economic Review*, **85**(2), 117–21.

Wagenaar, Alexander C. and Frederick M. Streff (1989), 'Macroeconomic conditions and alcohol-impaired driving', *Journal of Studies on Alcohol*, **50**(3), 217–25.

Wagstaff, Adam (1985), 'Time series analysis of the relationship between unemployment and mortality: a survey of econometric critiques and replications of Brenner's studies', *Social Science and Medicine*, **21**(9), 985–96.

2 The dynamics of health
*Andrew M. Jones, Nigel Rice and Paul Contoyannis**

1. The demand for health

Health has long been considered as a fundamental commodity in economic analyses; Michael Grossman (2000) cites Bentham as recognizing that the 'relief of pain' is one of the basic arguments in the utility function. Health was viewed both as an investment in human capital and as an output of a household production process by Grossman (1972a and b), the founding father of demand for health models. In the Grossman model, health is demanded both for utility reasons – it is good to feel well – and for investment reasons – to make more healthy time available for market and non-market activities.

Grossman developed a dynamic model for health, and solution of the dynamic optimization problem leads to optimal life-cycle health paths, gross investment in each period, consumption of medical care (which is seen as a derived demand) and time inputs in the gross investment function in each period. By comparing maximum lifetime utility for different lengths of life, it also allows endogenous determination of the length of life. Usually the comparative static and dynamic analyses are performed on sub-models where either the consumption benefits are assumed to equal zero (the investment model), or the investment benefits are assumed to equal zero (the consumption model).

In the investment model sharper predictions are available; this model results in a condition which determines the optimal stock of health in any period and shows that the rate of return on capital (or, marginal efficiency of capital, MEC) must equal the opportunity cost of capital.

Increases in the depreciation rate over time cause the optimal stock of health to decrease as the opportunity cost of capital increases. However, if the MEC curve is inelastic, gross investment grows over time. Thus the model predicts older people to have more sick time, to consume more medical care and devote more time to investment in health than younger people. An increase in the wage rate shifts the MEC to the right and steepens it simultaneously. Thus the demand for health capital rises. The demand for medical care also rises with the wage as gross investment increases. However, due to substitution incentives between medical care and time, the elasticity of medical care with respect to the wage is greater than that of health. The more educated would demand more health but, if the MEC elasticity with respect to education is less than one, less medical care.

We note in passing that wage effects and schooling effects on health are ambiguous in the pure consumption or mixed consumption-investments models. Theoretical extensions of the Grossman model have introduced uncertainty of health to the model. Compared to a model with certainty, the optimal level of the stock of health is larger and the optimal

* We are grateful to Cristina Hernandez-Quevedo and Teresa Bago d'Uva for their research assistance in preparing the empirical results for the ECHP. The ECHP UDB version of December 2003 was supplied by Eurostat.

quantities of investment are also larger in a pure investment model. A change in initial assets can cause a change in these quantities but the effects depend on how uncertainty influences earnings (see Grossman, 2000).

Another major issue in the demand for health literature concerns the impact of schooling on health (see Grossman, 2000). The question is: 'how much of the observed correlation in these variables is due to a causal effect of schooling on health?' Differences in time preference rates and the 'healthy student' and 'anticipated health' effects have been the focal points of discussion. Furthermore, even if the effect is causal, is it due to the impact of education on allocative efficiency, technical efficiency, or preferences (including the rate of time preference)? This is of course relevant for policy, as health-specific education may have large effects under some explanations but perform poorly under others.

2.   Reasons for persistence in health

Empirical analysis of health dynamics needs to address the question why some individuals experience persistently good health and others experience persistently poor health. To some extent this may reflect the nature of health problems: some illnesses are inherently chronic and long-lasting. Also a cumulative history of a range of health problems may have a direct influence on current health and on the effectiveness of medical care. These effects can be thought of as pure dynamics, often termed state dependence. But health problems may be persistent for other reasons. As predicted by the demand for health framework, an individual may have individual or socioeconomic characteristics that predispose them to poorer health and that linger over time. Factors such as education, material deprivation, childhood nutrition and environment may have a long-standing influence on an individual's health. Some of these factors may be observable, but others – such as ability, time preference and risk aversion – may be hard to control for, especially in the absence of longitudinal data.

These issues are exemplified by the debates over the association between health and socioeconomic status (SES): in particular health and education (see for example, Grossman, 2000; Smith, 2004) and health and income or wealth (see for example, Smith, 1999, 2004). Evidence of a positive association between health and SES is well-documented across many societies and periods (see for example, Smith, 1999; Deaton, 2003). But the causal mechanisms underlying this relationship are complex and controversial. There can be a direct causal link from SES to health, for example, through the direct influence of material deprivation on the production of health and on access to health care, or of education on the uptake and compliance with medical treatments. There can be a direct causal link from health to SES, for example, through the impact of health shocks on labour market outcomes such as unemployment, early retirement and earnings. But there may also be pathways that link health and SES through 'third factors', for example time preference rates, that do not imply any causal link.

A full discussion of the empirical literature on the relationship between health and SES – even that originating within economics – is beyond the scope of this chapter. Readers are referred to Adams et al. (2003) and the associated commentaries for a discussion of the methodological issues involved in identifying causal effects of income on health. The problem facing such analyses is to overcome the biases, caused by reverse causality and selection, by identifying a source of exogenous variation in income.

Meer et al. (2003) use inheritance as an instrument for wealth changes using the US Panel Study on Income Dynamics (PSID) from 1984–1999. They find a very small effect of changes in wealth requiring a quarter of a million dollar change to achieve an effect of around 2 percentage points in probability of excellent of good health. Frijters et al. (2004) use the unanticipated shift in permanent income for East German households, following the reunification of Germany, as a source of exogenous variation in income. Using the German Socioeconomic Panel (GSOEP) between 1991 and 1999 they find that, after controlling for heterogeneity, there is no evidence for a causal effect of income on health. Of course these findings do not rule out a cumulative and long-term relationship running from SES during childhood and early life to the gradient in adult health (see for example, Case et al., 2002; Smith, 2004).

3. Empirical analysis of the dynamics of health

Kerkhofs and Linderboom (1997) investigate the impact of changes in labour market status and work history on health. Recognizing that health changes with age and that individuals may experience shocks to their health that have permanent consequences for their future health, their empirical model incorporates health transitions by specifying a model in first-differenced form. By conditioning on a variable representing a health shock in the intervening years between the waves of data used, the authors control for previous health experiences. They report that the occurrence of a health shock causes large changes in individual health profiles.

As part of an analysis of inequalities in mental health, Hauck and Rice (2004) investigate health mobility. Concern focuses on the extent to which individuals migrate within the distribution of mental health and how this varies across socioeconomic groups. Using 11 waves of data from the British Household Panel Survey (BHPS), two regression-based approaches to estimating mobility are employed. The first method is based on the intra-unit correlation coefficient, $\rho = \sigma_\alpha^2/(\sigma_\alpha^2 + \sigma_\varepsilon^2)$ from an error components panel data model where σ_α^2 represents the variance of the unobserved individual effect and σ_ε^2 the variance of the idiosyncratic error component. The coefficient represents the correlation of health scores across periods of observation. Values of ρ close to unity indicate high persistence (low mobility) in health outcomes, whereas values of ρ close to zero are indicative of high random fluctuations resulting in high health mobility (low persistence). The second method is based on the estimated coefficient on lagged health status from a dynamic panel data model. The size of the estimated coefficient is informative about the degree of dependence between previous health and current health status. A coefficient close to zero indicates high mobility, whereas a coefficient close to unity indicates high persistence.

Hauck and Rice (2004) find evidence of substantial mobility in mental health with the extent differing systematically across socioeconomic groups. In general, mental health deteriorates with age and mental ill-health becomes more permanent in nature. Individuals from lower income groups are associated with greater mental ill-health, which exhibits greater persistence over time compared to individuals from higher income groups. Low educational attainment is also found to be associated with a greater reporting of mental health problems and greater persistence than that found for individuals from higher educational groups.

Investigating the association between socioeconomic status and health in older populations, by drawing on the health investment framework of Grossman's model, Salas (2002) specifies a dynamic model of the determinants of health which includes previous health status as an exogenous regressor. The model is estimated using two waves (1991 and 1995) of the BHPS and concentrates on a five-category self-assessed health variable (excellent, good, fair, poor, very poor), together with mortality, as the outcomes of interest. The results indicate a gradient over the categories of lagged self-assessed health status that appears statistically and substantively important – poor health status reported at time $t-1$ is a powerful predictive of poor health status at time t. The relationship between socio-economic status and survival is less well established leading the author to conclude that while, for the elderly, low socioeconomic position has a significant effect over a large range of the latent health variable, it might not have sufficient effect to push people past a 'death threshold'.

Buckley et al. (2004) also consider the relationship between socioeconomic position and health transitions in the older population. Using three consecutive years of data from the Canadian Survey of Labour and Income Dynamics (SLID), and dichotomizing an ordered categorical variable on reported health status into good or poor health, the authors estimate a probit model representing the probability of remaining in good health, given that an individual reported good health on entering the study period. Interest focuses on the relationship between income and health and in particular, the impact of long-term income. To this end, the authors construct a measure of household income standardized for age that it is claimed represents an indicator of lifetime income. The probability of remaining in good health for men in the highest quartile for both income and educational attainment is estimated to be 0.15 higher than men in the corresponding lowest quartiles. For women the difference in probabilities is greater, at 0.18.

Contoyannis, Jones and Rice (2004a) consider the determinants of a binary indicator for the existence of functional limitations using seven waves (1991–1997) of the BHPS. The model adopted allows for persistence in observed outcomes due to state dependence, unobservable individual effects (heterogeneity), and autocorrelation in the transitory error component. The length of the panel used allows state dependence – the influence of health history on current health – to be investigated with greater rigour than previous studies have allowed. Contoyannis et al. estimate static and dynamic panel probit models by Maximum Simulated Likelihood (MSL) and consider two approaches to dealing with the problem of initial conditions in models with unobserved effects and lagged dependent variables.

The results suggest that a sufficient parameterization for the error process in such longitudinal models comprises a random effects structure with the addition of a first-order autocorrelated error component. For both men and women they find that, in the models that do not allow for state dependence, the addition of a serially correlated error component reduces the proportion of variance explained by the individual unobserved effect. The magnitude of this reduction (10 per cent) is very similar to the effect of allowing for state dependence. This suggests that the proportion of variance due to time-invariant unobservable factors, and hence the amount of outcome persistence due to these factors, is overestimated in models that do not allow for dynamics. State dependence explains more of the persistence of functional limitations for men than for women, relative to the overall variance of latent health.

In a separate study, Contoyannis, Jones and Rice (2004b) explore the dynamics of self-assessed health, again drawing on data from the BHPS. The variable of interest is the same five-category ordered measure of self-assessed health used by Salas (2002) and, as with functional limitations, the BHPS reveals evidence of considerable persistence in individuals' health status. Two possible sources of this persistence are unobservable heterogeneity and state dependence. Contoyannis, Jones and Rice (2004b) develop an econometric model using a latent variable specification for self-assessed health. The models include measures of socioeconomic status together with the inclusion of lagged health states designed to capture state dependence. To deal with the initial conditions problem an attractively simple approach suggested by Wooldridge (2002) is used.

The sample data used consists of the first eight waves of the BHPS, and care is taken to investigate and control for the consequences of longitudinal attrition of sample respondents: attrition rates are higher among those who report very poor health at the previous wave of the panel. This health-related attrition may be a source of bias. To control for potential attrition bias inverse probablity weights are applied to the pooled ordered probit estimators. While there is evidence of health-related attrition in the data, the average partial effects of socioeconomic variables and of lagged health status are not influenced by sample attrition. This echoes earlier work by Kerkhofs and Lindeboom (1997), and is reinforced by further analysis of the BHPS and of the European Community Panel (ECHP) in Jones, Koolman and Rice (2004).

Contoyannis, Jones and Rice (2004b) present evidence of persistence in self-assessed health explained in part by state dependence, which is stronger amongst men than women, and by individual heterogeneity, with around 30–35 per cent of the unexplained variation accounted for by individual heterogeneity. As with functional limitations, there is evidence of a socioeconomic gradient by education and income.

4.　Mobility indices

Health economists have been at the forefront of developing analytic tools for the measurement and explanation of health inequalities. The concentration index of health on income (Wagstaff et al., 1989) is a widely adopted measure of relative income-related health inequality, and regression-based decomposition methods for the concentration index, of Wagstaff et al. (2003), have been used in a variety of settings and populations. While these methods have typically been applied to cross-sectional information, it is desirable that attention should be paid to the dynamics of health and their relation to socio-economic characteristics as revealed by longitudinal data.

Jones and López-Nicolás (2004) show that there are important features of health inequality that cannot be revealed by cross sectional data. Their starting point is provided by measurement tools from the income distribution literature. In order to approximate a measure of inequality in lifetime income, Shorrocks (1978) considered inequality in the distribution of individual incomes averaged over a sequence of time periods. In particular, he introduced the concept of income mobility to capture the degree to which income inequalities fade as the time interval over which the population is analysed extends. Jones and López-Nicolás (2004) show that this methodology can be a useful empirical tool for the analysis of health inequality over the long run. For example, a concern with inequalities in individuals' whole lifetime experience of health would mean taking an average over the whole lifespan.

Jones and López-Nicolás (2004) show that the long-run concentration index can be written as the sum of a weighted average of short-run concentration indices plus a term that captures the covariance between levels of health (y) and fluctuations in income rank (R) over time:

$$CI^T = \sum_t w_t CI^t - \frac{2}{NT\bar{\bar{y}}^T}\sum_i\sum_t (y_{it}-\bar{y}^t)(R_i^t - R_i^T) \quad \text{where} \quad w_t = \frac{\bar{y}^t}{T\bar{\bar{y}}^T}$$

This is a key result. Here it is presented in terms of the concentration index for socioeconomic inequalities in health, but the same idea also applies to the Gini coefficient for overall inequality in health or to extended Gini or concentration indices (see Wagstaff, 2002). The result shows that the concentration index (CI^T) for average health after T periods ($\bar{y}^T$) can be written down as the sum of two terms. The first term is a weighted sum of the concentration indices (CI^t) for each of the sub-periods (with weights equal to the share of 'total' health in each period). If the income ranking remains constant over time, a standard decomposition result for concentration indices implies that the concentration index for the average over time is equal to the (weighted) average of the concentration indices. However, income ranks may change over time. The second term captures the difference between period-specific income ranks and ranks for average income over all periods and their relationship to health. If people switch ranks significantly over the T periods and this is systematically and directly related to health, an inequality measure based on the average over the T periods would understate the total level of income-related inequality in health. Another way of seeing this is that using the average of short-run indices overestimates inequality.

It is useful to measure how much the longitudinal perspective alters the picture that would emerge from a series of cross-sections. Jones and López-Nicolás (2004) define an index of *health-related income mobility* as:

$$M^T = 1 - \frac{CI^T}{\sum_t w_t CI^t} = \frac{2}{N\sum_t \bar{y}^t CI^t}\left(\sum_i\sum_t (y_{it}-\bar{y}^t)(R_i^t - R_i^T)\right)$$

This is one minus the ratio by which the concentration index for the joint distribution of longitudinal averages differs from the weighted average of the cross-sectional concentration indices. An important feature of the mobility index is that it is invariant to linear transformations of the measure of health. This extends the result used in van Doorslaer and Jones (2003) that, if $y = \alpha + \beta x$, then $CI(y) = (\beta\mu_x/\alpha + \beta\mu_x)CI(x)$. Given that $\bar{y} = \alpha + \beta\bar{x}$, this result can be substituted into the expression for the mobility index to show that $M^T(y) = M^T(x)$. The implication of this property is that the problem of imposing the appropriate cardinal scaling, discussed in van Doorslaer and Jones (2003), is less of a restriction for the analysis of mobility indices: the results will be the same for any linear transformation of the health status measure.

Using a concentration index to measure income-related inequalities in health raises the possibility to incorporate an econometric model for health and to decompose inequality into the contributions of each of the regressors (Wagstaff et al., 2003). By analogy, Jones and López-Nicolás (2004) show how health-related income mobility can be decomposed into the contributions of covariates in an econometric model. The methods are illustrated by analysing the dynamics of income and mental health, as measured by the General Health Questionnaire (GHQ) index of psychological well-being in the first nine waves of the BHPS. The results reveal that, over eight years, adverse mental health becomes more concentrated among the poor. In particular, individual dynamics increase the absolute value of the concentration index of GHQ on income by 15 per cent for men and 5 per cent for women.

Lecluyse (2004) computes the mobility index proposed by Jones and López-Nicolás for a measure of self-assessed health (SAH), using the Panel Study of Belgian Households for 1994–2001. She applies the interval regression approach to the scaling of SAH, as suggested by van Doorslaer and Jones (2003), and finds a mobility index of 10 per cent over the eight years of the panel, suggesting that the short-run measures underestimate inequality by 10 per cent over the period.

To complement these earlier studies we present some new and previously unpublished findings based on the full eight waves, 1994–2001, of the *European Community Household Panel User Database* (ECHP-UDB) which was designed and coordinated by Eurostat. The ECHP is a multi-purpose annual longitudinal survey, based on a standardized questionnaire that involves annual interviewing of a representative panel of households and individuals of 16 years and older in each of the participating EU member states. We use data for the following 14 member states of the EU for the full number of waves available for each: Austria (waves 2–8), Belgium (1–8), Denmark (1–8), Finland (3–8), France (1–8), Germany (1–3), Greece (1–8), Ireland (1–8), Italy (1–8), Luxembourg (1–3), Netherlands (1–8), Portugal (1–8), Spain (1–8) and the United Kingdom (1–3).

In Table 2.1 we present comparative evidence on the long-run concentration indices (CI^T) and mobility indices (M^T) for self-reported health limitations. The two binary measures of health limitations have been labelled HAMP1 and HAMP2. The information comes from the variable PH003A: respondents are asked: 'Are you hampered in your daily activities by any physical or mental health problem, illness or disability?', with three possible answers: 1. Yes, severely; 2. Yes, to some extent; 3. No. We use two dummy variables to indicate either any limitation (HAMP1) or a severe limitation (HAMP2). The ECHP income measure is disposable household income per equivalent adult, using the modified OECD equivalence scale, deflated by PPPs and the CPI for each country. Total household income includes all net monetary income received by the household members during the reference year. The estimates are computed using the personal weights supplied with the ECHP-UDB.

The negative values of the long-run concentration indices show evidence of income-related inequalities in health throughout Europe, with health limitations concentrated among those with lower incomes. The mobility indices show that there is greater long-run income-related inequality in HAMP1 and HAMP2, than would be suggested by the average of short-run indices, for all countries. For the bulk of countries, which are observed for the full eight waves, health-related income mobility means that the long-run inequality in health is between 5 and 20 per cent greater than the short-run measure over eight years. The distinction between the short-run and long-run will be of interest to

Table 2.1   Long-run concentration indices (CI^T) and mobility indices (M^T) for the ECHP, 1994–2001

Country (waves)	CI^T		M^T	
	Any limitation (HAMP1)	Severe limitation (HAMP2)	Any limitation (HAMP1)	Severe limitation (HAMP2)
Austria (2–8)	−0.153	−0.187	−0.038	−0.023
Belgium (1–8)	−0.163	−0.304	−0.116	−0.110
Denmark (1–8)	−0.198	−0.378	−0.104	−0.043
Finland (3–8)	−0.108	−0.195	−0.061	−0.097
France (1–8)	−0.166	−0.223	−0.110	−0.101
Germany (1–3)	−0.089	−0.149	−0.040	−0.002
Greece (1–8)	−0.224	−0.291	−0.126	−0.129
Ireland (1–8)	−0.299	−0.424	−0.240	−0.209
Italy (1–8)	−0.119	−0.152	−0.202	−0.092
Luxembourg (1–3)	−0.155	−0.216	−0.126	−0.168
Netherlands (1–8)	−0.114	−0.202	−0.120	−0.104
Portugal (1–8)	−0.190	−0.274	−0.122	−0.174
Spain (1–8)	−0.182	−0.209	−0.100	−0.080
UK (1–3)	−0.185	−0.321	−0.062	−0.101

policy-makers whose ethical concern is with inequalities in long-run health. For example, the 'fair innings' perspective suggests that equity should be defined in terms of a person's lifetime experience of health (see for example, Williams and Cookson, 2000). The evidence provided so far, for the relatively short span of eight years, suggests that the gap between long-run and short-run inequalities may be substantial.

References

Adams, P., M.D. Hurd, D. McFadden, A. Merrill and T. Ribeiro, (2003), 'Healthy, wealthy, and wise? Tests for direct causal paths between health and socioeconomic status', *Journal of Econometrics*, **112**, 3–56.

Buckley, N.J., F.T. Denton, L. Robb and B.G. Spencer (2004), 'The transition from good to poor health: an econometric study of the older population', *Journal of Health Economics*, **23**, 1013–34.

Case, A., D. Lubotsky and C. Paxson (2002), 'Economic status and health in childhood: the origins of the gradient', *American Economic Review*, **92**, 1308–34.

Contoyannis, P., A.M. Jones and N. Rice (2004a), 'Simulation-based inference in dynamic panel probit models: an application to health', *Empirical Economics*, **29**, 49–77.

Contoyannis, P., A.M. Jones and N. Rice (2004b), 'The dynamics of health in the British Household Panel Survey', *Journal of Applied Econometrics*, **19**, 473–503.

Deaton, A. (2003), 'Health, inequality, and economic development', *Journal of Economic Literature*, **XLI**, 113–58.

Erbsland, M., W. Reid and V. Ulrich (1995), 'Health, health care, and the environment. Econometric evidence from Germany', *Health Economics*, **4**, 169–82.

Frijters, P., J.P. Haisken-DeNew and M.A. Shields (2004), 'Estimating the causal effect of income on health: evidence from post reunification East Germany', *Centre for Economic Policy Discussion Paper*, No. 465, Australian National University.

Grossman, M. (1972a), 'On the concept of health capital and the demand for health', *Journal of Political Economy*, **80**, 223–55.

Grossman, M. (1972b), *The Demand for Health: A Theoretical and Empirical Investigation*, New York: Columbia University Press for the National Bureau of Economic Research.

Grossman, M. (2000), 'The human capital model', in A.J. Culyer and J.P. Newhouse (eds), *Handbook of Health Economics*, Amsterdam: Elsevier, pp. 347–408.

Hauck, K. and N. Rice (2004), 'A longitudinal analysis of mental health mobility in Britain', *Health Economics*, **13**, 981–1001.

Jones, A.M. and A. López-Nicolás (2004), 'Measurement and explanation of socioeconomic inequality in health with longitudinal data', *Health Economics*, **13**, 1015–30.

Jones, A.M., X. Koolman and N. Rice (2004), 'Health-related attrition in the BHPS and ECHP: using inverse probability weighted estimators in nonlinear models', *Ecuity III Working Paper*, No. 18.

Kerkhofs, M. and M. Lindeboom (1997), 'Age related health dynamics and changes in labour market status', *Health Economics*, **6**, 407–23.

Lecluyse, A. (2004), 'Income-related health inequality in Belgium 1994–2001', *ECuity III Working Paper*, No. 28.

Meer, J., D.L. Millar and H.S. Rosen (2003), 'Exploring the health–wealth nexus', *Journal of Health Economics*, **22**, 713–30.

Salas, C. (2002), 'On the empirical association between poor health and low socioeconomic status at old age', *Health Economics*, **11**, 207–20.

Shorrocks, A. (1978), 'Income inequality and income mobility', *Journal of Economic Theory*, **19**, 376–93.

Smith, J.P. (1999), 'Healthy bodies and thick wallets', *Journal of Economic Perspectives*, **13**, 145–66.

Smith, J.P. (2004), 'Unravelling the SES health connection', *Institute for Fiscal Studies*, WP04/0.

Van Doorslaer, E. (1987), *Health, Knowledge and the Demand for Medical Care*, Maastricht, the Netherlands: Assen.

van Doorslaer, E. and A.M. Jones (2003), 'Inequalities in self-reported health: validation of a new approach to measurement', *Journal of Health Economics*, **22**, 61–87.

Wagstaff, A. (1986), 'The demand for health: some new empirical evidence', *Journal of Health Economics*, **5**, 195–233.

Wagstaff, A. (1993), 'The demand for health: an empirical reformulation of the Grossman model', *Health Economics*, **2**, 189–98.

Wagstaff, A. (2002), 'Inequality aversion, health inequalities and health achievement', *Journal of Health Economics*, **21**, 627–41.

Wagstaff, A., E. van Doorslaer and P. Paci (1989), 'Equity in the finance and delivery of health care: some tentative cross-country comparisons', *Oxford Review of Economic Policy*, **5**, 89–112.

Wagstaff, A., E. van Doorslaer and N. Watanabe (2003), 'On decomposing the causes of health sector inequalities with an application to malnutrition inequalities in Vietnam', *Journal of Econometrics*, **112**, 207–23.

Williams, A. and R. Cookson (2000), 'Equity in health', in A.J. Culyer and J.P. Newhouse (eds), *Handbook of Health Economics*, Amsterdam, the Netherlands: Elsevier, pp. 1863–910.

Wooldridge, J. (2002), 'Simple solutions to the initial conditions problem in dynamic, nonlinear panel data models with unobserved heterogeneity', *CEMMAP Working Paper*, CWP18/02.

3 Health and work of older workers
*Maarten Lindeboom**

1. Introduction

Health and work among older workers is not a new theme. In part it can be placed in the literature on the incentive effects of social security (see Hurd, 1990; Lumsdaine and Mitchell, 1999). An important conclusion of this literature is that financial incentives are very important for the retirement decision, but so is health. As a matter of fact, health appears to be the most important determinant of older persons' labour supply in a large number of studies. This result is, however, not undisputed. There are difficulties with the measurement of health, and empirical analyses are complicated by the fact that health and work are jointly determined. Quite a number of studies have addressed these issues, but there is still much controversy about how to measure health, how to deal with measurement errors and how to model the interrelation between health and work. This chapter aims to add to this discussion. I provide a framework for the interrelation between health and work and use this to discuss, assess and compare the most important contributions in the literature.

The literature on health and work includes the literature on health insurance and the labour market and the literature on the incentive effects of disability insurance programmes[1] (see Currie and Madrian, 1999; Gruber and Madrian, 2002; and Bound and Burkhauser, 1999 for this). This chapter focuses primarily on a part of the retirement literature that is concerned with the effect of health on work; little attention will be given to the literature on the effects of work on health. The model presented below could also be used to discuss issues involved in estimating the effect of work on health.

2. A model for health and work

The key variables of the model are the individual labour market status (S_{it}) and health status (H^*_{it}). S_{it} can be a dichotomous variable (work or not) or a more refined variable that distinguishes between various labour market states. Without being too explicit about the functional form of the labour supply model one could write:

$$\Pr(S_{it} = j | Z_{it}, H^*_{it}, \xi^j_i) = F_j(Z_{it}, H^*_{it}, \xi^j_i) \tag{3.1}$$

The vector Z includes variables like age, gender and education, but also previous labour market status,[2] previous health outcomes and measures for the incentives effects of social security, pension plans and health insurance coverage.

There is a huge literature on the effects of social security and pension plans on retirement behaviour (see Lumsdaine and Mitchell, 1999). Here it suffices to say that there is

---

*   The author wrote this chapter during his stay as the Netherlands Visiting Professor at the Department of Economics and the Institute of Social Research at the University of Michigan, Ann Arbor, USA.

a consensus that financial incentives are important for the retirement decision and that generous retirement schemes of the social security and pension system have induced many older workers to retire early, in the US, but even more so in Europe (see for example, Gruber and Wise, 1998). Gruber and Madrian (2002) conclude that health insurance is a central determinant of retirement decisions in the US.

Central for this chapter is the role of health H^*_{it}. Poor health may restrict workers in their ability to perform work tasks and may therefore induce people to retire early. Poor health may also change the value of leisure directly. The net effect is ambiguous. Moreover, health observed at advanced ages is an outcome of an individual's health endowed at birth, previous choices concerning health and human capital and shocks throughout life. This has two consequences. Firstly, work outcomes at advanced ages are also a result of previous outcomes regarding health and work. Relevant for the discussion here is that health and even elements of Z (in particular retirement opportunities and financial incentives)[3] may be endogenous for the retirement decision. Secondly, health and work are jointly determined and health should therefore be treated as an endogenous variable.

Ideally H^*_{it} should be a measure of an individual's capacity to perform his/her work (Bazzoli, 1985). In social surveys one usually has access to information on responses to questions like 'how do you rate your own health', 'does your health limit you in the kind and amount of work that you can do' and more objective indicators like the prevalence of chronic conditions, health care use, and so on. We use the generic symbol H_{it} for observed measures in surveys. The problem with subjective and objective measures of an individual's *general* health is that they are a noisy measure of the relevant work-related health. This will generally lead to a downward bias of the effect of health in (3.1).[4] In principle, a direct question regarding 'work-related health' would be perfect, but the responses to this question may be biased towards poor health for those out of work. There may be economic motives or individuals may rationalize inactivity by claiming that they can't work. *Justification bias* or *state-dependent reporting* will lead to an upward bias if not appropriately controlled for (see Bound, 1991). H^*_{it} is a latent variable and therefore researchers usually include an observed measure H_{it} in (3.1). As argued above, work and health outcomes may be generated jointly and a possible solution to this 'classical' endogeneity problem is to add a model for the impact of work on observed health:

$$H_{it} = H(S_{it}, H_{it-1}, X_{it}, \eta_i) \qquad (3.2)$$

Equation (3.2) is a health production function that relates current health to past health, possibly also current labour market status and a set of additional controls (X). The latter may include earlier labour market choices or health outcomes. η is an individual unobserved specific effect that may be correlated with the ξ^j of equation (3.1). We require an additional equation that relates unobserved health (H^*) to observed health (H) to close the model for health and work. The specifics of this 'reporting' model differ across applications and we therefore leave it implicit here.

Models for the production of health, such as Grossman (1972) and other models based on his seminal work can be used as a theoretical basis for the model above. The consequence of this interpretation is that it will be difficult to identify the causal effect of health on work and the other way around. With correlated unobserved specific heterogeneity (η and ξ^j) we require independent variation in one of the variables to assess its causal effect on the other, or some assumptions on the structure of the model.[5] Alternatively, one may employ fixed effects methods and estimate (3.1) and/or (3.2) separately.

3.   A review of the literature on the effect of health on work and the measurement of health

Early contributions of the effect of health on work

Early papers on this subject (for example, Quinn, 1977) already noted that the cross-sectional evidence regarding the impact of health on retirement should not be taken at face value. It was argued that self-reports were not reliable (for example, Lambrinos, 1981; Parsons, 1980) and that health should be treated as an endogenous variable (for example, Anderson and Burkhauser, 1985). The general response was to replace the subjective measure by measures believed to be less sensitive to justification bias, such as sickness absenteeism records (Burkhauser, 1979), observed future mortality of sample respondent (Parsons, 1980; Anderson and Burkhauser, 1985), more refined health indices derived from multiple indicators (Lambrinos, 1981; Bazzoli, 1985; Breslaw and Stelcner, 1987), or lagged health (Bazzoli, 1985). The general conclusion from these studies is that economic variables gain in importance and that health becomes less important in retirement models once more objective health measures are used. One interesting application is the study by Anderson and Burkhauser (1985). Their paper was the first to use a more objective health measure and at the same time control for the simultaneity between health and work. They found that the choice of health measure did not significantly influence the wage elasticity in the joint model, but that it did in a single equation retirement model. The health effects were much stronger when the subjective measure was used, regardless of whether the simultaneous nature of health and work was taken into account. From this one could at least conclude that endogeneity and measurement errors create different biases and that a more fundamental discussion is required to assess in what direction they work. Bound (1991) provided this.

Bound (1991) constructs a model for labour supply, wages and health. Reporting is assumed to be influenced by wages, rather than by labour market status. Bound shows that in his model each of the solutions proposed in the literature leads to different biases. The use of mortality as a proxy for true health will tend to underestimate the effect of health and overestimate the effect of financial incentives. If mortality is used to instrument subjective health, the impact of health will be correctly estimated in the labour supply model, but the effect of financial incentives will be overstated.[6] Lagged health does not account for changes in health between the time of measurement and the time of retirement and is therefore subject to the same criticism as other more objective indicators. The sign of the biases is ambiguous if a subjective health measure is included and treated as an exogenous variable. He makes two important final observations. First, external information is required to resolve the fundamental identification problem. Second, objective and subjective measures lead to biases in opposite directions and therefore one could use both to bound the actual effects of health and other variables on labour supply.

Studies on the reliability of self-reported and objective measures of health[7]

A simple test for the reliability of self-assessed measures is to compare the individual responses with objective medical reports on the individual's ability to perform work. There is evidence for justification bias or state-dependent reporting if the outcome varies across labour market states. The difficulty with this test is of course that one, in general, does not observe an accurate measure of the individual's 'true', work-related health. Alternatively, one could use an objective measure observed in the survey and relate these to the subjective responses for different groups in the labour market. In essence this is the approach taken by Kerkhofs and Lindeboom (1995), Kreider (1999) and O'Donnell (1999). They take the group of workers as a benchmark and use more objective health measures, such as observed chronic health disorders (Kreider, 1999; O'Donnell, 1999) or an outcome of a medical test score (Kerkhofs and Lindeboom, 1995) to filter out the bias relative to the group of workers.[8] The fundamental assumption is that the conditioning on objective health captures the direct effects of S on true health H^* and that therefore remaining systematic differences between subjective and objective measures across labour market states can be attributed to reporting behaviour.

The main problem with these approaches is that they will fail when there are unobservables that affect both health and work. In that case differences between workers and non-workers may reflect differences in reporting behaviour and other behavioural differences that may exist between workers and non-workers. To solve this, one needs to add a model for health.

Baker et al. (2004) use data from the Canadian National Population Health Survey (NPHS) and match these with administrative data from the Ontario Health Insurance Plan (OHIP) to assess the accuracy of self-reports on chronic conditions and objective medical records. They find that there are substantial errors in the self reports, that the errors are smaller for those in work and that the errors are larger when there is more room for personal subjective assessment. One may conclude from this that indicators for the prevalence of chronic conditions are not free of reporting errors either and that when used in labour supply models, this may lead to qualitatively similar biases when self-reports on general or work-related health are used.

Johansson and Skedinger (2004) use administrative data from the Swedish Public Employment System (PES) and survey data to examine the accuracy of health assessments. They argue that the official PES classification is also subject to systematic reporting errors. The PES has quantitative targets with respect to the placement of unemployed workers into jobs and it can more easily achieve this goal by placing individuals with low qualifications in subsidized jobs for disabled workers. They assume that the 'severity' of unemployment (measured by the accumulated months of unemployment) should have a stronger effect on the PES classification than on the individual self-report and find evidence for misreporting by PES officials.

Benitez-Silva et al. (2004) test the hypothesis of rational unbiased reporting of disability status. Their test is based on a comparison of the disability insurance administrators (SSA) award decision (a) with the measure for self-reported disability (d). The idea is that the SSA sets a standard of disability and that this standard becomes common knowledge (a social standard). If individuals exaggerate their health problems, then one would expect the rate of self-reported disability to exceed the fraction of those who are ultimately awarded benefits. It is concluded that for the US one can not reject the hypothesis that self-reported disability is an unbiased indicator of the SSA's award decision. It is interesting to contrast this finding with the study of Johansson and Skedinger (2004). Both studies compare official outcomes with self-reports, but come to different conclusions. The study of Benitez-Silva et al. (2004) takes the official outcome as the 'true' benchmark, whereas Johansson and Skedinger (2004) take the unemployment status and time spent in unemployment as the benchmark. The latter study seems to discredit the validity of the former's assumption, at least for Sweden. The results of both studies depend on untestable assumptions.[9] To 'solve' this, additional external information on the true health status is needed. The method proposed by King et al. (2004) and the application of this method by Kapteyn et al. (2004) are two interesting examples.

King et al. (2004) use vignettes to assess the relevance of systematic measurement errors in self-reports on health. The idea is that self-reports on disability may differ between different groups for health reasons and because people speak different 'languages'. Cultural differences, but also justification bias, may lead to differential reporting for a given level of true health. Health of hypothetical persons is described in vignettes and respondents' evaluations are used to identify the extent to which differences in self-reports between socio-demographic groups depend on reporting behaviour. Kapteyn et al. (2004) apply the method to Dutch and US data and find that about half of the difference between the self-reported rates of work disability in the two countries can be explained by reporting behaviour.

Empirical models for health and work

There is a set of papers that implicitly or explicitly use the conceptual model (3.1) and (3.2) of the previous section. Sickles and Taubman (1986) have a joint model for health and retirement in which health is allowed to affect work, but not the other way around.[10] They conclude that health plays a prominent role for the retirement decision. Stern (1989) constructs a latent variable model for labour supply, true health and reported health. Labour supply is influenced by unobserved true health, reported health depends on true health and labour supply, and unobserved true health depends on labour supply. It is possible to test for the endogeneity of health, but it is not possible to test separately for justification bias. Stern finds that both the subjective health measures have strong and independent effects on labour supply. He also finds that work-related health is an exogenous predictor of labour supply. Kerkhofs et al. (1999) estimate a retirement model with a range of different health constructs. These health constructs are derived from estimates of a model for health dynamics. They conclude that health and labour supply are endogenously related, that the size of the health effect crucially depends on the health measure used and that the effects of financial incentives are relatively insensitive to alternative specifications of health.

Retirement depends on financial incentives and true health in the retirement model of Dwyer and Mitchell (1998). They instrument true health with a range of more objective indicators. The idea is that one could use the objective indicators to correct for justification bias if the objective indicators are sufficiently correlated with true health. As argued previously, objective indicators of general health are likely to be imperfectly correlated with true work-related health. Moreover, this procedure only works if there are no direct effects of labour market status on the different response categories.[11] They find that health has a strong effect, but that the size of the effect varies with measures used, that self-rated health measures are exogenous and that they are not correlated with financial incentive variables. From the latter they conclude that there is no evidence in support of justification bias.[12]

Blau and Gilleskie (2001) estimate a model for transitions between labour market states and health. Their approach is to explore several alternative specifications of health, with each specification nested in the next one. The error terms of the health model and the work model (η and ξ in (3.1) and (3.2)) are stochastically related and estimated jointly. Health is found to be an important factor for the retirement decision and the most elaborate health specification gives the best fit of the model. They conclude that health and retirement models should avoid arbitrary specifications with a single measure of health and that health should be treated as an endogenous variable.

Bound et al. (1999) specify a model for transitions between work states and a dynamic model for health. Controlling for current health, past health can affect work decisions simply because it may take time to adjust working time. Moreover, with lagged health one can examine whether changes in health affect labour supply decisions, rather than the level of health. They construct a latent variable model for health that relates observed self-reported health to a set of detailed health measures. The set of detailed health measures are taken as exogenous for self-reported health. Estimates of this model are used to instrument self-reported health.[13] In this way one can correct for the endogenous nature of health, but this procedure does not necessarily eliminate the justification bias. To see this, suppose H is observed as an ordered response to K health categories:

$$H_i = k \Leftrightarrow c_{k-1} < I_i^* < c_k, \quad k = 1, \ldots, K \tag{3.3}$$

It matters whether the justification bias acts on the index function I^* or on the reporting thresholds c. The nature of the justification bias is that the individual response depends on labour market status and that it may affect different response categories in a different way. If this is the case, then one needs to model the thresholds c_l as a function of labour market states, rather then I^*. Bound et al. (1999) implicitly assume that the justification bias affects I^* (that is, that all c's shift in parallel). They find that health is important for labour supply behaviour and that respondents whose health has declined recently are more likely to leave the labour force. Lagged health affects labour force behaviour, even after controlling for current health. Disney et al. (2004) and Au et al. (2004) applied the method of Bound et al. (1999) to British and Canadian data, respectively and confirm the earlier results.

Lindeboom and Kerkhofs (2002) specify and estimate a model for work, health production and health reporting. The work model involves choices on work, or leaving the labour force via an employer-provided early retirement scheme, a disability insurance scheme or an unemployment insurance scheme. Past work choices affect health in the health production model. The health reporting model assumes that an individual's response to a health question depends on the true health H^*, but that justification bias leads to differential reporting via the response thresholds.

$$H_{it} = k \Leftrightarrow c_{k-1}(S_{it}) < H_{it}^* < c_k(S_{it}), \quad \text{for } k = 1, \ldots, K \tag{3.3'}$$

H^* is unobserved and it is assumed that it can be instrumented with an objective measure of health (H^0), and that this objective health measure acts as a sufficient statistic for the effect of work on true health:

$$E(H^*|H^0_{it}, S_{it}X^*_{it}, \eta^*_i) = E(H^*|H^0_{it}, X^*_{it}, \eta^*_i) = \alpha \cdot H^0_{it} + X^*_{it}\beta^* + v^*_i \qquad (3.4)$$

If (3.4) holds, then S should not play a role in (3.3), after that we have conditioned on H^0. If it does, then this can be interpreted as state dependent reporting.

Lindeboom and Kerkhofs (2002) estimate the health reporting model jointly with the model for work and health production. They find strong effects of financial incentives on work and that the different retirement options act as substitutes. Health has a strong effect on work choices and the biases in the self-reports are large and systematic for disability insurance recipients. The health production model reveals that increased work efforts eventually lead to worse health.

Some of the contributions above found health shocks to be important for work decisions. Some studies have focused on this in more detail.

McLellan (1998) studies how changes in health affect health insurance coverage and labour supply for middle-aged Americans. He uses detailed health information to define three broad classes of health problems: major health events that have acute and long-term functional implications; new chronic illnesses which are less likely to affect functional status today, but which may have substantial long-term implications; and accidents. He looks at determinants of these health factors and at the effects of these health factors on subsequent insurance coverage and labour supply. He finds that new health events of all kinds are more prevalent for individuals with low socioeconomic status. Major health events have large effects on retirement decisions, new chronic illnesses have a significant, though milder, effect on labour supply and accidents have no effect on labour supply.[14]

Riphahn (1999) investigates the effect of health shocks on employment and economic well-being of older German workers. She finds that a health shock increases the probability of leaving the labour force or becoming unemployed. The financial consequences of health shocks are relatively small. McGarry (2002) looks at the effect of health and changes in health on the individual's subjective probability of continued work. Health is treated as an exogenous regressor. She finds that subjective health has a strong impact on the subjective probability of continued work. The effect of subjective health remains large when more objective health measures are added to the model. She also finds that health changes are important for changes in retirement expectations.

Structural models for health and work
Estimates of the structural parameters of a behavioural model can be very powerful for the understanding of behaviour regarding labour and health, as well as for the evaluation of alternative policy proposals. Quite a few of these models have been developed and estimated in the retirement literature (for references see for example, Heyma, 2004). The contributions in the field of health and work are rare. Notable exceptions are Sickles and Yazbeck (1998) and Bound et al. (2005).

Sickles and Yazbeck (1998) specify and structurally estimate a model for the demand for leisure and the production of health for older males. They use a stochastic dynamic programming framework, where individuals are assumed to maximize lifetime utility subject to budget and time constraints and a health production function. Hours of leisure and levels of consumption of health-related and health-neutral goods and services are the choice variables in the model. They use an index for general health, derived from a range of subjective and objective health measures. They find that health positively influences the demand for leisure and that health-related consumption and leisure improve health.

The paper by Bound et al. (2005) looks at the interrelation between health, financial resources and labour supply for older men. The labour choices are staying in the career job, taking a bridge job, leaving the labour market and applying for disability insurance, and leaving the labour market and not applying for disability insurance. Latent true health depends on a range of detailed health indicators. As in Bound et al. (1999) it is assumed that the detailed health measures are strictly exogenous with respect to labour market choices and that the justification bias acts additively on the index function. Solving the dynamic programming model requires knowledge of the future path of the state variables, including the detailed health measures. It is assumed that these are not affected by labour market choices and that they remain constant. The authors find that both health and economic resources play an important role. Those in good health are unlikely to retire, unless their resources allow them to do so, but an individual in poor health is more likely to retire, regardless of available financial resources.

4.   Discussion and conclusions

The discussion on the interrelation between health and work among older workers is not over. Measurement issues remain important. Recent work suggests that we still have to learn more about the validity of health measures and that external information, from, for instance, vignettes can be very useful. Moreover, recent studies suggest that a measure should be used that acknowledges the different dimensions of health. Some of the studies suggested that, at later ages, changes in health become more important for work. Sudden, unanticipated, changes in health and variation in the timing of the occurrence of the health event may help in identifying the causal effect of health on work.[15]

This chapter has focused primarily on the effect of health on work at later ages. Recent research (Adams et al., 2003; Smith, 2004) suggests that this is the most important mechanism driving the association at later ages. There are, however, also studies that find that work outcomes at later ages are important for health (see for example, Kerkhofs and Lindeboom, 1997; Charles, 2002). Still much can be learned in this area. Health observed at later ages is the result of life cycle choices concerning work and health, and past health will influence current health. There is a growing literature that focuses on the effect of early life outcomes on later health and socioeconomic status (see for instance the literature reviewed in Case et al., 2005). Early life conditions are found to be very important for health and socioeconomic status at later ages. This is important for the interpretation of the effects found in the studies listed above and for public policy in an ageing society.

Notes

1.   Somewhat further related is the literature on the cross population comparability of health measures in social surveys. Here the issue is whether different (cultural) groups use different reference points when they respond to the same survey question (see King et al., 2004). We will discuss related issues when we focus on the validity of self-reports concerning the ability to work.

2. In this case the model concerns transitions between labour market states.
3. This would imply (for instance) that people with a great preference for leisure sort themselves into jobs that offer attractive retirement options. This relates to the discussion of the effect of health insurance (Gruber and Madrian, 2002; Currie and Madrian, 1999).
4. The attentuation bias will occur when the measurement error is not systematic.
5. An example of the former is an exogenous change in health, due to an unforeseen shock.
6. Note, once more, that this holds in this model where health reporting depends on wages. This result does not hold, for instance, in a model where health reporting depends on an individual's labour market status (Kerkhofs and Lindeboom, 1995).
7. We focus on the validity of self-reports concerning the ability to work. There is a literature on the cross-population comparability of health measures in social surveys. Here the issue is whether different (cultural) groups use different reference points when they respond to the same survey question (see King et al., 2004).
8. The idea is that workers have no incentives to report with error.
9. This also holds for the papers by Kerkhofs and Lindeboom (1995), Kreider (1999) and O'Donnell (1999).
10. They substitute H for H^* in (3.1) and take a reduced form specification for (3.2).
11. For this see below the discussion of Bound et al. (1999).
12. In their model, justification depends on the financial rewards, rather then on labour market status.
13. Dwyer and Mitchell (1998) use the same procedure.
14. We only list the most important results for this review. For more details on other findings we refer to McLellan (1998).
15. See for instance the paper by Abbring and van den Berg (2003), which deals with treatment effects in event history models.

References

Aarts, L.J.M. and Ph.R. de Jong (1992), *Economic Aspects of Disability Behavior*, Amsterdam: North-Holland.
Abbring, J.H. and G.J. van den Berg (2003), 'The nonparametric identification of treatment effects in duration models', *Econometrica*, **71**, 1491–517.
Adams, P., M. Hurd, D. McFadden, A. Merril and T. Ribeiro (2003), 'Healthy, Wealthy and Wise? Tests for direct causal paths between health and socio-economic status', *Journal of Econometrics*, **112**, 3–56.
Anderson, K.H. and R.V. Burkhauser (1985), 'The retirement–health nexus: A new measure of an old puzzle', *Journal of Human Resources*, **20**, 315–30.
Au, D., T. Crossley and M.W. Schellhorn (2004), 'The effect of health changes and long-term health on the work activity of older Canadians', IZA working paper 1281.
Baker, M., M. Stabile and C. Deri (2004), 'What do self-reported, objective, measures of health measure?', *Journal of Human Resources*, **39**(4), 1067–93.
Bazzoli, G. (1985), 'The early retirement decision: New empirical evidence on the influence of health', *Journal of Human Resources*, **20**, 214–34.
Benitez-Silva, H., M. Buschinski, H.M. Chan, S. Cheidvasser and J. Rust (2004), 'How large is the bias in self-reported disability?', *Journal of Applied Econometrics*, **19**(6), 649–70.
Blau, D. and D. Gilleskie (2001), 'The effect of health on employment transitions of older men', in S. Polacheck (ed.), *Worker Well-Being in a Changing Labor Market*, Amsterdam: JAI Press, pp. 35–65.
Bound, J. (1991), 'Self reported versus objective measures of health in retirement models', *Journal of Human Resources*, **26**, 107–37.
Bound, J. and R.V. Burkhauser (1999), 'Economic analysis on transfer programs targeted on people with disabilities', in O. Ashenfelter and D. Card (eds), *Handbook of Labor Economics*, vol. 3c, pp. 3417–528, Amsterdam: North-Holland, Elsevier.
Bound, J., M. Stinebrickner, T.R. and T. Waidmann (2005), 'Health, financial resources and the work decisions of older men', working paper, Department of Economics, University of Michigan.
Bound, J., M. Schoenbaum, T.R. Stinebrickner and T. Waidmann (1999), 'The dynamic effects of health on the labor force transitions of older workers', *Labour Economics*, **6**(2), 179–202.
Breslaw J. and M. Stelcner (1987), 'The effect of health on the labor force behavior of elderly in Canada', *Journal of Human Resources*, **22**(4), 490–517.
Burkhauser, R.V. (1979), 'The pension acceptance decision of older workers', *Journal of Human Resources*, **14**, 63–75.
Case, A., A. Fertig and C. Paxson (2005), 'The lasting impact of childhood health and circumstance', *Journal of Health Economics*, **24**(2), March, 365–89.
Charles, K. (2002), 'Is retirement depressing?: labor force inactivity and psychological well-being in later life', NBER working paper, 9033.

Currie, J. and B. Madrian (1999), 'Health, health insurance and the labor market', in O. Ashenfelter and D. Card (eds), *Handbook of Labor Economics*, vol. 3c, pp. 3309–416, Amsterdam: Elsevier, North-Holland.

Disney, R., C. Emmerson and M. Wakefield (2004), 'Ill health and retirement in Britain: A panel data-based analysis', IFS Working paper.

Dwyer, D. and O. Mitchell (1998), 'Health problems as determinants of retirement: are self-rated measures endogenous?', *Journal of Health Economics*, **18**, 173–93.

Grossmann M. (1972), 'On the concept of health capital and the demand for health', *Journal of Political Economy*, **82**, 223–55.

Gruber, J. and B. Madrian (2002), 'Health insurance, labor supply and job mobility: a critical review of the literature', NBER working paper, 8817.

Gruber, J. and D. Wise (1998), 'Social security and retirement: an international comparison', *The American Economic Review*, papers and proceedings of 110th Annual meeting of the American Economic Association, **88**(2), 158–63.

Heyma, A. (2004), 'A structural dynamic analysis of retirement behavior in the Netherlands', *Journal of Applied Econometrics*, **19**(6), 739–59.

Hurd, M. (1990), 'Research on the elderly: economic status, retirement, and consumption and savings', *Journal of Economic Literature*, **28**, 565–637.

Johansson, P. and P. Skedinger (2004), 'On the validity of objective measures of disability: evidence from a sample of Swedish jobseekers', IFAU working paper.

Kapteyn, A., J. Smith and A. van Soest (2004), 'Self reported work disability in the US and the Netherlands', RAND working paper WR-206.

Kerkhofs, M.J.M. and M. Lindeboom (1995), 'Subjective health measures and state dependent reporting errors', *Health Economics*, **4**, 221–35.

Kerkhofs, M.J.M. and M. Lindeboom (1997), 'Age related health dynamics and changes in labor market status', *Health Economics*, **6**, 407–24.

Kerkhofs, M.J.M., M. Lindeboom and J. Theeuwes (1999), 'Retirement financial incentives and health', *Labour Economics*, **6**, 203–27.

King, G., J. Murray, J. Salomon and A. Tandon (2004), 'Enhancing the validity and cross cultural comparability of measurement in survey research', *American Political Science Review*, **98**(1), 567–83.

Kreider, B. (1999), 'Latent work disability and reporting bias', *Journal of Human Resources*, **34**(4), 734–69.

Lambrinos, J. (1981), 'Health: a source of bias in labor supply models', *Review of Economics and Statistics*, **63**(2), 206–12.

Lindeboom, M. and M. Kerkhofs (2002), 'Health and work of the elderly: subjective health measures, reporting errors and the endogenous relationship between health and work', Tinbergen Institute working paper, 02-025/3.

Lumsdaine, R.L. and O.S. Mitchell (1999), 'New developments in the economic analysis of retirement', in O. Ashenfelter and D. Card (eds), *Handbook of Labor Economics*, 3(49), 3261–307.

McGarry, K. (2002), 'Health and retirement: do changes in health affect retirement expectations?', NBER working paper, 9317.

McLellan, M. (1998), 'Health events, health insurance and labor supply: evidence from the health and retirement survey', in D. Wise (ed.), *Frontiers in the Economics of Aging*, Chicago, University of Chicago Press, pp. 301–49.

O'Donnell, O. (1999), 'Employment, disability and work incapacity', working paper, University of Kent.

Parsons, D. (1980), 'The decline in male labor force participation', *Journal of Political Economy*, **88**, 117–34.

Quinn, J. (1977), 'Microeconomic determinants of early retirement: a cross sectional view of white married men', *Journal of Human Resources*, **12**, 329–46.

Riphahn, R. (1999), 'Income and employment effects of health shocks – a test case for the German welfare state', *Journal of Population Economics*, **12**(3), 363–89.

Sickles, R.C. and P. Taubman (1986), 'An analysis of the health and retirement status of the elderly', *Econometrica*, **54**, 1339–56.

Sickles, R.C. and A. Yazbeck (1998), 'On the dynamics of demand for leisure and the production of health', *Journal of Business and Economic Statistics*, **16**(2), 187–97.

Smith, J. (2004), 'Unraveling the SES Health Connection', IFS working paper, WP04/02.

Stern, S. (1989), 'Measuring the effect of disability on labor force participation', *Journal of Human Resources*, **24**, 361–95.

4 Using observational data to identify the causal effects of health-related behaviour
M. Christopher Auld

1. Introduction

The effect on health of behaviours such as smoking, drinking, illicit drug use, over-eating and exercise are of substantial interest to both academics and policy-makers. However, many of the results in the literature documenting how such behaviours affect health are based on correlations or partial correlations between behaviour and health. Because these correlations are almost always calculated from observational data, the health-related behaviours are not randomly assigned and therefore these correlations generally do not recover the magnitude or possibly even the sign of the underlying causal effect of interest. The research challenge then hinges on inferring causation from such observed patterns of behaviour and health.

Consider an example. Much of the literature on the effect of smoking on health considers a cross-section of the population consisting of information on smoking status and some measure of health along with other socio-demographic variables. Multivariate regression or a similar method is employed to estimate how much the health of smokers differs on average from the health of non-smokers, other observed factors being equal. This correlation can only be interpreted as an estimate of the causal effect of smoking on health under very restrictive and implausible assumptions: we would require that variation in health status unrelated to smoking is uncorrelated with variation in smoking status and that variation in health does not cause changes in smoking status. Indeed, the tobacco industry has argued that individuals who are genetically predisposed to smoke may also be genetically predisposed to poor health such that the correlation between poor health and smoking need not be attributed to causation from smoking to health. To recover the causal effect of interest (and empirically assess the credibility of such arguments), more complex and structured statistical models than partial correlations need to be employed.

This chapter focuses on the method of instrumental variables, the most common method used by health economists to infer causation in such situations. The chapter sketches classical results, considers recent developments on small-sample properties and on interpretation and estimation in the presence of heterogeneity in effects, and closes with discussion of two examples drawn from the health economics literature.

2. Instrumental variables estimation of causal effects

Suppose a researcher has access to a random sample of observations on a measure of health denoted H, a vector of socio-demographic characteristics X, and a measure of a health-related behaviour denoted D. For example, D may indicate the individual is a smoker, H may be a self-reported subjective health measure, and X may contain variables indicating age, ethnicity, sex and other such controls. The research question centres on the causal effect of the behaviour on health, by which we mean: if a given individual is induced to change behaviour exogenously, how will health be affected? (See Pearl, 2000 for an overview of the literature on causation.)

Classical instrumental variables estimation

The canonical econometric approach to estimating the effect of D on a measure of health H begins by specifying the conditional mean of H given D and X, commonly a linear specification such as:

$$H_i = X_i\beta + \delta D_i + u_i \tag{4.1}$$

where i indexes individuals, β is a vector of parameters and u_i is a zero-mean disturbance term. Interest generally centres on estimation of δ, the causal effect of the behaviour D on health, holding observed (X) and unobserved (u) determinants of health constant. The fundamental problem arising from the use of observational data is:

$$E(u_i|X_i, D_i)$$

generally depends on D_i (and possibly X_i). That is, even after conditioning on observed characteristics, unobserved determinants of health u generally vary with the health behaviour D. This covariance arises either because changes in health lead to changes in the behaviour or because unobserved characteristics affect both the behaviour and health.

Suppose for example that individuals in poor health are more likely to quit smoking, that is that there is *reverse causation* in this context. This mechanism induces positive covariance between u and D and might lead a researcher to underestimate the deleterious effects of smoking on health. To see this, consider the extreme case where only healthy people choose to smoke, and those made unhealthy for any reason, including smoking, choose to quit. In a cross-section a researcher would observe that healthy people tend to be smokers and may falsely conclude that smoking is beneficial for health! In addition, it is likely that there are determinants of both health and smoking which are not observed in the dataset, for example, individuals who heavily discount future outcomes may both tend to smoke and fail to engage in health-promoting behaviours. This *unobserved heterogeneity* across individuals implies that the correlation between behaviour and health, even after holding other factors X constant, does not generally recover the causal effect of the behaviour on health. The estimate of δ generated by ordinary least squares estimation of equations such as (4.1) generally tells us little or nothing about the causal effect of the behaviour on health.

Suppose the researcher observes a variable Z which is, according to economic theory or other compelling reasoning, correlated with the behaviour D after conditioning on X but uncorrelated with health after conditioning on both D and X. It is then possible to obtain a consistent estimator of δ. Formally, given that (X, Z) is of full rank, sufficient conditions for asymptotic identification are:

$$E[u|X, Z] = 0$$

$$\operatorname*{plim}_{n\to\infty} n^{-1}Z'D \neq 0 \tag{4.2}$$

where n is the sample size, E is the expectation operator, and plim denotes the probability limit operator. The first condition formalizes the requirement that the excluded instrument Z only affects the outcome y through its effect on D. The second condition requires that the instrument and endogenous regressor are asymptotically correlated. Intuitively, a change in Z changes the behaviour D without directly changing health, so it is *as if* changes in Z comprise randomized experiments: D is not randomly assigned, but Z is randomized with respect to H (conditional on X) and Z affects D. The researcher can proceed under these conditions to estimate causal effects despite the problems of reverse causation or unobserved heterogeneity inherent to observational data, because under these conditions changes in Z form a *quasi-experiment* and the behaviour is *quasi-randomized*. The linear instrumental variables estimate of the causal effect of D on H under model (4.1) is:

$$\hat{\delta}_{IV} = (\overline{D}'\,\overline{D})^{-1}\overline{D}'y \tag{4.3}$$

where

$$\overline{D} = \hat{D} - X(X'X)^{-1}X'\hat{D} \tag{4.4}$$

and $\hat{D}$ denotes the predicted values from the regression of D on (X, Z). The same expression is valid in the case where the model is *overidentified* by the use of more than one instrumental variable for D. Under conditions (4.2) and relatively weak regularity conditions $\hat{\delta}_{IV}$ is consistent and asymptotically normal,

$$\hat{\delta} \overset{a}{\sim} N[\delta, \sigma_0^2(\overline{D}'\overline{D})^{-1}] \tag{4.5}$$

where σ_0^2 is the variance of u_i, such that hypothesis testing can be carried out in a straightforward manner. More efficient estimates may be obtained in some cases by accounting for heteroscedasticity or serial correlation, see Davidson and MacKinnon (2004a, chapter 9).

The difficulty with instrumental variables estimation is not, however, deriving the efficient estimator in the presence of non-spherical disturbances or other such relatively mundane specification issues. Rather, the difficulty lies in finding instruments which are both *relevant* and *excludable*, that is, variables which both explain substantial variation in the behaviour D and which are only correlated with health because they are correlated with the behaviour. Since such variables are often difficult to find, the causal effect of behaviour on health remains a challenging research question. Other chapters in this Companion discuss use of instrumental variables in particular health-related applications. See also Angrist and Krueger (2001) for a survey of research exploiting natural experiments in economics more broadly.

Recent literature on finite-sample properties
It is common in econometrics to invoke asymptotic approximations even with fairly small sample sizes. Instrumental variables estimates are, however, often badly behaved even in surprisingly large samples, particularly if the excluded instruments (in the notation above, the variables in Z) do not explain much variation in the exogenous regressors. In these

cases asymptotic distributions such as (4.5) may be very poor approximations to the sampling distribution of the estimator.

First, instrumental variable estimates are generally not unbiased even when the model is correctly specified. Models which are exactly identified yield estimates with an infinite first moment, that is, it will not be uncommon to draw estimates which are far away from the population parameter. Overidentified models generally have finite first moments but the estimates will not generally be centred on the population value. Buse (1992) shows the instrumental variables estimates are biased in the same direction as the OLS estimates and that the finite sample bias increases with the degree of overidentification.

Second, if the excluded instruments do not explain substantial variation in the endogenous regressors – the instruments are weak – instrumental variables estimates may exhibit atrocious finite sample properties. Even very small correlation between the instruments and the error term in the equation of interest may cause very large inconsistencies (Bound, Jaeger and Baker, 1995). The asymptotic inconsistency of the instrumental variables estimate of δ relative to ordinary least squares is:

$$\plim_{n\to\infty} \frac{\hat{\delta}_{IV} - \delta}{\hat{\delta}_{OLS} - \delta} = \frac{1}{R^2} \frac{Cov(\bar{D}, u)}{Cov(\tilde{D}, u)} \tag{4.6}$$

where $\tilde{D} = D - X'(X'X)^{-1}X'D$ is the variation in D not attributable to X and R^2 is the population R^2 resulting from regression of $\tilde{D}$ on Z. That is, if after netting out the effect of X the excluded instruments Z explain little variation in D, any inconsistency resulting from invalid exclusion restrictions will be greatly exacerbated and the OLS estimate may be more accurate even if the treatment is highly correlated with the disturbance term.

Third, even if the instruments are truly exogenous such that the instrumental variables estimates are consistent, weak instruments nonetheless lead to finite sample distributions of the estimators which are vastly different from their asymptotic distributions: inference and confidence intervals based on asymptotics such as (4.5) may be very misleading. See Stock, Wright and Yogo (2002) for a survey of this literature. Alternate estimators, such as limited information maximum likelihood (LIML) or the jackknife instrumental variables estimator (JIVE) have been proposed as more well-behaved in the presence of weak instruments (for example, Blomquist and Dahlberg, 1999), but see Davidson and MacKinnon (2004b) for a critique of this proposal.

Instrumental variables problems in the health economics literature
Since health economists commonly use instrumental variables methods with observational data, problems inherent to instrumental variables estimation frequently arise in the health economics literature. Three papers drawing attention to problems arising from the use of instrumental variables methods are briefly discussed in this section.

Dranove and Wehner (1994) conducted an 'anti-test' of a common procedure to measure supplier-induced demand. They regressed number of childbirths by region on socioeconomic control variables and number of obstetricians, instrumenting number of obstetricians with variables such as hotel receipts argued in the literature to affect physician supply. They demonstrated that this procedure leads to the nonsensical conclusion that obstetricians induce demand for childbirths, and place the blame on invalid exclusion restrictions.

Auld and Grootendorst (2004) show that instrumental variables estimates of the estimable rational addiction model are severely biased towards finding evidence of rational addiction when time-series data are used. In an exercise similar in spirit to that of Dranove and Wehner (1994), they first show that estimation of the model using presumably non-addictive commodities such as milk, yields apparent evidence of addiction. They show through Monte Carlo simulation that finite-sample instrumental variables bias could explain such results.

Rashad and Kaestner (2004) argue that instrumental variables estimates of the effect of substance abuse on risky sexual behaviour are unconvincing because the instruments researchers have chosen are either weakly correlated with the risky behaviour or because the instruments are not validly excluded from the equation of interest.

3.   Estimation in the presence of heterogeneous effects
Relatively recently the econometrics literature has devoted considerable attention to a fundamental conceptual difficulty with instrumental variables estimation as discussed above. In our context, the problem arises when we acknowledge that different people will experience different effects on health from a given behaviour. If equation (4.1) is modified to allow the effect of D on H to vary across individuals:

$$H_i = X_i \beta + \delta_i D_i + u_i \tag{4.7}$$

observe that it is no longer sensible to discuss 'the' effect of the behaviour on health: every individual generally experiences a different effect, and the estimation problem centres on recovering properties of the distribution of δ_i, often certain conditional moments, as discussed below.

The interpretation of instrumental variables estimates
When the parameter of interest is unstable, interpretation of classical instrumental variables of equations such as (4.1) is problematic. Imbens and Angrist (1994) demonstrate that the instrumental variables estimator does not generally recover the mean of δ_i in the population or in the subpopulation who engage in the behaviour. Rather the IV estimator converges to a weighted average of causal effects where the weights are larger for respondents who vary the behaviour the most in response to changes in the instruments. In particular, if the instrument Z takes G different values, then under fairly general conditions the estimate of 'the' causal effect of D on H using Z as an instrument can be shown to converge to:

$$\hat{\delta}_{IV} \to \sum_{g=1}^{G} \lambda_g \delta_g \tag{4.8}$$

where δ_g is the local average causal effect of D on H in subpopulation g and the λ's are weights which depend on how much D varies with Z in subpopulation g. In stark contrast to the homogeneous case, the instrumental variables estimate admits no straightforward interpretation. Instrumental variables estimates must be interpreted carefully when response is heterogeneous because two researchers who both estimate correctly specified models and who both have access to genuinely quasi-randomized data will generally not estimate the same causal effect, even on average, if they use different instruments.

Suppose for example the health behaviour under study is smoking, and smoking is instrumented with the price of a pack of cigarettes. The argument above implies that the instrumental variables estimate of the effect of smoking is a weighted average of effects where the weights depend on the demand elasticity of smoking – individuals who present perfectly price inelastic demands, for example, contribute nothing to the estimate asymptotically. Consider a second related example: suppose instead of price the researcher uses an indicator for the event that the respondent's father smokes as an instrument for the respondent's smoking status. Then the result of Imbens and Angrist implies the instrumental variables estimate may be cleanly interpreted as the average causal effect of smoking on health among individuals who would smoke if their father smokes, but who would not otherwise smoke. A second researcher who used, say, the price of tobacco as an instrument would not generally recover the same estimate of the effect of smoking on health, even assuming the price of tobacco is also a valid instrument.

Concepts of average and marginal causal effects
In light of this problem researchers attempt to estimate some well-defined average effect, concepts of which are discussed recently by Imbens and Angrist (1994), Angrist, Imbens and Rubin (1996), Heckman (1997) and Aakvik, Heckman and Vytlacil (2005) among others. See Wooldridge (2002) chapter 18 for a textbook presentation and Manning (2004) for a simple exposition of estimation of heterogeneous causal effects. Heckman, Urzua and Vytlacil (2005) discuss classical and semi-parametric estimation of models with heterogeneous causal effects. In this section we consider expressions for the case where the 'treatment' D is binary, for example 'smoke' or 'does not smoke'.

The *average treatment effect* in the population for an individual with characteristics X_i is given by:

$$E[\delta_i|X_i] \tag{4.9}$$

and measures the effect of treatment on a randomly selected individual with characteristics X_i. This effect may be that which researchers commonly have in mind when they attempt to estimate 'the' effect of treatment. Alternatively a researcher may attempt to recover:

$$E[\delta_i|X_i, D_i = 1] \tag{4.10}$$

the effect of *treatment on the treated* for an individual with characteristics X_i; it measures the average effect of the behaviour on those who actually engage in the behaviour. Neither of these two effects is generally recovered by application of the instrumental variables estimator (4.3) (Heckman, 1997).

Economists are usually concerned with *marginal* causal effects: it is often irrelevant for economic calculations how the *average* person would respond to a change, rather what is important is how people near the margin are likely to change behaviour in response to changes in policy or other changes in incentives. These marginal causal effects may be explicitly characterized and estimated. The *local average treatment effect* (LATE) for an individual with characteristics X_i who would engage in behaviour D if the instruments were set to $Z = Z'$ but would not engage in the behaviour if the instruments were set to $Z = Z''$ is given by:

$$E[\delta_i | X_i, D(Z') = 1, D(Z'') = 0] \tag{4.11}$$

Notice that LATE is defined with respect to variation in a given instrument. Heckman and Vytlacil (2005) demonstrate that all of the above effects can be shown to be averages of the *marginal treatment effect* for an individual with characteristics X_i:

$$E[\delta_i | X_i, \varepsilon_i]$$

where ε_i is individual i's unobserved propensity to be treated.

These various causal effects only coincide if the conditioning on unobserved propensity to be 'treated' is irrelevant, which is only the case if selection into treatment is random with respect to the effect of treatment (Heckman, 1997). Since health economists rarely have reason to believe that the health impact of some behaviour will not affect an individual's propensity to engage in that behaviour, carefully considering underlying behavioural assumptions when developing and estimating empirical health models is critical.

Examples of estimating distributions of causal effects in health economics
Aakvik et al. (2003) estimated treatment effects on health for back pain patients using observational data from a low-key social insurance reform in Norway. Distance to the nearest hospital was used as an instrument in estimating different treatment effects. They find a positive effect of treatment of around six percentage points on the probability of leaving the sickness benefits scheme after allowing for selection effects and full heterogeneity in treatment effects. Based on simulations they find that there are sound arguments for expanding the multidisciplinary outpatient programme for treating back pain patients.

Auld (2005) estimates the effect of starting daily smoking behaviour early on the probability of smoking later in life. Here the health outcome H is an indicator for daily smoking in late adolescence and the 'treatment' D is daily smoking at or before age 14. The key question for policy purposes is not how much a randomly selected youth's smoking behaviour would be changed by early initiation but rather how much the smoking behaviour of youths likely to change early initiation status due to changes in policy is affected by early initiation. Tobacco prices at age 14 act as instruments. The results suggest that exogenously inducing a randomly selected youth to smoke by age 14 greatly increases the chances of smoking later in life. However, youths near the margin are much less affected by early initiation. Figure 4.1 illustrates the possibly dramatic differences between average and marginal causal effects: the figure shows the distribution (induced by variation in covariates) of the average effect of early initiation on subsequent

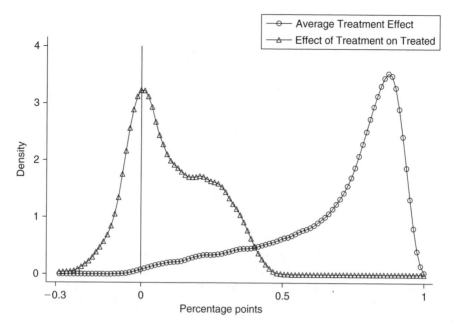

Note: Kernel density estimates of distributions of the Average Treatment Effect (ATE) and effect of Treatment on the Treated (TT) where the 'treatment' is early initiation into daily smoking and the outcome is subsequent smoking behaviour. The *x*-axis measures the percentage point increase in probability of late adolescent smoking caused by early initiation into smoking.

Source: Auld (2005).

Figure 4.1   Heterogeneous causal effect estimates

smoking probability and the distribution of the effect in the subpopulation of youths who did initiate early.

4.   Conclusions

Estimating the causal effect on health of behaviours such as substance abuse or exercise is difficult because these behaviours are rarely subject to experimental manipulation. Researchers must then use observational data, which poses the inherent challenges stemming from 'reverse' causation from health to behaviour and unobserved determinants of both health and behaviour confounding the relationship.

Health economists have most often chosen the method of instrumental variables to estimate causal relationships in the presence of these problems. In this chapter we have presented the reasoning underlying this method and emphasized recent literature documenting the conceptual and practical difficulties with this method. The most challenging problem is finding valid instruments, variables correlated with the behaviour but which only affect health through the behaviour under analysis. Recent literature shows that even small correlations between the proposed instruments and health can lead to very misleading estimates, and the instruments often used in the health economics literature are often subject to this criticism. Further, if the instruments are only weakly correlated with the behaviour, the estimator will have very poor finite sample properties and, again, health economists are often faced with the unpalatable prospect of trying to infer causation using such instruments.

The conceptual difficulty with classical instrumental variables estimation is revealed by the superficially innocuous observation that different people experience different health effects of the same behaviour. Recent econometric results demonstrate that canonical instrumental variables estimates are difficult to interpret once we allow for such heterogeneity in the causal effect of interest, generally only recovering a weighted average of causal effects rather than an easily interpreted average causal effect. Perhaps more troubling, two researchers who use the same data but different instruments will generally recover different estimates of 'the' causal effect of interest, even on average and even assuming each uses strong instruments which are validly excluded from the equation of interest.

Identifying causation from behaviour to health in future research hinges on finding quasi-experiments induced by nature or governments which involve large changes in behaviour without directly affecting health. Even when such experiments are exploited, researchers must carefully interpret instrumental variables estimates in the presence of heterogeneous effects or, preferably, employ models which explicitly characterize both the distribution of causal effects and the underlying behavioural model.

References

Aakvik, A., J. Heckman and E. Vytlacil (2005), 'Estimating treatment effects for discrete outcomes when responses to treatment vary: an application to Norwegian vocational rehabilitation programs', *Journal of Econometrics*, **125**, 15–51.

Aakvik A., T.H. Holmas and E. Kjerstad (2003), 'A low-key social insurance reform-effects of multidisciplinary outpatient treatment for back pain patients in Norway', *Journal of Health Economics*, **22**(5), 747–62.

Angrist, J. and G. Imbens (1994), 'Identification and estimation of local average treatment effects', *Econometrica*, **62**, 467–75.

Angrist, J. and A. Krueger (2001), 'Instrumental variables and the search for identification: From supply and demand to natural experiments', *Journal of Economic Perspectives*, **15**(4), 69–85.

Angrist, J., G. Imbens and D. Rubin (1996), 'Identification of causal effects using instrumental variables', *Journal of the American Statistical Association*, **91**, 444–55.

Auld, M.C. (2005), 'Causal effect of early initiation on adolescent smoking patterns', *Canadian Journal of Economics*, **38**(3), 709–34.

Auld, M.C. and P. Grootendorst (2004), 'An empirical analysis of milk addiction', *Journal of Health Economics*, **23**(6), 1117–35.

Blomquist, S. and M. Dahlberg (1999), 'Small sample properties of LIML and jackknife IV estimators: Experiments with weak instruments', *Journal of Applied Econometrics*, **14**, 69–88.

Bound, J., D. Jaeger and R. Baker (1995), 'Problems with instrumental variables estimation when the correlation between the instruments and endogenous regressors is weak', *Journal of the American Statistical Association*, **90**, 443–50.

Buse, A. (1992), 'The bias of instrumental variables estimators', *Econometrica*, **60**, 173–80.

Davidson, R. and J. MacKinnon (2004a), *Econometric Theory and Methods*, Oxford: Oxford University Press.

Davidson, R. and J. MacKinnon (2004b), 'The case against JIVE', working paper, Queen's University at Kingston.

Dranove, D. and P. Wehner (1994), 'Physician-induced demand for childbirths', *Journal of Health Economics*, **13**, 31–60.

Heckman, J. (1997), 'Instrumental variables: A study of implicit behavioral assumptions used in making program evaluations', *Journal of Human Resources*, **32**, 441–62.

Heckman, J. and E. Vytlacil (2005), 'Structural equations, treatment effects and econometric policy evaluation', *Econometrica*, **73**(3), 669–738.

Heckman, J., S. Urza and E. Vytlacil (2004), 'Understanding instrumental variables in models with essential heterogeneity', working paper, University of Chicago.

Imbens, G. and J. Angrist (1994), 'Identification and estimation of local average treatment effects', *Econometrica*, **62**(2), 467–76.

Manning, A. (2004), 'Instrumental variables for binary treatments with heterogeneous treatment effects: A simple exposition', *Contributions to Economic Analysis and Policy*.

Pearl, J. (2000), *Causality*, Cambridge: Cambridge University Press.

Rashad, I. and R. Kaestner (2004), 'Teenage sex, drugs and alcohol use: problems identifying the cause of risky behaviors', *Journal of Health Economics*, **23**(3), 493–504.

Stock, J.H., J.H. Wright and M. Yogo (2002), 'A survey of weak instruments and weak identification in generalized method of moments', *Journal of Business and Economic Statistics*, **20**, 518–29.

Wooldridge, J. (2002), *Econometric Analysis of Cross Section and Panel Data*, Cambridge, MA: MIT Press.

5 Economics of public health interventions for children in developing countries
David Bishai and Taghreed Adam

1. Introduction

We begin by defining what is meant by 'public health' and why public health interventions for children in developing countries deserve so much attention. After developing a theoretical framework we summarize the astounding accomplishments attributable to public health interventions for children over the last century. Finally we highlight some of the current issues in technology assessment in this area.

2. Theoretical framework

Individual vs. public interventions

Much of health economics focuses on the commodity of personal medical care in order to explore why markets for medical care function so dramatically differently from those for other commodities (Arrow, 1963; Rice, 1998). Yet it has long been understood that personal medical care played a relatively minor role in the 20th century mortality transition (McKeown, 1976). Improvements in the economic standard of living and especially in public health played a dominant role in the decline of child mortality in Europe historically and continue to dominate the decline of child mortality in developing countries (Jamison et al., 2004; Preston, 1975). *Public health* interventions are distinguished from personal medical care by two features: they are organized and implemented for entire populations; they require publicly coordinated financing. Public health interventions are not necessarily all preventive interventions. Some efforts in public health involve screening large populations in search of sick individuals who can be given treatment. Public health practice also includes strategic, publicly coordinated policy improvements that improve the availability of personal medical services to a population.

With this definition, it is clear that the tools of public economics can contribute to our understanding of public health interventions. Weisbrod (1960) and later Lave (1980) made important contributions to public health economics but there has been surprisingly little scholarship in this area in recent years. One extremely useful model of public health depicts its role in the household production of health. In this model there are three factors in the production of personal health, H: inputs from the physical environment, E; 'public health' inputs from government, Z; and private inputs from households, X (Mokyr, 1993).

$$H_{ij} = E + [G(B_j - \phi_j) \times Z] + [F(A_j - \varepsilon_{ij}) \times X_{ij}] \qquad (5.1)$$

where:
E is environment

G is the quality of government health production

B_j is best available public health technology in area j

ϕ_j is gap between best and actual in area j

Z is goods purchased by government

F is the quality of household health production

A_j is best available household technology in area j

ε_{ij} is gap between best and actual by i-th household in area j

X_{ij} is health inputs purchased by household i in area j.

The Mokyr production function highlights two very important features of public health. First because the household health inputs have opportunity costs, economic theory predicts possible 'crowd out' – reductions in household health investments if either government policies or environmental changes make household investments less necessary to maintain health. For example, residents of the Southeast US no longer invest in bed nets to control malaria, although they did 100 years ago when malaria was more prevalent. The second notable feature of the Mokyr model is its attention to the potential inefficiencies from deploying technologies that fall short of best practices. Given a decision to deploy scarce public resources, a public health planner can increase the impact of these resources by reducing the gap between best and current practice. Hence efforts in technology assessment in public health need to include not just the level of resources (Z) but also the quality of those resources adjusting for likely shortcomings from best practice (ϕ_j).

Market failures

Like other public goods, public health interventions are subject to potential under-provision, due to free-rider effects. The benefits of some (but not all) public health interventions are 'non-rival' in that benefits by one do not diminish the benefits by others; they are usually 'non-excludable', meaning it is impractical to set up barriers to exclude non-contributors. The properties of non-rivalry and non-excludability characterize public health interventions as 'public goods'. Classic examples are: basic sanitation, air and water quality, and epidemiologic surveillance. Each is of benefit to all members of society and each suffers from the classic problems of all public goods. These problems are perhaps exacerbated by the policy context for public health investments. Many governments allocate resources to public health from budgets earmarked for all health services including personal medical care. It is intuitive that the imperative to spend resources to alleviate current suffering of identified individuals often trumps what are often superior opportunities to save a future cohort of unidentified statistical lives via public health interventions. Welfare economists have been unable to settle whether the very human tendency to prefer saving identified lives over statistical lives is a feature of social welfare that should be honoured or ignored in favour of strict maximization of statistical lives (McKie and Richardson, 2003).

Intensive and extensive margins in public health

Public health practitioners frequently speak of the overall health effects of any public health intervention as a function of 'impact' $\times$ 'reach' (Habicht et al., 1999). Here 'impact' corresponds to the intensive margin and describes the average health benefit derived by each member of the population reached by a public health intervention. 'Reach' simply describes the proportion of the population served by an intervention and corresponds to the extensive margin. An extensive intervention like a public service advertisement might reach millions of viewers but have small impact, and an intensive intervention supplying home visitation for high risk pregnant women may not be easily scaled up. In contrast, developing countries often offer opportunities to scale up from low to high coverage of high impact interventions. The mortality-reducing impact of vitamin A supplementation is estimated at 30 per cent in a population suffering deficiency (Sommer et al., 1986). Measles vaccine can reduce child mortality by 46 per cent in a naive population (Koenig et al., 1990). Yet as interventions are scaled up in a population their impact on health and survival is likely to decline as less-frail individuals receive the services.

The historical role of public health interventions in mortality decline
Figure 5.1 shows the decline of infant mortality during the 20th century in 19 countries. Infant mortality declines have similar dynamics to capital accumulation, in that the detrended time series are non-stationary (Bishai, 1995). Indeed the social–cultural–economic forces that determine infant mortality are cumulative – short-term shocks endure in successive years. The revolution of the 20th century was that, in contrast to prior epochs, a long-term trend where reductions outweighed increases in infant mortality spread from Europe and North America to the entire world. Another indicator of improved health can be found in anthropometric records. Figure 5.2 shows heights attained by Americans over the 19th and 20th centuries – demonstrating a dramatic alteration in somatic form that Fogel terms 'technophysio-evolution' (Fogel and Costa, 1997). Together these figures indicate improvements in the health of children. Were these improvements due to medical care, economic development and nutrition, or public health interventions? Detailed analysis of the US experience shows that much of the decline in child mortality was due to reductions in communicable diseases (Cutler and Meara, 2001). However, effective medical treatments for these conditions were not developed until the 1940s, when penicillin and streptomycin became widely available. Clearly the initial phase of the mortality decline must have been spurred by factors other than medical care. McKeown judiciously cites the role of 'nutrition and hygiene' and implicates public health investments among the factors contributing to hygiene (McKeown, 1983).

Others have been relentlessly critical of McKeown's statements, preferring to misinterpret him as disregarding the role of public health interventions in contributing to hygiene (Szreter and Woolcock, 2004). Perhaps a lack of clarity over the words 'nutrition' and 'hygiene' can explain some of the confusion. In lay terms, 'child nutrition' can mean merely the oral intake of food – something that can improve through purely economic progress. However, in clinical terms, 'child nutrition' refers chiefly to the ability of a child to *absorb* nutrients – an ability that is impaired during recurrent bouts of illness. Reducing the incidence of infectious childhood diseases can contribute greatly to 'effective nutrition' by allowing nutrients to contribute to optimal growth. If economic opportunity affords children greater caloric intake, but stalled progress in hygiene keeps them in a state of near-perpetual disease, then in clinical terms their nutrition has not improved. The word 'hygiene' has also been sadly recast from its original use to describe the 'science of measures that prevent disease in populations' so that it now refers merely to personal practices such as bathing and wearing clean undergarments. In their original meaning,

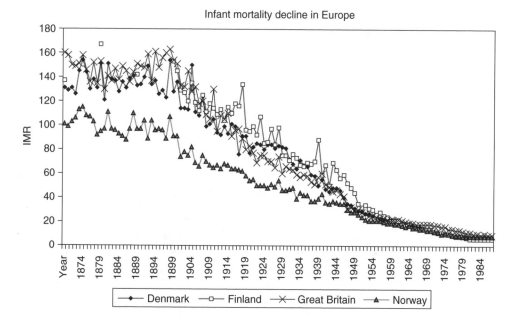

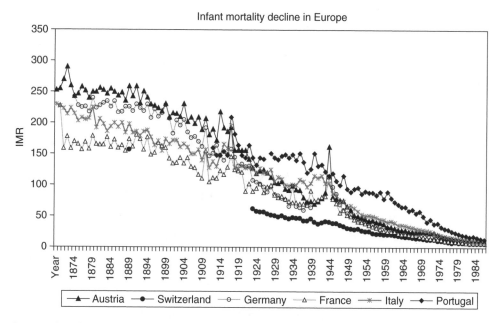

Source: Data from Pritchett and Summers (1996). Calculations by authors.

Figure 5.1   Twentieth century infant mortality decline in various regions of the world

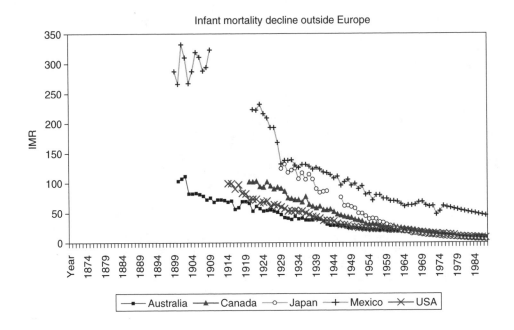

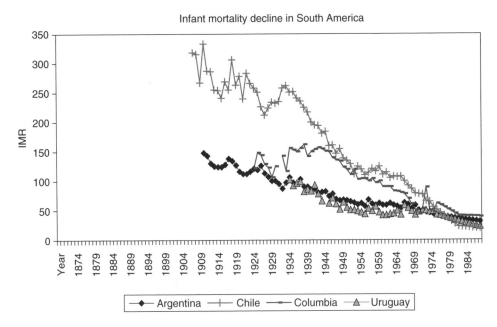

Figure 5.1   (*continued*)

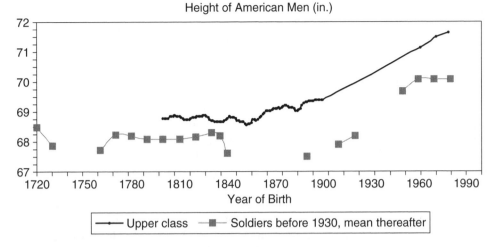

Notes: Squares indicate mean adult height in inches, with data based on soldiers prior to 1930 and a statistically representative sample thereafter. The solid line indicates the increase in height of a sample of upper class American men.

Source: John Komlos, personal communication.

Figure 5.2 *The increase in height of adult men in the US from 1720 to 1990*

nutrition and hygiene were indeed mutually responsible for improved child survival and both advanced through the dual force of public health improvements and economic development as contributors to the health improvements in the 20th century.

The modern evidence base for intervening
The uncertainty over the relative contributions to child survival from economic growth and public health interventions has led some to conclude that it is predominantly economic growth. These economic determinists believe that the best strategy is to focus on poverty reduction, and child health will take care of itself. Jamison shows that there is extensive variation in child death rates even among countries at the same level of PPP-adjusted GDP per capita. Clearly something other than GDP must be accounting for this variation (Jamison et al., 2004).

Caldwell (1986) has developed some insights about what sort of non-economic factors might be at work by specifically identifying countries where child survival is much higher (positive deviants) and much lower (negative deviants) than would be expected on the basis of GDP. Positive deviants in this analysis were Kerala State in India, Costa Rica and Sri Lanka. Negative deviants were Punjab and Kuwait. From an in-depth study of these countries Caldwell concluded that the positive deviants shared a culture of 1) female autonomy; 2) sufficient investment in health services and education; 3) wide accessibility (reach) of high quality health services; 4) broad nutritional adequacy; and 5) universal immunization. The negative deviants were predominantly Islamic societies with a lower degree of female autonomy.

3.   Disease control

We now discuss specific public health interventions that affect child health. We discuss these first starting with interventions at the level of the community, then at health facilities, then finally at the household level.

Community based interventions

Clean water   Difference-in-differences examination of US time series has shown that clean water supplies were a major contributor to the decline of typhoid fever as well as all-cause mortality (Cutler et al., 2004). Water chlorination offers substantial advantages in addition to filtration. The return on investment in the US has been estimated at 23 to 1 with a cost per life year of $500 in 2003 dollars (Cutler and Miller, 2004). One of the remaining challenges in maintaining clean water supplies in developing countries will be to ensure sufficient water pressure at all times to prevent backflow and to eliminate the thousands of cross-connections between sewage and the potable water supply. These cross-connections can occur at any place in the system – but are most likely to occur inadvertently in a household and can only be eliminated through a costly programme of regulation and regular inspection of premises.

Malaria control   At the community level this is of primary benefit to children. As noted in Table 5.1, residual spraying, draining swamps, and clearing vegetation are all relatively cost-effective.

Nutrition   Nutrition improves with development, but even greater child health benefits can be secured with food fortification – an intervention that only becomes feasible after the food industry is sufficiently concentrated (Bishai and Nalubola, 2002). Future developments in this area include breeding programmes to increase the nutrient quality for both vitamin A and iron of traditional cereals (International Food Policy Research Institute, 2005). Economic research can also inform food pricing policies (Behrman and Deolalikar, 1987). If more were known about the price elasticities of nutritious and non-nutritious foods, a strategic programme of Hicksian subsidies and taxes could be implemented to optimize child nutrition.

Improving the quality and accessibility of disease control

An important task for public health planners is implementing programmes and strategies to ensure the adequacy of clinical services. Public health policy-makers in developing countries have focused on both improving access and quality. Quality improvement of child health care facilities in developing countries has largely focused on training health workers and maintaining adherence to child health care guidelines. Chronic shortages of highly trained health care staff have led to the presence of fewer trained health workers delivering services in many dispensaries. Efforts to improve service quality can be extremely fragmented. There are sometimes separate initiatives to improve services for diarrhoea, respiratory illness, malaria, tuberculosis, family planning, nutrition, vaccinations and so on. Donor agencies tend to receive and disburse funds in blocks devoted to specific diseases. Health ministry efforts to allocate funds rationally by disease burden and programme efficacy can be subverted by the availability of these targeted 'vertical' programmes. While ministries of health can expand their ranks to accommodate separate bureaux for separate disease categories, a bottleneck occurs at the periphery. A lone nurse or clinical officer with only one year of post-secondary training is frequently the *only* representative of the health service for thousands of residents. These workers are over-tasked and under-trained. As disease-specific initiatives proliferate at the health ministry, each of them lands on the shoulders of the dispensary staff. Workers become responsible for everything from organizing local vaccination outreach visits, distributing latrine covers, selling bed nets, promoting family planning, measuring the monthly growth of infants, and so on, all while treating the citizens for the daily round of routine and less routine maladies. Just the time required to attend all of the official training sessions can greatly interfere with maintaining dependable services at the dispensary. An ethnographic study in Nepal during the 1980s noted how the peons at many of the facilities were often pressed into service as surrogate diagnosticians and therapists by villagers attempting to cope with the frequent absence of the official health workers who were forced to attend official meetings (Justice, 1983).

In the mid-1990s, the World Health Organization (WHO) began a worldwide initiative to develop an integrated threefold strategy to 1) Improve the quality of primary care services through the use of case management guidelines; 2) Improve the health system; 3) Improve family and community health practices (Gove, 1997; Tulloch, 1999). From an economic perspective, this strategy (known as Integrated Management of Childhood Illness (IMCI)) offers a principal advantage of compressing the seemingly endless cycle of health worker training sessions into a single 5 to 11-day training session. Improvements in several measures of service quality have been documented, particularly the proportion of children receiving antimicrobials when indicated (Armstrong Schellenberg et al., 2004; Gouws et al., 2004). Field studies of IMCI-trained workers have shown that improved health worker performance was achieved at similar levels of cost in Tanzania (Adam et al., 2005; Armstrong Schellenberg et al., 2004) and with negligible cost increases in Uganda (Mirchandani, 2005) when compared to routine care. There is also evidence that high coverage of good quality training was associated with reduction in under-five mortality (Armstrong Schellenberg et al., 2004). The IMCI strategy has been adopted in over 100 countries (Bryce et al., 2003); however, it is becoming apparent that implementation in most countries has emphasized the case management guidelines rather than the health system and community components of IMCI (Bryce et al., 2003).

Personal interventions: distributing the merit goods of public health
There are several classical public health strategies such as immunization that involve coordinated action to deliver bio-active agents or more basic health information to children and their families. These services can be considered merit goods both because they represent contagion and altruistic externalities, but also because most policy-makers believe that free market distribution systems would fail to deliver these services equitably or efficiently. The optimal mix of public health interventions as well as the composition of services varies greatly according to the local epidemiology and the local strengths of the health system. Information about the cost-effectiveness of particular interventions is thus regionally specific as well as time-sensitive. One of the challenges to informing choices in this area is the scarcity of original research as well as the variable quality of

Table 5.1 Public health interventions

Category	Description of Intervention	Area studied	Cost Effectiveness	Citation	Quality of Studies as % (100% = best)
Antimalarials	Mass chemoprophylaxis (with Maloprim)	The Gambia	The cost per child protected per season was US$2.84; the cost per childhood death averted was $143.	(Picard et al., 1992)	43%
Antiretrovirals	PMTCT followed by infant formula feeding	South Africa	Cost per life year gained: $88 to $331. With productivity losses due to HIV infection included, the programme would realize a cost savings to society of $1582 per infant HIV infection prevented.	(Soderlund et al., 1999, Wilkinson et al., 1998, Wilkinson et al., 2000)	87% 78% 84%
Immunization	Dengue vaccine	Southeast Asia	Cost per DALY: $50	(Shepard et al., 2004)	87%
Immunization	Cholera vaccine	Hypothetical refugee population	Cost per DALY: $2973	(Murray et al., 1998)	78%
Immunization	Rotavirus vaccine	Multiple	Cost per Death Averted: $69–$179	(Creese, 1986)	79%
Immunization	Hepatitis B vaccine	Mozambique	Cost per Death Averted: $1556–$3096	(Griffiths et al., 2005)	79%
Immunization	Measles vaccine	Multiple	Cost per Death Averted: $600 (Peru) $41 (Gambia); Cost per DALY: $5–$13 (Multiple)	(Sniadack et al., 1999) (Robertson et al., 1985) (Shepard et al., 1995)	43% 66% 75%
Immunization	Typhoid vaccine	Multiple	Cost per DALY: $20	(Shepard et al., 1995)	75%
Immunization	Pneumococcal vaccine	Multiple	Cost per DALY: $57	(Shepard et al., 1995)	75%
Immunization	DPT combination	Multiple	Cost per DALY: $78	(Shepard et al., 1995)	75%
Immunization	Meningococcal conjugate	Multiple	Cost per DALY: $1355	(Shepard et al., 1995)	75%

Category	Intervention	Location	Cost measure	Citation	%
Immunization	Yellow Fever	Nigeria	Cost per Death Averted: $1904	(Monath and Nasidi, 1993)	90%
Nutrition	Universal vitamin A supplementation	Philippines	Cost per Death Averted: $67	(Loevinsohn et al., 1997)	81%
Sanitation	Promoting handwashing with soap	Burkina Faso	Cost per Death Averted: $2792	(Borghi et al., 2002)	87%
Sanitation	Improving water quality	Hypothetical peri-urban (slum) area	Cost per DALY: $2–$1152	(Varley et al., 1998)	81%
Sanitation	Household latrine revision	Afghanistan	Cost per Death Averted: $2145	(Meddings et al., 2004)	71%
Vector Control	Insecticide treated nets	Africa	Cost per Death Averted: $2003–$2672	(Binka et al., 1997, Evans et al., 1997)	82% 76%
Vector Control	Insecticide treated nets	Africa	Cost per DALY: $4–10, $44, depending on methods	(Coleman et al., 1999, Goodman et al., 1999)	85% 91%
Vector Control	Residual spraying and case detection and treatment	Nepal	Cost per Death Averted: $1281–$33,181	(Mills, 1993)	94%
Vector Control	Social marketing of treated nets	Tanzania	Cost per Death Averted: $1560	(Hanson et al., 2003)	88%
Vector Control	Draining swamps, clearing vegetation, oil application	Zambia	Cost per Death Averted: $858	(Utzinger et al., 2001)	63%
AIDS prevention	Multiple	Low $ Middle Income	Cost per DALY: $5–$285	(Walker, 2003)	38%

published studies. The WHO has been working to remedy this limitation by combining existing epidemiological, demographic and cost data in a comprehensive and standardized way to make available regional estimates enable locally tailored estimates using the published results, databases and tools (World Health Organization, 2005b). Monte Carlo methods are used to convey the uncertainty in these estimates (Hutubessy et al., 2001, 2002).

4. Technology assessment

In order to review recent literature on technology assessment in public health we conducted a search of Medline, the Cochrane library and Google for articles assessing the cost-effectiveness of public health interventions for children in developing countries. Our goal was not to be universally comprehensive, but to represent the range of scholarship in this area in order to assess the quality of studies and their conformity with published guidelines (Drummond et al., 1997; Siegel et al., 1996). Readers interested in a more comprehensive review should consult the forthcoming volume on Disease Control Priorities (Jamison et al., forthcoming). The two-stage search strategy we used, first applied search terms: (cost-effectiveness or cost effectiveness or cost-benefit or cost benefit or cost or economic) + (child survival, child mortality). A supplementary search looked for: (cost-effectiveness or cost effectiveness or cost-benefit or cost benefit) + (immunization or immunization or diarrhoea or malaria or nutrition or HIV or integrated management of childhood illness). After obtaining 91 articles that fit these criteria we excluded all studies of clinical interventions detailing specific personal medical technologies, all studies that did not include a cost-effectiveness analysis, and all studies that were not relevant to child health to arrive at a final list of 43 studies.

We rated each article in four domains: Framework, Data and Methods, Results, and Discussion. Within each of the four domains we identified multiple items for examination and assigned each item 0 points for poor, 1 point for fair and 2 points for good. Representative items included *Framework* (perspective, population, time horizon . . . 8 items, 16 possible points); *Data and Methods* (identified outcomes, discount rates, data sources . . . 13 items, 26 possible points); *Results* (model validation, sensitivity analysis . . . 5 items, 10 points); and *Discussion* (implementation implications, distributive implications . . . 8 items, 16 points). The total possible points was 68 points.

Of the 43 studies evaluated, the average score was 75 per cent. There was remarkable consistency of studies across the four fields – studies that with superior scores for Framework also had superior scores for Data, Results and Discussion. Correlation statistics among the four fields ranged from 0.57 to 0.79.

Table 5.1 provides a summary of what can be learned about the economic performance of public health interventions for children in developing countries. The table is broken down into the category of the health intervention, a description of the intervention, and the applicable region, the cost-effectiveness outcome and the quality rating of the particular studies.

Cost-effective interventions

The technology assessment literature highlights multiple opportunities to achieve good health at low cost through these public health interventions. Notable interventions include immunizations, micronutrient supplementation and vector control. These interventions raise issues other than mere cost-effectiveness that bear examination.

Immunizations   Programmes to deliver the traditional six vaccinations (for polio, measles, tuberculosis, diphtheria, pertussis and tetanus) have been among the most successful and cost-effective interventions in public health. In the populations studied, programmes to distribute these vaccines had cost-effectiveness less than $100 per DALY (disability adjusted life years). Vaccine effectiveness is highest when population coverage is lowest and disease incidence is highest. As coverage increases past 80 per cent herd immunity begins to make the marginal benefit to a single individual approach zero. There has been little data until recently to indicate whether the marginal cost to raise coverage declines or increases as coverage increases. The recent availability of individual country reports on the cost of their vaccination programmes (World Health Organization, 2005a) makes it possible to study the correlation between costs and coverage. Figure 5.3 shows the relationship, and regression analysis confirms a coefficient of 0.78 in this relationship which is significantly less than 1. This can be interpreted to suggest that a 10 per cent increase in the number of covered children is associated with a less than 7.8 per cent increase in total costs consistent with increasing returns to scale. Large fixed costs in

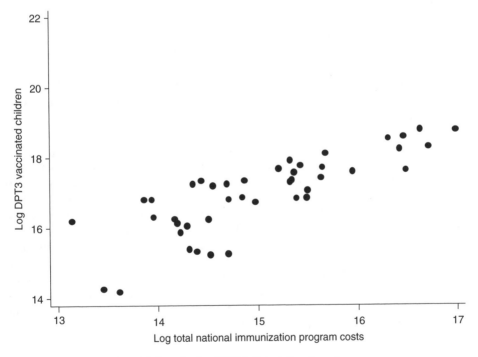

Source: Data from World Health Organization (2005a). Calculations by authors.

Figure 5.3   *Scatterplot of log DPT3 vaccinated children plotted against the log of grand total vaccination costs for 43 countries*

transportation and refrigeration equipment as well as staff training help to explain this pattern. Research suggesting the inefficiency of disease eradication efforts may need to revisit whether the marginal cost declines faster than marginal benefit as coverage increases towards 100 per cent (Geoffard and Philipson, 1997)

The frontier in vaccination includes not only the extension of the traditional six vaccines to cover large populations (especially in sub-Saharan Africa), but also the introduction of more recently developed vaccines for haemophilus influenza B (Griffiths et al., 2005), pneumococcal conjugate, and rotavirus. New, and as yet underutilized vaccines against strep pneumoniae and haemophilus influenza B will offer similar opportunities in coming years. Recent data from the Gambia suggest child mortality reductions of 16 per cent from a pneumococcal conjugate vaccine trial (Cutts et al., 2005).

Nutritional supplementation   Vitamin A distribution campaigns have been shown to produce mortality reductions as large as 30 per cent in populations with diminished intake of natural sources of vitamin A (Sommer et al., 1986b; West et al., 1991). The field effectiveness of vitamin A on child mortality depends critically on the way it is distributed. In community trials of vitamin A the nutrient is delivered to the home of every child every 6 months. In some countries, for example, Nepal, the national vitamin A programme continues with this distribution scheme. Nepal has seen a dramatic drop in child mortality and a notable equalization of formerly discordant death rates for boys and girls (Bishai et al., 2005). In contrast, in the Philippines a programme to distribute vitamin A to children from health facilities succeeded in improving vitamin A coverage from 27 per cent in 1993 to 79 per cent in 1998, but fell short of achieving a mortality impact. One explanation may be that mortality is concentrated among the most vulnerable children who were least likely to seek routine preventive care in a fixed site health facility. Poorer children were less likely to receive vitamin A in the Philippines during this period (Choi et al., forthcoming).

Control of vertically transmitted HIV   In areas of the world where HIV is prevalent, measures to prevent vertical transmission of HIV from mother to child can easily transcend clinical medicine as public health strategies are used to contribute to the success of this programme. One of the challenges has been to identify HIV positive women during their pregnancy in order to give them the anti-retroviral drugs at the time of labour. Earlier enthusiasm for mass treatment of all women in labour with anti-retrovirals has been tempered by concerns about toxicity. Emerging data suggests that single drug regimens to prevent vertical transmission can lead to higher likelihood of resistant viruses emerging, leading to the woman's later non-response to treatment if and when she undergoes the standard multi-drug treatment for treatment of advanced HIV disease (Jourdain et al., 2004). In response, vertical transmission regimens with multiple drugs are being developed which, though perhaps still cost-effective, will be more costly.

5.   Summary
Public health interventions for children have had an enormous contribution to the 20th century mortality transition. Developing countries will benefit from adapting these technologies to their local epidemiology and health system strengths. Economic contributions

to documenting the impact of public health and to technology assessment in this area have been of remarkably high quality. Future contributions of health economics lie in helping to solve the standard public goods problems that surround these technologies as well as helping to identify behavioural adaptations to public health policies at the level of households.

References

Adam, T., F. Manzi, J. Armstrong Schellenberg, L. Mgalula, D. de Savigny and D. Evans (2005), 'Does the integrated management of childhood illnesses cost more than routine care? Results from Tanzania', *Bulletin of the World Health Organization*, **83**(5), 369–77.

Armstrong Schellenberg, J.R., T. Adam, H. Mshinda, H. Masanja, G. Kabadi, O. Mukasa, T. John, S. Charles, R. Nathan, K. Wilczynska, L. Mgalula, C. Mbuya, R. Mswia, F. Manzi, D. de Savigny, D. Schellenberg and C. Victora (2004), 'Effectiveness and cost of facility-based Integrated Management of Childhood Illness (IMCI) in Tanzania', *The Lancet*, **364**(9445), 1583–94.

Arrow, K.J. (1963), 'Uncertainty and the welfare economics of medical care', *American Economic Review*, **53**(5), 941–73.

Behrman, J.R. and A.B. Deolalikar (1987), 'Will developing country nutrition improve with income? A case study of rural South India', *Journal of Political Economy*, **95**(3), 492–507.

Binka, F.N., O.A. Mensah and A. Mills (1997), 'The cost-effectiveness of permethrin impregnated bednets in preventing child mortality in Kassena–Nankana district of Northern Ghana', *Health Policy*, **41**(3), 229–39.

Bishai, D.M. (1995), 'Infant mortality time series are random walks with drift: are they cointegrated with socioeconomic variables?', *Health Economics*, **4**(3), 157–67.

Bishai, D. and R. Nalubola (2002), 'The history of food fortification in the US and its relevance for developing countries', *Economic Development and Cultural Change*, **51**(1), 37–53.

Bishai, D., S. Kumar, H.R. Waters, M. Koenig, J. Katz and K. West (2005), 'The impact of Vitamin A supplementation on mortality inequalities among children in Nepal', *Health Policy and Planning*, **20**(1), 60–66.

Borghi, J., L. Guinness, J. Ouedraogo and V. Curtis (2002), 'Is hygiene promotion cost-effective? A case study in Burkina Faso', *Tropical Medicine and International Health*, **7**(11), 960–69.

Bryce, J., S. el Arifeen, G. Pariyo, C. Lanata, D. Gwatkin and J.P. Habicht (2003), 'Reducing child mortality: can public health deliver?', *The Lancet*, **362**(9378), 159–64.

Caldwell, J. (1986), 'Routes to low mortality in poor countries', *Population and Development Review*, **12**(2), 171–220.

Choi, Y., D. Bishai and K. Hill (forthcoming), 'Socioeconomic differentials in Vitamin A supplementation: evidence from the Philippines', *Health Population and Nutrition*.

Coleman, P.G., C.A. Goodman and A. Mills (1999), 'Rebound mortality and the cost-effectiveness of malaria control: potential impact of increased mortality in late childhood following the introduction of insecticide treated nets', *Tropical Medicine and International Health*, **4**(3), 175–86.

Creese, A.L. (1986), 'Cost effectiveness of potential immunization interventions against diarrhoeal disease', *Social Science and Medicine*, **23**(3), 231–40.

Cutler, D.M. and E. Meara (2001), 'Changes in the distribution of mortality over the 20th Century', NBER Working Paper, 8556.

Cutler, D.M. and G. Miller (2004), 'The role of public health improvements in health advances: the 20th century United States', NBER Working Paper, 10511.

Cutts, F.T., S.M. Zaman, G. Enwere, S. Jaffar, O.S. Levine, J.B. Okoko, C. Oluwalana, A. Vaughan, S.K. Obaro, A. Leach, K.P. McAdam, E. Biney, M. Saaka, U. Onwuchekwa, F. Yallop, N.F. Pierce, B.M. Greenwood and R.A. Adegbola (2005), 'Efficacy of nine-valent pneumococcal conjugate vaccine against pneumonia and invasive pneumococcal disease in The Gambia: randomised, double-blind, placebo-controlled trial', *The Lancet*, **365**(9465), 1139–46.

Drummond, M., B. O'Brien, G. Stoddart and G. Torrance (1997), *Methods for the Economic Evaluation of Health Care Programmes* (Second Edition), London: Oxford University Press.

Evans, D.B., G. Azene and J. Kirigia (1997), 'Should governments subsidize the use of insecticide-impregnated mosquito nets in Africa? Implications of a cost-effectiveness analysis', *Health Policy Plan*, **12**(2), 107–14.

Fogel, R.W. and D.L. Costa (1997), 'A theory of technophysio evolution, with some implications for forecasting population, health care costs, and pension costs', *Demography*, **34**(1), 49–66.

Geoffard, P. and T. Philipson (1997), 'Disease eradication: private versus public vaccination', *American Economic Review*, **87**(1), 222–30.

Goodman, C.A., P.G. Coleman and A.J. Mills (1999), 'Cost-effectiveness of malaria control in sub-Saharan Africa', *The Lancet*, **354**, 378–85.

Gouws, E., J. Bryce, J.P. Habicht, J. Amaral, G. Pariyo, J.A. Schellenberg and O. Fontaine (2004), 'Improving antimicrobial use among health workers in first-level facilities: results from the multi-country evaluation of the integrated management of childhood illness strategy', *Bulletin of the World Health Organization*, **82**(7), 509–15.

Gove, S. (1997), 'Integrated management of childhood illness by outpatient health workers: technical basis and overview. The WHO Working Group on Guidelines for Integrated Management of the Sick Child', *Bulletin of the World Health Organization*, **75**, Suppl.1, 7–24.

Griffiths, U., E. d. D. Pascoal and G. Hutton (2005), 'Cost-effectiveness of introducing hepatitis B vaccine into the infant immunization schedule in Mozambique', *Health Policy and Planning*, **20**(1), 50–59.

Habicht, J.P., C.G. Victora and J.P. Vaughan (1999), 'Evaluation designs for adequacy, plausibility and probability of public health programme performance and impact', *International Journal of Epidemiology*, **28**(1), 10–18.

Hanson, K., N. Kikumbih, J. Armstrong Schellenberg, H. Mponda, R. Nathan, S. Lake, A. Mills, M. Tanner and C. Lengeler (2003), 'Cost-effectiveness of social marketing of insecticide-treated nets for malaria control in the United Republic of Tanzania', *Bulletin of the World Health Organization*, **81**(4), 269–76.

Hutubessy, R.C., R.M. Baltussen, D.B. Evans, J.J. Barendregt and C.J. Murray (2001), 'Stochastic league tables: communicating cost-effectiveness results to decision-makers', *Health Economics*, **10**(5), 473–7.

Hutubessy, R.C., R.M. Baltussen, T.T. Torres-Edejer and D.B. Evans (2002), 'Generalised cost-effectiveness analysis: an aid to decision making in health', *Applied Health Economics Health Policy*, **1**(2), 89–95.

International Food Policy Research Institute (2005), 'Breeding crops for better nutrition', Washington, DC: Harvest Plus. http://www.harvestplus.org/pdfs/brochure.pdf, 15 January, 2005.

Jamison, D.T., M. Sandbu and J. Wang (2004), 'Why has infant mortality decreased at such different rates in different countries?' Disease Control Priorities Project, Working Paper Number 21.

Jamison, D.T., D.B. Evans, G. Alleyne, P. Jha, J. Breman, A.R. Measham, M. Claeson, A. Mills and P.R. Musgrove (forthcoming), *Disease Control Priorities in Developing Countries* (2nd Edition), Oxford: Oxford University Press.

Jourdain, G., N. Ngo-Giang-Huong, S. Le Coeur, C. Bowonwatanuwong, P. Kantipong, P. Leechanachai, S. Ariyadej, P. Leenasirimakul, S. Hammer and M. Lallemant (2004), 'Intrapartum exposure to nevirapine and subsequent maternal responses to nevirapine-based antiretroviral therapy', *New England Journal of Medicine*, **351**(3), 229–40.

Justice, J. (1983), 'The invisible worker: the role of the peon in Nepal's health service', *Social Science Medicine*, **17**(14), 967–70.

Koenig, M.A., M.A. Khan, B. Wojtyniak, J.D. Clemens, J. Chakraborty, V. Fauveau, J.F. Phillips, J. Akbar and U.S. Barua (1990), 'Impact of measles vaccination on childhood mortality in rural Bangladesh', *Bulletin of the World Health Organization*, **68**(4), 441–7.

Lave, L. (1980), 'Economic evaluation of public health programs', *Annual Review of Public Health*, **1**, 255–76.

Loevinsohn, B.P., R.W. Sutter and M.O. Costales (1997), 'Using cost-effectiveness analysis to evaluate targeting strategies: the case of vitamin A supplementation', *Health Policy Plan*, **12**(1), 29–37.

McKeown, T. (1976), *The Modern Rise of Population*, New York: Academic Press.

McKeown, T. (1983), 'Hunger and history: the impact of changing food production and consumption patterns on society', *Journal of Interdisciplinary History*, **14**(2), 227–47.

McKie, J. and J. Richardson (2003), 'The rule of rescue', *Social Science Medicine*, **56**(12), 2407–19.

Meddings, D.R., L.A. Ronald, S. Marion, J.F. Pinera and A. Oppliger (2004), 'Cost effectiveness of a latrine revision programme in Kabul, Afghanistan', *Bulletin of the World Health Organization*, **82**(4), 281–9.

Mills, A. (1993), 'Is malaria control a priority? Evidence from Nepal', *Health Economics*, **2**(4), 333–47.

Mirchandani, G.G. (2005), 'The demand and supply of child health services in Uganda' Doctoral Dissertation.

Mokyr, J. (1993), 'Technological progress and the decline of European mortality', *American Economic Review*, **83**(2), 324–30.

Monath, T.P. and A. Nasidi (1993), 'Should yellow fever vaccine be included in the expanded program of immunization in Africa? A cost-effectiveness analysis for Nigeria', *American Journal of Tropical Medicine and Hygiene*, **48**(2), 274–99.

Murray, J., D.A. McFarland and R.J. Waldman (1998), 'Cost-effectiveness of oral cholera vaccine in a stable refugee population at risk for epidemic cholera and in a population with endemic cholera', *Bulletin of the World Health Organization*, **76**(4), 343–52.

Picard, J., A. Mills and B. Greenwood (1992), 'The cost-effectiveness of chemoprophylaxis with Maloprim administered by primary health care workers in preventing death from malaria amongst rural Gambian children aged less than five years old', *Transactions of the Royal Society of Tropical Medicine and Hygiene*, **86**(6), 580–81.

Preston, S.H. (1975), 'The changing relation between mortality and level of economic development', *Population Studies*, **29**(2), 231–48.

Pritchett, L. and L.H. Summers (1996), 'Wealthier is healthier', *The Journal of Human Resources*, **XXXI**(4), 841–68.

Rice, T. (1998), *The Economics of Health Reconsidered*, Chicago: Health Administration Press.

Robertson, R.L., S.O. Foster, H.F. Hull and P.J. Williams (1985), 'Cost-effectiveness of immunization in The Gambia', *Journal of Tropical Medicine and Hygiene*, **88**(5), 343–51.

Shepard, D.S., J.A. Walsh, E. Kleinau, S. Stansfield and S. Bhalotra (1995), 'Setting priorities for the Children's Vaccine Initiative: a cost-effectiveness approach', *Vaccine*, **13**(8), 707–14.

Shepard, D.S., J.A. Suaya, S.B. Halstead, M.B. Nathan, D.J. Gubler, R.T. Mahoney, D.N. Wang and M.I. Meltzer (2004), 'Cost-effectiveness of a pediatric dengue vaccine', *Vaccine*, **22**(9–10), 1275–80.

Siegel, J.E., M.C. Weinstein, L.B. Russell and M.R. Gold (1996), 'Recommendations for reporting cost-effectiveness analyses', *Journal of the American Medical Association*, **276**, 1339–41.

Sniadack, D.H., B. Moscoso, R. Aguilar, J. Heath, W. Bellini and M.C. Chiu (1999), 'Measles epidemiology and outbreak response immunization in a rural community in Peru', *Bulletin of the World Health Organization*, **77**(7), 545–52.

Soderlund, N., K. Zwi, A. Kinghorn and G. Gray (1999), 'Prevention of vertical transmission of HIV: analysis of cost effectiveness of options available in South Africa', *British Medical Journal*, **318**(7199), 1650–6.

Sommer, A., I. Tarwotjo, E. Djunaedi, K.P. West, Jr., A.A. Loeden, R. Tilden and L. Mele (1986), 'Impact of vitamin A supplementation on childhood mortality. A randomised controlled community trial', *The Lancet*, **1**(8491), 1169–73.

Szreter, S. and M. Woolcock (2004), 'Health by association? Social capital, social theory, and the political economy of public health', *International Journal of Epidemiology*, **33**(4), 650–67.

Tulloch, J. (1999), 'Integrated approach to child health in developing countries', *The Lancet*, **354**, Suppl. 2 SII16–20.

Utzinger, J., Y. Tozan and B.H. Singer (2001), 'Efficacy and cost-effectiveness of environmental management for malaria control', *Tropical Medicine International Health*, **6**(9), 677–87.

Varley, R.C., J. Tarvid and D.N. Chao (1998), 'A reassessment of the cost-effectiveness of water and sanitation interventions in programmes for controlling childhood diarrhoea', *Bulletin of the World Health Organization*, **76**(6), 617–31.

Walker, D. (2003), 'Cost and cost-effectiveness of HIV/AIDS prevention strategies in developing countries: is there an evidence base?', *Health Policy Plan*, **18**(1), 4–17.

Weisbrod, B.A. (1960), *The Economics of Public Health*, Philadelphia: University of Pennsylvania Press.

West, K.P., Jr., R.P. Pokhrel, J. Katz, S.C. LeClerq, S.K. Khatry, S.R. Shrestha, E.K. Pradhan, J.M. Tielsch, M.R. Pandey and A. Sommer (1991), 'Efficacy of vitamin A in reducing preschool child mortality in Nepal', *The Lancet*, **338**(8759), 67–71.

Wilkinson, D., K. Floyd and C.F. Gilks (1998), 'Antiretroviral drugs as a public health intervention for pregnant HIV-infected women in rural South Africa: an issue of cost-effectiveness and capacity', *AIDS*, **12**(13), 1675–82.

Wilkinson, D., K. Floyd and C.F. Gilks (2000), 'National and provincial estimated costs and cost effectiveness of a programme to reduce mother-to-child HIV transmission in South Africa', *South African Medical Journal*, **90**(8), 794–8.

World Health Organization (2005a), *Immunization Financing*, Geneva: WHO. http://www.who.int/immunization_financing/data/about/quality/en/, 15 January, 2005

World Health Organization (2005b), *WHO-CHOICE*, Geneva: World Health Organization. http://www3.who.int/whosis/menu.cfm?path=whosis,cea&language=english, 15 January, 2005

6 Health behaviours among young people
Don Kenkel

1. Introduction

Young people aged 12 to 20 are typically healthy and have little need for curative medical care. However, young people make important choices about health behaviours that have both immediate and longer-term consequences. The immediate consequences include some of the leading causes of death during adolescence: unintentional injuries (including deaths from motor vehicle crashes), homicide and suicide (CDC, 2004). Young people's sexual behaviour can result in sexually transmitted diseases and unwanted pregnancies. Over the longer term, young people's health behaviours may have important implications for their future health and economic well-being as adults. Tobacco use, obesity and alcohol consumption are leading causes of death (Mokdad et al., 2004). In many cases, these unhealthy behaviours are begun during adolescence. Although this does not necessarily mean that young people's health behaviours cause the adult behaviours, it is notable that tobacco use, obesity and alcohol consumption have strong elements of addiction or habit-formation. Young people's use consumption of alcohol and illicit substances may also reduce human capital formation, leading to lower lifetime income.

Empirical economic analysis contributes to our understanding of both the determinants and consequences of young people's health behaviours. This chapter selectively reviews recent contributions, with a particular focus on the challenges health economists face to develop policy-relevant estimates of cause-and-effect relationships.

2. The influence of prices, peers and parents: theoretical considerations

Empirical economic studies of young people's health behaviours are often guided by the standard theoretical approach developed to understand adults' preventive health choices (Kenkel, 2000). Before turning to empirical research, this section highlights three key influences on young people's health behaviours – prices, peers and parents – where advances in theoretical models might provide useful new guidance for future empirical analysis.

Market prices of health-related goods play a key role in the standard neoclassical model of consumer behaviour (Deaton and Muellbauer, 1980), the household production model of health behaviour (Grossman, 1972, 2000), and the model of rational addiction (Becker, Grossman and Murphy, 1991). But while standard economic models predict that young people's health behaviours will be responsive to price, they provide little guidance on the likely degree of responsiveness.

Peer and parental influences may make young people's substance use either more or less price-responsive. Liebenstein (1950) shows that consumer demand is more price-responsive when there are bandwagon effects. However, when there are 'snob effects', where the demand for a commodity is decreased when others are consuming it, consumer demand is less price-responsive. Peer and parental influences on adolescent substance use seem to be a combination of bandwagon and snob effects. For example, summarizing research on psychosocial risk factors in young people's smoking, a US Surgeon General's report concludes that '[s]moking initiation appears to be a component of peer associations and peer bonding in adolescence, as peer groups establish shared behaviours to differentiate themselves from other adolescents and from adults.' (USDHHS, 1994). If higher prices reduce substance use by peers and parents, there will be a bandwagon effect towards less adolescent substance use. But continuing to use the substance at higher prices might be a more effective way for members of a peer group to differentiate themselves from other adolescents and from their parents. In this case, a snob effect could operate making demand less price-responsive. Without knowing whether bandwagon effects or snob effects are more powerful, it is impossible to predict whether peer and parental influences make young people's substance use more or less price-responsive.

Further developing an economic model of the role of both prices and peer influences in young people's health behaviours could shed new light. To sketch a possible approach, make the strong assumption that both young people and adults want to be accepted by their peers: preferences for the commodity 'peer acceptance' are well-defined and unchanging over the life-cycle. However, suppose that young people face a more restricted household technology to produce peer acceptance. For example, market goods such as Nike athletic shoes or Marlboro cigarettes might be essential inputs into the production of acceptance into certain peer groups.[1] In this approach, young people's demand for unhealthy substances is a derived demand for an input into the production of peer acceptance.

Viewing substance demand as a derived demand sheds new light on the likely price-responsiveness.[2] The rules governing the price elasticity of derived demands date back at least to Marshall (1922). Two assumptions about the production of peer group acceptance are key: the degree of input substitutability; and the input's share of the total cost of producing peer acceptance. For example, if young people have limited or no ability to substitute other inputs in the production of peer acceptance, and if the cost of the substance is a relatively small share of the total cost of peer acceptance, the derived demand for the substance will be relatively inelastic with respect to its own price. That is, if few young people are discouraged from joining a given peer group by a hike in the price of the required 'cool' substance, their demand for the unhealthy substance will be inelastic. This approach to understanding the degree of price-responsiveness of youth health behaviours points to the need for empirical research into the production process of peer acceptance. Another need is for empirical research into peer group dynamics such as bandwagon and snob effects.

The approach sketched above of the role of prices and peers omits another key influence on young people's health behaviours – their parents. A more complete approach to modelling young people's health behaviours could build on modern theoretical models of the economics of the family. In standard economic models of the determinants of child health, parents are assumed to maximize a family utility function (Currie, 2000; Jacobson, 2000). These models adopt the common preference approach to family behaviour, where the family is treated as a single decision-making agent. More recent work treats family demands as the outcomes of bargaining games (Lundberg and Pollack, 1996). For example, Bolin, Jacobson and Lindgren (2001, 2002) extend the Grossman model of household health production to consider cases where spouses engage in Nash-bargaining or behave strategically. While they consider possible conflicts of interest between spouses, these models do not consider conflicts between parents and children – arguably a key omission if the approach is to be applied to families with adolescents rather than younger children. Such potential conflicts are central to Becker's (1974) model of a family with an altruistic parent and selfish children (the so-called 'rotten kids') and its extensions by Bruce and Waldman (1990, 1991). These models consider the influence of cash or in-kind transfers from parents on their children's behaviour. Becker (1996) also suggests that parents can make investments through channels such as church attendance to shape their children's preferences over consumption goods. Extending this approach to explicitly consider young people's health behaviours could provide new empirically testable predictions.

Moving in a somewhat different direction, theoretical work in behavioural economics rejects the standard rational-choice model of economics in favour of models that combine insights from both psychology and economics. The relevance of this line of research for future empirical analysis of young people's health behaviours remains to be seen. For example, as an alternative to Becker and Murphy's (1988) model of rational addiction, Gruber and Koszegi (2001) propose a behavioural economic model of smoking. O'Donoghue and Rabin (2001) discuss behavioural economic analysis of adolescent risky behaviours more generally. As is discussed in more detail in the chapter by Lakdawalla and Philipson in this Companion (Chapter 7), the behavioural model and the rational addiction model yield similar empirically testable predictions; however, the two models may have very different normative implications for policy.

3.   Empirical studies of the influence of price

Although more theory may provide useful guidance, the extent to which young people's health behaviours respond to changes in the prices of health-related goods is an empirical question. This is the focus of a great deal of older and more recent research. In a useful review, Grossman (2004) notes that a number of empirical studies find that young people's demand for substances including alcohol, cigarettes and cocaine is more price-responsive than adults' demand. However, not every study finds negative price effects. For example, in econometric specifications that control for state-level influences, Dee (1999) and DeCicca, Kenkel and Mathios (2002) fail to find evidence that young people's demands for alcohol and cigarettes (respectively) respond to price.

The central challenge for this line of empirical research is to find a suitable source of exogenous variation (that is natural experiments) to identify the price-responsiveness of young people's health behaviours. As Meyer (1995) emphasizes: 'If one cannot experimentally control the variation one is using [to identify a key parameter of interest], one should understand its source.' In many cases, the source of the variation in the prices of unhealthy substances is variation in taxes or other policies over time or across political units. Taxes and policies are not randomly set, but instead result from the political process. Increasingly, alcohol and cigarette excise tax hikes are explicitly motivated by public health concerns. Such tax hikes are also often coordinated with other alcohol control or tobacco control policy initiatives. The resulting variation in alcohol and tobacco prices may not identify causal effects, because higher prices will proxy for unobserved public sentiment and/or the other policies. For example, when DeCicca et al. (2004) include a direct measure of state anti-smoking sentiment in models of young people's demand for cigarettes, they find little evidence that higher prices discourage young people from smoking participation. Similarly, in models of young people's use of illicit substances, variation in the price of an illicit substance stemming from differences in law enforcement may tend to proxy for differences in public sentiment towards the illicit substances.

For these reasons, many economists are now sceptical of studies that rely on variation across states in the US to identify the impacts of taxes or other policies on individual behaviour. An alternative empirical strategy in US data is to include state fixed effects, thus relying on within-state variation for identification. Similarly, studies using data from other countries rely on time series variation to identify price effects; examples include studies of smoking initiation and cessation in Britain (Forster and Jones, 2001) and Spain (López-Nicolás, 2002). This strategy faces data and technical problems and a more fundamental problem. The data problem is that there is often relatively little within-state or within-country price variation, which makes it difficult to obtain precise estimates. The technical problem is that many studies of pooled cross-sections of states in the US neglect serial correlation. Bertrand, Duflo and Mullainathan (2004) show that this can result in inconsistent standard errors and lead researchers to incorrectly infer that a change in policy causes an outcome. The more fundamental problem is that unobserved influences are not necessarily fixed over time. In such a situation, within-state or within-country variation may proxy for changes in public sentiment or other unobserved influences.

The lesson for future work is not to be pessimistic about ever identifying the price-responsiveness of young people's health behaviours, but to search for contexts that provide useful sources of identifying variation. Lance and colleagues' (2004) study of adult demand for cigarettes in China and Russia provides an example where both cross-sectional and time series variation in prices appear to be useful sources of identification. Over the period studied, supply-side variation in cigarette prices appears to stem from different trends across communities in: privatization; the abandonment of price controls and supports; expansion or contraction of transportation infrastructure; and the production capacity of the cigarette industry. Because these trends in turn stem from fundamental reforms of the entire economies of China and Russia, there is less reason to suspect that they may be correlated with unobserved anti-smoking sentiment or policies. Given this potentially superior identification strategy, it is interesting that Lance et al. (2004) report very small price elasticities (in the range from 0 to −0.15) for adult cigarette demand, contradicting some previous research and many researchers' expectations about the elasticity of demand in poorer nations.

Exploiting within-country or within-state variation to identify the price-responsiveness of young people's health behaviours should also be viewed cautiously. But again, in some contexts such variation provides useful natural experiments. For example, Mohler-Kuo et al. (2004) study the impact of a natural experiment in Switzerland's markets for distilled spirits. A World Trade Organization agreement that took effect in July 1999 resulted in tax reform and increased competition among spirits importers. As a result, the retail prices of foreign spirits, which accounted for about half of spirits sales in Switzerland, fell by somewhere between 30 and 50 per cent. The empirical analysis by Mohler-Kuo et al. (2004) suggests that this price decrease resulted in an increase in spirits consumption and an increase in alcohol-related problems, especially among people 29 years old or younger. In another example where the price variation is plausibly exogenous, Sheu and colleagues

(2004) study the impact of a large increase in the real price of cigarettes within the state of California between 1996 and 1999. Unlike most previous research, their estimates suggest that the California price increase did not have an effect on smoking participation, but that it did have an effect on the level of cigarette consumption among potential smokers.

Given increased concern about obesity as a public health problem, health economists are also beginning to study the role of market prices in decisions about diet, exercise and obesity. Cawley, Markowitz and Tauras (2004) study the relationships between young people's decisions about body weight and smoking. Their findings suggest that girls have a stronger demand for thinness, which may make their smoking decisions less price-responsive than boys'. Chou, Grossman and Saffer (2004) estimate reduced-form models of the determinants of adult body mass index (BMI) and obesity. They find that higher prices for fast-food and full-service restaurants and for food at home have negative and statistically significant effects on BMI and obesity. The food price effects are identified using within-state variation and national variation over time. In this study, the controversial identification assumption is that national variation over time only influences BMI and obesity through the channel of food prices and other measured variables. Due to the omission of time trend measures as direct influences in their empirical models, the authors acknowledge that a conservative interpretation of their study is that 'we seek to explain trends in an accounting, rather than in a causal, sense' (Chou, Grossman and Saffer, 2004, p. 577). As in studies of substance use, the challenge for future studies of obesity among young people is to find suitable natural experiments to identify causal effects.

4.   Empirical studies of the influence of peers and parents

While the influence of prices is a long-standing focus of empirical health economics, an emerging line of research focuses on peer and parental influences on young people's health behaviours. Public health and social science research documents correlations between a young person's health behaviours and those of his or her peers. There are three reasons these correlations are not sufficient evidence of causal peer effects as defined in economic models. First, in what Manski (1993) calls the reflection problem, peer influences go both ways, so the young person's behaviours and those of his or her peers are simultaneously determined. Second, peer groups may be endogenously chosen based on individual preferences over risk, time and social deviancy. This creates a selection problem, where it is difficult to know whether a shared behaviour like substance use stems from the common preferences or from peer influences. Third, peers may experience unobserved common environmental factors such as family background, school, and market-level influences.

Eisenberg (2004) attempts to identify causal peer effects on young people's substance use by exploiting two types of natural experiments that create plausibly exogenous variation in peers. The first natural experiment is when a young person's substance-using friend moves away or graduates. Using data from the first two waves of AddHealth, Eisenberg finds some evidence that a young person's marijuana use, smoking, and binge drinking falls after a user-friend moves or graduates. However, the effects are weaker than some previous estimates suggest. The second natural experiment is when 12- and 13-year-olds attend schools with different grade spans, exposing them to peers of different ages. For example, a 13-year-old in a middle school environment is only exposed to younger children, but a 13-year-old in another school system can be exposed to adolescents up to the age of 18. Using data from the National Educational Longitudinal Survey, Eisenberg finds little evidence that substance use is higher among adolescents in schools with older peers.

Krauth (2004) uses a different identification strategy to study peer and selection effects on young people's smoking. His structural estimation approach addresses simultaneity by treating both the individual and group outcomes as endogenous. His empirical model also addresses the selection problem by using the degree of selection on observables as a proxy for the degree of selection on unobservables. If he assumes the same correlation in observables and unobservables among peers, Krauth's structural estimate of the peer effect is less than one-tenth as large as the benchmark estimate that fails to address simultaneity or selection. Although under weaker assumptions Krauth finds some evidence of peer effects, in general his results suggest weaker peer influences on smoking than commonly believed.

Turning to the influence of parents on young people's health behaviours, several recent studies explore the role of parents' time allocation. Anderson, Butcher and Levine (2003) use data from the National Longitudinal Survey of Youth (NLSY) 1979 to estimate the impact of maternal employment on children's weight. Their results suggest that a child is more likely to be overweight if his or her mother worked more hours per week over the child's life. Aughinbaugh and Gittleman (2004) also use data from the NLSY 1979 to study the relationships between maternal employment and the child's participation in a range of risky behaviours: smoking cigarettes, drinking alcohol, using marijuana and other drugs, engaging in sex, and committing crimes. In a similar study, Ruhm (2004) also uses the NLSY 1979 to study the effect of women's labour supply on children's smoking, drinking and body weight. These latter two studies provide somewhat mixed results, but both note the lack of statistical precision. Taking a different approach, Mathur and Freeman (2002) use a panel of state-level data to estimate the relationship between economic, social and demographic variables on young people's suicide rates. Their results are consistent with the argument that reductions in parental time, either through divorce or increased market work, tend to increase adolescent suicide rates.

Economic studies are also beginning to look at parental behaviours that may have more specific influences on their children's health behaviours. In yet another study that uses the NLSY 1979, Aizer (2004) finds that children with adult supervision after school are less likely to skip school, use alcohol or marijuana, steal something or hurt someone. Powell and Chaloupka (2005) use data from a 1996 survey of high school students to study the relationships between a range of parenting behaviours and teenagers' cigarette smoking. Like previous studies of young people's smoking, Powell and Chaloupka find that teens are more likely to smoke if their parents smoke. But even controlling for parental smoking, they find that other observed parenting behaviours such as home smoking rules also influence teen smoking.

The research reviewed above describes relationships between young people's health behaviours and their parents' endogenous choices related to employment, supervision and other behaviours. It is obviously very difficult to know if these studies have identified causal treatment effects of the parents' choices on youth behavioural outcomes. For example, maternal employment and the availability of adult supervision after school may reflect the economic circumstances of the family and other factors that also directly influence young people's health behaviours. Although Anderson, Butcher and Levine (2003), Aughinbaugh and Gittleman (2004), Ruhm (2004), and Aizer (2004) use the rich data available in the NLSY 1979 to control for many observable confounders, the concern remains that there may be important unobserved influences on young people's health behaviours that are correlated with the observed choices of parents. Similarly, although Powell and Chaloupka (2005) control for parental smoking, there may be important unobserved family background and attitude differences between the parents that adopt what Powell and Chaloupka term 'optimal' versus 'risky' parental behaviours. Further progress on these questions will once again require careful analysis of some natural experiment that provides a more plausibly exogenous source of identifying variation.

5.   The consequences of young people's health behaviours

Another body of empirical health economics research focuses on estimating the consequences of young people's health behaviours. In essence, these studies try to estimate the 'treatment effect' of the health behaviours on various outcomes. The outcomes include immediate consequences such as traffic fatalities, other health behaviours (such as the possibility that alcohol and drug use increase the probability of unsafe sex), and longer-term consequences such as decreased human capital formation.

Epidemiologic research documents strong statistical associations between young people's health behaviours and a wide range of adverse consequences. However, it is difficult to know whether these associations are causal in nature. First, the associations might reflect unobserved heterogeneity in characteristics such as time and risk preferences and tastes for socially deviant behaviour. Second, the associations might reflect reverse causality. For example, young people who plan otherwise unacceptable behaviour such as violence or promiscuous sex might consume alcohol to provide a psychological 'excuse'. Or, young people might drink or use other substances in response to problems like doing poorly in school. In principle, empirical studies could address some of these possibilities by using rich longitudinal data. In practice, such data are not often available, which leaves the question of causality open.

Empirical economic studies use two related strategies to explore whether there are causal relationships between young people's health behaviours and adverse consequences. The first approach uses instrumental variables (IV) methods to estimate the causal treatment effect of the health behaviour on an outcome of interest. In contrast, a second common approach is to estimate a reduced-form equation of the outcome variable as a function of market prices and other policy variables. Regardless of whether they use the structural IV approach or the reduced-form approach, studies of the impact of health behaviours need to address whether the variables used explicitly or implicitly as instruments are valid (see Chapter 4 by Auld in this Companion). For example, Rashad and Kaestner (2004) critique two recent studies that attempt to identify the causal impact of substance abuse on adolescent sexual behaviour, and conclude that the two studies use possibly invalid exclusion restrictions and a relatively weak set of IVs.

Carpenter (2005) provides new evidence on the role alcohol consumption plays in youths' risky sexual behaviour by exploiting a different source of identifying variation. He focuses on Zero Tolerance (ZT) laws that make it illegal for under-age drivers to have any noticeable amount of alcohol in their blood. Carpenter estimates reduced-form models of the impact of the ZT laws on state gonorrhoea rates by age group and race. In models that include state fixed effects, Carpenter finds that the adoption of a ZT law is associated with a statistically significant reduction in gonorrhoea rates among 15 to 19-year-old white males. The fact that there is no relationship between the ZT laws and gonorrhoea rates for slightly older males who were not affected by the laws provides confirmatory evidence that Carpenter has identified a causal effect. Carpenter is left with more puzzling results for white females. With the data he uses, he cannot estimate the structural relationship between drinking behaviour and risky sexual behaviour. Instead, it is necessary to infer some of the links in the causal chain from ZT laws to alcohol consumption to risky sexual behaviour to gonorrhoea rates.

6. Concluding comments

There is a great deal of exciting recent empirical research on the economics of young people's health behaviours. In addition to additional study of the roles of prices, peers and parents, more work is also needed on the impact of alcohol, cigarette and food advertising on young people's health choices (Saffer, 1998; Hastings et al., 2003). A recurring theme of this chapter has been the importance of finding suitable exogenous sources of variation to identify treatment effects. Although public policies often provide the natural experiments needed for identification, it is important to keep in mind that policy-relevance is not the only reason economists should be interested in young people's health behaviours. Fuchs (2000, p. 141) argues that the field of health economics faces two distinct missions: '(a) enhancing understanding of economic behaviour and (b) providing valuable input into health policy and health services research.' As I have argued elsewhere (Kenkel, 2000, p. 1713), health economics will ultimately provide the most valuable input by emphasizing the power of the economic approach to human behaviour.

Notes

1. As DeCicca, Kenkel and Mathios (2001) point out, this is consistent with the observed strong brand preferences among young smokers, and with observed differences in smoking rates and cigarette brand choices across racial/ethnic groups in the US.
2. I would like to thank Keith Bryant who provided very useful discussions of this approach.

References

Aizer, Anna (2004), 'Home alone: supervision after school and child behaviour', *Journal of Public Economics*, **88**, 1835–48.
Anderson, Patricia M., Kristin F. Butcher and Phillip B. Levine (2003), 'Maternal employment and overweight children', *Journal of Health Economics*, **22**, 477–504.
Aughinbaugh, Alison and Maury Gittleman (2004), 'Maternal employment and adolescent risky behaviour', *Journal of Health Economics*, **23**, 815–38.
Becker, Gary S. (1974), 'A theory of social interactions', *Journal of Political Economy*, **82**, 1095–117.
Becker, Garry S. (1996), *Accounting for Tastes*, Cambridge, Massachusetts: Harvard University Press.
Becker, Gary S. and Kevin M. Murphy (1988), 'A theory of rational addiction', *Journal of Political Economy*, **96**(4), 675–700.
Becker, Gary S., Michael Grossman and Kevin M. Murphy (1991), 'Rational addiction and the effect of price on consumption', *American Economic Review Papers and Proceedings*, **81**(2), 237–41.
Bertrand, Marianne, Esther Duflo and Sendhil Mullainathan (2004), 'How much should we trust differences-in-differences estimates?,' *Quarterly Journal of Economics*, **119**(2), 249–75.
Bolin, Kristian, Lena Jacobson and Bjorn Lindgren (2001), 'The family as the health producer – when spouses are Nash-bargainers', *Journal of Health Economics*, **20**, 349–62.

Bolin, Kristian, Lena Jacobson and Bjorn Lindgren (2002), 'The family as the health producer – when spouses act strategically', *Journal of Health Economics*, **21**, 475–95.
Bruce, Neil and Michael Waldman (1990), 'The Rotten-Kid Theorem meets the Samaritan's Dilemma', *Quarterly Journal of Economics*, **105**(1), 155–65.
Bruce, Neil and Michael Waldman (1991), 'Transfers in kind: why they can be efficient and nonpaternalistic', *American Economic Review*, **81**, 1345–51.
Carpenter, Christopher (2005), 'Youth alcohol use and risky sexual behaviour: evidence from underage drunk driving laws', *Journal of Health Economics*, **24**, 613–28.
Cawley, John, Sara Markowitz and John Tauras (2004), 'Lighting up and slimming down: the effects of body weight and cigarette prices on adolescent smoking initiation', *Journal of Health Economics*, **23**, 293–311.
Chou, Shin-Yi, Michael Grossman and Henry Saffer (2004), 'An economic analysis of adult obesity: results from the Behavioural Risk Factor Surveillance System', *Journal of Health Economics*, **23**(3), 565–87.
Currie, Janet (2000), 'Child health in developed countries', in Anthony J. Culyer and Joseph P. Newhouse (eds), *Handbook of Health Economics*, Amsterdam: Elsevier.
Deaton, Angus and John Muellbauer (1980), *Economics and Consumer Behaviour*, Cambridge: Cambridge University Press.
DeCicca, Philip, Donald Kenkel and Alan Mathios (2001), 'Racial differences in the determinants of smoking onset', *Journal of Risk and Uncertainty*, **21**(2/3), 311–40.
DeCicca, Philip, Donald Kenkel and Alan Mathios (2002), 'Putting out the fires: will higher taxes reduce the onset of youth smoking?', *Journal of Political Economy*, **110**(1), 144–69.
DeCicca, Phil, Donald Kenkel, Alan Mathios and Justine Shin (2004), 'Youth smoking, taxes, and anti-smoking sentiment', Working Paper, Department of Policy Analysis & Management, Cornell University.
Dee, Thomas (1999), 'State alcohol policies, teen drinking, and traffic fatalities', *Journal of Public Economics*, **72**(2), 289–315.
Eisenberg, Daniel (2004), 'Peer effects for adolescent substance use: do they really exist?', Working paper, University of California – Berkeley School of Public Health.
Forster, Martin and Andrew Jones (2001), 'The role of tobacco taxes in starting and quitting smoking: duration analysis of British data', *Journal of the Royal Statistical Society* (Series A) **164**, 517–47.
Fuchs, Victor R. (2000), 'The future of health economics', *Journal of Health Economics*, **19**, 141–57.
Grossman, Michael (1972), 'On the concept of health capital and the demand for health', *Journal of Political Economy*, **80**(2), 223–55.
Grossman, Michael (2000), 'The human capital model', in Anthony J. Culyer and Joseph P. Newhouse (eds), *Handbook of Health Economics*, Amsterdam: Elsevier, pp. 349–408.
Grossman, Michael (2004), 'Individual behaviour and substance use: the role of price', Working Paper 10948, National Bureau of Economic Research, Cambridge Massachusetts.
Gruber, Jonathan and Botond Koszegi (2001), 'Is addiction "rational"? Theory and evidence', *Quarterly Journal of Economics*, **116**(4), 1261–305.
Hastings, Gerard, Martine Stead, Laura McDermott, et al. (2003), 'Review of research on the effects of food promotion to children', Centre for Social Marketing, University of Strathclyde, UK.
Jacobson, Lena (2000), 'The family as producer of health – an extended Grossman model', *Journal of Health Economics*, **19**, 611–37.
Kenkel, Donald S. (2000), 'Prevention', in Anthony J. Culyer and Joseph P. Newhouse (eds), *Handbook of Health Economics*, Amsterdam: Elsevier, pp. 1675–720.
Krauth, Brian (2004), 'Peer and selection effects on youth smoking in California', Working paper, Simon Fraser University.
Lance, Peter M., John S. Akin, William H. Dow and Chung-Ping Loh (2004), 'Is cigarette smoking in poorer nations highly sensitive to price? Evidence from Russia and China', *Journal of Health Economics*, **23**(1), 173–89.
Liebenstein, Harvey (1950), 'Bandwagon, snob, and Veblen effects in the theory of consumer demand', *Quarterly Journal of Economics*, **64**, 183.
López-Nicolás, Angel (2002), 'How important are tobacco prices in the propensity to start and quit smoking? An analysis of smoking histories from the Spanish National Health Survey', *Health Economics*, **11**, 521–35.
Lundberg, Shelly and Robert A. Pollak (1996), 'Bargaining and distribution in marriage', *Journal of Economic Perspectives*, **10**(4), 139–58.
Manski, Charles F. (1993), 'Identification of endogenous social effects: the reflection problem', *Review of Economic Studies*, **60**(3), 531–42.
Marshall, Alfred (1922), *Principles of Economics*, 8th Edition, London: MacMillan.
Mathu, Vijay K. and Donald G. Freeman (2002), 'A theoretical model of adolescent suicide and some evidence from US data', *Health Economics*, **11**, 695–708.

Meyer, Bruce D. (1995), 'Natural and quasi-experiments in economics', *Journal of Business & Economic Statistics*, **13**(2), 151–61.

Mohler-Kuo, Meichun, Jurgen Rehm, Jean-Luc Heeb and Gerhard Gmel (2004), 'Decreased taxation, spirits consumption and alcohol-related problems in Switzerland', *Journal of Studies on Alcohol*, **65**(2), 266–73.

Mokdad A.H., J.S. Marks, D.F. Stroup and J.L. Gerberding (2004), 'Actual causes of death in the United States: 2000', *Journal of the American Medical Association*, **291**(10), 1238–45.

National Center for Health Statistics (2004), *Health, United States, 2004*, with chartbook on trends in the health of Americans, Hyatsville, Maryland.

O'Donoghue, T. and M. Rabin (2001), 'Risky behaviour among youths: some issues from behavioural economics', in Jonathan Gruber (ed.), *Risky Behaviour Among Youths*, Chicago: University of Chicago Press, pp. 29–68.

Powell, Lisa M. and Frank J. Chaloupka (2005), 'Parents, public policy, and youth smoking', *Journal of Policy Analysis and Management*, **24**(1), 93–112.

Rashad, Inas and Robert Kaestner (2004), 'Teenage sex, drugs and alcohol use: problems identifying the cause of risky behaviours', *Journal of Health Economics*, **23**(3), 493–503.

Ruhm, Christopher J. (2004), 'Maternal employment and adolescent development', Working Paper 10691, National Bureau of Economic Research, Cambridge, Massachusetts.

Saffer, Henry (1998), 'Economic issues in cigarette and alcohol advertising', *Journal of Drug Issues*, **28**(3), 781–93.

Sheu, Mei-ling, T eh-Wei Hu, Theodore E. Keeler, Michael Ong and Hai-Yen Sung (2004), 'The effect of a major cigarette price change on smoking behaviour in California: a zero-inflated negative binomial model', *Health Economics*, **13**, 781–91.

US Department of Health and Human Services (USDHHS) (1994), *Preventing Tobacco Use Among Young People: A Report of the Surgeon General*, Atlanta, Georgia: US Department of Health and Human Services, Public Health Service, Centers for Disease Control and Prevention, National Center for Chronic Disease Prevention and Health Promotion, Office on Smoking and Health.

7 Economics of obesity
Darius Lakdawalla and Tomas J. Philipson

1. Introduction
The recent rise in obesity has generated enormous popular interest and policy concern in developed countries where it is rapidly becoming one of the major health problems facing such nations. While obesity is most often conceived of as a problem of public health or personal attractiveness, it is very much an economic issue, of behaviour in response to incentives. As several economists have emphasized, the stubbornness of obesity's rise owes itself in large part to several intractable incentives favouring weight growth.

From an economic point of view, obesity poses three sets of issues that call for investigation. First, it is important to understand the nature and causes of the long-run historical trends in weight, and how they have been generated by changing economic incentives. Second, what are consequences of the growth in obesity, both in terms of health as well as other outcomes? And finally, though obesity may be a *private* health problem, what are the rationales for making it a *public* health problem to be addressed by government intervention.

We begin by discussing the short- and long-run historical trends in obesity, and then move to existing economic explanations of these empirical trends. Next, we discuss the impact of obesity on health and other outcomes. This motivates a discussion of whether and how obesity is a public policy problem, and the appropriate role for policy.

2. Trends in obesity and its determinants
The recent growth in obesity has been well-documented in the public health literature (Seidell and Deerenberg, 1994; VanItallie, 1996; Flegal et al., 1998; Mokdad et al., 1999, 2000; Flegal et al., 2002), and its magnitude has generated concern. Trends in healthy weight are measured either as body mass index (BMI) – a measure of height-adjusted weight equal to weight in kilogrammes divided by squared height in metres – or as the rate of obesity, where obesity is defined as having BMI greater than or equal to 30. Figure 7.1 depicts recent trends in BMI and obesity for adult males in the US (trends for females are extremely similar). It is based on data from the National Health Interview Survey, an annual repeated cross-section of the US population, surveying approximately 100 000 people every year. The survey asks respondents about, among many other things, their height and weight. This allows us to construct each respondent's body mass index and obesity status.

From 1976 to 2001, the rate of obesity more than doubled, rising from 7.9 per cent to 20.4 per cent. (For adult females, obesity rose from 9.6 per cent to 22.2 per cent.) Average height-adjusted weight also rose, as BMI went from 24.8 units in 1976 to 26.9 in 2001. Since the average adult male weighed 171 pounds in 1976, this corresponds to a 14.5 pound increase, holding height constant.

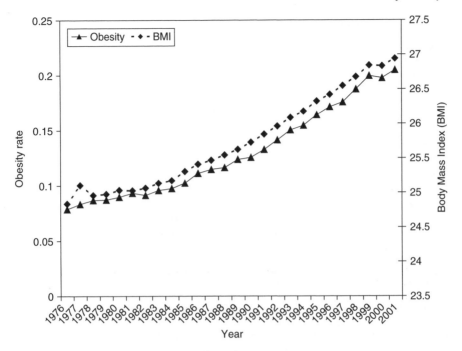

Source: Authors' calculations from National Health Interview Surveys.

Figure 7.1   Trends in obesity and BMI for US adult males, 1976–2001

While this increase is both significant and rapid, the last several decades are not anomalous in historical context. As Costa and Steckel (1995) have emphasized, weights have been rising for more than a century at least in the United States, or as far back as we have records. Costa and Steckel analyse growth in BMI from the US Civil War period to the 1990s.[1] There was pronounced growth in weight early in the 20th century, although the extreme weights in the tails of the distribution may be a more recent phenomenon. Height-adjusted weight for people in their 40s, the age group with the highest labour force attachment, has increased by nearly 4 units over this period. To put this into perspective, an increase of this magnitude in the height-adjusted weight of a 6-foot tall man would require a weight gain of approximately 30 pounds. Costa and Steckel interpret the long-run increase in weight as part and parcel of a long-run improvement in health and nutrition.

While weight is clearly the combined outcome of diet and exercise, the importance of both these factors is made clear by use of additional data. During the 20th century, weights rose even during periods where the total consumption of food did not. As Figure 7.2 illustrates, this secular growth in weight has been accompanied by only modest gains in calorie consumption.[2] Indeed, the immediate postwar period witnessed substantial growth in weight and *declining* consumption of calories. The lack of time-series correlation between calorie intake and weight suggests that an analysis of weight must account not only for food consumption, but also for changes in the strenuousness of work, both at home and in the market, caused by economic development.

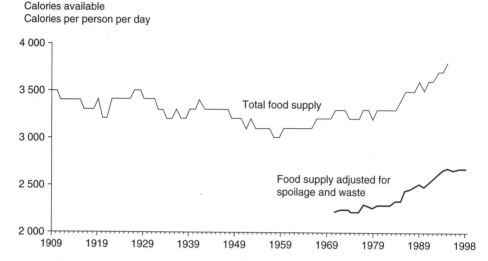

Source: USDA's Economic Research Service: reproduced from Putnam (2000, p. 10).

Figure 7.2   Trends in US calorie consumption, 1910–2000

3. Economic theories of obesity

Economists have taken several different theoretical approaches to the study of obesity. Neoclassical theories of weight include both addictive and capital investment models, which are quite complementary in explaining empirical patterns in weight and weight growth. As an alternative to the neoclassical theories, some have also developed behavioural theories of weight gain.

The neoclassical theory of weight

Philipson and Posner (1999), along with Lakdawalla and Philipson (2002), develop the capital investment model of weight. This is a dynamic model of weight in which individuals compare the lifetime costs and benefits of weight gain.[3] Weight is a durable capital good and the change of weight depends on both food intake and exercise. Eating provides an independent immediate flow of utility, without which weight gain would never be predicted to occur, while exercising can (but does not have to) produce disutility.

Significantly, utility also depends on an individual's level of weight. The individual's preference over his weight targets an ideal weight, W_0; this may or may not be the same as medically ideal weight, as an individual may consider other factors like appearance, in addition to health. Above this level, the individual considers himself to be overweight in the sense that he would pay for weight-loss, and below this level underweight in the sense of being willing to pay for weight gain.

The neoclassical theory of weight holds that the marginal benefit of eating today is equal to the current pleasure of eating, plus the present-discounted marginal utility (or disutility) of weight gain. Being overweight thus lowers the value of eating. The opposite is true for exercise. This leads to the natural implication that reductions in the price of food promote eating and weight gain, while reductions in the price of exercise do the reverse.

A less obvious implication is the natural complementarity of eating and exercise. Lakdawalla and Philipson emphasize the fact that food has become significantly cheaper since the late 1970s, and over the entire 20th century. A reduction in the price of food leads to weight gain; for individuals above their ideal weight (this is likely to be the modal case in the US), this raises the value of weight-control activities like exercise. This sheds some light on the rise in leisure-based exercise that has accompanied the recent growth in weight. Since the growth in exercise is second-order, it does not reverse the growth in weight. Therefore, cheaper food results in more eating, higher weight, *and* more exercise.

The neoclassical theory of weight stresses that technological change on the calorie supply and demand side provides natural interpretation of the overall time series. While food has become cheaper through technological change in agriculture, exercise has become more expensive, as work (at home and in the market) has become less physically demanding through technologies that at the same time raise productivity and lower calorie spending. The effects of scarcer exercise are quite analogous to the effects of food price reduction. As the implicit price of exercise rises, the result is less overall exercise, heavier weight, and *less* food consumption, as people substitute toward other forms of weight control. The declining price of food and the rising price of exercise have offsetting impacts on food consumption. Therefore, food consumption may rise or fall as weights rise; this is consistent with the 20th century data showing periods of both rising and falling food consumption, in spite of continual increases in weight and falling food prices.

The neoclassical weight model also yields important predictions about the relationship between income and weight. Health or 'closeness' to one's preference-defined ideal weight is likely to be a normal good. Therefore, richer people are more likely to spend resources moving in the direction of their ideal weight. This leads to a non-monotonic relationship between income and weight. For poor, underweight people, income growth leads to more food consumption and a drive to increase weight. However, among overweight people, additional income might lead to weight loss, as people strive to move towards ideal weight. This helps explain why, within rich countries, income raises weight among the poorest groups, but lowers it throughout the upper half of the income distribution. In addition, while income has a non-monotonic effect on weight within countries, it has a strong positive effect across countries, more than simply accounted for by aggregation. The impact of technology on weight is essential to interpret these two patterns, as across countries more sedentary but more productive technologies are used, causing both income and weight to rise. In poor countries today, as in rich countries historically, people get paid, rather than pay through leisure time, to exercise, making lower incomes associated with lower weight.

The neoclassical theory of weight has been tested in several contexts. Lakdawalla and Philipson (2002) provide evidence that the strenuousness of work has very large BMI effects and that career effects of jobs are on the order of magnitude of the long-run changes in weight. Using longitudinal data from the National Longitudinal Survey of Youth, they report finding that 14 years spent in the most sedentary job results in a BMI gain of 2 full units. Chou et al. (2004) analyse a wide variety of price effects and find that weight seems to rise with: lower relative prices of food at home, lower relative prices of fast-food and full-service restaurants, the wider availability of such restaurants, lower relative prices of alcohol, and higher relative prices of smoking.[4] Lakdawalla and Philipson (2002) report that about half the growth in weight since the late 1970s can be explained by the declining relative price of food. Lakdawalla et al. (2005) report similar findings for food quality, as opposed to quantity: increases in the relative prices of certain types of foods seem to increase the prevalence of deficiencies in nutrients from those foods. For example, when orange juice is more expensive, Vitamin C deficiency rises, and so on. Finally, Cutler et al. (2003) emphasize the declining time cost of preparing food, through technological change in food-processing.

Cawley (1999) discusses the implications of rational addiction on weight. Eating is addictive in the 'rational addiction' sense (see Becker and Murphy, 1988) that past eating raises the marginal utility of current eating. The neoclassical theory of weight stresses the dynamic costs of eating that flow from weight gain alone, but the addictive model adds to that characterization: additional food intake today makes it necessary to increase food intake in the future. This 'adjacent complementarity' implies that increases in the future price of food lead to current reductions in food intake, because current food intake shifts up the future demand for food.

In addition, Cawley studies a situation where weight gain damages an individual's stock of health and thus lowers utility. His framework thus involves two capital goods: weight and health. Significantly, the two capital goods trade off. Being heavier allows an individual to enjoy food consumption more, but it is also costly in that it damages health. Similarly, a greater stock of health improves welfare, but decreases the extent to which an individual enjoys eating. The presence of two opposed capital stocks leads to an important implication: in equilibrium, an addicted individual may exhibit cyclical fluctuation in weight. This leads to so-called 'binging and purging', which empirically characterizes the behaviour of people who are substantially overweight or obese. Levy (2002) derives a similar prediction from a dynamic model in which small perturbations of weight can lead to explosive oscillations.

In many respects, the neoclassical model and addiction model are complements, rather than substitutes. The addiction model explains an important non-steady state behaviour at the individual-level, particularly of behaviour by the severely overweight or obese. The neoclassical model focuses on explaining societal movements in weight over time and cross-sectional variation in weight. Both share the view that individuals are rational and forward-looking about their weight.

The behavioural theory of weight
Cutler et al. (2003) have explored a behavioural economics interpretation of weight and obesity. They argue that eating is addictive, but unlike Cawley, they argue that individuals have problems with self-control which prevents them from committing in advance to a consumption path for food, exercise and weight. Specifically, they assume that individuals do not discount the future exponentially, as a neoclassical consumer does, but instead quasi-hyperbolically (see Laibson, 1997; Gruber and Koszegi, 2001).

In particular, their one period ahead discount factor is $\beta\delta$, for β, $\delta < 1$, but their discount factor for t periods ahead is $\beta^t \delta$. The result is that the individual's marginal rate of substitution between today and tomorrow is $\beta\delta$, but the marginal rate of substitution between, say, next Wednesday and next Thursday is simply $\beta > \beta\delta$. Since the marginal rate of substitution over one period varies over time, the individual's decision-making is inconsistent, and the agent will always find it optimal to break with past consumption plans.

It is possible that individuals will mechanically and consistently violate their past plans for consumption. These individuals are called 'naive' time-inconsistent agents. However, repeatedly violating past consumption plans, time after time, may not constitute an equilibrium strategy, since an individual will soon learn not to formulate plans that will never be followed. Therefore, the literature on time-inconsistency also considers 'sophisticated' time-inconsistent agents, who recognize their incentive to deviate from consumption plans. Such individuals play a non-cooperative game with their future selves (Schelling, 1978); as a result, they value devices that will cause their future selves to commit to a particular consumption path, and dislike devices that facilitate deviation from prior plans.

Cutler et al. argue that this type of behaviour is important for understanding the recent growth in obesity, because much of the increase in calorie intake has come from a particular form of agricultural innovation: snack foods, prepared foods, and foods purchased from vending machines. They interpret such technological innovations as diminishing the possibility of self-control in a world with time-inconsistent agents. The presence of a ready-made snack food close at hand makes it more difficult for an individual to commit to eating less.

In spite of their very different structure, behavioural theories actually share quite a few commonalities with neoclassical ones; in general, it is extremely difficult to distinguish the positive predictions between a behavioural and a neoclassical theory of addiction. Both theories imply similar responses to price changes. Both argue that the most overweight people ought to respond most strongly to price changes, as appears to have occurred over the past several decades. Both can generate cyclical weight fluctuation, with the introduction of a health capital stock. Behavioural theories add a useful explanatory element: they help us understand why people seek self-control or commitment devices (for example, a Weight Watchers group) when they attempt to lose weight. However, they add less to understanding the overall time trends and differences across countries; differences in addictions seem implausible as an explanation why Africans are thinner than Americans. Addictions, similar to genes, affects the *elasticity* by which populations respond to the changed incentives discussed in the neoclassical model, but are not their cause.

4. The consequences of obesity

The theoretical framework for understanding obesity can be used to derive policy conclusions once we examine the public and private costs of obesity. The most easily quantifiable, and perhaps most important, cost of obesity is its effect on health. There have been both observational and clinical studies of the relationship between obesity and health; they suggest that obesity does adversely impact health, although the effects seem to vary in consistent ways.

Observational evidence on health

Numerous studies have found that obesity is associated with increased risk of hypertension, dyslipidemia, type 2 diabetes, coronary heart disease, stroke, gallbladder disease, osteoarthritis, respiratory disorders including sleep apnoea and asthma, and some types of cancer (National Institutes of Health, 1998). Hypertension prevalence also increases with BMI. Using nationally representative data from Wave III of the National Health and Nutrition Examination Survey, Brown et al. (2000) find that prevalence of high blood pressure (where high blood pressure is defined as mean systolic $BP \geq 140$ mm Hg or mean diastolic $BP \geq 90$ mm Hg) among adult men with $BMI < 25$ was 15 per cent, compared to 42 per cent for men with $BMI \geq 30$. For women, the prevalence of high blood pressure for the two ranges of BMI was 15 per cent and 38 per cent, respectively. The effect of BMI on blood pressure was greatest for men and women ages 20 to 59. Finally, studies have shown correlations between BMI and some types of cancer including colon, breast, endometrial and gallbladder (Garfinkel, 1986; Chu et al., 1991; Giovannucci et al., 1996; Brown et al., 2000).

In terms of overall medical spending, a recent estimate suggests that obesity alone is associated with \$75 billion (in 2003 dollars) of medical spending in the US (Finkelstein, Fiebelkorn and Wang, 2004), half of which comes from Medicare and Medicaid. Sturm (2002) found that non-elderly adults (18- to 65-year olds) who are obese ($BMI \geq 30$) incurred on average \$395 more in medical spending per year than those in the normal weight range.

Clinical evidence on health
While the observational evidence is voluminous and informative, it leaves open the possibility that obesity and poor health are caused by some third unobserved factor. Only experimental or quasi-experimental evidence can answer this question satisfactorily. To date, no economist or other social scientist has produced a quasi-experimental investigation of whether obesity affects health, but there are relevant clinical studies in the medical literature.

While not as reliable as experimental evidence, several studies have found that weight loss – voluntary or involuntary – reduces the risk of diabetes and hypertension, and improves health (Pamuk et al., 1992; Pamuk et al., 1993). More dependable are randomized clinical trials. Trials of behavioural changes have suggested that diet and exercise-induced weight loss reduces the risk of diabetes and hypertension, and improves health (Appel et al., 2003; Bray et al., 2003). Similar findings obtain for trials of pharmaceutically induced weight loss. The weight-loss drug sibutramine has been found both to lower weight and to reduce hypertension and diabetes prevalence (James et al., 2000; O'Meara et al., 2002).

Randomized clinical trials of weight-loss surgery[5] have also found it to have lifetime health benefits for the obese (Craig and Tseng, 2002). A larger, but non-randomized, trial – the Swedish Obese Subjects (SOS) study – also found similar results. While individuals had to agree to surgery, each was matched on the basis of various baseline characteristics to another individual in a control group that did not receive surgery. The study found virtually no weight loss in the control group, but a statistically significant loss of more than 16 per cent of body weight in the treatment arm (Sjostrom, 2003). This weight loss was accompanied by a significant reduction in the incidence of diabetes, hypertension and hyper-triglyceridaemia.

Labour market effects
The empirical analysis of weight gain has also addressed the labour market effects of weight. Cawley (2004) reports using an instrumental variables approach that body weight

lowers labour market wages for women, particularly white women, but not for men. He uses a sibling's weight as an instrument for an individual's own weight, by arguing that the vast majority of the within-family correlation is genetic rather than environmental. Baum and Ford (2004) show that the negative correlation between obesity and wages persists in panel data, even after family background and other covariates are controlled, but this approach cannot rule out unobserved heterogeneity to the extent that an instrumental variables strategy can. Similar relationships have been uncovered more generally between appearance and weight: more attractive people seem to earn more, whether from thinness or other factors (Hamermesh and Biddle, 1994; Averett and Korenman, 1996; Biddle and Hamermesh, 1998).

5. Obesity and public policy

From an economic point of view, the key question is whether the weight management decision involves external effects not accounted for by the individual. Clearly obesity is a private health problem, but is it also a public health problem in the sense of there being efficiency gains from weight reductions?

The neoclassical case for intervention

The neoclassical model of weight gain, either in its capital investment or addictive form, implies that externalities occur only if weight gain harms the welfare of other individuals. In the spirit of the early work by Keeler et al. (1989), Grossman and Rashad (2004) have argued that externalities are created by public health insurance pools. When individuals are publicly insured, as through Medicare or Medicaid in the US, increased weight can drive up average costs for the taxpayers who are financing these programmes. Those gaining weight are not likely to consider the effects they have on other taxpayers. Similar problems arise with private insurance when information or underwriting is incomplete: few insurers allow their premiums to vary with weight, but overweight people must then be passing costs along to others in the health insurance pool.

If public insurance is provided optimally, through the interaction of taxpayers and interest groups, taxpayers account for the health risks and behaviours of those in the public insurance pool, and are voluntarily covering their health expenditures. Problems may arise, however, if there are substantial fixed costs associated with changing public insurance programmes or institutions. If public intervention is to be justified by the neoclassical model, it must be because of these fixed costs. As emphasized by Grossman and Rashad (2004), these policies would best take the form of subsidies for exercise, since taxes on food intake would need to be highly non-linear in order to be effective. It is difficult to tax only excess calories; a blanket food tax affects even socially beneficial calorie intake. Conversely, a marginal increase in exercise always lowers weight and has social benefits, provided the individual is not underweight.

Many times observers, particularly in the policy community, who cite public health insurance costs as the rationale for public interventions into obesity purposely overlook what are potential offsetting fiscal effects of increased obesity, such as reduced spending on public annuity programmes. Such reduced fiscal spending due to increased mortality, as brought up by economists, is often viewed as absurd or irrelevant. However, neglecting it may simply reveal that fiscal effects are not the true rationale for an intervention, as taxpayers may actually save due to increased obesity, but it may be held up as a convenient substitute for other implicit rationales.

The behavioural case for intervention
While the behavioural economics case for policy intervention would appear to be stronger, it is actually considerably weaker. As Gruber and Koszegi (2001) and Cutler et al. (2003) have argued, there are gains to the provision of a self-control device when individuals are time-inconsistent in their health or other behaviours. However, this does not mean that governments have an advantage over the private sector in self-control. Indeed, savings behaviour was an initial area of the economic analysis of self-control, despite the fact that governments are not penalized for low savings and therefore have greater difficulties than individuals in controlling their debts. Any self-control device intrinsically restricts the choice set of a future individual; therefore, rather than Pareto-improving the welfare of a time-inconsistent individual, it simply redistributes welfare from future selves to earlier selves (Bhattacharya and Lakdawalla, 2004). While such policies may be adopted, they do not enhance efficiency in the Pareto sense. Policy-adoption under a behavioural theory requires that the policy-maker make a normative judgement about which 'self's' welfare is more important.

Notes
1. The figure's sources are documented completely in Costa and Steckel (1995).
2. The figure is based on US Department of Agriculture estimates of 'Calories available for human consumption'. For each agricultural commodity, the USDA estimates total output and subtracts exports, industrial uses and farm inputs (for example, feed and seed), to arrive at calories available from the given commodity. Total calories are computed by aggregating across all commodities. See Putnam and Allshouse (1999) for further details.
3. While the neoclassical theory tends to focus on the behaviour of well-informed individuals with rational expectations, there is some initial evidence that beliefs and information about obesity vary such that heavier people are less well-informed about the causes and consequences of weight gain (Kan and Tsai, 2004). It is difficult to draw firm conclusions from this research, however, since health knowledge tends to be positively correlated with incentives for good health.
4. Cawley et al. (2004) focus more specifically on the effect of smoking on weight: they show that adolescents, particularly females, sometimes initiate smoking as a method of weight control.
5. Two commonly used surgical procedures are gastric bypass, where a large portion of the stomach is bypassed to decrease the uptake of nutrients and fat, and vertical banded gastroplasty, which involves the restriction of oesophageal opening into the stomach.

References
Appel, L.J., C.M. Champagne, D.W. Harsha, L.S. Cooper, E. Obarzanek, P.J. Elmer, V.J. Stevens, W.M. Vollmer, P.H. Lin, L.P. Sretkey, S.W. Stedman and D.R. Young (2003), 'Effects of comprehensive lifestyle modification on blood pressure control: main results of the PREMIER clinical trial', *Journal of the American Medical Association*, **289**(16), 2083–93.
Averett, S. and S. Korenman (1996), 'The economic reality of the beauty myth', *Journal of Human Resources*, **31**(2), 304–30.
Baum, C.L. II, and W.F. Ford (2004), 'The wage effects of obesity: a longitudinal study', *Health Economics*, **13**(9), 885–99.
Becker, G.S. and K.M. Murphy (1988), 'A theory of rational addiction', *Journal of Political Economy*, **96**(4), 675–700.
Bhattacharya, J. and D. Lakdawalla (2004), *Time-Inconsistency and Welfare*, National Bureau of Economic Research, Inc, NBER Working Papers.
Biddle, J.E. and D.S. Hamermesh (1998), 'Beauty, productivity, and discrimination: lawyer's looks and lucre', *Journal of Labor Economics*, **16**(1), 172–201.

Bray, G.A., D.H. Ryan and D.W. Harsha (2003), 'Diet, weight loss, and cardiovascular disease prevention', *Current Treatment Options in Cardiovasc Medicine*, **5**(4), 259–69.

Brown, C.D., M. Higgins, K.A Donato, F.C. Rohde, R. Garrison, E. Obarzanek, N.D. Ernst and M. Horan (2000), 'Body mass index and the prevalence of hypertension and dyslipidemia', *Obesity Research*, **8**(9), 605–19.

Cawley, J. (1999), 'Obesity and addiction', Ph.D. Dissertation, University of Chicago, Department of Economics, Chicago, IL.

Cawley, J. (2004), 'Impact of obesity on wages', *Journal of Human Resources*, **39**(2), 451–74.

Cawley, J., S. Markowitz and J. Tauras (2004), 'Lighting up and slimming down: the effects of body weight and cigarette prices on adolescent smoking initiation', *Journal of Health Economics*, **23**(2), 293–311.

Chou, S.-Y., M. Grossman and H. Saffer (2004), 'An economic analysis of adult obesity: results from the Behavioral Risk Factor Surveillance System', *Journal of Health Economics*, **23**(3), 565–87.

Chu, S.Y., N.C. Lee, P.A. Wingo, R.T. Senie, R.S. Greenberg and H.B. Petersen (1991), 'The relationship between body mass and breast cancer among women enrolled in the Cancer and Steroid Hormone Study', *Journal of Clinical Epidemiology*, **44**(11), 1197–206.

Costa, D. and R. Steckel (1995), 'Long-term trends in health, welfare, and economic growth in the United States', National Bureau of Economic Research Historical Working Paper 76, Cambridge, MA: National Bureau of Economic Research.

Craig, B.M. and D.S. Tseng (2002), 'Cost-effectiveness of gastric bypass for severe obesity', *American Journal of Medicine* **113**(6), 491–8.

Cutler, D.M., E.L. Glaeser and J.M. Shapiro (2003), 'Why have Americans become more obese?', *Journal of Economic Perspectives*, **17**(3), 93–118.

Finkelstein, E.A., I.C. Fiebelkorn and G. Wang (2004), 'State-level estimates of annual medical expenditures attributable to obesity', *Obesity Research*, **12**(1), 18–24.

Flegal, K.M., M.D. Carroll, R.J. Kuczmarski and C.L. Johnson (1998), 'Overweight and obesity in the United States: prevalence and trends, 1960–1994', *International Journal of Obesity and Related Metabolic Disorders*, **22**(1), 39–47.

Flegal, K.M., M.D. Carroll, C.L. Ogden and C.L. Johnson (2002), 'Prevalence and trends in obesity among US adults, 1999–2000', *Journal of the American Medical Association*, **288**(14), 1723–27.

Garfinkel, L. (1986), 'Overweight and mortality', *Cancer*, **58**(8 Suppl), 1826–9.

Giovannucci, E., G.A. Colditz, M.J. Stampfer and W.C. Willett (1996), 'Physical activity, obesity, and risk of colorectal adenoma in women (United States)', *Cancer Causes Control*, **7**(2), 253–63.

Grossman, M. and I. Rashad (2004), 'The economics of obesity', *Public Interest*, (156), 104–12.

Gruber, J. and B. Koszegi (2001), 'Is addiction "Rational"? Theory and evidence', *Quarterly Journal of Economics*, **116**(4), 1261–303.

Hamermesh, D.S. and J.E. Biddle (1994), 'Beauty and the labor market', *American Economic Review*, **84**(5), 1174–94.

James, W.P., A. Astrup, N. Finer, J. Hilsted, P. Kopelman, S. Rossner, W.H. Saris and L.F. Van Gaal (2000), 'Effect of sibutramine on weight maintenance after weight loss: a randomised trial. STORM Study Group. Sibutramine Trial of Obesity Reduction and Maintenance', *The Lancet*, **356**(9248), 2119–25.

Kan, K. and W.-D. Tsai (2004), 'Obesity and risk knowledge', *Journal of Health Economics*, **23**(5), 907–34.

Keeler, E., W. Manning, J. Newhouse, E.M. Sloss and J. Wasserman (1989), 'The external costs of a sedentary life-style', *American Journal of Public Health*, **79**(8), 975–81.

Laibson, D. (1997), 'Golden eggs and hyperbolic discounting', *Quarterly Journal of Economics*, **112**(2), 443–77.

Lakdawalla, D.N. and T.J. Philipson (2002), 'Technological change and the growth of obesity', National Bureau of Economic Research Working Paper 8946, Cambridge, MA: National Bureau of Economic Research.

Lakdawalla, D., T. Philipson and J. Bhattacharya (2005), 'Welfare-enhancing technological change and the growth of obesity', *American Economic Review: AEA Papers and Proceedings*, **95**(3), May.

Levy, A. (2002), 'Rational eating: can it lead to overweightness or underweightness?', *Journal of Health Economics*, **21**(5), 887–99.

Mokdad, A.H., M.K. Serdula, W.H. Dietz, B.A. Bowman, J.S. Marks and J.P. Koplan (1999), 'The spread of the obesity epidemic in the United States, 1991–1998', *Journal of American Medical Association*, **282**(16), 1519–22.

Mokdad, A.H., M.K. Serdula, W.H. Dietz, B.A. Bowman, J.S. Marks and J.P. Koplan (2000), 'The continuing epidemic of obesity in the United States', *Journal of the American Medical Association*, **284**(13), 1650–1.

National Institutes of Health (1998), *Clinical Guidelines on the Identification, Evaluation, and Treatment of Overweight and Obesity in Adults*.

O'Meara, S., R. Riemsma, L. Shirran, L. Mather and G. ter Riet (2002), 'The clinical effectiveness and cost-effectiveness of sibutramine in the management of obesity: a technology assessment', *Health Technology Assessment*, **6**(6), 1–97.

Pamuk, E.R., D.F. Williamson, J. Madans, M.K. Serdula, J.C. Kleinman and T. Byers (1992), 'Weight loss and mortality in a national cohort of adults, 1971–1987', *American Journal of Epidemiology*, **136**(6), 686–97.

Pamuk, E.R., D.F. Williamson, M.K. Serdula, J. Madans, and T.E. Byers (1993), 'Weight loss and subsequent death in a cohort of US adults', *Annals Internal Medicine*, **119**(7 Pt 2), 744–8.

Philipson, T.J. and R.A. Posner (1999), 'The long-run growth in obesity as a function of technological change', National Bureau of Economic Research Working Paper 7423, Cambridge, MA: National Bureau of Economic Research.

Putnam, J.J. (2000), 'Major trends in US food supply: 1909–99', *Food Review*, **23**(1), 8–15.

Putnam, J.J. and J.E. Allshouse (1999), 'Food consumption, prices and expenditures, 1970–97', Economic Research Service, US Department of Agriculture Statistical Bulletin 965, Washington DC: Economic Research Service, US Department of Agriculture.

Schelling, T.C. (1978), 'Economics, or the art of self-management', *American Economic Review*, **68**(2), 290–94.

Seidell, J.C. and I. Deerenberg (1994), 'Obesity in Europe: prevalence and consequences for use of medical care', *Pharmacoeconomics*, **5**(Suppl. 1), 38–44.

Sjostrom, C.D. (2003), 'Surgery as an intervention for obesity. Results from the Swedish obese subjects study', *Growth Hormone and IGF Research*, **13**, S22–S26.

Sturm, R. (2002), 'The effects of obesity, smoking, and drinking on medical problems and costs. Obesity out-ranks both smoking and drinking in its deleterious effects on health and health costs', *Health Affairs (Millwood)*, **21**(2), 245–53.

VanItallie, T.B. (1996), 'Prevalence of obesity', *Endocrinology and Metabolism Clinics of North America*, **25**(4), 887–905.

8 Illicit drugs and drug-related crime
*Jody L. Sindelar and Todd A. Olmstead**

1. Introduction

Understanding the relationship between illicit drug use and crime is a critical first step in developing policies aimed at mitigating the costs to society of drug-related crime. Although illicit drug use harms both users (for example, loss of quality of life, premature death) and their families (for example, physical and emotional abuse), a substantial portion of the total cost of illicit drug use is borne by society in the form of externalities, especially drug-related crime. In the US, crime-related costs accounted for 62 per cent of the estimated $143 billion in societal costs due to illicit drug use in 1998 (ONDCP, 2001).[1] In Australia, crime-related costs accounted for 41 per cent of the estimated $6.1 billion in societal costs due to illicit drug use in 1998–99 (Collins and Lapsley, 2002). In Canada, 87 per cent of the societal cost per illicit opiate user ($45 000) in 1997 was due to crime victimization (45 per cent) and law enforcement/criminal justice system costs (42 per cent) (Fischer et al., 2001). And in Britain, 78 per cent of the societal cost per illicit drug user (£11 400) in 1996 was due to crime victimization and criminal justice system costs (Healey et al., 1998). While these estimated costs may not be comparable to each other due to variations in methods, and they may not be precise due to measurement issues, it is nevertheless clear that around the globe, the costs of drug-related crime are substantial.

This chapter focuses on the relationship between illicit drug use and crime. Section 2 provides background information on illicit drug use. Section 3 discusses the nature of the relationship between illicit drug use and crime. Section 4 discusses approaches to reduce the costs of both illicit drug use and drug-related crime. Section 5 concludes with a brief discussion of why we do not know more about either the relationship between drugs and crime or about the effects of policies on drug-related crime. Although we focus primarily on illicit drug use and crime in the US, we include results from other countries and, in any case, recognize that issues encountered in the US extend to other countries as well.

2. Background on illicit drugs

Whether a specific psychoactive drug is considered illegal depends on a variety of factors, including jurisdiction, purpose of use, amount in possession, age of user, activities undertaken by user while under the influence, and time period. Marijuana is the most widely used illicit drug in the US, but is legal in Holland in amounts up to 30 grams (Drug Policy Alliance, 2005). It is also legal in some US states (for example, California) if used by the sick and dying for medicinal purposes (Drug Policy Alliance, 2005). Similarly, many other

* The authors would like to acknowledge financial support from the National Institute on Drug Abuse (NIDA R01-DA14471)

drugs in the US are legal only with a prescription (for example, pain-relievers such as Vicodin and OxyContin) and are of concern here because they can substitute for some illegal drugs and can be characterized by similar maladaptive use. Some drugs are legal only to those above an age threshold. The legal drinking age for alcohol varies dramatically around the world, from 0 in China to 16 in France to 21 in the US. In addition, although possession and consumption of many drugs are legal, it may be illegal to perform certain activities while under the influence of these drugs. In the US, it is illegal to drive while under the influence of alcohol (thresholds for the definition of 'influence' vary from state to state). Finally, the laws determining whether a given drug is illegal are subject to change over time. Opium, morphine and cocaine were legally available in the US until the late 19th century when cities, states and the nation started passing laws restricting access. International agreements condemning opiates and cocaine were negotiated early in the 20th century (Musto, 1987).

In general, illicit drug users span the spectrum from the one-time or occasional user to those who abuse the drugs, to those who are dependent on them. Dependence is distinguished largely by tolerance and withdrawal symptoms, whereas abuse is distinguished by harmful use with knowledge of the persistent harms caused rather than meeting the criteria for dependence (American Psychiatric Association, 1994). In the US, information about illicit drug use is collected annually via the National Survey on Drug Use and Health (NSDUH), formerly called the National Household Survey on Drug Abuse, which groups illicit drugs into nine different categories: marijuana (including hashish), cocaine (including crack), heroin, hallucinogens (including LSD, PCP, peyote, mescaline, mushrooms, and 'Ecstasy'), inhalants (including amyl nitrite, cleaning fluids, gasoline, paint and glue) and non-medical use of prescription-type drugs (pain-relievers, tranquilizers, stimulants, and sedatives).[2] The 2003 NSDUH estimates that 8.2 per cent of Americans (19.5 million people) aged 12 or older are current illicit drug users (that is, they had used an illicit drug during the month prior to the survey), and 3.1 per cent (7.3 million people) were deemed to need treatment for abuse of or dependence on illicit drugs (SAMHSA, 2004).

Rates of use of illicit drugs vary by the drug in question as well as by many demographic factors, including age, gender, race, employment status and mental health. According to the 2003 NSDUH, marijuana is the most commonly used illicit drug in the US, used by 75 per cent of illicit drug users. Illicit drug use is strongly correlated with age, increasing with age until peaking in 18–20-year-olds (24 per cent), and then declining steadily after that. Men (10.0 per cent) are more likely to report illicit drug use than women (6.5 per cent). By race, illicit drug use is highest among American Indians and Alaska Natives (12.1 per cent) and lowest for Asians (3.8 per cent), with blacks (8.7 per cent), whites (8.3 per cent), and Hispanics (8.0 per cent) in between. By employment status, illicit drug use is highest for unemployed adults aged 18 or older (18.2 per cent), lowest for those employed full-time (7.9 per cent), and in between for those employed part-time (10.7 per cent). Adults aged 18 or older with a serious mental illness (SMI)[3] are more than twice as likely as adults without SMI to use illicit drugs (27.3 per cent vs. 12.5 per cent), and adults with SMI are more than four times as likely as adults without SMI to abuse or be dependent on illicit drugs (8.6 per cent vs. 2.0 per cent) (SAMHSA, 2004).

3.   Relationship between illicit drug use and crime

To craft effective policies that reduce both illicit drug use and drug-related crime, it is important to understand the relationships between drugs and crime. If illicit drug use is the root cause of crime, then prevention and treatment of drug use might be effective in stopping crime as well. The general consensus is that there is a very strong association between illicit drug use and crime, as evidenced both by high rates of illicit drug use among samples of criminals and by high rates of criminal behaviour among samples of illicit drug users. In the US, 55 per cent of convicted inmates held in local jails in 1996 said they used illegal drugs during the month prior to their offence (BJS, 1998), and 24 per cent of the estimated 1.4 million adults aged 18 or older on parole or supervised release from prison in 2003 were current illicit drug users (that is, they had used illicit drugs in the month prior to the survey), compared to 7.7 per cent among adults not on parole or supervised release (SAMHSA, 2004). In samples of illicit drugs users in Canada and Australia, 60–77 per cent of users reported criminal activity as a major or secondary source of income (Fischer et al., 2001; Hall et al., 1993).

Although it is clear that illicit drug use and crime are closely linked, there is less agreement about the nature of the association between these two social ills. Broadly speaking, researchers have offered four different explanations for the link between illicit drug use and crime: illicit drug use causes crime, crime causes illicit drug use, both crime and illicit drug use are caused by other factors (for example, abusive family environments, impoverished neighbourhoods), and, given that illicit drug users are a heterogeneous group, each of the previous explanations may be valid for different subgroups of users. Each of these four possibilities is discussed below.

Illicit drug use causes crime

In many countries, illicit drug use causes crime by definition, inasmuch as possession and sale of these drugs are illegal. Apart from this tautology, however, there are three reasons why illicit drug use may cause crime. First, users may commit crimes to generate income to finance their habit. Second, illicit drugs may change the nervous system in short- or long-term ways that predispose an individual to commit crimes. And third, inasmuch as activities involving illicit drugs (for example, manufacture, distribution, sales) are illegal, conflicts involving such activities must be resolved outside of the law, perhaps in violent ways.

The evidence supporting these three theories is compelling. Numerous studies report that the majority of crimes committed by illicit drug users are non-violent, income-generating offences such as shoplifting, burglary and forgery/fraud (Fischer et al., 2001; Haynes, 1998; Kaye et al., 1998). Moreover, criminals frequently claim that they committed their current offence to obtain money for drugs (BJS, 1999), and the frequency of such offences is reduced when individuals undergo treatment for their substance abuse (Jofre-Bonet and Sindelar, 2001; Gossop et al., 2000). There is evidence that some stimulant drugs (for example, cocaine, amphetamines) induce violent behaviour through their psychopharmacological properties (Davis, 1996; Giannini, et al., 1993; Post, 1986; Post and Kopanda, 1975, 1976). And in the US, the Federal Bureau of Investigations reported that 4.6 per cent of homicides, in which circumstances were known, were narcotics-related (that is, associated with drug trafficking, manufacturing, and so on) (BJS, 2005).

Crime causes illicit drug use
The theory that crime causes illicit drug use views drug-taking as an extension of a deviant lifestyle in which individuals become involved with whatever illegal activities are 'in vogue' – if not drugs, then it would be something else (Kaye et al., 1998; Bean and Wilkinson, 1988). In this view, individuals engaging in frequent illegal activities within criminal networks are exposed to other illegal behaviours, such as illicit drugs. Thus, the initiation of illicit drug use is through criminal networks (Fischer et al., 2001). Support for this view comes from the fact that, in many studies, the majority of user-criminals were criminals before they were users, suggesting that crime leads to illicit drug use (Best et al., 2001; Kaye et al., 1998; Bean and Wilkinson, 1988).

Both crime and illicit drug use are caused by other factors
Both crime and illicit drug use may be caused by other factors, including economic marginality, social isolation, family pathology, early childhood victimization, gaps in cognitive and emotional skills, and mental illness (Gossop et al., 2000; Haynes, 1998; Hall et al., 1993; Fagan, 1990; Hammersley et al., 1989; Clayton and Tuchfeld, 1982; McBride and McCoy, 1982). That is, societal, developmental and genetic factors may predispose individuals towards both illicit drug use and criminal behaviour. To the extent that these other factors cause both drug use and crime, complex changes have to take place to prevent drug use and crime from developing.

All of the above (users are a heterogeneous group)
The above explanations for the relationship between illicit drug use and crime are not mutually exclusive. Given the heterogeneity among illicit drug users (SAMHSA, 2004; Kaye et al., 1998; Shaffer et al., 1984), it is possible that each explanation is valid for particular drugs, for one or more subgroups of users, or for the same users at different times during their criminal and drug using careers. For example, when the order of initial illicit drug use and criminality are taken into account, Kaye et al. (1998) find significant differences in demographics, the nature and severity of criminal offences, and psychopathology across subgroups. Specifically, individuals who engage in criminal activity before their first use of illicit drugs are more likely to be young, male, diagnosed with antisocial personality disorder, and to commit violent and destructive crimes (for example, armed robbery, assault with a weapon, arson) than individuals who use illicit drugs before committing their first criminal offence. Such marked differences between the subgroups increase the likelihood of multiple valid explanations for the relationship between illicit drug use and criminality.

4. How to reduce the costs of illicit drug use and drug-related crime?
Society uses a wide variety of approaches to address the twin problems of illicit drug use and drug-related crime. Although no approach has been found to stop these problems, many approaches have been used, with varying degrees of effectiveness, to reduce the costs of illicit drug use and drug-related crime. Economists and others often delineate these approaches according to their impact on demand vs. supply, although some approaches operate on both dimensions and others are difficult to categorize into this simple taxonomy (Wilson, 1990). Approaches that primarily affect the demand for illicit drugs

include treatment, prevention and some criminal justice methods (for example, prison sentences incapacitate current users and deter would-be users). Interdiction and crop eradication are the most obvious methods to reduce the supply of illegal drugs, especially the inflow from foreign countries. Policing and prison sentences are aimed at suppliers as well, including local suppliers. Legalization, decriminalization and harm reduction take a different tack by suggesting that it is not drug use per se that harms society, but rather the current laws regarding drug use that harm society (Miron, 1991; Nadelmann, 1988). Each of these approaches is discussed below.

Demand

There are three primary approaches to reducing the demand for illicit drugs: treatment, prevention and raising the full cost of using illicit drugs. Treatment for drug abuse can be delineated into different modalities based on the type of therapy provided (for example, counselling vs. pharmacotherapy) as well as by the setting where therapy takes place (for example, inpatient, outpatient, prison-based).[4] Counselling is by far the most common type of therapy provided overall and is provided in all settings. Methadone maintenance is the most common type of pharmacotherapy, although new medications such as buprenorphine are becoming more prevalent. The majority of treatments take place in outpatient settings. Recommended duration of treatment varies, but two to four weeks is common in counselling-only facilities, whereas the duration of treatment in methadone maintenance programmes frequently exceeds one year. Therapeutic Communities are examples of long-term residential environments that are designed especially for hard-core heroin dependent criminals; individuals often live in these environments for more than a year (Institute of Medicine, 1990).

In general, the substance abuse treatment system is plagued by early dropout and recidivism among illicit drug users. This is not surprising, however, given that patients in substance abuse treatment frequently have a broad array of problems in addition to their drug use, including legal, family, social, medical, mental health and employment difficulties. Although treating these multiple problems makes treatment for substance abuse more successful, doing so is costly. Nevertheless, many types of treatment have been reported to be effective (McLellan et al., 1993, 1998; Hubbard et al., 1997), cost-effective (Sindelar et al., 2004; Jofre-Bonet et al., 2004; Sindelar and Fiellin, 2001) and cost-beneficial (French et al., 2000, 2002). Moreover, substance abuse treatment has been shown to reduce drug-related crime (Jofre-Bonet and Sindelar, 2001; Gossop et al., 2000). Unfortunately, there are many more people in need of treatment than actually receive treatment. In the US, for example, approximately 3.1 per cent of individuals aged 12 or older (7.3 million people) were deemed to need treatment for abuse or dependence on illicit drugs during 2003; however, only 0.5 per cent (1.1 million people) received treatment in specialty facilities for illicit drug problems (SAMHSA, 2004). This treatment gap is due both to insufficient resources to provide treatment to all who need it and to a lack of interest in treatment by some users.

A wide variety of methods are used to prevent illicit drug use. Specific methods targeted at potential drug users include anti-drug media campaigns, workplace drug testing, school-based prevention programmes, and community-based and family-based interventions. Although targeted prevention programmes have been shown to be effective, their impact is often limited and varies from programme to programme (National Research Council, 2001).[5] More general approaches aimed at broader social goals – reducing poverty, cleaning up neighbourhoods, eliminating gangs,[6] early education and after-school programmes – may also reduce illicit drug use. However, these general approaches are difficult to evaluate with respect to their effects on drug use and crime due to their long-term nature and widespread impacts. Such programmes are typically aimed at broader problems, and reduction in drug use and crime may be only two of many outcomes of concern.

The criminal justice system can also affect the demand for drugs and criminal acts through deterrence and incapacitation. Stiff penalties (for example, long incarcerations) on illicit drug use and sales achieve both deterrence and incapacitation (Kessler and Levitt, 1999). Incarceration is clearly effective in reducing crime on the streets. The degree to which deterrence is effective has not been precisely determined and is very difficult to establish. However, long prison sentences for possession and sales of illicit drugs, and ballooning prison populations have not substantially diminished drug use and drug-related crime (SAMHSA, 1997, 1999).

Supply
Illicit drugs are frequently imported from other parts of the world. Consequently, many countries use border interdiction to prevent illicit drugs from entering their country. Although interdiction efforts lead to large drug busts on occasion, measurement problems inhibit precise evaluation of the effectiveness (or cost-effectiveness) of this approach (National Research Council, 2001). In the US, for example, the amount of illicit drugs smuggled across national borders is unknown. Therefore, it is not possible to gauge the percentage of illegal drugs being interdicted nor the effectiveness of the interdiction programmes in reducing the amount of illicit drugs entering the country (USGAO, 1990). Nevertheless, the impact and the threat of interdiction are thought to vary by the drug. Marijuana, for example, is relatively bulky and is a lower priced drug, so it is easier to find in searches and there is less incentive to risk transporting. Thus interdiction could result in a relatively large reduction in the supply of marijuana. There is some evidence that interdiction has been more successful in reducing the supply of heroin than cocaine in the US (Moore, 1990). Finally, eradicating drug crops and encouraging alternative legal crops are other methods used around the world to reduce the supply of drugs.

The supply of illicit drugs can also be affected by the criminal justice system, inasmuch as stiff penalties for manufacturing, distributing, and selling illicit drugs both imprison individuals in the illicit drug supply chain and deter others from taking their place. Some have argued that more emphasis should be placed on local dealers as opposed to international interdiction (Kleiman and Smith, 1990).

Harm-reduction, legalization and decriminalization
Another set of approaches takes the view that it is not illicit drug use per se that harms society, but rather the system based on making drugs illegal that causes most of the harm (Miron, 1991; Nadelmann, 1988). Such approaches include harm-reduction, legalization and decriminalization. A needle-exchange programme is an example of an effective harm-reduction approach – intravenous drug use is not targeted, but the spread of disease

(along with its societal costs) is reduced (Kaplan and O'Keefe, 1993). Those favouring legalization or decriminalization believe that if certain drugs were legal (for example, marijuana), then the costs associated with the criminal justice system and the lives harmed by incarceration would be reduced greatly.

Combining approaches

Most of the approaches discussed above can be grouped into two general categories: health system interventions (for example, substance abuse treatment) and legal system controls (for example, incarceration, interdiction) (Anglin and Perrochet, 1998). It may be advantageous to integrate approaches from both categories to take full advantage of their complementary strengths. The hope is that these more comprehensive approaches will be more effective. For example, civil commitment, in which drug-dependent criminals are coerced into treatment, has been shown to be highly effective. In this case, treatment reduces drug use while the legal system enforces both treatment retention and programme compliance (Anglin and Perrochet, 1998).[7] Other combination approaches include treatment in prison and treatment for arrested drug-abusing juveniles (CASA, 2004; Belenko and Dembo, 2003).

5. Challenges for future research

Theory and evidence both suggest that illicit drug use and crime are entwined. Although researchers have made substantial progress mapping the complex causal pathways that link illicit drug use and crime, much remains unknown. Without a better understanding of this relationship, society is ill-equipped to determine the most cost-effective mix of approaches to stop illicit drug use and drug-related crime.

Significant challenges remain in determining both the underlying causal links between illicit drug use and crime and the most effective set of solutions to these social problems. For example, individuals frequently have multiple problems that are inextricably linked to illicit drug use and crime, including poor parenting, dangerous neighbourhoods, mental health problems and poor education. It is difficult in practice to ascertain which problems came first and the resolution of which would solve the other problems, or how many have to be solved simultaneously. Part of the difficulty is in gathering data to study these problems. Extant studies often rely on aggregate arrest data that under-report the frequency of actual occurrence and do not allow observation of individual characteristics. Moreover, self-reported individual-level data on drug use and crime are uncommon in surveys of general populations, and, in any case, are likely to miss the heavy drug users and criminals, to have reporting bias and to have very small cell sizes of criminals. Although samples of drug-users in treatment offer detailed data on key populations, these are not nationally generalizable and may be subject to recall bias.

Beyond the challenges of obtaining pure statistical information, it is difficult to establish situations that reveal the relative effectiveness of different policies, treatments and combinations thereof. Social experiments could be conducted to obtain this information; but to be truly informative, they would need to last many years (and therefore be expensive to conduct) and some might be considered unethical.

Despite the difficulties in developing and evaluating solutions to illicit drug use and drug-related crime, the search continues for evidenced-based treatments, policies and interventions. And there are successes. For example, new pharmaceutical and counselling-based treatments are being tested through clinical trials, new combinations of treatment and criminal justice are being developed, and there are ongoing productive debates about both harm reduction and sentencing guidelines for drug users.

Notes

1. Crime-related costs include health care costs of crime victims, productivity losses of both crime victims and incarcerated offenders, criminal justice system and other public costs (for example, police protection, legal adjudication, state and federal corrections), and private costs (for example, private legal defence, property damage for crime victims).
2. The National Survey on Drug Use and Health provides annual data on drug use in the US and is sponsored by the Substance Abuse and Mental Health Services Administration (SAMHSA), an agency of the US Public Health Service.
3. SMI is defined as 'having at some time during the past year a diagnosable mental, behavioural, or emotional disorder that met the criteria specified in the 4th edition of the Diagnostic and Statistical Manual of Mental Disorders (DSM-IV) (American Psychiatric Association, 1994) and that resulted in functional impairment substantially interfering with or limiting one or more major life activities (SAMHSA, 2004).'
4. Although detoxification programmes can be either inpatient or outpatient, these are not considered to be treatments per se.
5. For example, a stark lesson was learned in the US when a well-known school-based prevention programme was found to be ineffective after it was widely used for many years (Lyman et al., 1999).
6. See Levitt and Venkatesh (2000) for an interesting analysis of the economics of drug-selling by gangs.
7. Initially it was thought that only self-motivated individuals would have successful treatment outcomes, but mounting evidence suggests that coercion is equally, if not more effective (Anglin and Perrochet, 1998).

References

American Psychiatric Association (1994), *Diagnostic and Statistical Manual of Mental Disorders (DSM-IV)* (4th edn), Washington, DC: American Psychiatric Association.

Anglin, M.D. and B. Perrochet (1998), 'Drug use and crime: a historical review of research conducted by the UCLA Drug Abuse Research Center', *Substance Use and Misuse*, **33**(9), 1871–914.

Bean, P.T. and C. Wilkinson (1988), 'Drug taking, crime and the illicit supply system', *British Journal of Addiction*, **83**, 533–9.

Belenko, S. and R. Dembo (2003), 'Treating adolescent substance abuse problems in the juvenile drug court', *International Journal of Law and Psychiatry*, **26**(1), 87–110.

Best, D., L-H. Man, M. Gossop, J. Harris, C. Sidwell and J. Strang, (2001), 'Understanding the developmental relationship between drug use and crime: are drug users the best people to ask?', *Addiction Research and Theory*, **9**(2), 151–64.

Bureau of Justice Statistics (BJS) (1998), *Profile of Jail Inmates: 1996*, US Department of Justice, Office of Justice Programs, NCJ 164620, Washington, DC.

Bureau of Justice Statistics (BJS) (1999), *Substance Abuse and Treatment, State and Federal Prisoners: 1997*, US Department of Justice, Office of Justice Programs, NCJ 172871, Washington, DC.

Bureau of Justice Statistics (BJS) (2005), *Drugs and Crime Facts*, US Department of Justice, Office of Justice Programs, available at http://www.ojp.usdoj.gov/bjs/dcf/duc.htm.

CASA: The National Center on Addiction and Substance Abuse at Columbia University (2004), *Criminal Neglect: Substance Abuse, Juvenile Justice and the Children Left Behind*, New York: The National Center on Addiction and Substance Abuse (CASA) at Columbia University.

Clayton, R.R. and B.S. Tuchfeld (1982), 'The drug–crime debate – obstacles to understanding the relationship', *Journal of Drug Issues*, **12**(2), 153–66.

Collins, D.J. and H.M. Lapsley (2002), *Counting the Cost: Estimates of the Social Costs of Drug Abuse in Australia in 1998–9*, National Drug Strategy Monograph Series No. 49, Canberra, Commonwealth of Australia.

Davis, W. (1996), 'Psychopharmacologic violence associated with cocaine abuse: kindling of a limbic dyscontrol syndrome'?, *Progress in Neuro-Psychopharmacology and Biological Psychiatry*, **20**, 1273–300.

Drug Policy Alliance (2005), *Marijuana: The Facts*, available at http://www.drugpolicy.org/marijuana.

Fagan, J. (1990), 'Intoxication and aggression', in M. Tonry and J.Q. Wilson (eds), *Drugs and Crime*, vol. 13, University of Chicago Press, pp. 241–320.

Fischer, B., W. Medved, M. Kirst, J. Rehm and L. Gliksman (2001), 'Illicit opiates and crime: results of an untreated user cohort study in Toronto', *Canadian Journal of Criminology-Revue*, **43**(2), 197–217.

French M.T., H.I.J. Salome, J.L. Sindelar and A.T McLellan (2002), 'Benefit–cost analysis of addiction treatment: methodological guidelines and applications using the DATCAP and ASI', *Health Services Research*, **37**(2), 433–55.

French, M.T., H.J. Salome, A. Krupski, J.R. McKay, D.M. Donovan, A.T. McLellan and J. Durell (2000), 'Benefit–cost analysis of residential and outpatient addiction treatment in the State of Washington', *Evaluation Review*, **24**(6), 609–34.

Giannini, A.J., N.S. Miller, R.H. Loiselle and C.E. Turner (1993), 'Cocaine-associated violence and relationship to route of administration', *Journal of Substance Abuse Treatment*, **10**(1), 67–9.

Gossop, M., J. Marsden, D. Stewart and A. Rolfe (2000), 'Reductions in acquisitive crime and drug use after treatment of addiction problems: 1-year follow-up outcomes', *Drug and Alcohol Dependence*, **58**, 165–72.

Hall, W., J. Bell and J. Carless (1993), 'Crime and drug use among applicants for methadone maintenance', *Drug and Alcohol Dependence*, **31**, 123–9.

Hammersley, R., A. Forsyth, V. Morrison and J.B. Davies (1989), 'The relationship between crime and opioid use', *British Journal of Addiction*, **84**(9), 1029–43.

Haynes, P. (1998), 'Drug using offenders in South London: trends and outcomes', *Journal of Substance Abuse Treatment*, **15**(5), 449–56.

Healey, A., M. Knapp, J. Astin, M. Gossop, J. Marsden, D. Stewart, P. Lehmann and C. Godfrey (1998), 'Economic burden of drug dependency. Social costs incurred by drug users at intake to the National Treatment Outcome Research Study', *The British Journal of Psychiatry*, **173**(8), 160–65.

Hubbard, R.L., S.G. Craddock, P.M. Flynn, J. Anderson and R.M. Etheridge (1997), 'Overview of one-year follow-up outcomes in the Drug Abuse Treatment Outcome Study (DATOS)', *Psychology of Addictive Behavior*, **11**(4), 261–78.

Institute of Medicine (1990), *Treating Drug Problems – Volume 1: A Study of the Evolution, Effectiveness, and Financing of Public and Private Drug Treatment Systems*, Washington, DC: National Academy Press.

Jofre-Bonet, M. and J.L. Sindelar (2001), 'Drug treatment as a crime fighting tool', *The Journal of Mental Health Policy and Economics*, **4**(4), 175–88.

Jofre-Bonet, M., J. Sindelar, I. Petrakis, C. Nich, T. Frankforter, B.J. Rounsaville and K.Carroll (2004), 'Cost-effectiveness of disulfiram: treating cocaine use in methadone-maintained patients', *Journal of Substance Abuse Treatment*, **26**, 225–32.

Kaplan, E.H., and E. O'Keefe (1993), 'Let the needles do the talking! Evaluating the New Haven needle exchange', *Interfaces*, **23**(1), 7–26.

Kaye, S., S. Drake and R. Finlay-Jones (1998), 'The onset of heroin use and criminal behavior: does order make a difference?', *Drug and Alcohol Dependence*, **53**, 79–86.

Kessler D. and S. Levitt (1999), 'Using sentence enhancements to distinguish between deterrence and incapacitation', *Journal of Law and Economics*, **42**, 343–63.

Kleiman, M.A. and K.D. Smith (1990), 'State and local drug enforcement: In search of a strategy', in M. Tonry and J.Q. Wilson (eds), *Drugs and Crime*, vol. 13, University of Chicago Press, pp. 69–108.

Levitt, S. and S. Venkatesh (2000), 'An economic analysis of a drug-selling gang's finances', *Quarterly Journal of Economics*, **115**, 755–89.

Lyman, D.R., R. Milich, R. Zimmerman, S.P. Novak, T.K. Logan, C. Martin, C. Leukefeld and R. Clayton (1999), 'Project DARE: No effects at 10-year follow-up', *Journal of Consulting and Clinical Psychology*, **67**(4), 590–93.

McBride, D.C. and C.B. McCoy (1982), 'Crime and drugs – the issues and literature', *Journal of Drug Issues*, **12**(2), 137–52.

McLellan, A.T., I. Arndt, D. Metzger, G. Woody and C. O'Brien (1993), 'The effects of psychosocial services in substance abuse treatment', *Journal of the American Medical Association*, **269**(15), 1953–9.

McLellan, A.T., T.A. Hagan, K. Meyers, M. Levine, F. Gould, M. Bencivengo, J. Durell and J. Jaffe (1998), 'Supplemental social services improve outcomes in public addiction treatment', *Addiction*, **93**(10), 1489–99.

Miron, J. (1991), 'Drug legalization and the consumption of drugs: An economist's perspective', in M.B. Krauss and E.P Lazear (eds), *Searching for Alternatives: Drug-Control Policy in the United States*, Stanford, CA: Hoover Institution Press, Stanford University, pp. 68–76.

Moore, M.H. (1990), 'Supply reduction and drug law enforcement', in M. Tonry and J.Q. Wilson (eds), *Drugs and Crime*, vol. 13, University of Chicago Press, pp. 109–57.

Musto, D. (1987), *The American Disease: Origins of Narcotic Control*, New York: Oxford University Press, pp. 24–53.

Nadelmann, E.A. (1988), 'The great drug debate: the case for legalization', *Public Interest*, **92**: 3–17.

National Research Council (2001), *Informing America's Policy on Illegal Drugs: What We Don't Know Keeps Hurting Us*, Washington, DC: National Academy Press.
Office of National Drug Control Policy (ONDCP) (2001), *The Economic Costs of Drug Abuse in the United States: 1992–1998*, Executive Office of the President, Washington, DC.
Post, R.M. (1986), 'Psychiatric manifestations and implications of seizure disorders', in I. Extein and M.S. Gold (eds), *Medical Mimics of Psychiatric Disorders*, Washington, DC: American Psychiatric Press, pp. 35–91.
Post, R.M. and R.T. Kopanda (1975), Letter: 'Cocaine, kindling, and reverse tolerance', *The Lancet*, **1**(7903), 409–10.
Post, R.M. and R.T. Kopanda (1976), 'Cocaine, kindling, and psychosis', *American Journal of Psychiatry*, **133**(6), 627–34.
Shaffer, J.W., D.N. Nurco and T.W. Kinlock (1984), 'A new classification of narcotics addicts based on type and extent of criminal activity', *Comprehensive Psychiatry*, **25**(3), 315–28.
Sindelar, J.L. and D.A. Fiellin (2001), 'Innovations in treatment for drug abuse: solutions to a public health problem', *Annual Review of Public Health*, **22**, 249–72.
Sindelar, J.L., M. Jofre-Bonet, M.T. French and A.T. McLellan (2004), 'Cost-effectiveness analysis of addiction treatment: paradoxes of multiple outcomes', *Drug and Alcohol Dependence*, **73**(1), 41–50.
Substance Abuse and Mental Health Services Administration (SAMHSA) (1997), *Drug Abuse Warning Network Series: Year-End Preliminary Estimates from the 1996 Drug Abuse Warning Network*, Rockville, MD: US Department of Health and Human Services.
Substance Abuse and Mental Health Services Administration (SAMHSA) (1999), *National Household Survey on Drug Abuse: Main Findings 1997*, Rockville, MD: US Department of Health and Human Services.
Substance Abuse and Mental Health Services Administration (SAMHSA) (2004), *Results from the 2003 National Survey on Drug Use and Health: National Findings*, Office of Applied Studies, NSDUH Series H-25, DHHS Publication No. SMA 04-3964, Rockville, MD.
United States General Accounting Office (USGAO) (1990), 'Drug interdiction: funding continues to increase but program effectiveness is unknown', GAO/GGD-91-10, Washington, DC.
Wilson, J.Q. (1990), 'Drugs and crime', in M. Tonry and J.Q. Wilson (eds), *Drugs and Crime*, vol. 13, University of Chicago Press, pp. 521–45.

PART II

HEALTH CARE FINANCE, EXPENDITURE AND USE

9 The value of health insurance
John A. Nyman*

1. Introduction

What is the value of health insurance? Although the determination of value is the province of economists and economic analysis, economic thinking regarding how to evaluate health insurance has changed drastically over time. This, in turn, has led to dramatic swings in estimates of the value of health insurance. At present, this issue is controversial.

It is perhaps possible to identify three historical periods, corresponding to the analytical models that were ascendant at the time. In the first period, corresponding to the years from 1944 to 1968, the demand for health insurance was analysed as a demand for certainty. Under this model, health insurance appeared to have a moderately positive value. This was a period of expansion of state-sponsored health insurance programmes, such as the National Health Service Act of 1946 in the UK and the creation of Medicare and Medicaid in 1965 in the US.

A second period, from 1968 to around 1999, corresponds to a period of preoccupation with moral hazard. This preoccupation was due to the recognition that health insurance paid off not by transferring income in a lump sum, but by reducing the price. The economic analysis of the welfare implications of this feature implied that health insurance made consumers worse off. It was during this period that economists recommended cost sharing, utilization review, capitation, eliminating the tax subsidy in the US, and other provisions designed to reduce insurance coverage in order to reduce health care spending.

The third period corresponds to years from 1999 to the present; so far, a period of some turmoil. This period is characterized by a new analysis that challenges the previous understanding of the welfare consequences of moral hazard. The new theory recognizes that, for most of the more expensive medical procedures, only those who are ill would respond to the health insurance price reduction. Therefore, within the price reduction is an income transfer from those who remain healthy to those who become ill, and this income transfer is responsible for a large portion of the additional health expenditures that were deemed to be welfare-decreasing under the previous moral hazard model. The new analysis re-categorizes this portion of moral hazard as welfare-increasing, and as a result, health insurance once again has a positive value. In addition, this analysis suggests that for many, health insurance provides access to care that would otherwise be unaffordable, and as such, its value must also include the altruistic benefit that society derives from seeing that those who are seriously ill gain access to the necessary medical care.

This chapter reviews the literature on the value of health insurance. In the next three sections, it summarizes the analytical models of these three periods, the issues surrounding them, and the estimates of the value of insurance derived from each of them. We begin

*   Thanks to Bryan Dowd for helpful comments on this chapter. Any errors or oversights, however, remain mine alone.

with the value of health insurance derived from the demand for insurance as the demand for certainty.

2.   Demand for certainty

Theory
The history of thinking about how to evaluate insurance originates with Daniel Bernoulli ([1738] 1954) and the development of the concept of 'utility'. Bernoulli hypothesized that the utility or satisfaction that consumers derive from income increases with income, but at a decreasing rate. Bernoulli used an insurance example to illustrate utility, but stopped short of evaluating insurance. During the subsequent years, however, further develop-ment of the theory was frustrated by the failure to produce a physical measure of utility. We can probably trace the revival of interest in the analysis of the demand for insurance to von Neumann and Morgenstern (1944) and their development of a practical method for measuring utility as a function of income.

Friedman and Savage (1948) can be credited with laying out the theory of the demand for insurance in a clear and digestible form. According to this theory, consumers facing an uncertain loss of income or wealth have a choice between putting up with the situation or buying insurance. If y_1 is the original income level and a loss of $(y_1 - y_0)$ occurs with a probability of Π, then expected utility without insurance is:

$$Eu^u(y) = \Pi u[y_1 - (y_1 - y_0)] + (1 - \Pi)u(y_1).$$
$$= \Pi u(y_0) + (1 - \Pi)u(y_1). \qquad (9.1)$$

If y^* is the expected value of the income, such that the actuarially fair premium is $(y_1 - y^*)$, then expected utility of insurance with a payoff that covers the entire loss is:

$$Eu^i(y) = \Pi u[y_1 - (y_1 - y_0) + (y_1 - y_0) - (y_1 - y^*)] + (1 - \Pi)u[y_1 - (y_1 - y^*)]$$
$$= \Pi u(y^*) + (1 - \Pi)u(y^*) = u(y^*). \qquad (9.2)$$

If the consumer's utility function exhibits the standard concave or 'risk averse' functional form, then insurance produces a higher expected utility than no insurance. A consumer who purchases such insurance, according to Friedman and Savage (1948), is 'choosing certainty in preference to uncertainty' (p. 279). This paper established the demand for insurance as a demand for certainty.

Issues
The central issue here is whether it is appropriate to apply this theory to health insurance. In this model, medical care spending represents a loss in income or wealth, the same sort of loss that would occur if your house burned down. As a result, medical care spending can generate only a loss of utility. That is, the consumer is assumed to obtain utility only from spending on commodities other than medical care, not on medical care itself. Thus, this model does not recognize that at the onset of illness, preferences might change so that, when the consumer voluntarily gives up income in order to purchase medical care, the medical care makes him better off in that state.

Almost as important, in applying this model to medical care, it is assumed that the consumer would spend the same amount on medical care with insurance as without it. For example, a consumer with $50 000 in income who becomes ill without insurance spends $30 000 on medical care. According to this model, the same consumer who becomes ill with insurance also spends $30 000 on medical care, even though he knows that when he does, he will receive a $30 000 lump-sum income payment from the insurer, increasing his income by $30 000. In other words, the income elasticity of demand for medical care must be zero in order for the demand for health insurance to be a demand for certainty.

Furthermore, because this model specifies the insurance payoff as simply covering the consumer's medical care spending without insurance, it implies that all the medical care purchases that the ill consumer would want to make are within the consumer's budget constraint (or liquidity constraint, if wealth). Medical care purchases that would otherwise be unaffordable are simply not recognized by this model.

The interpretation of the demand for insurance as a demand for certainty stems from the specification of the consumer's problem as a *choice* between certainty and uncertainty. This is unusual because it does not recognize that the insurance contract is a commodity that people purchase, just like any other commodity. If the insurance contract were treated like other commodities, the demand for insurance would be related to the gain in utility from the insurance contract net of its price. Using equations (9.1) and (9.2), this net gain can be expressed as:

$$Eu^i(y) - Eu^u(y) = \Pi u(y^*) + (1 - \Pi)u(y^*) - [\Pi u(y_0) + (1 - \Pi)u(y_1)]. \qquad (9.3)$$

Collecting terms associated with the same states of the world yields:

$$Eu^i(y) - Eu^u(y) = \Pi[u(y^*) - u(y_0)] + (1 - \Pi)[u(y^*) - u(y_1)]. \qquad (9.4)$$

Thus, the net gain in utility from purchasing the insurance contract is the utility gained from the income transferred to the consumer if ill, net of the utility lost from paying the premium if healthy. Note that this specification would result in the same mathematical estimate of the value of insurance as the comparison of the expected utility equations in the original specification.

This specification, however, has nothing to do with certainty. Instead, it is consistent with the standard quid pro quo transaction that consumers make every day. This specification would have made clear that the demand for insurance is a demand for an income transfer when ill, and would leave open the possibility that this additional income could be spent on additional medical care. In contrast, the original *choice* specification brooked no possibility of purchasing additional medical care with the insurance payoff because to do so would have undermined the interpretation of the demand for insurance as a demand for certainty.

Estimates

To my knowledge, no empirical estimates of the value of health insurance were made during this period. Nevertheless, Arrow (1963) in his famous evaluation of the benefits of insurance during the run-up to the passage of the 1965 Amendments to the Social Security

Act in the US, made it clear that on the basis of this theoretical model, the value of health insurance is positive. Arrow writes that if consumers (1) maximize expected utility and (2) are normally 'risk-averters' (that is, they normally exhibit diminishing marginal utility of income or wealth), then full-coverage health insurance results in a welfare gain:

> Suppose . . . an agency, a large insurance company plan, or the government, stands ready to offer insurance against medical costs on an actuarially fair basis; that is, if the costs of the medical care are a random variable which mean m, the company will charge a premium m, and agree to indemnify the individual for all medical costs. Under these circumstances, the individual will certainly prefer to take out a policy and will have a welfare gain thereby (Arrow, 1963, p. 960).

Thus, Arrow did not distinguish health insurance from other forms, stating that under this model, '[t]he welfare case for insurance policies of all sorts is overwhelming' (Arrow, 1963, p. 961).

3.   Moral hazard welfare loss

Theory
The view that health insurance was valuable came to an end in 1968 with the publication of Pauly's equally famous 'comment' on Arrow's 1963 paper. Pauly (1968) observed that health insurance did not pay off with a lump sum payment as Friedman and Savage's model had implied, but instead it paid off by paying for the ill consumer's care. Pauly translated this payoff into theory as a reduction to zero in the price that insured consumers faced for medical care, resulting in a movement along the consumer's *pre-insurance* Marshallian demand for medical care. Consumers respond to the price reduction by consuming more health care – this is the moral hazard – but the true cost of the resources expended is still reflected in the market price. The value of the additional health care consumed, therefore, was less than its cost, and this represented a moral hazard welfare loss.

Issues
This theory made sense for the sort of medical care that all consumers might purchase whether ill or not. It did not, however, make sense for treatments that were directed at the seriously ill. For example, what healthy person would consider purchasing a coronary artery bypass procedure just because the price had fallen to zero? Pauly came to understand the limits of his analysis and, in a 1983 response to de Meza's (1983) paper that recognized that *lump-sum* insurance payoffs also generate additional medical care consumption, wrote that his original idea of the moral hazard welfare loss applied principally to:

> routine physicians' services, prescriptions, dental care and the like, [which] tend to occur in the case of minor illness. . . .
>   It is nevertheless true that the relevant theory, empirical evidence, and policy analysis for moral hazard in the case of serious illness has not been developed. This is one of the most serious omissions in the current literature (Pauly, 1983, pp. 82–3).

Thus, the moral hazard welfare loss only applies to insurance coverage of certain types of medical care, and the appropriate welfare analysis for additional consumption of the more serious medical procedures was not understood at the time.

Estimates

Empirical estimates of the value of insurance largely ignored these issues and proceeded by simply tacking Pauly's moral hazard welfare loss onto Friedman and Savage's gain from 'risk bearing'. These studies found that insurance, either in whole or in part, makes the consumer worse off because of the dominance of the moral hazard welfare loss.

Feldstein (1973) calculated the value of health insurance and concluded that the current level of health insurance used in the US – represented by an average co-insurance rate of about 33 per cent – was excessive and produced 'a very substantial welfare loss' (Feldstein, 1973, p. 275). To reduce this welfare loss, Feldstein recommended raising the average co-insurance rate to 67 per cent.

Feldstein and Friedman (1977) addressed the issue of the US tax treatment of employer-provided health insurance. The contributions that employers (and many employees) make for employee health insurance premiums are not subject to US income taxes. This represents a tax subsidy for health insurance compared with other consumer commodities that are purchased with fully taxed income. By increasing the demand for health insurance, the tax subsidy appears to decrease the average co-insurance rates for hospital insurance, and causes an additional welfare loss that is similar in magnitude to the loss from reducing the average co-insurance rate from 50 per cent to 33 per cent – about 25 per cent of total hospital expenditures in the US at the time (Feldstein and Friedman, 1977, p. 176). The tax subsidy also reduces the co-insurance rates for physician care, causing a similar welfare loss.

Manning et al. (1987) used RAND Health Insurance Experiment (HIE) data to estimate the welfare loss associated with buying additional health insurance. The authors compare health care spending under a 0 per cent co-insurance rate to spending under a 31 per cent average co-insurance rate (the average co-insurance of the HIE plan with a 95 per cent co-insurance rate until $1000 in out-of-pocket spending occurred and a 0 per cent rate for spending thereafter). They estimate a moral hazard welfare loss of between $37 and $60 billion (1984 dollars, out of about $200 billion in total health care spending) if the under-65 population were to become fully insured (0 per cent co-insurance instead of 31 per cent). The authors suggest that, because the benefit gained from increased risk-bearing is likely to be small, the purchase of this additional insurance decreases welfare (Manning et al., 1987, p. 270).

Feldman and Dowd (1991) also use data from the RAND HIE and make a similar calculation, but explicitly incorporate the benefits from risk bearing into the calculation. For the same change (from a 31 per cent co-insurance rate to a 0 per cent rate), the authors estimate a net welfare loss of between $33 billion and $109 billion (again in 1984 dollars and out of about $200 in total health care spending) for the under-65 population.

Manning and Marquis (1996) estimate the value of health insurance at various co-insurance rates and limits on out-of-pocket spending, compared with no insurance. The authors find that insurance with a 0 per cent co-insurance rate would generate a net welfare loss of $1424 per household in 1995 dollars compared with no insurance. Insurance with a 25 per cent co-insurance rate and a $4000 limit – the insurance coverage that is perhaps most similar to the insurance that is currently purchased in the US – generates a $131 welfare loss compared with no insurance. Of the alternatives considered, insurance with a 50 per cent co-insurance rate and no limits on out-of-pocket spending would be optimal.

4.   Demand for income transfers

Theory
Nyman (1999a, 1999b, 1999c, 2003a, 2003b) and Nyman and Maude-Griffin (2001)
suggest that a major source of value is missing from this conventional analysis of the value
of health insurance. This value stems from the additional health care that an insured consumer would purchase with the income that is transferred to him from those who remain
healthy, when he becomes ill. This income transfer makes health insurance very valuable
because it often allows the consumer to purchase medical care that he would not otherwise be able to afford on his present income or that is beyond his liquidity constraint.

The key to understanding this theory is to recognize that for much of medical care –
the serious medical care that is often associated with great pain and suffering, and also
with the saving of lives – the insurance price reduction would affect the behaviour of only
those who are ill. Again, what healthy person would opt to endure a liver transplant or a
course in chemotherapy just because the price dropped to zero? Because only the ill would
respond to the insurance price reduction on most types of medical care, the price reduction is the mechanism by which income is transferred from those who purchase insurance
and remain healthy. The additional care that is consumed because of this income transfer generates a welfare gain that must be accounted for in valuing health insurance.

To see this, consider Elizabeth who has just been diagnosed with breast cancer. Without
insurance, Elizabeth would purchase a $20 000 mastectomy procedure to rid her body of
the cancer. If she had purchased a fair insurance policy for $4000 that paid for her care, she
would have purchased the $20 000 mastectomy plus a $20 000 breast reconstruction procedure to correct the disfigurement caused by the mastectomy. Thus, the insurer would have
paid ($20 000 + $20 000 =) $40 000 out of the insurance pool on her behalf, of which,
($40 000 − $4000 =) $36 000 represents transfers of income from those who remain healthy.

The additional $20 000 breast reconstruction procedure represents the moral hazard,
but whether it is a welfare gain or a welfare loss depends upon Elizabeth's behavioural
response to the $36 000 income transfer. If Elizabeth had instead received a lump-sum
payment of $40 000 (that she could have spent on anything of her choosing) and she had
opted to purchase the breast reconstruction, then this additional procedure must be considered a welfare gain. If she would not have purchased the additional procedure with her
income plus the $40 000 lump-sum payment, then the moral hazard is a welfare loss in
keeping with the conventional theory.

This income transfer often allows the insured consumer to gain access to care that
would be unaffordable without insurance. For example, consider Nigel who has just been
diagnosed with liver failure. Nigel has $50 000 in assets, but the liver transplant that
he needs to stay alive costs $300 000. Without insurance, he would have to do without the
procedure because he cannot save the additional $250 000 and no one will lend him the
money because of the chance that he might not live to pay back the loan. Nigel, however,
could afford to have purchased health insurance coverage for liver transplants for $4, the
actuarially fair premium for a $300 000 transplant procedure that occurred with an annual
probability of 1/75 500 (since $300 000/75 500 = $4). The liver transplant would represent
moral hazard, but it also represents a welfare gain to the extent that Nigel would have been
willing to pay more than the $300 000 cost of the transplant with his original wealth of

$50 000 plus a transfer of ($300 000 – $4 =) $299 996 in income from the insurance pool. Government safety nets (such as Medicaid in the US) and charity perform this same function, so their presence would reduce the access value of health insurance, but probably not eliminate it (Thomas, 1994/1995).

In summary, the value of health insurance under this theory is derived from (1) the consumer surplus from the additional medical care purchases generated by the income transfer in the insurance payoff. Some of these medical care purchases may otherwise have been unaffordable and the *access* to needed medical care that the ill consumer gains also produces value stemming from (2) society's altruistic desire to see that those who are ill receive needed medical care. Thus, the additional health care generated by the income transfer represents both private and external welfare gains that were not recognized in the previous models and that must be accounted for in valuing insurance. The existence of an external gain suggests that not enough insurance is purchased privately and justifies government intervention. To this must be added (3) the traditional 'risk bearing' gain, which in the context of the new theory becomes 'the utility gain derived from the portion of the income transfer that is spent on other goods and services when ill'.

Subtracted from it is (4) the welfare loss from the portion of the moral hazard that is generated by using a price reduction, instead of a lump-sum payment, to pay off the insurance contract. This moral hazard welfare loss might simply represent a transaction cost, if all the other methods of transferring a certain amount of income to the ill would result in a greater loss. If so, its welfare consequences are irreducible and could simply be ignored.

Issues

Perhaps the most persistently voiced objection to this model is that, even though income is transferred to those who become ill and this increases some health care purchases, on the other end of the transaction, income is transferred away from those who remain healthy and this would potentially decrease some health care purchases. If the insurance premium is fair, the loss of income by the healthy equals income gained by the ill, and as a result, there is no net increase in income and there can be no net increase in health care expenditures.

The new theory, however, relies on the fact that for most health care, the loss of income by the healthy would not generate any reductions in consumption. For example, the loss of income (represented by the premium paid) by the *healthy* consumer would probably not result in the purchase of any fewer breast reconstructions, liver transplants, or coronary bypass procedures. That is, we can rely on the assumption that for most health care expenditures, the income elasticity exhibited by the healthy is zero.

Estimates

The new theory suggests that the additional health care consumed due to insurance should be evaluated according to the consumer's willingness-to-pay *after the insurance income transfer has occurred*. But Nyman (2003a, pp. 107–9) argues that even this willingness-to pay may be insufficient to capture the true value of health care for serious illnesses. As a result, Nyman (2003a, pp. 109–15) calculates the value of moral hazard based, not on how much the consumer would be willing to pay for the additional health care that the consumer purchases with the income transfer in insurance, but on how much the consumer would be willing to pay for the additional life years generated by that additional health care. He estimates the welfare gain that would occur from insuring the 40 million US citizens that were uninsured in 1999 in comparison to the cost of the additional health care. Valuing an additional life year at $100 000 and assuming that the additional health care when insured generates a 25 per cent reduction in the mortality rate, the additional $39 billion in moral hazard spending would have generated $123 billion worth of life expectancy. Thus, the welfare gain is $84 billion or about $2100 per person. This estimate includes the costs of all moral hazard but probably none of the benefits from the inefficient moral hazard. It also does not include the value from 'risk bearing', or the external value of health care access to society.

Miller, Vigdor and Manning (2004) use a similar approach. The authors calculate that health insurance 'is likely to produce gains in better health and longevity (valued at $65–$130 billion annually) well in excess of the incremental societal costs of increased use of services' (p. 162). Only about 2.5 per cent of the total value of insurance represents the value of 'risk bearing'.

Muennig, Franks and Gold (2005) conducted a cost-effectiveness analysis of health insurance and found that health insurance produced a quality-adjusted life year (QALY) in a 25-year-old at a cost of $35 500, and at lower costs for older people. If the willingness-to-pay for a QALY were $100 000, then the value of the additional care produced by health insurance would exceed its costs by at least $64 500.

Thus, current research suggests that health insurance has a large positive value that is derived mainly from the additional health care generated by insurance.

5. Conclusions
Health insurance represents the pre-purchase of medical care. As such, it represents the purchase of a large percentage of GDP. Understanding how consumers derive value from health insurance is, therefore, important. Estimates of its value, however, have swung from modestly positive based on the value of risk-bearing alone, to negative based on a moral hazard welfare loss, to greatly positive based mainly on the welfare gain from the additional purchases of medical care generated by the income transfer. That there have been such widely divergent views regarding the value of health insurance has probably not contributed to the confidence that others place on the pronouncements of economists. This suggests a need for additional debate, consensus building, and empirical research in order to reduce the variance in these estimates.

Perhaps the most persuasive empirical evidence regarding the value of health insurance is the extent to which health insurance is purchased voluntarily, or provided to the citizens of democratic states. This evidence, represented by the high proportion of US consumers who are insured and the high proportion of developed democracies that have some form of national health insurance, suggests that the value of health insurance is overwhelmingly positive. To hold that health insurance is welfare-decreasing would require that this evidence be explained away as well.

References
Arrow, Kenneth J. (1963), 'Uncertainty and the welfare economics of medical care', *American Economic Review*, 53, 941–73.

Bernoulli, Daniel (1738), 'Exposition of a new theory on the measurement of risk', trans. Louise Sommer (1954), *Econometrica*, **22**, 23–36.

de Meza, David (1983), 'Health insurance and the demand for medical care', *Journal of Health Economics*, **2**(1), 47–54.

Feldman, Roger and Bryan Dowd (1991), 'A new estimate of the welfare loss of excess health insurance', *American Economic Review*, **81**(1), 297–301.

Feldstein, Martin S. (1973), 'The welfare loss of excess health insurance', *Journal of Political Economy*, **81**, 251–80.

Feldstein, Martin and Bernard Friedman (1977), 'Tax subsidies, the rational demand for insurance, and the health care crisis', *Journal of Public Economics*, **7**, 155–78.

Friedman, Milton and L.J. Savage (1948), 'The utility analysis of choices involving risk', *Journal of Political Economy*, **56**(4), 279–304.

Manning, Willard G. and M. Susan Marquis (1996), 'Health insurance: the tradeoff between risk pooling and moral hazard', *Journal of Health Economics*, **15**(5), 609–40.

Manning, Willard G., Joseph P. Newhouse, Naihua Duan, Emmett B. Keeler, Arleen Leibowitz and M. Susan Marquis (1987), 'Health insurance and the demand for medical care: evidence from a randomized experiment', *American Economic Review*, **77**(3), 251–77.

Miller, Wilhelmine, Elizabeth Richardson Vigdor and Willard G. Manning (2004), 'Covering the uninsured: what is it worth?', *Health Affairs*, W4, 157–67.

Muennig, Peter, Peter Franks and Marthe Gold (2005), 'The cost effectiveness of health insurance', *American Journal of Preventive Medicine*, **28**(1), 59–64.

Nyman, John A. (1999a), 'The value of health insurance: the access motive', *Journal of Health Economics*, **18**(2), 141–52.

Nyman, John A. (1999b), 'The welfare economics of insurance contracts that pay off by reducing price', Department of Economics Working Paper No. 308, Minneapolis, US: University of Minnesota.

Nyman, John A. (1999c), 'The economics of moral hazard revisited', *Journal of Health Economics*, **18**(6), 811–24.

Nyman, John A. (2003a), *The Theory of Demand for Health Insurance*, Stanford, US: Stanford University Press.

Nyman, John A. (2003b), 'Health insurance theory: the case of the vanishing welfare gain', Department of Economics Working Paper No. 319, Minneapolis, US: University of Minnesota.

Nyman, John A. and Roland Maude-Griffin (2001), 'The welfare economics of moral hazard,' *International Journal of Health Care Finance and Economics*, **1**(1), 23–42.

Pauly, Mark V. (1968), 'The economics of moral hazard: comment', *American Economic Review*, **58**(3), 531–37.

Pauly, Mark V. (1983), 'More on moral hazard', *Journal of Health Economics*, **2**, 81–5.

Thomas, Kathleen (1994/1995), 'Are subsidies enough to encourage the uninsured to purchase health insurance? An analysis of underlying behavior', *Inquiry*, **31**, 415–24.

von Neumann, John and Oskar Morgenstern (1944), *Theory of Games and Economic Behavior*, Princeton, US: Princeton University Press.

10 Incentive and selection effects in health insurance
*Pierre-Yves Geoffard**

1. Introduction

Insurance partly covers income losses associated with unpredictable events. When individuals dislike risk, economic theory points out that risk pooling improves efficiency, since aggregate risk is in general more predictable than individual risks. Throughout history or across societies, the organization of insurance may take many forms: informal networks of solidarity in a community, formal mutual insurance arrangements within a group, publicly or privately provided group or individual contracts. Economic theory identifies two fundamental reasons why markets for insurance may fail to allocate resources efficiently (Stiglitz, 2000): asymmetries of information between different agents may (1) restrict the scope of mutually beneficial trades, and (2) create differences between private and social costs and benefits of some actions influencing the level of risk. However, theoretical results depend on the magnitude of informational asymmetries, and the empirical analysis of these effects has progressed less rapidly (Chiappori and Salanié, 2000).

Within the general field of insurance economics, health insurance shows some specific features, as pointed out in the seminal paper of Arrow (1963). An important feature is that health care consumption is determined by a complex decision process, in which both consumers (patients) and providers (doctors, hospitals . . .) may play an active role (see Chapter 24 by Rice in this Companion). Another important feature is that a key element in that process, patient's health, is costly to observe by a third party. Moreover, this is true both *ex post*, at the time of health care consumption, and *ex ante*, before the realization of the health risk, at the time of health insurance contracting.

This chapter presents an analysis of some problems created by the existence of *ex ante* and *ex post* asymmetries of information between patients and insurers. *Ex ante* asymmetries may induce self-selection behaviour by agents who can choose between different insurance contracts. *Ex post* asymmetries imply that insurance payments cannot depend on agents' health, and hence induce price distortions. These two problems are related, both theoretically and empirically. However, they call for different regulations.

Some preliminary remarks are needed about 'moral hazard'. The exact nature, the extent, and even the existence, of incentive effects on consumer demand for health care have been the object of debate among health economists (Nyman, 2002). Given that health insurance provides a partial coverage of health care costs, it generates a difference between the total cost and the price paid by the consumer. If the demand for health care is price elastic, then it may exceed the optimal level (Pauly, 1968; Feldstein, 1973). This analysis is essentially correct, but should not lead to the conclusion that health insurance induces a welfare loss. Indeed, the cost of this excessive consumption of health care should be balanced with the potentially important benefits of the better risk sharing

* This chapter has benefited from comments from Arnold Chassagnon, Paul Grotendoorst and John Nyman.

generated by insurance contracts covering income losses of risk averse agents (Cutler and Zeckhauser, 2000). The precise estimation of these benefits is difficult to assess, given the imprecision of empirical measures of risk aversion. Nevertheless, a global evaluation of costs and benefits of health insurance cannot be done without taking into account the income effects of health insurance (see Chapter 9 by Nyman in this Companion).

At a semantic level, the notion of '*ex post* moral hazard' is at odds with standard economic theory. Usually, in insurance economics as well as in contract theory, moral hazard refers to a situation in which the agent chooses an action, which is hidden to the principal. However, in health economics, the so-called '*ex post* moral hazard' refers to situations in which some information (namely, health state) is unobserved by the principal, and the action (health care) is observed by both parties. *Ex post* moral hazard stems from a hidden information, not a hidden action.

2. Theory

First best insurance with one or more risks

Where does the demand for insurance comes from? The immediate answer is that the marginal utility of income may depend on the realization of some risk. In a 'standard', expected utility model in which preferences only depend on wealth, risk is represented as a pure income loss. If the agent is risk averse, an income loss increases her marginal utility of income. In a Von Neumann–Morgenstern context, expected utility increases if the agent can equalize (or reduce differences in) marginal utilities in different states, and this takes the form of income transfers from states with high income to states with low income. This motivation determines the (*ex ante*) demand for insurance. Such contracts may be supplied by insurance firms which are typically assumed risk neutral, and trade is mutually beneficial. In this first best world, the optimal insurance contract offers a complete coverage to risk averse agents, and risk is totally transferred to risk neutral agents (insurance firms).

Yet, marginal utility of income may be affected by other events than income loss. An important case is health risk. Let us denote by $v(W, h)$ a VNM state-dependent utility index, taken as a function of income W and health h, and assume that there is a health risk, but no income risk (W is constant). *Ex ante* welfare is simply $E[v(W, \tilde{h})]$, where the expectation is taken over the distribution of h. When the cross derivative v_{Wh} is not zero, health shocks affect the marginal utility of income. In that case, a perfect insurance contract would take the form of monetary self-financed transfers $T(h)$ (i.e., such that $E[T(\tilde{h})] = 0$), that satisfy the efficient risk sharing condition: $v_W(W + T(h), h)$ must be independent of the realization of h.

Under the assumption $v_{Wh} < 0$, bad health (low value of h) increases v_W. This implies that insurance contracts that transfer income from states with large v_W (good health) to states with small v_W (bad health) increase *ex ante* welfare. Notice however that under the alternative assumption $v_{Wh} > 0$, an optimal insurance contract should transfer income from states with bad health to states with good health, in which income is more enjoyable.

Let us develop this point in a simple set-up. Assume that $v(W, h)$ is in fact the indirect utility function of some *ex post* decision problem. There exists a composite consumption good c, whose unit price is normalized to 1, and some composite health care good x, with unit price p. Preferences are represented by some utility function $u(c, x, h)$. Typically, bad health h increases the marginal rate of substitution between health care and consumption, $u_x/u_c(c, x, h)$. Thus v may be written as:

$$v(W, h) = \max_{x, c \mid px + c \leq W} u(c, x, h) \tag{10.1}$$

The first best allocation (*ex ante* and *ex post* efficient) is the solution to the following problem:

$$\max_{x(\cdot), c(\cdot) \mid E[px(\tilde{h}) + c(\tilde{h})] \leq W} E[u(c(\tilde{h}), x(\tilde{h}), \tilde{h})]$$

This first best allocation, denoted by $(C(h), X(h))$ is now characterized by two conditions:

- *Ex ante efficiency* still requires that the marginal utility of income is equalized across states of nature which, since the price of c is 1, imposes that $u_c(C(h), X(h), h)$ be independent of h (efficient risk sharing).
- *Ex post efficiency* requires that in each state h, the marginal rate of substitution u_x/u_c is equal to the relative price p (no price distortion).

If monetary transfers across states can depend on h, then this first best allocation may be implemented with a simple self-financed insurance scheme $T(h)$, defined by:

$$T(h) = \underbrace{pX(h) - E[pX(\tilde{h})]}_{\text{health care insurance}} + \underbrace{C(h) - E[C(\tilde{h})]}_{\text{consumption insurance}},$$

where in the *ex post* decision problem (10.1) W is replaced with $W + T(h)$. Such a scheme does not affect *ex post* prices, and makes the first best allocation (C, X) affordable. The monetary transfer may be decomposed in two parts: health care insurance transfers money such that in each state h, the desired level $X(h)$ is affordable; consumption insurance does the same for c. In a situation h in which a medical intervention is necessary (for example, in a life threatening condition), then the desired level $X(h)$ is very large, and hence the optimal transfer is also very large. In contrast, when health is good, the motivation for income transfer may rather be that the marginal utility of consumption may be large. Since for this first best insurance scheme T the marginal indirect utility of income v_W is independent of h, we also have that $T'(h) = -v_{Wh}/v_{WW}$. Hence it decreases with h if and only if v_{Wh} is negative (under the standard risk aversion assumption v_{WW}).

Second best insurance
However, such transfers must depend on h, which may be difficult to observe. A first best health insurance contract should specify the amount of money received by an individual in each health state she may be in. But the verification of h requires a medical examination, whose costs may be too large to be systematically undertaken. In practice, no health insurance contract takes this form, and actual contracts condition transfers on an indirect measure of health, namely health care expenditures x. This form of *reimbursement*

insurance induces some distortions with respect to first best efficiency. The transfer scheme now takes the form of some net payment $t(x)$ from the principal to the agent who declares that she spent x in health care. A feasibility condition is that t must be increasing with x (to be compatible with incentives to claim reimbursement). Full insurance would take the form $t(x) = px - P$, where P is the associated premium. But typical contracts include co-payments (with a constant co-payment rate $0 < k < 1$, $t(x) = (1 - k)px - P$), or deductibles ($t(x) = \max\{px - D, 0\} - P$, where D is the deductible; notice that co-payments are sometimes referred to as co-insurance), or other elements of cost-sharing.

The first source of inefficiency of such contracts is that, *ex ante*, they provide incomplete coverage. Under the standard assumption that the agent is risk averse and the insurer is risk neutral (or at least less risk averse than the agent), optimal risk sharing requires that all risk is borne by the insurer. *Ex ante* efficiency of the contract *decreases* with the magnitude of cost sharing (for example, with k or D).

The second source of inefficiency is that, *ex post*, they distort the price system faced by the agent. The marginal cost of health care, at the time h is revealed and the agent decides how to allocate her available income between x and c, is now $p - t'(x)$. *Ex post* efficiency *increases* with the magnitude of cost sharing. Under a constant co-payment rate, it is equal to $kp < p$, and with a deductible it is equal to p when p is below the deductible D, and 0 when it is above. This price distortion induces an excessive consumption of health care with respect to the first best one. This may also be interpreted as a negative externality of the agent's decision.

What form would a contract take that balances these two sources of inefficiency? The problem is simple to state, but quite difficult to solve. Formally, the second best optimal contract $t^*(\cdot)$ is a function that maximizes the expected utility $E[u(c(\tilde{h}), x(\tilde{h}), \tilde{h})]$, where for each h, $(c(h), x(h))$ is the solution to $\max_{cx} u(c, x, h)$ under the constraint $px + c \leq W + t^*(x)$, and $t^*(\cdot)$ is self-financed, that is $E[t^*(x(\tilde{h}))] = 0$.

This problem is studied by Blomqvist (1997) under the specification $u(c, x, h) = u_1(c) + u_2(x + h)$, and Vera-Hernández (2003) in an empirical perspective. The overall message is that the optimal contract is non linear: the co-payment rate should decrease with x (as in contracts with deductibles). The interpretation is clear if we have in mind two main elements.

First, monetary risks that induce a large *ex ante* cost if not insured are 'catastrophic' events, that occur with a low probability but lead to a very large income loss. For such events, risk averse agents are willing to pay large premiums (well above the fair premium equal to the average expected cost) to get rid of the risk.

Second, the price elasticity of the demand for health care may be important for small expenditures (especially for ambulatory care), but is probably close to zero for very costly medical interventions (as Nyman puts it, people do not demand a kidney transplantation because it is not expensive). Hence, a complete coverage of large expenditures is important for *ex ante* risk sharing efficiency, and may not induce any *ex post* price distortion, whereas a limited coverage of small expenditures tackles the *ex post* efficiency issue without 'too much' *ex ante* welfare loss.

This analysis leads to a simple message: in a world where health condition is not (perfectly) observable by the insurer, the optimal insurance contract needs to address the trade-off between risk sharing and incentives. It also provides some insights about the regulation of health insurance. First, notice that this trade-off affects private as well as public insurance programmes, and gives no decisive argument in favour of either form of organization. Second, efficiency may be improved if asymmetries of information are reduced. In practice, some insurers require medical examinations before some interventions.

Finally, this analysis points out that the trade-off between *ex ante* and *ex post* inefficiencies depends on two major elements: risk aversion, and price elasticity of medical care. Empirical measures such as coefficients of (relative and absolute) risk aversion are difficult to obtain, a main reason being that the expected utility framework underlying these measures may not be a good representation of actual attitudes towards risk (Starmer, 2000). Price elasticity of demand for medical care is also difficult to assess precisely, but the empirical health economics literature provides many measures. The following section provides a short introduction to this literature. For a more complete survey, the interested reader may refer to Zweifel and Manning (2000).

3. Empirical issues

In a very general way, price elasticity of demand may be measured by observing different (but comparable) individuals facing different prices. This creates a first difficulty: in health systems where the whole population is covered by the same contract (for example, in a national health system or with a universal social insurance), then all individuals face the same price system, and it is not possible to measure price elasticity. Another problem is raised when different schemes cover different populations. In many countries, employment linked social insurance covers workers and their families, and some means-tested public programme covers the rest of the population. Even though in general these two insurance schemes differ substantially in terms of coverage, individuals may have very different characteristics, making it difficult to infer price elasticity from differences in observed behaviour across groups.

A fundamental issue arises when there exist different contracts, but individuals may choose one contract. The observed price (or coverage) variation becomes endogenous, and comparing consumption behaviour of individuals with different insurance schemes may simply reveal that these individuals were different at the time they chose their contracts. This issue of self selection is a classic problem in many empirical studies based on historical data, especially for the evaluation of public programmes (Heckman, 2001; see also Jones, 2000).

In terms of estimation of incentive effects, the data may be ranked from best to worst, given the type of coverage variation: exogenous variation of coverage; endogenous variation of coverage; no variation of coverage.

In health economics, 'moral hazard' problems stem from the incapacity of the insurer to observe the agent's health at the time of health care consumption. Indeed, selection is a closely related problem, that stems from the difficulties for the insurer to observe the agent's health at the time of contract choice. Hence, even though this procedure cannot distinguish between the two potential effects, a positive correlation between coverage and expenditures provides a very robust test for the presence of informational asymmetries (Chiappori and Salanié, 2000). Empirically, such positive correlation is quite systematically obtained on health insurance data. However, it is important to separate both effects: measures of incentive effects need to control for selection effects.

Exogenous variation of coverage: the RAND Experiment

One important case in which endogenous selection may be ruled out is the Health Insurance Experiment. As Manning et al. (1987) recall, early empirical studies (for example, Phelps and Newhouse, 1972, 1974; Rosett and Huang, 1973; Scitovsky and Snyder, 1972) were unable to come to a consensus as to the magnitude of incentive effects. Expressed in terms of price elasticity of demand for health care, the estimates ranged from −2.1 to 0. Hence, the US government commissioned the RAND Corporation to undertake an important study, based on a controlled experiment. Almost 6000 individuals were randomly assigned to different health plans, that differed in terms of co-payment rate (from 0 to 95 per cent), and included a cap on annual out-of-pocket payments. These individuals were followed for up to 5 years; detailed information on health condition before and after the study was collected, as well as on health care consumption.

Given that the distribution of annual expenditures has a large weight at 0, and strongly differs for individuals who have been hospitalized, four equations were estimated: two probit equations (probability of positive expenditure, conditional probability of hospitalization), and two regressions under a log-normal specification. The results were presented in many articles, summarized in a main paper (Manning et al., 1987), and a book (Newhouse, 1993).

It measured an average price elasticity around −0.2. Table 10.1 presents the average health expenditure (and the 95 per cent confidence interval) as a function of co-payment rate. It shows a sharp decrease as co-payment rate increases from 0 (complete coverage) to 25 per cent, and slower decreases for larger levels of co-payment rates. Given the cap on annual expenditures, the price elasticity of demand for hospital care was more difficult to estimate. The analysis also showed a positive income effect on health care consumption, but the cross price-income elasticity was difficult to assess precisely.

Another important element of this study is that health outcomes were monitored. Even though consumption levels were very sensitive to coverage, health outcomes were not significantly different (after five years of follow-up), except for some specific health indicators (myopia, high diastolic pressure) among the lower income group, and for dental health. Based on these results, the authors estimated that around 20 per cent of total health care costs did not lead to significant health benefits, as measured by 'objective' (physiological) health indicators (however, this does not mean that such expenditures did not increase consumers' subjective utility).

Table 10.1   Annual health care expenditure, 1984 US$

Co-payment rate (%)	Health care expenditure
0	777 (711–843)
25	630 (572–688)
50	583 (518–648)
95	534 (479–589)

Source: Newhouse (1993)

Endogenous coverage

Though the RAND HIE has provided highly valuable information, it is important to obtain results in other contexts (other countries, more recent periods). Many empirical studies have attempted, in non-experimental contexts, to estimate incentive effects. Since in almost all cases, the source of variation is endogenous, it is important to control for such effects.

To clarify the different notions, let us introduce a one-period principal–agent model. *Ex ante*, the agent observes some private information θ about the distribution of her future health. She chooses an insurance contract among a given menu of contracts indexed by a real number g. A large value of g indicates better coverage (that is, small deductibles and co-payment rates). *Ex post*, the health state h is drawn from some distribution $f(h|\theta)$, observed by the agent, and some variable x (typically, health care expenditures) is observed by both parties. We also assume that all distributions are conditional on all observable variables. Let us denote by $G(.|g, h)$ the cumulative distribution function of x, conditional on coverage g and health status h. Better health leads to lower expenditures (ceteris paribus) in terms of first-order stochastic dominance; formally, this leads to $\partial G/\partial h(x|g, h) \geq 0$.

There is an incentive effect if x, *conditional* on h, increases with coverage g; formally, if $\partial G/\partial g(x|g, h) \leq 0$. There is a selection effect if the choice of coverage depends on the expected distribution of health, which (by Bayes' law) implies that the conditional distribution of h depends on the contract g; formally, if $\partial F/\partial h(h|g) \geq 0$.

For the principal (as well as, in many cases, for the econometrician), only g and x are observed. Typically, empirical studies show a positive correlation between coverage and expenditures: in this set-up, $\partial G/\partial g(x|g) \leq 0$. However, a standard problem in empirical contract theory (see, for example, Chiappori et al., forthcoming) is that a positive correlation between coverage and risk (as measured by insurance claims) may be due to selection, incentive, or both effects. Indeed, $G(x|g)$ is equal to: $E[G(x|g, \tilde{h})|g]$ and integrating this conditional expectation by parts leads to the following decomposition:

$$\frac{\partial G}{\partial g}[x|g] = \underbrace{\int_{\underline{h}} \frac{\partial G}{\partial g}[x|g, \tilde{h}] f(\tilde{h}|g)\, d\tilde{h}}_{A(g)} + \underbrace{\int_{\underline{h}} -\frac{\partial G}{\partial \tilde{h}}[x|g, \tilde{h}]\frac{\partial F}{\partial g}(\tilde{h}|g)\, d\tilde{h}}_{B(g)} \qquad (10.2)$$

If there is an incentive effect, then for any h, $\partial G/\partial g(x|g, h) \leq 0$ (holding health constant, a more extensive coverage induces more spending in health care), which implies that $A(g) \leq 0$. Recall that $\partial G/\partial h(x|g, h) \geq 0$ (holding coverage constant, better health leads to less spending). Hence, if there is a selection effect, then $\partial F/\partial h(h|g) \geq 0$ (a more extensive coverage reveals a worse expected distribution of health) implies $B(g) \leq 0$.

Empirical evidence

Direct evidence of selection effects is quite scarce, and there is no general consensus about the magnitude of such effects. Cutler and Reber (1998) present descriptive evidence of selection effects through the 'Harvard death spiral'. Cameron et al. (1988) find that socio-demographic and some health variables explain the choice of insurance, but do not test

Table 10.2   Estimated probability of death during the following year (per 1000)

	Deductible\Age	30	40	50	60
Women	230	0.95	1.66	3.35	7.70
	400	0.49	0.86	1.73	4.02
	≥ 600	0.34	0.60	1.20	2.80
Men	230	2.17	3.81	7.61	17.10
	400	1.12	1.97	3.97	9.09
	≥ 600	0.78	1.37	2.77	6.37

Source: Gardiol et al. (2005)

for the effect of unobservable variables. On the other side, Cardon and Hendel (2001) as well as Feldman and Dowd (1991) test for selection effects through unobservable variables and find no significant evidence.

Direct evidence of selection effects may be obtained by investigating a variable for which incentive effects are presumably absent (formally, for which $A(g) = 0$). Gardiol et al. (2005) study differences in mortality rates across individuals who have opted for different levels of coverage. As presented in Table 10.2, figures show that mortality rates for individuals with the largest coverage (the lowest deductible, SFr 230 per year) are three times larger than for individuals with the smallest coverage (the largest deductible, SFr 1500).

Controlling for selection effects
Econometric methods have been developed to take into account endogenous selection issues. A direct OLS regression would lead to biased estimates of incentive effects. One solution is to proceed in two steps. First, estimate a probit equation for insurance choice, and then replace in the equation for health care choice the coverage indicator with the inverse of the Mill's ratio from the first equation. Another solution is to use instrumental variables, but good instruments are not always available, especially on claims data which contain many observations but few variables (see for example, Cameron et al., 1988; Feldman and Dowd, 1991). Another solution is to estimate a recursive model for the demand for insurance and for health care. In such models, the unobserved health state h is in the residuals of both equations, and correlation indicates the presence of selection effects. If the model is identified (which requires use of exclusion restrictions), incentive effects are measured directly (see for example, Holly et al., 1998).

Other researchers use natural experiments, for which two comparable populations are followed up, and one (the test group) is subject to some exogenous contractual change, whereas the other (the control group) is not (for example, Chiappori et al., 1998). Difference in difference methods can then be used to estimate the size of incentive effects, but three conditions are necessary for such methods to be applied: the change must be exogenous; it must have affected the test but not the control group; no other relevant change must have affected the test group. One last idea is to use the specific features of many insurance contracts: given that in many cases the co-payment rate decreases with the amount of past expenditures (as it does with deductibles or cap on out-of-pocket payments), at any point in time the marginal cost of health care is affected by previous health events. When such events are exogenous (such as medical treatments for accidents), this provides an exogenous change in marginal prices (for example, Eichner, 1998).

All these studies find significant incentive effects. Overall, values of price elasticity of −0.2 for ambulatory care, closer to zero for in-patient care, as found by the RAND HIE, have not been seriously challenged by more recent research.

4. Policy implications

The policy implications of these empirical results are important. In the presence of incentive effects, the trade-off between risk sharing and incentives implies that regulatory rules such as mandatory co-payment rates or deductibles may improve welfare. Even though the optimal size of cost sharing is unknown, these regulations are used in some countries (for example, Switzerland, Belgium). Another open question is how such demand-side regulations interact with supply-side regulations (physician and hospital payment schemes). If selection effects are important, market failures may arise when insurers strategically respond to self-selection behaviour. This provides a rationale for mandatory insurance, for some form of contract standardization, for some redistribution across risk groups, and means that risk adjustment schemes (see Chapter 26 by Glazer and McGuire in this Companion) are an important element of a health system based upon competition among health insurers.

References

Arrow, Kenneth (1963), 'Uncertainty and the welfare effects of medical care', *American Economic Review*, 53, 941–73.
Blomqvist, Ake (1997), 'Optimal non-linear health insurance', *Journal of Health Economics*, 16, 303–21.
Cameron, A.C., P.K. Trivedi, Frank Milne and J. Piggot (1988), 'A microeconometric model of the demand for health care and health insurance in Australia', *Review of Economic Studies*, LV, 85–106.
Cardon, James and Igal Hendel (2001), 'Asymmetric information in health insurance: evidence from the National Medical Expenditure Survey', *RAND Journal of Economics*, 32(3), 408–27.
Chiappori, Pierre-André and Bernard Salanié (2000), 'Testing for asymmetric information in insurance markets', *Journal of Political Economy*, 108, 56–78.
Chiappori, Pierre-André, Franck Durand and Pierre-Yves Geoffard (1998), 'Moral hazard and the demand for physician services: first lessons from a French natural experiment', *European Economic Review*, 42, 499–511.
Chiappori, Pierre-André, Bruno Jullien, Bernard Salané and François Salanié (forthcoming), 'Asymmetric information in insurance: general testable implications', *RAND Journal of Economics*.
Cutler, David and Sarah Reber (1998), 'Paying for health insurance: the tradeoff between competition and adverse selection', *Quarterly Journal of Economics*, 113(2), 433–66.
Cutler, David and Richard Zeckhauser (2000), 'The anatomy of health insurance', in A. Culyer and J. Newhouse (eds), *Handbook of Health Economics*, Amsterdam: North-Holland, Elsevier.
Eichner, Matthew (1998), 'The demand for medical care: what people pay does matter', *American Economic Review Papers and Proceedings*, 88(2), 117–21.
Feldman, R. and B. Dowd (1991), 'A new estimate of the welfare loss of excess health insurance', *American Economic Review*, 81(1), 297–301.
Feldstein, Martin S. (1973), 'The welfare loss of excess health insurance', *Journal of Political Economy*, 81, 81–115.
Gardiol, Lucien, Pierre-Yves Geoffard and Chantal Grandchamp (2005), 'Separating selection and incentive effects: an econometric study of Swiss health insurance claims data', in P.-A. Chiappori and Ch. Gollier (eds), *Insurance Economics: Recent Advances*, Cambridge, MA: MIT Press.
Heckman, James (2001), 'Micro data, heterogeneity and the evaluation of public policy: Nobel Lecture', *Journal of Political Economy*, 109(4), 673–748.
Holly, Alberto, Lucien Gardiol, Gianfranco Domenighetti and Brigitte Bisig (1998), 'An econometric model of health care utilization and health insurance in Switzerland', *European Economic Review*, 42, 513–22.
Jones, Andrew (2000), 'Health econometrics', in A. Culyer and J. Newhouse (eds), *Handbook of Health Economics*, Amsterdam: North-Holland, Elsevier.

Manning, Willard G., Joseph P. Newhouse, Duan Naihua, Emmet B. Keeler, Arleen Leibowitz and Susan Marquis (1987), 'Health insurance and the demand for medical care: evidence from a randomized experiment', *American Economic Review*, **77**, 251–77.

Newhouse, Joseph P. (1993), *Free for All? : Lessons from the RAND Health Insurance Experiment*, Cambridge, MA: Harvard University Press.

Nyman, John A. (2002), *The Theory of Demand for Health Insurance*, Stanford, CA: Stanford University Press.

Pauly, Mark (1968), 'The economics of moral hazard', *American Economic Review*, **58**, 531–37.

Phelps, Charles E. and Joseph P. Newhouse (1972), 'Effects of coinsurance: a multivariate analysis', *Social Security Bulletin*, **35**(6), 20–9.

Phelps, Charles E. and Joseph P. Newhouse (1974), 'Coinsurance, the price of time, and the demand for medical services', *Review of Economics and Statistics*, **56**(3), 334–42.

Rosett, Richard and Lien Fu Huang (1973), 'The effect of health insurance on the demand for medical care', *Journal of Political Economy*, **81**, 281–305.

Scitovsky, Anne and Nelda Snyder (1972), 'Effect of coinsurance on use of physician services', *Social Security Bulletin*, **35**, 3–19.

Starmer, Chris (2000), 'Developments in non-expected utility theory: the hunt for a descriptive theory of choice under risk', *Journal of Economic Literature*, **38**, 332–82.

Stiglitz, Joseph (2000), 'The contributions of the economics of information to twentieth century economics', (Nobel Lecture), *Quarterly Journal of Economics*, **115**(4), 1441–78.

Vera-Hernández, Marcos (2003), 'Structural estimation of a principal-agent model: moral hazard in medical insurance', *RAND Journal of Economics*, **34**(4), 670–93.

Zweifel, Peter and Willard Manning (2000), 'Moral hazard and consumer incentives in health care', chap. 8 in A. Culyer and J. Newhouse, (eds), *Handbook of Health Economics*, Amsterdam: North-Holland.

11 Prescription drug insurance and reimbursement
Paul Grootendorst*

1. The gains from insurance

The headlines are familiar: prescription drug expenditures are burgeoning despite higher patient co-payments; many lack insurance to cover the high cost of new life-saving drugs; US drug insurers propose importing lower cost drugs *en masse* from Canada amid warnings from the pharmaceutical industry that research and development would suffer. Far from being solely of academic interest, understanding of the economics of drug insurance and reimbursement affords insights into many interesting policy issues.

To understand the issues, it is instructive to contrast the standard textbook model of the insurance market to the actual market. The expected utility model predicts that risk averse consumers – each facing the same probability p of a financial loss of $\$L$ associated with illness – are better off by paying a premium equal to the expected loss, $\$pL$, in exchange for compensation of $\$L$ should they become ill. Consumers' willingness to pay for insurance (net of pL) is greater, the more risk averse they are and the greater is the variance of losses (that is, the greater is L and the closer is p to 0.5). Hence, consumers' welfare gain from insuring against rare, catastrophic illness ('high variance' losses) exceeds that of insuring routine ailments ('low variance' losses).

The actual insurance market differs in several ways. First, premiums must exceed $\$pL$ to cover operating costs, including the cost of processing claims. The cost of insuring routine ailments would therefore exceed the cost of insuring catastrophic illness, even if the expected payouts for the two illnesses are identical. In the limit then, as $p \to 1$ and $L \to 0$, premiums will exceed consumers' willingness to pay for insurance. Many bio-pharmaceuticals, such as Remicade for rheumatoid arthritis, are both expensive (because of high unit prices and/or the need to take them indefinitely) and used to treat relatively rare disorders, so it is not surprising that drug insurance markets exist. But such drugs have been around only for the last several decades. What is surprising is that drug insurance existed during a time in which the scope for drugs to manage chronic health problems was limited, and drug spending correspondingly low.[1]

The answer is partly due to the tax treatment of employers' health plans for their employees. Drug and other health benefits are usually not taxable, whereas if the value of these benefits were instead paid as wages, they would be taxed. Such plans are therefore particularly valuable for employees facing high marginal tax rates and this raises questions about the distributional equity of this public subsidy. Using variation in tax rates across the provinces of Canada and the 1993 decision by the province of Quebec to begin taxing health benefits, Stabile (2001) and Finkelstein (2002) estimate that the

* Grootendorst is the recipient of a Research Career Award in Health Sciences from the Rx & D Health Research Foundation – Canadian Institutes of Health Research. He thanks Ernst Berndt, Tom Einarson, Joel Lexchin, Steve Morgan, John Nyman and Michael Veall for helpful comments.

elimination of the public subsidy would reduce the uptake of group insurance by about 20 per cent.

2.   Adverse selection

The employer provision of drug insurance also makes sense when we consider the implications of relaxing another restriction implicit in the standard model, that is all individuals share the same expected loss. In reality, consumers vary in p, L or both p and L in ways that are known to consumers but not insurers, making it costly to tailor premiums to individuals' risk. 'Sick' consumers – those whose expected loss exceeds the premium – are more likely to find insurance attractive and hence buy insurance than are the 'healthy' – those whose expected loss is less than the premium. The enrollee pool therefore tends to become dominated by the sick; attempts by insurers to recoup losses by raising premiums only exacerbates the problem as the remaining healthy opt out. Employer provision of drug insurance circumvents the problem by effectively requiring that healthy employees subsidize the premiums of their sick colleagues – those who wish to opt out must find employment elsewhere. Moreover, because insurers need only track total claims for purposes of setting premiums, operating costs are lower.

What are the insurance prospects for those who are not part of an employer (or other) group plan? One possibility is that insurers offer a menu of policies differing in premiums and deductibles. The policies are chosen such that those who expect to use lots of health care prefer the low deductible, high premium policies over the high deductible, low premium policies that the healthy prefer to purchase. In other words, the policies are chosen so that consumers reveal their expected losses by their choice of policy, allowing insurers to tailor coverage to individuals' risk (Rothschild and Stiglitz, 1976).

In this 'separating' equilibrium, information acquisition costs prevent the healthy from obtaining comprehensive coverage. Fortunately for the healthy, however, insurers are becoming increasingly sophisticated at predicting individuals' expected losses (Cawley and Philipson, 1999). For instance, the composition of glucose, enzymes, fats and various antibodies in a blood sample signals the presence of many risk factors.[2] Moreover, most spending is on drugs used to treat chronic conditions, such as elevated blood fat (hyperlipidemia) and pressure (hypertension), arthritis and depression (Morgan, 2004). Hence a patient's drug use history is an excellent predictor of future expenses (Coulson and Stuart, 1992); Pauly and Zeng (2003) note that drug use is among the most autocorrelated of all health services. Nevertheless, risk signalling is not costless: following Quebec's decision to tax health benefits, only 15 per cent of those who had lost employer coverage eventually acquired non-group coverage (Finkelstein, 2002).

The ability of insurers to predict risk is bad news for the sick: the actuarially fair premium for some will exceed their ability to pay. This raises the public policy question: should their premiums (or drug costs) be subsidized? The fact that many countries provide subsidies to those for whom drugs often constitute a large share of income – the aged and the indigent – suggests that equity concerns are important.[3] A prominent case in point is the recent decision to allocate $724 billion to extend drug subsidies to US seniors, only about half of whom have stable coverage (Pear, 2005; Reinhardt, 2001).

The targeting of subsidies on the basis of age (typically age 65+) raises questions of the incidence of the subsidy: are subsidies benefiting primarily low income seniors?

Alan et al. (2002) report that the introduction of Canadian provincial drug plans for seniors produced the largest benefits for the most affluent. Anecdotal evidence from drug plan managers suggests that higher income seniors are better able to get physicians to prescribe the latest drugs. In contrast to subsidies targeted at seniors, publicly funded catastrophic (large deductible) drug insurance for those under 65 appears to be mildly progressive (Alan et al., 2005). Apparently, the introduction of such subsidies has no impact on higher income households, who usually already have similar or better employer coverage, but represents an increase in coverage for lower income households who previously had little or no insurance.

3.   Moral hazard

A third restriction inherent in the standard model is that insurers can costlessly observe individuals' health and compensate claimants with lump-sum payouts L. If monitoring health is costly, however, insurers might instead reimburse drug expenditures (see Chapter 10 by Geoffard in this Companion). But reimbursement insurance, unlike lump-sum insurance, changes relative prices. Just as a fire insurance policy that covered the cost of a replacement home would increase demand for luxury homes, drug insurance increases demand for relatively expensive therapies.

Early treatments of this 'moral hazard' phenomenon emphasized the consumer-patient's role in driving up drug costs. Essentially, the price that the fully insured consumer faces for drugs is zero, prompting the consumer to expend less effort in illness or injury prevention (increasing p) and to 'demand' more drugs if ill (increasing L) compared to his non-insured counterparts. But the value of the additional drugs used is less than its resource cost, resulting in welfare loss (Pauly, 1968). Patient 'cost sharing' could help. The optimal patient charge would balance the benefits of insurance (in terms of risk reduction) against its cost (in terms of excessive drug use). A corollary is that the optimal patient charge is proportional to the price elasticity of drug use (η); if drug use does not depend on price (that is one's insurance status), then drugs should be fully insured (Zeckhauser, 1970).

Subsequent analysts, while not denying that patient-initiated moral hazard exists, emphasized the dominant role of the physician in diagnosis and treatment decisions. Patients, left to their own devices, might make serious mistakes. Therefore, most insured drugs can be used only with physician consent – hence the name 'prescription' drugs. This analysis yielded two insights. First, if patients have poor information about the properties of their drugs, an increase in patient charges may not lead them to relinquish selectively those drugs with the smallest expected health impact; hence patient charges might not necessarily be welfare improving.[4] Second, physician-initiated moral hazard might be as important as the patient-initiated variety. Because the physician treats drugs as a free input, she will select drugs based on perceived effectiveness or ease of use, not cost. Moreover, she might substitute drugs for her own time and other costly inputs. Indeed, prescribing rates and time spent per patient are negatively correlated (Davidson et al., 1994). If the patient is required to pay part of the drug cost and if the patient is cost conscious, the physician may be more likely to take drug cost into account. Nevertheless, attempts to curb moral hazard solely by targeting patients are likely to be ineffective, given the amount of physician influence in treatment decisions.

Nyman (Chapter 9 in this Companion) has further questioned the normative basis for evaluating the gains from insurance. The difference in drug costs incurred by the fully insured patient and what the patient would have purchased without insurance is, according to the standard model, undesirable. To be sure, some of this difference reflects the selection of substitutable drugs on the basis of perceived effectiveness or ease of use, regardless of cost. But some of this difference is also due to the income transfer to the insured ill patient, implicit in the reduction in drug prices, which makes the purchase of any of the substitutable drugs more affordable. This component of the difference, which presumably *is* desirable, would be likely to dominate if the drugs in question are costly.

Reimbursement insurance affects more than just the treatment choices of patients and physicians. Drug developers are more likely to introduce new drugs and charge more for them if end users do not bear the cost. As long as a new drug offers the slightest therapeutic advantage over existing drugs, it makes sense for fully insured patients to use it. The scope for drugs to treat health problems, and therefore the size of L, is likely to depend on the generosity of drug insurance. Scherer (2001) provides evidence consistent with this conjecture.

Pre-payment schemes

How could insurers combat moral hazard? In theory, insurers and physicians could agree on a treatment plan for every possible illness. Insurers would then pay out a lump sum L to cover the cost of these treatments should illness strike. In practice, this approach is difficult to implement. First, the contract would need to cover a very large number of contingencies due to the sheer number of different illnesses, differences in illness severity and progression, and uncertainties in diagnosis. Second, the physician could misrepresent the nature of the illness for financial gain. Finally, the contract would need to be renegotiated if there were material changes in medical technology or prices. To implement this approach, the gains from insurance would need to be sufficiently large so as to outweigh large transactions costs. That is perhaps why the system has been used to insure high variance losses, such as hospital care (the US Medicare programme introduced this approach in 1983 to pay for hospital care for its beneficiaries), but is not commonly used to insure drugs.

One way to circumvent the difficulties of negotiating illness-specific payouts is to give the physician (or other health provider) a budget with which to treat a group of patients for any illness that may arise over a period of time. At the end of the period, the physician keeps whatever money is left over (the 'residual'). The physician would therefore have an incentive to treat patients using the least costly mix of drug and other health services. While a promising approach, the potential problems are well known: physicians are likely to require additional compensation to accept income risk (the residual might be negative if their patients are atypically sick); physicians might 'cream-skim' (that is drop patients whose anticipated treatment costs exceed budgeted amounts); and physicians might reduce quality if it is difficult to distinguish low quality from 'bad luck' and/or if patient turnover is high (see Chapter 25 by Iverson and Lurås in this Companion). Prospective payment schemes of this sort are used in the US in the context of health maintenance organizations (HMOs) and in the UK in the context of general practitioner (GP) fundholding. Gosden and Torgerson (1997), in a review of the literature, report that fundholding appears to make GPs more cost conscious prescribers, a result corroborated by Domino and Salkever (2003) for US Medicaid HMOs. Little is known, however, about the attendant effects on the quality of care provided.

Schemes to affect prescribing behaviour

Physicians often have a choice of drugs to treat a given illness. For instance, diuretics, angiotensin converting enzyme inhibitors (ACEIs) and calcium channel blockers (CCBs) all manage uncomplicated hypertension. Diuretics are at least as effective as ACEIs and CCBs but are a fraction of the cost.[5] However, only 40 per cent of elderly beneficiaries of Pharmacare, the public drug plan for seniors and others in British Columbia (BC), Canada, receive diuretics as first line therapy for hypertension (Maclure et al., 1998). In an attempt to get physicians to become more cost conscious prescribers, drug insurers have used regulation, education, and in France, financial penalties for failure to prescribe according to guidelines.

A common regulatory tool is 'prior authorization' (PA) – the requirement that physicians justify why an expensive drug is required when cheaper alternatives exist. The evidence suggests that financial penalty and PA schemes change prescribing patterns and save money (Durand-Zaleski et al., 1997; Lexchin, 2002). For instance, Vioxx and Celebrex, introduced in 1999, are two selective cyclooxygenase-2 inhibitors (coxibs) used to manage arthritis pain and inflammation.[6] They are purported to have less gastro-intestinal toxicity compared to conventional analgesics, but are also more costly. The 22 US state Medicaid drug plans that implemented PA programmes for the coxibs during the period 1999–2003 reduced cost per analgesic prescription by about 20 per cent (Fischer et al., 2004). While they can save money, PA schemes might reduce patient access to beneficial drugs, and annoy doctors especially when the requirements for documentation are onerous and the appeals process cumbersome. The evidence on patient health impacts, while limited, suggests that these prescribing restrictions are largely innocuous (Lexchin, 2002).

Insurers have had much less success with educational initiatives targeted at prescribers. Unsolicited print materials and academic conferences without personalized attention simply don't work. However, interventions in which some effort is made to determine practice needs or to facilitate practice change can have a modest effect on prescribing and to a lesser extent, patient health (Oxman et al., 1995). In short, one can teach an old doc new tricks, but it's hard.

Patient cost sharing

The third method used to reduce drug costs – patient cost sharing – is ubiquitous. A variety of forms of cost sharing have emerged, including co-payment (a fixed fee per prescription), co-insurance (a proportion of ingredient cost and/or dispensing fee) and charges which vary with the number of prescriptions filled (for example deductibles and limits on total payouts). Patient charges also vary by drug. For instance, some insurers refuse to cover so-called 'lifestyle' drugs, such as drugs for erectile dysfunction. This amounts to 100 per cent co-insurance. Many public drug plans, such as those in Ontario (Ontario Ministry of Health, 1994) and Australia (Commonwealth of Australia, 1995), refuse to cover new drugs that do not offer sufficient therapeutic or cost advantages compared to existing therapies.[7] Alternatively, the insurer might provide more generous coverage to cheaper drugs within a drug class. For example, an insurer might limit reimbursement of branded and generic versions of the same drug to the price of the cheapest generic; any cost above that is borne by the patient. These product selection restrictions are commonplace. Less common are 'reference pricing' schemes wherein the insurer limits reimbursement of therapeutically similar, although chemically different drugs. For example, BC Pharmacare limits reimbursement of the 10 different ACEIs to about \$30/month. At this price, cheaper ACEIs are fully reimbursed; dearer ACEIs require patient contributions.[8] A variant of reference pricing is tiered cost sharing. Among private US insurers, drugs in the top tier typically require a \$30 co-payment for a month's supply, whereas bottom tier generic drugs usually require a \$5 co-payment (Gleason et al., 2005).

In addition to a money cost, consumers must pay a time cost for insured drugs. Traditionally this involved filling out forms and mailing these, along with receipts, to the insurer for reimbursement. Now most claims are processed electronically, at point of sale. This reduction in time cost had a remarkably large effect on drug use in BC (Grootendorst, 2005).

Most of the empirical evidence on the effects of traditional patient cost sharing on prescription drug use comes from observational studies of patient charges imposed by public drug plans in Canada, the US and UK, as well as within US HMOs. The evidence suggests that for most individuals, modest charges have a less than proportional effect on drug use: η is likely between -0.1 to -0.3 (Smith and Kirking, 1992; Gerdtham and Johannesson, 1996). The small response could reflect small income effects, limited substitution opportunities or high marginal valuation of health. The small response could also reflect patient adaptation to the cost sharing scheme. For instance, when faced with a co-payment, patients can economize by filling fewer, but larger prescriptions. Patients can mitigate the effects of dispensing fee co-insurance by patronizing mail order pharmacies and other low cost retailers (Berndt, 2002). If deductibles are used, once the deductible has been reached, drugs become free of charge. Ellis (1986) demonstrated that a forward-looking patient who expects to exceed the deductible would treat the marginal cost of all drugs used as zero – the deductible then affects drug use only through an income effect. Contoyannis et al. (2005) provide empirical evidence supporting this model.

Not surprisingly, η is larger for individuals who spend a larger share of their budgets on drugs – the sick poor (Lexchin and Grootendorst, 2004; Adams et al., 2001). For instance, the imposition of a limit of three reimbursed prescriptions per month by the New Hampshire Medicaid programme resulted in a 30 per cent reduction in the mean number of drugs used by (low income) schizophrenics (Soumerai et al., 1987). Proportionate reductions in drug use were even larger (46 per cent) in the sub-sample of multiple drug users. Depriving indigent schizophrenics of their medicines reduced Medicaid's drug bill by \$5 per person per month, but this was offset by increased use of other health services: overall expenditures increased by \$139 per month (Soumerai et al., 1994).

The health impacts of cost sharing depend on the price elasticity of drug use, the effectiveness of the drugs whose use is being deterred by the cost sharing and whether the drugs were used appropriately to begin with. This is illustrated by the analyses of the large cost sharing changes in the Quebec public drug plan. Prior to August 1996, all but the lowest income seniors paid a $2 co-payment (up to a $100 annual maximum). After this time seniors paid income-contingent premiums of $0–$175, and faced monthly deductibles of $8.33, with 25 per cent co-insurance, subject to income-contingent monthly maximums (from $16.67 to $62.50). Consistent with the literature, these sharp increases in charges did not result in particularly large drops in drug use: use of essential, life-saving medications (such as insulin, thyroid and anti-hypertensive drugs) dropped only 9 per cent, while use of less essential medications dropped 15 per cent. The relatively modest decline in essential drug use, however, resulted in substantially higher adverse event rates, including a 117 per cent increase in hospitalizations and doctors' visits and a 77 per cent increase in emergency department visits. Decreases in use of less essential drugs, on the other hand, did not result in such adverse events. Moreover, the relatively modest increases in charges targeted at welfare recipients produced larger proportionate reductions in drug use than observed for seniors and had comparable percentage increases in adverse event rates, even though the baseline adverse events rates were over double those for seniors (Tamblyn et al., 2001).

In contrast, Blais et al. (1999) found no adverse health impacts from the same charges applied to low income Quebec asthmatics. While asthma medications are usually deemed 'essential', these medications are known to be used inappropriately (Anis et al., 2001) so that reduced use would not be likely to affect health. Moreover, Blais et al. (2001) and Pilote et al. (2002) report that Quebec seniors' use of cardiac drugs and associated health outcomes were unaffected by the increase in patient charges; hence drugs used to treat more life threatening conditions appear less price sensitive.

Unlike conventional patient charges, reference pricing fully subsidizes lower cost medicines and, for those who meet exemption criteria, higher cost medicines as well. Reference pricing might therefore save money while avoiding the adverse patient health impacts associated with schemes that charge patients for all drugs. The most definitive evidence comes from the reference pricing programme introduced by BC Pharmacare, owing to the availability of patient-level drug and health services claims and health indicators data. Analyses of the impact of reference pricing applied to the ACEIs, CCBs and H_2-blockers suggest that drug plan savings were more than large enough to cover additional administrative costs (Schneeweiss et al., 2002, 2003, 2004; Hazlet and Blough, 2002; Grootendorst et al., 2002).[9] No deleterious effects on patient health were observed, although the health indicators – which are based on hospital admissions and mortality data – are likely to be insensitive to subtler changes in patient health related quality of life.

Drug price discounts
Drug manufacturers are able to exercise some market power owing to patent protection, differentiated products and/or price insensitive patients and prescribers. This has not gone unnoticed by drug insurers. Many large drug purchasers, such as the Australian national drug insurance scheme and US HMOs, secure price discounts in exchange for formulary listing (Wright, 2004; Scherer, 2000, p. 1325; Zaric and O'Brien, 2005). Not wanting to miss out on the action, the US Medicaid drug programme in 1993 demanded a 15 per cent discount off average wholesale prices, or access to the lowest price paid by any other purchaser in the US, whichever is greater. Although Medicaid initially enjoyed a windfall

gain, manufacturers eventually responded by increasing wholesale prices and reducing discounts (Congressional Budget Office, 1996), much to the chagrin of private insurers.[10]

Demands by insurers that they receive the best available price, although understandable, might reduce collective welfare in so far as they force drug manufacturers to charge identical prices to customers with different degrees of price sensitivity. For instance, if the US were to legalize drug imports from Canada, where drugs are cheaper in part because of lower incomes (Danzon and Furukawa, 2004), firms would eventually increase Canadian prices to US levels to stem the cross-border trade and thereby secure profits in the large US market. This would reduce both manufacturers' rents (and possibly R&D) and consumer surplus in the Canadian market.[11]

4.   Concluding comments

Prescription drug insurance schemes offer examples of how institutions have evolved to deal with the problems encountered with the provision of health insurance, namely adverse selection, moral hazard and the plight of the sick poor. Drug insurance is unique, however, in that institutional responses interacts with the pharmaceutical industry in ways that encourage or discourage technological development. The widespread adoption of reference pricing and schemes that reward drugs based on their productivity, such as those proposed by Hollis (2005), would dramatically reduce the payoff to drugs which offer only minor therapeutic advantages over incumbents, the so-called 'me-too' drugs. Conversely, attempts by drug payers to constrain prices on therapeutically novel 'blockbuster' drugs might inhibit the development of novel therapies, as sales from blockbusters have to repay the losses on the majority of drugs that don't even earn their capitalized R&D costs (Scherer, 2000, p. 1316).

Drug innovation might also affect drug insurance schemes. The continued development of costly biological drugs might make previously untreatable diseases treatable, or at least manageable, and hence create demand for insurance. Advances in genetic testing will make it easier to predict who will suffer losses in the future. Should this information be privileged, then adverse selection is likely to result. Conversely, if this information is public, this will limit the potential for risk pooling and exacerbate disparities in drug insurance coverage.

Notes

1. Berndt (2002, Table 2) reports that as the scope for drugs to treat problems has increased, so has the US drug insurers' share of prescription drug costs. The insurers' share increased from 3.5 per cent in 1965 to 73.4 per cent in 1998.
2. See, for example, http://www.amarillomed.com/howto.htm.
3. Equity concerns are not likely to be the only argument for public drug subsidies. If it were, then most developed countries would presumably have about the same public sector share of total drug spending. But this share varies markedly among OECD countries, from a low of 19 per cent (US) to a high of 94 per cent (Ireland) (OECD, 2004). It is also unlikely that this public subsidy variation is due to differences in externalities generated by the under-use of drugs that prevent the spread of infectious disease.
4. Evans (2002, page 25) also questions the normative basis for evaluating the welfare gains of health service use: 'In this technical meaning of "efficiency", the use of health care (or any other commodity) by people who are "unwilling" – which includes unable – to pay for it, is defined as "inefficient" regardless of the needs of the person or the effectiveness of the care. Conversely, use of care that is ineffective or even harmful by persons who are willing to pay for it (strikingly, even if they do not actually pay!) is defined as "efficient".'

5. For evidence on the efficacy of diuretics, ACEIs and CCBs, see: ALLHAT Officers and Coordinators for the ALLHAT Collaborative Research Group. The Antihypertensive and Lipid-Lowering Treatment to Prevent Heart Attack Trial (2002). The BC Therapeutics Initiative estimates the cost of 10 years' therapy (excluding dispensing fees) at maximum doses of a diuretic to be \$37 – substantially less than the cost of an ACEI (\$7139) or a CCB (\$7420). See http://www.ti.ubc.ca/pages/letter 47.htm
6. Vioxx was withdrawn from the market in September 2004 over cardiovascular safety concerns.
7. The prerequisite for the reimbursement of new drugs – evidence that they offer value for money – has spawned the field of 'pharmacoeconomics', the application of the tools of economic appraisal to new drugs (Drummond, Chapter 50 in this Companion). This area is ubiquitous, so many in the medical community consider 'health economics' and 'pharmacoeconomics' to be one and the same. Reinhardt (2001, 2004) has advocated that the US National Institutes of Health fund pharmacoeconomic analyses to guide reimbursement decisions.
8. Similar reimbursement limits have been applied to the CCBs, nitrates, H_2-blockers and NSAIDs. See http://www.healthservices.gov.bc.ca/pharme/sa/criteria/rdpcategoriesindex.html. Reference pricing and the use of pharmacoeconomic analyses to determine insurer reimbursement of medicines can be thought of as special cases of a reward system in which more productive drugs earn a larger share of a fixed reward fund (Hollis, 2005).
9. For literature reviews, see Lopez-Casasnovas and Puig-Junoy (2000) and Kanavos and Reinhardt (2003).
10. There are many other examples of externalities created by drug insurance: restrictions on the drugs reimbursed by large public insurers can reduce costs to private drug plans because of their durable influence on physician prescribing patterns (Wang et al., 2003). Conversely, a physician who is forced to keep track of the myriad formulary restrictions of all her patients might simply follow her own prescribing preferences (Berndt, 2002). Similarly, increases in the number of drug insurers increase the complexity of sorting out insurance claims (Reinhardt et al., 2004). The tax subsidies offered to private drug insurance can increase the number of physician visits because prescription drug use and physician visits are complements (Stabile, 2001). Conversely, the use of some prescription drugs can substitute for more costly hospitalization (Lichtenberg, 1996). (But see also Duggan (2005).) Insurance coverage of vaccinations and drugs that inhibit the spread of infectious disease will generate external benefits. Conversely, generous insurance of antibiotics might increase their use and propagate resistant strains of bacteria (Horowitz and Moehring, 2004). Widespread use of a particular drug might convey information about efficacy and safety to other patients and physicians. This can lead to dominance of one drug despite the availability of close substitutes (Berndt et al., 2003). Finally, expansions of public insurance designed to help the uninsured will also attract those who already have private insurance (Cutler and Gruber, 1996).
11. The parallel trade in pharmaceuticals in the European Union has also led to drug companies 'withholding or delaying launch of new products in traditional low-price countries of the EU, rather than accept prices that would invite parallel trade and hence erode the prices that they can earn in other larger markets' (Danzon, 1998, p. 300).

References

Adams, A.S., S.B. Soumerai and D. Ross-Degnan (2001), 'The case for a Medicare drug coverage benefit: a critical review of the empirical evidence', *Annual Review of Public Health*, **22**, 49–61.

Alan, S., T.F. Crossley, P. Grootendorst and M.R. Veall (2002), 'The effects of drug subsidies on out-of-pocket prescription drug expenditures by seniors: regional evidence from Canada', *Journal of Health Economics*, **21**(5), 805–26.

Alan, S., T.F. Crossley, P. Grootendorst and M.R. Veall (2005), 'Distributional effects of "general population" prescription drug programs in Canada', *Canadian Journal of Economics*, **38**(1), 128–48.

ALLHAT Officers and Coordinators for the ALLHAT Collaborative Research Group (2002), 'Major outcomes in high-risk hypertensive patients randomized to angiotensin-converting enzyme inhibitor or calcium channel blocker vs diuretic: the Antihypertensive and Lipid-Lowering Treatment to prevent Heart Attack Trial (ALLHAT)', *Journal of the American Medical Association*, **288**(23), 2981–97.

Anis, A.H., L.D. Lynd, X. Wang, G. King, J.J. Spinelli, M. Fitzgerald and T. Bai (2001), 'Double trouble: impact of inappropriate use of asthma medication on the use of health care resources', *Canadian Medical Association Journal*, **164**(5), 625–31.

Berndt, E.R. (2002), 'Pharmaceuticals in US health care: determinants of quantity and price', *Journal of Economic Perspectives*, **16**, 45–66.

Berndt, E.R., R.S. Pindyck and P. Azoulay (2003), 'Consumption externalities and diffusion in pharmaceutical markets: antiulcer drugs', *Journal of Industrial Economics*, **51**(2), 243–70.

Blais, L., A. Castilloux, J. Couture and J. LeLorier (1999), 'Impact of the Quebec cost sharing drug plan on asthmatic patients receiving social assistance', *Canadian Journal of Clinical Pharmacology*, **6**(1), 42.

Blais, L., J.M. Boucher, J. Couture, E. Rahme and J. LeLorier (2001), 'Impact of a cost-sharing drug insurance plan on drug utilization among older people', *Journal of the American Geriatric Society*, **49**(4), 410–14.

Cawley, J. and T. Philipson (1999), 'An empirical examination of information barriers to trade in insurance', *American Economic Review*, **89**(4), 827–46.

Commonwealth of Australia (1995), *Guidelines for the Pharmaceutical Industry on Preparation of Submissions to the Pharmaceutical Benefits Advisory Committee: Including Major Submissions Involving Economic Analyses*, Canberra: Australian Government Publishing Service.

Congressional Budget Office (1996), *How the Medicaid Rebate on Prescription Drugs Affects Pricing in the Pharmaceutical Industry*, Washington DC: CBO, Available at: http://www.cbo.gov/ftpdocs/47xx/doc4750/1996Doc20.pdf.

Contoyannis, P., J. Hurley, P. Grootendorst, S. Jeon and R. Tamblyn (2005), 'Estimating the price elasticity of expenditure for prescription drugs in the presence of non-linear price schedules: an illustration from Quebec, Canada', *Health Economics*, **14**(9), 909–23.

Coulson, N.E. and B. Stuart (1992), 'Persistence in the use of pharmaceuticals by the elderly: evidence from annual claims', *Journal of Health Economics*, **11**(3), 315–28.

Cutler, D.M. and J. Gruber (1996), 'The effect of Medicaid expansions on public insurance, private insurance, and redistribution', *American Economic Review*, **86**(2), 378–83.

Danzon, Patricia M. (1998), 'The economics of parallel trade', *PharmacoEconomics*, **13**(3), 293–304.

Danzon, P.M. and M.F. Furukawa (2004), 'Prices and availability of pharmaceuticals: evidence from nine countries', *Health Affairs*, **W3**, 521–36.

Davidson, W., D.W. Molloy, G. Somers and M. Bedard (1994), 'Relation between physician characteristics and prescribing for elderly people in New Brunswick', *Canadian Medical Association Journal*, **150**(6), 917–21.

Domino, M.E. and D.S. Salkever (2003), 'Price elasticity and pharmaceutical selection: the influence of managed care', *Health Economics*, **12**(7), 565–86.

Duggan, Mark (2005), 'Do new prescription drugs pay for themselves?: the case of second-generation antipsychotics', *Journal of Health Economics*, **24**(1), 1–31.

Durand-Zaleski, I., C. Conlin and C. Blum-Boisgard (1997), 'An attempt to save money by using mandatory practice guidelines in France', *British Medical Journal*, **315**(7113), 943–46.

Ellis, R. (1986), 'Rational behavior in the presence of coverage ceilings and deductibles', *The Rand Journal of Economics*, **17**(2), 158–75.

Evans, R.G. (2002), 'Raising the money: Options, consequences and objections for financing health care in Canada', Commission on the Future of Health Care in Canada Discussion Paper no. 27. Available at: http://www.hc-sc.gc.ca/english/care/romanow/hcc0493.html.

Finkelstein, Amy (2002), 'The effect of tax subsidies to employer-provided supplementary health insurance: evidence from Canada', *Journal of Public Economics*, **84**(3), 305–39.

Fischer, M.A., S. Schneeweiss, J. Avorn and D.H. Solomon (2004), 'Medicaid prior-authorization programs and the use of cyclooxygenase-2 inhibitors', *The New England Journal of Medicine*, **351**(21), 2187–94.

Gerdtham, U. and M. Johannesson (1996), 'The impact of user charges on the consumption of drugs: empirical evidence and economic implications', *PharmacoEconomics*, **9**(6), 478–83.

Gleason, P., B.W. Gunderson and K.R. Gericke (2005), 'Are incentive-based formularies inversely associated with drug utilization in managed care?', *The Annals of Pharmacotherapy*, **39**(2), 339–45.

Gosden, T. and D.J. Torgerson (1997), 'The effect of fund holding on prescribing and referral costs: a review of the evidence', *Health Policy*, **40**(2), 103–14.

Grootendorst, Paul (2005), 'The impact of an on-line pharmacy claims adjudication network on use and costs of prescription drugs: evidence from British Columbia Pharmacare', *Journal of Pharmaceutical Finance, Economics & Policy*, **13**(3), 27–39.

Grootendorst, P., L.R. Dolovich, A.M. Holbrook, A.R. Levy and B.J. O'Brien (2002), 'The impact of reference pricing of cardiovascular drugs on health care costs and health outcomes: evidence from British Columbia – volumes I: summary and II: technical report', *Social and Economic Dimensions of an Aging Population (SEDAP)*, working papers **s70**, **s71**. Available at: http://socserv.socsci.mcmaster.ca/sedap/p/sedap70.pdf and http://socserv.socsci.mcmaster.ca/sedap/p/sedap71.pdf.

Hazlet, T.K. and D.K. Blough (2002), 'Health services utilization with reference drug pricing of Histamine(2) receptor antagonists in British Columbia elderly', *Medical Care*, **40**(8), 640–49.

Hollis, Aidan (2005), 'An efficient reward system for pharmaceutical innovation', Mimeo, Department of Economics, University of Calgary. Available at: http://econ.ucalgary.ca/fac-files/ah/drugprizes.pdf.

Horowitz, J.B. and H. B. Moehring (2004), 'How property rights and patents affect antibiotic resistance', *Health Economics*, **13**(6), 575–83.

Kanavos, P. and U. Reinhardt (2003), 'Reference pricing for drugs: is it compatible with US healthcare?', *Health Affairs*, **22**(3), 16–30.

Lexchin, Joel (2002), 'Effects of restrictive formularies in the ambulatory care setting', *The American Journal of Managed Care*, **8**(1), 69–74.

Lexchin, J. and P. Grootendorst (2004), 'Effects of prescription drug user fees on drug and health services use and on health status in vulnerable populations: a systematic review of the evidence', *International Journal of Health Services*, **34**(1), 101–22.

Lichtenberg, Frank (1996), 'Do (more and better) drugs keep people out of hospitals?', *American Economic Review*, **86**(2), 384–88.

Lopez-Casasnovas, G. and J. Puig-Junoy (2000), 'Review of the literature on reference pricing', *Health Policy*, **54**(2), 87–123.

Maclure, M., C. Dormuth, T. Naumann, J. McCormack, R. Rangno, C. Whiteside and J.M. Wright (1998), 'Influences of educational interventions and adverse news about calcium-channel blockers on first-line prescribing of antihypertensive drugs to elderly people in British Columbia', *The Lancet*, **352**(9132), 943–78.

Morgan, S. (2004), 'Drug spending in Canada: recent trends and causes', *Medical Care*, **42**(7), 635–42.

OECD (2004), *Health Data*, Paris: OECD.

Ontario Ministry of Health (1994), *Ontario Guidelines for Economic Analysis of Pharmaceutical Products*, Toronto: Ontario Ministry of Health.

Oxman, A.D., M.A. Thomson, D.A. Davis and B. Haynes (1995), 'No magic bullets: a systematic review of 102 trials of interventions to improve professional practice', *Canadian Medical Association Journal*, **153**(10), 1423–31.

Pauly, M.V. (1968), 'The economics of moral hazard: comment', *American Economic Review*, **58**(3), 531–37.

Pauly, M.V. and Y. Zeng (2003), 'Adverse selection and the challenges to stand-alone prescription drug insurance', NBER working paper, **w9919**.

Pear, Robert (2005), 'Bush vows veto of any cutback in drug benefit', *New York Times*, 12 February.

Pilote, L., C. Beck, H. Richard and M.J. Eisenberg (2002), 'The effects of cost-sharing on essential drug prescriptions, utilization of medical care and outcomes after acute myocardial infarction in elderly patients', *Canadian Medical Association Journal*, **167**(3), 246–52.

Reinhardt, U.E. (2001), 'Perspectives on the pharmaceutical industry', *Health Affairs*, **20**(5), 136–49.

Reinhardt, U.E. (2004), 'An information infrastructure for the pharmaceutical market', *Health Affairs*, **23**(1), 107–12.

Reinhardt, U.E., P.S. Hussey and G.F. Anderson (2004), 'US health care spending in an international context', *Health Affairs*, **23**(3), 10–25.

Rothschild, M. and J.E. Stiglitz (1976), 'Equilibrium in competitive insurance markets: an essay on the economics of imperfect information', *Quarterly Journal of Economics*, **90**(4), 629–49.

Scherer, F.M. (2001), 'The link between gross profits and pharmaceutical R&D spending', *Health Affairs*, **20**(5), 216–20.

Scherer, F.M. (2000), 'The pharmaceutical industry', in J.P. Newhouse and A. Culyer (eds), *Handbook of Health Economics*, Amsterdam: Elsevier, pp. 1297–336.

Schneeweiss, S., C. Dormuth, P. Grootendorst, S.B. Soumerai and M. Maclure (2004), 'Net health plan savings from reference pricing for angiotensin-converting enzyme inhibitors in elderly British Columbia residents', *Medical Care*, **42**(7), 653–60.

Schneeweiss, S., S.B. Soumerai, M. Maclure, C. Dormuth, A.M. Walker and R.J. Glynn (2003), 'Clinical and economic consequences of reference pricing for dihydropyridine calcium channel blockers', *Clinical Pharmacology & Therapeutics*, **74**(4), 388–400.

Schneeweiss, S., A.M. Walker, R.J. Glynn, M. Maclure, C. Dormuth and S.B. Soumerai (2002), 'Outcomes of reference pricing for angiotensin-converting-enzyme inhibitors', *New England Journal of Medicine*, **346**(11), 822–29.

Smith, D.G. and D.M. Kirking (1992), 'Impact of consumer fees on drug utilisation', *PharmacoEconomics*, **2**(4), 335–42.

Soumerai, S.B., J. Avorn, D. Ross-Degnan and S. Gortmaker (1987), 'Payment restrictions for prescription drugs under Medicaid: effects on therapy, cost, and equity', *New England Journal of Medicine*, **317**(9), 550–56.

Soumerai, S.B., T.J. McLaughlin, D. Ross-Degnan, C.S. Casteris and P. Bollini (1994), 'Effects of limiting Medicaid drug-reimbursement benefits on the use of psychotropic agents and acute mental health services by patients with schizophrenia', *New England Journal of Medicine*, **331**(10), 650–55.

Stabile, Mark (2001), 'Private insurance subsidies and public health care markets: evidence from Canada', *Canadian Journal of Economics*, **34**(4), 921–42.

Tamblyn, R., R. Laprise, J.A. Hanley, M. Abrahamowicz, S. Scott, N. Mayo, J. Hurley, R. Grad, E. Latimer, R. Perreault, P. McLeod, A. Huang, P. Larochelle and L. Mallet (2001), 'Adverse events associated with prescription drug cost-sharing among poor and elderly persons', *Journal of the American Medical Association*, **285**(4), 421–29.

Wang, Y.R., M.V. Pauly and Y.A. Lin (2003), 'Impact of Maine's Medicaid drug formulary change on non-Medicaid markets: spillover effects of a restrictive drug formulary', *The American Journal of Managed Care*, **9**(10), 686–96.

Wright, D.J. (2004), 'The drug bargaining game: pharmaceutical regulation in Australia', *Journal of Health Economics*, **23**(4), 785–813.

Zaric, G.S. and B. O'Brien (2005), 'Analysis of a pharmaceutical risk sharing agreement based on the purchaser's total budget', *Health Economics*, **14**(8), 793–803.

Zeckhauser, R.J. (1970), 'Medical insurance: a case study of the tradeoff between risk spreading and appropriate incentives', *Journal of Economic Theory,* **2**, 10–26.

12 The economics of social health insurance
Peter Zweifel and Friedrich Breyer

1. Why social health insurance?

Most developed countries have some kind of collective financing for health services, either through taxes (for example the National Health Service (NHS) in the United Kingdom) or through their contributions to 'social' health insurance (henceforth: SHI). This type of insurance is usually characterized by mandatory membership, at least for the vast majority of the population, open enrolment and community rating, that is a prohibition to charge premiums related to individual risk. From a normative point of view, the institution of SHI can be defended on both efficiency and equity grounds, whereas positive economics can explain its existence in democracies on the basis of public choice models.

Efficiency reasons: characteristics of private health insurance markets
SHI may be efficiency-enhancing if it mitigates or even eliminates possible market failures.

(a) **Asymmetric information**: Ever since the seminal contribution by Rothschild and Stiglitz (1976), private competitive insurance markets are suspected to exhibit adverse selection due to asymmetric information. If the insured has more precise information on his individual risk distribution than the insurer, the only possible Rothschild–Stiglitz equilibrium is a separating equilibrium in which only the highest risks are offered complete coverage at actuarially fair premiums. Lower risks obtain more favourable terms but are rationed in terms of coverage. They would prefer to have more but this would make their contract attractive to unfavourable risks. Compared to such an equilibrium, SHI which forces all individuals into a pooling contract with partial coverage can achieve a Pareto improvement: high risks are made better off because they pay lower premiums for the mandated part of their coverage, whereas low risks benefit from improved total (social plus private) coverage (Newhouse, 1996). However, it is unclear to what extent asymmetric information on health risks is really a problem since medical exams may be used to determine the risk of an insured.

(b) **Altruism and free riding**: Altruistic rich members of society may be willing to subsidize the provision of health care to the poor if they are more interested in the health than in the subjective well-being of the poor (Pauly, 1970). Private charity is not suitable to reach an efficient allocation since donations to the poor, whether in cash or in kind, have a public-good characteristic because they increase the utility not only of the donor but also of other altruistic members of society. Either a tax-financed NHS or SHI with compulsory membership and contributions according to ability to pay solve this free-rider problem of potential donors.

(c) **Optimal taxation when health and income are correlated**: A related justification of SHI is derived from the theory of optimal taxation (for example, Cremer and Pestieau 1996). If abilities cannot be observed by tax authorities, the extent to which income taxation can be used for redistribution from the high-skilled to the low-skilled is limited because the high-skilled can always 'mimic' the low-skilled by reducing their labour supply. However, if there is a negative correlation between ability and the risk of illness, a mandatory SHI with community rating implicitly redistributes between the ability groups in the desired fashion and thus improves social welfare. It must be emphasized, however, that this justification departs from Paretian welfare economics by postulating a specific redistributive goal.

Equity reasons

A further and perhaps more compelling justification, also known as the 'principle of solidarity', relates to the achievement of equality of opportunity: people differ in their health risk already at birth, and some indicators of risk are readily observable. Moreover, with the rapid progress of genetic diagnostics and the spread of tests during pregnancy, the ability to measure individual health risks of newborns will become more and more pronounced. In private health insurance (PHI), these differences in risk immediately translate into differences in premiums so that those persons who are endowed by nature with a lower stock of 'health capital' and are thus already disadvantaged, have to pay a higher price for the same coverage on top of this. Behind the veil of ignorance, one would desire at least an equalization of the monetary costs of illness.

There are in principle two ways to achieve solidarity in health insurance (see Table 12.1). First, PHI premiums can be subsidized for those who would have to pay excessive contributions. The transfer could be on a current basis or a lump sum, equal to the estimated present value of future excess premiums over the whole expected lifespan of beneficiaries. Both have the important advantage of permitting full competition in PHI (or SHI), including insurers acquiring information about true risk. Besides means testing and the need to define a benchmark contract to determine the amount of the subsidy, the second

Table 12.1   Alternatives for achieving solidarity

Alternatives		Advantages	Disadvantages	References
Premium subsidy	Current transfer	Permits full competition in PHI (or SHI) both in premiums and products and full information on risk	Means testing; definition of benchmark contract	Pauly et al. (1992)
	Lump sum transfer for lifetime		Means testing; longevity risk shifted to beneficiaries	
Regulation: Community rating		Relieves public budget	Induces cream-skimming and RAS as secondary regulation	Van de Ven et al. (2000)

Note: RAS = risk adjustment scheme.

variant has the disadvantage of shifting the risk of longevity to beneficiaries. The alternative is a monopolistic SHI scheme with open enrolment and community rating that prevents differences in health risk from being translated into differences in contributions but induces cream-skimming and risk adjustment schemes (RAS, see below) as a secondary neutralizing regulation.

Public choice reasons
In PHI, redistribution occurs purely by chance, from consumers who did not suffer a loss during the life of the contract to those who do. By way of contrast, social insurance mixes in elements of systematic redistribution. The fact that contributions are not (or not fully) graded according to risk alone (OECD, 2004) serves to systematically redistribute wealth from high risks to low risks. In SHI, this redistribution not only affects wealth through its financing side but the benefit side as well, viz. medical services and health. This makes social health insurance an ideal means for a politician who seeks office (or re-election) by catering to the interests of groups who are sufficiently organized to have an effect on the outcome of an election (Gouveia, 1997; Hindriks and De Donder, 2003; Tullock, 2003). The redistributive effects of SHI can be described as follows.

(a) **Redistribution of wealth**: Using SHI as a vehicle for systematic redistribution has the important advantage that net payers have considerable difficulty determining the systematic component of redistribution. For example, when the contribution to SHI amounts to a payroll tax (as, for example, in Germany), high wage earners pay more for their health insurance. However, they are uncertain about the systematic redistribution component of their contribution because the expected value of their benefits may also be higher than average. This may have two reasons: preventive effort may be affected negatively by a higher wage, resulting in higher health costs, and demand for medical services may increase because short-term disability benefits usually increase with wages, creating a spillover moral hazard effect (Zweifel and Manning, 2000). Therefore, their higher contribution appears 'justified', masking a tax component which, if openly collected as a tax, would likely be opposed.

(b) **Redistribution of medical care**: There are two effects here. First, there is an income effect because some individuals who would have demanded less or no medical care without insurance coverage now demand a positive amount of it (Nyman, 2003 and Chapter 9 in this Companion). Indeed there is (macro) evidence suggesting that medical care is a normal good (Gerdtham, et al., 1992; Miller and Frech, 2004; Zweifel et al., 2005). Insurance coverage then amounts to an in-kind redistribution from the rich to the poor if the supply of medical services is not infinitely elastic and if the price elasticity of demand for medical care is not lower for the rich than the poor (which is doubtful, see Newhouse et al., 1993, ch. 11). However, there is also a price effect because health insurance boosts the 'true' willingness-to-pay (WTP) for medical care depending on the rate of co-insurance (Zweifel and Breyer, 1997, ch. 10). For example, if 'true' WTP is 100 and the rate of co-insurance is 25 per cent, observed WTP is 400.

(c) **Redistribution of health**: When it comes to health, altruism is probably more marked than with regard to income, although comparative evidence seems to be lacking (the methodology for measuring distributive preferences for health is still in its infancy, see Olsen 2000 and Chapter 36 by Dolan and Tsuchiya in this Companion). Therefore, politicians can claim to have a mission when seeking to guarantee 'health for all' (the famous slogan of the World Health Organization). Equal access to health insurance then may be seen as an important factor for securing equal access to medical care, and to the extent that medical care is effective at the margin (for which there is some evidence, see for example again Miller and Frech, 2004 and Lichtenberg, 2004) for securing equal health status (Culyer and Wagstaff, 1993).

If SHI indeed contributes to winning votes and increasing the chance of (re-)election of a democratic government, one would expect public expenditure for it to increase around election time. One piece of available evidence relates to two types of public expenditure by the Dutch government, expressed as GDP shares, between around 1956 and 1993, namely health (such as subsidies to hospitals) and tax contributions to social insurance in general. Van Dalen and Swank (1996), cited in Zweifel (2000a), find that while public expenditure on health does not vary around election time, transfers in favour of social insurance are systematically higher during the years prior, concurrent with, and after an election. The estimated effect is 13 per cent, for example an increase from 15 to 17 per cent of GDP. In addition, the share of the pensioners in the population is significantly related to both types of public expenditure. Nowadays pensioners are not poor in general, but they do go to the polls. The evidence thus is compatible with governments proposing social health insurance schemes to benefit pivotal voter groups.

2.   The supply of social health insurance
Governments (and public administrators) can be seen as the suppliers of social health insurance. This is true in systems of the National Health Service type, where in fact the government itself provides the insurance function while also acting as the organizer of medical care. This type will be called public health insurer. However, in a majority of industrialized countries, health insurers are not incorporated in the government's budget; they will be called (competitive) social health insurers.

Supply by a competitive social health insurer
Supply of health insurance can be characterized by several dimensions (Zweifel, 2005), such as comprehensiveness of the benefit package, the amount of loading included in the premium, the degree of vertical integration of health care providers, the amount of effort devoted to risk selection and to innovation, and the degree of seller concentration. Arguably, the two crucial decision variables for public policy are effort devoted to innovation and effort devoted to risk selection. The first type of effort results in new benefits covered but also, and even more importantly, in a better control of *ex post* moral hazard (that is, moral hazard given that illness has occurred). Developing managed care alternatives or contracts with no-claims bonuses are examples of such costly efforts. The second type of efforts is often called 'cream-skimming', an activity that has no social value (assuming that the threat of being found to be a high risk does not induce preventive effort on the part of consumers). Note that cream-skimming is of interest only to the extent that premiums do not fully reflect true risk, which is typically the case; otherwise, expected

profit margins would equalize across risk types, making high risks (because of higher pre-miums paid) no less attractive than low risks (Zweifel and Eisen, 2002, ch. 5.5.2).

Given uniformity of premiums, risk adjustment schemes (RAS) in SHI are designed to redress the balance between innovation and cream-skimming effort by meting out a financial sanction to health insurers with an above-average share of low risks and using the proceeds to support those with an above-average share of high risks. However, RAS are not likely to fully achieve this purpose because innovation typically attracts younger, better-educated consumers. These individuals show up as low risks with the innovator, who has to pay into the risk adjustment scheme. Thus, while RAS discourage risk selec-tion, they discourage innovation as well. Indeed, the experience of those countries that have introduced competition between social health insurers combined with RAS (such as Germany, the Netherlands and Switzerland) has been somewhat disappointing. Health insurers have been rather slow launching new products; of course, they may have been hampered by regulation in addition to the RAS (Beck et al., 2003), although they seem to achieve substantial savings net of risk selection effects (Lehmann and Zweifel, 2004).

Supply by a public health insurer
Since the manager of a public insurance scheme is a public official, the full set of inter-actions between a politician, a bureaucrat and a voter should be specified in principle (as for example in Alesina and Tabellini, 2004; Coates et al., 2004; see also Boldrin and Rustichini, 2000 and Hammond and Knott, 1996); for a comparative description of regu-lation of social health insurers, see Maarse et al. (2004). Here, the discussion is limited to two institutional features.

A first difference from competitive SHI is that a public insurer typically is not allowed to build major reserves. Reserves are also unnecessary because its economic survival is assured by the government. This means that a public official who deviates from a balanced budget is at risk of being demoted. Second, a monopoly enrolling the entire population has no reason to exert any risk selection effort. On the other hand, innovation cannot attract low risks but only helps to keep the budget balanced. Therefore, the expectation is that public health insurers exert less effort in innovation than do (competitive) private ones.

3.   The design of an optimal health insurance contract

The efficiency reasons given above for the existence of SHI with compulsory membership can be convincing only if the design of the SHI contract is in some sense 'optimal' from the point of view of the representative consumer (see for example Zweifel and Breyer 1997, ch. 6). In view of the tendency towards full coverage of most SHI schemes, an issue of particular importance are the circumstances justifying co-payments, that is deviations from full coverage of health care expenditures.

(a) **Administrative costs**: Co-payment provisions can be called for to save administrative costs such as costs of handling claims. For this reason, and assuming expected utility maximization on the part of consumers, it is optimal to exclude partially or entirely expenditures on health care items that occur frequently but in limited amounts, such as minor medications (Mossin, 1968). More specifically, if administrative costs are proportional to the expected volume of health expenditures, a feature of the optimal insurance contract is a fixed deductible (Arrow, 1963).

(b) **Non-insurable loss**: Illness typically involves not only monetary costs but also non-monetary losses such as pain and suffering. Optimal health insurance equalizes marginal utility of wealth in all states of nature but this is not equivalent to full coverage if there are complementarities between non-monetary and monetary losses. In particular, if marginal utility of wealth is lower in the case of illness than in good health (due, for example, to reduced ability to enjoy expensive types of consumption), optimal health insurance does not fully reimburse the monetary loss (Cook and Graham, 1977).

(c) **Ex-ante moral hazard**: If the insurer cannot observe preventive effort on the part of the insured, a high degree of coverage reduces the incentive for prevention. Hence there is a trade-off between risk spreading through insurance and maintaining incentives to keep the risk of illness low. This trade-off leads to a premium function which is convex in the degree of coverage, such that full coverage should be particularly expensive (Ehrlich and Becker, 1972). In SHI such a premium function is nowhere observed, although it could be easily administered because consumers cannot circumvent the convex schedule by purchasing many insurance contracts with limited coverage and low premiums.

(d) **Ex-post moral hazard**: If the insurer could observe the health status of the insured, the optimal type of health insurance would provide indemnity payments, that is the insurance payment would not depend on the insured's health care expenditure. With asymmetric information, however, linking reimbursement to expenditure is inevitable. Still, co-payment provisions are needed to fend against overconsumption of medical care. The optimal co-payment rate is higher the more price elastic the demand for the particular type of medical services (Spence and Zeckhauser, 1971, see also Zweifel and Breyer 1997, ch. 6, and Chapter 10 by Geoffard in this Companion). Empirical evidence, for example from the RAND Health Insurance Study (Manning et al., 1987), shows that there is a small, albeit statistically significant, price elasticity of demand for most medical services (for a survey of the evidence, see Zweifel and Manning, 2000).

4.   Comparative outcomes

Having discussed the demand for social health insurance (section 1) and the two sources of supply of this type of insurance (section 2), one would ideally want to determine the equilibrium outcome and compare it with the optimal contract as described in section 3. However, there are more dimensions to the product than just quantity and price. In the following, some tentative inferences will be drawn as to the equilibrium values of some of these dimensions, depending on whether competitive health insurers or a monopolistic public insurer is in charge.

Moral hazard

Some writers argue that public health insurers are more successful in controlling moral hazard. Indeed, compulsory membership combined with a monopoly provides the supplier with full power to implement a scheme that minimizes moral hazard, for example by asking for medical reports that make health status observable and imposing indemnity insurance (Zweifel and Breyer, 1997, ch. 6). However, as shown in section 3 above, given lack of observability, a rate of co-insurance smaller than one is optimal, which leaves room for moral hazard. Politicians in fact tend to mandate very low rates of co-insurance, possibly for fear of consumers irrationally choosing excessive cost sharing and then either going broke over medical bills or hurting their health due to insufficient care.

By way of contrast, the theoretical argument developed in section 2 suggests that competing health insurers may exert at least as much innovative effort for reducing cost (possibly through controlling moral hazard) than their public counterparts. Indeed, one typically observes a wide range of rates of cost sharing offered and accepted in PHI (see for example, Van de Ven and van Praag, 1981 or Zweifel, 1992). Also, competitive social health insurers stagger (if permitted) their cost sharing parameters, matching them with premium reductions, in order to cater to the variety of preferences among their clientele (Felder and Werblow, 2003; Zweifel, 1982). In sum, it may well be that problems of moral hazard are induced by regulation imposed on SHI rather than the choice between the competitive and monopoly schemes.

Risk selection
In an unregulated private health insurance market, high risks pay higher premiums for the same level of coverage than do low risks. Community rating in SHI prevents this, making 'cream-skimming' attractive, which in turn runs counter to the aim of open enrolment.

There are a number of options for complementary regulation designed to limit risk selection (see Table 12.2 and Chapter 26 by Glazer and McGuire in this Companion). The first is a central fund running an RAS, as discussed above. *Ex ante* equalization of expected health care expenditures has the crucial advantage of preserving incentives for cost control but is resisted by risk-averse insurers. The classical alternative is re-insurance, where competitive experience-rated premiums largely conserve direct insurers' incentive for cost control. However, its transaction costs are frequently high because re-insurers must assess risks ceded and monitor contracts. Finally, regulation may prescribe a high-risk pool, in which expenditures of the x per cent most expensive insured (which are identified on the basis of past experience) are covered by the central fund. Being targeted to the very high risks, this saves on transaction costs but conserves incentives to select favourable risks at the low end of the cost distribution.

Rationing
Rationing can occur in two ways. First, *explicit rationing* means that the extent of coverage of a health insurance plan is not fully comprehensive. For example, certain types of health care services such as medications or dental care may be excluded or there may be age limits for the coverage of specific types of services such as organ transplants. Explicit rationing provisions have the advantage of allowing the purchase of supplementary private health insurance contracts for the services not covered within SHI, but the disadvantage of making these limitations transparent. Therefore, explicit rationing is not very popular among politicians who fear to lose the support by those groups of voters who are particularly interested in having the excluded services covered. In contrast, *implicit rationing* involves the use of additional instruments such as global budgets to constrain

Table 12.2   *Alternatives for neutralizing insurers' incentive to skim the cream (given uniform premiums)*

Alternatives		Advantages	Disadvantages	References
RAS	*ex ante*	Preserves incentives for cost control	Exposes little diversified insurers to risk	Ellis and van de Ven (2000)
	ex post	Relieves insurers of risk	Undermines incentives for cost control	
Re-insurance	*ex post*	Competitive re-insurance premiums conserve direct insurers' incentive for cost control; exposes insurers to some risk	High transaction cost	
High-risk pool	*ex ante*	Reduced transaction cost; largely conserves incentives for cost control; exposes insurers to some risk	Conserves incentive to select risks at the low end of cost distribution	Van Barneveld et al. (1996)
	ex post	Reduced transaction cost; conserves some incentive for cost control; relieves insurers of risk		

the level or growth of total SHI expenditures. These measures are more popular among politicians because they can keep the appearance of comprehensive coverage but still contain expenditure growth. On the downside, implicit rationing puts health care providers under permanent pressure to meet an ever-increasing demand for services with constant or only slowly growing budgets. This conflict is usually solved by resorting to the 'five D's': deterrence, deflection, dilution, delay, denial (Hunter, 1997, p. 22).

5. Future challenges
Both competitive and public SHI are facing important future challenges (see for example Lindbeck, 1995; Jacobs and Goddard, 2002).

Cost of dying
It is well known by now that much of an individual's lifetime health care expenditure occurs during the last two years of life (Lubitz and Riley, 1993; Zweifel et al., 1999; Seshamani and Gray, 2004; Zweifel et al., 2005). This fact has spurred a debate on rationing based on an age criterion (see, for example, Callahan, 1987; Williams, 1997; Breyer and Schultheiss, 2002). However, rationing means disregard of individual preferences. A more efficient alternative would be a contract design that induces self-rationing by the insured (for example through increased cost sharing or experience rating of premiums) in the face of low chances of success. The question then arises of whether public or competitive SHI is more prone to developing such contracts; both may rely on the government to impose rationing.

'Umbrella' policies

Health risks are not the only risks confronting individuals during their lifetime. From their point of view, it would be efficient to combine weakly, or even better negatively correlated risks in one contract in order to achieve a degree of risk diversification that the insurer could honour through a lower combined premium (Zweifel, 2000b). For example, for females, auto liability risks are lower but financial health risks higher than for males, and combining the two would result in a reduced total premium. However, this gain in efficiency could be wiped out if the insurer writing such an 'umbrella' policy were to take advantage of the reduced premium elasticity of the consumer to increase its monopoly mark-up.

International purchasing

Contrary to, for example, life insurance, health insurers can be understood as 'wholesale' purchasers of health care services on behalf of their clients, who then make their choice of individual provider. Traditionally, both the public insurer and competitive insurers were legally bound to purchase domestically, with exceptions within the European Union (Hermans and Berman, 1998). Would a public health insurer dare to break away from this rule, thus simultaneously exposing the entirety of domestic providers to international competition?

Technological change in medicine

New therapies are continually being developed, and at the going insured price, there is demand for almost all of them. Health insurers are challenged to weigh the additional benefits against the additional costs (weighted by the probability of use) on behalf of their clients. Competitive health insurers may be under some pressure to perform such calculations; if, however, they are uniformly mandated to include an innovation in their benefit package, they cannot gain a competitive advantage from doing so. A substitute may be the estimation of WTP from surveys in the guise of market experiments which expose respondents to the premium increase that is caused by the inclusion of the new product or therapy (see, for example, Telser and Zweifel, 2002). However, it is not clear whether either public or competitive social health insurer acting in concert have much incentive to generate and heed such information.

In sum, while important challenges are confronting health insurers regardless of type, economic theory and empirical investigations contribute to providing answers to at least some of the pertinent questions.

References

Alesina, A. and G. Tabellini (2004) 'Bureaucrats or politicians?', National Bureau of Economic Research, NBER Working Paper No.10241.
Arrow, K.J. (1963), 'Uncertainty and the welfare economics of medical care', *American Economic Review*, **53**, 941–73.
Beck, K., S. Spycher, A. Holly and L. Gardiol (2003), 'Risk adjustment in Switzerland', *Health Policy*, **65**(1), 63–74.
Boldrin, M. and A. Rustichini (2000), 'Political equilibria with social security', *Review of Economic Dynamics*, **3**(1), 41–78.
Breyer, F. and C. Schultheiss (2002), ' "Primary" rationing of health services in ageing societies – a normative analysis', *International Journal of Health Care Finance and Economics*, **2**, 247–64.

Callahan, D. (1987), *Setting Limits. Medical Goals in an Aging Society*, New York: Simon and Schuster.
Coates, D., B.R. Humphreys and M. Vachris (2004), 'More evidence that university administrators are utility maximizing bureaucrats', *Economics of Governance*, Special Issue, **5**(1), 77–101.
Cook, P.J. and D.A. Graham (1977), 'The demand for insurance and protection: the case of irreplaceable commodities', *Quarterly Journal of Economics*, **91**, 143–56.
Cremer, H. and P. Pestieau (1996), 'Redistributive taxation and social insurance', *International Tax and Public Finance*, **3**, 281–95.
Culyer, A. J. and A. Wagstaff (1993), 'Equity and equality in health and health care', *Journal of Health Economics*, **12**, 431–57.
Ehrlich, I. and G.S. Becker (1972), 'Market insurance, self-insurance and self-protection', *Journal of Political Economy*, **80**, 623–48.
Ellis, R.P. and W.P.M.M. van de Ven (2000), 'Risk adjustment in competitive health plan markets', in: A.J. Culyer and J.P. Newhouse (eds), *Handbook of Health Economics*, Vol. 1A, Amsterdam: Elsevier, pp. 755–845.
Felder, S. and A. Werblow (2003), 'Der Einfluss von freiwilligen Selbstbehalten in der gesetzlichen Krankenversicherung: Evidenz aus der Schweiz (The influence of voluntary deductibles in social health insurance: evidence from Switzerland)', *Schmollers Jahrbuch: Zeitschrift für Wirtschafts- und Sozialwissenschaften/Journal of Applied Social Science Studies*, **123**, 235–64.
Gerdtham, U.G., B. Jönsson and J. Søgaard (1992), 'An econometric analysis of health care expenditure: a cross section study of OECD countries', *Journal of Health Economics*, **11**, 63–84.
Gouveia, M. (1997), 'Majority rule and the public provision of a private good', *Public Choice*, **93**, 221–44.
Hammond, T.H. and J.H. Knott (1996), 'Who controls the bureaucracy? Presidential power, congressional dominance, legal constraints, and bureaucratic autonomy in a model of multi-institutional policy-making', *Journal of Law, Economics, and Organization*, **12**, 119–66.
Hermans, H.E.G.M. and P.C. Berman (1998), 'Access to health care and health services in the European Union: regulation 1408/71 and the E111 process', in: R. Leidl (ed.), *Health Care and Its Financing in the Single European Market*, Amsterdam: IOS Press, pp. 324–43.
Hindriks, J. and P. De Donder (2003), 'The politics of redistributive social insurance', *Journal of Public Economics*, **87**, 2639–60.
Hunter, D.J. (1997), *Desperately Seeking Solutions: Rationing Health Care*, London: Longman.
Jacobs, R. and M. Goddard (2002) 'Trade-offs in social health insurance systems', *International Journal of Social Economics*, **29**, 861–75.
Lehmann, H. and P. Zweifel (2004), 'Innovation and risk selection in deregulated social health insurance', *Journal of Health Economics*, **23**, 997–1012.
Lichtenberg, F.R. (2004), 'Sources of US longevity increase, 1960–2001', *Quarterly Review of Economics and Finance*, **44**, 369–89.
Lindbeck, A. (1995), 'Hazardous welfare state dynamics', *American Economic Review*, **85**(2), 9–15.
Lubitz, J.B. and G.F. Riley (1993), 'Trends in Medicare payments in the last year of life', *New England Journal of Medicine*, **328**, 1092–96.
Maarse, H., A. Paulus and G. Kuiper (2004), 'Supervision in social health insurance: a four-country study', *Health Policy*, available online 2 September 2004.
Manning, W.G. et al. (1987), 'Health insurance and the demand for medical care. Evidence from a randomized experiment', *American Economic Review*, **77**, 251–77.
Miller, R.D. Jr. and H.E. Frech III (2004), *Health Care Matters. Pharmaceuticals, Obesity, and the Quality of Life*, Washington DC: AEI Press.
Mossin, J. (1968), 'Aspects of rational insurance purchasing', *Journal of Political Economy*, **76**, 553–68.
Newhouse, J.P. and The Insurance Experiment Group (1993), *Free for All? Lessons from the RAND Health Insurance Experiment, A RAND Study*, Cambridge and London: Harvard University Press.
Newhouse, J.P. (1996), 'Reimbursing health plans and health providers: efficiency in production versus selection', *Journal of Economic Literature*, **34**, 1236–63.
Nyman, J.A. (2003), *The Theory of Demand for Health Insurance*, Stanford: Stanford University Press.
OECD (2004), *The OECD Health Project – Towards High-Performing Health Systems*, Paris.
Olsen, J.A. (2000), 'A note on eliciting distributive preferences for health', *Journal of Health Economics*, **19**, 541–50.
Pauly, M.V. (1970), 'The efficiency in the provision of consumption subsidies', *Kyklos*, **23**, 33–57.
Pauly, M.V., P. Danzon, P. Feldstein and J. Hoff (1992), *Responsible National Health Insurance*, Washington DC.: American Enterprise Institute.
Rothschild, M. and J.E. Stiglitz (1976), 'Equilibrium in competitive insurance markets: an essay on the economics of imperfect information', *Quarterly Journal of Economics*, **90**, 630–49.

Seshamani, M. and A. Gray (2004), 'A longitudinal study of the effects of age and time to death on hospital costs', *Journal of Health Economics*, **23**, 217–35.

Spence, A.M. and R.J. Zeckhauser (1971), 'Insurance, information, and individual action', *American Economic Review*, Papers and Proceedings, **61**, 380–87.

Telser, H. and P. Zweifel (2002), 'Measuring willingness-to-pay for risk reduction – an application of conjoint analysis', *Health Economics*, **11**, 129–39.

Tullock, G. (2003), 'The origin of the rent-seeking concept', *International Journal of Business and Economics*, **2**, 1–8.

Van Barneveld, E.M., R.C.J.A. van Vliet and W.P.M.M. van de Ven (1996), 'Mandatory high-risk pooling: an approach to reducing incentives for cream skimming', *Inquiry*, **33**, 133–43.

Van Dalen, H.P. and O.A. Swank (1996), 'Government spending cycles: ideological or opportunistic?', *Public Choice*, **89**, 183–200.

Van de Ven, W.P.M.M. and B.M.S. van Praag. (1981), 'The demand for deductibles in private health insurance: a probit model with sample selection', *Journal of Econometrics*, **17**, 229–52.

Van de Ven, W.P.M.M., R.C.J.A. van Vliet, F.T. Schut and E.M. van Barneveld (2000), 'Access to coverage for high risks in a competitive individual health insurance market: via premium rate restrictions or risk-adjusted premium subsidies?', *Journal of Health Economics*, **19**, 311–39.

Williams, A. (1997), 'Rationing health care by age – the case for', *British Medical Journal*, **314**, 822–5.

Zweifel, P. (1982), 'Demand for supplementary health insurance in Switzerland: a theoretical and empirical investigation', *Geneva Papers on Risk and Insurance*, **7**(24), 207–36.

Zweifel, P. (1992), *Bonus Options in Health Insurance*, Boston: Kluwer.

Zweifel, P. (2000a), 'The division of labor between private and social insurance', in: G. Dionne (ed.), *Handbook of Insurance*, Boston: Kluwer, chapter 28.

Zweifel, P. (2000b), 'The future division of labour between private and social health insurance', *Journal of Health Care Finance*, **26**(3), 38–55.

Zweifel, P. (forthcoming), 'The supply of voluntary health insurance in developing countries', mimeo, SOI University of Zurich, in: A. Preker (ed.), *Voluntary Health Insurance in Developing Countries*, Washington: World Bank.

Zweifel, P. and F. Breyer (1997), *Health Economics*, New York: Oxford University Press.

Zweifel, P. and R. Eisen (2002), *Versicherungsökonomie (Insurance Economics)*, 2nd edn, Heidelberg: Springer.

Zweifel, P. and W.G. Manning (2000), 'Moral hazard and consumer incentives in health care', in: A.J. Culyer and J.P. Newhouse (eds), *Handbook of Health Economics*, Vol. 1A, Amsterdam: Elsevier, pp. 409–59.

Zweifel, P., S. Felder and M. Meier (1999), 'Ageing of population and health care expenditure: a red herring?,' *Health Economics*, **9**, 485–96.

Zweifel, P., L. Steinmann and P. Eugster (2005), 'The Sisyphus syndrome in health care revisited', *International Journal of Health Care Finance and Economics*, **5**, 127–45.

13 Competition and health plan choice
Bryan Dowd and Roger Feldman

1. A brief overview of the health plan choice literature

In the late 1960s, Paul Ellwood and Walter McClure began advancing the idea of health plans competing for consumers on the basis of price and quality. Early advocates of market reform envisioned a market structure with unique pairings of health care providers and health plans, for example, closed panel or non-overlapping provider networks (Havinghurst and Hackbarth, 1979). Competition among health plans thus would 'trickle-down' and discipline the market for health care services, as well.

A decade later, Alain Enthoven (1978) articulated a similar role for health plans within the context of a broader national health insurance proposal. In retrospect, one of the most interesting aspects of Enthoven's proposal was his ability to assume broad acceptance of the notion that private health plans plausibly could serve as effective brokers between consumers and health care providers. The concept of competing private health plans found its way into the US Medicare programme in 1982 as a demonstration project, and by 1985 was a permanent part of the programme.

The original vision of competing private health plans evolved gradually into the concept of managed competition – a prescription for health insurance offerings by public and private 'sponsors' that included the offering of multiple health plans, the provision of information on plan choices to consumers, and consumers who paid the marginal cost of more expensive health plans out of their own pocket. The exposition of the managed competition model generated research interest in the model's performance. Early studies focused on estimates of the price elasticity of health plan choice and the effect of offering multiple health plans on the total cost of employment-based insurance. If health plan competition was to be the primary mechanism for allocating health care resources, then it was important to know how sensitive consumers were to differences in health plan premiums, controlling for other characteristics of the plan.

During the 1980s, there was no general agreement about the importance of premiums in the consumer's choice among competing health plans. In the US, the Congressional Budget Office needed reliable estimates of the parameters in health plan choice models to predict the budgetary effects of various health care reform proposals. Anecdotal evidence suggested that consumers placed a high value on their relationship to their personal physician. Would loyalty to specific physicians be strong enough to attenuate the premium-price elasticity of choice among health plan with non-overlapping provider networks?

Prior to 1989, there were a number of studies of health plan choice, but none that controlled for the fact that employees in a firm face different constraints on their choice sets. Single employees with children and married employees whose spouses are not working must choose among only family coverage plans or leave their spouse and children uninsured, while single employees without children presumably choose only among single coverage plans. For other employees, the choice set is ambiguous. Generally, survey data did not contain enough information to assign employees to the proper choice set (for example, only single coverage plans or only family coverage plans). Even when that was possible, however, most analysts chose to examine only two choices at a time, rather than the full choice set facing the employee. Analysts typically chose a health plan they believed to be the closest alternative to the one picked by the respondent.

In 1989, Feldman et al. published an analysis of health plan choice using individual employee data from 17 firms in the Minneapolis-St. Paul metropolitan area. The data set contained information on all health plans offered to employees and enough personal characteristics to develop sub-samples of employees who faced similar choice sets (for example, family coverage only or single coverage only). In addition to estimating health plan choice models based on the full set of choices and the correct specification of the choice set, the authors were able to investigate the degree to which health plan choices were equally substitutable with regard to unobserved characteristics. The authors found that these improvements in the analysis resulted in price elasticity estimates within groups of similar health plans that were several times larger in absolute value than those found in previous studies, while estimates based on mis-specified choice sets were similar to the earlier estimates. This study lent empirical support to the idea that premium-based competition among health plans was a plausible mechanism for allocating health care resources. It also refined the assessment of antitrust cases involving competing health plans. Mergers between health plans of low consumer substitutability were viewed as less harmful than mergers between health plans of higher substitutability.

Over the next 15 years, additional studies were added to the literature. Some of these studies used individual level data, while others used the market shares of health plans as the dependent variable. Price-elasticity estimates have varied from one study to another (Scanlon, Chernow and Lave, 1997). We now have premium-price elasticity estimates for the elderly population in the US (Dowd, Feldman and Coulam, 2003; Atherly et al., 2004), but no national premium-price elasticity estimate for the non-elderly US population.

Although much of the early work on health plan choice took place in the US where private health plans are more numerous, recent interest in health plan choice and market competition in Europe has generated additional studies. Schut, Greb and Wasem (2003) analysed plan choice data from the social health insurance programmes of Germany and the Netherlands. They found that the price elasticity of plan choice was large (in absolute value) in Germany and larger for the non-elderly than for the elderly. Price elasticities in the Netherlands were numerically small and not statistically different from zero.

2.   Methods used to study health plan choice
There are two types of health plan choice studies: those that use individual level data and those that use aggregate or market share data. Both approaches have inherent limitations.

Individual level data
The most common approach to modelling the consumer's health plan choice problem is the conditional logit model of McFadden (1974). In that model, the *i*th consumer's

expected utility from selecting the *j*th alternative is expressed as a function of character-istics of the alternative:

$$U_{ij} = X_j\beta + v_{ij} \tag{13.1}$$

where: U_{ij} = the *i*th ($i = 1, \ldots, N$) consumer's utility for the *j*th ($j = 1, \ldots, M$) alternatives
X_j = a vector of $k = 1, \ldots, K$ characteristics of the choice
v_{ij} = a random error term specific to the consumer and the choice
β = a vector of coefficients

Characteristics of the consumer, such as health status, are introduced by interacting consumer characteristics with observed plan characteristics or a dummy variable representing each plan as follows:

$$U_{ij} = X_j\beta + \sum_{k=1}^{K}\sum_{s=1}^{S}X_{jk}X_{is}\beta_{ks} + v_{ij} \tag{13.2}$$

where X_{is} = a vector of $s = 1, \ldots, S$ characteristics of the consumer.

If the v_{ij} are identically and independently distributed (IID) Gumbel then the likelihood that the *i*th consumer will choose the *j*th alternative is:

$$P_{ij} = \frac{\exp\left(X_j\beta + \sum_{k=1}^{K}\sum_{s=1}^{S}X_{jk}X_{is}\beta_{ks} + v_{ij}\right)}{\sum_{m=1}^{M}\exp\left(X_m\beta + \sum_{k=1}^{K}\sum_{s=1}^{S}X_{mk}X_{is}\beta_{ks} + v_{im}\right)} \tag{13.3}$$

The assumption that the v_{ij} are frequently independent is problematic because some choices may be closer substitutes than others, and in that case the analyst must turn to nested or mixed logit models or multinomial probit models (Greene, 2003). In all of these non-linear models, the derivative of P_{ij} with respect to X_j varies not only with respect to the value of X_j, but with respect to the values of all other variables in the model, as well. As a result, the values of the explanatory variables at which the derivative is evaluated become important.

Elasticities must be reported carefully. The own premium-price elasticity is:

$$\varepsilon_{ij} = \frac{\partial P_{ij}}{\partial \text{premium}_j} \frac{\text{premium}_j}{P_{ij}}$$

In a simple model with no interaction terms of the form $X_{jk}X_{is}$,

$$\frac{\partial P_{ij}}{\partial X_{jk}} = (\beta_k)(P_{ij})(1 - P_{ij}) \tag{13.4}$$

And so the own premium-price elasticity is:

$$\varepsilon_{ij} = \beta_{\text{premium}}(1 - P_{ij})\text{premium}_j \tag{13.5}$$

The derivative of P_{ij} with respect to the premium of the lth plan is

$$\frac{\partial P_{ij}}{\partial X_{lk}} = -(\beta_k)(P_{ij})(P_{il})$$

and thus the cross-price elasticity is:

$$\varepsilon_{ij} = \frac{\partial P_{ij}}{\partial \text{premium}_l} \frac{\text{premium}_l}{P_{ij}}$$

or:

$$\varepsilon_{ij} = -\beta_{\text{premium}}(P_{il})\text{premium}_l$$

There are usually two premiums to consider. The first is the total premium, and the second is the premium paid out-of-pocket by the consumer. These two are not the same because the employer or the government usually pays part of the premium on behalf of the consumer. The models are usually estimated using the consumer's out-of-pocket premium on the assumption that out-of-pocket premiums are the relevant variable from the consumer's perspective. This interpretation assumes that the employee's wages or other fringe benefits are not adjusted when the employee chooses a health plan receiving a higher or lower employer premium contribution. Elasticities are frequently calculated from the health plan's perspective, however, and the health plan controls only the total premium. In that case, analysts use the total premium in equation (13.5).

Market share data
In some cases, data on individual consumers are not available. Instead, the analyst observes the market shares of health plans. The term 'market share' can be confusing, because the word 'market' is used two different ways. A health plan's market area usually refers to the entire geographic area in which the plan operates, or in the case of antitrust law, plausibly could operate.

The second type of market for health plans is defined by the homogeneity of the consumer's choice set. If all the employees of a firm are offered the same set of health plans, then we speak of the market share of each plan as the proportion of employees in the firm that chooses each plan. In this section, we are using the second definition of a health plan market.

Analyses of market shares also are derived from the logit model. As before, the probability that the jth plan is chosen is:

$$P_j = \frac{e^{X_j\beta}}{\sum_{m=1}^{M} e^{X_m\beta}}$$

and the ratio of the probability of the jth plan to the kth plan is:

$$\frac{P_j}{P_k} = \frac{\dfrac{e^{X_j}}{\displaystyle\sum_{m=1}^{M} e^{X_m\beta}}}{\dfrac{e^{X_k}}{\displaystyle\sum_{m=1}^{M} e^{X_m\beta}}} = e^{(X_j - X_k)\beta}.$$

Interpreting P_j as the proportion of consumers who choose the jth plan, P_j becomes the market share of the jth plan (MS_j). Adding a stochastic error term and taking the natural log of the ratio of the market shares of the two plans yields the following estimated equation:

$$\ln\left(\frac{MS_j}{MS_l}\right) = (X_j - X_l)\beta + u_{jl}$$

There are a number of important questions raised by these discrete choice models. The first is the interpretation of premium coefficients. If all the relevant characteristics of the choice were included among the explanatory variables, then the coefficient on premiums should be infinite. Analysts usually assume that some characteristics of the plan are unobserved to the analyst and lead to product differentiation. These unobserved characteristics of the choice are incorporated into the logit error term.

Recently, the mathematical treatment of the error term has come under scrutiny (Berry, 1994). The construction of the error term in a standard conditional logit model implies that each new choice brings a new, unobserved plan characteristic to the choice set. Any new plan that enters the market is predicted to have a non-zero market share, even if it is identical to an existing plan. Because each plan adds a new characteristic, the characteristic space never becomes saturated as the number of plans increases. That feature of the model has important implications for the estimated welfare effects of adding new competitors to the market. In addition, the model can identify cross-price elasticities even in data where changes in relative prices are not observed (Ackerberg and Rysman, 2002). Research continues on these problems, but it is still in the early stages of development, and to our knowledge has not been incorporated into the health plan choice literature.

3. Recent variations on the basic choice model

Harris, Schultz and Feldman (2002) developed an interesting variant of the standard conditional logit model. In the standard model, the estimated coefficients are the weights in the consumer's utility function associated with the observed health plan characteristics, while the data are the characteristics themselves (in addition to data on the choice set and an indicator for the specific choice made by the consumer). Harris, Schutlz and Feldman turned the problem on its head, using the consumer's reports of the 'importance' of various plan characteristics as data and interpreting the estimated coefficients as the average values of the plan characteristics. This approach has an important advantage over the traditional approach, because it can be applied to characteristics of the plan that are difficult to measure, such as the quality of care offered by providers associated with the plan.

A second important variation on the basic model involves the addition of characteristics of consumers to the model. The consumer characteristics of greatest current interest are measures of the consumer's health status or expected level of health expenditures. The effect of health status on health plan choice is viewed most usefully in the context of the literature on risk segmentation. As Feldman and Dowd (2000) note, the early literature on risk segmentation by health plan assumed that segmentation of risk was a welfare-enhancing goal because it removed a price distortion imposed by applying the same unit price of coverage to consumers of varying underlying risk (Rothschild and Stiglitz, 1976).

During the 1980s, however, the tone of the health policy literature changed, and risk segmentation began to be viewed as a problem, in fact, the 'Achilles heel' of managed competition among multiple competing health plans (Robinson et al., 1991). Much of the concern over risk segmentation was driven by a model (usually informally stated) that health plans somehow would not be compensated fully for the cost of enrollees with higher expected health care costs. As a result of this supply-side price distortion, health plans might fail to offer benefits that attracted high-risk consumers who gladly would pay their own actuarially fair premium for those benefits. In the limiting case, a health plan that attracted high-risk enrollees might actually be driven from the market in a 'death spiral' (Cutler and Zeckhauser, 1998).

The true culprit in this theory is neither multiple competing health plans, nor even risk-based health plan choice, however. Instead, it is the constraint, commonly imposed by both public and private purchasers, that health plans must charge the same premium to enrollees regardless of their health risk. In the US, this constraint is applied at the employer level or at the county level in the Medicare programme. The problem could be solved, or at least attenuated, by allowing plans to risk-rate enrollees within a market. In theory, the efficient market shares for each plan could be obtained through application of appropriate risk-based cross-subsidies (for example, 'risk adjustments') among health plans.

Suppose that high-risk consumers do prefer some characteristics of health plans more than low-risk consumers. If some of the characteristics valued by high-risk consumers are unobserved and positively correlated with premiums, then high-risk consumers might appear to be less sensitive to out-of-pocket premium differentials than low-risk consumers. Strombom, Buchmueller and Feldstein (2002) found that the out-of-pocket premiums had a smaller effect on health plan choice for consumers who were chronically ill. However, Parente, Feldman and Christianson (2004) found the opposite result: consumers who reported having one or more chronic illnesses were more sensitive to out-of-pocket premiums than those who did not report having a chronic illness.

Feldman and Schultz (2004), using the same approach as the earlier study by Harris, Schultz and Feldman (2002), treated consumers' stated preferences as proxies for the utility of various plan characteristics. They found that healthy and sick consumers did not have different preferences for low premiums. Given these different findings, at the present time it is fair to say that we don't know whether high-risk consumers have different preferences than low risks.

A third variation on the standard choice model is the model of plan switching. The vast majority of health plan choice studies use cross-sectional data. The assumption underlying inference from the model is that the distribution of consumers across alternatives in cross-sectional data reflect accurately the choices that consumers would be observed to make in response to changes in the same set of plans' characteristics over time. The difficulty with this assumption is the possibility of omitted variables bias. Many plan characteristics that are important to consumers are unobserved by the analyst, but may be correlated with observed characteristics, especially premiums. If, over time, the plan alters the observed characteristic while leaving the unobserved characteristic unchanged, the coefficient on the observed characteristic will not provide an accurate estimate of the consumer's response to that change.

Another reason for a discrepancy between cross-sectional and time series estimates is simply that consumers may require several iterations of plan choice to obtain or process information about changes in plan characteristics. This effect could produce a degree of 'stickiness' in the consumer choices observed in time series data.

These issues can be investigated, though not entirely resolved, by assembling a panel data set in which the observed characteristics of a fixed set of plan choices change over time. If the results from the panel data mirror the results from cross-sectional data, then we could conclude that (1) consumers adjust instantaneously to changes in observed plan characteristics, and (2) the correlation of observed and unobserved characteristics either is negligible or remains constant over time, perhaps due to some structural constraint. Time series studies of plan choice are usually referred to as studies of plan switching. Buchmueller and Feldstein (1997) were able to study plan switching in a group of University of California employees. Buchmueller and Feldstein found that plan switching was quite sensitive to changes in out-of-pocket premiums. Increases in premium differentials of less than $10 were associated with a five-fold difference in the probability of switching plans. This finding suggests that the stickiness of health plan choices may be negligible.

In addition to the studies that analyse 'real world' data from health plan markets, there is an experimental literature on health plan choice. In a typical experimental study, subjects are presented with a carefully designed set of alternatives and asked to indicate their stated choice (Louviere, Hensher and Swait, 2000). Stated choice models are widely used in situations where real-world choice data are inadequate or incomplete because of failure to measure key constructs or because independent variation in plan attributes is lacking. In one such experimental study, Harris, Dennis and Pippin (2002) found that most subjects preferred a lower-quality health plan with unrestricted provider choice to a high-quality plan that restricts provider choice. The disadvantages of such studies are that the well-designed hypothetical choices may not be available in the real word, and the usual caveat that stated preferences may not predict actual choices.

4.   Health plan choice and the market for health care services

The transaction that provides the rationale for the entire health care system is not the transaction between the consumer and the health plan, but the interaction between the consumer and the health care provider in the market for health care services. The market for health care services is characterized by market failure in the form of poor information, restricted entry and distorted prices. The appeal of competing health plans has always relied upon the assumption that health plans have the ability to address consumers' problems of market failure in the health care services market. Health plans, in theory, can obtain competitive prices from providers, collect information on provider quality and exclude lower quality providers from their networks, and encourage the substitution of more cost-effective medical personnel up to the limits allowed by law.

However, health plans must serve two masters. They must balance the demands of their enrollees and large purchasers, for example, employers or the government, against the constraints imposed by the supply side of the health care services market. During the 1990s the managed care industry in the US suffered a severe, though perhaps largely symbolic, public relations setback referred to as the 'managed care backlash'.[1] The adverse reaction to aggressively managed care in the US has contributed to increased interest in 'consumer directed' health plans. These are plans that typically feature large deductibles and minimal management of care by the insurer. As their name suggests, the purported advantage of these plans is increased consumer autonomy in the choice of providers and treatment options. Health plans with large deductibles are not a new idea, of course, and historically have been an attractive option for consumers seeking lower premiums, particularly in the individual insurance market.

Pauly and Nicholson (1999) attribute the managed care backlash to an untenable mixture of higher risk enrollees seeking low out-of-pocket costs with low-risk enrollees seeking low premiums. High-deductible plans could suffer the same fate, if low-risk enrollees seeking lower premiums mix with higher risk enrollees seeking to escape aggressively managed care. The only published study of choice of consumer-directed health plans found that enrollees tended to be higher income, rather than lower or higher health status (Parente, Feldman and Christianson, 2004).

The choice between managed care and consumer-directed health plans is one of the most interesting aspects of the evolving US health care system because it provides an empirical test of different models of consumer agency in the market for health care services. Can consumers, in consultation with their physicians, make the most efficient choices, or do efficient choices require a third party with large datasets and perhaps some purchasing power, as well? If a third party is required, will its role merely be to provide information to consumers or will it broker transactions between consumers and providers?

5.   Health plan choice and the market for health insurance

Although this chapter has focused primarily on the health plan choice literature, there is related literature that addresses the environment in which health plan choices are presented to consumers. Maxwell and Temin (2002) describe two different types of health insurance purchasing strategies that employers might adopt: managed competition and 'industrial purchasing'. The managed competition strategy has several elements including multiple health plan choices; a fixed employer contribution to premiums regardless of the plan chosen by the employee; and some degree of integration of organizations that finance and deliver health care.

In contrast, employers adopting the industrial purchasing model often substitute health plan competition for entry to the firm for competition for individual employees. Among the 500 publicly traded companies in the US with the largest revenues in 1998, Maxwell and Temin found that only 9.6 per cent offered multiple plans and set a fixed employer contribution to premiums. Maxwell and Temin did not find a significant association of purchasing strategies and premiums.

Vistnes, Cooper and Vistnes (2001) developed a two-stage model that incorporated both the competition by health plans to enter the firm, and competition for employees among plans that gained entry. Analysing data from the 1996 Medical Expenditure Panel Survey – Insurance Component (MEPS-IC), the authors found that offering multiple health plans combined with a fixed contribution to premiums resulted in lower total premiums than offering a single health plan. In other words, managed competition dominated industrial purchasing. Vistnes, Cooper and Vistnes' results are consistent with those of Schut, Greb and Wasem, who attribute the difference in price elasticities in Germany and the Netherlands, in part, to Netherlands employers' practice of paying a fixed percentage of the premium, while in Germany, employees are more likely to face the marginal cost of more expensive plans (Schut, Greb and Wasem, 2003). Enthoven (2003) offered a scathing rebuke of US employers for failing to adopt the managed competition strategy.

6. Summary

The future of the health plan choice literature is linked to developments in the broader discrete choice literature. The anomalies of the conditional logit model are causing economists and econometricians to reconsider both the theory and estimation methods used to analyse discrete choice problems, and it is reasonable to expect important advances in both areas in the near future.

The intersection of health plan choice and competition in the market for health care services seems more uncertain, at least in the US. While the importance of plan choice in Europe increases, much of the rhetoric in the US places increased emphasis on direct consumer interactions with providers. Currently, it is unclear whether health care is more like the ready-to-eat breakfast cereal industry or more like the individual stocks in a mutual fund manager's portfolio, the tradesmen working for a general contractor, or the candidates of a political party. In the latter three examples, there is an organization that acts as the consumer's agent to arrange multiple transactions and solve multiple forms of market failure, especially the problem of poor information. Of course, many consumers prefer to pick their own stocks, be their own general contractor and write in their own political candidates. Ultimately, the market will sort out these different approaches to allocating health care resources. One may supplant the other, or the two approaches may find a peaceful, but competitive, coexistence.

Notes

1. The managed care backlash generated a substantial literature. The January/February 1998 issue of *Health Affairs* contained several review articles, and the entire October 1999 issue of the *Journal of Health Politics, Policy and Law* was devoted to the topic. Another analysis is found in Zelman, Walter A. and Robert A. Berenson (1998), *The Managed Care Blues and How to Cure Them*, Georgetown University Press: Washington, DC, pp. 121–2.

References

Ackerberg, Daniel A. and Marc Rysman (2002), 'Unobserved product differentiation in discrete choice models: estimating price elasticities and welfare effects', NBER Working Paper No. W8798. http://ssrn.com/abstract=301419

Atherly, Adam, Bryan E. Dowd and Roger Feldman (2004), 'The effect of benefits, premiums, and health risk on health plan choice in the Medicare program', *Health Services Research*, **39**(4), 847–64.

Berry, Steven T. (1994), 'Estimating discrete-choice models of product differentiation', *Rand Journal of Economics*, **25**(2), 242–62.

Buchmueller, Thomas C. and Paul J. Feldstein (1997), 'The effect of price on switching among health plans', *Journal of Health Economics*, **16**(2), 231–47.

Cutler, David M. and Richard J. Zeckhauser (1998), 'Adverse selection in health insurance', in Alan Garber (ed.), *Frontiers in Health Policy Research: Volume 1*, Cambridge, MA: MIT Press, pp. 1–31. Also see Feldman, Roger and Bryan E. Dowd (1991), 'Must adverse selection cause premium spirals?' *Journal of Health Economics*, **10**(3), 349–58.

Dowd, Bryan E., Roger Feldman and Robert Coulam (2003), 'The effect of health plan characteristics on Medicare + Choice enrollment', *Health Services Research*, **38**(1) Part 1, 113–36.

Ellwood, Paul M., Nancy N. Anderson, James E. Billings, Rick J. Carlson, Earl J. Hoagberg and Walter McClure (1971), 'Health maintenance strategy', *Medical Care*, **9**(3), 291–8.

Enthoven, Alain C. (1978), 'Consumer-choice health plan: first of two parts', *New England Journal of Medicine*, **298**(12), 630–58; and 'Consumer-choice health plan: second of two parts', *New England Journal of Medicine*, **298**(13), 709–20.

Enthoven, A. (2003), 'Employment-based health insurance is failing: Now what?', *Health Affairs Web Exclusive*, W3-237-W3–249.

Feldman, Roger and Bryan E. Dowd (2000), 'Risk segmentation: goal or problem?', *Journal of Health Economics*, **19**(4), 499–512.

Feldman, Roger and Jennifer Schultz (2004), 'Consumer demand for guaranteed renewability in health insurance', *Journal of Consumer Policy*, **27**(1), 75–97.

Feldman, Roger, Michael Finch, Bryan E. Dowd and Steven Cassou (1989), 'Demand for employment-based health insurance plans', *The Journal of Human Resources*, **24**(1), 115–42.

Greene, William H. (2003), *Econometric Analysis* (5th edn), Upper Saddle River, NJ: Prentice Hall, pp. 727–8.

Harris, Katherine M., J.M. Dennis and C. Pippin (2002), 'Patient differences in the willingness to trade physician access for health plan quality: evidence from a national survey', Santa Monica, CA: RAND Corporation.

Harris, Katherine, Jennifer Schultz and Roger Feldman (2002), 'Measuring consumer perceptions of quality differences among competing health benefit plans', *Journal of Health Economics*, **21**(1), 1–17.

Havinghurst, Clark C. and Glenn M. Hackbarth (1979), 'Private cost containment', *New England Journal of Medicine*, **300**(23), 1296–305.

Louviere, J.J., D.A. Hensher and J.D. Swait (2000), *Stated Choice Models: Analysis and Application*, Cambridge, UK: Cambridge University Press.

Maxwell, James and Peter Temin (2002), 'Managed competition versus industrial purchasing of health care among the Fortune 500', *Journal of Health Politics, Policy & Law*, **27**(1), 6–30.

McFadden, Daniel (1974), 'Analysis of qualitative choice behavior', in Paul Zarembka (ed.), *Frontiers in Econometrics*, New York, NY: Academic Press, pp. 105–42.

Parente, Stephen T., Roger Feldman and Jon B. Christianson (2004), 'Employee choice of consumer driven health insurance in a multi-plan, multi-product setting', *Health Services Research*, Part II, **39**(4), 1091–111.

Pauly, Mark V. and Sean Nicholson (1999), 'The adverse consequences of adverse selection', *Journal of Health Politics, Policy and Law*, **24**(5), 921–30.

Robinson, James C., Harold S. Luft, Laura B. Gardner and Ellen M. Morrison (1991), 'A method for risk-adjusting employer contributions to competing health plans', *Inquiry*, **28**(2), 107–16.

Rothschild, M. and J. Stiglitz (1976), 'Equilibrium in competitive insurance markets: an essay on the economics of imperfect information', *Quarterly Journal of Economics*, **90**(4), 629–49.

Scanlon, Dennis P., Michael Chernew and Judith R. Lave (1997), 'Consumer health plan choice: current knowledge and future directions', *Annual Review of Public Health*, **18**, 507–28.

Schut, Frederik T., Stefan Greb and Juergen Wasem (2003), 'Consumer price sensitivity and social health insurer choice in Germany and the Netherlands', *International Journal of Health Care Finance and Economics*, **3**(2), 117–38.

Strombom, Bruce A., Thomas C. Buchmueller and Paul J. Feldstein (2002), 'Switching costs, price sensitivity and health plan choice', *Journal of Health Economics*, **21**(1), 89–116.

Vistnes, Jessica P., Philip F. Cooper and Gregory S. Vistnes (2001), 'The effect of competition on employment-related health insurance premiums', *International Journal of Health Care Finance and Economics*, **1**(2), 159–87.

14 Empirical models of health care use
Partha Deb and Pravin K. Trivedi

1. Background

In many studies of the use of medical care services, utilization is measured as a count variable taking only non-negative integer values. In such cases, for example, the number of visits to a doctor, number of hospital stays or the number of prescription medicines, the sample is concentrated on a few small values, the distribution is substantially skewed and the distribution of counts is intrinsically integer-valued and non-negative. In addition, these counts include both non-users and users, with the former group usually consisting of a non-trivial fraction of the sample reporting zero use. This 'zeros problem', which generates a non-linearity in the response to determinants of use, is a significant econometric complication that has motivated a variety of specification and estimation strategies.

Typical analyses of health care use analyse the role of its potential determinants and are focused on the effects of these determinants on the expected number of events. There are, however, practical and policy-related applications in which predictions of the distributions of event-counts or probabilistic statements regarding the distributions are of interest. In many applications, the determinants of health care use are treated as if they are exogenous variables. However, this is not always the case; two leading examples of potentially endogenous variables in such models, central to the economics of the utilization of health care services, are price and insurance effects. When individuals choose health insurance plans, insurance status and service-level, out-of-pocket prices are likely to be endogenous. This problem is ubiquitous in the US system where most individuals purchase insurance via employer-sponsored health care plans and where others can choose to purchase private insurance coverage independently; it also exists in certain countries in Europe and elsewhere in mixed public–private systems where individuals can purchase private insurance supplemental to that provided in the universal public plan. In either case, the plan is not exogenously assigned, which may lead to self-selection. Self-selection, which may take the form of favourable or adverse selection, arises because optimizing individuals, possessing knowledge of their own health attributes, proclivities and economic constraints, select plans accordingly. Therefore, these attributes, which partly determine the individual's choice of health plans, also affect their expected utilization of services. Consequently, insurance status and prices of services cannot be treated as exogenous. Instead, identification of the causal impact of insurance on health care use requires joint modelling of insurance choice and use of care.

The objective of successful identification and consistent estimation of these key parameters faces several challenges, many of which are the subject of current research. In this article we summarize the leading issues in econometric analyses of the use of health care services based on individual-level cross-section data. We consider first the case of exogenous regressors, and then the more general model with endogenous regressors.

2.   Methods 1: exogenous covariates

The Poisson regression model, derived from the Poisson distribution for the number of occurrences of the event provides a natural starting point for analyses of count data. The first two moments of the distribution are $E[y] = \mu$, and $V[y] = \mu$. The regression model is derived by parameterizing the relation between the mean μ and predictors x. The standard assumption uses the exponential mean parameterization with K linearly independent covariates,

$$\mu_i = \exp(x_i'\beta), \quad i = 1, \ldots, N.$$

Because $V[y_i|x_i] = \exp(x_i'\beta)$ the regression is intrinsically heteroscedastic.

The Poisson property of equality of mean and variance, that is the equidispersion property, is usually too restrictive for counts of health care use. Most measures of health care use display overdispersion, with conditional variance exceeding the conditional mean. In many applications a Poisson density predicts the probability of a zero count to be considerably less than is actually observed in the sample, which reflects the failure of the equidispersion. This is termed the 'excess zeros problem', as there are more zeros in the data than the Poisson predicts.

The phenomenon of overdispersion has several explanations. In count data it may be due to unobserved heterogeneity. Counts are viewed as being generated by a Poisson process, but the researcher is unable to correctly specify the rate parameter of this process. Hence the rate parameter is itself modelled as a random variable whose variation is partly induced by unobserved factors that are assumed to be uncorrelated with observed covariates. The resulting model is a mixture model. If the unobserved heterogeneity is multiplicative and has an independent gamma distribution, then the marginal distribution of event counts is the widely-used negative binomial (NB) model. Unlike the Poisson, the NB model allows for overdispersion as its conditional variance exceeds the conditional mean. In applications, however, the NB often underpredicts the number of zeros, especially for measures such as number of doctor visits, with a substantial fraction of zeros and a long right tail. In response to these concerns, a number of modified Poisson alternatives have been developed in the literature, which we describe below. In practice, it is desirable to consider and compare its adequacy with these modified Poisson alternatives.

Hurdle or two-part models

Overdispersion may also arise because the process generating the first event may differ from the process determining later events. In modelling the usage of medical services, the two-part model (TPM) has served as a methodological cornerstone of empirical analysis. The first part of the TPM is a binary outcome model that describes the determinants of use versus non-use. The second part describes the distribution of use conditional on some use. Although in health economics the term 'two-part model' has been used predominantly to refer to models of health expenditures, the structure of the TPM is equally applicable for discrete or continuous outcomes. The TPM for count data has, on the other hand, often been referred to as a hurdle model (Mullahy, 1986). This leads to a modified model for count data. Suppose the zeros are determined by the density $f_1(.)$, so that $\Pr[y = 0] = f_1(0)$. The positive counts come from the truncated density

$f_2(y|y>0)=f_2(y)/(1-f_2(0))$, which is multiplied by $\Pr[y>0]=1-f_1(0)$ to ensure that probabilities sum to unity. Then

$$g(y)=f_1(0) \quad \text{if } y=0$$
$$=f_2(y)(1-f_1(0)) \quad \text{if } y>0.$$

This reduces to the standard model only if $f_1(.) = f_2(.)$. Thus, in the modified model, the two processes generating the zeros and the positives are not constrained to be the same. Additional flexibility results from being able to choose suitable component densities that improve on the Poisson; for example, one could use a NB density for the positive counts, thus allowing for two sources of overdispersion. Note that while the motivation for this model is to handle excess zeros, it is also capable of modelling too few zeros.

The appeal of the TPM is partly driven by an important feature of the demand for medical care, which is the high incidence of zero usage. For example, approximately 30 per cent of typical cross-sectional samples of non-institutionalized individuals in the United States report no outpatient visits in the survey year. The TPM is also well supported empirically, with explanatory variables often playing different roles in the two parts of the model. The appeal of the TPM in health economics is also based on its connection to a principal–agent model (see, for example, Zweifel, 1981). In this framework, it is argued, the decision to seek care is largely the patient's (the principal) whereas the physician (the agent) determines utilization on behalf of the patient once initial contact is made (this argument is well motivated in Manning et al., 1981; Pohlmeier and Ulrich, 1995; Gerdtham, 1997). Finally, because maximum likelihood estimation of the hurdle model involves separate maximization of the two terms in the likelihood, one corresponding to the zeros and the other to the positives, the TPM is easy to estimate and typically does not suffer from computational instabilities.

Pohlmeier and Ulrich (1995) develop a TPM based on the NB distribution and estimate its parameters for counts of GP and specialist visits using data from the German Socioeconomic Panel. They find strong evidence favouring the TPM over Poisson and NB models and conclude that contact and frequency decisions are governed by different stochastic processes, hence should be modelled using a TPM. Gerdtham (1997) examines the issue of horizontal inequity in delivery of health care using a TPM model and data from Sweden. The paper rejects the hypothesis of no inequity because income and size of community of residence have significant effects on utilization.

Zero-inflated models

A second modified count model is the zero-inflated model. This supplements a count density $f_2(.)$ with a binary process with density $f_1(.)$. If the binary process takes value 0, with probability $f_1(0)$, then $y=0$. If the binary process takes value 1, with probability $f_1(.)$, then y takes count values $0,1,2,\ldots$ from the count density $f_2(.)$. This lets zero counts occur in two ways: as a realization of the binary process and as a realization of the count process when the binary random variable takes value 1. In the context of health care use, suppose the binary process determines whether or not an individual participates in the market for health care services, that is, distinguishing between those who have demand for medical care from those who do not. Suppose, in addition, that the count process determines the use of health care services among those who have demand. Then the appropriate statistical model is the zero-inflated model. The density is

$$g(y) = f_1(0) + (1 - f_1(0))f_2(0) \quad \text{if } y = 0$$
$$= (1 - f_1(0))f_2(y) \quad \text{if } y > 0.$$

Regression models typically let $f_1(.)$ be a logit model and $f_2(.)$ be a Poisson or negative binomial density. Like the hurdle or TPM, the zero-inflated model is capable of modelling too many or too few zeros, which can be verified by checking the first-order condition for likelihood maximization.

Although the zero-inflated model provides a natural way to introduce extra zeros, it is considerably less used as compared to the TPM. We speculate this is because the computational task is considerably more complex than the TPM as the binary and count parts of the model cannot be estimated separately. If the regression specifications for the binary and count have the same covariates, then identification of parameters of the binary and count parts separately can be a difficult problem in small to medium sized samples.

Chang and Trivedi (2003) find that the zero-inflated Poisson and negative binomial models used to analyse Vietnamese health care utilization data considerably improve the fit of the Poisson regression. Wang (2003) estimates a zero-inflated negative binomial regression model using data from the Australian Health Survey and it provides a plausible explanation for the relatively large fraction of 'permanent' non-users of health care services.

Latent class models
Overdispersed counts can also be modelled using a discrete representation of unobserved heterogeneity. This generates the finite mixture class of models, and a particular subclass of this is the latent class models (LCM).

Within the LCM class the density of y is a linear combination of $m, m \geq 2$, different densities, where the jth density is $f_j(y|\theta_j), j = 1, \ldots, m$. Thus an m-component finite mixture is

$$g(y|\theta) = \sum_{j=1}^{m} \pi_j f_j(y|\theta_j), \quad 0 \leq \pi_j \leq 1, \quad \sum_{j=1}^{m} \pi_j = 1.$$

Here the components of the mixture are assumed, for generality, to differ in all their parameters. Less general formulations assume that only some parameters differ across the components.

Plausibly, different classes of users of health care services exist if the population is split by the latent health status of individuals. Note that, although surveys typically have some measures of health status, and administrative data considerably richer diagnosis-based measures, few would argue that these data contain adequate information on the severity of the illnesses, for example, among latent dimensions of health status. The healthy sub-population, perhaps the majority, might account for low average demand, whereas those who are ill may account for high average demand. When the observed health status is imperfectly observed, the finite mixture model may do a good job of separating subpopulations.

The LCM is an attractive candidate for modelling health care use for a number of reasons. First, it provides a flexible and parsimonious method of modelling the data.

Each mixture component provides a local approximation to some part of the true distribution. Second, the LCM is semiparametric in the sense that it does not require any distributional assumptions for the mixing variable. Third, in many cases the latent classes may correspond to specific subpopulations of relevance from the viewpoint of public policy; for example healthy and sick, or high users and low users, in which case the finite mixture characterization has a natural interpretation. However, this is not essential. A caveat is that the LCM may fit the data better simply because outliers, influential observations, or contaminated observations, present in the data, are captured by the additional components of the LCM model. Hence it is desirable that the hypothesis of LCM should be supported both by a priori reasoning and by meaningful a posteriori differences in the behaviour of latent classes. Finally, the approach can flexibly incorporate departures from random sampling, for example as in on-site and truncated samples, by substituting component densities that capture such departures (Lourenço and Ferreira, 2004).

A preference for the LCM over TPM in the context of models of the use of health care services may also be because the sharp dichotomy between users and non-users may not be tenable in the case of typical cross-sectional datasets. In these data, health care events are recorded over a fixed time period and not over an episode of illness. Note that the TPM is motivated by the principal–agent model over an episode of illness. The LCM provides a more tenable distinction for typical cross-sectional data, distinguishing between an 'infrequent user' and a 'frequent user' of medical care, the difference being determined by health status, attitudes to health risk, and choice of lifestyle.

Practical limitations of LCM include: lack of theoretical guidance on specifying the number of components; inability to distinguish reliably between some of insufficiently-different components; the computational difficulties due to the multiple maxima in the likelihood function. The usual practice is to start with a few components and then add additional components if the fit of the model is significantly improved by doing so. Information criteria are often used to select between models with a different number of components.

Deb and Trivedi (1997) estimated NB, TPM and LCM models of use for a number of types of services in a study of medical care demand by the elderly in the US. Using a variety of tests, they conclude that the LCM is superior to the TPM for most types of services and speculate that the source of latent heterogeneity might be unobserved health status. Deb and Trivedi (2002) compare TPM and LCM models in a re-examination of data from the RAND Health Insurance Experiment. They also find that LCM performs better than TPM in most cases. Because heterogeneity due to insurance status can be ruled out in the RAND study, the authors argue that the case for health status as the source of latent heterogeneity is strong. Jiménez-Martín et al. (2002), using data from the European Community Household Panel, estimate demand for physician services equations for 12 European countries. They find that LCM is preferred to TPM for visits to GPs while the opposite is true for visits to specialists.

3.   Methods 2 – endogenous covariates
We now consider complications that arise from the presence of endogenous regressors in a model of counts. Neglecting endogeneity means that estimates will not be consistent. A leading example of an endogenous regressor in the context of the use of health care

services is insurance status. In the simplest case, this might be a binary variable that takes the value 1 if the subject is insured, and zero otherwise. The full model then consists of two equations, a binary choice model for insurance and a count model for health care use. More generally, we may have a multinomial choice model for insurance (if the choice is between three or more insurance plans) and a count model for utilization (see Deb and Trivedi, 2004). If self-selection or adverse selection is an important feature of individual behaviour then modelling interdependence between use ('outcome') and insurance choice ('treatment') is very important. The econometric challenge in these cases is to specify the precise manner in which the interdependence between the use and choice equations arises, and to control for the interdependence in estimation.

As is well-known, in the linear instrumental variable (LIV) approach the outcome equation is estimated after specifying instruments, denoted W, defined as variables that are correlated with treatments, but uncorrelated with the outcomes, conditional on other exogenous variables (see Chapter 4 by Auld in this Companion). That is, valid instruments are those that impact on outcomes solely through the treatment variables. Important advantages of LIV are well documented (see Angrist, 2001). Under appropriate conditions they include consistent estimation, computational simplicity, and an absence of strong distributional assumptions. Such models have been used in models of health care use when insurance is binary. Linearization of the models for use and insurance can be justified (Angrist, 2001). However, extensions of such models to the case in which the treatment is multinomial do not exist. In addition, ignoring the discreteness of the count and the substantial mass at zero, often leads to poorly fitting models.

Among non-linear models, for consistent estimation, the literature suggests two broad estimation approaches. The first is a limited information ('semiparametric') approach based on non-linear instrumental variables (NLIV) or generalized method of moments (GMM); see Mullahy (1997). The second is a fully parametric approach that makes distributional assumptions about all endogenous variables (see Terza, 1998; Deb and Trivedi, 2004). Terza also provides a two-step approach that mimics the linear two-stage least squares estimator in which the endogenous variable is replaced by a fitted value from a reduced form.

The first approach begins with a moment condition. Then, assuming that there are enough moment conditions available, the GMM or NLIV estimation is feasible. But for non-linear and limited dependent variable models, the advantages of NLIV methods are less well understood (Angrist, 2001; section 2). First, efficient estimation is computationally awkward because optimal non-linear instruments are hard to find (Amemiya, 1985). Second, in implementing this approach the discrete nature of the variable is ignored and the model is treated like any other non-linear model with an exponential mean. This is likely to lead to a substantial loss of goodness of fit.

In contrast to GMM and two-step approaches, Munkin and Trivedi (2003) and Deb and Trivedi (2004) develop a joint parametric model of counts with insurance plan variables as regressors and a choice model for the insurance plans. Endogeneity arises from the presence of correlated unobserved heterogeneity in the outcome (count) equation and the binary choice equation. Their model has the following structure:

$$\Pr(Y_i = y_i | \mathbf{x}_i, \mathbf{d}_i, \mathbf{I}_i) = f(\mathbf{x}_i'\beta + \gamma\mathbf{d}_i + \lambda\mathbf{I}_i)$$

$$\Pr(\mathbf{d}_i = 1 | \mathbf{z}_i, \mathbf{I}_i) = g(\mathbf{z}_i'\alpha + \delta\mathbf{I}_i).$$

Here $\mathbf{I}_i$ is a vector of latent factors reflecting unobserved heterogeneity and λ and δ are associated vectors of factor loadings. The joint distribution of selection and outcome variables, conditional on the common latent factors, can be written as

$$\Pr(Y_i = y_i | \mathbf{x}_i, \mathbf{d}_i, \mathbf{I}_i) = f(\mathbf{x}_i'\beta + \gamma\mathbf{d}_i + \lambda\mathbf{I}_i) \times g(\mathbf{z}_i'\alpha + \delta\mathbf{I}_i)$$

because (y, D) are conditionally independent.

The problem in estimation arises because the $\mathbf{I}_i$ are unknown. Although the $\mathbf{I}_i$ are unknown, assume that the distribution of $\mathbf{I}_i$, h, is known and can therefore be integrated out of the joint density, that is,

$$\Pr(Y_i = y_i, d_{ij} = 1 | \mathbf{x}_i, \mathbf{z}_i) = \int [f(\mathbf{x}_i'\beta + \gamma\mathbf{d}_i + \lambda\mathbf{I}_i)g(\mathbf{z}_i'\alpha + \delta\mathbf{I}_i)]h(\mathbf{I}_i)d\mathbf{I}_i$$

The unknown parameters of the model may be estimated by maximum likelihood. The main problem of estimation, given suitable specifications for f, g and h, is the fact that the integral does not have, in general, a closed form solution. A simulated log-likelihood function for the data can then be defined and maximized as in Deb and Trivedi (2004).

The above approach is equally applicable to multiple treatments and multiple outcomes, discrete or continuous. The limitation comes from the burden of estimation which is very heavy compared with an IV type estimator.

It is also possible to specify the error structure of our model using discrete distributions, often called the discrete factor model, as described by Mroz (1999). There are two advantages to such an approach. First, because such models are latent class models, they are semi-parametric and the discrete distributions can, in principle, approximate any continuous distributions. Second, because such models replace the integration with summation, their likelihood functions are considerably simpler to compute. There is one substantial drawback of such a specification. Because the discrete factor model is a finite mixture model, its likelihood function is known to have multiple maxima (Lindsay, 1995), a feature more likely to be encountered in applications involving multiple treatments and non-linear outcomes.

4.   Which parameters?

In many non-linear models including the models for count data described here, direct interpretation of coefficients is difficult. In such cases, marginal effects can be calculated as functions of estimated parameters and data. The effect of covariates such as insurance status can be measured using the framework of the potential outcome model (POM).

Let D_i be a $(1,0)$ binary indicator of insurance status, and let y_{1i} denote use when insured, and y_{0i} denote use when uninsured. In the framework POM, we interpret D_i as an indicator of treatment. Assume that every element of the target population is potentially exposed to the treatment. Then the triple $\{(y_{1i}, y_{0i}, D_i, i = 1, \ldots, N)\}$ forms the basis of treatment evaluation, with y_{1i} measuring the response if receiving treatment, and y_{0i} when not receiving treatment. Since the receipt and non-receipt of treatment are mutually exclusive states for individual i, only one of the two measures is available for any given i, and the unavailable measure is the counterfactual. The effect of the cause D on the outcome of individual i is measured by $(y_{1i} - y_{0i})$. The average causal effect of $D_i = 1$, relative to $D_i = 0$, is measured by the average treatment effect (ATE): $ATE = E[y|D = 1] - E[y|D = 0]$ where expectations are with respect to the probability distribution over the target population (see chapters by Auld (Chapter 4), and Polsky and Basu (Chapter 43) in this Companion for further discussion of ATEs).

The POM framework is simpler to apply if treatment is randomly assigned. But in observational data, random assignment of treatment is generally not a reasonable assumption. Then for consistent estimation of ATE it is necessary to control for possible correlation between the outcomes and treatment. However, if we do so, then ATE, or any other interesting quantile of the distribution of treatment effects, can be estimated, although one may need to resort to simulation in order to do so (see Deb and Trivedi, 2004).

5. Conclusion

In this chapter we have summarized the leading issues in econometric analyses of the use of health care services based on individual-level cross-section data, both for the case of exogenous regressors and for the case with endogenous regressors. We have drawn from studies on the demand for medical care using counts of service use by Cameron et al. (1986), Chang and Trivedi (2003), Deb and Trivedi (1997, 2002), Gerdtham (1997), Kenkel and Terza (2001), Jiménez-Martín, Labeaga and Martínez-Granado (2002), Mullahy (1997), Munkin and Trivedi (1999, 2003), Pohlmeier and Ulrich (1995), Schellhorn (2001), Windmeijer and Santos-Silva (1997), and Winkelmann (2004).

The literature on count data models with endogenous regressors is still nascent and an active area of research. For example, while there are numerous applications of modified count-data models in the context of exogenous regressors, there are few applications when one or more regressor is endogenous. In addition, we have not described extensions of these models to panel data, another area in which the literature is growing.

References

Amemiya, T. (1985), *Advanced Econometrics*, Cambridge: Harvard University Press.
Angrist, J.D. (2001), 'Estimation of limited dependent variable models with dummy endogenous regressors: simple strategies for empirical practice: reply', *Journal of Business and Economic Statistics*, **19**, 27–8.
Cameron, C., P.K. Trivedi, F. Milne and J. Piggot (1988), 'A microeconometric model of the demand for health care and health insurance in Australia', *Review of Economic Studies*, **55**, 85–106.
Chang, F.-R. and P.K. Trivedi (2003), 'Economics of self-medication: theory and evidence', *Health Economics*, **12**, 721–39.
Deb, P. and P.K. Trivedi (1997), 'Demand for medical care by the elderly in the United States: a finite mixture approach', *Journal of Applied Econometrics*, **12**, 313–36.
Deb, P. and P.K. Trivedi (2002), 'The structure of demand for health care: latent class versus two-part models', *Journal of Health Economics*, **21**, 601–25.
Deb, P. and P.K. Trivedi (2004), 'Specification and simulated likelihood estimation of a non-normal treatment-outcome model with selection: application to health care utilization', *Working Paper*.
Gerdtham, U.-G. (1997), 'Equity in health care utilization: further tests based on hurdle models and Swedish micro data', *Health Economics*, **6**, 303–19.
Jiménez-Martín, S., J.M. Labeaga and M. Martínez-Granado (2002), 'Latent class versus two-part models in the demand for physician services across the European Union', *Health Economics*, **11**, 301–21.
Kenkel, D.S. and J. Terza (2001), 'The effect of physician advice on alcohol consumption: count regression with an endogenous treatment effect', *Journal of Applied Econometrics*, **16**, 165–84.

Lindsay, B.J. (1995), *Mixture Models: Theory, Geometry, and Applications*, NSF-CBMS Regional Conference Series in Probability and Statistics, Vol. 5, IMS-ASA.

Lourenço, O.D. and P.L. Ferreira (2004), 'The impact of non-monetary factors on the primary care utilization in Portugal: finite mixture models applied to on-site and truncated samples', working paper.

Manning, W.G., J.P. Newhouse, N. Duan, E.B. Keeler, A. Leibowitz and M.S. Marquis (1987), 'Health insurance and the demand for medical care: evidence from a randomized experiment', *American Economic Review*, **77**, 251–77.

Mello, M.M., S.C. Stearns and E.C. Norton (2002), 'Do Medicare HMOs still reduce health services use after controlling for selection bias?', *Health Economics*, **11**, 323–40.

Mroz, T.A. (1999), 'Discrete factor approximations in simultaneous equation models: estimating the impact of a dummy endogenous variable on a continuous outcome', *Journal of Econometrics*, **92**, 233–74.

Mullahy, J. (1986), 'Specification and testing of some modified count data models', *Journal of Econometrics*, **33**, 341–65.

Munkin, M.K. and P.K. Trivedi (1999), 'Simulated maximum likelihood estimation of multivariate mixed-Poisson regression models, with application', *Econometrics Journal*, **2**, 29–48.

Pohlmeier, W. and V. Ulrich (1995), 'An econometric model of the two-part decisionmaking process in the demand for health care', *The Journal of Human Resources*, **30**, 339–61.

Schellhorn, M. (2001), 'The effect of variable health insurance deductibles on the demand for physician visits', *Health Economics*, **10**, 441–56.

Terza, J.V. (1998), 'Estimating count data models with endogenous switching: sample selection and endogenous treatment effects', *Journal of Econometrics*, **84**, 129–54.

Wang, P. (2003), 'A bivariate zero-inflated negative binomial regression model for count data with excess zeros', *Economics Letters*, **78**, 373–8.

Windmeijer, F. and J. Santos-Silva (1997), 'Endogeneity in count data models: an application to demand for health care', *Journal of Applied Econometrics*, **12**, 281–94.

Winkelmann, R. (2004), 'Health care reform and the number of doctor visits – an econometric analysis', *Journal of Applied Econometrics*, **19**, 455–72.

Zweifel, P. (1981), 'Supplier-induced demand in a model of physician behaviour', in J. van der Gaag and M. Perlman (eds), *Health, Economics, and Health Economics*, Amsterdam: North-Holland, pp. 245–67.

15 The unofficial health care economy in low- and middle-income countries
Tim Ensor and Robin Thompson

1. Introduction

There is a growing realization that a simple dichotomy between public and private funding and provision of health care is not sufficient to explain health care systems in many countries, particularly those in low- and middle-income economies (Ensor and Witter, 2001). Much, in some cases most, activity occurs at the nexus of the public and private sectors: services that are officially financed publicly are delivered on a quasi-private basis within public facilities and out of hours by public doctors in their own clinics. Unofficial payments can be defined as those given to providers outside official channels for services that should be covered by the (public) health care system (Lewis, 2000). Sometimes unofficial systems for delivering these services are extremely sophisticated with groups of clinicians and administrators colluding in the delivery of services by unofficial means.

Unofficial activity can be placed in the broader context of the strategies used by staff within the health sector to supplement incomes. Illicit activities such as kickbacks on public procurement contracts, fraud and theft of materials from public establishments will not be considered. It is acknowledged, however, that low salaries and poor governance, which are seen to be important in determining unofficial activity, may also be key in explaining the level of these activities.

2. The extent and nature of unofficial payments

There is now a burgeoning literature on the existence of various types of unofficial payments and activity within, and alongside, the public health sector (Killingsworth et al., 1999; Lewis, 2000; Thompson and Witter, 2000). One review article compares the prevalence of payments in 12 transition countries (Lewis, 2000). Estimates, based on an affirmative answer to the question 'did you have to make an additional payment?', ranged from a low of 21 per cent in Bulgaria to more than 90 per cent in Armenia. Amounts spent varied from $14 per capita in Bulgaria to more than $68 in Kyrgyzstan (1995 PPP dollars). Studies suggest that in transition countries payments are much more prevalent in hospitals than in out-patient settings (Lewis, 2000; Kutzin, 2001; Balabanova and McKee, 2002). Payment for drugs are the most common form of unofficial payments although payments to doctors are also extremely common and dominant in countries such as Bulgaria, Poland and Albania (Hotchkiss et al., 2004).

Outside transition countries unofficial payments for health are recorded in many low- and middle-income systems including China, Cambodia, Bangladesh, Nepal, Uganda and Latin America (Killingsworth et al., 1999; McPake et al., 1999; Di Tella and Savedoff, 2001a; Akashi et al., 2004; Borghi et al., 2004). In Dhaka charges are so significant that the unofficial costs of a normal birth can exceed the costs of a delivery in a comparable

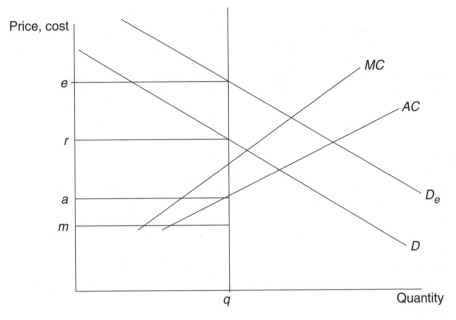

Figure 15.1   Unofficial payments and monopoly provision

private facility (Nahar and Costello, 1998). In Hungary, payments assumed a pseudo-legal status where clinicians are expected to declare unofficial payments to the tax author-ities (Gaal and McKee, 2004).

One outlet for unofficial activity is dual practice, where public practitioners maintain a private clinical practice. Dual practice is extremely common in low- and middle-income countries. It is often seen as a way of retaining workers who would otherwise have left the sector but also results in doctors spending less time on public duties while referring patients to their private clinics, a debate also common across Western Europe (Gonzalez, 2004). There is at present limited empirical evidence to support either view, although some studies have been initiated (Berman and Cuizon, 2004).

A number of reasons can be identified for substantial or growing unofficial payments. In transition economies particularly, unrealistic state guarantees combined with declines in public funding have led to a substantial gap between what is promised by the state and what can actually be delivered (Thompson and Witter, 2000). This can be illustrated diagrammatically by assuming that public services have a commitment to deliver a given amount of medical treatment (which fixes q) for an agreed public budget ($m \cdot q$ – see Figure 15.1). If the budget per unit (m) falls below the average cost of services (a) then providers may respond by attempting to treat fewer patients or by reducing quality of services (Ensor, 2003). In order to maintain quality, patients are forced to contribute to the costs of their care by both buying medical supplies and contributing to the basic incomes of medical staff through unofficial payments. The ability to augment incomes through unofficial payments may prevent workers leaving for more lucrative employment. It is also possible that public positions gain staff greater prestige in the private sector than if they devoted all their time to private activities. Where information signals on quality are imperfect, the public position of a practitioner may serve as a proxy indicator and help build up a practitioner's client base. Much of the focus in the health economics and systems literature has been on the strategies employed by clinicians to cope with low relative wages. McPake et al. (1999), for example, consider three such strategies including informal payments, and also the outside sale of drugs and misappropriation of formal user charges. A similar framework is used by Bloom, who considers a wider framework that allows for the offsetting impact of incentives, regulation and professional ethics (Bloom et al., 2000).

The theory of 'inxit' (a contrived term implying exit behaviour without leaving the organization) has been offered as an alternative strategy for public health workers and patients who are unable to influence their work environment but who lack alternative choices should they leave the public sector (Gaal and McKee, 2004). As a consequence they collude through unofficial transactions in order to boost medical incentives and obtain improved quality care. Patients involved in these transactions are crucial to the sustenance of the public sector which lacks sufficient budget to properly finance public care commitments. Forcing patients and providers to accept the choice of free care in the public sector or paying for care in the private sector could be counter-productive in that it could lose quality-seeking staff and patients who force improvements in standards and so lead to the development of a two-tier service.

Even though individual physicians may compete with each other within the same institution for unofficial payments, specialization and collusion leads to the persistence of monopoly power even in large institutions. Thompson describes how department heads organize their staff to collect specified amounts from patients based on perceived willingness to pay (Thompson, 2004). This enables staff to exploit a near-monopoly position by demanding payment for service over and above their cost. The maximum level of this unofficial rent-seeking can be represented as the distance between the cost and demand curve $(r-a)$ in Figure 15.1. Further payments can be extracted through price discrimination as in Bangladesh, for example, where patients are offered a choice between shared and single occupancy rooms (cabins) and open wards. Those choosing to pay for rooms are then assumed to have identified themselves (self-selected) as relatively wealthy, and larger unofficial payments for the medical treatment are demanded (Killingsworth et al., 1999).

A further type of behaviour is where a public physician offers an additional service to a patient that is not available unless a payment is made. If these services are provided by staff unofficially, they can be characterized as shifting the demand curve rightwards to $D_e(e-r)$. Thompson describes a series of scenarios based on qualitative interviews where doctors extract payments from patients through implicit promises of enhanced service (Thompson, 2004). Enhancements include smaller stitches after surgery, immediate surgery rather than prolonged pain relief, and physician visits during weekends.

An important issue is whether unofficial payments affect the poor or the rich more severely. There is some suggestion of a 'Robin Hood effect', where the rich pay to cross-subsidize the poor. Recent empirical evidence challenges this view. In Hungary a study computed Kakwani (a measure of the progressivity of financing) indices for unofficial payments at various levels of the system (Szende and Culyer, 2005). The study found that payments are highly regressive. In Kazakhstan, Thompson's work suggests that the rich pay more, simply because they get higher quality services (Thompson, 2004). At the same time the necessity to make payments causes delays in seeking treatment, which impacts disproportionately on the poor.

3.   Theoretical approaches to modelling unofficial markets

Modelling the relationship between provider and consumer as a way of explaining unofficial activity has led to a number of distinctive approaches. These range from a corruption approach, which views payments mainly as a deadweight loss resulting from poor governance; contracting theories, which view unofficial activity as an ethically neutral phenomenon that arises from imperfect information between client, principal and agent; and consumer theories, which place the paying client in a more active role of seeking better quality service.

Corruption approaches to unofficial markets
The view of payments as a deadweight loss that inhibits the ability of health systems to convert inputs into improved health outcomes is implicit in studies that have investigated the impact of unofficial payments, bribes and other measures of 'corruption' on outcomes. One study, for example, found that increasing levels of unofficial activity had a significant negative impact on health status as measured by child and infant mortality (Gupta et al., 2000). One conclusion is that increasing spending on health may well be wasted without improved system transparency and governance.

A similar idea is implicit in the assessment of incentives resulting from unofficial activity. This is based around the individual calculation of expected income resulting from unofficial activity (Rijckeghem and Weber, 1997). Expected income from indulging in unofficial activity, compared to guaranteed government income without unofficial payment, is given as:

$$E(Y) = (1 - p)(CB + W_g) + p(W_p - f) \gtrless W_g$$

where p is the probability of detection followed by punishment, W_g is the wage in government employment, CB is the number of unofficial (or corrupt) acts multiplied by the level of income from each act, W_p is the wage in private sector or alternative employment should the act lead to loss of employment and f is the value of any sanction that results from being caught. The probability of being caught and punished is vital to this formulation. If this is zero or close to zero then it is easy to see that expected income collapses to $CB + W_g$ where workers always choose unofficial payments. A low value for p also means that increasing the public sector wage is rendered ineffectual as a way of lowering unofficial activity. Indeed, given that public sector jobs are often purchased (applicants make one-off or regular payments to secure a job) it may even increase illicit activity by encouraging more corrupt people to apply for employment (Di Tella and Savedoff, 2001b).

The above model was tested in a series of studies in Latin America, undertaken in Venezuela, Peru, Argentina, Bolivia and Colombia, employing various indices of unofficial activity in individual hospitals (Di Tella and Savedoff, 2001a). Although there are some differences across the studies, several common conclusions emerged. The studies generally found that increasing the formal wage has a relatively small or insignificant impact on activity. Conversely increasing the ability to penalize activities reduces the likelihood of unofficial activity. In the Colombian study it was shown that having a fixed term as opposed to a permanent contract, so making it easier to get rid of staff in the event of an unofficial act being exposed, appeared to have a negative impact on unofficial behaviour.

Studies in other contexts have found that increasing civil servant salaries do have an impact on illicit activity (Rijckeghem and Weber, 1997). Rather different formulations of the expected income problem have also been formulated. As with the Latin American studies an income maximizing strategy is proposed, but alongside a second fair wage hypothesis that suggests that employees exploit opportunities for unofficial behaviour only when their own official income falls short of a basic subsistence level. The Rijckeghem and Weber study was unable to show which hypothesis is favoured empirically.

The latter hypothesis is a specific version of a more general utility approach where individual utility from employment is described as a function of both financial rewards, such as wages and unofficial payments, and non-financial rewards, such as individual reputation, job satisfaction and personal ethics. This has been used to model the motivations and constraints to supplier induced demand but has wider application to unofficial markets (Evans, 1974). With a trade-off between financial and non-financial motivations, the demand for unofficial income may be moderated by values such as integrity and reputation in the community. As official income falls, unofficial income becomes marginally more valuable. Further research is needed to explore the nature of and extent of these trade-offs at different levels of income.

Contracting approaches

The alleged inefficiency of informal payments can be challenged where consumers take a more active part in the contract with the provider. A recent model assumes that providers alone observe the severity of the illness while both payer and patient observe the level of treatment (Vaithianathan, 2003). Provider utility is assumed to be a function of both income and health gain of patients. Since patients place a high value on high intensity treatment, small side-payments can induce more treatment than is appropriate. Purchasers may, however, structure contracts to take account of side-payments by introducing incentives that encourage providers to deliver mild treatment to all patients irrespective of severity, so containing costs. Within this incentive structure patients offering side-payments are treated differently. Payments from patients with the severe form of the illness are accepted since benefits to providers outweigh the additional costs. In contrast payments from those suffering from the mild form of the disease are not accepted since providers, while receiving income, do not gain the same level of utility from patient health gain. Hence contracts might be used to ensure that unofficial payments only induce additional care where it is advantageous to patients.

In a similar vein (Gonzalez, 2004) examines the conditions under which dual practice increases or decreases efficiency under different contract scenarios. On the basis that the prestige, and therefore earnings, in private (dual) practice increase if patients are cured quickly, the model suggests that, in certain circumstances, dual practice increases the effort in reaching a correct diagnosis and treating seriously ill patients. This enhances reputation.

A weakness with both of these models is that they make no allowance for income distribution and the ability to make payments. Neither has been empirically validated.

Consumer choice of quality

The specific link between quality and payments has been explored in a supply-side model of vertical differentiation with price discrimination (Thompson and Xavier, 2002). Demand is the result of patients' perceptions of quality, their associated preferences for a given level of quality and the prices charged. Some patients are willing to pay informally for services that should normally be provided free, as they perceive it will improve the quality of care received. A patient chooses the high quality treatment rather than the low quality one if net utility obtained from higher quality minus the cost is higher than that obtained with the low quality public service.

The model was tested using data from a survey of surgical patients treated in hospitals in Almaty (Thompson, 2004). Two proxy indicators of technical quality were used: length of wait in the admissions department and length of stay in hospital. In the first case it is assumed that shorter waits are indicative of better quality. In the latter it was assumed that longer stays equate with better quality treatment. This assumption may be considered strange in the context of most of the OECD countries, where shorter, not longer stays are generally desired. In Kazakhstan and other transition countries it is argued that longer stays are usually preferred because follow-up care on leaving hospital is often of poor quality and transport networks are more limited. The study found that longer stays are indeed associated with greater payment controlling for severity of illness and other factors such as age and income.

4. Policy implications of unofficial payments and the need for further research

Delineating the types of payment is of more than academic interest. It may also influence whether a particular policy is effective in controlling unofficial activity. If payments mainly arise from monopolistic opportunities for rent extraction then stronger penalties with better monitoring may be successful in forcing monopolistic practitioners into line. A rent-seeking (corruption) approach to payments tends to emphasize the need to increase sanctions and the probability of detection. Several studies conducted in South America emphasize the importance of improved voice of patients through hospital boards, other forms of scrutiny in the governance of hospitals and also a well-developed private sector offering alternative services for patients (Di Tella and Savedoff, 2001a).

Where salaries are below reservation or subsistence wages, however, increasing penalties are likely to drive better workers into the private sector or alternative non-clinical employment. In these circumstances any improvement in governance must be accompanied by an increase in financial incentives from public or formal out-of-pocket sources. Unless considerably more funding is made available from the government, it is likely that this will require a concentration of funding on fewer staff and services financed by the state.

Improving knowledge of entitlements and clearly defining the level of payments expected through more formalized arrangements may help to reduce the level of unofficial activity. Several countries have attempted to formalize funding arrangements at the same time as rationalizing the services financed by the state. In Kyrgyzstan, user payments were formalized in two regions as part of the development of a single payer reform. An evaluation was undertaken that compared total patient payments before and after the reform in both the intervention regions and other regions of the country (Kutzin et al., 2003). Regression analysis suggested that, in the institutions introducing co-payments, not only did informal payments decline by more than 50 per cent, but the total of patient informal and formal payments also fell. In Cambodia efforts to formalize payments have been mixed. At a national Maternal and Child Health Centre some evidence suggests that formalizing payments has reduced unofficial fees and boosted overall utilization rates (Akashi et al., 2004).

While a considerable number of studies now demonstrate the importance of unofficial health care markets in many low- and middle-income countries, research on policy formulation remains at an early stage. The theoretical contracting frameworks, supported by some empirical observation, suggest that the efficiency of unofficial payments is not straightforward. Testing these models in different countries would help to determine the conditions under which payments become inefficient and the extent to which government regulation, perhaps through contracting, could help re-direct unofficial effort. A search for new instruments to control payments is also suggested by the current paucity of policy instruments actually used in practice. A related area for further investigation is the extent to which dual practice impedes or promotes public sector commitments to financing and providing services. Of particular empirical interest is the extent to which non-financial incentives of public service offset the lower financial incentives on offer.

In most transition and developing countries unofficial payments are not isolated events but part of the public sector culture, going well beyond the health sector into other areas of government activity. The endemic nature of this activity means that changes to individual incentive structures may well be insufficient without further and perhaps dramatic changes. It has been suggested that unofficial (or corrupt) activities have only two stable equilibria, either where all or none are affected (Bardhan, 1997). There continues to be a substantial gap in knowledge on how the endemic nature of this activity can be overcome. Most theoretical and empirical work has assumed a static cultural environment. Yet environments are dynamic, and an exploration of the way in which changes have made unofficial activity more or less acceptable in the past could help in understanding what conditions are required in low- and middle-income countries today.

A final line of inquiry is to examine to what extent payments are seen by patients as indicators of quality, gifts as part of a cultural solidarity system, or required payments to ensure service delivery (Gaal and McKee, 2005). Such investigation requires interpretations and insights from beyond economics, but economic theory still provides a framework for helping to analyse motivations for payments, which can be used to structure responses.

References

Akashi, H., T. Yamada, E. Huot, K. Kanal and T. Sugimoto (2004), 'User fees at a public hospital in Cambodia: effects on hospital performance and provider attitudes', *Social Science & Medicine*, **58**(3), 553–64.

Balabanova, D. and M. McKee (2002), 'Access to health care in a system transition: the case of Bulgaria', *International Journal of Health and Planning Management*, **17**, 377–95.

Bardhan, P. (1997), 'Corruption and development: a review of issues', *Journal of Economic Literature*, **35**(3), 1320–46.

Berman, P. and D. Cuizon (2004), 'Multiple public–private jobholding of health care providers in developing countries: An exploration of theory and evidence', London: Harvard School of Public Health for DFID Health Systems Resource Centre.

Bloom, G., L. Han and X. Li (2000), 'How health workers earn a living in China', IDS Working Paper 108, Brighton: Institute for Development Studies.

Borghi, J., T. Ensor, B.D. Neupane and S. Tiwari (2004), 'Coping with the burden of the costs of maternal health', Kathmandu: Nepal Safer Motherhood Project, part of HMGN Safe Motherhood Programme, Options, DFID and HMGN.

Di Tella, R. and W.D. Savedoff (eds) (2001a), *Diagnosis Corruption: Fraud in Latin America's public hospitals*, Washington: Latin American Research Network, Inter-American Development Bank.

Di Tella, R. and W.D. Savedoff (2001b), 'Shining light in dark corners', in R. Di Tella and W.D. Savedoff (eds), *Diagnosis Corruption: Fraud in Latin America's public hospitals*, Washington: Latin American Research Network, Inter-American Development Bank.

Ensor, T. (2003), 'Informal payments for health care in transition economies', *Social Science & Medicine*, **58**(2), 237–46.

Ensor, T. and S. Witter (2001), 'Health economics in low income countries: adapting to the reality of the unofficial economy', *Health Policy*, **57**, 1–13.

Evans, R.G. (1974), 'Supplier-induced demand: some empirical evidence and implications', in M. Perlman (ed.), *The Economics of Health and Medical Care*, London: Macmillan.

Gaal, P. and M. McKee (2004), 'Informal payment for health care and the theory of "INXIT" ', *International Journal of Health Planning & Management*, **19**, 163–78.

Gaal, P. and M. McKee (2005), 'Fee-for-service or donation? Hungarian perspectives informal payment for health care', *Social Science & Medicine*, **60**(7), 1445–57.

Gonzalez, P. (2004), 'Should dual practice be limited? An incentive approach', *Health Economics*, **13**(6), 505–24.

Gupta, S., H. Davoodi and E. Tiongson (2000), 'Corruption and the provision of health care and education services', Working Paper 116, Washington: International Monetary Fund.

Hotchkiss, D.R., P.L. Hutchinson, A. Malaj and A.A. Berruti (2004), 'Out-of-pocket payments and utilisation of health care services in Albania: evidence from three districts', Bethseda, Maryland, PHRplus, Abt Associates.

Killingsworth, J., N. Hossain, Y. Hedrick-Wong, S.D. Thomas, A. Rahman and T. Begum (1999), 'Unofficial fees in Bangladesh: price, equity and institutional issues', *Health Policy and Planning*, **14**(2), 152–63.

Kutzin, J. (2001), 'A descriptive framework for country-level analysis of health care financing arrangements', *Health Policy*, **56**(3), 171–204.

Kutzin, J., T. Meimanaliev, A. Ibraimova, C. Cashin and S. O'Dougherty (2003), *Formalizing Informal Payments in Kyrgyz Hospitals: Evidence from Phased Implementation of Financing Reforms*, International Health Economics Association Conference 2003, San Francisco, USA.

Lewis, M. (2000), 'Who is paying for health care in Eastern Europe and Central Asia? ', Washington: Human Development Sector Unit, Europe and Central Asia Region, World Bank.

McPake, B., D. Asiimwe, F. Mwesigye, M. Ofumbi, L. Ortenblad, P. Streefland and F. Turinde (1999), 'Informal economic activities of public health workers in Uganda: implications for quality and accessibility of care', *Social Science & Medicine*, **49**(7), 849–65.

Nahar, S. and A. Costello (1998), 'The hidden cost of "free" maternity care in Dhaka, Bangladesh', *Health Policy and Planning*, **13**(4), 417–22.

Rijckeghem, C.V. and B. Weber (1997), 'Corruption and the rate of temptation: do low wages in the civil service cause corruption?', Research Department WP/97/73, Washington, IMF Working Paper.

Szende, A. and A.J. Culyer (forthcoming), 'The inequity of under-the-counter payments for health care: the case of Hungary', *Health Policy*.

Thompson, R. (2004), 'Informal payments for emergency hospital care in Kazakstan: an exploration of patient and physician behaviour', York: Department of Economics, University of York: 205 pp.

Thompson, R. and S. Witter (2000), 'Informal payments in the former Soviet Union: implications of policy', *International Journal of Health Planning and Management*, **15**, 169–87.

Thompson, R. and A. Xavier (2002), 'Unofficial payments for acute state hospital in Kazakhstan: a model of physician behaviour with price discrimination and vertical service integration', Licos Discussion Paper 124/2002, Leuven, LICOS Centre for Transition Economics.

Vaithianathan, R. (2003), 'Supply-side cost sharing when patients and doctors collude', *Journal of Health Economics*, **22**, 763–80.

16 Trade in health services: current challenges and future prospects of globalization
Richard Smith

1. Globalization and health

Globalization is a term that encapsulates many different phenomena peculiar to the late twentieth and early twenty-first centuries. Advances in travel and telecommunications have facilitated a greater mixing of people, customs and cultures, and more rapid cross-border flows of goods and services, people and capital, and ideas and information. For some this heralds increasing standards of living for all. For others it brings greater exploitation of poor countries and the destruction of indigenous cultures. What is clear, however, is that this is a process that is continuing apace, and will have significant effects on health and health care (Yach and Bettcher, 1998a; 1998b).

The influence of globalization on health is complex, with multiple direct and indirect linkages between factors of globalization and the proximal and distal determinants of health, illustrated in Figure 16.1.

In the lower half, the standard influences on health are illustrated: risk factors, representing genetic predisposition to disease, environmental influences on health, infectious disease and other factors; household economy, representing factors associated with human capital and the investment in health by individuals/households; health services, representing the impact of goods and services consumed principally to improve health status; and the national economy, representing the meta-influences of government structures and general economic well-being. The range of inter-linkages between these factors is also illustrated.

In the upper half, the influences of factors outside the national economy are illustrated. For example, there are a wide variety of aspects of globalization that will impact directly upon risk factors for health, including: an increased exposure to infectious disease through the rapid cross-border transmission of communicable diseases; increased marketing of unhealthy products and behaviours; and increased environmental degradation as a result of increased industrialization. Many of these factors may be considered externalities and have, to a greater or lesser extent, public good attributes. These global externality and public good aspects of, and impacts on, health are not considered further here, but are covered in detail elsewhere (Smith, 2003; Smith et al., 2003; 2004b).

Globalization will also affect health through influences upon the national economy. There is an extensive literature concerning the relationship between health and wealth. Thus, to the extent that globalization influences economic growth, and the distribution of positive and negative aspects of this growth, it will also influence health.

Finally, globalization will affect health through the direct provision and distribution of health-related goods, services and people, such as access to pharmaceutical products,

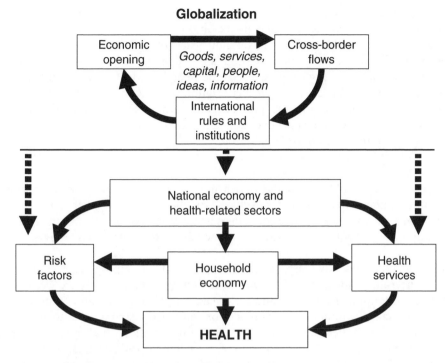

Figure 16.1 Schematic outline of globalization and health

health-related knowledge and technology (for example, new genomic developments) and the movement of patients and professionals (WHO/WTO, 2002). It is this aspect of globalization – increased liberalization of *trade in health services* – that is the subject of this chapter.

This is not to suggest that other aspects of globalization are not of importance for health, but that trade in health services will command increasing importance over the next decade because: (i) although international trade in general is growing, trade in services is an increasing proportion of this overall growth; (ii) the health sector is already being affected by liberalization in other areas of services trade (such as finance, which affects health insurance) and will become more so as health services are themselves being opened up to international trade; and (iii) many countries see health as a sector where they have a comparative trade advantage (mainly due to lower labour costs) (Adlung, 2002).

A final factor promoting the development of trade in health services has been the World Trade Organization (WTO) negotiations specifically aimed at the further liberalization of trade in *services*: the General Agreement on Trade in Services (GATS) (Blouin et al., 2005). The GATS provides an international legal structure for such trade.

2. Trade in health services

The GATS – initiated during the 1994 Uruguay Round of WTO negotiations – extends the objectives of the GATT (General Agreement on Tariffs and Trade) system, concerning trade in goods, to trade in services (see http://gats-info.eu.int/). These objectives are to ensure transparency, consistency and predictability in international economic policies through creating a credible, reliable and binding system of international trade rules, ensuring an equitable treatment of exporters, stimulating economic activity and promoting economic development, through progressive trade liberalization (Adlung and Carzaniga, 2001). Its philosophical basis is that liberalization will encourage a global increase in efficiency, through the traditional economic arguments relating to comparative advantage, ensuring consumers continued product availability and reducing the economic power of individual economic operators (Chanda, 2002).

The GATS is framed around four 'modes' of supply:

1.   Cross-border supply – where the service, not supplier/consumer, crosses a border;
2.   Consumption abroad – where consumers cross borders but suppliers do not;
3.   Commercial presence – where companies invest in foreign service sectors; and
4.   Temporary movement of providers – where human resources cross borders.

Although countries may liberalize trade outside GATS, it imposes a *structure* and *discipline* concerning trade on a *multilateral* basis. Countries select the service sector(s) they wish to open to foreign suppliers, and then make a legal commitment concerning trade within this sector – within individual modes or combined – stating what treatment suppliers will receive (Article XVII). The impact of liberalization on each sector therefore depends upon the nature of these commitments (Adlung and Carzaniga, 2005).

The benefit of GATS in stimulating increased world trade is in securing stability and predictability through their legally enforceable and indefinitely binding nature. Although changes to commitments can be made after three years have elapsed (Article XXI), these entail compensation (offering new commitments in other sectors to restore the previous balance of commitments) if these changes will impact adversely upon other countries. This binding nature has, however, raised concerns that GATS threatens to outpace the ability of governments to adjust to globalization, let alone guide it (Price and Pollock, 1999; Pollock and Price, 2000). In this respect there are three specific aspects of importance.

First, GATS applies to services provided in competition, thus excluding services provided in the 'exercise of government authority'. Whilst health services not supplied competitively fall outside GATS, if there is a combination of public *and* private providers then the public providers *are* covered by GATS. This is significant, as many health sector reform programmes have introduced some element of commercialization. Second, sectors which are opened may contain qualifications, such as limitations to foreign equity investment, size limitations on facilities or exclusion from subsidy. However, GATS requires as an absolute general obligation that members extend to all other members the best treatment that they give to their most favoured trading partner (the most favoured nation (MFN) obligation in Article II). Third, GATS does not affect member rights concerning market regulation for social policy purposes, such as universal access to care, but it could affect what *type* of regulations are allowed. For example, the 'necessity test' allows governments to deal with economic and social problems as they wish, *provided* that the measures/regulations are not more trade restrictive or burdensome than necessary – obviously much depends here on how 'necessary' is defined (Nielson, 2005).

Current negotiations on GATS commitments, begun in February 2000, were finalized in January 2005 (information on GATS negotiations is available at http://gats-info. eu.int/). In general the number of sectors committed is positively related to the level of economic development, although there are anomalies with respect to the health sector. Here commitments are lower than any other sector except education, yet far more *developing* than developed countries have made commitments in health. This is illustrated in Table 16.1.

For instance, Canada has no commitments in health, the USA and Japan have only committed in one sub-sector, whereas the least developed countries – such as Burundi, Gambia and Zambia – have made commitments in all four sub-sectors. However, the low overall level of commitments is suggested as being because: many countries simply ratified already existing trade arrangements, which in health are historically low; health is seen by pace setters for trade – the USA and EU – as of less comparative economic value (compared with telecommunications or financial services for example); and for most countries health is an area of significant government involvement (Adlung and Carzaniga, 2005). Current, and especially future, rounds of negotiations are therefore expected to yield much greater levels of commitments as these barriers are overcome, and it is therefore timely to examine the current understanding and status of trade in health services, using the GATS structure.

Mode 1: cross-border supply of services
Mode 1 – where the service crosses a border but the producer and consumer (mainly provider to client, but also provider to provider, government to client and government to provider) do not – is synonymous with e-health, which has arisen from advances in information and telecommunications technologies (WHO, 1997a; 1997b). For instance, China provides hospital diagnostic services via electronic means to Macao, Taiwan and other countries (Lethridge et al., 2005). However trade in this mode ranges from medical transcription and health insurance, through web-based education and training, to data storage and usage. For example, a growing number of universities offer internet based educational courses, and there are a number of medical information services on the internet to help doctors and consumers (most obviously those such as Medline, but the WHO has recently initiated the 'Health InterNetwork' which provides access to high quality, relevant and timely health information, and facilitates communication and networking among public health care workers, researchers and policy-makers).

Trade within this mode presents several opportunities: increased health care delivery to remote and under-serviced areas; alleviating (some) human resource constraints in service delivery; enabling more extensive and cost effective disease surveillance; improving quality of diagnosis and treatment; and upgrading skills, by disseminating knowledge through interactive electronic means (Yach, 1998). However, there are risks that such capital-intensive activity may divert resources from basic preventive and curative services, and that by potentially catering to the urban affluent it may adversely impact on equity of access to services. The primary concern, though, is that electronic trade requires appropriate telecommunications and power infrastructure, which has led to developments in this mode being almost exclusively within developed countries (in Africa, for example, the cost of internet access is around five times that in OECD countries) (Yach, 1998).

Table 16.1   Specific commitments of WTO members on individual health services

Members	Medical and dental s.	Nurses, midwives etc.	Hospital services	Other Human health s.
Albania	x	x	x	x
Antigua and Barbuda	x			
Armenia	x	x	x	x
Australia	x			x
Austria	x	x	x	x
Barbados	x			
Belize	x			x
Bolivia			x	
Botswana	x	x		
Brunei Darussalam	x			
Bulgaria	x			
Burundi	x		x	x
China	x			
Chinese Taipei			x	x
Congo RP	x			
Costa Rica	x		x	
Croatia	x	x	x	x
Czech Republic	x			
Dominican Rep.	x		x	x
Ecuador			x	
EC (12)	x	x	x	
Estonia	x		x	x
Finland		x		
Gambia	x	x	x	x
Georgia	x		x	x
Guyana	x			
Hungary	x		x	x
India			x	
Jamaica	x	x	x	
Japan			x	
Jordan	x	x	x	x
Kuwait			x	x
Kyrgyz Rep.	x	x	x	x
Latvia	x	x	x	
Lesotho	x	x		x
Lithuania	x	x	x	
Macedonia	x	x	x	x
Malawi	x	x	x	

Notes: No commitments: Argentina, Aruba, Bahrain, Brazil, Canada, Chile, Colombia, Cuba, Cyprus, Egypt, Gabon, Ghana, Guinea, Haiti, Honduras, Hong Kong (China), Iceland, Indonesia, Israel, Kenya, Korea (Rep. of), Liechtenstein, Macau, Malta, Mauritius, Morocco, New Zealand, Nicaragua, Nigeria, Paraguay, Peru, Philippines, Romania, Solomon Islands, Sri Lanka, Thailand, Tunisia, United Arab Emirates, Venezuela. EC Member States are counted individually.

Table 16.1   (continued)

Members	Medical and dental s.	Nurses, midwives etc.	Hospital services	Other Human health s.
Malaysia	x		x	x
Mexico	x	x	x	
Moldova	x	x	x	
Norway	x	x		
Oman	x		x	
Pakistan	x		x	
Panama			x	
Poland	x	x	x	
Qatar	x			
Rwanda	x			
Saint Lucia			x	
Senegal	x			
St. Vincent			x	x
Sierra Leone	x	x	x	
Slovak Republic	x			x
Slovenia	x		x	
South Africa	x	x		
Swaziland	x		x	
Sweden	x	x		
Switzerland	x			
Trinidad and Tobago	x		x	
Turkey			x	
USA			x	
Zambia	x	x	x	x
TOTAL	**54**	**29**	**44**	**17**

In this sense, globalization could extend the development gap, as the comparative advantage in e-health, as a capital-rather than labour-intensive industry, is unlikely to lie with developing countries, unless they find niche areas of competency. One such area may be the export of health-related services such as medical transcription, health insurance processing and data mining/storage, which have proved a success in India, where it is estimated that over 25 000 people are employed in industries in these sectors (WTO, 1998).

Aside from physical infrastructure, there are also unresolved issues concerning delivery infrastructure, legal frameworks, quality assurance and certification at a global, as well as national, level. There are also a range of other legal, and ethical, issues that arise, including privacy and consumer protection (see, for example, http://www.ifpma.org/ Appendix.htm).

Mode 2: consumption abroad

Mode 2 – where the consumer crosses a border to receive a service – is predominantly associated with the movement of patients from their country of domicile to the country providing the service. However, it also covers the movement of health professionals to receive education abroad, tourists who incidentally need medical care abroad, migrant workers and cross-border commuters (Lethridge et al., 2005).

Mode 2 accounts for the greatest proportion of trade in health services, since the only formal decision a nation makes is whether to allow its citizens to go abroad for medical care, with an estimated average of 1.3 per cent of total travel expenditures in 2002 being spent on health care (ranging from 0.2 per cent in Poland to 2.4 per cent in Romania) (Interagency Task Force on Service Statistics, 2002). However, it is a fundamental mode in another respect, as it is to capture, or redirect, this trade that is the basis for commitments in other modes.

For the consumer, travelling abroad *explicitly* to consume care is a result of a combination of disparities in quality, availability, cost, and/or cultural familiarity. For instance, although one may naturally think of Harley Street or the Mayo Clinic in this respect, countries such as Kuwait and Saudi Arabia are developing world-class hospitals and medical schools to attract patients. But decisions by developing countries to attract or retain patients don't necessarily have to replicate world-class facilities; as cross-border flows from the US to Mexico indicate (Moss and Felkner, 1994). Some countries attract additional consumers by developing or expanding specialized facilities, such as Thailand (Wattana and Supakankunti, 2002), India (Waldman, 2003), Chile (Francisco, 2002) and Australia (Diaz Benavides, 2002). Groote Schuur hospital in Cape Town recently developed an arrangement to treat between 500 and 1000 British patients who need heart operations to reduce waiting lists in the UK (Cleary and Thomas, 2002).

Broadly speaking, trade within this mode is argued to offer exporting countries the opportunity to generate foreign exchange earnings to increase resources for health, as well as to upgrade health infrastructure, knowledge and standards. For instance, Cuba receives around 25 000 foreign patients annually for treatment, yielding around US$30 million (see http://www.cubanacan.cu/espanol/turismo/salud/index.htm). For importing countries (when patients leave a country it is importing health care) there are possible benefits of overcoming shortages of physical and human resources in speciality areas, and for patients to receive more affordable treatment. However, consumers who go abroad for care usually pay out of pocket, as government or private insurance plans will generally not pay except for an emergency, and there is the risk that this will create a dual market structure, widening the gap between rich and poor. There is also a concern that such trade will divert resources from the public health system, and generate an outflow of foreign exchange (for importing countries) (Lethridge et al., 2005).

Mode 3: commercial presence/foreign direct investment
Mode 3 – where foreign companies invest in service provision within another – primarily concerns the establishment of hospitals, clinics, diagnostic and treatment centres, nursing homes and training facilities through foreign direct investment (FDI); usually in the form of cross-border mergers/acquisitions or joint venture/alliance (Woodward, 2001). For instance, the Apollo Group in India is currently investing some US$4billion in 15 new hospitals in Malaysia, Nepal, Sri Lanka and elsewhere (Waldman, 2003). However mode 3 also covers foreign commercial presence in the management of health facilities and allied services, medical and paramedical education, health insurance and medical-related information technology (Smith, 2004).

Mode 3 is one of the most 'popular' modes for commitments to be sought, as it is seen as generating additional resources for investment in the upgrading of infrastructure and technologies, thus reducing the burden on public resources, as well as creating employment opportunities and raising standards of care, management and availability (Zhang and Felmingham, 2002; ODI, 1997). However, there are associated costs. Significant public investments are often required to attract FDI (for instance, in travel infrastructure), and where public funds/subsidies are used there is the potential for diversion of resources from the public health sector. The presence of foreign-owned enterprises, in developing countries especially, may lead to the development of a two-tier structure of health care establishments, with the wealthy receiving high quality care at private/foreign establishments and the poor receiving lower quality care in public/domestic establishments. This differential system may be exacerbated by the 'internal brain drain', whereby the high quality health professionals are tempted away from the public/domestic sector to the private/foreign sector providers, as well as 'cream-skimming' by these private/foreign institutions aimed at the wealthiest consumers (Smith, 2004).

It is worth noting, though, that FDI is, by definition, only relevant to the *private* market. To this extent it is unlikely to *cause* a two-tier system, although may well exacerbate an existing one; it is therefore important to differentiate the 'foreign' from the 'commercial' element in considering the impact of mode 3. Further, there is no standard definition of what *constitutes* FDI. For instance, where proportion of foreign ownership is used, this ranges from as little as 10 per cent to well over 50 per cent. Similarly, there is often no distinction made between 'for profit' versus 'not for profit' FDI, such as where non-resident nationals of a country may wish to improve the situation in their homeland rather than necessarily seeking large profits. Factors such as these create considerable uncertainty in what is measured as FDI as well as determining the performance of FDI (Woodward, 2001).

Mode 4: temporary movement of providers
Mode 4 covers cross-border movements of doctors, nurses and other medical professionals, such as paramedics, midwives and physiotherapists, as well as non-medical personnel, such as managers. It includes those employed by a foreign company abroad, but also employees of a foreign company sent to fulfil a contract with a host country client, employees of a foreign company established in the host country, business visitors and the self-employed (Nielson, 2002).

This is an area of services trade that has considerable history as people seek to capitalize on wage differentials between countries, search for better working conditions and standards of living, and professional exposure, training and qualifications. It also reflects the market response to demand and supply imbalances between countries, although country response varies – some encourage outflow, others create impediments (Winters et al., 2002). Indeed, mode 4 was introduced to GATS partly as a result of pressure from developing countries who felt that movement of capital (mode 3) should be balanced by movement of labour (Nielson, 2002).

At present, commitments under mode 4 are minor, relating to highly skilled migration. Main exporters are Caribbean states, the Philippines, South Africa, Bangladesh and India. Eastern Europe, Canada and, to a lesser extent, the UK, Sweden, Australia and

New Zealand also export skilled health workers to other developed countries (Ouaked, 2002). For example, in the 1970s the Philippine government established the Philippine Overseas Employment Administration specifically to promote migrant labour as a means of reducing unemployment and earning foreign exchange, with approximately 43 000 (33 000 women) health professionals temporarily migrating in 2002 (Ouaked, 2002).

The main importing countries are the UK, United States, Australia, Canada and Norway, which are characterized by having shortages of health professionals and an ageing workforce. For example, it is estimated that 26 500 nurses were imported by the USA during 1997–2000, with some 100 000 foreign trained nurses living there in 2000 (Buchan et al., 2003).

For the host country, importing foreign personnel helps meet a shortage of health care providers, improve access and quality, and contain cost. For countries 'exporting' personnel there are perceived benefits from the promotion of professional knowledge exchange, leading to a skills upgrade, as well as gains from remittances and transfers. However, exporters may find a shortage of skilled health professionals, decreasing the capacity of health services to deliver health care, increasing the cost of recruitment and retention, and lowering consumer and worker morale. If temporary becomes permanent, the 'brain drain' of skilled personnel, associated loss of subsidized training and financial capital invested, and possible adverse effects on equity, availability and quality of services are further risks. Although both developing and developed countries experience highly skilled migration, for developed countries there is more *circulation* between countries; most return to their country of origin and migration represents a small proportion of the labour market. For developing countries, these factors do not apply (Martin, 2003).

3.   Current challenges and future prospects

Globalization means one can no longer view a nation's health, or evaluate interventions and policies, in isolation from other nations or sectors (Woodward and Smith, 2003). Greater interdependence of nations presents challenges in maintaining national health sovereignty and security (Fidler et al., 2005). International legal systems, such as GATS, both heighten this tension and bring in to sharp relief more general issues facing the globalization of health care in the twenty-first century: for instance, the need to develop *global* health governance (Krajewski, 2003). Currently, institutions and systems are designed around dealing with domestic organizations, issues and disputes. Increasing globalization, such as trade in health services, will generate cross-national issues and disputes and it is less clear how these will be resolved, and at what cost (Chanda, 2002). Similarly, international trade is associated with commercial involvement, and there is concern about 'privatization by stealth' in public health systems, and the perpetuation of inequalities in systems already containing significant commercial involvement (Pollock and Price, 2000). A further issue is the balance to be struck between economic indicators, such as growth and balance of payments, and health; it is quite possible for some countries to see the exportation of health services, contributing to the economy, as of higher priority than their populations' health status (Adlung and Carzaniga, 2001).

Of course, if, and when, these challenges are met and overcome, international trade creates the prospect for increased global well-being through securing the benefits of comparative advantage in the production and provision of health services. Through concentrating the production of services where capital and labour are most efficiently employed, more services overall will be able to be produced for given resource inputs (Krugman and Obstfeld, 1997). This should assist developing countries in improving population health and alleviating poverty through a healthier workforce, and for developed countries should ease cost pressures and waiting lists. Compared to other services sectors, health is one sector where developing countries in particular are argued to stand to gain most, through importing under mode 3 and exporting under modes 1 and 4 (Chanda, 2002).

However, the debate, at present, is polemical; there is little direct empirical evidence to substantiate many of the claims for or against increased liberalization of the health sector (Gobrecht et al., 2003). In this respect, the key challenge for health economics is to develop means to establish empirically the potential health and economic impact of trade liberalization (Chanda and Smith, 2005). For example, even the most basic information of how to measure the degree to which a country (health sector) is 'open' to trade is undeveloped (Findlay and Warren, 2000). Nevertheless, some progress in developing suitable methodologies in these areas is being made (Smith and Adil, 2005).

At present it is therefore important that countries do not engage in hasty liberalization; and especially so under GATS. The potential consequences are significant, and although these may be positive, they may also be negative, and under GATS they would be legally enshrined. In simple terms, using a common market adage, countries are advised to 'try before you buy' – sampling liberalization unilaterally outside GATS before making GATS commitments (Smith et al., 2005).

4. Health economics and globalization

Whilst international trade in health services generates specific demands on health economics, it also exemplifies the wider challenge that globalization presents to health economics. For example, the interrelationship between national health care systems and the rest of the world means that empirical research, conceptual and methodological developments and policy advice can no longer be viewed in isolation (Smith, 2003). To take a simple example, cost-effective measures to contain resistance to antibiotics will be negated if international travel leads to the importation of resistance from elsewhere (Smith and Coast, 2002; 2003). Similarly, the interaction between health and other economic sectors will have to be accounted for. To take another simple example, the impact of SARS on health was marginal, yet the impact on the travel and tourism sectors – even of those countries not infected – was significant (Smith and Sommers, 2003; Smith and Drager, 2005). There will also be greater examination of the balance between health and economic indicators (Sachs, 2001). For instance, expenditure in health care may no longer be seen as purely 'consumption', but also as investment. For example, in genomics, developments are pursued not simply to increase the health of the domestic population, but also with a view to export earnings (Smith et al., 2004a).

Within the wider economics discipline, health economics has increasingly become associated with 'micro' economics; exemplified by the concentration of the majority of research and policy endeavours focusing on economic evaluation and market analyses of incentive systems and reforms (Tudor-Edwards, 2001). Globalization heralds a challenge to this balance. If health economics is to remain relevant to the development of health care and policy within the twenty-first century, it will require a greater emphasis to be placed on the macroeconomics of health (care), and a greater involvement and collaboration with untraditional bedfellows, such as trade, commerce and international relations.

References

Adlung, R. (2002), 'Health services in a globalizing world', *EuroHealth*, **8**, 18–21.
Adlung, R. and A. Carzaniga (2001), 'Health services under the General Agreement on Trade in Services', *Bulletin of the World Health Organization*, **79**, 352–64.
Adlung, R. and A. Carzaniga (2005), 'Update on GATS negotiations', in C. Blouin, N. Drager and R. Smith (eds), *Trade in Health Services, Developing Countries and the GATS*, Washington DC, USA: The World Bank, in press.
Blouin, C., N. Drager and R. Smith (eds) (2005), *Trade in Health Services, Developing Countries and the GATS*, Washington DC, USA: The World Bank, in press.
Buchan, J, T. Parkin and J. Sochalski (2003), *International Nurse Mobility: Trends and Policy Implications*, Geneva: World Health Organization.
Chanda, R. (2002), 'Trade in health services', *Bulletin of the World Health Organization*, **80**, 158–361.
Chanda, R. and R. Smith (2005), 'Trade in health services and GATS: a framework for policy makers', in C. Blouin, N. Drager and R. Smith (eds), *Trade in Health Services, Developing Countries and the GATS*, Washington DC, USA: The World Bank, in press.
Cleary, S. and S. Thomas (2002), *Mapping Health Services Trade in South Africa*, Capetown, SA: University of Capetown.
Diaz Benavides, D. (2002), 'Trade policies and export of health services: a development perspective', in N. Drager and C. Viera (eds), *Trade in Health Services: Global, Regional and Country Perspectives*, Washington DC, USA: PAHO-WHO.
Fidler, D., N. Drager, C. Correa and O. Aginam (2005), 'Making commitments in health services under the GATS: legal dimensions', in C. Blouin, N. Drager and R. Smith (eds), *Trade in Health Services, Developing Countries and the GATS*, Washington DC, USA: The World Bank, in press.
Findlay, C. and T. Warren (eds) (2000), *Impediments to Trade in Services: Measurement and Policy Implications*, London, UK and New York, USA: Routledge.
Francisco, L. (2002), 'The case of the Chilean health system, 1983–2000', in N. Drager and C. Viera (eds), *Trade in Health Services: Global, Regional and Country Perspectives*, Washington DC, USA: PAHO-WHO.
Gobrecht, J., R. Smith and N. Drager (2003), 'Measuring trade in health services', *Globalization, Trade and Health Working Paper*, Geneva: World Health Organization.
Interagency Task Force on Service Statistics (2002), *Manual on Statistics of International Trade in Services*, Geneva: OECD.
Krajewski, M. (2003), 'Public services and trade liberalization: mapping the legal framework', *Journal of International Economic Law*, **6**, 341–67.
Krugman, P. and M. Obstfeld (1997), *International Economics: Theory and Policy*, Reading, UK: Addison-Wesley.
Lethridge, J., D. Singh, R. Smith and D. Warner (2005), 'Trade in health services under the four modes of supply: review of current trends and policy issues', in C. Blouin, N. Drager and R. Smith (eds), *Trade in Health Services, Developing Countries and the GATS*, Washington DC, USA: The World Bank, in press.
Martin, P. (2003), *Sustainable Migration Policies in a Globalising World*, Geneva: International Institute for Labour Studies.
Moss, K. and M. Felkner (1994), 'Patient transfers along the US–Mexico border', *Public Affairs Comment, Lyndon B. Johnson School of Public Affairs*, **40**.
Nielson, J. (2002), 'Movement of People and the WTO', *Working Paper on Migration*, Geneva: OECD.
Nielson, J. (2005), '10 steps before making commitments in health services under the GATS', in C. Blouin, N. Drager and R. Smith (eds), *Trade in Health Services, Developing Countries and the GATS*, Washington DC, USA: The World Bank, in press.
ODI (1997), 'Foreign direct investment flows to low-income countries: a review of the evidence', *Briefing Paper No. 1997(3)*, London, UK: Overseas Development Institute.
Ouaked, S. (2002), 'Transatlantic roundtable on high-skilled migration and sending countries issues', *International Migration*, **40**, 153–64.
Pollock, A. and D. Price (2000), 'Rewriting the regulations: how the World Trade Organisation could accelerate privatization in health care systems', *The Lancet*, **356**, 1995–2000.

Price, D. and A. Pollock (1999), 'How the World Trade Organisation is shaping domestic policies in health care', *The Lancet*, **354**, 1889–92.
Sachs, J. (2001), 'Macroeconomics and health: investing in health for economic development', *Report of the Commission on Macroeconomics and Health*, Geneva: World Health Organization (http://www.cmhealth.org/).
Smith, R. (2003), 'Global public goods and health', *Bulletin of the World Health Organization*, **81**, p. 475.
Smith, R. (2004), 'Foreign direct investment and trade in health services: a review of the literature', *Social Science and Medicine*, **59**, 2313–23.
Smith, R. and M. Adil (2005), 'Measuring the globalisation of health services: a possible index of openness of country health sectors to trade', *Globalization, Trade and Health Working Paper*, Geneva: World Health Organization.
Smith, R. and J. Coast (2002), 'Antimicrobial resistance: a global response', *Bulletin of the World Health Organisation*, **80**, 126–33.
Smith, R. and J. Coast (2003), 'Resisting resistance: thinking strategically about antimicrobial resistance', *Georgetown Journal of International Affairs*, **IV**, 135–41.
Smith, R. and N. Drager (eds) (2005), *The Rapid Assessment of the Economic Impact of Public Health Emergencies of International Concern: the case of SARS*, Geneva: World Health Organization (in press).
Smith, R. and T. Sommers (2003), *Assessing the Economic Impact of Communicable Disease Outbreaks: the Case of SARS*, Geneva: World Health Organization.
Smith, R., C. Blouin and N. Drager (2005), 'Trade in health services and the GATS: what next?', in C. Blouin, N. Drager and R. Smith (eds), *Trade in Health Services, Developing Countries and the GATS*, Washington DC, USA: The World Bank, in press.
Smith, R., R. Beaglehole, D. Woodward and N. Drager (eds) (2003), *Global Public Goods for Health: a Health Economic and Public Health Perspective*, Oxford: Oxford University Press.
Smith, R., H. Thorsteinsdóttir, A. Daar, R. Gold and P. Singer (2004a), 'Genomics knowledge and equity: a global public good's perspective of the patent system', *Bulletin of the World Health Organization*, **82**, 385–9.
Smith, R., D. Woodward, A. Acharya, R. Beaglehole and N. Drager (2004b), 'Communicable disease control: a "global public good" perspective', *Health Policy and Planning*, **19**, 271–8.
Tudor-Edwards, R. (2001), 'Paradigms and research programmes: is it time to move from health care economics to health economics?', *Health Economics*, **10**, 635–49.
Waldman, A. (2003), 'Indian heart surgeon took talents home', *New York Times*, 10 May, p. 3.
Wattana, S. and S. Supakankunti (2002), 'International trade in health services in the Millennium: the case of Thailand', in N. Drager and C. Viera (eds), *Trade in Health Services: Global, Regional and Country Perspectives*, Washington DC, USA: PAHO-WHO.
WHO (1997), *Health Informatics and TeleMedicine*, Geneva: World Health Organization.
WHO/WTO (2002), *WTO Agreements and Public Health: a joint study by the WHO and the WTO Secretariat*, Geneva: World Health Organization.
Winters, L., T. Walmsley, Z. Wang and R. Grynberg (2002), 'Negotiating the liberalisation of the temporary movement of natural persons', University of Sussex Department of Economics: Discussion Paper 87.
Woodward, D. (2001), *The Next Crisis? Direct and Equity Investment in Developing Countries*, London: Zed Books.
Woodward, D. and R. Smith, (2003), 'Global public goods for health: concepts and issues', in R. Smith, R. Beaglehole, D. Woodward and N. Drager (eds), *Global Public Goods for Health: a Health Economic and Public Health Perspective*, Oxford: Oxford University Press, pp. 3–29.
WTO (1998), *Special Studies: Electronic Commerce and the Role of the WTO*, Geneva: World Trade Organization.
Yach, D. (1998), 'Telecommunications for health – new opportunities for action', *Health Promotion International*, **13**, 339–47.
Yach, D. and D. Bettcher (1998a), 'The globalisation of public health I: threats and opportunities', *American Journal of Public Health*, **88**, 735–8.
Yach, D. and D. Bettcher (1998b), 'The globalisation of public health II: the convergence of self-interest and altruism', *American Journal of Public Health*, **88**, 738–41.
Zhang, Q. and B. Felmingham (2002), 'The role of FDI, exports and spillover effects in the regional development of China', *The Journal of Development Studies*, **38**, 157–78.

PART III

EQUITY IN HEALTH AND HEALTH CARE

17 Decomposition of inequalities in health and health care

*Owen O'Donnell, Eddy van Doorslaer and Adam Wagstaff**

1. Introduction

Most of the economic literature on distributional issues in the health field has focused on the measurement of inequity and inequality along different dimensions – see Wagstaff and van Doorslaer (2000) for a review. Recently, however, the focus has shifted from measurement towards explanation of inequity and inequality using decomposition methods. Decomposition can be used to understand not only the sources of inequality at a point in time but also the reasons for changes and cross-country differences in inequalities.

Depending upon the purpose of the analysis and the conception of justice, one might be interested in explaining total inequality in a health sector variable or only that part of inequality that is systematically related to some measure of socioeconomic status (SES).[1] To date, most applications of decomposition methods have sought to explain income-related inequality in a health sector variable. This chapter concentrates on this type of inequality but in the final section we describe a technique that decomposes changes in the full distribution of a variable. This allows one to explain changes in both total health inequality and in SES-related health inequality.[2]

The basic idea of decomposition is that inequality in the variable of interest, y, reflects, at the minimum, inequalities in various associated factors, x. All decomposition methods provide a way of weighting these inequalities. In the next section, we show how income-related inequality in health, as measured by the concentration index, can be decomposed directly from linear regression. We then turn to Oaxaca-type decompositions that allow for an additional source of income-related inequality, namely that the association between y and the x's may vary with income. The decomposition of change in the full distribution of health, presented in the final section, allows for variation in the effects of the x's across the distribution of health itself.

2. Decomposition of a concentration index via linear regression

The concentration index is a measure of income-related inequality in a health variable (Wagstaff et al., 1991). Wagstaff et al. (2003) show how income-related inequality can be explained through decomposition of the concentration index. For any linear additive regression model of health or health care (y) such as

$$y = \alpha + \sum_k \beta_k x_k + \varepsilon, \tag{17.1}$$

* The findings, interpretations and conclusions expressed in this chapter are those of the authors and do not necessarily represent those of the World Bank, its Executive Directors, or the countries they represent.

the concentration index for y, C, can be written as:

$$C = \sum_k (\beta_k \bar{x}_k / \mu) C_k + GC_\varepsilon / \mu, \quad (17.2)$$

where μ is the mean of y, $\bar{x}_k$ is the mean of x_k, C_k is the concentration index for x_k (defined analogously to C) and GC_ε is the generalized concentration index for the error term (ε). Equation (17.2) shows that C is equal to a weighted sum of the concentration indices of the k regressors, where the weight for x_k is the elasticity of y with respect to x_k ($\eta_k = \beta_k(\bar{x}_k/\mu)$). The residual component – captured by the last term – reflects the inequality in health that is not explained by systematic variation in the regressors by income, which should approach zero for a well-specified model.

Wagstaff et al. (2003) also proposed two approaches to explaining changes in inequality over time. A first approach is to apply an Oaxaca-type decomposition (Oaxaca, 1973). This can also be used to examine differences in inequality across cross-sectional units (see for example, van Doorslaer and Koolman, 2004). Applying Oaxaca's method to (17.2) gives,

$$\Delta C = \sum_k \eta_{kt}(C_{kt} - C_{kt-1}) + \sum_k C_{kt-1}(\eta_{kt} - \eta_{kt-1}) + \Delta(GC_{\varepsilon t}/\mu_t), \quad (17.3)$$

where t indicates time period and Δ denotes first differences. It is well known that the Oaxaca decomposition is not unique (see section 3), with an alternative being to weight the difference in concentration indices by the first period elasticity and weight the difference in elasticities by the second period concentration index.

This approach allows one to decompose change in income-related inequality in health into changes in inequality in the determinants of health, on the one hand, and changes in the elasticities of health with respect to these determinants, on the other. But it does not allow one to disentangle changes going on within the elasticities. To address this limitation, Wagstaff et al. (2003) consider the total differential of equation (17.3), allowing for changes *in turn* in the regression parameters, the means and the concentration indices of the regressors. The change in the concentration index can be approximated (for small changes) by,

$$dC = -\frac{C}{\mu}d\alpha + \sum_k \frac{\bar{x}_k}{\mu}(C_k - C)d\beta_k + \sum_k \frac{\beta_k}{\mu}(C_k - C)d\bar{x}_k + \sum_k \frac{\beta_k \bar{x}_k}{\mu}dC_k + d\frac{GC_\varepsilon}{\mu}.$$

$$(17.4)$$

Note that the effect on C of a change in β_k, or in $\bar{x}_k$, depends on whether x_k is more or less unequally distributed than y. This reflects two separate channels of influence – the direct effect of the change in β_k (or $\bar{x}_k$) on C, and the indirect effect operating through μ. An increase in inequality in x_k (that is, C_k) will increase the degree of inequality in y. The impact is an increasing function of β_k and $\bar{x}_k$, and a decreasing function of μ.

Example
Wagstaff et al. (2003) applied all three decomposition methods to explain the level and change in income-related inequality in child malnutrition in Vietnam in 1993 and

1998. Malnutrition is measured by the height-for-age z-scores (HAZ) of children less than 10 years old.[3] A summary of the results is presented in Table 17.1. The (negative) concentration indices in the last row of the first two columns show that there was inequality in HAZ to the disadvantage of the poor in each year and that this inequality increased over time. The entries in the other rows of the first two columns are derived from equation (17.1) and give, for each year, the total contribution of each determinant to the HAZ concentration index. In each year, most of the income-related inequality in HAZ is explained by household consumption (the measure of socioeconomic status) and by commune level correlates of both malnutrition and income.

The remaining columns of Table 17.1 give the results of decomposing the change in the concentration index by both the total differential and the Oaxaca-type approaches. Estimates of the percentage contribution of each determinant to the total change in C (3rd from last and last columns) are broadly similar across the two methods with some important discrepancies. The Oaxaca-type method attributes more of the change to household consumption, while the differential approach gives more weight to changes occurring at the commune level. From the individual components of the total differential method (columns 4–6), we see that while changes in the means and concentration indices of the determinants of malnutrition have, on balance, tended to increase income-related inequality in HAZ, the opposite appears to be true of changes in the regression coefficients.

Extensions

One is often interested in income-related inequality in a health sector variable after standardizing for correlates of income, such as age, gender or 'need' for health care. The regression decomposition method (equation. (17.1)) is a convenient way of making such standardization. One simply needs to deduct the contributions of the standardizing variables (included in the regression along with others) from total inequality. Van Doorslaer, Koolman and Jones (2004) have demonstrated that this is equivalent to a two-step approach to standardization. One advantage of the approach is that, by controlling for factors other than the standardizing variable in the regression, there is less risk of omitted variable bias contaminating the standardization (Gravelle, 2003). A second advantage is that the analyst can duck the contentious issues of defining 'justified' and 'unjustified' inequality. The full decomposition results can be presented and the user can choose on which factors to standardize. This approach has been used to measure and decompose age–sex standardized income-related inequalities in self-reported health in Canada (van Doorslaer and Jones, 2003), in 13 European countries (van Doorslaer and Koolman, 2004), to compare England, Wales and Scotland over the period 1979–1995 (Gravelle and Sutton, 2003), and to investigate the causes of changes in mental health in Great Britain (Wildman, 2003).

The decomposition method relies on linearity of the underlying regression model. When the model is inherently non-linear, a few options remain. The model has a latent variable representation, that is linear in the regressors (as in ordered response or survival models) and one can proceed by decomposing inequality in the latent construct. Examples include van Doorslaer and Gerdtham (2003), who decompose the log of the hazard rate in a survival model of Swedish adults. However, if interest lies in decomposing the degree of inequality in the *observed* measure of health or health care, and not its

Table 17.1   Decomposition of levels and change in concentration index. Height-for-age z-scores of children <10 years, Vietnam 1993–98

| | Decomposition of concentration index | | Decomposition of *change* in concentration index | | | | | | |
| | | | Total differential approach | | | | | Oaxaca-type approach | |
	1993	1998	β's	Means of x's	CIs	Total	%	Total	%
Child's age (in months)	0.023	0.030	0.003	0.011	-0.002	0.012	-57%	0.007	-30%
Child's age squared	-0.019	-0.025	0.003	-0.010	0.001	-0.006	29%	-0.006	26%
Child = male	0.000	0.001	0.001	0.000	0.000	0.001	-5%	0.001	-3%
Household consumption	-0.035	-0.052	-0.005	-0.005	-0.002	-0.011	52%	-0.016	74%
Safe drinking water	-0.001	-0.004	-0.002	0.000	0.000	-0.003	14%	-0.003	16%
Satisfactory sanitation	-0.004	-0.003	0.003	-0.002	0.000	-0.003	-5%	0.001	-5%
Years schooling hhold. head	-0.001	-0.001	0.001	0.000	0.000	0.001	0%	0.000	1%
Years schooling mother	-0.003	0.000	0.005	0.000	-0.001	0.000	-19%	0.003	-11%
Fixed commune effects	-0.035	-0.047	0.000	-0.014	-0.010	-0.025	119%	-0.012	55%
'Residual'	0.000	-0.001				0.005	-24%	0.005	-24%
Total	-0.075	-0.102	0.010	-0.021	-0.016	-0.021	100%	-0.022	100%

Source: Tables 2, 3 and 4 from Wagstaff *et al.* (2003)

propensity, then it becomes essential to obtain a linear version of the non-linear specification. Van Doorslaer et al. (2004), for instance, have used the 'partial effects' representation of non-linear count models to assess the degree of horizontal inequity in health care use in 12 European countries. This representation has the advantage of being a linear additive model of actual utilization, but it only holds by approximation, and its error term includes, in addition to the estimation error, an approximation error which depends on the choice of estimation method for the partial effects. Obtaining standard errors for the various components of the decomposition requires bootstrapping. An example is provided in van Doorslaer and Koolman (2004).

3. Decomposition of a difference in means

The decomposition in the previous section has the merit of decomposing inequalities in health across the entire income distribution. The disadvantage is that it assumes the same regression coefficients for everyone. This disadvantage can be overcome if one is prepared to divide the income distribution into only two groups (poor and non-poor, say) and to restrict attention to differences between them in the mean of some health sector variable. Under these conditions, the Oaxaca (1973) decomposition is applicable.[4] Differences in group-means of the outcome variable are decomposed into between-group differences in the means of determinants, on the one hand, and differences in the effects of these determinants, as represented by the coefficients of the underlying regression model. For example, the higher prevalence of diarrhoea among poor children may be due not only to the fact that poor households are less likely to have piped water but also to poor households' deficiency in knowledge about how to get the maximum health benefits from piped water.

Assume we have two groups, the poor and non-poor, and the regression model underlying the outcome variable y is (intercepts are suppressed for simplicity):

$$y_i = \begin{cases} \beta^{poor} x_i + \varepsilon_i & \text{if poor} \\ \beta^{non\text{-}poor} x_i + \varepsilon_i & \text{if non-poor} \end{cases} \tag{17.5}$$

In Figure 17.1, the non-poor are assumed to have a more *advantageous* regression line. At each value of x, the outcome, y, is better for the non-poor. In addition, the non-poor are assumed to have a higher mean of x. The result is that, on average, the poor have a lower value of y than the non-poor. This gap can be expressed in two (equally valid) ways, which differ according to how differences in covariates and coefficients are weighted:

$$y^{non\text{-}poor} - y^{poor} = \Delta x \beta^{poor} + \Delta \beta x^{non\text{-}poor} \tag{17.6}$$

where $\Delta x = x^{non\text{-}poor} - x^{poor}$ and $\Delta \beta = \beta^{non\text{-}poor} - \beta^{poor}$, or as

$$y^{non\text{-}poor} - y^{poor} = \Delta x \beta^{non\text{-}poor} + \Delta \beta x^{poor}. \tag{17.7}$$

The decompositions in equations (17.6) and (17.7) can be seen as special cases of a more general decomposition[5]

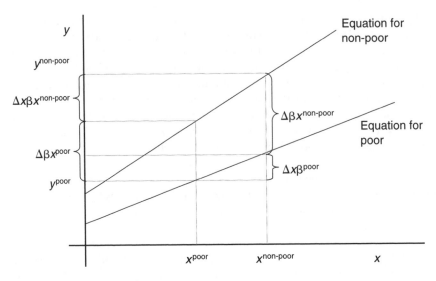

Figure 17.1   Oaxaca decomposition

$$y^{\text{non-poor}} - y^{\text{poor}} = \Delta x \beta^{\text{poor}} + \Delta \beta x^{\text{poor}} + \Delta x \Delta \beta$$
$$= E + C + CE \tag{17.8}$$

so that the gap in outcomes can be thought of as deriving from a gap in endowments (E), a gap in coefficients (C), and a gap arising from the interaction of endowments and coefficients (CE). Equations (17.6) and (17.7) are special cases, where the interaction effect is placed in the contribution of the difference in coefficients and in covariates respectively. We can also write Oaxaca's decomposition as a special case of a general decomposition:

$$y^{\text{non-poor}} - y^{\text{poor}} = \Delta x[D\beta^{\text{non-poor}} + (1 - D)\beta^{\text{poor}}] + \Delta \beta[x^{\text{non-poor}}(1 - D) + x^{\text{poor}}D]. \tag{17.9}$$

where I is the identity matrix and D a matrix of weights. In the simple case, where x is a scalar, I is equal to one, and D is a weight equal to 0 in the first decomposition, (17.6), and 1 in the second, (17.7). In the case where x is a vector, we have

$$D = 0 \quad \text{(Oaxaca eqn (17.6))} \tag{17.10}$$
$$D = I \quad \text{(Oaxaca eqn (17.7))} \tag{17.11}$$

Cotton (1988) suggested weighting the differences in the x's by the mean of the coefficient vectors, which is obtained from (17.9) by defining,

$$\text{diag}(D) = 0.5 \quad \text{(Cotton)} \tag{17.12}$$

where $\text{diag}(D)$ is the diagonal of D. Reimers (1983) suggested weighting the coefficient vectors by the proportions in the two groups, so that if f_{NP} is the sample fraction in the non-poor group, we have

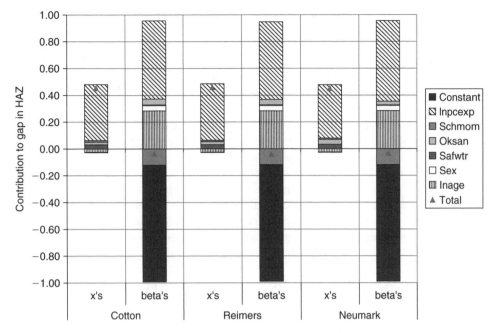

Notes: Regressions include the log of the child's age in months (lnage), a dummy indicating whether the child in question is male (sex), dummies indicating whether the child's household has safe drinking water (safewtr) and satisfactory sanitation (oksan), the years of schooling of the child's mother (schmom), and the natural logarithm of household per capita consumption (lnpcexp).

Figure 17.2   Oaxaca-type decompositions of difference in mean height-for-age z-scores between non-poor and poor children, Vietnam 1998

$$\text{diag}(D) = f_{NP} \quad \text{(Reimers)}. \tag{17.13}$$

Neumark (1988) defines yet another decomposition by making use of coefficients from a pooled regression, β^P:

$$y^{\text{non-poor}} - y^{\text{poor}} = \Delta x \beta^P + [x^{\text{non-poor}}(\beta^{\text{non-poor}} - \beta^P) + x^{\text{poor}}(\beta^P - \beta^{\text{poor}})] \quad \text{(Neumark)}. \tag{17.14}$$

Example
Figure 17.2 shows the results of using the Cotton, Reimers and Neumark weighting schemes to decompose the difference in the mean HAZ of poor and non-poor children (<10 years) in Vietnam in 1998.[6] The mean HAZ among children living below Vietnam's poverty line in 1998 was -1.86, compared to a mean of -1.44 among children living above the poverty line. The covariates included in the regression model are the same as in Table 17.1 above. The triangles in Figure 17.2, which indicate the overall contributions of the x's and the β's, show that the bulk of the gap in malnutrition arises from differences in the x's not the β's. The difference in per capita household consumption is by far the

most influential covariate in explaining the gap. Although the aggregate contribution of differences in coefficients is close to zero, this is due to offsetting effects from different β's. The poor have a higher intercept in the HAZ equation, but this is largely offset by the, perhaps surprising, fact that the consumption effect is weaker for the poor. The results are robust to the weighting scheme employed in the decomposition.

Extension
The approach can be extended to explain change in an outcome gap. For example, one might be interested in why an outcome has improved less markedly among the poor. In the framework of equation (17.5), possible explanations are: (i) the poor experienced less advantageous changes in the x's; (ii) changes in the x's mattered less for the poor since they face a worse set of coefficients linking the determinants to the outcome; (iii) the poor experienced less advantageous changes in the β's; (iv) changes in the β's mattered less to the poor since they had worse determinants to start with. Formally, the 'excess' growth of y experienced by the non-poor can be decomposed as follows (cf. Makepeace et al., 1999):

$$\Delta[y^{\text{non-poor}}] - \Delta[y^{\text{poor}}] = B_1 + B_2 + B_3 + B_4, \tag{17.15}$$

where

$B_1 = (\Delta x^{\text{non-poor}} - \Delta x^{\text{poor}})\beta_t^{\text{non-poor}},$

$B_2 = (\beta_t^{\text{non-poor}} - \beta_t^{\text{poor}})\Delta x^{\text{poor}},$

$B_3 = (\Delta\beta^{\text{non-poor}} - \Delta\beta^{\text{poor}})x_{t-1}^{\text{non-poor}},$ and

$B_4 = (x_{t-1}^{\text{non-poor}} - x_{t-1}^{\text{poor}})\Delta\beta^{\text{poor}},$ where t indicates time period.

Terms B_1–B_4 correspond respectively to (i)–(iv) above.

Wagstaff and Nguyen (2004) employed this decomposition to understand why in Vietnam between 1993 and 1998 child mortality appears to have fallen less among the poor than among the better off. They used survey data from 1993 and 1998 to estimate hazard models for the survival of children born in the ten years prior to each survey. Covariates are assumed to be linearly related to the negative of the natural log of the hazard rate. A restricted model in which $\Delta\beta$ is assumed constant across poor and non-poor is not rejected, so B_3 in (17.15) is zero. The remaining three terms are roughly equal. B_1 is largely due to the greater increase in health service coverage of the non-poor. B_2 is mostly due to the larger impacts on mortality of the non-poor of health services and safe water. B_4 is largely due to the lower per capita consumption of the poor, which meant that the slight increase in the coefficient on consumption between 1993 and 1998 made for a larger improvement in survival prospects of non-poor children.

4.   Decomposition of change in a distribution
So far, we have concentrated on decomposition of income-related inequality in health. As mentioned in the introduction, one may be interested in explaining total inequality in health and changes in this over time. One option would be to choose some decomposable

measure of health inequality, for example, the Gini index, and proceed in a fashion similar to that described above for the concentration index. When examining changes over time, concentrating on a summary statistic is convenient but risks obscuring important differences in the evolution of a variable across the full range of its distribution. It will not reveal differences in the explanations for changes occurring at the bottom, middle and top of the distribution. An alternative approach is to decompose change in the full marginal distribution and, consequently, any parameter of this distribution.

A variety of methods have been developed in the labour economics literature to decompose change in the full distribution of wages (DiNardo et al., 1996; Donald et al., 2000; Fortin and Lemieux, 2000; Gosling et al., 2000; Machado and Mata, 2005). O'Donnell et al. (2005) use the method of Machado and Mata to explain the change in the distribution of HAZ in Vietnam between 1993 and 1998. In the spirit of Oaxaca, the method decomposes the change in the marginal distribution of y into that part due to changes in the distributions of covariates (x) and that due to changes in the effects of these covariates.

Conditional distributions, required to construct the counterfactual densities, are estimated by quantile regression (QR). This allows for variation in the correlations between y and x across the (conditional) distribution of y. Such heterogeneity is advantageous when one is particularly interested, as with malnutrition, in effects other than those at the conditional mean of the distribution, which are given by OLS.

Construction of marginal distributions that are consistent with the estimated conditional distributions is achieved as follows (Machado and Mata, 2005). First, for each time period (t), QR coefficients are estimated at a random sample of m quantile points. Second, a random sample of m sets of covariates is selected for each t. Then, a random sample of size m from the marginal distribution at time t is given by combining the randomly sampled covariates at t with the QR coefficients at t. Counterfactual distributions are constructed by combining the QR coefficients with the sampled covariates from the *other* time period.

Let $f(y(t))$ be the empirical density of y at t that is estimated directly from the data. Let $f^*(y(t))$ be the estimated marginal density constructed to be consistent with the QR estimated conditional density. The estimate of the marginal density that would have prevailed in $t=0$ if covariates had been distributed as in $t=1$ is denoted by $f^*(y(0); x(1))$. Then, the change in any summary statistic of the distribution, $\alpha(\ )$, can be decomposed as follows:

$$\underbrace{\alpha(f^*(y(1))) - \alpha(f^*(y(0); x(1)))}_{\text{coefficients}}$$

$$\alpha(f(y(1))) - \alpha(f(y(0))) = + \underbrace{\alpha(f^*(y(0); x(1))) - \alpha(f^*(y(0)))}_{\text{covariates}} + \text{residual} \qquad (17.16)$$

The first and second terms on the RHS are the contributions of change in the coefficients and covariates respectively. The residual is due to the difference between the empirical densities and the marginal densities estimated using the QR coefficients. This is an extension to the Oaxaca method that allows decomposition of changes in any parameter of the distribution and not only the mean. Like Oaxaca, the decomposition requires a particular weighting scheme. In (17.16), the coefficient contribution is weighted by period 1

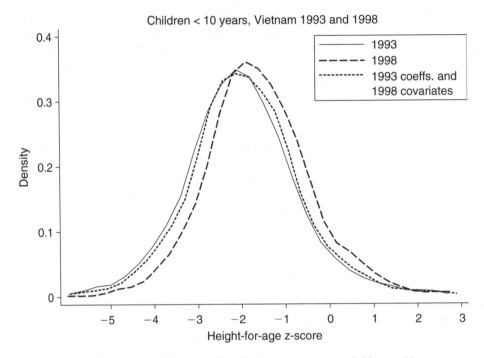

Figure 17.3   Estimated distributions of height-for-age z-scores, children <10 years, Vietnam 1993 and 1998

values of covariates and the covariate contribution by period 0 values of the coefficients. Weights can be reversed and robustness checked.

Example
We decompose the change between 1993 and 1998 in the distribution of HAZ among Vietnamese children (<10 years). For consistency with the HAZ decompositions presented in the previous sections, we use a more restrictive specification of the regression function than is employed in O'Donnell et al. (2005).[7] The size of the random samples (m) is set at 4500, slightly less than the smallest of the two survey samples.

Figure 17.3 shows a marked rightward shift in the HAZ distribution between 1993 and 1998. The counterfactual illustrates how HAZ would have been distributed if its relationships with covariates were as in 1993 but those covariates were distributed as in 1998. This counterfactual density is much closer to the 1993 estimated distribution than it is to the 1998 distribution, indicating that changes in coefficients explain most of the observed shift in the distribution.

In Table 17.2 we see that HAZ increased across the range of the distribution but, in relative terms, the increases are greater at the top of the distribution. The resultant increase in inequality is evident in the increase in the absolute value of the coefficient of variation. The final three columns give, for each statistic, the proportionate contribution of changes in the covariates, the coefficients and the residual term (as in equation (17.16)). Again

Table 17.2   Decomposition of change in summary statistics of distribution of height-for-age z-scores of children <10 years, Vietnam 1993–98

	1993	1998	change	Proportionate contribution to change of		
				covariates	coefficients	residual
10th quantile	−3.55	−3.02	0.53	0.1881	0.7761	0.0358
25th quantile	−2.82	−2.36	0.46	0.1672	0.7550	0.0779
Median	−2.07	−1.70	0.37	0.0997	0.8455	0.0549
75th quantile	−1.30	−0.92	0.38	0.0845	0.7871	0.1283
90th quantile	−0.48	−0.11	0.37	0.0553	0.7716	0.1731
Mean	−2.04	−1.61	0.4269	0.0989	0.8239	0.0772
Coefficient of variation	−0.6620	−0.7907	−0.1287	−0.0587	0.9448	0.1139
Concentration index	−0.0770	−0.0975	−0.0205	0.7210	0.7884	−0.5094

we see that changes in coefficients explain most of the changes in HAZ. But relative contributions are not constant across the distribution or statistics. Covariates account for 18.8 per cent of the increase in HAZ at the 10th quantile point but only 5.5 per cent at the 90th quantile. Changes in coefficients explain almost 95 per cent of the increase in the coefficient of variation.

As we saw in Table 17.1, the absolute value of the concentration index rises, indicating greater disparities in HAZ between rich and poor children.[8] The decomposition suggests that the change in covariates alone would give rise to a change in the concentration index that is 72 per cent of the actual change. The equivalent figure for a change in coefficients is 78 per cent. The two figures are reconciled through a very large (negative) residual term. These results are inconsistent with those presented in Table 17.1, which suggest that changes in (OLS) coefficients would have reduced income-related inequality had this not been more than offset by changes in the means and concentration indices of the covariates. Besides general differences in the estimation and decomposition methods, a possible explanation for the inconsistency is the omission of commune fixed effects from the quantile regressions. As a result, changes in correlated unobservable commune level effects, shown to be important in Table 17.1, will be picked up as changes in coefficients in the decomposition presented in Table 17.2.

Extensions
The method can be extended to identify the contribution of a particular covariate. Machado and Mata (2005) propose a procedure that gives the effect of changing the distribution of a covariate along with all its observable and unobservable correlates. One may want to hold, at least, observable correlates constant. O'Donnell et al. (2005) do this by exploiting panel data. Standard errors of the contributions can be obtained by bootstrapping (Machado and Mata, 2005; O'Donnell et al., 2005).

5. Concluding remarks
There is a wide range of potential health sector applications of the decomposition methods that have been developed in the income inequality and labour economics' literatures.[9] This review is not comprehensive in coverage of the applications that have been undertaken nor in drawing attention to all potentially fruitful applications. Jones and López-Nicolás (2004) extend the regression-based decomposition of the concentration index to a longitudinal setting, distinguishing between short-term inequality and the covariance between income and health through time (see Chapter 2 by Jones, Rice and Contoyannis in this Companion). The same principle could be used to decompose total health inequality into 'temporary' and 'permanent' components. Wan (2004) generalizes the regression-based decomposition method for application to any inequality measure with few restrictions on the underlying regression model. This is a potentially fruitful way of generalizing the Wagstaff et al. (2003) decomposition of the concentration index.

Notes

1. For differing opinions as to the relative merits of measuring total or socioeconomic inequality in health, see, for example, Gakidou et al. (2000) and Braveman et al. (2000). On the relationship between the two approaches, see Wagstaff and van Doorslaer (2004).
2. For brevity, we will often use 'health' as an abbreviation of 'health sector variable'.
3. A z-score is the deficit of a child's height from the mean height of a child of the same age and gender in a well nourished population divided by the standard deviation in that population. The reference population is well-nourished American children.
4. This method would be directly applicable if one was interested in, for example, gender or ethnic group differences in some health sector variable.
5. This notation is from Ben Jann's help file for his Stata decompose routine.
6. Further details are to be found in Technical Note #15 at http://www.worldbank.org/povertyandhealth.
7. Given the use of quantile regression, we are not able to allow for fixed commune effects, as was done in decomposition of the concentration index. Instead, we include an urban dummy and region dummies. Otherwise, the specification is as in Table 17.1.
8. The concentration indices in Table 17.2 differ slightly from those in Table 17.1 due to slight differences in the definition of the samples.
9. See Heshmati (2004) for a review of decomposition methods in the field of income inequality.

References

Braveman, P., N. Krieger and J. Lynch (2000), 'Health inequality and social inequalities in health', *Bulletin of the World Health Organization*, **78**(2), 232–5.

Cotton, J. (1988), 'On the decomposition of wage differentials', *Review of Economics and Statistics*, **70**(2), 236–43.

DiNardo, J., N. Fortin and T. Lemieux (1996), 'Labour maket institutions and the distribution of wages, 1973–92', *Econometrica*, **64**, 1001–44.

Donald, S., D. Green and H. Paarsch (2000), 'Differences in the distribution of wages between Canada and the United States: an application of a flexible estimator of a distribution function in the presence of covariates', *Review of Economic Studies*, **67**, 609–33.

Fortin, N. and T. Lemieux (2000), 'Rank regressions, wage distributions and the gender gap', *Journal of Human Resources*, **XXXIII**, 610–43.

Gakidou, E., C. Murray and J. Frenk (2000), 'Defining and measuring health inequality', *Bulletin of the World Health Organization*, **78**(1), 42–54.

Gosling, A., S. Machin and C. Meghir (2000), 'The changing distribution of male wages in the UK', *Review of Economic Studies*, **67**, 635–66.

Gravelle, H. (2003), 'Measuring income related inequality in health: standardization and the partial concentration index', *Health Economics*, **12**(10), 803–19.

Gravelle, H. and M. Sutton (2003), 'Income related inequalities in self assessed health in Britain: 1979–1995', *Journal of Epidemiology and Community Health*, **57**(2), 125–9.

Heshmati, A. (2004), 'A review of decomposition of income inequality', *IZA Discussion Paper 1221*, Bonn, Institute for the Study of Labor.

Jones, A. and A. López-Nicolás (2004), 'Measurement and explanation of socioeconomic inequality in health with longitudinal data', *Health Economics*, **13**, 1015–30.

Jones, A., N. Rice and P. Contoyannis (2006), 'The dynamics of health', in A.M. Jones (ed.), *Elgar Companion to Health Economics*, Cheltenham, UK and Brookfield, US: Edward Elgar.

Machado, J. and J. Mata (2005), 'Counterfactual decomposition of changes in the distribution of wages using quantile regression', *Journal of Applied Econometrics*, **20** (in press).

Makepeace, G., P. Paci, H. Joshi and P. Dolton (1999), 'How unequally has equal pay progressed since the 1970s', *Journal of Human Resources*, **34**(3), 534–56.

Neumark, D. (1988), 'Employers' discriminatory behavior and the estimation of wage discrimination', *Journal of Human Resources*, **23**(3), 279–95.

Oaxaca, R. (1973), 'Male–female wage differentials in urban labor markets', *International Economic Review*, **14**, 693–709.

O'Donnell, O., A. López-Nicolás and E. van Doorslaer (2005), 'Decomposition of changes in the distribution of child nutritional status using quantile regression: Vietnam, 1993–98' mimeo, University of Macedonia, Thesssaloniki, Greece.

Reimers, C.W. (1983), 'Labor market discrimination against hispanic and black men', *Review of Economics and Statistics*, **65**(4), 570–9.

van Doorslaer, E. and U.-G. Gerdtham (2003), 'Does inequality in self-assessed health predict inequality in survival by income? Evidence from Swedish data', *Social Science and Medicine*, **57**(9), 1621–9.

van Doorslaer, E. and A.M. Jones (2003), 'Inequalities in self-reported health: validation of a new approach to measurement', *Journal of Health Economics*, **22**, 61–87.

van Doorslaer, E. and X. Koolman (2004), 'Explaining the differences in income-related health inequalities across European countries', *Health Economics*, **13**(7), 609–28.

van Doorslaer, E., X. Koolman and A.M. Jones (2004), 'Explaining income-related inequalities in health care utilisation in Europe', *Health Economics*, **13**(7), 629–47.

Wagstaff, A. and E. van Doorslaer (2000), 'Equity in health care financing and delivery', in A.J. Culyer and J.P. Newhouse (eds), *Handbook of Health Economics*, Amsterdam: North Holland, pp. 1803–62.

Wagstaff, A. and E. van Doorslaer (2004), 'Overall versus socio-economic inequality in health: a measurement framework and two empirical illustrations', *Health Economics*, **13**(3), 297–301.

Wagstaff, A. and N. Nguyen (2004), 'Poverty and survival prospects of Vietnamese children under Doi Moi', in P. Glewwe, N. Agrawal and D. Dollar (eds), *Economic Growth, Poverty and Household Welfare: Policy Lessons from Vietnam*, World Bank: Washington DC.

Wagstaff, A., E. van Doorslaer and N. Watanabe (2003), 'On decomposing the causes of health sector inequalities with an application to malnutrition inequalities in Vietnam', *Journal of Econometrics*, **112**(1), 207–23.

Wagstaff, A., P. Paci and E. van Doorslaer (1991), 'On the measurement of inequalities in health', *Social Science and Medicine*, **33**, 545–57.

Wan, G. (2004), 'Accounting for income inequality in rural China: a regression based approach', *Journal of Comparative Economics*, **32**, 348–63.

Wildman, J (2003), 'Income related inequalities in mental health in Great Britain: analysing the causes of health inequality over time', *Journal of Health Economics*, **22**(2), 295–312.

18 Economic studies of equity in the consumption of health care

Hugh Gravelle, Stephen Morris and Matt Sutton

1. Introduction

Ensuring that the consumption of health care is equitable is a key objective of many health care systems. There is a considerable economic literature on the measurement and decomposition of inequity that is reviewed in the chapter by O'Donnell, van Doorslaer and Wagstaff in this Companion (Chapter 17) and several empirical studies that compare levels of inequity across European (van Doorslaer, Koolman and Jones, 2004), OECD (van Doorslaer, Masseria et al., 2004) and Asian (see Chapter 19 by Rannan-Eliya and Somanathan in this Companion) countries.

In this chapter, we emphasize that economic study of equity in health care consumption requires both empirical analysis and value judgements. Ensuring that the empirical analysis is appropriate relies on econometric models of consumption patterns that are valid for the data available and the decision-making processes involved. Since econometric studies are discussed elsewhere, in Chapter 14 by Deb and Trivedi in this Companion, we set out a welfare maximization model that motivates analysis of equity, emphasize the value judgements that are required, and highlight some empirical problems that are frequently encountered. We illustrate these issues using a recent study of equity in England.

2. Welfare maximization, equity and need

It is important to distinguish between *inequality* and *inequity*. There is *inequality* in consumption when different individuals receive different amounts of care. Inequity, on the other hand, implies that individuals do not receive the amounts of care that they *need*. Therefore, in defining inequity it is usual to distinguish between *need variables* that 'ought' to affect use of health care and *non-need variables* that 'ought not'.

A further important distinction is between *horizontal* and *vertical* inequity. There is *horizontal inequity* when use is affected by non-need variables, so that individuals with the same level of the needs variables consume different amounts of care. There is *vertical equity* when individuals with different levels of the needs variables consume 'appropriately' different amounts of health care.

The labelling of variables, such as age, as need or non-need is crucial to testing for horizontal and vertical inequity. The 'ought' and 'appropriately' in the definitions of horizontal and vertical equity clearly rest on value judgements, but they also rest on positive assessments of the relationships between variables and about their effects on health. There is considerable debate about the meaning of 'need' and whether equity concerns should relate to health status, the amount of health care received, or access to health care (see Wagstaff and van Doorslaer (2000) and Williams and Cookson (2000) for surveys of the arguments.)

In this chapter we concentrate on the interplay of value and positive judgements and the equity interpretation of the observed relationship between use and individual characteristics. We start by setting out a simple welfare maximization model which yields horizontal and vertical equity as necessary conditions for an optimal allocation.

Suppose we make the value judgment that the consumption of health care by individuals matters only because of its effects on individual welfare. Let v_i be the welfare accruing to an individual i from her utilization of care:

$$v_i = v(y_i, \mathbf{x}_i, c_i) = (\alpha_0^o + \alpha_1^o x_{1i} + \alpha_2^o x_{2i} - \alpha_3^o c_i) y_i - \tfrac{1}{2}\phi y_i^2 \qquad (18.1)$$

where y_i is utilization by individual i, and $\mathbf{x}_i$ is a vector of individual characteristics. c_i is the cost of accessing the service which may depend on the individual's characteristics, such as location, and on the configuration of supply. Variables are defined so that all coefficients are non-negative.

Our concern may be highly paternalistic, so that v_i need not reflect the preferences of individual i. We assume that v_i has the same functional form across individuals. It reflects the value judgement that the welfare of individuals depends only on their characteristics, not their identities, so that two individuals with the same y_i, $\mathbf{x}_i$ and c_i characteristics generate the same welfare. We could interpret v_i as the health of the individual or some increasing function of it.

The characteristics $\mathbf{x}_i$ which affect the social value of health care v_i may include measures of morbidity and some types of socioeconomic non-morbidity variables which influence the benefits derived from care, for example the type and condition of accommodation or the composition of the individual's household. Thus the value of a longer hospital stay for a patient with a hip fracture may depend on whether they live in a bungalow or at the top of tower block with unreliable lifts and whether they have able-bodied people living with them. The form of v_i (the coefficients α_j^o) also reflects factual judgements about the effect of care on different types of individuals. When v_i is some function of health it incorporates beliefs about the effects of health care on health.

Suppose that the health policy problem is to choose levels of individual utilization to maximize an aggregate welfare function subject to the constraint that total utilization cannot exceed supply (S):

$$W = \sum_i v(y_i, \mathbf{x}_i, c_i) \quad s.t. \quad \sum_i y_i \leq S \qquad (18.2)$$

The additive form of the welfare function reflects a judgement that the marginal welfare for one individual from increased utilization is independent of the level of utilization or welfare of other individuals. The welfare function is also neutral between individuals: each individual's welfare receives the same weight.

Socially optimal utilization is characterized by the equality of the social marginal value of utilization across all individuals:

$$\frac{\partial W}{\partial y_i} = \frac{\partial v_i}{\partial y_i} = (\alpha_0^o + \alpha_1^o x_{1i} + \alpha_2^o x_{2i} - \alpha_3^o c_i) - \phi y_i = \lambda^o(S, \mathbf{x}, \mathbf{c}), \qquad (18.3)$$

where λ^o is the marginal value of utilization (the Lagrange multiplier from the welfare problem (18.2)) and depends on total supply and on the distribution of individual characteristics and access costs. With this simple welfare function we can solve (18.3) for the optimal use of each individual as:

$$y_i^* = \alpha_0 + \alpha_1 x_{1i} + \alpha_2 x_{2i} - \alpha_3 c_i - \lambda(S, \mathbf{x}, \mathbf{c}) \qquad (18.4)$$

where $\alpha_j = \alpha_j^o / \phi$, $\lambda = \lambda^o / \phi$. We can label the characteristics $(\mathbf{x}_i, c_i)$ of individual i which affect the amount of care she ought to have as *need variables*. Her optimal consumption is not however determined solely by her own characteristics: the fact that resources are scarce means that optimal use by one individual depends, via λ, on the needs characteristics of all other individuals and on the supply of care available.

The optimal allocation is characterized by *horizontal equity*: individuals with the same policy-relevant characteristics – the same levels of their needs variables – will receive the same treatment. Note that because we assume that access cost affects the marginal welfare from utilization ($\alpha_3 \neq 0$) then individuals with the same $\mathbf{x}_i$ characteristics may receive different treatment.

The optimal allocation also implies *vertical equity* or the appropriately different treatment of those with different needs. Thus the 'appropriate' difference in use between individuals i and j with different levels of the needs variables is:

$$y_i^* - y_j^* = \alpha_1(x_{1i} - x_{1j}) + \alpha_2(x_{2i} - x_{2j}) - \alpha_3(c_i - c_j). \qquad (18.5)$$

Now suppose that the true model of actual, rather than optimal, utilization is:

$$y_i = \beta_0 + \sum_{j=1}^{2} \beta_j x_{ji} - \beta_3 c_i + \sum_{j=1}^{2} \gamma_j z_{ji} + \varepsilon_i \qquad (18.6)$$

ε_i is a random error. The z_{ji} are non-need characteristics of the individual that affect their consumption of health care but ought not to. Examples might include income, education, gender and ethnicity, depending on value judgements.

Actual utilization may differ from optimal utilization for a variety of reasons:

(i) $\varepsilon_i \neq 0$. If x_1 and x_2 are the only needs variables then individuals with the same needs variables receive different amounts of care. Our attitude to such variations may depend on whether the effect is persistent: if the expected value of the error for each individual across time periods is zero, we might feel that the realized error in any particular period is not important. On the other hand, if the individual error has a non-zero expectation across periods we might feel that this was horizontally inequitable: there is some unobserved time invariant characteristic of individuals which affects their use and ought not to.

(ii) $\gamma_j \neq 0$. Use is affected by non-need variables, such as income. Hence there is horizontal inequity: individuals with the same needs receive different treatment.

(iii) $\beta_j \neq \alpha_j$. Use does not vary appropriately with need variables, so that there is vertical inequity. Vertical inequity does not imply horizontal inequity: individuals with the same level of needs variables may receive the same amount of health care.

(iv) $\beta_0 \neq \alpha_0 - \lambda(S, \mathbf{x}, \mathbf{c})$. The base level of use is inappropriate which implies that $(\alpha_1 - \beta_1)\bar{x}_1 + (\alpha_2 - \beta_2)\bar{x}_2 - (\alpha_3 - \beta_3)\bar{c} \neq 0$ and so $\beta_j \neq \alpha_j$ for some j. Hence, there is vertical inequity but there need not be horizontal inequity.

3.   Common problems in empirical analyses of inequity

We discuss three issues that arise in attempting to test for inequity in the consumption of health care: the distinction between need and non-need variables; the implications of omitted variables; and identifying horizontal and vertical inequity.

Distinguishing between need and non-need variables
Suppose that the best-fitted model of individual health service use is

$$y = b_0 + b_1\text{morbidity} + b_2\text{age} + b_3\text{supply} + b_4\text{income} + b_5\text{gender} \qquad (18.7)$$

where *gender* is a dummy variable taking the value one if the individual is male and zero otherwise. The *supply* variable might be the number of hospital beds or the number of clinicians per head of population in the area in which the individual lives.

The equity implications from an empirical model like (18.7) depend on value judgements about which variables are need variables. Hence, although (18.7) may look like the estimated equation for the true model (18.6), to avoid pre-judging the issue we have written the estimated coefficients as b_j rather than as $\hat{\beta}_j$ or $\hat{\gamma}_j$.

(i)   Suppose we believe that use of health care should be based solely on health status, which is captured fully by the morbidity variable. Then there is horizontal inequity if, holding morbidity constant, use varies with any of the other four variables, which by assumption are non-need variables. For example, there is horizontal inequity with respect to income if $b_4 \neq 0$.

(ii)   For some types of health care, such as screening, one may feel that morbidity is not a needs variable but that gender is. Thus one would not interpret a gender effect on use of cervical screening as inequity whereas one might for screening for colorectal cancer. Thus the equity interpretation may depend on the definition and level of aggregation of the utilization variable. If y_i was, say, the cost of all health care consumed by i we would have to know how large a proportion of total cost was accounted for by cervical screening.

(iii)   Some value judgements are more contentious than others. For example, the judgement that income ought to have no direct effect on use is less contested than the judgements about the appropriate effect of age. Williams (1997) has suggested that entitlement to health care should decline with age since capacity to benefit declines and because older individuals have achieved more of their 'fair innings' of life expectancy. On this view b_2 should be negative. Others might argue that if morbidity measures capture all the potential for an individual to benefit from health care then age ought to have no effect ($b_2 = 0$). Alternatively, providing more care to older individuals, even if it is less effective, can be seen as a sign of social solidarity or as a means of compensating the elderly for other disadvantages. These latter arguments imply that use should increase with age: $b_2 > 0$.

(iv)   The supply variable differs from the other variables in the utilization equation in that inequality and inequity in access are of policy interest in their own right. Indeed, some commentators have argued that policy should be directed at variations in access rather than in use (Mooney et al., 1991). It would be possible to test for horizontal inequity in access by regressing supply on morbidity, age, income, ethnicity and other variables. Non-zero coefficients on the non-need variables such as income or ethnicity would then be evidence of horizontal inequity in access. Here we consider only whether the coefficient on the supply variable in the utilization equation provides evidence about horizontal inequity in utilization.

Typically individuals in areas with greater supply have greater utilization ($b_3 > 0$). Suppose one believes that the reason individuals have greater use if they live in areas with greater supply is that they have lower access costs in the form of shorter distances to travel or shorter waiting times. If, as in (18.4), one also makes the value judgement that use ought to be greater when access costs are lower, because the individual's net benefit from use is thereby greater, then supply factors are need variables, and $b_3 > 0$ is not an indication of horizontal inequity. Alternatively, if one believes that use of health services should not be affected by access costs, then supply factors are non-need variables, and $b_3 > 0$ is evidence of horizontal inequity. The latter view would imply that two patients with the same morbidity should have the same number of GP visits, irrespective of whether they live very close to a general practice or whether they live in a remote area and would incur heavy access costs.

Omitted variables

Inevitably, many of the datasets used in the empirical literature have incomplete observations of need, access cost, and non-need variables. Many general population surveys have only a very limited range of health variables, typically just categorical self-reported health or limiting illnesses. Such surveys usually have a richer set of socioeconomic variables so that the problem of missing non-need variables may be less serious. Most surveys have very poor or no information on access costs since these depend, *inter alia*, on the details of health service configuration in the areas where individuals live. If the survey provides area identifiers it is possible to link the individual with supply characteristics as a proxy for their access costs. But typically surveys only have highly aggregated geographic identifiers, such as a region, whereas it is the local supply conditions that determine an individual's access costs.

Suppose we believe that the only need variable is morbidity and that the measured morbidity variable does not capture all aspects of morbidity. Suppose that the unobserved components of morbidity are negatively correlated with income. Then, if income has no direct effect on use, the coefficient on income will reflect its negative correlation with unobserved morbidity and so ought to be negative. The estimated coefficient on income will reflect its direct effect on use, which ought to be zero for horizontal equity, and the negative correlation between income and unobserved morbidity. Hence if $b_4 = 0$ or $b_4 > 0$ there is horizontal inequity with respect to income. If $b_4 < 0$ we cannot draw any conclusion about inequity unless we make much stronger factual judgements about the strength of the correlation between income and unobserved morbidity, and about how large the effect of unobserved morbidity on use ought to be. The same argument would hold for age. Even if one accepted the Williams' (1997) argument that age ought not to affect use, it is likely that age is positively correlated with unobserved morbidity, so that an observed positive coefficient on age does not imply pro-old horizontal inequity.

Suppose we believe that access cost is not a need variable and we observe that the estimated coefficient on supply is positive: $b_3 > 0$. This is not necessarily an indication of horizontal inequity. There is some debate in the resource allocation literature about whether supply is correlated with omitted need variables (Carr-Hill et al., 1994; Gravelle et al., 2003). If it is, the positive coefficient on supply in the utilization model is not evidence for horizontal inequity in consumption, since supply is acting as a proxy for unobserved need variables in addition to any direct effect of supply via access costs. The richer the health measures and other need variables in the data set, the less likely it is that the estimated positive effect of supply on consumption could be attributed to omitted need variables.

Identifying horizontal and vertical inequity
We used our simple theoretical model above to bring out the relationship between horizontal and vertical inequity, but distinguishing them empirically is more problematic. Testing for vertical inequity requires strong additional judgements about the way consumption ought to vary amongst individuals with different needs, which implies both value judgements about relative merits and positive judgements about the effect of health care on individuals with different levels of need. As a consequence, most empirical studies of equity in use of services do not investigate the magnitudes of the estimated coefficients on need variables, and concentrate instead on horizontal inequity by testing for significant effects of the non-need variables and constructing measures of the extent of horizontal inequity based on these coefficients.

Separation of horizontal from vertical inequity may be misleading because each has distributional consequences for the population groups identified by the other. A negative correlation between morbidity and income, for example, means that pro-healthy vertical inequity will tend to benefit those on higher incomes. Conversely, pro-poor horizontal inequity will tend to mean that the sick have higher than expected levels of consumption. Therefore, if there is vertical inequity, studies that focus only on horizontal inequities with respect to income will only pick up part of the extent to which health care consumption varies inequitably with income.

Many studies of horizontal inequity focus on the relationship between use and non-need variables after controlling or standardizing for need. The coefficients on the need variables may not be reported or discussed. This is a pity because a number of useful analyses of the coefficients on need variables are possible:

(i)   A necessary but not sufficient test for vertical equity is whether higher levels of need (usually represented by more severe morbidity) are associated with higher levels of health care consumption (Abasolo, Manning and Jones, 2001). The analyst does not have to specify just how use ought to increase with need. All that is required is that those in greater need should get more care.

(ii)   In an extension of this approach, Sutton (2002) analysed the morbidity–consumption correlation at different levels of morbidity and found a negative correlation at high levels of morbidity. Assuming a linear relationship between levels of morbidity and need then provided a method for testing for vertical inequity and measuring its distributional consequences.

(iii) In multi-country and multi-period comparisons, coefficients on need variables can be compared and inequity-levels measured using different reference coefficients, such as unit-specific values, the all-sample average, the most progressive distribution and so on.

(iv)   Interactions between the need and non-need variables can be included. If, for example, the morbidity coefficients vary across income groups, this indicates that a vertical equity assumption is inappropriate and patterns of inequity cannot be separated simply into horizontal and vertical aspects.

4.   An empirical example – equity in health care consumption in England

To illustrate some of the points we have made, we present a subset of results from a study of equity in health care consumption in England (Morris et al., 2005). The analysis was based on pooled data from three years (1998–2000) of the Health Survey for England (HSE) with a total sample size of 50 977 observations. The data set has two merits: a large set of morbidity variables and good quality small area health care supply measures, both of which are important in reducing the risk of omitted variable bias.

Binary measures of GP consultations, out-patient visits, day case treatment, and in-patient stays were regressed on the available morbidity, demographic, socioeconomic and supply measures. Table 18.1 presents the estimated effects of the health variables, as measures of need. Worse levels of self-reported general health are associated with greater utilization for all types of care so that the basic test for vertical inequity is passed. Having a limiting long-standing illness increases out-patient visits and in-patient stays significantly. Worse psychosocial health (captured by the GHQ-12 score) is generally associated with more consumption, but there is evidence that consumption declines at the highest levels of psychological morbidity for three types of health care. With the long-standing illnesses, all the conditions, with the exception of infectious diseases, have a significant and positive impact on at least one form of use, though musculoskeletal illness significantly decreases in-patient stays.

Table 18.2 shows the estimated effects of the socioeconomic status variables on use. Increases in income lead to fewer GP visits, though the coefficient is not significant at the 5 per cent level. For out-patient, day case and in-patient treatment, increases in income result in greater utilization and the effects for out-patient visits are statistically significant at the 5 per cent level. Education has no significant association with day case or in-patient treatment. Those with lower education attainment are more likely to visit their GP. For out-patient visits there is also evidence that differences in education have an effect on utilization but there is no clear gradient relative to the effect of a degree.

The impact of ethnicity on health service use varies across ethnic groups and types of health care. Non-whites are generally more likely to consult GPs relative to whites, though the effect is significant only for the Indian group. Non-white groups are less likely to have an out-patient visit. None of the individual ethnic categories are significant in the day

Table 18.1   Effect of health measures on health service utilization

	GP consultations		Out-patient visits		Day case treatment		In-patient stays	
	Marg. Eff.	t	Marg. Eff.	t	Marg. Eff.	z	Marg. Eff.	z
Crude self-reported health measures								
Self-reported general health [a]								
Good	0.022	5.72	0.041	7.68	0.011	3.41	0.008	2.20
Fair	0.066	9.38	0.121	13.95	0.030	6.26	0.041	7.65
Bad	0.083	5.56	0.206	13.59	0.055	6.69	0.073	7.80
Very bad	0.131	5.09	0.264	11.35	0.075	5.58	0.217	12.96
Limiting long-standing illness	0.001	0.11	0.065	6.91	0.007	1.74	0.033	6.68
Type of long-standing illness								
Neoplasms and benign growths	0.023	1.04	0.307	13.72	0.076	6.12	0.108	7.94
Endocrine and metabolic	0.055	4.42	0.133	9.05	0.012	1.83	0.005	0.73
Mental disorders	0.035	2.18	0.013	0.74	-0.005	-0.66	-0.005	-0.62
Nervous system	0.017	1.27	0.060	4.01	0.017	2.33	-0.004	-0.59
Eye complaints	-0.015	-1.00	0.178	9.10	0.033	3.42	0.007	0.83
Ear complaints	0.015	1.06	0.088	4.41	0.031	3.33	0.004	0.45
Heart and circulatory	0.049	5.01	0.075	6.27	0.010	1.89	0.024	3.98
Respiratory system	0.042	5.40	0.045	4.65	0.007	1.45	0.006	1.17
Digestive system	0.034	2.74	0.109	7.20	0.048	6.21	0.017	2.31
Genitourinary system	0.029	1.68	0.172	8.23	0.074	7.30	0.031	3.11
Skin complaints	0.050	3.10	0.074	3.99	0.031	3.28	-0.003	-0.37
Musculoskeletal system	0.002	0.24	0.067	6.44	0.014	2.65	-0.011	-2.16
Infectious disease	0.052	0.95	-0.007	-0.11	-0.005	-0.18	-0.008	-0.29
Blood and related organs	0.035	1.09	0.178	5.04	0.051	2.60	0.001	0.05
Other complaints	0.017	0.31	0.062	1.05	0.057	1.82	0.004	0.12

GHQ-12 score[b]

1	0.020	3.19	0.027	3.49	0.012	3.07	0.026	5.18
2	0.028	3.39	0.040	3.69	-0.005	-0.92	0.033	5.39
3	0.034	3.28	0.037	2.90	0.011	1.69	0.036	4.85
4	0.058	4.08	0.058	3.83	0.026	3.40	0.046	5.42
5	0.055	3.49	0.047	2.66	0.011	1.37	0.016	1.77
6	0.007	0.42	0.088	4.25	0.011	1.21	0.042	3.87
7	0.048	2.29	0.053	2.40	-0.005	-0.53	0.022	1.90
8	0.037	1.62	0.072	2.77	0.015	1.29	0.041	3.12
9	0.069	2.80	0.084	3.24	0.028	2.34	0.062	4.42
10	0.074	2.96	0.083	3.36	0.034	2.72	0.077	5.18
11	0.082	2.94	0.110	3.90	0.021	1.65	0.060	3.85
12	0.070	2.46	0.081	2.77	0.042	3.30	0.047	3.33

Notes:
The models also control for age, gender, indicators of the supply of health care, co-morbidities, and socioeconomic status.
[a] The baseline category is 'Very good'.
[b] The baseline category is 0.

Table 18.2 Effect of socioeconomic variables and ethnicity on health service utilization

	GP consultations		Out-patient visits		Day case treatment		In-patient stays	
	Marg. Eff.	t	Marg. Eff.	t	Marg. Eff.	z	Marg. Eff.	z
Log(Income)	−0.005	−1.47	0.011	2.66	0.002	1.01	0.003	1.40
Economic activity[a]								
Going to school or college full time	−0.038	−3.54	−0.032	−2.36	−0.023	−3.69	−0.038	−5.58
Permanent long-term sickness	0.018	1.13	0.093	5.70	0.019	2.63	0.046	5.13
Retired from paid work	0.010	1.09	0.033	2.86	0.004	0.75	0.040	6.02
Looking after the home	0.017	2.13	−0.030	−3.27	−0.006	−1.32	0.050	8.51
Waiting to take up paid work	0.019	0.39	0.112	1.85	0.052	1.54	0.010	0.29
Looking for paid work	−0.027	−1.96	−0.020	−1.07	−0.010	−1.00	0.000	−0.04
Temporary sickness or injury	0.143	2.84	0.138	2.56	0.025	1.13	0.163	5.05
Doing something else	−0.013	−0.51	−0.013	−0.34	0.007	0.34	0.066	2.82
Education[b]								
Higher education less than a degree	0.007	0.85	0.023	1.92	0.001	0.15	0.014	2.18
A-level or equivalent	0.014	1.72	0.009	0.80	−0.001	−0.22	0.005	0.83
GCSE or equivalent	0.014	2.00	0.020	2.09	0.001	0.11	0.008	1.46
CSE or equivalent	0.021	1.96	0.021	1.56	0.008	1.11	0.004	0.56
Other qualification	0.032	2.66	0.041	2.64	0.000	0.05	0.003	0.33
No qualification	0.015	1.82	−0.003	−0.31	−0.006	−1.11	0.000	0.04
Ethnic group[c]								
Black Caribbean	−0.006	−0.41	−0.011	−0.60	0.010	0.91	−0.009	−0.94
Black African	0.009	0.40	−0.007	−0.26	0.013	0.80	0.013	0.88
Black Other	0.057	1.03	0.019	0.34	0.006	0.20	−0.016	−0.74
Indian	0.030	2.25	−0.009	−0.72	−0.009	−1.17	−0.002	−0.27
Pakistani	0.022	1.43	−0.065	−4.43	−0.016	−1.87	0.004	0.39
Bangladeshi	0.029	1.16	−0.085	−3.24	0.015	0.84	−0.020	−1.08
Chinese	−0.014	−0.60	−0.122	−3.88	−0.020	−1.20	−0.039	−2.38
Other non-white ethnic group	0.012	0.78	−0.043	−2.63	−0.002	−0.16	0.014	1.14

Notes:
The models also control for age, gender, morbidity and indicators of the supply of health care. Social class was also included but was never significant.
[a] The baseline category is In Paid Employment.
[b] The baseline category is Degree.
[c] The baseline category is White.

case model. There are no significant differences in the probability of an in-patient stay across ethnic groups with the exception of the Chinese whose probability of use is smaller than Whites'.

The permanently sick, those with temporary sickness or injury and the retired are more likely to use health services relative to individuals in paid employment. Since the analysis already allows for age, the retirement category is likely to pick up those who have retired early on health grounds. The results for these three categories may suggest that the observed morbidity variables do not capture the full effect of morbidity on consumption or that some of these groups attend for non-health reasons, such as sickness certification.

The example demonstrates inequality in the use of health care services with respect to income, ethnicity, employment status and education. The interpretation of the findings as evidence of inequity requires both value and factual judgements. If there are unobserved morbidity variables that are positively related to low socioeconomic status, or if we believe that low socioeconomic status groups justifiably visit the GP for non-health reasons, the pro-poor inequality in GP consultations is not evidence for pro-poor horizontal inequity. But with analogous assumptions in respect of out-patient visits, the findings suggest statistically significant pro-rich inequity. The results also indicate that non-white groups have higher than expected use of GP services, but lower than expected use of hospital services. The interpretation is complicated by potentially unobserved cultural differences, which may legitimately affect the use of health services. We might expect these unobserved cultural factors to have a smaller impact on use of hospital services, since doctors exert more influence over hospital utilization than over GP utilization. If so, the study results are evidence for horizontal inequity for ethnic minorities in the case of hospital services. In the case of vertical equity, the example provides some evidence that the basic test is not passed for psychosocial disorders and some long-standing illnesses.

5. Concluding remarks

We have emphasized that interpreting observed inequalities in health care consumption as inequity requires good-quality data, careful empirical analysis and value judgements. We have shown how a simple welfare maximization problem can generate horizontal and vertical equity as necessary conditions, but we have highlighted the implied assumptions about the effect of health care on health, the irrelevance of individual preferences and the comparative value of individuals. Each of these is subject to challenge and would change the way in which we analyse equity in health care.

In addition to these issues, we highlighted the empirical problems that are frequently encountered. These include the difficult decisions that must be made about the classification of variables into need and non-need categories, the implications of omitted variables (particularly need variables) and the problems of separating horizontal and vertical aspects of inequity when the need and non-need variables are correlated.

We used an example from a recent study to demonstrate some of the issues involved. We discussed the estimated effects of the need variables and, although they pass some basic tests for vertical equity, highlighted the differences across diseases and types of health care. In considering the effects of non-need variables we found some evidence that may suggest omitted variable bias even with a particularly rich dataset on morbidity.

The potential for such bias forces us to make some assumptions about the probable correlations between unobserved morbidity and the non-need variables.

References

Abasolo, I., R. Manning and A. Jones (2001), 'Equity in utilization of and access to public-sector GPs in Spain', *Applied Economics*, **33**, 349–64.

Carr-Hill, R., T.A. Sheldon, P.C. Smith, S. Martin, S. Peacock and G. Hardman (1994), 'Allocating resources to health authorities: development of methods for small area analysis of use of inpatient services', *British Medical Journal*, **309**, 1046–49.

Gravelle, H., M. Sutton, S. Morris, F. Windmeijer, A. Leyland, C. Dibben and M. Muirhead (2003), 'A model of supply and demand influences on the use of health care: implications for deriving a "needs-based" capitation formula', *Health Economics*, **12**, 985–1004.

Mooney, G., J. Hall, C. Donaldson and K. Gerrard (1991), 'Utilisation as a measure of equity: weighing heat', *Journal of Health Economics*, **10**, 475–80.

Morris, S., M. Sutton and H. Gravelle (2005), 'Inequity and inequality in the use of health care in England: an empirical investigation', *Social Science and Medicine*, **60**, 1251–66.

Sutton, M. (2002), 'Vertical and horizontal aspects of socio-economic inequity in general practitioner contacts in Scotland', *Health Economics*, **11**, 537–49.

van Doorslaer, E., X. Koolman and A.M. Jones (2004), 'Explaining income-related inequalities in doctor utilisation in Europe', *Health Economics*, **13**, 629–47.

van Doorslaer, E., C. Masseria and the OECD Health Equity Research Group Members (2004), 'Income-related inequality in the use of medical care in 21 OECD countries', OECD Health Working Papers 14, DELSA/ELSA/WD/HEA(2004)5.

Wagstaff, A. and E. van Doorslaer (2000), 'Equity in health care finance and delivery', in Anthony Culyer and Joseph Newhouse (eds), *Handbook of Health Economics*, vol. 1, Amsterdam: Elsevier.

Williams, A. (1997), 'The rationing debate: rationing health care by age: the case for', *British Medical Journal*, **314**, 820–24.

Williams, A. and R. Cookson (2000), 'Equity in health', in Anthony Culyer and Joseph Newhouse (eds), *Handbook of Health Economics*, vol. 1, Amsterdam: Elsevier.

19 Equity in health and health care systems in Asia
Ravindra Rannan-Eliya and Aparnaa Somanathan

1. Introduction
This chapter reviews the empirical research on equity in health systems in Asia, much of which has been informed and motivated by earlier work in Europe. The emphasis is on the findings for developing countries of Asia. The results for the high-income Asian economies, such as Japan, Hong Kong, Korea and Taiwan, typically resemble those for European countries, but it is in developing Asia that significant contrasts with the developed country literature emerge.

Definitions of equity
As a concept, equity has multiple meanings – for few of which there is universal agreement – and it can be applied to a variety of measures or objects of interest. The reader is referred to the comprehensive discussion by Wagstaff and van Doorslaer (2000) of the concept of equity in health economics. This chapter will generally follow their treatment of equity, and confine itself to consideration of the following types of equity in Asian health systems: (i) equity in health status, (ii) equity in financing of health services, (iii) equity in the delivery of health services, and (iv) equity in terms of risk protection.

Development of empirical analysis of equity in Asian health systems
Systematic empirical work on equity in health systems in Asia does not have as extensive a history as in Europe or the OECD generally. Historical evidence of socioeconomic and sub-national differentials in health status, as proxied by mortality, exists for several countries with good mortality data from the early part of the twentieth century, such as Japan, Sri Lanka and Malaysia (Mosk and Johansson, 1986; Meegama, 1986). However, empirical analysis of equity in health systems commenced only in the 1970s, with several pioneering and independent studies of benefit incidence of government health spending in countries, such as Malaysia and Sri Lanka (Meerman, 1979; Alailima and Mohideen, 1983), and with other studies of socioeconomic and geographical inequalities in health status and health care utilization in Japan (Hasegawa, 2001). Since the early 1990s, there has been a substantial expansion in the empirical work in countries at all income levels, and in all three areas of equity in financing, delivery and health status.

In the area of equity in health status, outside the high-income economies of Japan, Korea, Taiwan and Hong Kong SAR, researchers have made the greatest progress in revealing differentials in child mortality (Gwatkin et al., 2000; Gwatkin, 2001). A large number of studies have examined the incidence of public health spending in most countries, and an emerging interest in the literature since 2000 has been a concern with equity in financing. This latter concern has not only been with progressivity of financing, but also with the impact on household welfare of catastrophic health expenses. A recent feature of this literature has been a comparative perspective, with researchers collaborating on multi-country regional studies, which is best exemplified by the Equitap study (www.equitap.org), an EU-sponsored collaboration involving 17 research groups in Asia and Europe.

What makes the emergence of this regional literature so illuminating and distinctive from the pioneering comparative work in Europe is the wide diversity in health care systems and levels of development found in Asia, and the continuing transformation of many national health systems. This provides a potentially rich evidence base for examining which attributes of systems ultimately matter for health equity, as well as opportunity to examine the impact of major system changes on overall equity. This has been exploited in recent years, by several authors in China, Korea, Thailand and Taiwan, who have examined the impact of major financing changes on overall equity (Liu et al., 1999; Liu et al., 2002; Lu, forthcoming).

2.   Empirical evidence

Inequalities in health status
Empirical assessment of income-related inequalities in health status in low- and middle-income Asia has not been as extensive as in Europe, largely because of the lack of appropriate data, such as vital registration systems that are reliable and comprehensive (and encode proxies for socioeconomic status) outside the advanced Asian economies, and some unusual demographic surveillance sites, such as Matlab in Bangladesh (Bhuiya et al., 2001). In addition, the other potential data source for assessing health inequalities – population surveys – presents particular problems in the poorer Asian countries. Few of these surveys have collected objective health indicators in tandem with income measures, and most use subjective health indicators based on self-reporting to simple questions (as opposed to more systematic instruments, such as the SF-36). This approach is particularly problematic, since in many of the poorer countries, richer individuals typically report greater levels of sickness than the poor, which is neither intuitively reasonable nor consistent with other objective evidence. For illustrations of this from Bangladesh, Nepal and Sri Lanka see Institute of Policy Studies (2003). In India, there is an inverse relationship between objective indicators of state-level mortality and self-reported sickness rates, as noted by Sen (2002). Recognition of this problem by the WHO has led to an approach that uses reporting on vignettes to anchor reported own health (Tandon et al., 2001), although it should be noted that such methods are yet to be universally accepted, and are difficult to apply to most existing datasets.

In the absence of systematic data on health status inequalities in the overall population, the major empirical advance in the past five years has arisen from the development of methods, based on principle component analysis, to formulate asset indices as proxies for income level in surveys lacking such direct measures (Filmer and Pritchett, 2001). These methods have enabled researchers to exploit the widely available Demographic and Health Surveys (DHS). This has contributed greatly to the knowledge on differentials in child and maternal health in most low-and middle-income Asian countries with DHS data (Gwatkin, 2000; Gwatkin et al., 2000). The evidence for differentials in infant and child mortality rates from DHS are summarized in Table 19.1. Sharp income gradients exist for both measures of health status, with differentials greatest in countries where the

Table 19.1   Infant and child mortality rates in the Asian region

	Quintiles					Concentration index
	First	Second	Third	Fourth	Fifth	
Infant mortality rates						
Bangladesh (1996/97)	96	99	97	89	57	−0.066
India (1992/93)	109	106	90	66	44	−0.149
Indonesia (1997)	78	57	51	39	23	−0.195
Nepal (1996)	96	107	104	85	64	−0.060
Pakistan (1990/91)	89	109	109	96	63	−0.051
Philippines (1998)	49	39	34	25	21	−0.156
Sri Lanka (2000)	26	23	16	13	17	−0.126
Vietnam (1997)	43	43	35	27	17	−0.143
Under-five mortality rates						
Bangladesh (1996/97)	141	147	135	122	76	−0.084
India (1992/93)	155	153	120	87	54	−0.169
Indonesia (1997)	109	77	70	52	29	−0.210
Nepal (1996)	156	164	155	118	83	−0.096
Pakistan (1990/91)	125	147	135	115	74	−0.083
Philippines (1998)	80	61	50	33	29	−0.191
Sri Lanka (2000)	33	24	16	13	19	−0.153
Vietnam (1997)	63	52	42	38	23	−0.159

Source: Gwatkin et al. (2000), except for Sri Lanka from authors' own estimates.

mortality rates are highest. However, it should be noted that some significant data gaps remain, principally in China, Thailand and Malaysia.

Equity in health care utilization
The lack of data on reliable measures of health status in much of Asia has impeded assessment of horizontal equity in health care utilization. Analysis of whether equal treatment for equal need (ETEN) is achieved requires information on the individual's health status with which to standardize his or her utilization of services (Wagstaff and Van Doorslaer, 1991). As a result, most empirical work to date on equity in health care use in the region has not been standardized with respect to need, outside of Japan, Korea, Taiwan and Hong Kong. In the latter territories, empirical studies reveal patterns of health care use similar to that reported from most European nations: pro-poor gradients in overall medical care use, but a flat or pro-rich gradient when standardized for need (Yang and Kwon, forthcoming; Lu, forthcoming; Leung and Tin, forthcoming).

With the caveat that lack of standardization of use according to need is a major limitation, almost all of the empirical work to date has found evidence of significant pro-rich differentials in receipt of medical treatment in most of low- and middle-income Asia, particularly in countries where out-of-pocket payments are significant (Data International, 1998; Gao et al., 2002; Gao et al., 2001; Hotchkiss et al., 1998). Empirical studies have only revealed two consistent exceptions, where the income gradient is flat

Table 19.2   Concentration indices for utilization of in-patient and out-patient services in the Asian region

	Hospital in-patient care	Hospital out-patient care	Ambulatory out-patient care
Bangladesh (1999/2000)	0.336	0.064	−0.021
China (Gansu province) (2003)	0.296	0.043	NA
Hong Kong (2002)	−0.381	−0.323	0.009
Indonesia (2001)	0.424	0.341	−0.017
India (1995/96)	0.361	0.150	0.118
South Korea (1998)	−0.218	NA	−0.098
Nepal (1995/96)	−0.010	−0.010	0.010
Sri Lanka (1996/97)	0.010	−0.041	0.153
Thailand (2002)	0.222	0.083	−0.001
Taiwan (2001)	−0.117	−0.018	−0.027

Notes:
(a) Includes public and private sector services
(b) Unstandardized with respect to need

Source: Equitap Study results (forthcoming)

or reversed, namely Malaysia and Sri Lanka (Meerman, 1979; Institute of Policy Studies, 2003)

In Europe, an important finding has been of differences in the patterns of use of general practitioners and hospital specialists (Wagstaff and van Doorslaer, 2000). However, such differentials are of little interest in most of Asia, where general practitioners generally don't play the gate-keeping role they do in some European health systems. What has been of more interest in developing Asia has been examining differentials in use between public and private providers, because in the absence of social insurance in most countries, direct public provision of services is the mechanism by which public financing typically is delivered. Numerous country studies have examined choice of provider by income level in China (Gao et al., 2002; Gao et al., 2001) and elsewhere in Asia.

The most recent results from the Equitap Study (Somanathan and Rannan-Eliya, 2005) and from analysis of DHS data by Gwatkin et al. (2000) are summarized in Tables 19.2 and 19.3. The distribution of use of public and private hospital in-patient care services is highly pro-rich in most of Asia, with the richest one-fifth of the population accounting for 30–40 per cent of all services. The only exceptions are Sri Lanka, Hong Kong and Malaysia (not shown) where the poor have proportionately greater access to government hospital services. These patterns are reflected in Gwatkin et al.'s findings that the use of hospital services for child delivery is heavily concentrated among high-income groups in most low- and middle-income countries, with the exception of Sri Lanka and some states in India. Out-patient care use, particularly when publicly funded and provided, on the other hand is found to be less regressive than in-patient care in much of Asia, although not always pro-poor. Utilization of public sector ambulatory care services is typically the most progressive in all settings.

Table 19.3   Concentration indices for utilization of maternal and child health services in the Asian region

	Medically assisted deliveries	Delivery in a public facility	Sought medical treatment if ill	Seen in a public facility among those medically treated
Bangladesh (1996/97)	0.534	0.476	0.140	0.131
India (1992/93)	0.351	0.321	0.057	−0.009
Indonesia (1997)	0.262	0.345	0.153	−0.043
Nepal (1996)	0.449	0.496	0.084	0.104
Pakistan (1990/91)	0.488	0.521	0.079	0.015
Philippines (1998)	0.265	0.244	0.087	−0.148
Vietnam (1997)	0.129	0.190	0.068	0.048

Source: Gwatkin et al. (2000)

Gwatkin et al.'s work indicates that a fairly progressive distribution of public sector health care services in countries like Sri Lanka, the Philippines and Vietnam is associated with a more progressive distribution in the likelihood of any medical care being sought for child delivery, Acute Respiratory Infections (ARIs), diarrhoea and so on. This suggests that in most resource-constrained countries, achieving a pro-poor distribution of publicly-funded services is key to achieving a progressive distribution of all medical services overall, which justifies the concentration by researchers on the distribution of public services.

Benefit incidence analysis
Benefit incidence analysis examines the extent to which government spending for health reaches the poor. There is a well-established tradition of such work in developing Asia, reflecting the predominance of general revenue funding as a mechanism for financing health care in the public sector, starting with Meerman's (1979) study of government social spending in Malaysia, and a similar study in Sri Lanka by Alailima and Mohideen (1983). Other comprehensive national studies have been conducted in the past decade in several countries, including Bangladesh and Sri Lanka (Institute of Policy Studies, 2003), Indonesia (Lanjouw et al., 2001), Thailand, Kyrgyz Republic (Makinen et al., 2000) and Hong Kong (Rannan-Eliya and Somanathan, 1999). The study by Mahal et al. (2001) of most Indian states is of particular note, in that it shows that the variation between states in India is as great as within Asia, with the distribution of spending between pro-poor in some states, and pro-rich in others. Far fewer benefit incidence studies are reported from social insurance-dominated countries, largely because the incidence of government tax spending is harder to interpret in them.

More recently, the Equitap Study has provided comparative benefit incidence results for eight Asian countries, which are summarized in Figures 19.1 and 19.2 (O'Donnell et al., 2003). In general, these results largely reflect the pattern of public sector utilization in countries, and confirm findings from earlier studies of pro-rich inequalities in most countries. In Hong Kong and Sri Lanka, where the distribution of public sector in-patient care is progressive, the distribution of public subsidies for in-patient care is pro-poor.

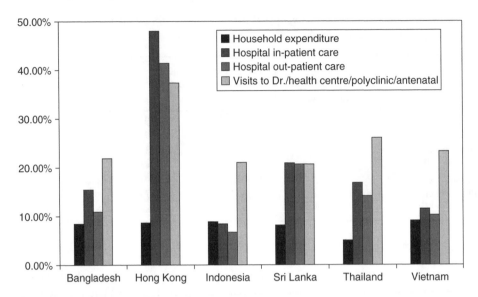

Source: Equitap Study results (forthcoming).

Figure 19.1   Poorest quintiles' shares of public health subsidy by category of care

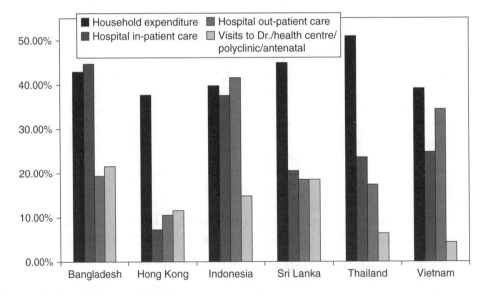

Source: Equitap Study results (forthcoming).

Figure 19.2   Richest quintiles' shares of public health subsidy by category of care

In Indonesia where the use of government health care services is concentrated among the rich, the distribution of public sector health subsidies is regressive. It is interesting to note that Hong Kong, Malaysia and Sri Lanka, which are found to have most progressive distribution of public health subsidies, are unusual within Asia as being the three countries that are most committed to the practice of providing health services free on a universal basis, without explicit targeting of the poor. Their positive experience may be linked to their commitment to universality, and provides some justification for their reliance on indirect means to voluntarily shift richer patients to the private sector through the use of consumer quality differentials.

Vertical equity and progressivity in health care financing
Empirical measurement of the progressivity of health care financing mechanisms in Asia has only received significant attention in the past decade. The existence of multiple financing mechanisms, the substantive role of direct payments in most low- and middle-income countries, and lack of accurate data on the share of financing of each mechanism render the task of assessing the overall progressivity of Asian health care systems more challenging than in Europe. In Europe and most OECD countries, more than 80 per cent of financing is either from public sources or organized private sources, for which administrative data are readily available. Direct payments typically account for less than 10 per cent of total funding, in contrast to much of Asia where it ranges from 20–80 per cent of total funding. Since there is considerable uncertainty over the actual share of direct payments in total financing in many countries (for example, estimates of private, mostly household, expenditure in India range from 2 per cent to 4 per cent of GDP), estimates of the overall progressivity of financing systems are highly susceptible to the assumptions made about the relative shares of each source.

The Equitap study attempted to deal with this in its comparative analysis by using wherever possible national health accounts-type data to fix the relative shares. Its estimates of the progressivity indices for 13 countries in Asia are summarized in Table 19.4 (O'Donnell et al., 2004). In high-income Japan, Korea and Taiwan, where health care is primarily financed through social insurance, the rich pay more in absolute terms but less as a proportion of incomes. On the other hand, in Hong Kong where public funding is from general revenue taxation, overall system financing is progressive. This result confirms earlier findings in Europe about the greater progressivity of general revenue financing relative to social insurance. Direct, and to a lesser extent, indirect taxes tend to be strongly progressive compared to social insurance contributions which are levied as a fixed proportion of earnings.

The findings from Europe that out-of-pocket or direct payments represent a regressive financing method hold true only for high-income economies in Asia. In contrast, in low- and middle-income countries in Asia, direct payments absorb a proportionately larger share of rich households' resources. In low-income settings where health insurance coverage is not universal, better-off households pay out-of-pocket for more or better health care, while the poor simply forgo care or seek care in the public sector. So in low- and middle-income Asia, the distribution of direct payments is typically progressive, although to the extent that it reflects greater of use of services and greater access to such services by the rich, it does not imply an equitable outcome. In fact, in localities where access

Table 19.4   Kakwani progressivity indices: country and source

	Direct taxes	Indirect taxes	Social insurance	Private insurance	Direct payments	Total financing
Bangladesh (1999/2000)	0.552	0.111	NA	NA	0.219	0.214
China (2000)	0.152	0.040	0.235	NA	−0.017	0.040
Hong Kong (1999/2000)	0.386	0.119	NA	0.040	0.011	0.166
Indonesia (2001)	0.196	0.074	0.306	(a)	0.176	0.174
Japan (1998)	0.095	−0.223	−0.041	(b)	−0.269	−0.069
South Korea (2000)	0.268	0.038	−0.163	NA	0.012	−0.024
Kyrgyz Republic (2000)	0.074	−0.096	−0.034	NA	0.264	0.125
Nepal (1995/96)	0.144	0.114	NA	NA	0.053	0.063
Philippines (1999)	0.381	0.002	0.205	0.120	0.139	0.163
Punjab, India (1999/2000)	NA	0.058	NA	(a)	0.046	0.049
Sri Lanka (1996/97)	0.569	−0.010	NA	(a)	0.069	0.085
Taiwan (2000)	0.244	0.040	−0.075	0.205	−0.078	−0.029
Thailand (2000)	0.510	0.182	0.180	0.004	0.091	0.197

Notes:
(a) Allocated as direct out-of-pocket payments
(b) No data

Source: Equitap Study results (forthcoming).

barriers are minimal, such as urban Thailand (Pannarunnothai and Mills, 1997), studies have reported a regressive pattern of payments.

Catastrophic and poverty impact of health care expenditures
The failure of health systems in developing countries, and in Asia particularly, to protect individuals against the catastrophic economic impacts of illness has received increasing attention in the policy and research literature in the past decade (Pradhan and Prescott, 2002; Xu et al., 2003). However, as noted by Rannan-Eliya and de Mel (1997), this issue was identified, and impacted actual policy in Sri Lanka as early as the late-1930s. This has been driven by the increasing evidence from countries such as China (Yuan and Wang, 1998), Vietnam (Wagstaff and van Doorslaer, 2001) and Bangladesh, that inadequate risk protection by health systems is often a major cause of impoverishment, and was reinforced by the economic crises in the late-1990s, which exacerbated existing deficiencies in health systems, such as Indonesia's (Pradhan and Prescott, 2002). The findings of the Equitap study (van Doorslaer et al., 2005) represent the first major attempt to generate comparative evidence on the catastrophic and poverty impact of direct payments for a large number of Asian countries. These reveal considerable differences between countries, even at the same income level. More importantly, they show a strong positive association between direct payments share in total finance and the risk of financial catastrophe (van Doorslaer et al., 2005; Wagstaff and van Doorslaer, forthcoming), although the correlation is weaker for total consumption than for non-food consumption (Figure 19.3). This points to the critical importance of increasing public financing in many countries to reduce reliance on direct payments.

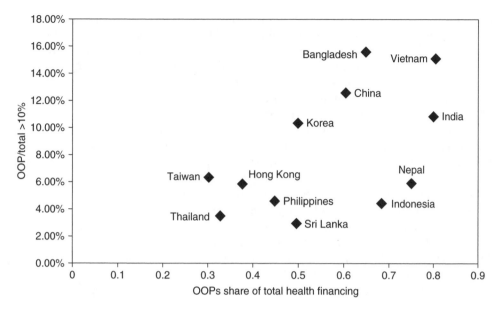

Source: Equitap Study results (forthcoming).

Figure 19.3 *Share of households with out of pocket expenses (OOPs) share of total household expenditures > 10 per cent and OOPs share of total health financing*

Interestingly, high levels of direct payments do not necessarily translate into high catastrophic impact for the poor. When defined as a proportion of total expenditures in a given time period, both the incidence and intensity of catastrophic impact are concentrated empirically among the better-off households in almost all countries examined. This finding must be qualified by noting that high expenditure flows for the wealthy may not be as catastrophic for them, given that such households typically have greater access to savings and other mechanisms for smoothing consumption, and their decision to make payments as opposed to using free public care is typically by choice. However, when catastrophe is defined as a share of non-food expenditures, financial catastrophe is no longer concentrated among better-off households. As food shares decline at higher levels of overall consumption, direct payments are a heavier burden on lower income households' non-food consumption. The risk of health care expenditures driving households below the poverty level is significant in countries such as Bangladesh, Nepal and to a lesser extent China and Vietnam, where a large proportion of households have living standards close to subsistence level.

Similarities and differences to European work
Much of the current established knowledge on the determinants of health systems equity is derived from the extensive work conducted by research collaborations in Europe in the past two decades (Wagstaff and van Doorslaer, 2000). The recent empirical work in Asia, in countries with a far greater diversity of income levels, has validated the broad

conclusions of this work with respect to the relative benefit of taxation and social insurance for progressivity of financing (Table 19.4). In Asia, as in Europe, health care financing in the social insurance countries (Japan, Korea, Taiwan) is regressive, whilst in the predominantly tax-financed countries (Thailand, Hong Kong, Kyrgyzstan, Sri Lanka), it is typically proportional or mildly progressive. In Asia, direct taxation is generally progressive; however, unlike in Europe, in the middle- and low-income economies of Asia indirect taxation is typically progressive also.

The major difference between Asia and Europe lies in the impact of private financing on progressivity. In middle- and low-income Asia, direct payments are found to be progressive, and the privately-financed systems in Asia (Nepal, India, Indonesia) are not found to be regressive, and in fact are mildly progressive. This contrast is explained by a distinct difference between European and most Asian systems (exceptions are Japan, Korea, Taiwan). In most of developing Asia, health care provision is generally by separately-funded and uncoordinated public and private sectors, with most of the population entitled in theory to subsidized public care, but also entitled to opt for private services. Most direct payments are associated with use of private services, and use of these is voluntary. The wealthier can better afford higher quality private care, and choose to pay for it or for higher volumes of service, thus giving direct payments a mostly progressive profile.

3.   A typology of health systems according to financing and delivery/equity performance

The diversity of findings for equity in Asian health systems should not surprise. The region contains the widest diversity of types of economic and social systems, and levels of economic development. If anything, the differences with Europe, and the variations within Asia, suggest that it is Europe that is the global exception in its relative homogeneity. However, within this diversity, it is possible now to begin to identify a typology based on distinct national clusters of health system organization and performance with respect to equity.

Social insurance systems with effective universal access

In these countries (Japan, Korea, Taiwan, Mongolia, Kyrgyz), public sources of financing account for half or more of the total, virtually all citizens are covered by a national social insurance system, access to services is effectively universal, and major variations in equity in financing and delivery are mostly explained by differences in insurance tax schedules and levels of co-payments.

Predominant tax systems with effective universal access

In these countries (Malaysia, Sri Lanka, Hong Kong, Thailand), public sources of financing account for half or more of the total, virtually all citizens are eligible to use subsidized public services, actual access to services is effectively universal, and relative rates of use of medical services are high. In general, variations in equity of financing and delivery are mostly explained by specific details of tax schedules, and the extent to which wealthier individuals opt out of public provision to obtain additional levels of care from private provision. In practice, public in-patient services are relatively equally and preferentially utilized by all income levels, except the top decile, whilst public out-patient service use shows a negative income gradient, with private use increasing conversely. In these countries, government health spending is pro-poor in its incidence, in a pattern which is consistent with the optimizing implications of the theoretical model of public financing of public goods distribution suggested by Besley and Coate (1991).

Mixed systems involving tax and direct payments, but ineffective universal access
In these countries (Bangladesh, Indonesia, Nepal, most states in India), direct payments account for more than half of total financing, and although all citizens are nominally eligible to use subsidized public services, actual access to services is not universal. This lack of effective and equitable access to public services is driven by a number of factors, including geographical distance from too few fixed facilities, high levels of official and unofficial user charges, and low levels of health awareness and understanding of the benefits of professional medical treatment. Consequently, although financing may be progressive, health care utilization is pro-rich, and government health spending is not pro-poor, particularly in the case of in-patient services. Unofficial user charges in public sector facilities in these countries are a pervasive problem, and a disincentive for use of public facilities by the poor. In most of these cases, the high prevalence of such informal charging reflects not only inadequate public budgets, but also historical traditions of legitimized rent-seeking by public officials (Killingsworth and Thomas, 2003; Ensor and Thompson, Chapter 15 in this Companion).

Transition economies
The former socialist economies in Asia (China, Vietnam, central Asian republics), excepting Mongolia, represent a special case. They generally had achieved high levels of service access through public financing during the socialist period, but did not maintain predominant public financing during their transition to market economies. In the case of the central Asian republics, the gap in public funding was replaced by a mix of official and unofficial fees in public facilities, and in China and Vietnam by predominant reliance on official fees in public facilities. In these countries, particularly in rural areas of China and Vietnam, financial barriers to medical care for the poor can be substantial, and significant inequities in health care use and health care outcomes have emerged in the past two decades. In China, where rural hospitals are mostly funded from user charges, this has resulted in a high level of non-use of medical services by the poor sick, and high levels of catastrophic impoverishment as a result of medical treatment. Mongolia is a notable exception in that it shifted to a predominantly general-revenue funded social insurance system in the mid-1990s, which appears to have been effective in maintaining equity in access and also protecting its rural population from catastrophic impoverishment as a result of sickness.

4.   Questions and future agenda
The past decade has seen considerable advances in the empirical work on equity in Asian health systems, particularly of a comparative nature in the past five years. We now have a reasonably comprehensive profile of equity in financing and delivery in most major Asian countries, although detailed analyses are still needed in many states and provinces of India and China, the two countries with large subnational variations. Assessment of health care status differentials has been largely limited to Japan, and to child mortality

differences in low- and middle-income Asia. Clearly, extending this work to look at inequity in adult morbidity and mortality is needed, but will require significant method-ological and data developments. However, it could be argued that this ought not to be a priority for the immediate future, since we already know that inequalities in health out-comes are likely to exist in the adult population, accompanying the known inequalities in health care use, and better understanding the latter may be more useful.

For most of low- and middle-income Asia, use of medical services is either pro-rich or only approximately equal by income level. So whilst the issue of equity of use in relation to need is important to further improve equity in countries such as Japan, Korea, Taiwan and Hong Kong, it is not of critical importance in the others at the current time.

The issue that is most pronounced in the region is the failure of many health systems to protect the poor against financial catastrophe following illness. This does not appear to be the simple consequence of low incomes, since there are large variations in national performance at the same income level, and some low-income countries are able to protect their populations. Moreover, there are clear differences between countries in the extent to which subsidized public services reach the poor, and this is the main correlate of overall equity in access to services. The findings to date point to the importance of system factors in determining overall outcomes, but also point to the need to better under-stand the institutional particularities which explain why some countries do well and others do not.

References

Alailima, Patricia J. and Faiz Mohideen (1983), 'Health sector commodity requirements and expenditure flows', Unpublished report, Colombo, Sri Lanka: National Planning Department.

Besley, Timothy and Stephen Coate (1991), 'Public provision of private goods and the redistribution of income', *American Economic Review,* **81**(4), 979–84.

Bhuiya, Abbas, Mushtaque Chowdhury, Faruque Ahmed and Alayne M. Adams (2001), 'Bangladesh: an inter-vention study of factors underlying increasing equity in child survival', in T. Evans, M. Whitehead, F. Diderichsen, A. Bhuiya and M. Wirth (eds), *Challenging Inequities in Health,* New York, NY: Oxford University Press.

Data International (1998), *Bangladesh National Health Accounts 1996/97,* Dhaka, Bangladesh: Health Economics Unit, Ministry of Health and Family Welfare.

Filmer, Deon and Lant Pritchett (2001), 'Estimating wealth effects without income data or expenditure data – or tears: Educational enrollment in India', *Demography,* **38**(1), 115–32.

Gao, Jun, Shenglan Tang, Rachel Tolhurst and Keqing Rao (2001), 'Changing access to health services in urban China: implications for equity', *Health Policy and Planning,* **16**(3), 302–12.

Gao, Jun, Juncheng Qian, Shenglan Tang, Bo Eriksson and Erik Blas (2002), 'Health equity in transition from planned to market economy in China', *Health Policy and Planning,* 17 (Supplement 1), 20–9.

Gwatkin, Davidson R. (2000), 'Health inequalities and the health of the poor: What do we know?', *Bulletin of the World Health Organization,* **78**, 3–17.

Gwatkin, Davidson R., Shea Rutstein, Kiersten Johnson, Rohini Pande and Adam Wagstaff (2000), *Socio-eco-nomic Differences in Health, Nutrition, and Population,* Washington, DC, USA: World Bank, HPN/Poverty Thematic Group.

Hasegawa, Toshiko (2001), 'Japan: historical and current dimensions of health and health equity', in T. Evans, M. Whitehead, F. Diderichsen, A. Bhuiya and M. Wirth (eds), *Challenging Inequities in Health,* New York, NY: Oxford University Press.

Hotchkiss, David R., Jeffrey J. Rous, Keshav Karmacharya and Prem Sangraula (1998), 'Household health expenditures in Nepal: implications for health care financing reform', *Health Policy and Planning,* **13**(4), 371–83.

Institute of Policy Studies, Sri Lanka (2003), 'Equity in financing and delivery of health services in Bangladesh, Nepal, and Sri Lanka', in A.S. Yazbeck and D.H. Peters (eds), *Health Policy Research in Asia: Guiding Reforms and Building Capacity,* Washington, DC, USA: World Bank.

Killingsworth, James R. and Stephen Thomas (2003), 'Responding to unofficial fees through appropriate analytical frameworks', paper presented at International Health Economics Association 4th World Congress, San Francisco, USA.

Lanjouw, Peter, Menno Pradhan, Fadia Saadah, Haneen Sayed and Robert Sparrow (2001), 'Poverty, education and health in Indonesia: who benefits from public spending', *World Bank Working Paper 2739*.

Leung, Gabriel M. and Keith Y.K. Tin (forthcoming), Equal treatment for equal need in a post-colonial, advanced Chinese mixed medical economy', paper presented at International Health Economics Association World Congress, 10–13 July 2005, Barcelona, Spain.

Liu, Yuanli, William C. Hsiao and Karen Eggleston (1999), 'Equity in health and health care: the Chinese experience', *Social Science and Medicine*, **49**, 1349–56.

Liu, Gordon G., Zhongyun Zhao, Renhua Cai, Tetsuji Yamada and Tadashi Yamada (2002), 'Equity in health care access to: assessing the urban health insurance reform in China', *Social Science and Medicine*, **55**, 1779–94.

Lu, Jui-fen Rachel (forthcoming), 'Horizontal inequity in medical care utilization – further examination of the impact of Taiwan's National Health Insurance program', paper presented at International Health Economics Association Association World Congress, 10–13 July 2005, Barcelona, Spain.

Mahal, Ajay, Janmejaya Singh, Farzana Afridi, Vikram Lamba, Anil Gumber and V. Selvaraju (2001), 'Who benefits from public health spending in India', December 10, 2000, New Delhi: National Council of Applied Economic Research.

Makinen, M., H. Waters, M. Rauch, N. Almagambetova, R. Bitran, L. Gilson, D. McIntyre, S. Pannurothai, A.L. Prieto, G. Ubilla and S. Ram (2000), 'Inequalities in health care use and expenditures: empirical data from eight developing countries and countries in transition', *Bulletin of the World Health Organisation*, **78**(1), 55–65.

Meegama, A. (1986), 'The mortality transition in Sri Lanka', in *Determinants of Mortality Change and Differentials in Developing Countries: The Five-Country Case Study Project*, New York, USA: United Nations.

Meerman, Jacob (1979), *Public Expenditure in Malaysia: Who Benefits and Why*, New York, USA: Oxford University Press.

Mosk, Carl and S. Ryan Johansson (1986), 'Income and mortality: evidence from modern Japan', *Population and Development Review*, **12**(3), 415–40.

O'Donnell, Owen, Aparnaa Somanathan, Eddy van Doorslaer, Ravi P. Rannan-Eliya, Piya Hanvoravongchai, Mohammed Nazmul Huq, Gabriel M. Leung, Keith Tin and Chitpranee Visasvid (2003), 'The distribution of benefits from public health care in some Asian countries', Equitap Working Paper Number 3, Colombo, Sri Lanka.

O'Donnell, Owen, Eddy van Doorslaer, Ravi P. Rannan-Eliya, Aparnaa Somanathan, Shiva Raj Adhikari, Baktygul Akkazieva, Deni Harbianto, Shamsia Ibragimova, Charu C. Garg, Piya Hanvoravongchai, Alejandro N. Herrin, Mohammed N. Huq, Anup Karan, Soon-man Kwon, Gabriel M. Leung, Jui-fen Rachel Lu, Yasushi Ohkusa, Badri Pande, Rachel Racelis, Keith Tin, Laksono Trisnantoro, Chitpranee Vasavid, Quan Wan, Bong-Min Yang and Yuxin Zhao (2004), 'Who pays for health care in Asia?', Equitap Working Paper Number 1, July, Colombo, Sri Lanka: Equitap Project.

Pannarunnothai, Supasit and Anne Mills (1997), 'The poor pay more: health relative inequality in Thailand', *Social Science and Medicine*, **44**(12), 1781–90.

Pradhan, Menno and Nicholas Prescott (2002), 'Social risk management options for medical care in Indonesia', *Health Economics*, **11**, 431–46.

Rannan-Eliya, Ravi P. and Nishan de Mel (1997), *Resource Mobilization for the Health Sector in Sri Lanka*, Data for Decision Making Publication, Boston, MA, USA: Harvard School of Public Health.

Rannan-Eliya, Ravi P. and Aparnaa Somanathan (1999), 'Estimates of domestic health expenditures 1989/90 to 1996/97', Special Report No. 1 (Harvard Health Care Financing Study Report), Hong Kong SAR: Health and Welfare Bureau.

Sen, Amartya (2002), 'Health: perception versus observation', *British Medical Journal*, **324**(7342), 860–1.

Somanathan, Aparnaa and Ravi P. Rannan-Eliya (2005), 'Who uses health care in Asia?', Equitap Working Paper Number 3, Colombo, Sri Lanka: Equitap Project.

Tandon, Ajay, Christopher Murray and J.A. Salomon (2001), 'Statistical methods for enhancing cross-population comparability', GPE Discussion Paper Series, Geneva, Switzerland: World Health Organization.

van Doorslaer, Eddy, Owen O'Donnell, Aparnaa Somanathan, Ravi P. Rannan-Eliya, Charu C. Garg, Piya Hanvoravongchai, Alejandro N. Herrin, Mohammed Nazmul Huq, Gabriel M. Leung, Jui-fen Rachel Lu, Badri Pande, Rachel Racelis, Sihai Tao, Keith Tin, Chitpranee Visasvid, Bong-Min Yang and Yuxin Zhao (2005), 'Paying for health care in Asia: Catastrophic and poverty impact', Equitap Working Paper Number 2, Colombo, Sri Lanka: Equitap Project.

Wagstaff, Adam and Eddy Van Doorslaer (1991), 'On the measurement of horizontal inequity in the delivery of health care', *Journal of Health Economics*, **10**(2), 169–205.

Wagstaff, Adam and Eddy van Doorslaer (2000), 'Equity in health care finance and delivery', in A.J. Culyer and J.P. Newhouse (eds), *Handbook of Health Economics*, Amsterdam, Netherlands: Elsevier Science BV.

Wagstaff, Adam and Eddy van Doorslaer (2001), 'Paying for health care quantifying fairness, catastrophe, and impoverishment, with applications to Vietnam, 1993–1998', Working Paper Series Number 2715, Washington, DC, USA: World Bank.

Wagstaff, Adam and Eddy van Doorslaer (forthcoming), 'Catastrophe and impoverishment in paying for health care: with applications to Vietnam 1993–1998', *Health Economics*.

Xu, Ke, D.B. Evans, Kei Kawabata, R. Zeramdini, Jan Klavus and Christopher J.L. Murray (2003), 'Household catastrophic health expenditure: a multicountry analysis', *The Lancet*, **362**, 111–17.

Yang, Bong-min and Soonman Kwon (forthcoming), 'Horizontal equity in health care utilization in South Korea', paper presented at International Health Economics Association World Congress, 10–13 July 2005, Barcelona, Spain.

Yuan, C. and Z. Wang (1998), 'Treatment and financial loss of catastrophic diseases among rural farmers', *Medicine and Society,* **3**, 627–30.

PART IV

ORGANIZATION OF HEALTH CARE MARKETS

20 Hospital competition and patient choice in publicly funded health care
Richard Cookson and Diane Dawson*

1. Introduction

Public funding makes up around 70–85 per cent of total health expenditure in almost all large high-income OECD countries (Figure 20.1), and has done since the 1960s. The two exceptions are Switzerland and the USA, where the figures are 56 per cent and 44 per cent respectively.

Since the late 1990s, several tax-funded, publicly administered national health care systems in Europe – including England, Denmark, Sweden and Norway – have extended patient choice with the aim of reducing waiting times and, to a lesser extent, improving quality of care. Implicit in policy discussions about choice in all of these countries are assumptions about the nature of hospital competition. England is perhaps unusual in explicitly linking the introduction of patient choice with a desire for more competition.

The scope for effective hospital competition driven by patient choice is restricted in health care. This is due to the multiplicity of informational problems facing the patient, including uncertainty of demand and asymmetric information about both product need and product quality (Newhouse, 2002). The scope is further restricted by political constraints on the market, which are shaped by voters' special concerns about equity in health care (Enthoven, 1999). Political constraints are particularly powerful in countries with predominantly publicly funded health care systems. This was highlighted in the 1990s, when Finland, Italy, Spain, Sweden, New Zealand and the United Kingdom all tried, largely ineffectually, to introduce hospital competition driven by third party payers (Savas et al., 1998).

A different approach is health plan competition and enrollee choice, the subject of Chapter 13 by Dowd and Feldman in this Companion. However, the political constraints on competition between public insurance plans are severe. One problem is that, due to concerns for equity of access, governments are reluctant to allow differences in premiums to reflect differences in coverage or quality. In addition, evidence from the Czech Republic, Israel, the Russian Federation, the Netherlands, Switzerland and the USA suggests that health plan competition generates strong financial incentives to 'cream-skim' low risk enrollees (Chintz et al., 1998, *Economist* 2004). Most European health care systems reflect the principle of 'solidarity': a health care system is organized and managed on the basis of universal access, without risk selection, based on income-related premia or tax finance with no significant differences in the benefit package available to people (Jost et al., forthcoming; Reinhardt, 1997).

* We would like to thank Shelley Farrar, Julian Le Grand and Alan Maynard for helpful comments on an earlier draft, together with participants at the UK Health Economists' Study Group Meeting in Oxford, January 2005, and a seminar at the University of York.

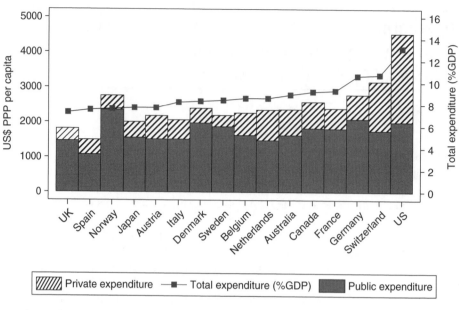

Note: [1]GDP > US$150bn and GDP per capita > US$10 000.

Source: OECD Health Data 2003, 3rd edition.

Figure 20.1   Public, private and total health expenditures in 2000 for large high-income OECD countries[1]

In this chapter we are concerned with patient choice as a policy instrument for stimulating hospital competition, not a policy goal. Patient choice is often advocated as a policy goal involving the 'customization' or 'personalization' or 'responsiveness' of health services given heterogeneity in patient preferences (Appleby et al., 2003).

2.   Economic theory of hospital competition

Definition and objectives of hospital competition

Stigler defines competition as 'a rivalry between individuals (or groups or nations) that arises whenever two or more parties strive for something that all cannot obtain' (Stigler, 1987). Our interest is in one form of competition that historically has been rare in publicly funded health care: product market competition between hospitals to attract patients and the associated public funding, under conditions where money follows the patient.

Why might introducing this form of competition help to improve health care performance? Following Vickers (1995), we can identify two general arguments:

1.   More efficient behaviour by providers. Providers facing competition have an incentive to eliminate organizational slack to maintain or increase their surplus (Leibenstein, 1966).

2.   New entry by efficient providers and exit of inefficient providers. Providers unable or unwilling to behave efficiently may fail to break even and thus exit the market (Nelson and Winter, 1982).

In addition, it is sometimes argued that competition may be a spur to innovation that yields long-run efficiency gains (Schumpeter, 1943) although this is particularly controversial in health care (Weisbrod, 1991).

Table 20.1   Attributes of the regulatory environment that may influence the nature and intensity of hospital competition

Supply-side		Demand-side			
		Less patient choice		More patient choice	
Reimbursement	Impediments to entry and exit	Less payer choice	More payer choice	Less payer choice	More payer choice
No price regulation	High	Beveridge pre-1990s	NHS 1991–97	Bismark pre-2000s	
	Low		US managed care		
Fixed price	High		Bismark post-2000s?	Scandinavia post-1990s	
	Low			NHS post-2003	

The regulatory environment

The nature of hospital competition depends crucially upon the regulatory environment. Table 20.1 sets out the main relevant attributes of the regulatory environment under four headings: (i) price regulation, (ii) supply-side impediments to entry and exit, (iii) degree of patient choice and (iv) degree of payer choice. Quality of care, defined broadly in terms of all attributes of care valued by patients, is also regulated in most countries (see Chapter 30 by Smith and Street in this Companion). Quality regulation may constrain product market competition and, if explicit incentives are awarded for comparative performance, may introduce what we might call 'league table' competition.

Price regulation pervades health care (Newhouse, 2002). Historically, publicly funded systems have reimbursed hospitals on the basis of global budgets or block contracts based largely on last year's costs adjusted for inflation. Under such conditions, product market competition is impossible as money does not follow the patient. Prior to the 1980s, retrospective reimbursement was common in the USA, whereby the insurer paid whatever bill was presented. Under those conditions, providers competed not by lowering prices but by over-investing in high-tech facilities to attract doctors who refer and admit patients – known as the 'medical arms race' (Robinson and Luft, 1985). To strengthen cost containment incentives, many publicly funded health systems – following US Medicare in the 1980s – are introducing a degree of fixed price regulation based on local versions of

Diagnosis Related Groups (DRGs). Regulation of this kind restricts price competition but allows non-price competition on quality.

Economies of scale in hospital care may give rise to a degree of local natural monopoly. In addition, supply-side impediments can arise from a variety of government actions that influence market structure and conduct. These include:

1. Public funding limits that result in aggregate capacity constraints and long waiting lists (Chalkley and Malcomson, 1998).
2. Entry and exit regulations that limit the number of providers and/or the threat of new entry ('contestability') (Baumol et al., 1982).
3. Labour and capital market regulations that limit provider ability to compete through hiring, firing and capital investment.
4. Discretionary political interventions to subsidize failing providers which result in 'soft' rather than 'hard' budget constraints (Kornai et al., 2003).
5. Weak antitrust regulation that facilitates consolidation and collusion (Gaynor and Vogt, 2000, Federal Trade Commission and Department of Justice, 2004).

Finally, it is important to distinguish between payer-driven and patient-driven competition (Dranove et al., 1993). Although payer and patient choice may co-exist, there comes a point at which there is a trade-off between the two. In particular, if the payer is to have effective choice over price – that is the ability to negotiate discounts with selected providers in return for channelling business their way, known as 'selective contracting' – then they must be able to restrict or influence patient choice.

Imperfect competition with no price regulation
Perfect competition is rarely observed in any market (Stiglitz, 1989). In some cases, however – such as hospitals in metropolitan areas of the USA – hospital competition may be tolerably well characterized by its close counterpart of monopolistic competition (Dranove and Satterthwaite, 2000). The two distinguishing assumptions of this family of models are: (1) that the provider has a small degree of market power due to product differentiation, that is, provider-level demand is elastic but not perfectly elastic, and (2) that there are sufficiently large numbers of firms to ignore competitors' strategic reactions to price and output decisions. Elastic provider-level demand may be implausible in the case of emergency services (Chalkley and Malcomson, 1998), but is compatible with the inelastic market-level demand that characterizes most health services.

In general, monopolistic competition (compared with unregulated monopoly) will tend to lower prices and improve quality. The effect on any given quality attribute will depend upon the corresponding elasticity of demand and marginal cost of production. It may also depend upon the non-monetary benefit to the provider of improving quality due to benevolence and/or long-run reputation concerns (Chalkley and Malcomson, 2000).

However, it is typically reasonable to assume that price and quality are both imperfectly observed by the health care consumer. This feature can be incorporated into the classic model of monopolistic competition to yield important insights (Dranove and Satterthwaite, 1992). First, competition can sometimes harm quality. Consumer demand may be more responsive to accurately perceived changes in price than to poorly perceived changes in quality. Second, competition can improve accurately perceived aspects of quality while harming poorly perceived dimensions.

The main drawback with monopolistic competition is the assumption of large numbers of providers. Publicly funded payers often rely upon a small number of local hospitals. In such cases, entrants and incumbents are likely to pay close attention to each other's potential strategic reactions. Classic Cournot duopoly and oligopoly theory may apply in some such cases, yielding similar outcomes to monopolistic competition. In other cases, however, dynamic oligopoly models may be required to analyse strategic behaviour (Shapiro, 1989; Joskow, 1975).

Non-price competition under fixed price regulation
Most of the literature on non-price competition under fixed price regulation relates to the US Medicare 'prospective payment system' introduced in 1980 (Joskow, 1983; Pope, 1989). Fixed price regulation is an important form of 'yardstick' competition (Shleifer, 1985). Typically the fixed price for a Diagnostic Related Group of services is based on some average of the costs or charges of all hospitals. The objective is to create incentives for monopoly providers to reduce costs (and/or increase activity) by eliminating organizational slack and monopoly pricing. It also generates three perverse incentives: (i) to over-admit patients with expected cost below the fixed price ('creaming'), (ii) to offer low quality to patients with expected cost above the fixed price ('skimping'), and (iii) to under-admit patients with expected cost above the fixed price ('dumping') (Ellis, 1998). Furthermore, if the price is set 'too low' then quality will also be too low – since once the provider has eliminated organizational slack, it can only cut costs by lowering quality.

The effects of patient choice on quality and waiting times
Payers may have better information than patients on technical aspects of quality – for example health outcomes. The patient may have better information on other aspects – for example responsiveness of nursing staff. Under these conditions, non-price competition driven by patient choice of provider may be a more effective way of improving some aspects of quality than purchaser–provider contracting.

Patient choice of provider can play a quite different role in relation to waiting times. Patient choice – like payer choice – can help to reduce waiting times, and encourage convergence in waiting time between providers, by matching referrals with spare capacity. This is because, in the absence of patient or payer choice, primary care physicians may fail to refer patients to routine providers with the lowest waiting times. This agency failure may arise if the physician bears the search and switching costs but does not reap the rewards of a lower waiting time.

In its role of stimulating non-price competition, patient choice can have exactly the opposite effect on waiting times: it can increase overall waiting times and lead to divergence between providers. The divergence problem is that top quality hospitals (like top quality restaurants) will have longer waiting times. The perverse effect on overall waiting times may arise because effort to increase activity and reduce waiting time will attract patients from other providers – the more patient choice, the more rapidly – thus pushing waiting time back up again. This may act as a perverse incentive because providers want to keep their waiting times low, at least in performance-managed publicly funded health systems (Siciliani, 2005).

Effects of competition on geographical equity of access

The current UK Prime Minister has claimed that patient-driven hospital competition will reduce inequalities of access: 'Choice mechanisms enhance equity by exerting pressure on low-quality or incompetent providers' (Tony Blair, 23 January 2003). However, quality and access may tend to diverge if the strength of competitive incentives varies geographically – for example, between metropolitan and rural areas. In near-monopoly rural areas, low-cost providers may simply pocket their surplus without improving quality, while high-cost providers may face insolvency – causing potential access problems. Effects of this kind were observed under fixed price regulation of the US airline industry in the 1970s (Joskow, 1983). A second source of divergence is that providers may face 'unavoidable' differences in the marginal costs of producing different quality attributes – that is, not attributable to inefficiency – for example heterogeneity in individual physician productivity.

3.   Evidence on hospital competition and patient choice in publicly funded systems

United States

There is clear evidence from the US that payer-driven price competition has substantially reduced prices, costs and excess capacity since the mid-1980s, following the rise of managed care (Zwanziger and Melnick, 1988; Dranove and White, 1994; Keeler et al., 1999; Dranove and Satterthwaite, 2000). A recent study of selective contracting in California from 1983–97 suggests that for-profit plans may have been somewhat more effective drivers of this price competition than non-profit plans (Zwanziger et al., 2000).

Evidence on quality of care is more limited and contradictory (Romano and Mutter, 2004; Robinson, 2000). To date, the most rigorous econometric studies are Kessler and McClellan (2000) and Gowrisankaran and Town (2003). They are based on analysis of patient-level data on costs and outcomes. They measure competition using a modified Herfindahl–Hirshman Index of concentration (Hay and Morris, 1991) and address the endogeneity of actual patient flows by estimating predicted patient flows from exogenous characteristics of hospitals and patients.

Kessler and McClellan find that, after 1991, hospital competition improved quality of care as measured by one-year mortality rates and re-admission rates following admission for acute myocardial infarction (AMI). In this respect, its findings conflict with those of other US studies suggesting that competition has a negative or negligible effect on quality (Shortell and Hughes, 1988; Volpp and Buckley, 2004; Volpp et al., 2003; Sari, 2002). Gowrisankaran and Town, using risk adjusted mortality rates for AMI and pneumonia as measures of quality, find that the impact of competition on quality differs by method of payment. Vigorous competition for (fixed price) Medicare patients was associated with higher mortality rates, while increased competition for HMO patients (negotiated contracts) was associated with reduced mortality rates.

England

The NHS 'internal market' in England from 1991–97 was an attempt to introduce hospital competition into a publicly funded health care system. Le Grand et al. (1998) is a systematic review of the evidence up to 1997. Since then, a number of studies at national level have attempted to control for selection and other biases in earlier studies (for example, Croxson et al., 2001; Dowling, 2000; Dusheiko et al., 2004; Propper et al., 2004; Propper and Soderlund, 1998; Propper et al., 1998; Propper et al., 2002).

Hospital competition was driven by two main public payers: District Health Authorities and General Practice Fundholders. The former were ineffective drivers of competition. This is usually attributed to poor information, weak incentives (for example financial savings could not be rolled over to the next financial year) and political constraints on 'destabilizing' local hospitals (Le Grand et al., 1998). Well-established effects of General Practice Fundholding include:

- Reduced hospital prices for non-emergency treatment (Propper, 1996; Propper and Soderlund, 1998)
- Reduced waiting times for non-emergency treatment (Dowling, 2000; Propper et al., 2002; Dusheiko et al., 2004)
- Reduced referral rates (Gravelle et al., 2002; Dusheiko et al., 2003)
- A one-off reduction in prescribing costs (Gosden and Torgerson, 1997).

In addition, one study found that price competition may have slightly reduced hospital quality of care as measured by 30-day mortality rates following AMI admission (Propper et al., 2004). There was no evidence that fundholding practices engaged in 'cream-skimming' of low-cost patients (Le Grand et al., 1998). Finally, there is no reliable evidence on one of the most politically sensitive aspects of the reforms: their administrative costs (Le Grand, 2002).

From 2002, the NHS in England has been introducing reforms designed (among other things) to encourage hospital competition and patient choice. There is some early evidence from a regional trial of these reforms, the London Patient Choice Project (LPCP) from 2002–4. This offered patients likely to wait more than nine months for certain elective procedures the choice of another hospital within the metropolitan area, and achieved an acceptance rate of 66 per cent (Dawson et al., 2004). Central to this high uptake was (1) the existence of alternative providers with substantially lower waiting times due to recent investment in new capacity and (2) that LPCP subsidized search and switching costs by providing information, and organizing and paying for transport. 'Exporting' hospitals did not lose money if patients accepted the offer of choice, and so were not competing with the 'importing' hospitals. The role of patient choice was thus to match demand with excess capacity, rather than to stimulate non-price competition.

Other countries
Many low- and middle-income countries have a high proportion of public funding, especially the formerly communist countries of Central and Eastern Europe and the Commonwealth of Independent States. However, competition within the publicly funded sector is not (yet) a live issue in such countries, since it would require prohibitively expensive infrastructure investment in cost accounting and quality monitoring systems.

Several high-income countries outside the US and UK have experimented with hospital competition (Ranade, 1998). However, evidence on such experiments tends to be descriptive: there is limited econometric evidence attempting to quantify the effects of competition after controlling for potential biases.

Denmark since the early 1990s and Norway and Sweden more recently have offered patients choice of any hospital in the country. Studies report little patient movement and no sign of competition (Williams and Rossiter, 2004). Two comments are common. First, patients are reluctant to travel outside their local area due to search and travel costs (Goddard and Hobden, 2003). Second, historic reimbursement regimes made it unattractive for hospitals to expand capacity and attract non-resident patients. These countries are now introducing an element of DRG pricing at the margin of historic budgets. As in England, however, there remain powerful political constraints on closing failing hospitals (Norwegian Ministry of Finance, 1999; Vrangbaek and Bech, 2004).

Brouwer et al. (2003) report on three experiments to facilitate cross-border patient movement in the border regions of the Netherlands. In spite of efforts to reduce switching costs, however, the response was low. Evidence on willingness to travel within the Netherlands to reduce waiting times also suggests a low elasticity of demand.

Most of the 'Bismark' health care systems in Europe with employer-based social insurance schemes (Austria, Belgium, France, Germany, Luxembourg and Switzerland), have long had unrestricted patient choice of provider but limited hospital competition. France and Germany – the two highest-spending of the Bismark countries – are currently trying to reduce patient choice in order to contain costs (Rodwin and Le Pen, 2004).

Finally, a small but growing literature uses discrete choice modelling based on revealed and stated preference data from various countries (for example Cyprus and Zambia) to estimate patient demand for different quality attributes in terms of time, money or distance prices (Hanson et al., forthcoming; Hanson et al., forthcoming, Burge et al. 2005). So far, this literature has tended to find that patient demand is more responsive to non-technical aspects of quality – such as interpersonal and amenity attributes – than technical aspects such as the type and intensity of clinical treatment.

4.   Political constraints on competition

Publicly funded health care takes equity of access as a primary objective. Competition between providers is only considered as a means of securing more cost-effective delivery of an equitable health care system. This means there is a trade-off between the productive efficiency that competition may produce, and equity. This trade-off is of major importance for publicly funded health care and of peripheral importance in privately funded health care. How countries manage this trade-off is complex but three issues dominate the literature:

1.   Budget constraints may be 'soft' even where competition between providers is introduced. This weakens the incentive effects of competition and possible efficiency gains.
2.   Rent-seeking behaviour and 'corporatism' may restrict the willingness and ability of governments to impose the sanctions of competition on producers of public services.
3.   Where quality is difficult to measure and services are delivered to vulnerable people, 'intrinsic' motivation of providers is important and can be crowded out by competition.

The most common form of hospital competition being introduced into publicly funded health care is prospective payment at fixed DRG prices (Langenbrunner et al., 2005). In countries where health care for the majority of the population is publicly funded, this type of yardstick competition is in its infancy and there is no evidence available on cost or equity. In order for a fixed price reimbursement regime to generate incentives to improve productive efficiency, the threat of bankruptcy must be credible. Past research on the impact of reform in publicly funded health systems suggests this is rarely the case. Whether municipalities, county councils or national governments are responsible for funding health care, there is a reluctance to allow local providers to close; indirect ways of funding deficits are found and budget constraints are perceived as soft (Norwegian Ministry of Finance, 1999; Mossialos and Le Grand, 1999).

The economic literature on 'rent-seeking' examines how producer interests use the political process to gain protection from competition (Cullis and Jones, 1998; Tirole, 2000). This public choice literature treats actors, such as the medical profession or hospital administrators, as pursuing their own self-interest in seeking protection from market forces. A different slant on the same issue has long been discussed in the politics literature under the heading of 'corporatism' (Ogus, 1994). This reflects a political tradition that producer interests must be accommodated in the shaping of public policy to the extent that they can block major policy initiatives. Consensus is required before things can change. This is particularly strong in Germany where powerful associations of doctors, hospitals and sickness funds all participate in policy-making and have prevented many pro-competition reforms being introduced. France is another country that has faced similar impediments to reform (Rodwin and Le Pen, 2004).

In stark contrast to models of rent-seeking by opportunistic professional groups is the literature on a 'public sector ethos' where it is assumed that part of the motivation of health sector worker (doctor, nurse, administrator) is the satisfaction that they are doing something socially desirable. More effort is produced than could be explained by pay and long-term career concerns alone. If so, productive efficiency could fall if competition erodes or 'crowds out' the intrinsic motivation of public service workers. That is, in Le Grand's colourful terminology, public service workers may turn from 'knights' into 'knaves' (Le Grand, 2003; Frey and Oberholzer-Gee, 1997). This may harm productive efficiency in two ways: first, increased 'shirking', and second, reduced co-operation with employees of competing organizations in contributing towards public goods such as clinical networks. The argument about crowding out of intrinsic motivation applies to all 'extrinsic' financial and non-financial motivations for improved performance – including, for example, fee-for-service versus salary payment for consultants, or for-profit versus not-for-profit ownership of providers – and does not apply exclusively to the incentives arising from competition.

5. Conclusions

Routine data on quality of care is limited and competition is difficult to measure. However, it is clear from this brief overview that:

1. Theoretical models of payer-driven price competition appear to have the predicted effects on costs, prices and perverse incentives, although most of this evidence is from the US.

2. In predominantly publicly funded systems, competition tends to be stifled by political constraints related to system-level cost control and solidarity.
3. Neither theory nor evidence give clear guidance about the effect of competition – payer or patient-driven – on different dimensions of quality or equity.

Most theoretical models of competition do not take account of important political constraints on hospital markets. Nor is there much analysis of patient-driven as opposed to payer-driven competition. Given increasing public policy focus on hospital competition and patient choice, these are clearly priorities for future research.

The current frontier for research is improving measures of quality of care and modelling the impact of competition on delivering quality. A related issue is the impact of patient choice on hospital performance under different regulatory environments. Claims are often made about the impact of patient choice on quality of care. Unfortunately, neither theory nor evidence is available to support such claims. This is an important gap in the economics literature required to inform public policy.

References
Appleby, J., A. Harrison and N. Devlin (2003), *What is the Real Cost of more Patient Choice?*, London: Kings Fund.
Baumol, W., E, Panzar and R. Willig (1982), *Contestable Markets and the Theory of Industry Structure*, New York: Harcourt Brace.
Brouwer, W., J. van Exel, B. Hermans and A. Stoop (2003), 'Should I stay or should I go? Waiting lists and cross-border care in the Netherlands', *Health Policy*, **63**(3), 289–98.
Burge, P., N. Devlin, J. Appleby, C. Rohr and J. Grant (2005), 'London Patient Choice Project Evaluation: A model of patients' choices of hospital from stated and revealed preference choice data', RAND Europe.
Chalkley, M. and J.M. Malcomson (1998), 'Contracting for health services with unmonitored quality', *Economic Journal*, **108**(449), 1093–110.
Chalkley, M. and J.M. Malcomson (2000), 'Government purchasing of health services', in A. Culyer and J.P. Newhouse (eds), *Handbook of Health Economics*, Amsterdam, New York: Elsevier, pp. 847–90.
Chintz, D., A. Preker and J. Wasem (1998), 'Balancing competition and solidarity in health care financing', in R.B. Saltman, J. Figueras and C. Sakellarides (eds), *Critical Challenges for Health Care Reform in Europe*, Buckingham and Philadelphia: Open University Press, pp. 55–77.
Croxson, B., C. Propper and A. Perkins (2001), 'Do doctors respond to financial incentives? UK family doctors and the GP fundholder scheme', *Journal of Public Economics*, **79**(2), 375–98.
Cullis, J. and P. Jones (1998), *Public Finance and Public Choice*, Oxford: Oxford University Press.
Dawson, D., R. Jacobs, S. Martin and P. Smith (2004), *Evaluation of the London Patient Choice Project: system wide impacts. Report to the Department of Health*, University of York.
Dowling, B (2000), *GPs and Purchasing in the NHS*, Aldershot: Ashgate.
Dranove, D. and M.A. Satterthwaite (1992), 'Monopolistic competition when price and quality are imperfectly observable', *Rand Journal of Economics*, **23**(4), 518–34.
Dranove, D. and M.A. Satterthwaite (2000), 'The industrial organization of health care markets', Volume 1B, in A. Culyer, and J.P. Newhouse (eds), *Handbook of Health Economics*, Amsterdam; New York and Oxford: Elsevier Science, pp. 1093–139.
Dranove, D. and W.D. White (1994), 'Recent theory and evidence on competition in hospital markets', *Journal of Economics and Management Strategy*, **3**(1), 169–209.
Dranove, D., M. Shanley and W.D. White (1993), 'Price and concentration in hospital markets – the switch from patient-driven to payer-driven competition', *Journal of Law & Economics*, **36**(1), 179–204.
Dusheiko, M., H. Gravelle, and R. Jacobs (2004), 'The effect of practice budgets on patient waiting times: allowing for selection bias', *Journal of Health Economics*, **13**, 941–58.
Dusheiko, M., H. Gravelle, R. Jacobs and P. Smith (2003), 'The effects of budget on doctor behaviour: evidence from a natural experiment', Centre for Health Economics Technical Report 26. Downloadable via http://www.york.ac.uk/inst/che/tech.htm.
The Economist, (2004), 'Survey: health care finance: new remedies', www.economist.com/displaystory.cfm?story_id=2896030, 15 July.

Ellis, R.P. (1998), 'Creaming, skimping and dumping: provider competition on the intensive and extensive margins', *Journal of Health Economics*, **17**, 537–55.

Enthoven, A. (1999), *In Pursuit of an Improving National Health Service*, London: Nuffield Trust.

Federal Trade Commission and Department of Justice (2004), *Improving Health Care: A Dose of Competition*, Washington, DC: Federal Trade Commission and Department of Justice.

Frey, B. and F. Oberholzer-Gee (1997), 'The cost of price incentives: an empirical analysis of motivation crowding out', *American Economic Review*, **87**, 746–55.

Gaynor, M. and W.B. Vogt (2000), 'Antitrust and competition in health care markets Volume', 1B, in A. Culyer, and J.P. Newhouse (eds), *Handbook of Health Economics*, Amsterdam; New York: Elsevier, pp. 1405–87.

Goddard, M. and C. Hobden (2003), *Patient Choice: a review. Report to the Department of Health*, York: Centre for Health Economics.

Gosden, T. and D. Torgerson (1997), 'The effect of fundholding on prescribing and referral costs: a review of the evidence', *Health Policy*, **40**, 103–14.

Gowrisankaran, G. and R.J. Town (2003), 'Competition, payers, and hospital quality', *Health Services Research*, **38**(6), Part I.

Gravelle, H., M. Dusheiko and M. Sutton (2002), 'The demand for elective surgery in a public system: time and money prices in the UK National Health Service', *Journal of Health Economics*, **21**(3), 423–49.

Hanson, K., W.C. Yip and W. Hsiao (forthcoming), 'The impact of quality on the demand for outpatient services in Cyprus', *Health Economics*.

Hanson, K., B. McPake, P. Nakamba and L. Archard (forthcoming), 'Preferences for hospital quality in Zambia: results from a discrete choice experiment', *Health Economics*.

Hay, D.A. and D.J. Morris (1991), *Industrial Economics and Organisation: Theory and Evidence*, Oxford: Oxford University Press.

Joskow, P. (1975), 'Firm decision-making processes and oligopoly theory', *American Economic Review*, **65**(2), 270–79.

Joskow, P. L. (1983), 'Reimbursement policy, cost containment and non-price competition', *Journal of Health Economics*, **2**(2), 167–74.

Jost, T., D. Dawson and A. den Exter (forthcoming), 'The role of competition in health care: a Western European perspective', *Journal of Health Politics, Policy and Law*.

Keeler, E. B., G. Melnick and J. Zwanziger (1999), 'The changing effects of competition on non-profit and for-profit hospital pricing behavior', *Journal of Health Economics*, **18**(1), 69–86.

Kessler, D. P. and M. B. McClellan (2000), 'Is hospital competition socially wasteful?', *Quarterly Journal of Economics*, **115**(2), 577–615.

Kornai, J., E. Maskin and G. Roland (2003), 'Understanding the soft budget constraint', *Journal of Economic Literature*, **41**(4), 1095–136.

Langenbrunner, J., E. Orosz, J. Kutzin and M. Wiley (2005), 'Purchasing and paying providers', in J. Figueras, R. Robinson and E. Jakubowski (eds), *Purchasing to Improve Health System Performance*, Maidenhead: Open University Press, pp. 236–64.

Le Grand, J. (2002), 'Further tales from the British National Health Service', *Health Affairs*, **21**(3), 116–28.

Le Grand, J. (2003), *Motivation, Agency, and Public Policy: Of Knights and Knaves, Pawns and Queens*, Oxford and New York: Oxford University Press.

Le Grand, J., N. Mays and K. Mulligan (eds) (1998), *Learning from the NHS Internal Market: a Review of the Evidence*, London: King's Fund Publishing.

Leibenstein, H. (1966), 'Allocative efficiency versus x-efficiency', *Americal Economic Review*, **56**, 392–415.

Mossialos, E. and J. Le Grand (1999), *Health Care and Cost Containment in the European Union*, Aldershot: Ashgate.

Nelson, R. and S. Winter (1982), *An Evolutionary Theory of Economic Change*, Cambridge, MA: Harvard University Press.

Newhouse, J.P. (2002), *Pricing the Priceless: A Health Care Conundrum*, Cambridge and London: Walras-Pareto Lectures, MIT Press.

Norwegian Ministry of Finance (1999), *Hospital Owners' Use of Comparative Costs Information in Determining Hospitals' Budgets*, Iceland: Norwegian Ministry of Finance.

Ogus, A.I. (1994), *Regulation: Legal Form and Economic Theory*, Oxford: Clarendon Press.

Pope, G.C. (1989), 'Hospital nonprice competition and medicare reimbursement policy', *Journal of Health Economics*, **8**(2), 147–72.

Propper, C. (1996), 'Market structure and prices: The responses of hospitals in the UK National Health Service to competition', *Journal of Public Economics*, **61**(3), 307–35.

Propper, C. and N. Soderlund (1998), 'Competition in the NHS internal market: an overview of its effects on hospital prices and costs', *Health Economics*, **7**(3), 187–97.

Propper, C., S. Burgess and K. Green (2004), 'Does competition between hospitals improve the quality of care? Hospital death rates and the NHS internal market', *Journal of Public Economics*, **88**(7–8), 1247–72.

Propper, C., B. Croxson and A. Shearer (2002), 'Waiting times for hospital admissions: the impact of GP fundholding', *Journal of Health Economics*, **21**(2), 227–52.

Propper, C., D. Wilson and N. Soderlund (1998), 'The effects of regulation and competition in the NHS internal market: the case of general practice fundholder prices', *Journal of Health Economics*, **17**(6), 645–73.

Ranade, W. (eds) (1998), *Markets and Health Care: A Comparative Analysis*, Harlow, Essex: Addison Wesley Longman.

Reinhardt, U.E. (1997), *Accountable Health Care: is it Compatible with Social Solidarity?*, London: Office of Health Economics.

Robinson, J. and H. Luft (1985), 'The impact of hospital market structure on patient volume, average length of stay and the cost of care', *Journal of Health Economics*, **4**, 333–56.

Robinson, R. (2000), 'Managed care in the United States: a dilemma for evidence-based policy?', *Health Economics*, **9**(1), 1–7.

Rodwin, V.G. and C. Le Pen (2004), 'Health care reform in France – The birth of state-led managed care', *New England Journal of Medicine*, **351**(22), 2259–62.

Romano, P.S. and R. Mutter (2004), 'The evolving science of quality measurement for hospitals: implications for studies of competition and consolidation', *International Journal of Health Care Finance and Economics*, **4**,131–57.

Sari, N. (2002), 'Do competition and managed care improve quality?', *Health Economics*, **11**(7), 571–84.

Savas, S., I. Sheiman, E. Tragekes and H. Maarse (1998), 'Contracting models and provider competition', in R.B. Saltman, J. Figueras and C. Sakellarides (eds), *Critical Challenges for Health Care Reform in Europe*, Buckingham: Oxford University Press, pp. 157–78.

Schumpeter, J.A. (1943), *Capitalism, Socialism and Democracy*, New York: Harper and Row.

Shapiro, C. (1989), 'Theories of oligopoly behavior', 1, in R.L. Schmalensee, and R.D. Willig (eds), *Handbook of Industrial Organization*, Elsevier, pp. 329–414.

Shleifer, A. (1985), 'A theory of yardstick competition', *Rand Journal of Economics*, **16**(3), 319–27.

Shortell, S.M. and E.F. Hughes (1988), 'The effects of regulation, competition, and ownership on mortality rates among hospital inpatients', *New England Journal of Medicine*, **318**(17), 1100–07.

Siciliani, L. (2005), 'Does more choice reduce waiting times?', *Health Economics*, **14**(1), 17–23.

Stigler, G.J. (1987), 'Competition', in J. Eatwell, M. Milgate and P. Newman (eds), *The New Palgrave: A Dictionary of Economics*, Basingstoke and Hampshire: Palgrave Macmillan, pp. 531–5.

Stiglitz, J.E. (1989), 'Imperfect information in the product market', in R.L. Schmalensee, and R.D. Willig (eds), *Handbook of Industrial Organization*, Elsevier.

Tirole, J. (2000), *Incentives and Political Economy*, Cambridge: Cambridge University Press.

Vickers, J. (1995), 'Concepts of competition', *Oxford Economic Papers*, **47**(1), 1–23.

Volpp, K.G.M. and E. Buckley (2004), 'The effect of increases in HMO penetration and changes in payer mix on in-hospital mortality and treatment patterns for acute myocardial infarction', *American Journal of Managed Care*, **10**(7), 505–12.

Volpp, K.G.M., S.V. Williams, J. Waldfogel, J.H. Silber, J.S. Schwartz and M. V. Pauly (2003), 'Market reform in New Jersey and the effect on mortality from acute myocardial infarction', *Health Services Research*, **38**(2), 515–33.

Vrangbaek, K. and M. Bech (2004), 'County level responses to the introduction of DRG rates for "extended choice" hospital patients in Denmark', *Health Policy*, **67**(1), 25–37.

Weisbrod, B.A. (1991), 'The health care quadrilemma: an essay on technological change, insurance, quality of care, and cost containment', *Journal of Economic Literature,* **29**(2), 523–52.

Williams, J. and A. Rossiter (2004), *Choice: the Evidence*, London: Social Market Foundation.

Zwanziger, J. and G.A. Melnick (1988), 'The effects of hospital competition and the Medicare PPS program on hospital cost behavior in California', *Journal of Health Economics*, **7**(4), 301–20.

Zwanziger, J., G.A. Melnick and A. Bamezai (2000), 'The effect of selective contracting on hospital costs and revenues', *Health Services Research*, **35**(4), 849–67.

21 Models of negotiation and bargaining in health care

Pedro Pita Barros and Xavier Martinez-Giralt

1. Introduction

Under traditional health insurance arrangements, citizens were covered by some insurance scheme (either public or private). When sick, insurance arrangements allowed citizens to go to a health care provider, pay the price of the care received and be reimbursed later. Alternatively, the care provider could be owned by the insurer (like in integrated national health systems) and the patient paid nothing at the moment of consumption. In such arrangements, providers would freely set their prices or have no price to set at all (in an NHS-like system).

Recent developments in health care financing include independent institutions that negotiate (bargain) the prices with the financing institution. This is true with respect to health maintenance organizations (HMOs), managed care in general, but also in national health systems where decentralization and the split between provision and financing was implemented.

In this scenario, negotiation over contractual terms, including prices as one major element, becomes a relevant issue in the analysis of performance of health care systems. Both empirical and theoretical analyses have been produced, and are reviewed below.

This chapter reflects our views and preferences. It does not aim to be an encyclopaedic view of the existing literature on bargaining in health care. Instead, we try to motivate the reader for the new developments associated with explicit bargaining between third-party payers and providers of health care (a relationship which is, in itself, only one of many that exist in the health care sector).

Bargaining theory has a long tradition in the literature. However, it is only recently that this approach has found space in the analysis of the health care sector. The recognition of the strategic interaction among agents in the health care sector (patients, providers and third-party payers) came with the application of models borrowed from the industrial organization tradition since the 1970s. It was in the early 1990s when a step forward was taken with the eruption of the models of bargaining. In many situations the health care sector has the structure of a bilateral monopoly/oligopoly. In this context, bargaining becomes the natural way to approach the interactions among agents.

* We benefited from the comments and suggestions of Miguel Gouveia, Andrew Jones, Inés Macho-Stadler, Mónica Oliveira, Pau Olivella and David Pérez-Castrillo. The financial support of Fundación BBVA, and projects SAPIENS grant 37762/01 (Pedro P. Barros) and 2001SGR-00162, and BEC2003-01132 (Xavier Martinez-Giralt) is gratefully acknowledged. The opinions expressed herein are those of the authors and do not necessarily represent those of the institutions to which they are affiliated. Responsibility of errors and omissions remains with the authors.

Most economic analyses of contract design in health care in fact assume that the party that moves first, typically the payer, makes a take-it-or-leave-it offer to the provider. We take here a broader view, looking at other types of negotiation procedures. We do not discuss issues related to contract design, which are taken up in the chapter by Chalkley in this Companion (Chapter 22).

We focus here on models of explicit bargaining between two parties, which we call the *payer* and the *provider*. On theoretical grounds, simple bargaining models can have their results transposed in a straightforward way: higher bargaining power and higher alternative-option values from providers originate higher prices. Therefore, a first empirical question comes to mind: how strong are providers? Or, put in another way, financing institutions/payers are, usually, large relative to providers although the latter can have a natural exclusive 'catchment area' (in geographic terms or medical speciality). Then, what is the effect on prices from moving to an explicit bargaining situation? This being a relevant question, it is certainly not the only one. The special setting of health care markets brings to attention the optimal design of the negotiation procedure. In particular, timing and format of negotiations between payers/financing institutions and health care providers may lead to distinct outcomes.

We discuss first the main theoretical background, emphasizing recent work. Afterwards, we review some of the 'small' empirical literature on bargaining in health care. We conclude with directions for future research.

2.   Models of bargaining in health

The basic model (see for example, Osborne and Rubinstein (1990), or Binmore et al. (1986) for nice presentations) has a single third-party payer bargaining with a single provider over the division of a surplus S. The Nash bargaining solution is a price p such that:

$$p^* = \arg\max_p \Omega = V(p)^\delta \Pi(p)^{1-\delta} \qquad (21.1)$$

where $V(p)$ is the surplus for the third-party payer ($V'(p) < 0$), $\Pi(p)$ is the profit for the provider ($\Pi'(p) > 0$), and δ is a parameter related to the relative bargaining power of the third-party payer. Whenever the total surplus $S = V(p) + \Pi(p)$ is constant, the Nash bargaining solution entails

$$V(p^*) = \delta S \qquad (21.2)$$

Thus, the greater the bargaining power, the greater the share of surplus captured. This simple model does not allow for outside options. The Nash bargaining solution has been extended to the situation where the parties have an alternative in case of breakdown of negotiations. Suppose that the third-party payer has an alternative value of $\bar{V}$ and the provider has a profit $\bar{\Pi}$ when negotiations fail. Then, the generalized Nash bargaining solution corresponds to

$$p^* = \arg\max_p \Omega = \left(V(p) - \bar{V}\right)^\delta \left(\Pi(p) - \bar{\Pi}\right)^{1-\delta} \qquad (21.3)$$

Taking again the case of a fixed total surplus, S, the Nash bargaining outcome implies:

$$V(p^*) = \bar{V} + \delta(S - \bar{\Pi} - \bar{V}) \tag{21.4}$$

That is, the third-party payer is assured of its outside option value, $\bar{V}$, plus a share δ of the total surplus at stake, given by the overall surplus S, deducted from the assured outside option values to each side, $\bar{V}$ and $\bar{\Pi}$. These outside option values also drive the outcome of the bargaining process. In particular, the higher the outside value of the third-party payer (the provider), the lower (the higher) the equilibrium price will be.

The Nash bargaining solution is rooted on a set of four axioms placing the emphasis on efficiency, that is, the patient who can only be given a small health improvement will receive less of the health care budget than a patient with potential to achieve a large health improvement. A useful illustration supporting this solution and other alternatives can be found in Clark (1995) and Cuadras-Morato et al. (2001).

The empirical papers reviewed below can be interpreted in this simple framework, as they attempt to identify the sources of the third-party payer bargaining power (high δ), or of the provider (low δ), or the impact of increasing $\bar{V}$/decreasing $\bar{\Pi}$. The theoretical works by Gal-Or (1997, 1999a, 1999b), Barros and Martinez-Giralt (2004, 2005a, 2005b), Milliou et al. (2003) and Fingleton and Raith (2005) elaborate on this bargaining model by providing more structure, mainly to functions $V(\cdot)$, $\Pi(\cdot)$ and $\bar{V}$, $\bar{\Pi}$. The particular market structures assumed to contextualize the bargaining process allow discussion of different aspects. These are the impact (i) of product differentiation across providers and (ii) of mergers between providers in the outside values. Gal-Or (1999b) and Milliou et al. (2003) discuss the role of vertical mergers between hospitals and physician practices in increasing the bargaining power of the latter vis-à-vis third-party payers. In Gal-Or (1997, 1999a), Barros and Martinez-Giralt (2004, 2005a, 2005b) and Fingleton and Raith (2005), the interest is in the way the bargaining is organized, which originates different values for these parameters, as discussed below.

The next logical step is, in our view, to use the bargaining model to discuss the particular institutional arrangement for bargaining. In particular, two sorts of choices seem relevant to consider. On the one hand, we have the choice between the bargaining game and the use of 'any willing provider' clauses. The other one is whether it is preferable to negotiate with each provider on a one-to-one basis, or to do it with an association of providers.

Both institutional arrangements can be found in practice. The 'any willing provider' approach has been debated mainly in the United States, where the enactment of 'any willing provider' laws by some states has been taken to the Supreme Court, and has been upheld by a recent decision. These laws require managed care organizations to announce contractual conditions to providers (prices, quality, and so on). A provider that accepts such conditions can enrol in the network of the managed care organization. But also in some European countries we can find the use of 'any willing provider' dispositions. Empirical work on the implications of the 'any willing provider' laws by Carroll and Ambrose (2002), Glazer and McGuire (1993), Morrisey and Oshfeldt (2004), Vita (2001), have been complemented by the novel theoretical treatment of Barros and Martinez-Giralt (2004). We address the question of how a third-party payer (for example, an insurer) decides what providers to contract with. Two different mechanisms are studied and their properties compared. A first mechanism consists in the third-party payer setting up a bargaining procedure with both providers. The second mechanism is the 'any willing provider' where the third-party payer announces a contract and every provider freely decides to sign it or not. The main finding is that the decision of the third-party payer depends on the surplus to be shared. When it is relatively high, the third-party payer prefers the 'any willing provider' system. When, on the other hand, the surplus is relatively low, the third-party payer will select a negotiated solution.

The analysis of 'any willing provider' clauses and its comparison with pure bargaining situations suggests that depending on the underlying context, namely, surplus to be shared, either one can lead to lower prices. This imposes further demands on empirical work related to impact of such laws. It also raises econometric issues: countries, states or third-party payers may introduce them because they fulfil the conditions to get lower prices that way. This endogeneity issue has not yet been tackled in empirical work, to our knowledge.

As to the second issue dealing with the convenience of bargaining with an association, we do find in several European countries examples of centralized negotiations of third-party payers (national health services, health plans or insurers) with associations of providers. For example, in several instances, third-party payers negotiate prices of health care services with providers. We show that a third-party payer may prefer to deal with a professional association than with the sub-set constituted by the more efficient providers, and then apply the same price to all providers. The reason for this is the increase in the bargaining position of providers. The more efficient providers are also the ones with higher profits in the event of negotiation failure. This allows them to extract a higher surplus from the third-party payer.

In this respect, the general literature on bargaining, mostly with applications to the labour market, provides rationales for providers to join forces and to negotiate as a single entity vis-à-vis the third-party payer. The direct application of most bargaining theory results to health care settings faces a difficulty: the existence of market interaction between participants in one side of the negotiation (*the provider*). This often makes, in health care, the value of one negotiation to be conditional on the outcome of some other (simultaneous) negotiation(s). Firm–union bargaining issues have similarities, allowing for useful analogies to health care settings. For example, Davidson (1988) considers unionized oligopolistic industries where wage can be negotiated at the firm level or at the industry level. In the former case, workers of each firm are represented by independent and separate unions, while in the latter case there is a single union representing all workers in the industry. This multi-payer set-up is also used by Gal-Or (1997) to study the way third-party payers select providers to contract with. She considers two differentiated providers and finds that when consumers' valuation of accessing a full set of providers is small (large) relative to the degree of differentiation between payers, both payers choose to contract with only one (both) of the providers. Petrakis and Vlassis (2000) provide a model of endogenous determination of the firm–union bargaining. According to the relative bargaining power of the unions, they choose to negotiate over wages only or over wages and employment as well. Barros and Martinez-Giralt (2005a) note that a feature present in countries with a national health service is the co-existence of a public and a private sector. Often, the public payer contracts with private providers while holding idle capacity. We argue that the public sector may opt to have idle capacity as a way to gain bargaining power vis-à-vis the private provider, under the assumption of a more efficient private than the public sector.

Chae and Heidhues (2004) point out that when studying negotiations within and across groups, it is essential to define the preferences of the group. Their analysis provides a theoretical foundation for treating groups as single decision-makers and generalizes the Nash bargaining model. Cai (2004) studies the bargaining structure of a game of complete information where a player bargains sequentially with a number of passive players to implement a project. It turns out that in equilibrium, the probability of the project getting implemented decreases with the number of passive players and their bargaining power. Finally, Stole and Zwiebel (1996a, 1996b) and Wolinsky (2000) examine the effects of union bargaining on employment and other organizational design issues. This line of research is also related to other work, namely by Horn and Wolinsky (1988) and Inderst and Wey (2003). They show that as each supplier acts on the incremental surplus, under decreasing surplus function, doubling the incremental surplus is smaller than the entire surplus, which provides an incentive for providers to join forces and gain bargaining power in input markets.

However, at least equally relevant is to know under which circumstances the third-party payer itself prefers to bargain with an association, or not. This will depend on the change in the outside option value for providers. Barros and Martinez-Giralt (2005b) show that by negotiating with an association, the third-party payer dilutes the outside option value of the more efficient providers. The more efficient providers are the ones that have more to gain from a bilateral bargaining process. The change in their bargaining power, measured by the outside option value, can more than compensate the willingness to take up lower prices due to higher efficiency.

A different line of research proposed by Jelovac (2002) studies the financing of pharmaceutical products in a national health system where negotiations between the public financing agency and pharmaceutical laboratories are affected by the conditions on the demand side, in particular, by the level of co-payments. Wright (2004) also contributes to this discussion, focusing on the Australian regulation system for drug introduction, and the price bargaining process for new drugs.

3.   Evidence on bargaining outcomes

Even though explicit negotiations exist in countries with national health services (like the UK and Canada) and with private insurance-oriented systems (like the United States), a crucial difference can be found (on brief and recent comparison of UK and US health systems see: Quam and Smith (2005) on the differences in insurance systems; Ham (2005) on differences in values and politics; Starfield (2005) on organizational differences; and Feachem and Sekri (2005) on integrated health care). In national health services, negotiations often take place between third-party payers (the Government or health plans) and professional associations (like medical associations). This sets the negotiation in terms of bilateral monopoly. On the other hand, health maintenance organizations, like the ones that emerged in the United States, use negotiations with providers in a competitive setting. The third-party payer uses the outside option it has, looking for an alternative provider, to put pressure upon providers and obtain lower prices.

There is a recent line of literature looking at the empirical impact of negotiation (bargaining) processes between providers and insurers/third-party payers of health care. The first empirical issue addressed is whether managed care organizations are able to obtain advantageous conditions through bargaining. The debate has one side claiming that lower costs associated with managed care are the outcome of quality degradation. The other side claims that lower costs are due to the ability of managed care organizations to obtain lower prices from providers. The existing evidence favours the last interpretation over the former (see Cutler et al. (2000); Ho (2004); Maude-Griffin et al. (2001); Melnick et al. (1992); and Sieg (2000), among others).

Also in the UK NHS, changes in bargaining power seem to have produced visible effects. One of the main policy experiments in the UK, the fundholding GPs, implied an important shift of bargaining power towards GPs, especially those that were fundholders. The empirical research looking at hospital discrimination (favouritism for patients associated with fundholders) can also be used to address the impact of bargaining power shifts. According to Propper et al. (2002), the fundholding GPs were able to obtain lower waiting times for their patients. The ability of GP fundholders to channel money is a reinforcement of their bargaining position vis-à-vis hospitals, and prompted better conditions for the patients of GP fundholders. Thus, understanding 'time' as a sort of *price* in a health system where monetary prices are administratively fixed, the increased bargaining power of GPs, created by the different institutional arrangement (fundholding), has lowered the price/time paid (as a side note, concerns over risk selection issues led to the elimination of the fundholding system, to be substituted by primary care groups).

Since lower prices are obtained by payers, a second empirical question arises: the source of the bargaining power of insurers and providers. Theory suggests that size and the existence of outside options do increase a side's bargaining strength. The studies on the sources of bargaining power in health care can be divided into two lines: one looking at bargaining power of third-party payers; the other one detailing the bargaining power of providers, usually hospitals. On the latter line of empirical research, Brooks et al. (1997, 1998) and Town and Vistnes (2001) look at hospital competition, and ownership type, as sources of bargaining power. Their findings conform well to what we should expect (see above): competition between hospitals to attract health plans and patients reduces their bargaining power, and lower prices are observed. Moreover, the increased HMO penetration over time was associated with a decrease in hospitals' bargaining power.

With respect to third-party payers, the available evidence suggests that availability of alternatives is a more significant source of bargaining power than size alone. Availability of alternatives has the meaning, for health care third-party payers, of ability to channel patients to different providers. Studies by Ellison and Snyder (2001), Pauly (1998), Sorensen (2003) and Staten et al. (1988) give empirical support to this view. Pauly (1998) noted that size did not preclude small managed care organizations from obtaining significant discounts from hospitals. Sorensen (2003) takes a step further and finds that the ability of third-party payers to direct patients to designated providers has a greater impact than size.

It should also be apparent that some of the theoretical testable predictions are yet to be taken to the data.

4. Directions for future research

Health economics has radically changed its 'toolbox' in the last 25 years. It was the recognition of the strategic behaviour of the agents interacting in the health care sector that brought the view of the industrial organization field into the analysis. More recently, since the mid-1990s, an explicit recognition of the particular interactions between the different *types* of players (patients, providers and third-party payers) has introduced bargaining theory among the tools of analysis. We attempt here to provide a quick overview of the problems tackled so far. Although bargaining theory is widely developed, the health care sector contains enough peculiarities preventing a direct application of the results already obtained in other sectors like, for example, the labour market. Some distance has been travelled, but there is much further to go. We mention several issues that still require intense research efforts.

One relevant dimension is the timing of the negotiation, especially when the payer has to deal with several providers. Then, it may choose to negotiate simultaneously with all interested providers, to do it sequentially (each provider at a time) or to use mechanisms like 'any willing provider' clauses. These alternative scenarios have clear implications for the modelling of the information available to the negotiating parties. Also, one should take into account that asymmetric information in negotiation games may reveal information.

The protocol of the bargaining game also has consequences for the capacity of the third-party payer to dilute bargaining power of providers in order to try to bias the outcome of the negotiation. This may, obviously, lead to policy-relevant insights. Along this line, we can put forward a counter-intuitive conjecture based on Barros and Martinez-Giralt (2005b). This is that allowing entry by efficient providers can be harmful if negotiations are not done under the umbrella of an association.

Another issue that, to our knowledge, has not yet been fully examined is the bargaining over price and (observable) quality. This implies a multi-dimensional bargaining problem. A first step, in the context of drug prices, can be found in Wright (2004), though quality is assessed and not subject to negotiation, in the process of price determination.

Many of the relevant relations between third-party payers and providers are repeated ones, and often bargaining occurs repeatedly over time. How this repeated nature does (or does not) change the bargaining outcome in health care provision is yet to be discussed.

We also feel that empirical analysis of bargaining outcomes in European countries is also warranted, as they occur mostly in the context of bilateral monopoly, with providers organized in professional associations. Of course, we are aware that gathering the relevant information will be a formidable task.

Last but not least, in a somewhat different direction, a recent trend in the organization of the health care sector is given by the so-called private finance initiatives (PFI) in the UK, Portugal and other countries. The implementation of these public–private partnership programmes demands careful negotiation leading to the contract design, and the definition of what is included in the contract of one entity and what remains to the other one.

Overall, the spread of instances of explicit bargaining/negotiations between third-party payers and providers should lead to the need of both positive and normative theoretical approaches and further empirical work.

References

Barros, P.P. and X. Martinez-Giralt (2004), 'Selecting negotiation processes with health care providers', Barcelona Economics Working Paper 30.

Barros, P.P. and X. Martinez-Giralt (2005a), 'Bargaining and idle public sector capacity in health care', *Economics Bulletin*, **9**, 1–18.

Barros, P.P. and X. Martinez-Giralt (2005b), 'Negotiation advantages of professional associations in health care', *International Journal of Health Care Finance and Economics*, **5**, 1–14.

Binmore, K.G., A. Rubinstein and A. Wolinsky (1986), 'Non-cooperative models of bargaining', in R.J. Aumann and S. Hart (eds), *Handbook of Game Theory with Economic Applications*, Amsterdam: North-Holland, vol. 1, chapter 7.

Brooks, J.M., A. Dor and H.S. Wong (1997), 'Hospital–insurer bargaining: an empirical investigation of appendectomy pricing', *Journal of Health Economics*, **16**(4), 417–34.

Brooks, J.M., A. Dor and H.S. Wong (1998), 'The impact of physician payments on hospital–insurer bargaining in the US', in D. Chinitz and J. Cohen (eds), *Governments and Health Care Systems: Implications of Differing Involvements*, London: John Wiley and Sons.

Cai, H. (2004), 'Uncertainty and commitment in multilateral bargaining', mimeo.

Carroll, A. and J. Ambrose (2002), 'Any willing provider laws: their financial effect on HMOs', *Journal of Health, Politics, Policy and Law*, **27**(6), 927–45.

Chae, S. and P. Heidhues (2004), 'A group bargaining solution', *Mathematical Social Sciences*, **48**, 37–53.

Clark, D. (1995), 'Priority setting in health care: an axiomatic bargaining approach', *Journal of Health Economics*, **14**, 345–60.

Cuadras-Morato, X., J.L. Pinto-Prades and J.M. Abellan-Perpiñan (2001), 'Equity considerations in health care: the relevance of claims', *Health Economics*, **10**, 187–205.

Cutler, D., M. McClellan and J.P. Newhouse (2000), 'How does managed care do it?', *Rand Journal of Economics*, **31**(3), 526–48.

Davidson, C. (1988), 'Multiunit bargaining in oligopolistic industries', *Journal of Labor Economics*, **6**(3), 397–422.

Ellison, S.F. and C.M. Snyder (2001), 'Countervailing power in wholesale pharmaceuticals', MIT Working Paper.

Feachem, R.G.A. and N.K. Sekri (2005), 'Moving towards true integration', *British Medical Journal*, **330**, 787–8.

Fingleton, J. and M. Raith (2005), 'Career concerns of bargainers', *Journal of Law, Economics, and Organization*, **21**, 179–204.

Gal-Or, E. (1997), 'Exclusionary equilibria in health care markets', *Journal of Economics & Management Strategy*, **6**(1), 5–43.

Gal-Or, E. (1999a), 'Mergers and exclusionary practices in health care markets', *Journal of Economics & Management Strategy*, **8**, 315–50.

Gal-Or, E. (1999b), 'The profitability of vertical mergers between hospitals and physician practices', *Journal of Health Economics*, **18**, 623–54.

Glazer, J. and T.G. McGuire (1993), 'Should physicians be permitted to "balance bill" patients?', *Journal of Health Economics*, **11**, 239–58.

Ham, C. (2005), 'Money can't buy you satisfaction', *British Medical Journal*, **330**, 597–9.

Ho, K. (2004), 'Selective contracting in the medical care market: explaining the observed equilibria', Harvard University, mimeo.

Horn, H. and A. Wolinsky (1988), 'Worker substitutability and patterns of unionization', *Economic Journal*, **98**, 484–97.

Inderst, R. and C. Wey (2003), 'Market structure, bargaining, and technological choice', *Rand Journal of Economics*, **34**(1), 1–19.

Jelovac, I. (2002), 'On the relationship between the negotiated prices of pharmaceuticals and the patients copayments', CREPP WP 2002/04, University of Liège.

Maude-Griffin, R., R. Feldman and D. Wholey (2001), 'A Nash bargaining model of the HMO premium cycle', mimeo.

Melnick, G.A., J. Zwanziger, A. Bamezai and R. Pattison (1992), 'The effects of market structure and bargaining position on hospital prices', *Journal of Health Economics*, **11**(3), 217–33.

Milliou, C., E. Petrakis and N. Vettas (2003), 'Endogenous contracts under bargaining in competing vertical chains', CEPR Discussion Paper 3976.

Morrisey, L. and R.L. Ohsfeldt (2004), 'Do "Any Willing Provider" and "Freedom to Choose" laws affect HMO market share?', *Inquiry*, **40**, 362–74.

Osborne, M. and A. Rubinstein (1990), *Bargaining and Markets*, San Diego: Academic Press.

Pauly, M. (1998), 'Managed care, market power and monopsony', *Health Services Research*, **33** (5), 1439–40.

Petrakis, E. and M. Vlassis (2000), 'Endogenous scope of bargaining in a union–oligopoly model: when will firms and unions bargain over employment', *Labour Economics*, **7**, 261–81.

Propper, C., B. Croxson and A. Shearer (2002), 'Waiting times for hospital admissions: the impact of GP fund-holding', *Journal of Health Economics*, **21**(2), 227–52.

Quam, L. and R. Smith (2005), 'What can the UK and US systems learn from each other', *British Medical Journal*, **330**, 530–33.

Sieg, H. (2000), 'Estimating a bargaining model with asymmetric information: evidence from medical malpractice disputes', *Journal of Political Economy*, **108**(5), 1006–21.

Sorensen, A.T. (2003), 'Insurer–hospital bargaining: negotiated discounts in post-deregulation Connecticut', *The Journal of Industrial Economics*, **51**(4), 469–90.

Starfield, B. (2005), 'Why is the grass greener?', *British Medical Journal*, **330**, 727–9.

Staten, M., J. Umbeck and W. Dunkelberg (1988), 'Market share/market power revisited: a new test for an old theory', *Journal of Health Economics*, **7**(1), 73–83.

Stole, L.A. and J. Zwiebel (1996a), 'Intrafirm bargaining under nonbinding contracts', *Review of Economic Studies*, **63**, 375–410.

Stole, L.A. and J. Zwiebel (1996b), 'Organizational design and technology choice under intra-firm bargaining', *American Economic Review*, **86**(1), 195–222.

Town, R. and Vistnes, G. (2001), 'Hospital competition in HMO networks', *Journal of Health Economics*, **20**(4), 733–53.

Vita, M.G. (2001), 'Regulatory restrictions on selective contracting: an empirical analysis of "Any Willing Provider" regulations', *Journal of Health Economics*, **20**, 951–66.

Wolinsky, A. (2000), 'A theory of the firm with non-binding employment contracts', *Econometrica*, **68**, 875–910.

Wright, D.J. (2004), 'The drug bargaining game: pharmaceutical regulation in Australia', *Journal of Health Economics*, **23**(4), 785–813.

22 Contracts, information and incentives in health care
Martin Chalkley

1. Introduction

This chapter has three aims. The first is to provide a short and non-technical overview of the key ideas and concepts that are a part of the large and growing literature in economics concerned with how health care can best be, or 'better be', purchased. That literature draws on an even more extensive literature concerned with how contracts can be written so as to provide appropriate incentives, and so a part of this chapter will touch upon general issues in respect of contracts and incentives. Second, because the central concerns of contract and incentive theory even *applied* to health care can seem very *theoretical* and abstract, this chapter aims to provide some insight into how theory guides an interpretation of developments in policy towards actual health care systems, particularly the hospital sector and most especially in regard to the adoption of *prospective payment systems*. Third, it aims to give a sense of what is the unfinished business in respect of contracts and incentives in health care. This final task is naturally subjective and will of necessity be biased towards my own interests and recent research. This chapter is not a review of the literature, which is a task that is simply too vast to be attempted here. The interested reader can refer to Laffont and Martimort (2001) for a comprehensive overview of the contracts and incentives literature and to Chalkley and Malcomson (2000) and McGuire (2000) for a guide to the relevant literatures in the context of health care.

A recent search utilizing www.scholar.google.com yielded approximately 50 000 hits on the keywords 'contracts' and 'incentives', nearly 20 000 of which survived the addition of 'health' and 'care'. Perhaps the first question that needs to be addressed is why the terms *contracts* and *incentives* have come to characterize so much of the discussion surrounding health care systems, and in particular the reform of health care delivery. At least part of the explanation must lie in the relevance of the analysis in understanding the real concerns that exist regarding the performance of health care systems. An approach to health care markets that can rationalize ever-increasing real unit costs, highlights an inherent tension between cost control and hidden aspects of *quality* and at least in some demonstrable ways has been able to suggest effective remedies – claims for contract and incentive theory that this chapter will seek to justify is perhaps an obvious growth area of economics.

From the perspective of the theory, many of the elements of health care that give rise to contracting and incentive issues pervade many other services. In particular, asymmetric information wherein the provider of a service knows much more about what is to be supplied than the purchaser, is a pervasive feature of health care, legal services, accountancy and many other professional services. Neither is insurance and the resultant schism between receiving a service and paying for it – termed *third party payment* – unique to health care. But the extent to which, at least in most developed economies, these two features occur together does single health care out. A further issue is that in health care there is a much greater degree of public funding and this has a relevance because whereas excessive transfers (rents and profits) between private economic agents may be objected to on moral grounds, they do not give rise to the same concerns regarding deadweight welfare loss due to taxation as arise when the transfer is from a public payer.

2. Contracts and incentives

General issues

It is possible to have many different legal, economic or philosophical definitions of a contract but for the purposes of this chapter the simple idea that a contract is a formal statement of the linkage between what will be paid for a task (or tasks) and observable aspects of the performance of that task will suffice. Whereas it is possible to write almost whatever one wishes into a contract, in order to be useful in ensuring that a task is carried out as desired it must be possible to enforce the contract. Enforcement requires in turn appropriately empowered enforcers, and those enforcers need to be able to ascertain whether or not the terms of the contract have been met. It is not enough that the parties to the contract observe the outcome: in the jargon of contracting we require that the aspects of performance that are written in the contract are *verifiable* to the enforcer.

In terms of economic analysis it is important to recognize that a contract signifies delegated decision-making. Hence, the economic actor performing the task (usually called the *agent*) is doing so on behalf of, or to the benefit of, another economic actor (usually called the *principal*) who is then going to reward them, and we can thus invoke *principal–agent* models. Different methods of reward imply potentially different incentives to perform the task. So why is there ever a problem in getting incentives right? Why not just structure the contract to say 'do this how I want it done, or else'? Principal–agent analysis suggests not one, but two general problems. The first problem is easy to grasp – the task itself, or some aspects of it, may not be verifiable. This gives rise to what is termed a *moral hazard* or *hidden action* problem. Somewhat more subtle, is what is termed the *hidden information* problem. This arises when some uncertainty affects the performance of a task such that it would be desirable to condition payment on the resolution of that uncertainty. The alternative, discussed below, is to pay more than is strictly necessary. If the agent observes the resolution of uncertainty and the principal does not, an incentive problem arises that is different from simply ensuring that the agent performs the task appropriately – they must also correctly reveal their information.

Of course in many circumstances it is simply not going to be possible to get everything right – to solve both moral hazard and hidden information issues – and interest then centres upon what forms of contract can achieve the second-best outcome, and what that second-best entails.

There is one further distinction to draw before going on to see how all this plays out in the context of health care. Often in economic analysis a contrast is drawn between efficiency issues and distributional issues, and a similar distinction arises in the context of contracts. Broadly speaking, moral hazard is concerned with efficiency. There is often a way of performing the task that maximizes the joint surplus of principal and agent but moral hazard gets in the way and distorts choice away from that outcome. In such circumstances, even when the rest of society is not directly affected, we may be concerned about the loss of economic value and the waste of resources. In its simplest form, hidden information can be reduced to a matter of distribution in that one resolution of the information problem is simply to, in essence, ignore it. Here the principal pays enough that whatever the resolution of uncertainty, the agent carries out the task (and there is no moral hazard). Whilst it might be tempting to think of hidden information as a distributional issue, this is far too simplistic. First in any practical situation hidden information and hidden actions are interwoven; second, if agents seek to maximize their informational advantage we have *rent-seeking* and therefore inefficiency and third, as is often the case in health care, where the principal is a public agency the payment of economic rents requires additional taxation that imposes burdens elsewhere in the economic system.

Moral hazard and hidden information in health care
Henceforth, the task that will be considered is that of delivering health care; we will use the term *purchaser* in place of principal and the term *provider* in place of agent. As noted in the Introduction there is a degree of consensus that in delivering health care, providers have discretion which can impact upon either or both quality and cost. In the literature it is traditional to think about there being two *decisions* that providers make in respect of *quality*, henceforth q, and *cost-reducing effort*, henceforth e. The first of these requires little comment save to say that, in practice, quality of health care is considered to be multi-faceted. The second decision captures the idea that in delivering health care there are things that can be done, or left undone, that impact upon cost without necessarily affecting quality. For example, medical supplies can be conserved or wasted. With two aspects to health care decisions, in the jargon of the literature, there is a *multi-task* principal–agent problem.

The key issues can be understood by restricting attention to the case of treating a single patient and assuming the two decisions combine to yield our provider a payoff of $p - v(q, e) - c(q, e)$, where P is the payment that will be received from the purchaser. It is easiest to think about $c(.)$ as constituting the observable monetary costs of carrying out treatment whilst $v(.)$ might be comprised of other unobserved costs (or indeed benefits) expressed in monetary terms. With these interpretations it is natural to assume that $v_e > 0$ (effort is unpleasant to the provider), $c_e < 0$ (but works to reduce monetary costs) and $c_q, v_q > 0$ (quality is in all senses of the word costly to produce). Meanwhile the purchaser, who is typically a third party payer, can be assumed to have some intrinsic concern about quality of care, captured by a payoff function $b(q)$ and a dislike of paying captured by $-(1 + \alpha)P$ where α is some dis-benefit over and above the transfer to the provider that may reflect, for example, deadweight welfare loss.

This simple set-up helps in understanding the incentive properties of different payment schemes. The provider can be modelled as maximizing $P - v(q, e) - (q, e)$ and the purchaser can set P to reflect any verifiable outcome of health care delivery. In the present setting the only potentially verifiable outcomes are whether treatment is carried out and how much it costs. In the first case the payment P is just a fixed sum – a price per patient treated, or *prospective payment* because it can be set in advance of treatment occurring – and the provider will want to balance the benefits and costs of q and e on the margin which requires $-v_e - c_e = 0$ and $-c_q - v_q = 0$. There is no problem with the first of these requirements and it corresponds in most circumstances with exactly what a well-meaning social planner would try and implement, but the second condition cannot be satisfied if quality is always costly. This suggests that, when faced with a fixed price contract, the provider will endeavour to economize on quality as much as possible. Thus, the first key idea from the application of contracts and incentives to health care is that fixed price arrangements provide incentives to keep costs down but may compromise incentives to provide high quality care.

Turning now to conditioning payment upon cost, one possibility is to set $P = (1 + m)c(.)$., where the 'mark-up' m ensures that the provider is compensated for their unobserved costs $v(.)$. Balancing marginal benefits and costs now leads the provider to want to set $mc_e - v_e = 0$ and $mc_q - v_q = 0$. In principle, the second of these requirements is not problematic and we can conclude that paying a mark-up over costs gives a strong incentive towards higher quality – in fact rather too strong in that it is certainly possible that the provider will want to push quality higher than is socially desirable. However, the first condition cannot be satisfied under the assumptions, and the implication is that there is no incentive to raise e above whatever the minimum level is. Here is a second key idea: paying for health care according to what it costs inflates that cost.

The implications of this approach may appear very obvious but they have been generalized to settings which are much more complex. The central idea is enduring – fixed prices for health care help contain costs – and a significant extension to this is the notion that fixed prices might be consistent with achieving a socially appropriate level of quality. This works by allowing for the fact that under fixed prices that pay a surplus over costs, providers have an incentive to attract more patients. Enhanced service quality is one way that they might endeavour to do this, so that high prices become a driver of quality when patient demand reflects quality. The analysis above can be modified to illustrate this idea by allowing for a probability that a patient will arrive to be treated and that this probability depends on quality, hence $p(q)$ multiplies the expression for the provider's objective. It is straightforward to show in this case that the condition for choosing a positive level of quality can be satisfied. There is one particular implication of this that will be discussed further below: it provides a reason why prices should not simply reflect average costs.

The framework above can be adapted to illustrate the essence of a hidden information problem by assuming that there are two different kinds of patients – high cost and low cost – and dropping the quality variable. With these modifications the expected (observable and unobserved) costs of treating a randomly selected patient is $\beta c^h(e) + (1 - \beta)c^l(e) + v(e)$ where β is the proportion of patients in the population that are the high cost type. Hidden information is reflected in the assumption that only the provider can determine whether a patient is going to be high or low cost.

One contract that could be used here is again a fixed price per patient treated, but unless the price is set high enough, the provider might choose not to treat high cost patients at all. This is called *dumping* in the literature. Dumping may not actually mean forcing people away but it may entail trying to persuade them that they are better off seeking treatment elsewhere. Dumping can be avoided by setting a price $P^h = c^h(e) + v(e)$ and because this is a fixed price, there will be no problem in terms of incentives for cost-reducing effort. However, the purchaser will be paying more than the actual costs that the provider incurs in treating patients – when n patients are treated the excess payment will be $n(1 - \beta)(c^h - c^l)$. This sum is a pure surplus or *rent* for the provider.

The approach taken here and in the previous section illustrates the apparent dichotomy between moral hazard (inefficiency) and hidden information (rent) problems. In the present case the health care decisions are correct (and efficiently produced) but the provider pays too much for them.

Amongst the most popular and intensively researched contract models are ones that have sought to understand how the situation that has just been described can be improved upon. One obvious possibility is to attempt to discriminate between hospitals who treat a large number of high cost patients and those who treat only a few. The problem is the private nature of information. If the purchaser conditions payment upon average cost, the provider has an incentive to economize on effort so that average cost ceases to be an accurate signal of case-mix. However, with care it is possible to stop this distortion of the cost signal. As long as the provider is rewarded more (in terms of rent per patient) the lower is its cost, and it will want to keep costs low. In fact one can think about a payment system that in effect asks the provider to state its case mix (its β) and rewards it by giving it a price that depends on its reports that is $P(\beta)$. This sort of arrangement of necessity reduces incentives towards cost-reducing effort, but it is worth doing that at the margin provided one makes a sufficient saving in terms of the rent that has to be paid. Thus, such a payment system is second-best optimal and trades off rent and productive (that is cost) efficiency. This idea has been explored in many different contexts but one problem is that the optimal payment contracts derived on the basis of theory do not appear to materialize in health care practice. Some possible reasons for this will be discussed below.

3.   Policy implications of fixed prices

Fixed price contracts have become increasingly popular in health care. In the US since the 1980s they have been used in the Medicare and some aspects of Medicaid publicly funded systems under what is called a *prospective payment system (PPS)*. They have been in, and out, and then again in fashion in the British (or latterly English) National Health Service (NHS), first under what were termed *cost per case* contracts and now encapsulated in the *Payment by Results* proposals. In both of the US and UK systems a fixed payment is set for each patient falling into a particular category – *Diagnosis Related Group (DRG)* in the US, or *Health Resource Group (HRG)* in the UK. There are many other examples of health care systems moving towards prospective payment systems.

From the perspective of the theory that was set out above, the benefit of these types of arrangements is that they efficiently decentralize cost control decisions by making decision-makers within hospitals residual claimants over any cost savings they implement.

In this section, two ideas will be explored further, from a practical, policy oriented perspective. The first, which follows from a consideration of moral hazard, is that carefully set fixed price contracts may achieve appropriate quality of care. The second is that, where there are large variations in case mix, there may be substantial savings in moving away from fixed prices.

Appropriate prices

Much has been made in the literature of exploring the extent to which the risk of poor service quality under fixed price systems may be managed through setting prices at an appropriate level. 'Appropriate' here means that a provider is sufficiently incentivized to attract extra patients such that they improve service quality to do that. Unfortunately this means that price setting is a non-trivial exercise. From the perspective of theory, unit costs, the marginal benefit of quality and the responsiveness of patients/consumers to variations in quality all need to be factored in to the price-setting decision.

All of these are potentially challenging to discover and can be expected to vary from treatment to treatment, from hospital to hospital and from area to area. The practical difficulties in setting prices to reflect even cost variations are extensively discussed by Newhouse (2002). Hence, when relying upon prices to provide incentives towards greater quality, there is no simple rule for determining those prices. Furthermore, this issue does not go away when there is competition between hospitals. The problem is that both cost and revenue depend upon quality in such a system (low quality may drive away patients but it also lowers cost) and it is thus perfectly possible that low quality, low volume providers can survive in a competitive market place.

The conclusion is a somewhat uncomfortable one for policy-makers wanting simple and 'clean' rules for price setting in health care markets. It is that the current state of knowledge of health care systems would not seem to offer the information necessary to set prices in an appropriate (from a theoretical perspective) way. However, information about health care delivery is improving all the time and it is possible to speculate as to where further investment might be most productive. Considerable efforts are already being made to refine estimates of costs and to identify cost 'drivers' – see, for example, the chapters by Raikou and McGuire (40), and Manning (41) in this Companion. At the same time the evaluation of health care interventions – the measurement of valuation of quality – continues apace as witnessed by the chapters by Donaldson, Mason and Shackley (Chapter 37), and Ryan, Gerard and Currie (Chapter 38) in this Companion. The missing pieces of the jigsaw are how responsive patients/consumers are to variations in *perceived* quality and how those perceptions may differ from society's view of what constitute the appropriate dimensions of health care quality. The developments in the analysis of competition between health plans reported elsewhere in the chapters by Dowd and Feldman (Chapter 13), and Cookson and Dawson (Chapter 20), have a crucial role to play here.

Defining services

Turning now to the potential benefits identified on the basis of theory for allowing prices to reflect *ex post* costs, a first observation is that the sophisticated mechanisms identified by contract theory do not appear likely to be implemented any time soon. The practical difficulties, over and above those already highlighted in determining fixed prices, appear insurmountable and the risks (of a return to uncontrolled cost inflation) are probably too great. So what value can a policy-maker adduce from these sophisticated models? One useful insight that they offer is in respect of the social losses implied by fixed price arrangements when there is uncertainty about costs. Recall that in the simple example discussed above, the rent that accrued to providers was $n(1 - \beta)(c^h - c^l)$ which can be interpreted as indicating that the more variable are costs, particularly the higher are costs for the most complex treatments, the worse things will be. Fortunately there is not total ignorance regarding health care costs even if disentangling the various cost drivers is challenging. To give some idea of the magnitude that may be involved it is necessary only to review some published sources of data. For example, Medicare data is very revealing. It is often the case that the top 1 per cent most expensive cases within a DRG constitute more than 35 per cent of the overall cost of that DRG – admittedly as reported by the hospitals themselves. Such dispersion at the top end suggests that there could be substantial savings in the order of 15–30 per cent of health care costs from adopting a fully optimal contract mechanism. Of course not all of this is a social saving. Taken literally, the theory suggests that this is largely a matter of transfers. In practice rent-seeking behaviour can waste real resources so in this sense the cost transfer understates social welfare costs but on the other hand pure transfers may not seem so troubling – these will be transfers to those working in the health care professions – except that there are welfare costs of taxation. One third (a reasonable figure for deadweight loss) of one quarter of health care costs is nevertheless a considerable sum.

As already suggested, fully optimal partial cost sharing contracts do not seem a practical solution – at least not given the current state of knowledge of health care systems – but figures of this magnitude certainly make some refinement at least worth investigating.

One productive avenue is to think carefully about how broad a category of treatment is covered within a single payment category. Even rough and ready calculations suggest that there may be considerable value of seeking out the most heterogeneous DRGs/HRGs and attempting to refine payments within those. This suggests that there is valuable and urgent work to be done on refining the understanding of the determinants of hospital costs and how these can be apportioned to the treatment of patients within different DRGs/HRGs.

4.   Conclusion

The theory of contracts, information and incentives continues to have a substantial impact upon both the theory and practice of managing health care providers. In essence, payment systems can be viewed as managing incentive problems that arise from hidden actions and hidden information that seem to characterize much of health care delivery. The central idea that fixed prices generate incentives to restrain cost has been important in the development of fixed price, prospective payment systems. The theory helps in understanding how those systems might develop to better reflect the objectives of ensuring appropriate quality of care and so as to avoid excessive payment in the presence of asymmetric information regarding case mix.

There are, however, some important omissions that are being suggested by current empirical research. One omission concerns variations in the behaviour of health care providers. Empirical analysis, of the kind summarized in the chapter by Propper and Wilson (Chapter 31) in this Companion, indicates that after controlling for case-mix, health care providers exhibit different behaviour in respect of treatments that they deliver. Such variation has been subject to very little scrutiny from the perspective of its implications for what might constitute an appropriate menu of incentive contracts to offer. A second omission involves the motivation of health care professionals. The theory described in this chapter has been modified to reflect a broader spectrum of motivation than simple self-interest. But the theory tends to treat motivation itself as exogenous, that is independent of the context in which decisions are made and, in particular, of the payment mechanism. This does not accord well with much of what is being learned from behavioural and experimental economics research as reported by Rabin (2002). We do not have, as yet, a convincing economic theory of professions. To whom do health care professionals owe their allegiance and why? What influences professional motivation? Without answers to these questions there is a real risk that adherence to the simple tenets of the theory of incentives and contracts might end up damaging something – unselfishness on the part of health care providers – that it would be valuable to preserve.

References

Chalkley, M.J. and J.M. Malcomson (2000), 'Government purchasing of health services', in A.J. Culyer and J.P. Newhouse (eds), *Handbook of Health Economics*, Amsterdam: Elsevier, chapter 15, pp. 847–90.

Laffont, J.J. and D. Martimort (2001), *The Theory of Incentives: The Principal Agent Model*, Cambridge MA: Princeton University Press.

McGuire, T.G. (2000), 'Physician agency', in A.J. Culyer and J.P. Newhouse (eds), *Handbook of Health Economics*, Amsterdam: Elsevier, chapter 9, pp. 461–536.

Newhouse, J.P. (2002), *Pricing the Priceless: A Health Care Conundrum*, Cambridge MA: MIT Press.

Rabin, M. (2002), 'A perspective on psychology and economics', *European Economic Review*, **46**, pp. 657–85.

23 Contracting-out health service provision in resource- and information-poor settings
Natasha Palmer and Anne Mills

1. Introduction

The 'make or buy' question (Williamson, 1985) in relation to the provision of publicly-funded health services is posed frequently in resource-poor settings. Should a public bureaucracy be responsible for the provision of health services to the general public, or should the government contract-out the service provision function, while retaining responsibility for funding (Mills, 1997)? Whilst this is a direct echo of debates in developed countries such as the UK, the different motivations and context of such a policy in countries which are both resource- and information-poor suggest that the approach, outcomes and implications are likely to diverge from those in wealthier settings. This chapter explores these issues, gives examples of the range of contracts and their uses, discusses how they can be evaluated and the nature of the evidence base, and identifies policy implications and research needs.

Three key features of such settings affect the landscape for policy implementation, with implications for the type of contracts that can feasibly be used, and the manner in which they are likely to operate. First, whilst in many developed countries contracts are used as a mechanism to reshape service delivery, usually between existing parts of a public sector bureaucracy, resource-poor settings often employ them as a way of expanding service provision and bringing in new providers. Such providers are independent private entities, in contrast to the developed country providers who are not necessarily privately owned or profit-maximizing (Bartlett and Le Grand, 1993). Second, the public sector bureaucracy is usually weak and overstretched (Bennett and Mills, 1998), with implications for its capacity both to provide services and to fulfil a stewardship role and act as informed purchaser (WHO, 2000). Lack of government capacity also implies that the problem of 'hidden information' (where uncertainty affects the performance of a task: see Chapter 22 by Chalkley in this Companion) will be considerable for resource-poor governments who lack information on the cost and quality of public and private service provision. Third, most low-income country governments are dependent to a considerable degree on external finance, and this means that the agenda of the donor community can play a role in determining national policy: in effect the donor may be the purchaser, at least during the period of project funding. Indeed, contracting-out service delivery to the private sector appears to be primarily favoured by the donor community rather than by countries: research recently undertaken for the UK Government's Department for International Development (DFID) has suggested that many governments actively distrust the for-profit private sector (Palmer, 2005). A further implication of the involvement of international funding agencies is that it can open the local market to international contractors such as international non-government organizations (NGOs).

2. The motivation for contracting-out

Whether espoused by donor or government, the rationale for contracting-out service provision to the private sector is varied, ranging from the theoretical to the pragmatic. Theoretically, the arguments are broadly similar to those put forward within the approach known as 'New Public Management' in developed countries (Walsh, 1995). The main objective is to improve efficiency of service provision and it is argued that either making clinics and hospitals residual claimants on revenues (Milgrom and Roberts, 1992; Gauri et al., 2004), or exposing them to competitive markets through the establishment of renewable and competitive contracts, will achieve this aim. The idea of giving incentives to providers by making them more autonomous is less relevant in resource-poor settings, where providers are often private and autonomous. These private providers are commonly thought to be more efficient than public providers, though evidence on this, certainly at primary care level, is equivocal (Mills et al., 2004).

Pragmatically, a number of arguments have favoured contracting-out policies. One key argument is that in many settings, public provision has failed altogether, or has widespread technical inefficiencies. For example poor drug supply systems result in health facilities lacking drugs for a good part of the year; poor human resource management and remuneration systems result in high rates of health worker absenteeism and poor service quality (Hanson et al., 2003). Allocative efficiency is also judged to be poor: expenditure is skewed to hospitals, with low levels of coverage of highly cost-effective interventions such as immunization and treatment of under-fives. There are also widespread inequalities: resource allocation (both funding and staff) favours urban areas. Thus there is scepticism on the willingness and ability of the public sector to improve technical and allocative efficiency through direct provision and hierarchical management.

Global attention has been focused on public sector failings by the establishment in 2000 of the UN Millennium Development Goals (MDGs), including such targets as reduction of under-five mortality by two thirds, and by the rapidly increasing international funding available to tackle diseases such as HIV/AIDS and malaria. Interventions exist which can help achieve the MDG targets, but coverage is low. For example, if use of proven effective childhood services rose from current levels to 99 per cent, under-five deaths could fall by 63 per cent (Jones et al., 2003). Multilateral and bilateral agencies tasked with a goal of poverty eradication are thus seeking ways of rapidly 'scaling up' health services in a context of limited government capacity (Wagstaff and Claeson, 2004). Contracting-out offers a means of getting round limited government absorptive capacity and resistance to changing resource allocation patterns.

Another pragmatic argument is that resources already exist in the private sector both locally and globally and can be rapidly mobilized through contracts. Such resources include solo private practitioners, drug sellers, private hospitals, and NGOs such as church providers. The latter may already receive government subsidies, but without a formal contract. Evidence abounds that the majority of care-seeking, even for an important public health issue such as TB, is within the private sector (Uplekar et al., 2001), so these providers are widely acceptable to the population – usually more so than public providers.

Finally, it is argued that NGOs are better suited to delivering certain types of services, notably socially and politically sensitive ones such as those related to HIV/AIDs.

This is rooted in the belief that NGOs are more experienced and appropriate for working at community level, dealing with marginalized or at-risk populations, and addressing topics too sensitive for the government, such as illegal drug use.

Given these various contexts and motivations, the most common contractual arrangements are with private sector individuals, groups and organizations (for-profit or not-for-profit) and for the provision of particular services and functions, across a defined geographical area. We refer to this as 'selective' contracting with the private sector, because even in its most extensive form (for example district-wide contracting in some parts of Cambodia) it still falls short of a universal system. While the purchaser is officially the government (national or local), in practice the contract is often initiated, funded and regulated by an external donor. In some cases the donor may be instrumental in creating the local public agency that acts as the purchaser.

3. Approaches to contracting-out service provision in resource-poor settings

A range of different types of services and functions can be contracted-out (Table 23.1). Recent years have seen a particular growth of contracting services to NGOs. Examples include contracting-out the management of public facilities, for example in Cambodia, Afghanistan, Pakistan and Bangladesh; contracting community nutrition or health workers, for example in Senegal and Madagascar (Marek et al., 1999); and contracting-out a variety of preventive and palliative services related to HIV/AIDS, such as targeted services for high risk groups in Pakistan and India, and home-based care in South Africa. More traditionally, there have also been contracts with church hospitals in rural areas of many African countries, for example Uganda, Malawi, Nigeria and Lesotho.

Contracts vary considerably in formality and design. In some cases the contract is little more than the formalization of a subsidy from government to ensure that private

Table 23.1   Services that may be contracted out

Category	Examples
Personal health services	hospital facility
	primary care facility
	specific service
	laboratory tests
Public health services	vector control
	nutrition programme
Non-clinical services	pharmacy
	catering
	laundry
	cleaning
	maintenance
	security
Management functions	facility management
	personnel recruitment and employment
	purchasing

providers continue to provide services in under-served areas. In others, requirements may be more extensively specified, and payment may contain a performance-based element.

4.   Contract evaluation

Are any or all of these types of contract a good idea? This question is difficult to answer, and remarkably few attempts have been made to address it comprehensively. Contracts can be evaluated both directly and indirectly. Direct evaluation can attempt to look at the performance of providers, or results achieved in terms of volume, efficiency and equity of service provision. These studies are difficult to conduct rigorously and few have been done. They are often hindered by the need to have similar data on the 'counterfactual', or the efficiency and equity of service provision by any alternative provider, who may not actually operate in the same setting. This means that there needs to be careful assessment of the study context in order to understand whether findings are more widely relevant.

Where this type of research is not possible, indirect methods of evaluation can still be used. In the early days of the UK's quasi-market reforms, Bartlett and Le Grand (1993) suggested that a theoretical analysis can be undertaken that specifies the conditions that services need to meet if they are to succeed, and then a preliminary empirical assessment made of the extent to which these conditions appear to have been met in practice. A second indirect line of enquiry examines the nature of contracts in practice, and whether they operate in the manner specified or foreseen (Abramson, 1999; Palmer and Mills, 2003; Palmer and Mills, 2005). This literature draws on Macauley (1963) and MacNeil's (1978) work showing how contracts tend to become more relational and less transactional over time. In particular, it is suggested that contracts for health in resource-poor settings will tend to be relational where there are difficulties in specifying the services to be delivered and a lack of competition in the award of contracts (Palmer and Mills, 2005). This has implications for the way in which contracts will influence providers, and the ability of contracts to provide transparency and improve the efficiency or quality of service delivery. Since contracts are often justified on the grounds that they are an effective mechanism for providing incentives or controlling providers, questioning whether this appears to be the case is an indirect way of assessing the value of contracting-out.

The appropriate type of evaluation depends on the rationale for the contract in the first place. For example, a contract may be introduced to increase access to services rapidly and efficiently, to create incentives for existing providers to become more efficient, or to buy services that otherwise could not be provided by the public sector. Knowing to what extent contracting-out has been successful in each case implies a different type of evaluation. For example, where contracts are used to scale-up services where there is no public provision or to purchase services which the public sector is not able to provide, it is irrelevant to compare relative cost and efficiency between public and private providers. If a contract is made with private providers on the grounds that they will be more efficient, evaluation needs to compare their relative efficiency with that of possible alternative providers.

A further issue facing evaluation is what is feasible in terms of data collection or data availability. Many contracts in resource-poor countries have not been in place for very long, or the lack of data on service delivery can make it impossible to evaluate. An exception to the latter is the large externally funded contracting arrangements, some of which have provided a vehicle for research.

5.   Examples of recent evaluations of contracting out

This section summarizes the evidence base on contracting-out, selecting the most comprehensive recent attempts to evaluate the performance of providers and the nature of contractual relationships.

Two models of contracting for the delivery of district health services were piloted in rural Cambodia during 1998–2001 as part of a project funded by the Asian Development Bank. Districts were selected randomly and assigned either to 'contracting-out' (two districts), 'contracting-in' (three districts), or controls (four districts). Under contracting-out, NGOs were given full responsibility for the delivery of specified services in a district, including drug procurement and hiring and firing of staff. Under contracting-in, NGOs worked within the existing system to strengthen district administrative structures. Control districts received no external support except a small subsidy towards service delivery. Equity as well as coverage targets for primary health care services were explicitly included in contracts. Pre- and post-intervention household and facility survey data are available for evaluation of service delivery (Schwartz and Bhushan, 2004a; 2004b). Coverage of primary care services in all districts substantially increased over the study period. Based on the household and facility survey 2.5 years after contracts started, all contracted districts outperformed control districts in terms of pre-defined coverage indicators such as immunization and attended deliveries. Contracted-out models outperformed contracted-in. Much of the increase in health care utilization in contracted districts was attributed to increased use by households of low socioeconomic status – children in the poorest 50 per cent of households in the contracted districts were more likely to be fully immunized than those living in similar households in districts served by the government model of service provision (Schwartz and Bhushan, 2004b). However, there may have been different resource flows to the different districts, and the differences observed could be attributed to this. In addition it is unclear to what extent the NGOs that held these few contracts would be able to replicate this performance over a larger scale, or could be substituted by other NGOs.

A similar comparison between NGO and public sector service delivery has been attempted in Bangladesh (Mercer et al., 2004). During 1998–2003, the Bangladesh Population and Health Consortium, supported by DFID, funded NGOs to deliver an essential package of services through their own clinics. NGOs reported their activities quarterly and their performance was evaluated using indicators such as the vaccination status of children and deliveries attended by a qualified person. Similarly compiled data from public sector clinics were not available, so to evaluate the performance of the NGOs, the authors compared selected health indicators with the latest estimates for Bangladesh, some of which covered earlier time periods. NGO data indicated high coverage of reproductive and child health services, and low levels of child mortality, in comparison to the rest of Bangladesh. Given the absence of any baseline data, it is not clear whether this was inherent to the areas where the NGOs were operating, although the authors attempted to control for this by tracking mortality rates: these demonstrated a clear drop since the commencement of contracts.

In the late 1980s, the Costa Rican government introduced a number of market-like mechanisms including the contracting of provision to health care cooperatives, which are founded by employees of primary care clinics. Cooperatives are autonomous legal entities which receive a yearly capitation fee based on the local population size. A recent analysis compared health outputs amongst the cooperatives with traditional and comparable public sector facilities (Gauri et al., 2004) using panel data from 1990–1999. They found that cooperative clinics had significantly more generalist visits per capita and significantly fewer specialist visits per capita than traditional clinics; they also performed fewer lab tests and prescribed fewer drugs. This suggests that cooperatives were reducing costs, and the authors concluded that overall they were not under-servicing according to tracers of the per capita rate of emergency visits and first-time patients, which were similar to those in traditional clinics. The authors pointed out that the differences could be due to unobserved variables that systematically differed between the cooperative areas and areas of public provision, differences in the population, or differences in the organizational culture of those facilities that converted to cooperatives.

Abramson (2001) studied the operation of this same contract between the Costa Rican Social Security Fund and one cooperative, COOPESALUD, in terms of how contract performance was measured by use of indicators. She found that although a series of targets and indicators were well established and the objectives of the contract well articulated, the data gathered did not provide quantifiable measures of impact, and evaluation results tended to be superficial. Often targets were stressed in terms of population-based goals, but the real population was not reliably known, and providers had no incentive to exceed these targets.

In South Africa, in order to inform policy on the desirability of contracting with private providers, a study compared the performance of different models of primary care provision (Mills et al., 2004). Public sector clinics, private clinics, and private providers (clinics and GPs) under contract to the public sector, were all evaluated. Performance was defined as a combination of technical quality of service delivery, acceptability to users, and cost. Some private providers (contracted GPs and a chain of private clinics) were found to deliver services at similar or lower overall cost than the public sector. The acceptability of private sector providers to users was much higher, notably of those who were not yet under contract to government. Some private contracted GPs were perceived to be offering a second-rate service to state patients, and the study speculated whether or not the private clinic chain, if contracted to serve public patients, would be able to maintain current quality standards.

The study also evaluated the nature of contractual relationships between the state and private providers, and found that formal aspects such as design, monitoring and resort to sanctions offered little control over the nature of the contractual outcome. In a contract with private GPs, individual, social and professional factors, and motivation played an important role in determining the nature of service delivery under the contract (Palmer and Mills, 2003). A comparison of three different contracts showed that an urban-based private sector contract for a sub-set of primary care services operated very differently from rural public sector contracts which attempted to provide broader health care coverage. Important environmental influences on contracts were highlighted, including the nature of the market, scope of services and involvement of a public purchaser (Palmer and Mills, 2005). The study suggests that service delivery under contract can be relatively unpredictable in a situation where contracts are not, or cannot be, closely specified. The lack of government capacity to specify and monitor contracts closely in many resource-poor settings emphasizes the importance of this point.

Performance-based contracting has been suggested as one way of better aligning incentives so that problems of 'hidden information' are lessened, and the need for costly and difficult monitoring of performance reduced. Eichler et al., (2001) reported the findings of a pilot scheme in Haiti (funded by the US Agency for International Development (USAID)) which introduced performance-based contracts for NGOs providing basic health services. Under the new system, which replaced a system of straightforward reimbursement for NGO expenditure, a portion (5 per cent) of the NGOs' historical budget was withheld, but the opportunity was offered to earn that plus an additional 5 per cent if performance targets were met. A one-year pilot showed marked improvements in performance. This type of approach is also being used in a pilot scheme for contracting with Ugandan NGO hospitals (funded by the World Bank), and in extensive contracting with NGOs to deliver a basic health service package in Afghanistan (funded by World Bank and USAID). In these settings, the extent to which the incentive of a performance bonus will alter the behaviour of providers is not yet clear.

6.   Policy implications

The above studies almost all suggest that contracting-out services can lead to improvement in service provision. However, caution is needed in assuming this holds everywhere, for three main reasons. Firstly, studies examine contracting-out in very specific settings, with little attention paid to the context in which they operate. This makes it very difficult to know to what extent the same benefits will be seen in different settings. In particular, some contracts apparently improved service delivery dramatically, but were introduced where public provision was virtually absent (for example Cambodia). Whether contracted-out services outperform a functioning public sector cannot be answered in such settings. In other studies there are problems of attributing the relative merits of contracted-out service delivery to the contracts per se, as opposed to unobserved factors.

Secondly, many contracting arrangements are externally funded, with strong design and management input, and of limited duration. Evaluations of locally initiated and managed arrangements, such as in Costa Rica and South Africa, found that the contract did not appear to have a strong influence on service delivery and that many other aspects of the purchaser and provider were more important. This echoes some of the findings of long-term contractual relationships in developed countries (Flynn and Williams, 1997). As yet there is no information on what might happen to externally funded and initiated contracting arrangements once the period of external funding ends.

Thirdly, most contracting-out is at the moment still only on a small scale, and it is unclear to what extent private providers currently involved are representative of a larger pool of potential contractors. There are uncertainties over whether there are enough technically capable and motivated NGOs or private providers to cover all parts of a country, and how limited competition might affect contract performance over time. The studies cited above demonstrate some of the difficulties in comprehensively evaluating the performance of contracts in resource-poor settings. If contracting-out is seen as an alternative to public sector provision, there is a need for some comparison between the two types of provider, but data on public sector service delivery is very scarce. Another problematic area is separating out delivery of a useful service such as community outreach from its roots in NGO provision: certain services currently delivered by NGOs are successful, but they may be equally so if they were delivered by government.

7. Further research

There remains a large agenda of further research. If the desirability of contracting-out as a reform prescription is to be established, a focus on the relative performance of different providers and contracting models needs to be complemented by better understanding of the dynamics of purchaser and provider relationships and contract management, and of the nature and size of local and global markets for contractors.

A further issue is the impact of contracting on the broader health system. A key difference in the types of contracts described here from those in an internal market is that both contracts and providers may be numerous and small scale, with little standardization across a country. This runs the risk of fragmenting the health system and possibly creating substantial differences in provision from place to place. Other issues to consider include how referrals operate in a contracted-out arrangement, how accountability can be guaranteed with a number of small-scale providers, and lastly the transaction costs of managing contracts in a resource-poor environment. There is no evidence on these issues.

In resource- and information-poor settings, external support (both financial and technical) commonly supports the purchasing role. It is as yet unclear what would occur if this support is withdrawn, whether governments can continue contracting on their own, and whether it is cost-effective for them to do so. One option which requires evaluation is contracting-out the purchasing function to a technically strong, independent body.

Governments often face a choice of type of provider. For example in South Africa, private GPs, NGOs, and commercial firms are all options for being contracted to deliver primary care. In the future, we may see not only NGOs competing for contracts, but also commercial contractors, such as those that compete for contracts in other sectors. On theoretical grounds, there may be a basis for preferring not-for-profit providers in a context of weak purchasing capacity. It is generally assumed that non-profit organizations are more trustworthy and motivated to provide services in the public benefit, but these assumptions require empirical testing.

References

Abramson, W. (1999), 'Public/private partnerships for contracting of primary health care services', Bethesda, MD: PHR project Abt Associates Inc.

Abramson, W. (2001), 'Monitoring and evaluation of contracts for health service delivery in Costa Rica', *Health Policy and Planning*, 16(4), 404–11.

Bartlett, W. and J. Le Grand (1993), 'The theory of quasi-markets' in J. Le Grand and W. Bartlett (eds), *Quasi Markets and Social Policy*, Basingstoke: Macmillan.

Bennett, S. and A. Mills (1998), 'Government capacity to contract: health sector experience and lessons', *Public Administration and Development*, 18, 307–26.

Eichler, R., P. Auxila and J. Pollock (2001), 'Output-based health care: paying for performance in Haiti', World Bank Private Sector and Infrastructure Network, Note Number 236 Washington DC: World Bank.

Flynn, R. and G. Williams (1997), *Contracting for Health*. Oxford: Oxford University Press.

Gauri, V., J. Cercone and R. Briceno (2004), 'Separating financing and provision: evidence from 10 years of partnership with health cooperatives in Costa Rica', *Health Policy and Planning*, 19(5), 292–301.

Hanson, K., K. Ranson, V. Oliveira-Cruz and A. Mills (2003), 'Expanding access to health interventions: a framework for understanding the constraints to scaling-up', *Journal of International Development*, 15(1), 1–14.

Jones, G., R.W. Steketee, R.E. Black, Z.A. Bhutta and S.S. Morris (2003), 'How many child deaths can we prevent this year?', *The Lancet*, 362(9377), 65–71.

MacNeil, I. (1978), 'Contracts: adjustment of long-term economic relations under classical, neo-classical and relational law', *North Western University Law Review*, **72**, 854–905.

Macauley, S. (1963), 'Non contractual relations in business: a preliminary study', *American Sociological Review*, **28**(1), 55–67.

Marek, T., I. Diallo, B. Ndiaye and J. Rakotosalama (1999), 'Successful contracting of prevention services: fighting malnutrition in Senegal and Madagascar', *Health Policy and Planning*, **14**(4), 382–89.

Mercer, A., M. Hossain Khan, M. Daulatuzzaman and J. Reid (2004), 'Effectiveness of an NGO primary health care programme in rural Bangladesh: evidence from the management information system', *Health Policy and Planning*, **19**(4), 187–97.

Milgrom, P. and J. Roberts (1992), *Economics, Organisation and Management*, New Jersey: Prentice-Hall.

Mills, A. (1997), 'Improving the efficiency of public sector health services in developing countries: Bureaucratic versus market approaches', in C. Colclough (ed.), *Marketizing Education and Health in Developing Countries: Miracle or Mirage?*, Oxford: Clarendon Press.

Mills, A., N. Palmer, L. Gilson, D. McIntyre, H. Schneider, E. Sinanovic and H. Wadee (2004), 'The performance of different models of primary care provision in Southern Africa', *Social Science and Medicine*, **59**, 931–43.

Palmer, N. (2005), 'Non state providers of basic services; the health sector', presentation to DFID sponsored workshop on non-state providers of basic services, Dubai, 17–18 January.

Palmer, N. and A. Mills (2003), 'Classical versus relational approaches to understanding controls on a contract with independent GPs in South Africa', *Health Economics*, **12**, 1005–20.

Palmer, N. and A. Mills (2005), 'Contracts in the real world: case studies from Southern Africa', *Social Science and Medicine*, **60**(11), 2505–14.

Schwartz, B. and I. Bhushan (2004a), 'Cambodia: using contracting to reduce inequity in primary health care delivery', HNP Discussion Paper: reaching the poor program paper no. 3. Washington DC: World Bank.

Schwartz, B. and I. Bhushan (2004b), 'Improving immunization equity through a public–private partnership', *WHO Bulletin*, **82**(9), 661–67.

Uplekar, J., V. Pathania and M. Ravigione (2001), 'Private practitioners and public health: weak links in tuberculosis control', *The Lancet*, **358**, 912–16.

Wagstaff, A. and M. Claeson (2004), *The Millennium Goals for Health: Rising to the Challenges*, Washington DC: World Bank.

Walsh, K. (1995), *Public Services and Market Mechanisms. Competition, Contracting and the new Public Management*, Basingstoke: Macmillan.

WHO (2000), *World Health Report 2000: Health Systems: Improving Performance*, Geneva: World Health Organization.

Williamson, O. (1985), *The Economic Institutions of Capitalism*, Oxford: Oxford University Press.

PART V

PROVIDER REIMBURSEMENT, INCENTIVES AND BEHAVIOUR

24 The physician as the patient's agent
Thomas Rice

1. Introduction

It has been long recognized that the physician plays a major role in the health care system, not only acting as the patient's 'agent' but also as a key stakeholder in any discussions of changing a country's health care structure and policy. Before the advent of health insurance (the so-called 'third party') physicians faced no external impediments in treating their patients: they performed the services that they saw fit, and charged what they liked, taking into account what the market would bear. Both public and private insurance intervenes in this relationship because most physician payments are governed by the insurer.

As a result, physicians and their organizations have been instrumental in calling for policies that affect public and private insurers themselves, which in turn can greatly influence the foundations of national health care systems. Depending on the particular country in question, physicians and their organizations have been instrumental in determining the ratio of specialists to generalists, the relative fees paid for different services, what other professions can practise medical care, as well as policing their colleagues to help ensure that adequate quality care is delivered to the population.

Thus, in their role as a trusted patient agent, physicians as a group have amassed a great deal of influence. What, then, is the nature of this agency relationship? First and foremost, it is to assist the patient in medical decision-making. But in addition, the physician acts as an agent for the insurers that provide their monetary compensation, and for society, which is concerned about both medical outcomes and the cost of providing services.

Physicians typically must engage in a delicate balancing act. Like almost everyone else, they are influenced by 'selfish' economic motives. They must grapple with the tension of doing what is best for the patient while at the same time maximizing their own utility. It is this tension that is responsible, in large measure, for various efforts to 'fine tune' payment schemes, with the goal of making it advantageous for the physician to behave in a way that is in the patient's, insurer's and society's best interest. As will be shown, this ideal is impossible to fully achieve but efforts are underway to better align payment to encourage quality and control costs.

2. Theories of agency and physicians' economic behaviour

Agency theory

Agency theory addresses the relationship between two parties: a principal and an agent. In medical care, the patient is the principal. Because the patient typically lacks sufficient medical knowledge to specify what treatments should be carried out – and oftentimes, lacks the authority to do so (for example, patients cannot operate on themselves nor can they write drug prescriptions) – he or she relies on one or more medical professionals to act as agent(s). Although agents do not have to be physicians, the latter normally assume this role because they tend to be the most thoroughly trained in medical matters, and also possess the legal authority to prescribe medications and treat medical problems.

Economics is concerned with specifying the contract between the principal and the agent, so as to ensure that the principal receives what he or she seeks at the lowest possible cost. This is no easy matter, however, given inherent uncertainty about the future, and the multitude of possible outcomes in almost any transaction. There are several characteristics of health care markets that complicate matters even further:

- Whereas normally agents would be expected to act solely to maximize their own utility, in medical care we assume that physicians also care deeply about the welfare of their patients.
- As suggested above, physicians are really quadruple agents: for the patient, for themselves, for the insurer that pays for the service, and for society as a whole (Blomqvist, 1991). Each of these principals has their own set of objectives that they are trying to fulfil. It is difficult to imagine how one set of actions by an agent could possibly maximize four different sets of utility functions.
- Medical care is fraught with uncertainty, making it particularly difficult to determine, even after the fact, whether a physician has indeed been a good agent. This is aggravated by the fact that the actions of even an excellent physician may not be sufficient to restore a patient to good health. Compare that to, say, a roofer. One can usually tell the quality of a roofing job as soon as there is a hard rain.

To amplify on the first two bullet points, coming up with a successful payment system would seem to depend, first, on understanding and explicating the goals and motivations of all parties involved: physicians, patients, insurer and society (Mooney and Ryan, 1993). Second, one needs to consider the extent to which physicians can indeed be good agents for the other parties. As discussed by Gafni et al. (1998), who consider the agency relationship between the physician and patient, this could take two forms: (a) the physician seeks to understand the patient's utility function, so as to make medical decisions that are in the latter's best interest, or (b) the patient makes the medical decisions, with the physician assuming the role of providing the necessary medical information to the patient. These authors suggest that (b) is more feasible, noting, however, that the vast majority of writing on the topic has assumed (a) to be the norm.

There is one other related impediment to developing a successful physician compensation system related to the third bullet point: information asymmetry. This is typically defined as occurring when one party (here, the agent or physician) has more information than another party (here, the principal or patient). The success of an agency relationship depends, crucially, on the principal being able to determine whether the agent has met expectations (Rochaix, 1998). But if physicians have an information advantage, as their training and experience would indicate, and also have motivations that go beyond those of the patient (for example, making more money), then the agency relationship becomes all the more difficult. Compensation systems need to reward physicians for revealing their knowledge to the patient, both to help the latter in making certain medical decisions as well as to allow for the assessment of whether the physician has done a good job representing the patient's interest.

Out of this morass, insurers and society must come up with a compensation system for physicians, some of the choices of which are discussed next.

Physician compensation systems

Traditionally, contracts with physicians have been specified in one of three ways or some combination: fee-for-service, capitation and salary. Under *fee-for-service* systems, physicians are paid an additional amount of money for each service they provide. Although it may seem that this automatically provides motivation to increase the volume of services, the incentive is actually somewhat more complicated. First, there is an incentive to increase volume only if the payment for providing the services exceeds the physician's cost, including his or her time. Second, even if payments exceed costs, the physician will not necessarily have an economic incentive to treat the patients of a particular insurer if there are multiple insurers that pay different amounts. This is because the patients covered by one insurer are effectively competing against the patients of other insurers for the attention of the physician. With this caveat in mind, it is safe to say that in general, fee-for-service provides an incentive to physicians to deliver more services. This implies that it will also result in higher medical care spending for insurers and for society.

Although the incentives of fee-for-service with respect to the quantity of services provided are fairly clear, the same cannot be said about its anticipated effect on the quality of care provided. On the one hand, better quality is encouraged in that physicians do not have an incentive to withhold services. But on the other hand, physicians may provide too many services under fee-for-service which not only wastes resources, but could actually cause harm to the patient. There are no estimates available on the proportion of services provided that are actually harmful, but estimates on the portion of services that are not medically necessary range as high as 30 per cent (Schuster et al., 1998).

Capitation provides incentives that are diametrically opposed to those of fee-for-service. Under a full capitation system, physicians receive a fixed amount of money for providing services to a patient for a particular period of time, including the cost associated with referrals to hospitals or specialists, as well as the ordering of tests. Although it may seem that this will result in an economic incentive to provide as little care as possible per patient, and to maximize the number of patients under the physician's care, it turns out again that the incentives are somewhat more complicated. It is true that under-providing services will result in more money for the physician in the short-run, but it may be a counterproductive strategy over time. This is because patients are likely to gravitate away from physicians who, they believe, are not giving them the attention that they deserve. As was the case in fee-for-service, the impact of capitation on quality depends, in large measure, on whether capitation is placed on a system characterized by over-provision vs. under-provision.

Salary provides a fixed income to a physician over a particular time period. In some ways, it may be viewed as a compromise between fee-for-service and capitation. There is not an inherent incentive under salary to provide too many, or too few, services to a particular patient. For that reason it may be argued that salary provides an incentive to provide high-quality care, since a physician that does not have an incentive to over- or under-provide may then deliver an appropriate level of services. The problem with salary concerns the lack of economic incentives to provide care efficiently. A physician who is lazy may provide little care, and one that is not dedicated may provide poor care. Because of this, systems relying on salary (such as group and staff model HMOs in the United States) tend to supplement it with subsidiary incentive schemes.

In fact, any of the three payment methods can be, and often are, linked with such schemes. In general, fee-for-service payment is linked with incentives to economize; capitation, with incentives to provide adequate quality; and salary, with productivity incentives. Thus, additional incentives are designed to help quell some of the problems inherent in particular payment systems. To give an example, an organization that provides a salary to a physician may also provide bonuses, depending on whether the physician provides a quantity of services per week that is deemed sufficiently productive – or a penalty if the physician does not.

Further complicating this is that sometimes insurers do not pay physicians directly. Take the case of independent practice association (IPA)-type HMOs in the United States. Most of these use a 'three-tier' payment scheme. For example, an employer that provides the IPA to its employees pays a capitation fee per member per month to the IPA. The IPA, in turn, pays its member physicians. Oftentimes, the IPA does not pay its physicians through capitation, using instead fee-for-service. In order to help ensure that physicians do not provide too many costly services, or make too many costly referrals, the IPA may withhold a percentage of the physicians' revenue each year, and not return it if: (a) physicians have unduly high hospitalization rates; or (b) physicians have unduly low referral rates to specialists. Such withholdings may be based on an individual physician's performance, or the performance of the physician group as a whole.

This moves us to the central question: is there evidence of the superiority of any particular form of physician compensation in terms of its success in making physicians better agents for the various principals involved, and most notably, patients? This is considered next.

3.   Physicians' economic behaviour: evidence

Fee-for-service
Much of the research on this topic has been done as part of an effort to determine if (and to what extent) physicians can 'induce' demand for the services they provide. It is generally thought that if physicians do have this power, and if they take advantage of it, then fee-for-service payment is flawed: too many services will be provided by physicians, who are seeking to maximize their incomes rather than the patient's welfare or society's objective to use resources efficiently.

There is far too much literature on this topic – much of it peripheral to the matter at hand – to be discussed here. For a review of some of the key issues through the early 1990s, see Labelle et al. (1994); for a more recent treatment, see Bickerdyke et al. (2002). One test of demand inducement is to determine how physicians in a fee-for-service system respond to changes in the payments they receive. One might expect that, without demand inducement, physicians would provide fewer services when they face a decline in payment because their income would be lower. But with demand inducement, they might behave differently by providing a greater number, or more intensive, services in the wake of payment reductions, so as to recoup lost income.

Most, but certainly not all, of the evidence on demand inducement using these methods supports its existence. There is still much controversy, in part because the data and methods available are often not sufficiently convincing. In that regard, Dranove and Wehner (1994) used two-stage least squares techniques on cross-sectional supply and utilization data to analyse a situation where one would not expect to find much if any demand inducement – childbirth – and found it anyway, which, they assert, calls 'into question the validity of the . . . approach' (p. 61).

Starting with some US-based studies, researchers from the Urban Institute found that Californian physicians increased the quantity and intensity of services provided to Medicare beneficiaries in response to a freeze in programme payment rates during the early 1970s (Holahan and Scanlon, 1979; Hadley et al., 1979). In another set of studies, the present author found that physicians in urban areas of Colorado who faced declines in their Medicare payment rates during the late 1970s compared to their non-urban colleagues, increased the intensity of medical and surgical services, and the amount of surgery provided and laboratory tests ordered (Rice, 1983). Other researchers have found that physicians responded to Medicare payment rate freezes during the mid-1980s by increasing the quantity and/or intensity of surgery, radiology, and special diagnostic tests (Mitchell et al., 1989).

A study of the Canadian experience through the early 1980s showed that provinces that were least generous in raising physician payment rates over time experienced the greatest increase in the volume and intensity of services provided (Barer et al., 1988). Unlike most other studies, this one could not be criticized for ignoring changes in patient out-of-pocket costs because during this period Canadians received services without any co-payments. In contrast, one confounding factor in most US studies is that reduced physician payment rates often result in lower patient co-payments (for example, the patient pays 20 per cent of charges). Thus, if the physician provides more services after the payment reduction, it is possible that part of the reason is that patient demand increased as a result of lower co-payments.

There has been some counter-evidence, however. A study using data from some of the Canadian provinces found little relationship over a dozen years between utilization of specific procedures and their fees (Hurley et al., 1990). Some studies of Medicare payment rate reductions for so-called 'overvalued procedures' (mainly surgery and testing) in the late 1980s found little evidence that physicians increased the quantity of services provided (Escarce, 1993a; 1993b). Other studies of the same payment reductions do find evidence of volume increases in the wake of Medicare payment reductions, however (Physician Payment Review Commission, 1993).

Perhaps a good summary of the state of the art is provided by Jeremiah Hurley and Roberta Labelle (1995, p. 420), who conclude, 'It appears that, in response to economic considerations . . . physicians *can* induce demand for their services, they *sometimes do* induce demand, but that such responses are neither automatic nor unconstrained. Further, physicians do not always respond in ways that can be predicted' (italics in original).

Capitation and salary

Although there has not been a great deal of research on the impact of these incentives, most studies find them to be at least somewhat effective, and sometimes very effective, in controlling utilization and expenditures (see Chapter 25 by Iversen and Lurås in this Companion for further discussion of capitation). Beginning with the US, in one study of

Wisconsin employees enrolled in an IPA, a change from fee-for-service to capitation payment (with physicians sharing in the financial risk of hospitalization and speciality costs) resulted in an 18 per cent increase in primary care visits, along with a 45 per cent decline in referrals to specialists outside the IPA. In addition, there was a 16 per cent decrease in hospital admissions and a 12 per cent drop in length of stay (Stearns et al., 1992).

Similarly, in a study of an Illinois IPA, physicians were switched from fee-for-service payment with a 15 per cent withholding (returned at end of year if utilization is kept below a target) to capitation payment with bonuses for reduced hospitalization and shared financial risk for speciality referral costs. It was found that specialist costs increased 2 per cent in the year after the change, after rising by 12 per cent in the previous year. Hospital outpatient service costs declined 7 per cent, after increasing 12 per cent in the previous year. But there was little change in in-patient hospital utilization (Ogden et al., 1990).

In Europe, Mooney relates an interesting study on the power of incentive reimbursement. He reports on a study from Denmark in which physician payment methods were altered rather dramatically (Mooney, 1994; Krasnik et al., 1990). In October 1987, general practitioners in Copenhagen changed from fully capitated payment to payment based partly on capitation and partly on fee-for-service, to conform with physicians in the rest of the country. This new system resulted in the ability of general practitioners (GPs) to make extra money for consultations, prescriptions, certain procedures and tests, and some other procedures. It was found that the provision of services that provided extra fees increased substantially, and there was a large decrease in referrals to specialists and hospitals. From this, Mooney (1994, p. 127) concludes that '[t]here clearly is considerable discretion on the part of GPs in how they act and remuneration systems can push them to go one way or another in how they treat their patients and whether they treat them themselves or refer them on in the system'.

The chapters by Iversen and Lurås (25), Ettner and Schoenbaum (27) and Grabowski and Norton (28) in this Companion discuss how changing physician payment methods affects the quality of care provided. Somewhat parallel information exists in a review of studies from the US that compare the quality of care in HMOs vs. fee-for-service. A review of studies published between 1997 and 2001 by Miller and Luft (2002, p. 657) shows that, 'Quality-of-care findings for HMO plans were roughly comparable to those of non-HMO plans. Of forty-seven findings from thirty-seven articles, fourteen were predominantly favourable with respect to HMOs and fifteen were predominantly unfavourable.'

There is now much interest in developing 'mixed' payment systems, ones that are neither fee-for-service or capitation, but rather, include aspects of each. In this regard, James Robinson (2001) has written:

> There are many mechanisms for paying physicians; some are good and some are bad. The three worst are fee-for-service, capitation, and salary. Fee-for-service rewards the provision of inappropriate services, the fraudulent upcoding of visits and procedures, and the churning of 'ping-pong' referrals among specialists. Capitation rewards the denial of appropriate services, the dumping of the chronically ill, and a narrow scope of practice that refers out every time-consuming patient. Salary undermines productivity, condones on-the-job leisure, and fosters a bureaucratic mentality in which every procedure is someone else's problem (p. 149).

It is in this sobering context that we conclude with some implications for paying physicians in a way that will encourage them to perform as good agents for patients and society.

4.   Implications for paying physicians

Up till now, relatively little progress has been made in developing payment systems that both encourage physicians to act as a good agent towards society by controlling costs, as well as good agents to patients by providing high quality care. Perhaps the most promising developments in this regard are so-called 'pay-for-performance' schemes. These are discussed here, but it should be kept in mind that most are very new and are, as yet, largely untested.

There are many examples of pay-for-performance initiatives in the United States, but they tend to be so new that there has been little in the way of systematic evaluation of their impacts. They focus on quality, by tying part of a physician's (or hospital's) remuneration to meeting specified quality performance thresholds. Thus, it is not clear that such systems will do much to control costs. In the short-term, they are more likely to *redistribute* existing revenues from low-quality to high-quality providers. In the longer term, however, they could generate savings to the extent that they encourage the provision of cost-effective preventive services, and if they lead, say, to lower rates of re-hospitalization.

Rosenthal and colleagues (2004) summarize over 30 such schemes that currently are in place in the US that cover more than 20 million insurance enrollees. In most, performance measures are based on clinical outcomes, processes such as provision of recommended preventive services, and patient satisfaction – or a combination of these. Typically, a certain portion of a physician's payment from an insurer (for example, 1 per cent or 5 per cent) is based on meeting the quality goals. Financial incentives can be of either the 'carrot' variety (bonuses) or 'stick' (penalties or withholdings). Needless to say, developers of these arrangements face major challenges in collecting, compiling, and disseminating the necessary information on quality performance.

Thus, further experimentation and research is greatly needed before one can be confident in touting any particular method of paying physicians that can meet the often conflicting goals of physicians, insurers, patients and society at large.

References

Barer, M.L., R.G. Evans and R.J. Labelle (1988), 'Fee controls as cost control: tales from the frozen north', *The Milbank Quarterly*, **66**(1), 1–64.
Bickerdyke, I., R. Dolamore, I. Monday and R. Preston (2002), 'Supplier-induced demand for medical services', Productivity Commission Staff Working Paper, Canberra, Australia.
Blomqvist, A. (1991), 'The doctor as double agent: information asymmetry, health insurance, and medical care', *Journal of Health Economics*, **10**, 411–32.
Dranove, D. and P. Wehner (1994), 'Physician-induced demand for childbirths', *Journal of Health Economics*, **13**, 61–73.
Escarce, J.J. (1993a), 'Effects of lower surgical fees on the use of physician services under Medicare', *Journal of the American Medical Association*, **269**(19), 2513–18.
Escarce, J.J. (1993b), 'Medicare patients' use of overpriced procedures before and after the Omnibus Budget Reconciliation Act of 1987', *American Journal of Public Health*, **83**(3), 349–55.
Gafni, A., C. Charles and T. Whelan (1998), 'The physician–patient encounter: the physician as a perfect agent for the patient versus the informed treatment decision-making model', *Social Science and Medicine*, **47**(3), 347–54.
Hadley, J., J. Holahan and W. Scanlon (1979), 'Can fee-for-service reimbursement coexist with demand creation?', *Inquiry*, **16**(3), 247–58.

Holahan, J. and W. Scanlon (1979), 'Physician pricing in California: price controls, physician fees, and physician incomes from Medicare and Medicaid', Grants and Contracts Report, Pub. No. 03006, Washington, DC: US Health Care Financing Administration.

Hurley, J. and R. Labelle (1995), 'Relative fees and the utilization of physicians' services in Canada', *Health Economics*, **4**(6), 419–38.

Hurley, J., R. Labelle and T. Rice (1990), 'The relationship between physician fees and the utilization of medical services in Ontario', *Advances in Health Economics and Health Services Research*, **11**, 49–78.

Krasnik, A., P.P. Groenewegen, P.A. Pedersen, P. von Scholten, G. Mooney, A. Gottschau, H.A. Flierman and M.T. Damsgaard (1990), 'Changing remuneration systems: effects on activity in general practice', *British Medical Journal*, **300**(6741), 1698–701.

Labelle, R., G. Stoddart and T. Rice (1994), 'A re-examination of the meaning and importance of supplier-induced demand', *Journal of Health Economics*, **13**, 347–68.

Miller, R.H. and H.S. Luft (2002), 'HMO plan performance update: an analysis of the literature, 1997–2001', *Health Affairs*, **21**(4), 63–86.

Mitchell, J.B., G. Wedig and J. Cromwell (1989), 'The Medicare physician fee freeze: what really happened?', *Health Affairs*, **8**(1), 21–33.

Mooney, G. (1994), *Key Issues in Health Economics*, New York City, US: Harvester Wheatsheaf.

Mooney, G. and M. Ryan (1993), 'Agency in health care: getting beyond first principles', *Journal of Health Economics*, **12**, 125–35.

Ogden, D., R. Carlson and G. Bernstein (1990), 'The effect of primary care incentives', *Proceedings from the 1990 Group Health Institute*, Washington, DC: Group Health Association of America.

Physician Payment Review Commission (1993), *Annual Report to Congress*, Washington, DC.

Rice, T.H. (1983), 'The impact of changing Medicare reimbursement rates on physician-induced demand', *Medical Care*, **21**(8), 803–15.

Robinson, J.C. (2001), 'Theory and practice in the design of physician payment incentives', *Milbank Quarterly*, **79**(2), 149–77.

Rochaix, L. (1998), 'The physician as perfect agent: comment', *Social Science and Medicine*, **47**(3), 355–6.

Rosenthal, M.B., R. Fernandopulle, H.R. Song and B. Landon (2004), 'Paying for quality: providers' incentives for quality improvement', *Health Affairs*, **23**(2), 127–41.

Schuster, M.A., E.A. McGlynn and R.H. Brook (1998), 'How good is the quality of health care in the United States?', *Milbank Quarterly*, **76**(4), 517–63.

Stearns, S., B. Wolfe and D. Kindig (1992), 'Physician responses to fee-for-service and capitation payment', *Inquiry*, **29**(4), 416–25.

25 Capitation and incentives in primary care
Tor Iversen and Hilde Lurås

1. Introduction

Capitation means a (risk-adjusted) fixed fee for each person who receives medical care from a certain organization or a certain physician. The concept may be related to primary care both through the revenue system for primary care organizations and through the payment system for an individual general practitioner (GP).[1] In this chapter we primarily focus on capitation as a component in the payment system for GPs, and in particular capitation payment related to a list of people. First, we give a brief description of primary care and discuss the key role of GPs. Then we review recent theoretical models and empirical findings in the literature. For this purpose we have searched Econlit and Medline.

Our selection of literature has two important restrictions. First, literature published before 1999 is ignored, irrespective of the relevance for capitation in primary care. Readers interested in the early literature are referred to Scott (2000). Second, the focus is on capitation as a component of a payment system in primary care. Hence, literature that studies the effect of economic incentives is ignored if capitation is not treated as an explicit payment component. We first review studies that explicitly consider how capitation is expected to influence the quality of the GP's services in general. Next, we review studies of potential effects of capitation on the quantity of care provided by general practitioners irrespective of whether the quantity adds to quality or not. The distinction between quality and quantity of medical care is often not quite clear. Following McGuire (2000) quality can be interpreted as a non-contractible (cannot be used as a basis for payment) input into the production of medical care. Hence, with negligible co-payment the quality of health care increases with the quantity of a service until the health effect at the margin is zero.

We also present studies on the effect of capitation on referrals and selection of patients to the practice. Finally, we review some of the literature on capitation in the revenue system for primary care organizations and, in particular, present theoretical and empirical results from the fundholding experiment in the UK. A final section presents some ideas for future work in this field.

2. Primary care

General practitioners are the first-level providers of health care, that is they are the population's gateway to the health care sector. During episodes of illness GPs give general advice on health and illness, arrange follow-ups, order tests, prescribe medication, write medical certificates and refer patients to medical specialists. A majority of patients receive all their treatments in primary care, but GPs also use their broad and general medical knowledge to sort out cases that are expected to benefit from treatment by medical specialists. Their role in the first level of the health care sector and their role as medical filters for secondary health care – or the gatekeeper role – are the reasons why GPs hold a key position in the health care system.

A key factor determining GPs' behaviour is patients' health and diagnosis. But even if demand for GP services mainly reflects patients' need for health care, the organization of the health care system – both the organization of general practice and the organization of the specialist health care – influences demand and utilization of GPs' services. In Arrow's seminal paper (Arrow, 1963) he points out how uncertainty influences the health care market, and according to Wennberg (1982 and 1984) uncertainty is the most important factor influencing physicians' behaviour. When the basis of knowledge is weak, the medical profession may disagree on the proper ways to use various medical interventions. Therefore, *the* right treatment for a certain diagnosis often does not exist (Enthoven, 1990). The existence of medical practice variation and the fact that GPs have superior medical information compared with that of patients, give rise to agency problems in primary care.

Eisenberg (1986) contends that physicians' motivation can be divided into: concern for patients, concern for the social good and self-interest. Hence, in addition to a concern for patients' health and welfare, possible arguments in the utility function for GPs are the interests of society and the GP's own income, leisure, workload and medical skills. The classification of economic models of GP behaviour made by Scott (2000) is based on this division. Several authors have reviewed the literature on whether GPs' treatment of patients is influenced by the organization of general practice and by the way GPs are paid (see Scott, 2000; McGuire, 2000 and Chapter 24 by Rice in this Companion). While the results from theoretical models compare a GP's treatment of patients under a certain payment system with a socially optimal medical treatment, the empirical results are more ad hoc and inaccurate.

It seems that paying doctors on a fee-for-service basis encourages the provision of services. Fee-for-service may even imply an incentive to provide more than an optimal quantity of services from a patient's point of view. Per capita payment, on the other hand, provides incentives to compete for patients, but it also provides incentives to minimize efforts by referring and prescribing to reduce one's own workload. Capitation payment may also imply an incentive for selection behaviour, that is in order to increase capitation income the GP selectively attracts healthy people with small health care need to their list. Salaried GPs cannot increase their income by providing more services to patients: they receive the same income irrespective of their effort during the consultation. Salaried payment may therefore lead to lower levels of tests and referrals compared with fee-for-service, but it may also adversely affect the GP's productivity (see for instance Gosden et al., 2003; 2001; 1999; Scott, 2000; Scott and Hall, 1995; Donaldson and Gerard, 1989; Kristiansen and Mooney, 1993; Maynard et al., 1986 and Chapter 24 by Rice in this Companion).[2]

Newhouse (1992, 2002) argues that because the market mechanism for establishing optimal prices does not operate in the health care sector, prices paid to the provider may not reflect the costs. Paying GPs on a fee-for-service basis may therefore be costly to the insurer. On the other hand, because capitation may imply selection behaviour, fee-for-service is required to prevent GPs from cream-skimming (Lurås, 2004). According to Newhouse et al. (1989) adjustment of the capitation component only accounts for roughly 10 per cent of the explainable variance in treatment cost across people. This is the reason why Newhouse (1992) suggests that capitation payment usually does not account for patient heterogeneity, and he suggests a mixed (blended) reimbursement scheme (Newhouse, 1996).

On average, Danish GPs receive 2/3 of their income from fee-for-service and 1/3 from capitation (Christiansen, 2002; Davis, 2002). The fee-for-service component makes it possible to influence GPs' service provision and the capitation component has a potential for creating more population-related care, greater continuity of care, less doctor shopping and more patient loyalty to GPs and GP loyalty to patients (Mooney, 2002), and according to Christiansen (2002, p. 111): 'The Danish system comes close to what Newhouse (1992) found was an optimal system in an imperfect world'. A similar payment system has been practised in Norway since the implementation of a nationwide list patient system in 2001. Similar systems are proposed in other European countries, for instance Croatia (Hindle and Kalanj, 2004) and Estonia (Lember, 2002).[3] Dutch GPs also face a payment system based on fee-for-service and capitation, but the composition is different from the Danish and the Norwegian systems. The payment is based on a two-tiered system depending on patients' income: the GP receives fee-for-service payment from the 30 per cent highest-income privately insured patients and a capitation fee for Sickfund-insured patients (70 per cent lowest income). But although fee-for-service and capitation might prompt GPs to make different medical decisions there are few differences in care received by privately insured and Sickfund-insured (Van Weel, 2004).

Prior to the fundholding initiative in the UK general practice faced conflicting goals: there was a monetary incentive to expand the number of patients on a practice list but, simultaneously, an interest in minimizing the workload and expenditure within the practice. Rather than providing the medical treatment in his own practice, it was profitable for a GP to refer patients for treatment in the specialist health care. Hence, GPs had little incentive to economize on the services they demanded for their patients (Moon et al., 2002). The introduction of fundholding was one way of addressing a shortcoming in the NHS' ability to contain costs.

In the UK fundholding system the Health Authority (HA) delegated an annual budget to larger general practices (fundholders) and made them responsible for purchasing elective procedures at hospitals for their listed patients (Wyke et al., 2003). A number of other countries have introduced primary care-based capitation, fund pooling and budget holding either as experiments or as an overall policy. For instance, in Germany there is an overall expenditure cap for pharmaceutical prescribing (Delnoij and Brenner, 2000) and in the US more than half of HMO enrollees belong to health plans that contract with primary care physician (PCP) groups on a predominantly capitated basis (Harvard Managed Care Industry Center Group, 2002; see also Glied (2000)).

It seems that capitation-based budgeting could have a major impact on reducing hospitalization, length of hospital stay and out-patient activity, and as such contains incentives for the efficient use of services. However, there may be concerns about whether such budgeting has a negative influence on the quality of care and whether GP organizations which are primarily funded by capitation may give rise to a selection of healthy people to the practice. These concerns are related to the potential problems of risk sharing among the insurer, provider (physician) and patient.

In the US there is an increasing interest in aligning the incentives faced by individual physicians with the incentives faced by the physician organizations through payments from insurers. According to Robinson and Casalino (2002), the alignment of the payment system for individual GPs and the revenue system for physician organizations is fundamental for achieving efficiency in an organization as a whole. Paying the organization capitation and the individual physician fee-for-service is an example of misalignment (see also Pedersen et al., 2000). The focus in Europe, on the other hand, is more on capitation-based budgets as a way of strengthening the GP's role and contributing to cost containment and efficient use of services (Davis, 2002; Wyke et al., 2003; Lewis and Gilliam, 2000). One example is the fundholding experiment and Primary Care Trusts[4] in the UK.

3.   Recent studies of capitation as a component in the payment system for GPs

Effects on the quality of health services
Gravelle (1999) and Gravelle and Masiero (2000) study theoretically the properties of capitation contracts in providing high-quality health care. In Gravelle (1999) profit-maximizing GPs compete for patients. A patient's utility is increasing in quality and decreasing in contract price and distance to the GP. A GP's level of quality is assumed to be common knowledge and GPs are competing for patients via the level of quality they offer. An increase in the capitation fee makes the marginal patient more valuable to GPs and encourages them to raise quality in their competition for patients.

That patients have a correct observation of quality is a dubious assumption to make, and is modified in a two-period model by Gravelle and Masiero (2000). Two practices are located at each end of a street. Patients are located uniformly along the street and have preferences for a short distance to the GP and a high quality of GP services. Patients are *ex ante* identical except for location and age. An elderly patient has already been listed with a GP and has perfect knowledge of that particular GP, while he is assumed to have acquired no additional information about the other practice. An increase in the capitation fee is shown to increase the equilibrium quality even when patients also care about distance, have imperfect information about quality and face switching costs.

The waiting time from the booking of a consultation until the consultation takes place is a specific quality indicator. In Iversen and Lurås (2002) the starting point is that GPs differ with regard to quality characteristics that are part of their personality, and hence, considered to be exogenous. GPs with an unfavourable personality have to offer relatively more of other quality characteristics to attract patients. It is predicted that only physicians with quality characteristics perceived as inferior by patients are willing to embark on costly waiting time reductions. Because of variation among physicians in these quality characteristics, the market equilibrium is likely to show a range of waiting times. This hypothesis is supported by results from a study of Norwegian general practitioners.

An empirical study by Sorbero et al. (2003) points to the possibility that quality of care may be compromised under capitation. Based on the administrative enrolment and encounter data from four physician organizations in 1994 and 1995, the results show that controlled for patient age and sex, and physician-fixed effects, patients with chronic conditions and capitated primary care physicians are 36 per cent more likely to switch physician than similar patients with physicians paid on a fee-for-service basis.

In a questionnaire survey mailed to randomly selected physicians Williams et al. (1999) investigated whether physicians' diagnostic and treatment approaches to depressive disorders differ according to physician speciality and extent of capitation payment. A substantial proportion of the physicians reported treatment approaches that were consistent with high quality care. Approaches varied more by speciality than by type of depressive disorder or extent of capitation. However, organizational barriers, such as time for an adequate case history and the affordability of mental health professionals differed by degree of capitation. The authors conclude that the organization and financing of health care affects physician practices in complex ways and deserves further investigation.

By means of a mail survey to a random sample of the American Academy of Family Physicians, Shen and colleagues (2004) also conclude that payment mechanisms have significant effects on clinical decision-making. In this study physicians are asked to make treatment decisions in a hypothetical family practice setting that includes patients insured by both fee-for-service and capitated risk-sharing payment plans. After reading each scenario, physicians are asked what clinical decision they would make and how bothered they are with the decision they make. The term 'bother' is defined as a global measure of discomfort or distress in decision-making. The results show that physicians are significantly more 'bothered' when they make clinical decisions under capitation payment.

Effects on quantity of health services
In Iversen and Lurås (2000a) and Iversen (2004) the quantity of services that GPs provide is the focus. In a mixed capitation and fee-for-service payment system, physicians who are experiencing a shortage of patients are predicted to increase the number of services they provide to each patient in order to increase their income. Since patients are likely to be rationed with regard to the number of services the popular GPs provide, some patients are willing to stay with the less popular GPs who provide the extra services that may or may not contribute to the quality of health care. In the empirical analysis of a panel of Norwegian GPs the authors show that GPs who experience a shortage of patients have a higher income per listed person than GPs with enough patients.

Effects on referral rate
Barros and Martinez-Giralt (2003) study the effect of the payment system on referrals and the preventive care provided by a primary care centre. Their model consists of two agents: a primary care centre and a hospital. Even if prevention and treatment costs are partially compensated, the effort to reduce referrals to hospitals is at the minimum value under capitation because of an externality resulting from the referral decision. The referral rate is likely to be smaller with fee-for-service than with capitation. Also capitation-based integrated management is expected to decrease the number of referrals since the referral decision is now internalized.

In Iversen and Lurås (2000b) the results are similar, but the mechanisms are somewhat different. In their model a GP both chooses his preferred number of patients and the referral rate. Capitation encourages a higher referral rate and more regular patients than fee-for-service since a higher income can be obtained for the same effort. Hence, because of the referral externality the GP shifts costs to the specialist sector. The predictions are supported in an empirical analysis with data comparing the referral rate before and after the introduction of a capitation component in the payment system for GPs.

This result is in accordance with a study of the influence of gatekeeping arrangements and capitated physicians' payment on the speciality referral process in primary care (Forrest et al., 2003). The authors conclude that capitated physicians appear to shift the balance toward more referrals made for discretionary indications. The findings from structured focus group interviews with Norwegian GPs by Carlsen and Norheim (2003) confirm these results. The doctors generally perceived themselves as less concerned with the gatekeeper role under (partial) capitation, and felt it more important to provide better services and keep patients satisfied.

4.   Recent studies of capitation as a component in the revenue system for primary care organizations

Gravelle et al. (2002) and Dusheiko et al. (2003) study the effect of the UK fundholding scheme on hospital elective admission rates. To make predictions of the effect of fund-holding on the number of elective admissions, a model for practice decisions under fund-holding, non-fundholding and Primary Care Trust (PCT) budgetary regimes is developed. Practices are heterogeneous with respect to valuing patients' benefits and the distaste for fundholding. After the abolition of the fundholding system the number of admissions among the previous fundholders is expected to increase because of the decline in the marginal cost of an admission. The conclusion from the empirical study is that gate-keeping practices will reduce their elective admissions by a modest but not negligible amount when confronted with a budget and explicit prices.

A third study of the impact of GP fundholding on hospital admission rates is Croxson et al. (2001). This study makes use of the fact that the fundholders' budgets were based on their activity in the year before they became fundholders. Hence, the fundholders have an incentive to increase the number of referrals in the year that precedes the initial year of fundholding. The results show that fundholders have a rise in elective admissions prior to becoming a fundholder. The authors conclude that fundholders respond to financial incentives.

GP organizations primarily funded by capitation may give rise to a selection of healthy people to the practice, and there may be some potential problems regarding risk sharing among the insurer, provider (physician) and patient. Fairchild et al. (2000) explore this issue by interviewing physicians at an Academic Medical Centre (AMC) regarding patients facing catastrophic illness who sometimes request specialists. Under capitation payment primary care physicians (PCP) have an incentive to refer patients to local specialists and not to AMCs which generally are more expensive and with whom the capitation-based integrated management may not have a working relationship. This forces some patients to terminate their existing PCP and enrol with PCPs affiliated with the AMC to which they wish to be referred. The shift creates a financial burden for the AMC and their affiliated physicians, and the authors suggest that risk-adjusted capitation payment based on health status and the disease burden of its population to a certain extent may compensate for this problem.

Some studies investigate and discuss methods of need-based capitation. Hutchinson et al. (2000) and Baines and Parry (2000) develop needs adjustment formulas for prescribing budgets and conclude that all fail to measure needs adequately. For a review of the literature on optimal risk adjustment, see Chapter 26 by Glazer and McGuire in this Companion.

Rice et al. (2000) derive a need-based capitation formula for allocating prescribing budgets to health authorities and primary care groups. They use regression analysis and find that a need gradient based on permanent sickness, percentage of dependants in no-career households, percentage of students, percentage of births on practice lists, together with supply characteristics explained 41 per cent of the variation in prescribing costs per prescribing unit.

To develop an allocation formula that provides equal access to equal need, Gravelle et al. (2003) apply a utilization approach. The utilization approach for measuring need rests on the assumption that use of health care is determined by demand and supply, and that need is an important determinant of demand. The authors' modelling strategy is innovative, and the authors conclude that 'we believe that if the aim is to allocate resources so that there is equal access to equal need the utilisation approach we have outlined is currently the best of the available imperfect alternatives'.

5.   Conclusion – ideas for further work

Equity and efficiency are important challenges in health policy. Capitation payment linked to registration of a person on a GP's list provides incentives for continuity of care, and it implies that a GP has an obligation to provide care for persons on the list and do what is in their best interests. But as we have noted in the previous sections, capitation payment has some disadvantages; quality may be compromised (although theoretical and empirical studies seem to diverge here), quantity may be lower and referrals to specialists higher than with other payment systems, and it has a built-in risk of selection behaviour (see also Van Weel and Del Mar, 2004; Robinson et al., 2004, Lewis and Gilliam, 2000; Eggleston, 2000). Correspondingly, a capitation-based revenue system has some good and some poor characteristics. It may lead to cost containment and efficient allocation between primary and specialist care, but it may also give rise to poor quality, selection behaviour and involve problems regarding risk sharing (see also Pena-Dolhun et al., 2001; Bodenheimer et al., 1999; Engstrom et al., 2001). Based on conclusions from the literature, it seems that the results so far are insufficient as a basis for guiding policy-makers in their efforts to design optimal payment systems and optimal revenue systems.

To some extent this is also related to the fact that the overall objectives of public policy for primary care are not quite clear. Unless it is known what objectives a system should attain, it is less meaningful to design regulatory and payment systems. A related problem is the GP's objective function. With poor knowledge of its content, the basis for making solid predictions of behaviour is insufficient.

In general, the payment system and the revenue system should aim at protecting GPs against financial risk without inducing an inefficiently high level of health service use (Ellis and McGuire, 1990 and Chapter 22 by Chalkley in this Companion). Without appropriate protection against financial risk, GPs may engage in risk shifting by means of patient selection and provide care of inferior quality. Needs-adjusted capitation budgeting and a mixed payment system of capitation and fee-for-service are all important policy instruments in achieving the optimal balance between patient selection and inefficiency in health care. Important challenges to future research are therefore to gain more knowledge about the optimal composition of capitation and fee-for-service in a mixed payment system for GPs and whether other payment components should supplement this mixture. In this connection the various trials with pay-for-performance, as reviewed by Ettner and Schoenbaum in this Companion (Chapter 27), may offer a promising path.

Notes

1. A physician working in primary care is denoted general practitioner (GP) or primary care physician (PCP). In the following we will use the term general practitioner (GP).
2. See also Binderman (2001) who presents a case study of Dr Jones with the purpose of giving GPs a broad understanding of underlying business cycles in their practice that will (p. 68): 'bring about incremental changes in most practices'.
3. See also Gillett et al. (2001) who discuss capitation and primary care in Canada, and Van Weel and Del Mar (2004) who discuss how Australian GPs should be paid.
4. From April 1999 the fundholding system was replaced by Primary Care Groups that were later transformed into Primary Care Trusts (PCT) that all practices in a particular area have to join.

References

Andersen, T.F. and G. Mooney (eds) (1990), '*The Challenge of Medical Practice Variation*', London: Macmillan.

Arrow, K.J. (1963), 'Uncertainty and the welfare economics of medical care', *American Economic Review*, **53**, 941–73.

Baines, D.L. and D.J. Parry (2000), 'Analysis of the ability of the new needs adjustment formula to improve the setting of weighted capitation prescribing budgets in English general practice', *British Medical Journal*, **320**, 288–90.

Barros, P.P. and X. Martinez-Giralt (2003), 'Preventive health care and payment systems', *Topics in Economic Analysis & Policy*, **3**(1), 1–21.

Binderman, J. (2001), 'Variables affecting the financial viability of your practice: a case study', *Journal of Medical Practice Management*, **17**(2), 64–8.

Bodenheimer, T., B. Lo and L. Casalino (1999), 'Primary care physicians should be coordinators, not gatekeepers', *Journal of the American Medical Association*, **281**(21), 2045–9.

Carlsen, B. and O.F. Norheim (2003), 'Introduction of the patient-list system in general practice: changes in Norwegian physicians' perception of their gatekeeper role', *Scandinavian Journal of Primary Health Care*, **21**, 209–13.

Christiansen, T. (2002), 'Organization and financing the Danish health care system', *Health Policy*, **59**,107–18.

Croxson, B., C. Propper and A. Perkins (2001), 'Do doctors respond to financial incentives? UK family doctors and the GP fundholder scheme', *Journal of Public Economics*, **79**, 375–98.

Davis, K. (2002), 'The Danish system through an American lens', *Health Policy*, **59**, 119–32.

Delnoij, D. and G. Brenner (2000), 'Importing budget systems from other countries: what can we learn from the German drug budget and the British GP fundholding?' *Health Policy*, **52**, 157–69.

Donaldson, C. and K. Gerard (1989), 'Paying general practitioners: shedding light on the review of health services', *Journal of Royal College of General Practitioners*, March.

Dusheiko, M., H. Gravelle, R. Jacobs and P. Smith (2003), 'The effects of budgets on doctors' behaviour: evidence from a natural experiment', CMPO Working Paper Series No. 03/064, University of Bristol.

Eggleston, K. (2000), 'Risk selection and optimal health insurance–provider payment systems', *The Journal of Risk and Insurance*, **67**, 173–96.

Eisenberg, J.M. (1986), 'Doctors' decisions and the cost of medical care', Ann Arbor, MI: Health Administration Press.

Ellis, R.P. and T.G. McGuire (1990), 'Optimal payment systems for health services', *Journal of Health Economics*, **9**, 375–96.

Engstrom, S., M. Foldevi and L. Borgquist (2001), 'Is general practice effective? A systematic literature review, *Scandinavian Journal of Primary Health Care*, **19**(2),131–44.

Enthoven, A.C. (1990), '*Health Plan: The Only Practical Solution to the Soaring Cost of Medical Care*', Addison-Wesley, Reading, M.A.

Fairchild, D.G., A.J. Sussman, T.H. Lee and T.A. Brennan (2000), 'When sick patients switch primary care physicians: the impact on AMCs participating in capitation', *Academic Medicine*, **75**(10), 980–85.

Forrest, C.B., P. Nutting, J.J. Werner, B. Starfield, S. von Schrader and C. Rohde (2003), 'Managed health plan effects on the specialty referral process: result from the Ambulatory Sentinel Practice Network referral study', *Medical Care*, **41**, 242–53.

Gillett, J., B. Hutchinson and S. Birch (2001), 'Capitation and primary care in Canada: financial incentives and the evolution of health service organizations', *International Journal of Health Services*, **31**(3), 583–603.

Glied, S. (2000), 'Managed care' in Anthony J. Culyer and Joseph P. Newhouse (eds), *Handbook of Health Economics*, Volume 1, Amsterdam: Elsevier Science, pp. 707–53.

Gosden, T., L. Pedersen and D. Torgerson (1999), 'How should we pay doctors? A systematic review of salary payments and their effect on doctor behaviour', *QJM*, **92**, 47–55.

Gosden, T., B. Sibbald, J. Williams, R. Petchey and B. Leese (2003), 'Paying doctors by salary: a controlled study of general practitioner behavior in England', *Health Policy*, **64**(3), 415–23.

Gosden, T., F. Forland, I.S. Kristiansen, M. Sutton, B. Leese, A. Giuffrieda, M. Sergisin and L. Pedersen (2001), 'Impact of payment method on behaviour of primary care physicians: a systematic review', *Journal of Health Services Research and Policy*, **6**(1), 44–55.

Gravelle, H. (1999), 'Capitation contracts: access and quality', *Journal of Health Economics*, **18**, 315–40.

Gravelle, H. and G. Masiero (2000), 'Quality incentives in a regulated market with imperfect information and switching costs: capitation in general practice', *Journal of Health Economics*, **19**, 1067–88.

Gravelle, H., Dusheiko, M. and M. Sutton (2002), 'The demand for elective surgery in a public system: time and money prices in the UK National Health Service', *Journal of Health Economics*, **21**, 423–49.

Gravelle, H., M. Sutton, S. Morris, F. Windmeijer, A. Leyland, C. Dibber and M. Muirhead (2003), 'Modeling supply and demand influences on the use of health care: implications for deriving a need-based formula', *Health Economics*, **12**, 985–1004.

Harvard Managed Care Industry Center Group (2002), 'Managed care: an industry snapshot', *Inquiry*, **39**(3), 207–20.

Hindle, D. and K. Kalanj (2004), 'New general practitioner formula in Croatia: is it consistent with worldwide trends?', *Croatian Medical Journal*, **45**(5), 604–10.

Hutchinson, B., J. Hurley, S. Birch, J. Lomas, S.D. Walter, J. Eyles and F. Stratford-Devai (2000), 'Needs-based primary medical care capitation: development and evaluation of alternative approaches', *Health Care Management Science*, **3**(2), 89–99.

Iversen, T. (2004), 'The effects of a patient shortage on general practitioners' future income and list of patients', *Journal of Health Economics*, **23**, 673–94.

Iversen, T. and H. Lurås (2000a), 'Economic motives and professional norms: the case of general medical practice', *Journal of Economic Behavior and Organization*, **43**, 447–71.

Iversen, T. and H. Lurås (2000b), 'The effect of capitation on GPs' referral decisions', *Health Economics*, **9**, 199–210.

Iversen, T. and H. Lurås (2002), 'Waiting time as a competitive device: an example from general medical practice', *International Journal of Health Care Finance and Economics*, **2**, 189–204.

Keating, N.L., B.E. Landon, J.Z. Ayanian, C. Borbas and E. Guadagnoli (2004), 'Practice, clinical management, and financial arrangements of practicing generalists', *Journal of General Internal Medicine*, **19**, 410–18.

Kristiansen, I.S. and G. Mooney (1993), 'Remuneration of GP services: time for more explicit objectives? A review of the systems in five industrialised countries', *Health Policy*, **24**, 203–12.

Lember, M. (2002), 'A policy of introducing a new contract and funding system of general practice in Estonia', *International Journal of Health Planning Management*, **17**(1), 41–53.

Lewis, R. and S. Gilliam (2000), 'Doctors' pay. What seems to be the trouble?', *Health Service Journal*, **110**(5715), 28–30.

Lurås, H. (2004), 'General Practice. Four Empirical Essays on GP Behaviour and Individuals' Preferences for GPs', Working Paper 2004:1, Health Economic Research Programme (HERO), University of Oslo.

Maynard, A., M. Marinker and D. Pereira Gray (1986), 'The doctor, the patient and their contract III. Alternative contracts: are they viable?', *British Medical Journal*, **292**, 1438–40.

McGuire, T.G. (2000), 'Physician agency' in Anthony J. Culyer and Joseph P. Newhouse (eds), *Handbook of Health Economics*, Volume 1, Amsterdam: Elsevier Science, pp. 462–536.

Moon, G., J. Mohan, L. Twigg, K. McGrath and A. Pollock (2002), 'Catching waves: the historical geography of the general practice fundholding initiative in England and Wales', *Social Science and Medicine*, **55**, 2201–13.

Mooney, G. (2002), 'The Danish health care system: it ain't broke . . . so don't fix it', *Health Policy*, **59**, 161–71.

Newhouse, J.P. (1992), 'Pricing and imperfections in the medical care marketplace', in P. Zweifel and H.E. Freck (eds) *Health Economics Worldwide*, Kluwer Academic Publishers, pp. 3–22.

Newhouse, J.P. (1996), 'Reimbursing health plans and health providers: efficiency in production versus selection', *Journal of Economic Literature*, **34**, 1236–63.

Newhouse, J.P. (2002), *Pricing the Priceless. A Health Care Conundrum*, Cambridge, MA: The MIT Press.

Newhouse, J.P., W.G. Manning Jr, E.M. Keeler, E.M. Sloss (1989), 'Adjusting capitation rates using objective health measures and prior utilisation', *Health Care Financing Review*, **10**(3), 41–54.

Pedersen, C.A., E.C. Rich, J. Kralewski, R. Ferldman, B. Dowd and T.S. Bernhardt (2000), 'Primary care physician incentives in medical group practices', *Archives of Family Medicine*, **9**, 458–62.

Pell, J. and S. William (1999), 'Do nursing home residents make greater demands on GPs? A prospective comparative study, *British Journal of General Practice*, **49**(444), 527–30.

Pena-Dolhun, E., K. Grumbach, K. Vranizan, D. Osmond and A. Bindman (2001), 'Unlocking specialists' attitudes toward primary care gatekeepers', *Journal of Family Practice*, **50**(12), 1032–7.

Rice, N., P. Dixon, P.C. Lloyd and D. Roberts (2000), 'Derivation of a need based capitation formula for allocating prescribing budgets to health authorities and primary care groups in England: regression analysis', *British Medical Journal*, **320**, 284–8.

Robinson, J.C. and L.P. Casalino (2002), 'Reevaluation of capitation contracting in New York and California', *Health Affairs* – web exclusive.

Robinson, J.C., S.M. Shortell, R. Li, P.C. Casalino and T. Rundall (2004), 'The alignment and blending of payment incentives within physician organizations', *Health Services Research*, **39**(5), 1589–606.

Scott, A. (2000), 'Economics of general practice' in Anthony J. Culyer and Joseph P. Newhouse (eds), *Handbook of Health Economics*, Volume 1, Amsterdam: Elsevier Science, pp. 1175–200.

Scott, A. and J. Hall (1995), 'Evaluating the effects of GP remuneration problems and prospects', *Health Policy*, **31**, 183–93.

Shen, J., R. Andersen, R. Brook, G. Kominski, P.S. Albert and N. Wenger (2004), 'The effect of payment method on clinical decision making: physician responses to clinical scenarios, *Medical Care*, **42**(3), 297–302.

Sorbero, M.E.S., A.W. Dick, J. Zwanziger, D. Muhamel and N. Weyl (2003), 'The effect of capitation on switching primary care physicians', *Health Services Research*, **38**(1), 191–209.

Stepanikova, I. and K.S. Cook (2004), 'Insurance policies and perceived quality of primary care among privately insured patients: do features of managed care widen the racial, ethnic and language-based gaps?', *Medical Care*, **42**, 966–74.

Van Weel, C. (2004), 'How general practice is funded in the Netherlands', *The Medical Journal of Australia*, **181**(2), 110–11.

Van Weel, C. and C.B. Del Mar (2004), 'How should GPs be paid?', *The Medical Journal of Australia*, **181**(2), 98–9.

Wennberg, J. (1982), 'Professional uncertainty and the problem of supplier-induced demand', *Social Science & Medicine*, **16**, 811–24.

Wennberg, J. (1984), 'Dealing with medical practice variations: a proposal for action', *Health Affairs*, Summer 1984, 6–32.

Williams, J.W. Jr., K. Rost, A.J. Dietrich, M.C. Gotti, S.J. Zyzanski and J. Cornell (1999), 'Primary care physicians' approach to depressive disorders. Effects of physician speciality and practice structure', *Archives of Family Medicine*, **8**(1), 58–67.

Wyke, S., N. Mays, A. Street, G. Bevan, H. McLeod and N. Goodwin (2003), 'Should general practitioners purchase health care for their patients? The total purchasing experiment in Britain', *Health Policy*, **65**, 243–59.

26 Optimal risk adjustment
Jacob Glazer and Thomas G. McGuire

1. What is optimal risk adjustment?

When a provider is paid using risk adjustment, the price paid to the provider is conditioned on observable characteristics of the enrollee or patient. For example, if a primary care physician accepts responsibility for providing all necessary medical services to an enrollee for a year, the capitation payment to the physician might be based on the enrollee's age, with older enrollees having higher payments associated with them because they are expected to cost more (see Chapter 25 by Iversen and Lurås in this Companion.) Methods of risk adjustment are concerned with how much more to pay the physician for an older enrollee than for a younger enrollee.

Two approaches to addressing this question have been taken in the economic literature. *Conventional risk adjustment* sees the goal of risk adjustment as to pay providers as close as possible to the amount the enrollee is expected to cost. If an older enrollee is expected to be twice as expensive as a younger enrollee, conventional risk adjustment would pay twice as much for the older enrollee. Many factors other than age matter for expected costs. Research on conventional risk adjustment is statistical and data oriented. Researchers seek to find the right combination of variables (referred to as risk adjustors) to include in regression models so that the explained variation in health care costs is high, without relying on risk adjustors that are difficult to collect in practice or can be manipulated by providers seeking to increase revenue. The premise behind this research – sometimes regarded to be so obvious as to not require justification or analysis – is that the health care market in question will function better the better job the regression model can do in predicting health care costs of enrollees.

Optimal risk adjustment methods also yield an answer to how much more to pay for an older enrollee but by a different method. *Optimal risk adjustment* views risk adjustment as a set of incentives aimed to induce providers to behave in accordance with some well defined objective. Calculating the optimal risk adjustment begins with an explicit assumption about the functioning of price in the relevant market and a model that relates the terms of that price (for example, the payment for young and old) to the behaviour of providers and patients (for a general treatment of these issues, see Chalkley, Chapter 22 in this Companion). The economic objective (usually efficiency) is also stated explicitly. Then, using principal–agent methods, the optimal risk adjustment is derived as the prices for young and old which maximize the efficiency of the health care market. Notice, therefore, that the term 'optimal risk adjustment' does not refer to particular weights, but rather to a procedure by which the optimal weights are obtained. Optimal risk adjustment also relies on data, but the optimal weights are not in general regression coefficients, but a more complex function involving an economic maximization.

In this review, we introduce the ideas behind optimal risk adjustment by stating explicitly the different types of problems in health care markets we expect risk adjustment to address. We then consider, for each of these problems, whether conventional risk adjustment is a good approach to solution, and whether a different approach to risk adjustment would be superior. We will see that for almost any problem in health care markets, conventional risk adjustment is dominated by another risk adjustment mechanism and that the superior mechanism depends on the specifics of the problem it tries to address. Optimal risk adjustment is better thought of as a methodological approach than a particular form of 'answer'. The challenge for proponents of the idea of optimal risk adjustment is to translate ideas from economic theory into concrete improvements in the way risk adjustment is done in practice, a topic we address at the close of the chapter.

2.   Problems in health care markets that risk adjustment may help address

The ideas presented here apply to a number of different health care markets, including physician and hospital payment. To keep the discussion simple, we will confine examples to the market for competing health plans. The settings we have in mind include the private health insurance market in the US where employers decide what to pay health plan options for employees, the US Medicare programme where beneficiaries choose between regular (fee-for-service) Medicare and competing health plans paid by capitation, and public sector health insurance in a number of countries where the national or local governments pay health plans a capitation payment for each enrollee.

Risk adjustment is intended to deter certain unwanted health plan behaviours (Cutler and Zeckhauser, 2000; Van de Ven and Ellis, 2000; Geoffard, Chapter 10 in this Companion) which can be grouped into three categories: (i) individual access problems, (ii) group access problems, and (iii) quality distortions. In what follows we will discuss each of these problems and how risk adjustment is supposed to address them.

Ensuring individual access
If a health plan knows that the expected cost of an identifiable enrollee will be more (or less) than the capitation payment the plan receives, the plan might take actions that discourage (or encourage) enrolment by the individual. For example, suppose an employer paid the same amount to a health plan for any employee who joined the plan, irrespective of the age, gender, or any other characteristic of the employee. The plan could anticipate that older workers are going to be more expensive, and discriminate against them in the enrolment process. In the extreme the plan could simply deny the application of an older worker.

If the capitation payment to the plan is related to the expected cost of enrollees based on observable characteristics such as age, the plan has no motive to discriminate against the old. The plan might still have a motive to discriminate on the basis of other things it might know about the person that are not captured in the risk adjustment formula. For example, suppose the plan knows that more educated enrollees demand more health care services, but the payment formula does not include an adjustment for education. Then, the plan has a motive to discriminate against the educated in enrolment.

This individual level discrimination is the problem conventional risk adjustment is best suited to fixing. Indeed, under a certain set of assumptions about the nature of the individual access problem, it can be shown that conventional risk adjustment is also 'optimal', in other words, maximizes efficiency in the market. Suppose inefficiency exists whenever the (risk-adjusted) payment made for a potential enrollee deviates from the actual cost the enrollee would incur. In particular, suppose that the magnitude of the inefficiency is proportional to the square of the difference between the payment and the actual cost. In this case, risk adjustment derived from a least squares regression will minimize the magnitude of the inefficiency (by minimizing the residual sum of squares) and therefore be identical to the optimal risk adjustment. In other words, the loss function in terms of economic efficiency is identical to the statistical loss function minimized by a 'least squares' regression.

This is not a particularly plausible formulation of inefficiency related to individual access, and more reasonable ones imply that even with respect to individual access, conventional risk adjustment is not the efficient way to do risk adjustment. First, the loss function is probably not symmetric. Underpayments may be worse in terms of an inefficiency than overpayments of the same magnitude. It may be that underpayment results in an access problem but overpayment does not result in 'too much' access. Second, a gap between payment and actual cost is not really the problem. Plans react only to what they expect, so since a plan cannot forecast costs exactly, minimizing a function related to the gap between payments and actual costs is not the right objective; it is the gap between payment and the costs the plan expects an enrollee to incur that leads to access problems. To quantify this gap for a particular risk adjustment formula requires specification of what the plan's expectations are. An asymmetric loss function and specification of what a plan might know have been incorporated in risk adjustment research designed to contend with individual access in work by Shen and Ellis (2002), who assume that a health plan can deny enrolment to an applicant if the plan expects costs to exceed payment. (The loss function in this chapter is thus highly asymmetric. There is no efficiency loss if payment exceeds expected cost.) In their empirical analysis of the individual access problem using employer data, a form of optimal risk adjustment based on simple age–gender adjustment is superior to conventional risk adjustment based on more variables. Thus, in general, conventional risk adjustment is not 'optimal' for dealing with individual access.

Although ensuring individual access is a major rationale for conventional risk adjustment, it is not clear that individual access is even much of a problem in practice. In the contracts that employers have with their health plans, and in regulations imposed by public payers in the US and other countries, health plans are required to maintain 'open enrolment'. In a conference on the use of risk adjustment by private payers in the US, employers' representatives believed that these contract features adequately addressed the individual access problem (Glazer and McGuire, 2001). Medicare also requires 'open enrolment' for contracting plans. If a plan takes Medicare enrollees it must accept any who apply. Similar regulations against individual discrimination apply to this problem in public payment systems in other countries as well.

Ensuring group access

Risk adjustment has also been used to deal with access problems at the group level. In the US, health plans decide if they wish to contract with a private employer or with a public programme such as Medicare. Once they do, they must take all applicants as we just noted. But if the plan anticipates drawing an 'adverse selection' of the risks from the potential applicant pool, risk adjustment of the payments may ameliorate any plan concern about adequate payment. Analysis of this issue leads to important insights about risk adjustment.

Consider first the situation of a private employer, small in the local market for health plans, and wishing to offer employees choice of plans to be paid by capitation. If the employer offers only one plan, no risk adjustment is necessary. With two or more plans, the employer and the plans might be concerned that the distribution of health care cost risks might not be evenly distributed among the plans. Employers enter into contracts with health plans to pay them for enrollees but virtually never use risk adjustment in these contracts (Glazer and McGuire, 2001), conventional or otherwise. It is the average capitation payment to a plan that matters both to the plan and to the employer, so negotiations around the contract concern this average payment. Data confirm that negotiated prices characterize this market; employers pay different prices to different plans for the same coverage, and different employers pay a plan different prices for the same coverage (Glazer and McGuire, 2002a). It may seem irrational for a plan to accept the same price for an old as for a young worker, but as long as the average has been determined appropriately in negotiation, there is no reason from either party's point of view to do any risk adjustment at all. Private markets in the US continue to disregard the call by some researchers for employers to use risk adjustment to address problems of adverse selection, and the ability of negotiated average prices to solve both sides' problems in private markets is probably the major reason why.

Medicare, and public payers in most countries, faces a different problem. A large national programme is not in a position to negotiate plan by plan but must set rules that apply nationally. In this case, risk adjustment may be a partial solution to inducing plans fearing selection to contract with Medicare. However, even in this case conventional risk adjustment is not in general the optimal mechanism. As shown in Glazer and McGuire (2000), if 'sicker' individuals prefer to join one plan and 'healthier' individuals prefer to join another plan, then unless the risk adjustors are perfectly correlated with the individuals' 'health status', optimal risk adjustment calls for 'overpaying' for some individuals and 'underpaying' for the other, relative to the conventional risk adjustment rates. That is, if, for example, age is used as the only risk adjustor and age is correlated, but not perfectly, with individuals' health status (that is, some old individuals are healthy and some young individuals sick) then unless risk adjustment 'overpays' for the old and 'underpays' for the young, plans that attract (a share above the population's share of) the sick individuals may not break even. Furthermore, in a surprising result, the lower the correlation between age and health status, the higher should be the overpayment for the elderly and the under-payment for the young in order for all plans to break even.

Ensuring the efficient quality of care
In situations where competing health plans are prevented from denying enrolment to particular individuals due to open enrolment provisions, plans can still seek to attract and deter enrollees with certain characteristics by setting various dimensions of the quality of services. This is termed service-level selection and links risk adjustment with incentives to plans to provide the efficient quality of health care.

It has long been recognized that plans have an incentive to over-provide some services and under-provide others in order to deter and attract enrollees with certain characteristics

(Newhouse, 1996; Van de ven and Ellis, 2000). This 'plan manipulation' in the terminology of Cutler and Zeckhauser (2000), emerges when plans compete on the basis of service quality in an environment of prospective payment and potential adverse selection (Glazer and McGuire, 2000). Frank et al. (2000) use data from a Medicaid public payer in the US to show that plans have an incentive to distort the quality of different services to affect patterns of enrolment. Recent papers confirm the predictions that plans will differentially distort quality choices (Cao and McGuire, 2003; Mello et al., 2002).

In this context, risk adjustment can alter a plan's incentives and balance the incentives to provide care attractive to both low-cost potential enrollees (such as primary care) and to high-cost enrollees (care for a chronic disease such as diabetes). Conventional risk adjustment can improve incentives over no risk adjustment by increasing the payment for higher cost persons, but optimal risk adjustment can do better. The approach taken in the optimal risk adjustment literature in this context is to view the plan as making a decision about how tightly to ration the various services the plan provides. A 'service' might be primary care, cardiac care, maternity care, and so on. Tighter rationing means lower cost and lower quality of care. By explicitly recognizing the financial incentives a plan has to set quality differentially, and relating these to the parameters of the risk adjustment formula, the weights on the available adjustors can be chosen so as to achieve the desired balance of incentives.

When a plan decreases the stringency of rationing on a service, that is, increases the level of spending on a service, costs are affected because spending goes up for existing enrollees and because spending is incurred on enrollees newly attracted by the spending increase. The idea of optimal risk adjustment is to make sure that, for all services a plan is making a decision about, from those used mostly by the healthy and cheap to those used mostly by the sick and costly, these cost increases are balanced against revenue gains to the same degree. This is done by recognizing that new enrollees have a payment made on their behalf and the terms of that payment are described by the risk adjustment parameters. There is thus a relation between the marginal cost and marginal revenue for each of the services in a plan. Balancing incentives across services essentially amounts to an equation for each service, the level of rationing being the variable and the risk adjustment weights being the parameters.

Glazer and McGuire (2002b) characterize optimal risk adjustment in a market where competing health plans choose the quality of their bundle of services and show that it depends on the first and second moments of the distribution of health care utilization patterns by service in the population. To equalize incentives to ration all services, the covariance of the risk adjusted payment with the use of every service must track the covariance of the total predicted costs associated with the increase in use of the service. Intuitively, the optimal risk adjustment formula must have the property that by spending on a service, the cost consequences to a plan relate to the revenue consequences in the same way for all services. It is important to stress that the result for optimal risk adjustment says how a given average payment should be risk adjusted, but does not answer the question of how high or low on average the payment should be.

A key assumption in this approach is that a plan sets rationing at the service level, and does not customize rationing for each individual. Ma (2003) and Jack (2004) have both pointed out that profit maximization implies that a plan would prefer to ration services person by 'type' of person, and Jack (2004) has incorporated this feature into a model of optimal risk adjustment. Glazer and McGuire (2000) justify their assumption by appealing to separate objectives of the managers and the physicians in a plan. A manager would prefer doctors to ration more tightly to the sicker (more costly) patients. Doctors in each clinical area in models of service-level rationing are viewed as being given a budget, and doing the best they can to maximize the health benefits to their pool of patients. This behaviour implies that the shadow price of rationing across patients within a service area is the same, but because the managers set the budgets, the level of rationing differs across clinical areas.

The optimal risk adjustment emerges as a set of linear equations, one for each service, with unknowns equal to the variables available for risk adjustment. An interesting feature of this optimal risk adjustment scheme is that the number of parameters available for risk adjustment could be greater or less than the number of services a plan is deciding about. (Some risk adjustment systems have scores of weights.) If the number of available risk adjustment parameters is larger than the number of services whose quality the plan decides on, there may be many risk adjustors that achieve optimality in the sense of incentive balance across services. Glazer and McGuire (2002b) label and characterize 'minimum variance' optimal risk adjustment as the solution to the optimal risk adjustment formula that minimizes the symmetric loss function in the square of deviations between payments and actual costs. The 'second best' optimal risk adjustment, when the number of risk adjustment parameters is less than the number of services, has not yet been described in the literature.

3.   Optimal risk adjustment and the practice of risk adjustment

What promise does the economic research on optimal risk adjustment hold for the practice of risk adjustment policy in the US and other countries? As we noted above, formal risk adjustment of any stripe, conventional, optimal, or otherwise, does not appear to be needed in private employer markets in the US, where employers or their representatives choose the plans they contract with and negotiate the average rates. In contrast to other payment reforms initiated by Medicare in the areas of both physician payment and hospital payment, where the private sector followed Medicare's lead, this is not happening in the area of risk adjusted payment for health plans.

Remaining in the US context, Medicare is in the process of phasing in more detailed risk adjustment based on diagnoses from hospital discharges from the previous year, a revision based on an improvement in the form of conventional risk adjustors used in this programme. The major problem in Medicare at this point is what has been referred to above as the 'group access' problem, the issue of inducing health plans to offer enrolment to Medicare beneficiaries. This is mostly a payment level, not a payment mix, issue. Private markets address the group problem by negotiation; Medicare substitutes regulation, and since the Balanced Budget Amendment (BBA) of 1998, there are new regulations raising the levels in counties in which the old formula has led to low payment levels, and limiting the level and growth of payments in counties in which the old formulas led to high payments. Medicare is a large payer, so its risk adjustment formula matters (as the literature on service level selection attests) but in Medicare, the policy action is primarily in the level of payment. Similar observations apply to Medicaid programmes administered by states in the US.

The larger is a payer in relation to the market for health plans, the more risk adjustment matters; indeed, the more payment policy matters across the board. Medicare is an intermediate case, large, but not the whole market. Economic analysis of risk adjustment matters most, therefore, in countries or settings with a one-payer system, such as in the national plans of the Netherlands, Germany, Israel or Switzerland. Although each country is a special case, and has a complex set of regulations affecting the quality and access choices of plans, the economics of risk adjustment finds its most ready application in these settings. Thinking of optimal risk adjustment as an approach or a method leads to the following simple conclusion: economic researchers should set up a simple model of the health plan market in each country, regard the weights on the risk adjusters as the variables, and characterize the optimal weight.

In light of the widespread concern for the quality of care in many countries, it is important to consider what role risk adjustment might play in promoting quality. Obviously, if the question is the overall level of funding of the health care system, risk adjustment, which raises the payment for one person by lowering it for another, is not the issue. Risk adjustment can affect the relative incentives to provide quality of different types of health care services.

References

Cao, Z. and T.G. McGuire (2003), 'Service-level selection by HMOs in Medicare', *Journal of Health Economics*, **22**, 915–31.

Cutler, D. and R. Zeckhauser (2000), 'The anatomy of health insurance', in: A. Culyer and J. Newhouse (eds), *Handbook of Health Economics*, Amsterdam: North-Holland.

Frank, R.G., J. Glazer and T.G. McGuire (2000), 'Measuring adverse selection in managed health care', *Journal of Health Economics*, **19** (November), 829–54.

Glazer, J. and T.G. McGuire (2000), 'Optimal risk adjustment of health insurance premiums: an application to managed care', *American Economic Review*, **90** (4, September), 1055–71.

Glazer, J. and T.G. McGuire (2001), 'Private employers don't need formal risk adjustment', *Inquiry*, **38**(3), 260–69.

Glazer, J. and T.G. McGuire (2002a), 'Multiple payers, commonality and free-riding in health care: Medicare and private payers', *Journal of Health Economics*, **21**, 1049–69.

Glazer, J. and T.G. McGuire (2002b), 'Setting health plan premiums to ensure efficient quality in health care: minimum variance optimal risk adjustment', *Journal of Public Economics*, **84**, 153–73.

Jack, William (2004), 'Optimal risk adjustment in a model with adverse selection and spatial competition', Unpublished.

Ma, Ching-to Albert (2003), 'Managed care and shadow price', *Health Economics Letters*, **7**(3), 17–20.

Mello, M.M., S.C. Stearn and S.C. Norton (2002), 'Do Medicare HMOs still reduce health services use after controlling for selection bias?', *Health Economics*, **20**(11), 323–40.

Newhouse, J.P. (1996), 'Reimbursing health plans and health providers: selection versus efficiency in production', *Journal of Economic Literature*, **34**(3), 1236–63.

Shen, Y. and R.P. Ellis (2002), 'Cost minimizing risk adjustment', *Journal of Health Economics*, **21**(3), 515–30.

Van de Ven, W.P. and R.P. Ellis (2000), 'Risk adjustment in competitive health plan markets', in: A. Culyer and J. Newhouse (eds), *Handbook of Health Economics*, Amsterdam: North Holland.

27 The role of economic incentives in improving the quality of mental health care
Susan L. Ettner and Michael Schoenbaum

1. Introduction

Inadequate quality, while of general concern in the health care sector, may be an even greater problem in the area of mental health care. Past studies have shown that patients with mental disorders frequently remain undiagnosed; when diagnosed, remain untreated; and when treated, do not receive guideline-concordant treatment (Borus et al., 1988; Fifer et al., 1994; Ormel et al., 1990; Simon and Vonkorff, 1995; Von Korff et al., 1987; Wells et al., 1999; Young et al., 2001). Many factors underlie this low quality of care, including poor patient and provider knowledge about mental disorders and appropriate treatment; social stigma, which inhibits patient and provider communication; and organizational and financial characteristics of the health care and health insurance systems (Kilbourne et al., 2004). Moreover, mental disorders may directly undermine patients' ability to act rationally in an economic sense, by causing cognitive and perceptual deficits, excessive pessimism, low energy and other problems. Thus patients may be unaware of the likely costs and benefits of various treatment options; may be unable to discern quality of care even after treatment has been provided; and, particularly for patients with severe and persistent mental illness such as schizophrenia, may even be unaware of having a disorder at all. Patients with mental health problems may also lack familial ties and social support systems, reducing the availability of people who could act as their agents in health care decisions. Under such circumstances, patients are unlikely to make utility-maximizing choices.

In the absence of adequate information, patients rely on other players in the health care system, such as providers, health plans and purchasers, to serve as agents in representing patients' interests; in effect, the health insurance benefit or provider–patient relationship becomes a type of implicit contract to help patients in circumstances when they may not fully represent their own interests (see, for instance, Chapter 24 by Rice in this Companion). As is typical of principal–agent relationships, however, these players all face different sets of incentives that may influence their actions. Ultimately, the quality of mental health care is determined by the interactions of these various actors, so it is important to understand what incentives each group faces and how these incentives can be modified to promote efficient outcomes.

Patients make choices about the quantity and type of services obtained, as well as the type of provider used. The RAND Health Insurance Experiment demonstrated that under fee-for-service insurance, the price elasticity of demand for mental health care was substantially higher than that for medical care, suggesting that patients respond strongly to cost-sharing requirements. This responsiveness frequently leads to under-utilization – and over-utilization – of services, relative to clinical guidelines and societal cost-effectiveness.

Mental health benefits also help to determine the specialty of the treating provider, which in turn is associated with the quality of care received. For example, rates of appropriate psychotropic medication management are higher among patients treated by psychiatrists than those treated in primary care, yet most health plans have higher cost-sharing and stricter benefit limits for mental health specialty care than for general or specialty medical care.

Quality of care is most directly affected by health care providers, including psychiatrists, generalist physicians, psychologists, and psychiatric social workers, and by delivery institutions such as psychiatric and general hospitals. While altruism and professionalism are strong motivations determining the behaviour of providers, the amount and form of financial remuneration (for example, salary, capitation, fee-for-service, performance-based payment) also affects behaviour, especially when providers are themselves poorly-informed about the evidence base for the treatment decision. As noted by the Institute of Medicine (2001), the incentives inherent in the reimbursement system may not encourage – or indeed may actually discourage – quality improvement efforts, even among the best-motivated professionals.

Health plans affect quality of care through cost-sharing terms (including co-payments, co-insurance, deductibles, stop-loss provisions, and benefit limits), methods for contracting providers, the specific providers with whom they contract, use of utilization management tools such as preauthorization requirements and utilization review, and other methods. These details are jointly determined with the amount of the premium or capitated payment that plans are paid for covering each beneficiary, as well as by any incentives built into that payment, for example, the risk borne for excess patient costs, or performance bonuses.

Health care purchasers influence quality indirectly, through their choice of which insurance products to offer beneficiaries. However, they may have considerable influence over the details of these products, particularly in the case of large purchasers and those bearing the financial risk of insurance themselves ('self-insured' purchasers). The incentives facing health care purchasers vary. For example, in the US, most health care purchasers are employers or government programmes. Employers have a direct interest in the health of their beneficiaries, to promote productivity and minimize absenteeism and disability; and they have an indirect interest, because health benefits are part of a broader compensation package intended to attract and retain the types of employees the firm wants. For government programmes, beneficiaries are one constituency of interest, but policy-makers are also influenced by the political interests of voters who – except in the case of Medicare – are mainly not programme beneficiaries.

In the rest of this chapter, we focus primarily on the incentives facing health care providers, because they most directly influence quality of care and thus have been a particular focus of efforts to promote quality using economic incentives. However, we also consider the perspectives of other stakeholders, because incentives must be aligned throughout the health system in order to be effective and efficient. As discussed below, the existing theoretical and especially empirical literature on financial incentives to promote health care quality is quite limited and very little of it focuses on mental health. As appropriate, however, we comment on issues relating to mental illness or mental health care organization that are particularly relevant for considering programmes to incentivize quality.

2. 'Real world' applications

The 'first generation' of financial incentives in health care was focused principally on controlling cost rather than promoting quality or efficiency. Among other means of cost containment, capitation, utilization review and selective contracting based on the physician's historical utilization patterns were used by the newly emerging managed health and managed behavioural health companies. Historically, these incentives were implemented in ways that were either independent of quality or that actually inhibited quality. We therefore focus on a 'second generation' of financial incentives that aim to improve health care quality through 'value-based purchasing' and 'pay for performance'. This second generation is motivated by a desire to improve clinical outcomes as an end in itself – and by a perception that clinically suboptimal care is economically inefficient and that quality improvement may be one path to controlling costs.

Several national organizations in the US have developed prominent 'value-based purchasing' initiatives to assist consumers and health care purchasers in choosing plans based on 'value' rather than on cost per se: the National Committee for Quality Assurance (NCQA), the Joint Commission on Accreditation of Health Care Organizations (JCAHO) and the National Business Coalition on Health (NBCH). Each is a private, not-for-profit organization. NCQA started an accreditation programme for managed care organizations (MCOs) in 1991 and regularly issues report cards based on its Health Plan Employer Data and Information Set (HEDIS). HEDIS is a set of standardized performance measures, including depression-related measures, used to compare MCOs in terms of their quality, access to care and member satisfaction. JCAHO is perhaps best known for evaluating and accrediting health care providers, but it also evaluates and accredits health and behavioural health plans with respect to specific standards for improving their health care quality and safety. NBCH is a member-based organization of employer-based health coalitions. Its major tool is the eValue8 system (National Business Coalition on Health, 2004), which uses a standard annual survey to collect information from health plans on benchmarks in a variety of areas, including behavioural health, and creates standardized performance reports for its members to use in evaluating quality.

An increasing number of 'real world' examples of pay-for-performance programmes can be found in both the US and the UK. Rosenthal et al. (2003) describe many of the quality-based compensation programmes that have been implemented by health plans in recent years. The Leapfrog Group for Patient Safety, a consortium of private and public health care purchasers founded in 2000, has developed an 'Incentive and Reward Compendium', which documents all financial and non-financial incentive programmes being carried out in the US (The Leapfrog Group, 2005). As of February 2005, this website listed 89 initiatives, although not all of these involved explicit financial incentives. Listed programmes that involved pecuniary rewards (and in some cases, penalties) encompass a wide range of performance measures, including health outcomes, quality of care scores, patient satisfaction, investment in information systems and care management tools, professional contributions to the medical group, prescribing patterns and preventive screening rates.

The US Centers for Medicare and Medicaid Services (CMS) recently introduced several demonstration programmes involving financial incentives to promote quality (CMS, 2005). The Premier Hospital Quality Incentive Demonstration gives financial incentives to about 300 hospitals based on 34 quality indicators related to five clinical conditions. Hospitals scoring in the top 10 per cent receive a 2 per cent bonus payment and those scoring in the next 10 per cent receive a 1 per cent bonus, while hospitals that do not meet certain quality standards after two years are subject to payment reductions. The three-year Physician Group Practice Demonstration, which is being pilot-tested with ten large physician practices, allows physicians who reduce Medicare costs to retain part of the savings as a bonus and earn back another part of the savings if they meet certain quality targets. Other Medicare demonstrations use set-asides for quality incentive payments based on clinical performance measures, focusing on areas such as the use of health information technology; patient safety, reduction in small-area variations and the use of culturally appropriate care; disease management for beneficiaries with advanced heart failure and/or complex diabetes; end-stage renal disease services; disease management for severely chronically ill Medicare beneficiaries and dual Medicare–Medicaid beneficiaries; and care management for high-cost beneficiaries.

In 2004, the UK government signed a contract with family practitioners in the National Health Service (NHS) that will provide more than $1.8 billion in bonuses for high-quality care (Roland, 2004). Family practitioners earn points based on clinical indicators, which are process and intermediate outcome measures related to ten chronic conditions; organizational indicators, which include records and information about patients, communication with patients, education and training, management of medicines and management of physicians' practices; patient experience, measured by the use of patient surveys and length of consultations; and prompt access to services. A provider earning the maximum points possible would earn an additional $77 000 per year. The NHS set aside more than 20 per cent of its previous family practice budget for bonuses under this plan, making it the largest quality incentive programme to date (Roland, 2004).

The most widely publicized demonstrations focusing on mental health are the 'incentive grants' funded through the Robert Wood Johnson Foundation's programme on 'Depression in primary care: linking clinical and system strategies' (Robert Wood Johnson Foundation, 2005). This five-year, $12 million programme began in July 2000 and has funded eight projects which are currently being evaluated. Its goal is to overcome the barriers to diagnosis and guideline-concordant treatment of depression in the primary care sector by combining an effective clinical model of quality improvement with changes in the incentives and organizational arrangements necessary to support the clinical model. The financial incentives offered to providers vary widely across the eight projects, ranging from minimal incentives to paying providers to spend an extra 15 minutes with depressed patients.

3. Empirical evidence
Gibbons (1998) and Prendergast (1999) provide useful overviews of the general economic theory underlying pay-for-performance. Most of the published research on financial incentives in health care is also conceptual rather than empirical (Berwick, 1996; Conrad and Christianson, 2004; Dudley et al., 2004; Glass et al., 1999; Grignon et al., 2002; Robinson, 2001; Tufano et al., 1999) or focuses on the 'first generation' of economic incentives (for example, the impact of capitation on costs) rather than the 'second generation' of incentives designed to improve quality. Although a full review of the literature on

financial incentives and health care quality is outside the scope of this chapter, prior reviews include Dudley et al. (1998), Armour et al. (2001), National Health Care Purchasing Institute (2001), Maio et al. (2003), and Rosenthal and Frank (2004). These studies have noted variability in existing empirical evidence regarding the effect of financial incentives and the general lack of a substantial evidence base in this area. Performance-based bonuses have been associated with higher immunization rates (Fairbrother et al., 1997; 1999; 2001; Hemenway, 1994; 1995; Kouides et al., 1998), increased use of ACE inhibitors and HbA1c assessments (Chung et al., 2003), and lower Caesarean section rates (Hanchak, 1997), but not patient satisfaction (Hanchak, 1997), quality of diabetes care (Keating et al., 2004) or cancer screening rates (Hillman et al., 1998).

Almost none of the literature on financial incentives and quality of care has focused on mental health. Goldberg (1999) describes the financial incentives affecting integration of primary and specialty care for mental disorders. Similarly, Dewa et al. (2001) discuss the likely effectiveness of fee-for-service, capitation and blended payment in promoting a 'shared-care' approach to treating mental disorders. Frank et al. (2003) describe institutional barriers to the adoption of quality improvement interventions in mental health. In a rare empirical study in this area, Sturm and Wells (1998) provide data suggesting that improving provider knowledge is a more efficient way to improve quality of care than changing financial incentives, although only payment type (prepaid vs. fee-for-service) was examined. We know of no published study examining the impact of performance bonuses on the quality of mental health care.

4.   Designing and evaluating economic incentives to improve quality

Although performance-based payment systems are most commonly used to reward productivity or penalize clinicians for high patient utilization, they are increasingly being tied to quality measures (National Health Care Purchasing Institute, 2001). JCAHO (2004) noted that, although financial incentives are likely to be among the most powerful tools available for changing provider behaviour, pay-for-performance programmes are still largely untested, and that payment for patient education, continuity of care and integration of services – all particularly critical issues in behavioural health – is often inadequate.

In practice, the effectiveness of financial incentives to providers to improve quality is likely to depend heavily on the choice of who is being incentivized, how the incentive is structured, which behaviours are incentivized for which patients, and how the behaviour is measured and risk-adjusted. The choices of who to incentivize for which behaviours, and how to incentivize them, are not always independent. Many health care professionals play a role in the delivery of mental health services – psychiatrists, primary care physicians, psychologists, psychiatric social workers – and mental disorders are treated in both the primary care and specialty sectors. In specialty settings, patients often present with a diagnosis and are relatively sick, so quality hinges on appropriate, active treatment; while primary care providers may need to be incentivized to screen and diagnose patients, and to monitor or refer them to specialty care (Frank et al., 2003). Also, mental health specialists are more likely than primary care providers to be in solo (or small group) practice and paid on a fee-for-service basis. The insurance setting matters in choosing which behaviours to incentivize. For example, the ability to incentivize greater continuity of mental health care between the primary care and specialty sectors will be diminished when behavioural health specialty care is 'carved out' of the services provided by the health plan (Frank et al., 2003).

In prioritizing the services to incentivize, the number of patients likely to be affected, existence of accepted performance measures and clinical guidelines and potential for quality improvement should all be considered (National Health Care Purchasing Institute, 2001). Within mental health, psychotherapy and pharmacotherapy are the two main treatment modalities, yet there are many aspects of these modalities that could be intervened on (for example, the type of psychotherapy, drug class or drug dosage). Provider incentives generally must also be tailored to a target disease. While interventions focusing on a particular disease run the risk of diverting resources away from other conditions, a 'one-size-fits-all' intervention is unlikely to exist. For example, while analogous incentives may help improve care for adults with depression and children with attention deficit and hyperactivity disorder, since both conditions are common and generally treatable in primary care settings, significantly different strategies may be required to improve care for schizophrenia, which is rarer and requires more in-patient and specialty care as well as comprehensive social services.

Possible financial incentive models include quality bonuses, at-risk compensation, performance fee schedules, quality grants, reimbursement for care planning and variable cost-sharing for patients (National Health Care Purchasing Institute, 2002). For example, in a fee-for-service system, total compensation for the services provided to the patient is $R*V$, where R is the per-visit rate paid to the provider and V is the total number of visits during the treatment episode. A bonus $B(O)$ that depends on the provider's performance (O) can be paid as an add-on to the base fee per visit (total compensation $= (R + B(O))*V$) or as a lump-sum bonus for the episode (total compensation $= R*V + B(O)$). The former approach gives providers an incentive to provide additional services, which might reduce cost-efficiency but be beneficial if patients typically receive inadequate levels of care. If the bonus is determined by the average performance of a *group* of providers, the bonus can be expressed as:

$$B\left(\sum_{i=1}^{N} O_i/N\right),$$

where O_i is the performance of provider i and N is the number of providers in the group.

As group size increases, the bonus resulting from a given improvement in provider j's behaviour grows smaller. Thus there are trade-offs between administrative feasibility and optimizing incentives. For example, bonuses are frequently calculated based on the performance of an entire provider group rather than of individual providers. While this method simplifies performance measurement, it clearly dilutes the incentives, especially in large practices. Choices for the incentive also include the magnitude and frequency of the bonus. Typical performance-based bonuses are only 5 per cent of the provider's total compensation, which may not provide sufficient motivation for change, especially if the bonus comes from a single health plan accounting for only a modest proportion of the provider's total caseload.

Some providers may be resistant to the idea of having part of their compensation depend on their performance, especially if they do not agree with the practices being incentivized or if they believe adequate performance measurement and/or case mix adjustment is not possible (see, for instance, the chapters by Glazer and McGuire (26) and Smith and Street (30) in this Companion). Not all providers accept the premise of evidence-based medicine (Shojania and Grimshaw, 2005), that is, that research findings should drive the treatment of individual patients, especially in the area of mental health (Tanenbaum, 2005). Providers may also be reluctant to participate in programmes in which compensation depends in part on patient behaviour. This may be particularly important for mental disorders, since they directly affect patient behaviour in ways that may inhibit adherence to treatment recommendations, complicating the interpretation of data once they have been collected. Some areas may be more vulnerable than others to confounding of provider with patient behaviour. The ability to risk adjust adequately in order to put the providers on a 'level playing ground' is a particular concern when better patient outcomes, rather than process, are being rewarded.

Thus any pay-for-performance programme depends critically on the ability to measure and interpret performance (see the chapters by Smith and Street (30) and by Propper and Wilson (31) in this Companion). Some behaviours can be readily measured through the use of claims data (for example, the type of drug prescribed), while others may require primary data collection (for example, type of psychotherapy delivered) or cannot be readily measured at all (for example, the quality of the patient–clinician interaction during psychotherapy). In practice, incentive programmes in which performance can be measured using automated data are more likely to be used and sustained than those that require collection of primary data (for example, medical chart review or patient surveys). In the words of the Joint Commission on Accreditation of Healthcare Organisations (2004), the 'implementation and success of the programmes rests on the timely creation and deployment of an electronic health infrastructure that facilitates the collection, transmittal and analyses of the performance data that will drive the programmes.'

Finally, institutional barriers may limit the ability to pilot-test whether economic incentives are a viable means to improving quality of mental health care. Although the cost of *evaluating* the impact of reimbursement incentives is not relevant to long-term sustainability of incentive-based programmes to improve quality, the cost of running the programme itself is. While in theory such programmes can be made cost-neutral by penalizing low-quality providers in order to reward high-quality providers, in reality, providers are typically unwilling to risk a pay cut for the chance to receive a bonus. Thus, for instance, provider acceptance for the current NHS experiment was facilitated by the fact that the UK substantially increased the overall health care budget, so that total compensation paid to the family practitioners was not viewed as a 'zero-sum game' in which low-quality providers would lose in absolute terms.

Furthermore, transactions costs associated with running incentive-based programmes, such as the cost of measuring and monitoring quality, can be substantial. Health plans have strong concerns about implementing pilot incentives programmes using research funds and then having to discontinue the programme once the funding stops, so they sometimes opt not to get involved in such studies to begin with. Also, it may not be possible to randomize providers to incentives programmes, leading to selection bias in evaluating the effects of such programmes if provider groups who care more about quality are more likely to adopt reimbursement strategies that reward high-quality providers (or conversely, if groups with a bad track record are more motivated to change the system).

5.   Conclusions

Economic incentive programmes are a promising avenue for improving the quality of mental health care in both medical and specialty settings. However, considerable new research is needed to develop best practices in this area. Prior studies have described possible unintended consequences of pay-for-performance programmes, including the potential for 'gaming' the system, patient cream-skimming and dumping, and 'crowd-out,' that is, focusing on the incentivized behaviour at the expense of other desirable behaviours (Rosenthal and Frank, 2004). To date, however, we know of little empirical evidence regarding such issues; indeed, the main limitation of existing pay-for-performance programmes appears to be their relative weak incentives, and the resulting lack of effectiveness.

In describing the factors influencing the effectiveness of financial incentives in improving the delivery of care, the National Health Care Purchasing Institute (2002) identified the degree of trust between the physicians and the individuals and organizations implementing the incentives; the size of the incentive; the consumer's knowledge of the provider's performance; the perceived and actual accuracy of the data on which the incentives are based; recognition of the need for change among physicians; the medical leaders' degree of support for the incentives programme; the physicians' knowledge and understanding of the incentives; and the simplicity and directness of the incentive programme. Future research should focus on developing feasible, empirically tested approaches for designing economic incentive programmes that address these various factors.

Financial incentives may also be complemented by non-pecuniary incentives, such as public recognition of high-quality providers or a preferential referral system (Casalino et al., 2003; National Health Care Purchasing Institute, 2002). Providers may also be motivated by a reduction in administrative and regulatory burden (for example, via automatic authorization for more visits under a 'gate-keeping' system) or the receipt of continuing medical education credits. When provider knowledge is weak, it may also be desirable to reinforce economic incentives with training; for example, the effectiveness of a programme of incentives for primary care providers to prescribe anti-depressants at therapeutic dosages may be increased by training in appropriate dosage levels. Given the high societal cost associated with current patterns of health care for many common conditions – including prevalent, disabling and treatable mental disorders – progress towards developing effective economic incentive programmes may have high societal returns.

References

Armour, B.S., M.M. Pitts, R. Maclean, C. Cangialose, M. Kishel, H. Imai and J. Etchason (2001), 'The effect of explicit financial incentives on physician behavior', *Archives of Internal Medicine*, **161**, 1261–6.

Berwick, D.M. (1996), 'Payment by capitation and the quality of care', *New England Journal of Medicine*, **335**(16), 1227–31.

Borus, J.F., M.J. Howes, N.P. Devins, R. Rosenberg and W.W. Livingston (1988), 'Primary health care providers' recognition and diagnosis of mental disorders in their patients', *General Hospital Psychiatry*, **10** (5), 317–21.

Casalino, L., R.R. Gillies, S.M. Shortell, J.A. Schmittdiel, T. Bodenheimer, J.C. Robinson, T. Rundall, N. Oswald, H. Schauffler and M.C. Wang (2003), 'External incentives, information technology, and organized processes to improve health care quality for patients with chronic diseases', *Journal of the American Medical Association*, **289**(4), 434–41.

Centers for Medicare & Medicaid Services (2005), 'Medicare "Pay for Performance (P4p)" Initiatives', http://www.cms.hhs.gov/media/press/release.asp?Counter=1343, 31 January.

Chung, R.S., H.O. Chernicoff, K.A. Nakao, R.C. Nickel and A.P. Legorreta (2003), 'A quality-driven physician compensation model: four-year follow-up study', *Journal for Healthcare Quality*, **25**(6), 31–7.

Conrad, D. and J.B. Christianson (2004), 'Penetrating the "black box": financial incentives for enhancing the quality of physician services', *Medical Care Research and Review*, **61**(3), 37S–68S.

Dewa, C.S., J.S. Hoch and P. Goering (2001), 'Using financial incentives to promote shared mental health care', *Canadian Journal of Psychiatry*, **46**(6), 488–95.

Dudley, R.A., R.H. Miller, T.Y. Korenbrot and H.S. Luft (1998), 'The impact of financial incentives on quality of health care', *The Milbank Quarterly*, **76**(4), 649–86.

Dudley, R.A., A. Frolich, D.L. Robinowitz, J.A. Talavera, P. Broadhead and H.S. Luft (2004), 'Strategies to support quality-based purchasing: a review of the evidence', technical review 10 (prepared by the Stanford University of California San Fransisco Evidence-Based Practice Center under Contract No. 290-02-0017), Rockville, MD: Agency for Healthcare Research and Quality.

Fairbrother, G., S. Friedman, K.L. Hanson and G.C. Butts (1997), 'Effect of the vaccines for children program on inner-city neighborhood physicians', *Archives of Pediatric and Adolescent Medicine*, **151**(12), 1229–35.

Fairbrother, G., K.L. Hanson, S. Friedman and G.C. Butts (1999), 'The impact of physician bonuses, enhanced fees, and feedback on childhood immunization coverage rates', *American Journal of Public Health*, **89**(2), 171–5.

Fairbrother, G., M.J. Siegel, S. Friedman, P.D. Kory and G.C. Butts (2001), 'Impact of financial incentives on documented immunization rates in the inner city: results of a randomized controlled trial', *Ambulatory Pediatrics*, **1**(4), 206–12.

Fifer, S.K., S.D. Mathias, D.L. Patrick, P.D. Mazonson, D.P. Lubeck and D.P. Buesching (1994), 'Untreated anxiety among adult primary care patients in a health maintenance organization', *Archives of General Psychiatry*, **51**(9), 740–50.

Frank, R.G., H.A. Huskamp and H.A. Pincus (2003), 'Aligning incentives in the treatment of depression in primary care with evidence-based practice', *Psychiatric Services*, **54**(5), 682–7.

Gibbons, R. (1998), 'Incentives in organization', *Journal of Economic Perspectives*, **12**(4), 115–32.

Glass, K.P., L.E. Pieper and M.F. Berlin (1999), 'Incentive-based physician compensation models', *Journal of Ambulatory Care Management*, **22**(3), 36–46.

Goldberg, R.J. (1999), 'Financial incentives influencing the integration of mental health care and primary care', *Psychiatric Services*, **50**(8), 1071–5.

Grignon, M., V. Paris, D. Polton, A. Couffinhal and B. Pierrard (2002), 'Influence of physician payment methods on the efficiency of the health care system', Paris: Commission on the Future of Health Care in Canada.

Hanchak, N.A. (1997), 'A performance-based compensation model for obstetricians/gynecologists', *Clinical Obstetrics and Gynecology*, **40**(2), 437–45.

Hemenway, D. (1994), 'Economics of childhood immunization', *Journal of Policy Analysis and Management*, **32**, 519–23.

Hemenway, D. (1995), 'Financial incentives for childhood immunization', *Journal of Policy Analysis and Management*, **14**(1), 133–9.

Hillman, A.L., K. Ripley, N. Goldfarb, I. Nuamah, J. Weiner and E. Lusk (1998), 'Physician financial incentives and feedback: failure to increase cancer screening in Medicaid managed care', *American Journal of Public Health*, **88**(11), 1699–701.

Institute of Medicine (2001), 'Crossing the quality chasm: a new health system for the 21st Century', Washington, DC.

Joint Commission on Accreditation of Healthcare Organizations (2004), 'Joint commission establishes national principles to guide pay-for-performance programs', http://www.jcaho.org/news+room/news+release+archives/jcaho_112204.htm, 2 December.

Keating, N.L., M.B. Landrum, B.E. Landon, J.Z. Ayanian, C. Borbas, R. Wolf and E. Guadagnoli (2004), 'The influence of physicians' practice management strategies and financial arrangements on quality of care among patients with diabetes', *Medical Care*, **42**(9), 829–39.

Kilbourne A.M., H.C. Schulberg, E.P. Post, B.L. Rollman, B.H. Belnap and H.A. Pincus (2004), 'Translating evidence-based depression management services to community-based primary care practices', *Milbank Quarterly*, **82**(4), 631–59.

Kouides, R.W., N.M. Bennett, B. Lewis, J.D. Cappuccio, W.H. Barker and F.M. LaForce (1998), 'Performance-based physician reimbursement and influenza immunization rates in the elderly. The primary care physicians of Monroe County', *American Journal of Preventative Medicine*, **14**(2), 89–95.

Maio, V., N.I. Goldfarb, C. Carter and D.B. Nash (2003), 'Value-based purchasing: a review of the literature', The Commonwealth Fund, Jefferson Medical College, Thomas Jefferson University, Philadelphia.

National Business Coalition on Health (2004), 'About Evalue8, Overview', http://wwww.evalue8.org/eValue8/about/overview.cfm, 7 February 2005.

National Health Care Purchasing Institute (2001), 'The growing case for using physician incentives to improve health care quality': National Health Care Purchasing Institute, The Robert Wood Johnson Foundation.

National Health Care Purchasing Institute (2002), 'Provider incentive models for improving quality of care', National Health Care Purchasing Institute, The Robert Wood Johnson Foundation.

Ormel, J., W. Van Den Brink, M.W.J. Koeter, R. Giel, K. Van Der Meer, G. Van De Willige and F.W. Wilmink (1990), 'Recognition, management and outcome of psychological disorders in primary care: a naturalistic follow-up study', *Psychological Medicine*, **20**(4), 909–23.

Prendergast, C. (1999), 'The provision of incentives in firms', *Journal of Economic Literature*, **37**(1), 7–63.

Robert Wood Johnson Foundation (2005), 'Depression in primary care: linking clinical and system strategies', http://www.wpic.pitt.edu/dppc/, 25 July.

Robinson, J.C. (2001), 'Theory and practice in the design of physician payment incentives', *The Milbank Quarterly*, **79**(2), 149–77.

Roland, M. (2004), 'Linking physicians' pay to the quality of care – a major experiment in the United Kingdom', *New England Journal of Medicine*, **351**(14), 1448–54.

Rosenthal, M.B. and R.G. Frank (2004), 'Is there an empirical basis for quality-based incentives in health care?', unpublished manuscript.

Rosenthal, M.B., R. Fernandopulle, H.R. Song and B. Landon (2003), 'Paying for quality: an assessment of recent efforts to align provider incentives with the quality improvement agenda', unpublished manuscript, Harvard School of Public Health.

Shojania, K.G. and J.M. Grimshaw (2005), 'Evidence-based quality improvement: the state of the science', *Health Affairs (Millwood)*, **24**(1), 138–50.

Simon, G. and M. VonKorff (1995), 'Recognition, management, and outcomes of depression in primary care', *Archives of Family Medicine*, **4**(2), 99–105.

Sturm, R. and K.B. Wells (1998), 'Physician knowledge, financial incentives, and treatment decisions for depression', *Journal of Mental Health Policy and Economics*, **1**(2), 89–100.

Tanenbaum, S.J. (2005), 'Evidence-based practice as mental health policy: three controversies and a caveat', *Health Affairs (Millwood)*, **24**(1), 163–73.

The Leapfrog Group (2005), 'Compendium search', http://ir.leapfroggroup.org/compendium/compendiumsearch.cfm, February.

Tufano, J.T., D.A. Conrad and S.Y. Liang (1999), 'Addressing physician compensation and practice productivity', *Journal of Ambulatory Care Management*, **22**(3), 47–57.

Von Korff, M., S. Shapiro, J.D. Burke, M. Teitlebaum, E.A. Skinner, P. German, R.W. Turner, L. Klein and B. Burns (1987), 'Anxiety and depression in a primary care clinic. Comparison of diagnostic interview schedule, general health questionnaire, and practitioner assessments', *Archives of General Psychiatry*, **44**(2), 152–6.

Wells, K.B., M. Schoenbaum, J. Unutzer, I.T. Lagomasino and L.V. Rubenstein (1999), 'Quality of care for primary care patients with depression in managed care', *Archives of Family Medicine*, **8**(6), 529–36.

Wells, K.B., C.D. Sherbourne, M. Schoenbaum, N. Duan, L.S. Meredith, J. Unutzer, J. Miranda, M.F. Carney and L.V. Rubenstein (1999), 'Can managed, primary care practices improve quality and outcomes of care and employment status of depressed patients? Results from a randomized trial', Working Paper No. P-143-Rev, Santa Monica, CA: The Depression Patient Outcomes Research Team (PORT).

Young, A.S., R. Klap, C.D. Sherbourne and K.B. Wells (2001), 'The quality of care for depressive and anxiety disorders in the United States', *Archives of General Psychiatry*, **58**(1), 55–61.

28 Nursing home quality of care
*David C. Grabowski and Edward C. Norton**

1. Introduction

Nursing home quality of care continues to be an important public policy issue in spite of prolonged public outcry and government commissions addressing this issue. Often the number of nurses per resident is low and the staff turnover rate is high. Residents may develop new health problems after admission from physical restraints and missed medications. Amenities that are public goods within a nursing home – including the food, activities and public spaces – are too often sub-standard. Nursing home quality of care is of public concern because a high fraction of the elderly will live in a nursing home eventually, and the government pays for more than half of all nursing home costs. Therefore, economists have long studied the causes and potential policy responses to low quality nursing home care.

The recent academic interest in nursing home quality of care is driven by important new government policies aimed at improving quality of care and structural changes in the long-term care market that affect how nursing homes compete. We first review these major policies and trends. This research has also benefited from newly available data sets, which we summarize briefly. Finally, the bulk of this chapter synthesizes the economic literature on nursing home quality of care published primarily since 2000, when a chapter on long-term care in the *Handbook of Health Economics* was published (Norton, 2000).

This review is limited to the recent economic literature on the US long-term care system because there is relatively little published on other countries. For recent research on long-term care outside the US, see Carmichael and Charles (2003), Forder and Netten (2000), Lindeboom et al. (2002), O'Neill et al. (2000) and Portrait et al. (2000). We hope that researchers will explore similar issues in other countries.

2. Background

This section provides an overview of the nursing home industry and reviews recent economic, policy and demographic trends that may have implications for nursing home quality.

Financing and payment of nursing home services
A significant portion of nursing home care in the US is publicly paid. Medicaid accounts for roughly half of all nursing home expenditures and Medicare accounts for about 12 per cent (National Center for Health Statistics, 2003). Over the past three decades, both the Medicaid and Medicare programmes have dramatically changed how they pay nursing homes, which ultimately affects the quality of care.

* We are grateful to R. Tamara Konetzka, John Nyman, David Stevenson and Courtney H. Van Houtven for providing extremely helpful suggestions on an earlier draft.

In the mid-1970s, the Federal government required state Medicaid programmes to pay nursing homes retrospectively. Under a retrospective system, payment is determined after the provision of care and is based on the costs incurred by the facility. In contrast, under a prospective system, rates are set in advance of care and are independent of actual costs incurred by the facility. After the Federal government relaxed its Medicaid policy in the late 1970s, states moved towards prospective payment. By 2002, only two states still used a retrospective system (Grabowski et al., 2004). Prospective payment, however, gives a disincentive to admit sicker patients. Therefore, prospective payment systems typically case-mix adjust payments, paying higher rates for patients requiring more resources. In 1979, only three states used case-mix systems, but by 2002, 32 states employed these methods (Swan et al., 2000; Grabowski et al., 2004). Over this same period, the nominal average Medicaid per diem increased from $38.61 to $117.73, for a real increase of 23 per cent. However, there was substantial variation in the level of payment both across states and within states over time.

The recent repeal of the Boren Amendment and the economic recession both may have implications for the generosity of state Medicaid payment. As part of the Balanced Budget Act (BBA) of 1997, Congress repealed the 1980 Boren Amendment, which had required Medicaid payment to be sufficient to maintain certain quality of care standards. The repeal put less pressure on states to increase Medicaid payment rates. However, real Medicaid payment rates continued to increase in the majority of states through 2002 even during the recession (Grabowski et al., 2004), because states relied on alternative Medicaid funding sources such as tobacco settlement dollars (GAO, 2003).Nevertheless, given the current state budget shortfalls (National Conference of State Legislatures, 2003), the coming years may result in cuts to Medicaid payment rates if states cannot uncover additional sources of revenue.

The BBA of 1997 also fundamentally changed how Medicare paid nursing homes. Starting in 1998, Medicare paid nursing homes using a prospective payment system (PPS) instead of a cost-based payment system. In addition, overall payment levels were initially lowered under PPS, then increased again through subsequent legislation. Changes to both the marginal and the average payment rate may affect quality of care for all residents (Zinn et al., 2003; Konetzka, Norton, and Stearns, 2004).The lower Medicare payments were largely responsible for more than 10 per cent of facilities nationwide filing for Chapter 11 bankruptcy.

3.   Market characteristics

Demand-side
The rapid rise in the number of elderly over the next few decades will greatly increase demand for all types of long-term care, including informal care (Van Houtven and Norton, 2004). However, two demographic trends are already influencing the demand for services. The mortality rate has fallen by about one per cent per year since 1950, so elderly people are living longer (Cutler, 2001). In particular, the mortality rate for elderly men is falling faster than for women, narrowing the longevity gender gap. Disability rates among the elderly are also declining (Manton et al., 1993; Cutler, 2001).Therefore, people are living longer and living healthier (Manton and Gu, 2001). Lakdawalla and Philipson

(2002) argue that these trends help explain much of the decline in the relative growth in nursing home use seen since 1970. If informal care from spouses is a substitute for formal nursing home care, and if there is a compression in morbidity, and if wives spend less time widowed, then the demand for nursing home care will fall.

Supply-side

Although economists have traditionally assumed a binding bed constraint in the market for nursing home care (for example, Scanlon, 1980), there is evidence that certificate of need (CON) and moratoria policies have become less important over time. First, many states have repealed CON laws over the 1980s and 1990s (Grabowski et al., 2003). Second, there has been a significant decline in nursing home occupancy rates over the last two decades, even in states with CON and moratoria policies. The national occupancy rate was 92.9 per cent in 1977, 91.8 per cent in 1985 and 87.4 per cent in 1995 (Strahan, 1997). Given this shift, the traditional nursing home model, which assumes a binding bed constraint, may no longer be relevant for today's nursing home market.

Market competition

Several recent market-wide changes may also affect the quality of nursing home care. On the Medicare side, the adoption of prospective payment for hospital care in 1983, which provided an incentive for hospitals to discharge patients 'sicker-and-quicker' to hospital-based skilled nursing home units, had profound effects on the nursing home industry. The proportion of hospital-based nursing homes rose from 5.7 per cent in 1987 to 11.4 per cent in 1996 (Rhoades and Krauss, 1999). Additionally, many nursing home chains began to specialize in the post-acute marketplace with chain ownership growing by 15 per cent between 1985 and 1995 (Strahan, 1997). With the shift to Medicare PPS for nursing home care, there was widespread bankruptcy in the nursing home industry, particularly among hospital-based and chain facilities. About 20 per cent of hospital-based nursing facilities exited the market by 2000 (MedPAC, 2002; Dalton and Howard, 2002).

Although the lion's share of long-term care research is on nursing homes, alternative and less expensive forms of care have become more popular over the last decade. These substitutes include home health care, assisted living and board and care homes, adult day care, and hospice care. One reason for the expansion of options is the increase in public funding. Both Medicare and Medicaid have increased expenditures on home health care substantially since the early 1990s (Anderson et at., 2003). The Supreme Court's Olmstead decision in 1999 further encouraged this growth by prohibiting states from unnecessarily institutionalizing individuals if their needs could be reasonably met in a community setting (Van Houtven and Domino, 2005).

There are three implications of this trend. Any policy question about overall quality of care for elderly persons must encompass a broad spectrum of types of care, not just nursing home care. Additionally, nursing homes have become more specialized. The average severity of illness in nursing homes has increased because the less disabled elderly are seeking less expensive forms of care. Finally, the growth in assisted living and other substitutes may explain much of the decline in nursing home occupancy rates.

Quality assurance and measurement

Congress passed the landmark Omnibus Budget Reconciliation Act of 1987 (OBRA87), which was implemented in 1990 and consisted of three broad requirements. First, all nursing homes must provide at least eight hours of registered nurses per day, conduct background checks on nursing aides, and provide in-house training for nurses' aides. Second, regulations shifted from health processes to health outcomes. Nursing homes must assess residents' health periodically with a standard health-based instrument. Third, the survey and inspection process was changed to be more uniform and less predictable, with greater penalties for infractions. All these changes were intended to improve the quality of care (Kumar and Norton, 2004).

Two significant data developments, which increased research interest in this sub-field, were an outgrowth of OBRA87. First, the Centers for Medicare and Medicaid Services (CMS, previously known as the Health Care Financing Administration) became more rigorous in collecting data on Medicaid- and Medicare-certified facilities through the Online Survey Certification and Reporting (OSCAR) system, which contains facility-level measures on processes of care (for example physical restraints), outcomes (for example, pressure ulcers), staffing and deficiencies. OSCAR also contains information on facility characteristics such as number of beds, occupancy rate, payer mix, ownership status, and chain affiliation. From a research perspective, strengths of the OSCAR system include the panel framework and the public availability of the data. Limitations include the reporting of data at the facility-level, accuracy of certain variables (for example, staffing measures), and lack of information on payment rates.

The second major development under OBRA87 was the requirement that Medicaid- and Medicare-certified nursing homes begin collecting minimum dataset (MDS) assessments on all residents. The MDS instrument contains over 350 discrete data elements including socio-demographic information, numerous clinical items ranging from degree of functional dependence to cognitive functioning, and a checklist for staff to indicate the presence of the most common geriatric diagnoses. Assessments are performed on admission, upon significant change in health status, and at least quarterly, giving multiple assessments of the same individual over time. The strengths of the MDS are the resident-level focus and the quarterly panel framework. Unfortunately, economists have not yet widely used the MDS because privacy concerns resulted in a long and complex data acquisition process with CMS, at least initially.

Other survey datasets that hold some promise for examining the nursing home industry include the National Nursing Home Survey, the Medical Expenditure Panel Study-Nursing Home Component, the National Long-Term Care Survey, and the Health and Retirement Study. The first two datasets are nationally based samples of nursing homes and their residents while the latter two are community-based samples that track transitions into nursing homes. Medicare cost reports are a source of information on skilled nursing homes. Medicaid cost reports are useful for studies of a single state, but are hard to compare across states.

Researchers have used these new datasets to develop innovative new quality measures. Outcome measures have improved from facility-level proxies for quality such as staffing (Gertler, 1992) and government-cited violations (Nyman, 1985) to resident-level pressure ulcers (Grabowski et al., 2004) and the use of anti-psychotic medications (Mor et al.,

2004). Facility-level quality indicators derived from the MDS are now used by surveyors in the field and can be downloaded from the web. Moreover, the availability of repeated observations on residents and homes has allowed researchers to employ panel data methods that address unobserved heterogeneity.

4.   Literature review
After a brief summary of the early US literature, this section reviews the more recent work from the US on the effect of Medicaid payment rates and methods, Medicare payment, certificate of need regulation, ownership type, and terminations on nursing home quality.

Prior literature
The health economics literature on nursing home quality of care in the 1980s and 1990s was largely based on Scanlon's model (1980) in which nursing homes face two markets. One market is for private residents with downward sloping demand, and the other is for Medicaid residents who are insensitive to price. Scanlon's empirical work (1980) presented the evidence that the Medicaid side of this market could be characterized nationally by an excess demand. Certificate of need and construction moratoria policies had constrained growth in the supply of nursing home beds, and nursing homes preferred to admit the higher paying private patients. As a result, when a bed shortage existed, it was the Medicaid patients who would be excluded.

At the time, many non-economists thought that the problem of quality in nursing homes could only be solved by raising Medicaid reimbursement rates. By incorporating a quality variable into Scanlon's model, Nyman (1985) showed that raising Medicaid rates in a market with excess demand would result in nursing homes facing a reduced incentive to use quality of care to compete for the private patients. Several prominent papers confirmed this inverse relationship between Medicaid reimbursement level and quality of care (Nyman, 1985; Gertler, 1989; Dusanksy, 1989; Gertler, 1992). Nyman (1988a, 1989) proposed that this outcome would be spurious if tight markets eliminated an observable measure of quality – the occupancy rate – to inform consumers. Other papers focused on the method of reimbursement instead of the level. Cohen and Spector (1996) found that states with flat-rate reimbursement had lower staffing ratios than states with cost-based reimbursement. Norton (1992) showed that cost-mix adjusted reimbursement with incentives for quality improvement lead to improved health outcomes.

Level of Medicaid payment
The recent decline in nursing home occupancy rates, repeal of CON laws in certain states, and emergence of improved data, have all contributed to a renewed interest in the relationship between Medicaid payment and nursing home quality. Unlike the earlier research on this issue, results from more recent studies have generally found a modest positive relationship between state Medicaid payment rates and nursing home quality. Higher payment rates have been found to be associated with fewer pressure ulcers (Grabowski and Angelelli, 2004), more staffing (Grabowski, 2001b), fewer hospitalizations (Intrator and Mor, 2004), fewer physical restraints (Grabowski, Angelelli and Mor, 2004), less feeding tube use and fewer government-cited deficiencies (Grabowski, 2004). In terms of the size of the effect, these studies indicate a payment-quality elasticity in the range

0.1 to 0.7, depending on the quality measure. For example, a 10 per cent increase in Medicaid payment reduced pressure ulcers by roughly 2 per cent (Grabowski, 2004; Grabowski and Angelelli, 2004). Importantly, across all recent studies, there is virtually no support for a negative relationship between the Medicaid payment level and quality.

In an attempt to bridge the two generations of this literature, Grabowski (2001a) replicated data, methods and quality measures from Gertler (1989) to identify the underlying source of the different findings. When the methods and quality measures from the earlier study were applied to more recent data, Medicaid payment was found to be positively associated with quality. Changes in the marketplace – not alternative data or methods – explain the different findings across the two generations of studies. However, using national data from the earlier time period, Grabowski also found that Gertler's New York results did not generalize to the entire US. Thus, the earlier result may have been only relevant for a minority of states or markets where CON laws were particularly binding.

Method of Medicaid payment
Quality of nursing home care may depend not only on the level of Medicaid payment but also on the method. Research has focused on two aspects of Medicaid payment systems: whether they are cost-based and whether they are case-mix adjusted. Towards the first issue, there is evidence that staffing is higher under a cost-based system (Cohen and Dubay, 1990; Cohen and Spector, 1996; Grabowski, 2002a). This result is intuitive because a cost-based system rewards additional staffing with higher revenue. As Nyman (1988b) has argued, however, although a cost-based system encourages nursing homes to spend more, it does not necessarily reward the provision of higher quality. In support of this point, there is no evidence that payment method significantly affects process- or outcomes-based measures of quality (Cohen and Spector, 1996; Grabowski, 2002a). However, given the minority of states that use pure cost-based systems today, lack of precision may be an issue in the failure to detect a significant effect.

The literature consistently finds that Medicaid case-mix payment systems are associated with higher resident acuity (for example, Arling and Daneman, 2002; Norton, 1992; Thorpe et al., 1991). However, findings have not been consistent on the effect of these systems on nursing home quality. After accounting for a higher acuity patient mix, most studies have not found that staffing increased under case-mix adjusted payment (Feder and Scanlon, 1989; Butler and Schlenker 1989; Cohen and Dubay, 1990; Grabowski, 2002b). In terms of process- and outcome-based measures of quality, studies have generally found no significant difference in quality (Butler and Schlenker, 1989; Grabowski, 2002b), but there is evidence that hospitalizations (Arling and Daneman, 2002) and tube feedings (Feder and Scanlon, 1989) increased under case-mix payment.

Medicare payment
Prospective Medicare payment might reduce quality of care for two reasons (Cutler, 1995, Norton et al., 2002). First, elimination of marginal payment reduces expenditures on quality at the margin (White, 2003; Wodchis, 2004). Second, because average revenues declined, the average effect is expected to be the same as the marginal effect. Facilities that experience average payment decreases have fewer resources to be spent on quality of care for all. Konetzka and colleagues (2004) studied how Medicare PPS affected both staffing

and regulatory deficiencies using data from before and after the change in regulation. These measures of quality of care are for the entire nursing home, not just Medicare residents. Even though Medicare residents comprise less than 10 per cent of all residents nationwide, changes in the type and level of payment may spill over to other residents. Both measures of quality decreased under Medicare PPS, though the results were stronger for staffing. The implications are that quality of care is responsive to the level of public funding even for Medicare payment, which often funds a relatively small percentage of residents.

Certificate of need

The importance of CON and construction moratoria for nursing home quality hinges on whether these laws bind. Although data from the late 1960s through the early 1980s argued that CON acted as a binding constraint and created excess demand for Medicaid beds (for example, Scanlon, 1980), subsequent research has questioned the applicability of this finding for today's nursing home market. Grabowski and colleagues (2003) found that states that repealed CON and moratoria laws did not experience an increase in Medicaid expenditures relative to states that did not repeal these laws. Similarly, Gulley and Santerre (2003) found that the presence of CON laws did not affect the availability of nursing home care across markets. Taken together with the national trend towards lower occupancy rates over the last two decades, these findings provide support for the idea that CON and moratoria are no longer binding constraints in most nursing home markets.

It is not altogether surprising that recent work generally finds these policies to be unrelated to the quality of care. Two sets of findings support this conclusion. First, Grabowski and Castle (2004) found that market tightness, a proxy for how much CON and moratoria bind, was generally unrelated to outcome- and process-based quality measures. Second, as noted above, most recent work examining Medicaid payment rates and quality has not found support for the negative relationship predicted under the excess demand model. However, CON may still impede quality competition for Medicaid recipients in a minority of nursing home markets. Grabowski and Angelelli (2004) found that Medicaid payment rates were associated with fewer pressure ulcers nationally, but when the model was restricted to the tightest nursing home markets (roughly 27 per cent of the sample), a higher payment rate was not significantly associated with fewer pressure ulcers. Thus, if CON and moratoria are still relevant for today's nursing home sector, it is only for a small number of homes.

Ownership type

In contrast to the hospital industry, two-thirds of all nursing homes are for-profit. In both industries, the mix of for-profit and non-profit firms has led to studies of how ownership affects costs, quality and access to care. In nursing homes, the primary concern is the existence of asymmetric information about quality. Consumers, especially the frail elderly with no close family support, may have trouble discerning quality within a nursing home, and may not have the ability to shop among nursing homes (Spector et al., 1998).

Several recent papers promote the idea that non-profit status is a signal of quality. Chou (2002) looked at differences in quality of care, measured by death and adverse health outcomes, between for-profit and non-profit nursing homes and between residents who had close family. She found that the differences between ownership types were greater when there was asymmetric information, meaning that no spouse or child visited within one month of admission. Grabowski and Hirth (2003) looked at the related issue of how the share of non-profit nursing homes in the market affected quality of care. They argue that a greater percentage of non-profit nursing homes would have competitive spillover effects, which is what they found after controlling for the endogeneity of non-profit market share. Konetzka, Yi, Norton and Kilpatrick (2004) found that financial incentives in treatment decisions (hospitalizations for pneumonia) varied both by ownership and by resident payer source.

Publicizing quality information
The regulation process may also encourage quality of care by providing information to consumers. Information about quality deficiencies is publicly available and must be posted in all nursing homes (Angelelli et al., 2003). If consumers use this information to make informed decisions about nursing home entry, then public information may help to improve quality. Nursing homes with many deficiencies are more likely to go out of business, either voluntarily or non-voluntarily, than those with few deficiencies (Angelelli et al., 2003). In related research, homes with greater physical restraint use are also more likely to close, although this finding was not robust to other process- and outcome-based quality measures (Castle, 2005). Thus, there is some qualified evidence that information improves quality by removing the worst offenders. However, terminations, even of the lowest quality nursing home, may still have adverse consequences. When these nursing homes terminate, access to care is reduced for some populations, typically those living in the poorest communities (Mor et al., 2004). Therefore, information about quality of care may improve quality for remaining nursing homes while reducing access for some.

5.   Conclusion
Newly available datasets on nursing homes and new market and regulatory conditions have allowed economists to revisit old research questions and tackle new problems. The market conditions under which increases in Medicaid payment led to lower quality have disappeared. The standard relationship that higher payment improves quality now holds as occupancy rates have fallen. Clinical measures of health outcomes have been used to study how a wide variety of market and policy variables affect quality of nursing home care. The availability of good quality measures is expanding. We hope and expect that this area of research will remain fruitful for years to come, both in the US and in other countries.

References
Anderson, W.L., E.C. Norton and W.H. Dow (2003), 'Medicare maximization by state Medicaid programs: effects on Medicare home care utilization', *Medical Care Research and Review*, **60**(2), 201–22.
Angelelli, J., V. Mor, O. Intrator, Z. Feng and J. Zinn (2003), 'Oversight of nursing homes: pruning the tree or just spotting bad apples?', *Gerontologist*, **43**(2), 67–75.
Arling, G. and B. Daneman (2002), 'Nursing home case-mix payment in Mississippi and South Dakota', *Health Services Research*, **37**(2), 377–95.
Butler, P.A. and R.E. Schlenker (1989), 'Case-mix payment for nursing homes: objectives and achievements', *The Milbank Quarterly*, **67**(1), 103–36.
Carmichael, F. and S. Charles (2003), 'The opportunity costs of informal care: does gender matter?', *Journal of Health Economics*, **22**(5), 781–803.

Castle, N.G. (2005), 'Nursing home closures and quality of care', *Medical Care Research and Review*, **62**(1), 111–32.

Chou, S.Y. (2002), 'Asymmetric information, ownership and quality of care: an empirical analysis of nursing homes', *Journal of Health Economics*, **21**(2), 293–311.

Cohen, J. and L. Dubay (1990), 'The effects of Medicaid payment method and ownership on nursing home costs, case-mix, and staffing', *Inquiry*, **27**(2), 183–200.

Cohen, M.A. and W.D. Spector (1996), 'The effect of Medicaid payment on quality of care in nursing homes', *Journal of Health Economics*, **15**(1), 23–48.

Cutler, D.M. (1995), 'The incidence of adverse medical outcomes under prospective payment', *Econometrica*, **63**(1), 29–50.

Cutler, D.M. (2001), 'Declining disability among the elderly', *Health Affairs*, **20**(6), 11–27.

Dalton, K. and H.A. Howard (2002), 'Market entry and exit in long-term care: 1985–2000', *Health Care Financing Review*, **24**(2), 17–32.

Dusansky, R. (1989), 'On the economics of institutional care of the elderly in the US: the effects of change in government payment', *Review of Economics*, **56**, 141–50.

Feder, J. and W. Scanlon (1989), 'Case-mix payment for nursing home care: lessons from Maryland', *Journal of Health Politics, Policy and Law*, **14**(3), 523–37.

Forder, J. and A. Netten (2000), 'The price of placements in residential and nursing home care: the effects of contracts and competition', *Health Economics*, **9**(7), 643–57.

GAO (2003), 'Medicaid nursing home payments: states' payment rates largely unaffected by recent fiscal pressures', Pub. no. GAO-04-143, Washington: GAO.

Gertler, P.J. (1989), 'Subsidies, quality, and the regulation of nursing homes', *Journal of Public Economics*, **38**, 33–52.

Gertler, P.J. (1992), 'Medicaid and the cost of improving access to nursing home care', *Review of Economics and Statistics*, **74**(2), 338–45.

Gertler, P.J. and D.M. Waldman (1992), 'Quality-adjusted cost functions and policy evaluation in the nursing home industry', *Journal of Political Economy*, **100**(6), 1232–56.

Grabowski, D.C. (2001a), 'Medicaid payment and the quality of nursing home care', *Journal of Health Economics*, **20**(4), 549–70.

Grabowski, D.C. (2001b), 'Does an increase in the Medicaid payment rate improve nursing home quality?', *Journal of Gerontology: Social Sciences*, **56B**(2), S84–93.

Grabowski, D.C. (2002a), 'A multi-part model approach to examining Medicaid payment methods and nursing home quality', *Health Services and Outcomes Research Methodology*, **3**(1), 21–39.

Grabowski, D.C. (2002b), 'The economic implications of case-mix Medicaid payment for nursing home care', *Inquiry*, **39**(3), 258–78.

Grabowski, D.C. (2004), 'A longitudinal study of Medicaid payment, private-pay price and nursing home quality', *International Journal of Health Care Finance and Economics*, **4**(1), 5–26.

Grabowski, D.C. and J.J. Angelelli (2004), 'The relationship of Medicaid payment rates, bed constraint policies, and risk-adjusted pressure ulcers', *Health Services Research*, **39**(4), 793–812.

Grabowski, D.C. and N.G. Castle (2004), 'Nursing homes with persistent high and low quality', *Medical Care Research and Review*, **61**(1), 89–115.

Grabowski, D.C. and R.A. Hirth (2003), 'Competitive spillovers across nonprofit and for-profit nursing homes', *Journal of Health Economics*, **22**(1), 1–22.

Grabowski, D.C., J.J. Angelelli, and V. Mor (2004), 'Medicaid payment and risk-adjusted nursing home quality', *Health Affairs*, **23**(5), 243–52.

Grabowski, D.C., R.L. Ohsfeldt and M.A. Morrissey (2003), 'The effects of CON repeal on Medicaid nursing home and long term care expenditures', *Inquiry*, **40**(2), 146–57.

Grabowski, D.C., Z. Feng, O. Intrator and V. Mor (2004), 'Recent trends in state nursing home payment policies', *Health Affairs*, **W4**, 363–73.

Grabowski, D.C., J.J. Angelelli and V. Mor (2004), 'Medicaid payment and risk-adjusted nursing home quality measures', *Health Affairs*, **23**(5), 243–52.

Gulley, O. David and Rexford E. Santerre (2003), 'The effect of public policies on nursing home care in the United States', *Eastern Economic Journal*, **29**(1), 93–104.

Intrator, O. and V. Mor (2004), 'Effect of state Medicaid payment rates on hospitalizations from nursing homes', *Journal of the American Geriatrics Society*, **52**(3), 393–8.

Konetzka, R.T., E.C. Norton and S.C. Stearns (2004), 'Medicare prospective payment and nursing home quality of care', University of Chicago working paper.

Konetzka, R.T., D. Yi, E.C. Norton and K.E. Kilpatrick (2004), 'Effects of Medicare payment changes on nursing home staffing and deficiencies', *Health Services Research*, **39**(3), 463–87.

Kumar, V. and E.C. Norton (2004), 'OBRA 1987 and quality of nursing home care', UNC at Chapel Hill Working paper.

Lakdawalla, D. and T. Philipson (2002), 'The rise in old-age longevity and the market for long-term care', *American Economic Review*, **92**(1), 295–306.

Lindeboom, M., F. Portrait and G.J. van den Berg (2002), 'An econometric analysis of the mental-health effects of major events in the life of older individuals', *Health Economics*, **11**(6), 505–20.

Manton, K.G. and X.L. Gu (2001), 'Changes in the prevalence of chronic disability in the United States black and nonblack population above age 65 from 1982 to 1999', *Proceedings of the National Academy of Sciences of the United States of America*, **98**(11), 6354–9.

Manton, K.G., E. Stallard and K. Liu (1993), 'Forecasts of active life expectancy – policy and fiscal implications', *Journals of Gerontology*, **48**, 11–26.

Medicare Payment Advisory Commission (MedPAC) (2002), *Report to Congress*, Washington: MedPAC.

Mor, V., J.S. Zinn, J.J. Angelelli, J.M. Teno and S.C. Miller (2004), 'Driven to tiers: Socioeconomic and racial disparities in the quality of nursing home care', *Milbank Quarterly*, **82**(2), 227–56.

National Center for Health Statistics (2003), *Health, United States, 2003*, Hyattsville, Maryland: National Center for Health Statistics.

National Conference of State Legislatures (2003), *State Budget Update: April 2003*, Washington: NCSL.

Norton, E.C. (1992), 'Incentive regulation of nursing homes', *Journal of Health Economics*, **11**(2), 105–28.

Norton, E.C. (2000), 'Long-term care', in A.J. Culyer and J.P. Newhouse (eds), *Handbook of Health Economics*, vol. IB, New York, NY: Elsevier Science, pp. 956–94.

Norton, E.C., C.H. Van Houtven, R.C. Lindrooth, S.T. Normand and B. Dickey (2002), 'Does prospective payment reduce inpatient length of stay?', *Health Economics*, **11**(5), 377–87.

Nyman, J.A. (1985), 'Prospective and cost-plus Medicaid payment, excess Medicaid demand, and the quality of nursing home care', *Journal of Health Economics*, **4**(3), 237–59.

Nyman, J.A. (1988a), 'Excess-demand, the percentage of Medicaid patients, and the quality of nursing home care', *Journal of Human Resources*, **23**(1), 76–92.

Nyman, J.A., (1988b), 'Improving the quality of nursing home outcomes: are adequacy- or incentive-oriented policies more effective', *Medical Care*, **26**, 1158–71.

Nyman, J.A. (1989), 'Excess demand, consumer rationality, and the quality of care in regulated nursing homes', *Health Services Research*, **24**(1), 105–27.

O'Neill, C., L. Groom L, A.J. Avery, D. Boot and K. Thornhill (2000), 'Age and proximity to death as predictors of GP care costs: results from a study of nursing home patients', *Health Economics*, **9**(8), 733–38.

Portrait, F., M. Lindeboom and D. Deeg (2000), 'The use of long-term care services by the Dutch elderly', *Health Economics*, **9**(6), 513–31.

Rhoades, J. and N. Krauss (1999), *Nursing home trends, 1987 and 1996, MEPS Chartbook* 3, AHCPR Pub. No. 99–0032.

Scanlon, W.J. (1980), 'A theory of the nursing home market', *Inquiry*, **17**, 25–41.

Smits, H.L. (1984), 'Incentives in case-mix measures for long-term care', *Health Care Financing Review*, **6**(2), 53–9.

Spector, W.D., T.M. Selden and J.W. Cohen (1998), 'The impact of ownership type on nursing home outcomes', *Health Economics*, **7**(7), 639–53.

Strahan, G.W. (1997), 'An overview of nursing homes and their current residents: data from the 1995 National Nursing Home Survey', *Advance Data*, No. 280, National Center for Health Statistics, Centers for Disease Control and Prevention, US Department of Health and Human Services.

Swan, J.H., C. Harrington, W. Clemena, R.B. Pickard, L. Studer and S.K. deWit (2000), 'Medicaid nursing facility reimbursement methods: 1979–1997', *Medical Care Research and Review*, **57**(3), 361–78.

Thorpe, K.E., P.J. Gertler and P. Goldman (1991), 'The Resource Utilization Group System: its effect on nursing home case-mix and costs', *Inquiry*, **28**(4), 357–65.

Van Houtven, C.H. and M.E. Domino (2005), 'Home and community-based waivers for disabled adults: program versus selection effects', *Inquiry*, **42**(1), 43–59.

Van Houtven, C.H. and E.C. Norton (2004), 'Informal care and health care use of older adults', *Journal of Health Economics*, **23**(6), 1159–80.

White, C. (2003), 'Rehabilitation therapy in skilled nursing facilities: effects of Medicare's new prospective payment system', *Health Affairs (Millwood)*, **22**(3), 214–23.

Wodchis, W.P. (2004), 'Physical rehabilitation following Medicare prospective payment for skilled nursing facilities', *Health Services Research*, **39**(5), 1299–318.

Zinn, J.S., V. Mor, O. Intrator, Z. Feng, J. Angelelli and J.A. Davis (2003), 'The impact of the prospective payment system for skilled nursing facilities on therapy service provision: a transaction cost approach', *Health Services Research*, **38**(6) Part 1, 1467–85.

29 Direct to consumer advertising
W. David Bradford and Andrew N. Kleit*

1. Introduction

Historically, pharmaceutical advertising has been done largely through 'detailing' – promotion directly from the manufacturer to the physician, either through visits by representatives or contacts by pharmacists. This mode of promotion, along with advertisements in clinical journals, is still the mainstay in most of the world. However, New Zealand and the United States stand out as significant exceptions to this general practice, in that these two countries permit relatively free direct to consumer advertising (DCA) for pharmaceutical products that are only available by prescription.

In the US this trend began during the mid-1980s and accelerated in the 1990s. Before August 1997, broadcast ads were permitted only to mention either the name of a drug or a disease against which a drug was effective, but not both. After August 1997, the US Food and Drug Administration (FDA) relaxed the rules governing television advertising of prescription pharmaceutical products and pharmaceutical companies were allowed to mention both the disease and drug brand name in US advertisements (as long as a brief list of side-effects was mentioned and a 1–800 number or World Wide Web site was provided with more detailed information). Spending for DCA for prescription drugs went from $596 million in 1995 to an estimated $2.5 billion by 2000. This has led to a great deal of concern in the medical profession, from health care insurers and managed care organizations, and among policy-makers. However, the literature that exists – both by economists and health services researchers – is currently divided on the issue.

This chapter reviews the broad issues addressed in the literature to date. We begin with a brief historical review. Following that, we examine the general economic literature on advertising that is most relevant to DCA, and then explore the conceptual literature regarding the impact of DCA on clinical care and the agency relationships between patients and physicians. Finally, we survey existing empirical studies of DCA. The chapter concludes with a summary of what we currently know, and where future research may be most fruitfully directed.

2. Historical background

For most of the world, the issue of direct to consumer advertising (DCA) for prescription drugs is largely moot. For example, both the European Union and Canada officially prohibit the practice (Palumbo and Mullins, 2002). Only New Zealand and the United States sanction DCA. The market for DCA is most developed in the United States, where such promotion has been used for at least a decade and a half. The advertising was initially placed in print media. (The first such promotional effort was placed by British

*   This chapter was funded by grants from the Agency for Healthcare Research and Quality (1 R01 HS011326-01A2) and from the National Heart Lung and Blood Institute (1 R01 HL077841-01).

manufacturer Boots Pharmaceuticals on behalf of their then-prescription ibuprofen product, Rufen (Pines, 1999).

As the practice grew, the FDA requested a voluntary moratorium of the practice in 1982 until it could issue guidelines. These guidelines were issued in 1985, and simply asserted that pharmaceuticals should adhere to the same rules for advertising as governed physicians. Technically, this meant that the ads must include the product generic name, a brief list of side-effects and contra-indications, must relate only material facts, and must not be false or misleading. In practice, pharmaceuticals and the FDA interpreted the regulations to also hold that broadcast ads could also not mention both the name of the product and the clinical benefits that were claimed for it. For example, an early television advertisement for Claritin could only mention the name of the product, and did not inform consumers that the product was a treatment for hay fever that did not generally cause drowsiness.

In August 1997, the FDA issued new guidelines with respect to broadcast DCA. Since that time DCA on television and radio has been permitted to reveal both the name of the product and clinical benefit as long as 'adequate provision' was made to fully inform the consumer of side-effects and contra-indications via a toll-free telephone number, World-Wide-Web address, or reference to a complete print advertisement. Figure 29.1 shows the trend in DCA spending since 1989 (Palumbo and Mullins, 2002). One thing that should be noted is that the sharp rise in DCA began several years before the August 1997 regulatory change. In that sense, the easement in regulatory strictures by the FDA should

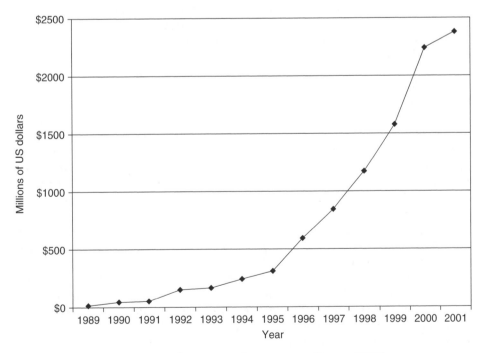

Figure 29.1   Spending of DCA in the United States, in millions of $US

perhaps be seen as a reaction to a change in DCA behaviour, rather than a cause of the change. One issue that is hidden in the series, however, is the sharp increase since 1995 in the proportion of DCA that is targeted at television as compared to radio and print media. For example, in 1994 television ads accounted for only 13.5 per cent of all DCA promotion; by 2000 that proportion had risen to 63.8 per cent (Frank et al., 2002).

3.   Economic literature on advertising relevant to DCA

Advertising is paid, non-personal presentation of goods, services, or ideas, and as such is different from personal selling and publicity. Consumers also expect that advertisements are self-promoting communications (Fisher and Anderson, 1990). Advertising is designed to move individuals through stages in the buyer process, that is, awareness, interest, evaluation, trial and adoption (Arens, 1998). The controllable variables in advertising are to whom the message is sent, when the message is sent, what is said, and how often the message is communicated. Each of these variables will have an impact on advertising effectiveness (Aaker and Stayman, 1990).

The literature on the economic impact of advertising is long and well-established. Much of the current economic literature on this issue cites work by Nelson (1970, 1974) as its antecedent. Nelson asserts that there are two classes of products in the market – those where consumers can evaluate the quality by examination before purchase and those where consumers can evaluate the quality only after purchase and consumption. The former class of goods he labels 'search' goods, the latter, 'experience' goods. Nelson then analyses the characteristics of advertising for each kind of good and finds that in general, sellers have an incentive to provide accurate information. In addition, Nelson finds that market forces tend to encourage the most advertising for the highest quality goods.

In a related – and also widely cited – paper, Klein and Leffler (1981) further expand the range of efficient advertising by pointing out that consumers will tend to believe information provided by competitive firms in adverts, since the incentives in many circumstances are for truth-telling. This is because firms that invest large amounts in advertising of brands – even when the products are experience goods – would be unlikely to recoup the costs if the advertising is misleading, which would produce disappointment associated with consumption that would preclude repeat purchases. The more a firm sinks into advertising, the higher the potential losses from false advertising, and the more likely consumers are to believe the ad. In this case, the advertisement serves as a performance bond. One important fundamental of all of this research is that the product in question can be evaluated with some positive probability in terms of quality or performance at some point, either before or after purchase.

Several areas specific to health care have been examined in terms of the impact of advertising. Most notably, there is a series of papers which have discussed the impact of advertising on the ophthalmologic market in the sale of prescription eyeglasses. Benham (1972) first investigated the question of whether advertising would enhance or harm the efficiency of a market that was regulated in other areas. Since there is physician licensure, presumably the concern for entry by low-quality providers is ameliorated. Benham then asks whether the remaining rationale for eliminating advertising is justified. He finds that advertising tends to be associated with lower prices for prescription eyeglasses. Kwoka (1984) also finds that the inverse relationship between advertising and price holds even in the (regulated) prescription eyeglasses market. Finally, Rizzo and Zeckhauser (1990) explore the same question. Unlike Benham and Kwoka they find that the consequences of advertising in the (general) physician services market tends to harm entry, and works to the advantage of well-established physicians (though they are the group that appears to advertise the least).

4.   The impact of DCA on agency relationships

The beginnings of the current policy debate may date from Masson and Rubin (1985). In a brief communication in a major medical journal, they make several points about the merits of consumer advertising for pharmaceuticals. First, advertising may cause consumers to realize that they do indeed have a disease. Advertisements by Pfizer, for example, apparently caused many people to realize that the thirst they were suffering from was a symptom of diabetes. Similarly, advertising may reveal to consumers that a new treatment may exist for a condition currently being treated by another drug. The consumer may then respond by asking their physician for a prescription for the new drug. This care-seeking effect remains one of the main arguments advanced by those who advocate on behalf of DCA.

One of the recurring themes among critics of DCA is that the practice should intrude on the agency relationship between physicians and patients. Fundamentally, the issue has merit – if physicians are hired as agents by patients to make decisions regarding diagnoses and treatment using their superior medical knowledge, the question is what new information can be added by DCA? The problem with this simple criticism is that since there are few comprehensive models of physician/patient interactions concerning prescribing, we know very little *theoretically* about the efficiency of the agency relationships, with or without DCA. Thus, observing that DCA tends to increase prescribing is uninformative (from a welfare perspective) unless we knew that prescribing was optimal (or too low/high) to begin with.

A few published studies have made a beginning at empirically understanding prescribing behaviour. Coscelli (2000) uses a panel of clinical observations on Italian patients over a two-year period, which permits identification of both within-patient and within-physician effects. She finds that patients and physicians collectively express preferences for brand differences within a single therapeutic class (despite the generally high clinical substitutability between drugs in the class). This suggests a high level of habit-driven behaviour by physicians in prescribing. Lundin (2000) investigates a similar question using Swedish data, and reaches similar conclusions – that there is high persistence in prescribing, and that the fact that patients respond to changes in deductible when there are no associated changes in the real product price suggests moral hazard generally permeates the market. Interestingly, neither of these papers is able to determine whether DCA would improve or worsen the moral hazard problem. If physicians are responding to patient preferences, then DCA clearly can be used to influence prescribing patterns.

In the US, where DCA is most developed, there are relatively few studies that examine the determinants of prescribing behaviour. One set of unpublished results can be found in a series of studies conducted by the FDA, based on surveys of physicians and patients. These surveys elicit information about the underlying factors that prompt patients to seek care, and how responses to DCA affect the patient–physician interaction. While DCA is reported as a reason for patients seeking care (approximately 5 per cent of patients report that some DCA was a factor in the decision to seek care), other factors dominate the process (for example, pre-existing conditions play a role in 62 per cent of visits while 50 per cent of visits are prompted by acute onset of illness). However, patients also report that if they ask for a specific brand of drug by name, they received the prescription 49 per cent of the time, while the physician recommended a different brand 34 per cent of the time, and recommended no prescription at all only 13 per cent of the time (Aikin, 2003).

5.   Empirical literature on DCA

Studies using pre-1997 data
The studies on the impact of advertising in the prescription pharmaceutical market that have been published to date have tended to yield conflicting results. There is an arm of this literature that is generally supportive of advertising in this market, such as Telser's (1975) and Leffler's (1981) work. Keith (1995) finds that patient suggestions regarding pharmaceuticals (aspirin for cardiovascular disease) are important determinants in prescription decisions, and that advertising tends to lead to more appropriate care as a consequence. In this, Keith is advancing an argument mentioned above by Masson and Rubin (1985) which posits several mechanisms that could lead to positive impacts from advertising on the efficiency of the pharmaceutical market (including that it might encourage people to associate symptoms with a disease and seek care, or that it might alert people to treatments they were previously unaware of, which would encourage them to seek care).

Not all economists, however, are so sanguine about the prospects of positive welfare effects from prescription pharmaceutical advertising. Hurwitz and Caves (1998) find that – on balance – promotional activities by pharmaceutical firms tend to have the effect of preserving market share for existing products and slowing the penetration of new compounds in the market. King (1996) uses monthly sales data in the ulcer drug market to test the effect that marketing efforts have on the industry. He finds that marketing by a firm causes the demand for the firm's own products to become more inelastic, and tends to hamper product diversification. Similarly, Rizzo (1999) finds that direct to consumer advertising significantly reduced price elasticity in the market. A reduction in price elasticity would increase opportunities for supra-competitive pricing.

Studies on post-1997 period using survey data
There are a variety of studies that examine DCA through the lens of survey data. For example, using a Scott-Levin dataset, Gonul et al. (2000) examine the sentiments of both patients and physicians toward DCA. They find that patients with chronic needs and parents of children with health needs are positively disposed toward DCA, while older patients are more trusting of physicians. They also find that more experienced physicians, physicians with larger caseloads, and physicians with more exposure to DCA are likely to be supportive of such advertising. Sumpradit et al. (2002) conducted a study in 1998 of 1102 consumers with respect to DCA. Being afflicted with chronic conditions and having positive attitudes toward DCA were associated with the consumers' willingness to talk with doctors about the advertised drugs. Sumpradit et al. also find that consumers who asked for prescriptions tended to agree that DCA made prescription drugs appear harmless and helped them make their own decision.

Weissman et al. (2003) conducted a national telephone survey of 3000 adults in 2002 concerning the effects of DTCA. They found that 35 per cent of those surveyed had had a physician visit where DCA was discussed. More than half of those patients reported that their physician took action other than prescribing the relevant advertised drug. The survey found no difference in health effects between those who were prescribed the advertised drug and those who did not. The authors assert that their results indicate positive findings for DCA, along the lines of Masson and Rubin (1985), as there is some evidence that DCA drew ill patients into their physicians' offices, and there was no evidence of drugs being improperly prescribed.

They followed up this study with a survey of physicians published the following year. In that study, they found that physician attitudes toward DCA are mixed. However, using a survey of Arizona physicians who were randomized into one of eight different hypothetical vignettes, Zachry et al. (2003) find physicians were quicker to become annoyed with repeated patient questioning when the reason was DCA compared to patients who got their information from medical publications. This negative attitude reinforces results from earlier survey studies, which found that nearly 80 per cent of physicians had a negative attitude toward DCA (Lipsky and Taylor, 1997), and that a large percentage of patients would react negatively (either expressing disappointment or seeking a new physician) if they were denied a prescription that they asked about after having seen it advertised (Bell et al., 1999).

Several authors published editorials responding to the Weissman et al. paper. Bodenheimer (2003), Gahart et al. (2003) and Avorn (2003) all express scepticism that DCA can be relied upon to support the beneficial welfare effects that are claimed in the primary research cited above. This scepticism is largely driven by doubts surrounding the accuracy of information presented in ads, the capacity of patients to process complex clinical information, and the lack of control groups in the Weissman et al. study. Calfee (2003), on the other hand, is more supportive of the positive findings of Weissman et al. and Dubois (2003). Calfee finds the work persuasive due to its emphasis on the informational content of any advertisement and notes that the results of those two studies are quite consistent with the research on advertising in general in the economics literature.

Studies on the post-1997 period using aggregate data
The post-1997 era has presented an opportunity for examination of the new policy regime in the US for DCA, and much of the literature has been focused on the FDA policy shift. As Zachry and Ginsburg (2001), point out, however, there is a paucity of studies that examine the actual impacts of DCA. The earliest of these use aggregate (usually national) data.

In one of these studies, Dubois (2003) examines the impact of DCA through the lens of variation in procedure and drug use. He notes previous evidence that there is a wide variety geographically in the use of various medications, and suggests such variations imply underserved population. Dubois cites several sources that indicate that variations have declined since the relaxation of DCA regulations, perhaps implying that DCA is conveying important medication information to previously underserved populations. Calfee et al. (2002) study whether the August 1997 policy change at FDA increased the demand for the statin class of drugs. However, the authors are unable to find any significant short run direct effect. Their regressions are based on monthly data from IMSHealth and Scott-Levin for a 58-month period. They found that advertising did not have a statistically significant impact on aggregate prescriptions filled. According to the authors, 'it may only be possible to detect the effect of DCA on consumer demand with disaggregated data that links a patient's cholesterol treatment history with the timing of DCA expenditures'. In a second test, Calfee et al. attempt to determine if advertising causes patients to visit their doctor for a check-up. Once again, advertising is found to be statistically insignificant (again, not reported). In a final test, Calfee et al. (2002) found that 'emerging success' increased the demand for the relevant cholesterol-fighting drugs. They had some evidence that television ads aided adherence, which in turn improved success, which in turn increased demand.

One other study has examined the role of DCA in aggregate prescribing patterns in the US; Rosenthal et al. (2003) use data on pharmaceutical spending, DCA, and professional detailing from two marketing research firms. They find that DCA has a generally positive effect, though the parameters are very imprecisely measured.

Studies on the post-1997 period using survey data
Authors who have studied DCA using aggregate data have generally been unable to find consistently significant advertising effects. Those authors note that the question is one that is best attached using patient or practice level micro-data. Unfortunately, there are few published studies with access to such data; however, several studies have recently been presented at professional meetings, and may soon find their way into the peer-reviewed literature. Zachry et al. (2002) use the National Ambulatory Medical Care Survey (United States data) to correlate prescribing for several drug classes with monthly national DCA data. They find conflicting results, with national DCA having a positive impact on prescribing for some drug classes/brands, and having a negative effect for others. This lack of consistency may be due to the nature of the data (only a few observations per physician practice sampled, and only national advertising data).

In a recent session of the American Economic Association Annual Conference (January 2005, in Philadelphia, PA) three papers on DCA using patient micro-data were presented. Iizuka and Jin (2005) presented a study using multiple years of the National Ambulatory Medical Care Survey which found that DCA tended to increase the number of visits provided by physicians, though had no effect on actual prescribing. In that same session, Bradford et al. (2005) presented research which examined the impact of DCA for COX-2 inhibitors on a three-year panel of monthly patient micro-data taken from a nationally distributed sample of 81 primary care practices. Their preliminary results found that advertising increased the proportion of patients in each practice seeking care for osteoarthritis (the condition for which the COX-2 inhibitors are the primary treatment) and also found that advertising for one brand (Vioxx) increased the prescribing for both itself and its major competitor (Celebrex). Finally, Kenkel et al. (2005) presented a research approach for examining the content of DCA in the print media.

6. Summary
The issue of what impact DCA has on the behaviour of patients and physicians is of much more than academic importance. In the US approximately half of state Medicaid

programmes rely upon formularies in order to control excessive pharmaceutical spending. Even moderate changes in prescribing for a small number of products can lead to dramatic changes in Medicaid spending. For example, the increase in per-prescription costs (from $39 in 1998 to $49 in 2000) accounted for almost half of the total increase in Medicaid spending in North Carolina over that period, while increases in the use of only six drugs accounted for almost a quarter of that rise (Iizuka and Jin, 2005). On a national level, the US Congress has passed legislation that provides a pharmaceutical benefit to Medicare recipients in the United States beginning in 2006. As advertising for prescription pharmaceuticals is more frequently aimed at patients, then the ability of the US Medicare system to control prescribing through formularies or utilization management may be compromised, and current estimates of the new pharmaceutical costs may prove conservative.

In addition, important medical interests worldwide have expressed profound concern over the practice of DCA by pharmaceutical companies. National (for example, Canadian) systems and multinational organizations (for example, the European Union) are coming under increased pressure to permit expansion of some forms of DCA in their jurisdictions. While there has been some study of the issue, researchers currently do not have a consistent answer to the question of whether DCA has a major impact on health care markets, and if so, whether the effect is welfare-enhancing or welfare-reducing. Studies that rely on survey methods find evidence of an effect, though they cannot quantify it. Studies aimed at quantifying the effect using aggregate data have proved inconclusive. Additional work is needed using patient-level data – ideally relying on panel datasets that can control for both patient and physician heterogeneity. While such work is currently underway, little of it has yet been published.

References

Aaker, D. and D. Stayman (1990), 'Measuring audience perceptions of commercials and relating them to ad impact', *Journal of Advertising Research*, **30**(4), 7–17.

Aikin, K. (2003), 'Direct-to-consumer advertising of prescription drugs: patient survey results', in *Direct-to-Consumer Promotion: FDA Public Meeting*, Washington DC.

Arens, W. (1998), *Contemporary Advertising*, 7th edn, Columbus: McGraw-Hill.

Avorn, J. (2003), 'Advertising and prescription drugs: promotion, education and the public's health', *Health Affairs*, Supplemental Web Exclusives W3, pp. 104–8.

Bell, R., M. Wilkes and R. Kravitz (1999), 'Advertisement induced prescription drug requests: patients' anticipated reactions to a physician who refuses', *Journal of Family Practice*, **48**(6), 446–52.

Benham, L. (1972), 'The effect of advertising on the price of eyeglasses', *Journal of Law and Economics*, **15**(2), 337–52.

Bodenheimer, T. (2003), 'Perspective: two advertisements for TV drug ads', *Health Affairs*, Supplemental Web Exclusives W3, pp. 112–15.

Bradford, W.D., A. Kleit, P.J. Nietert, T. Steyer, T. McIlwain and S. Ornstein (2005), 'The impact of direct to consumer advertising for prescription drugs on physician prescribing behavior', presented at American Economic Association Annual Meeting: Philadelphia.

Calfee, J. (2003), 'What do we know about direct-to-consumer advertising of prescription drugs', *Health Affairs*, Supplemental Web Exclusives W3, pp. 116–19.

Calfee, J., C. Winston and R. Stempski (2002), 'Direct to consumer advertising and the demand for cholesterol reducing drugs', *Journal of Law and Economics*, **45**(2, pt. 2), 673–90.

Coscelli, A. (2000), 'The importance of doctors' and patients' preferences in the prescription decision', *Journal of Industrial Economics*, **42**(3), 349–69.

Dubois, R. (2003), 'Pharmaceutical promotion: don't throw the baby out with the bath water', *Health Affairs*, Supplemental Web Exclusives W3, pp. 96–103.

Fisher, C. and C. Anderson (1990), 'Hospital advertising: does it influence consumers?', *Journal of Health Care Marketing*, **10**(4), 40–46.

Frank, R., E.R. Berndt, J. Donohue, A. Epstein and M. Rosenthal (2002), *Trends in Direct-to-Consumer Advertising of Prescription Drugs*, Washington, DC: Kaiser Family Foundation, pp. 1–14.

Gahart, M., L.M. Duhamel, A. Dievler and R. Price (2003), 'Examining the FDA's Oversight of Direct-to-Consumer Advertising', *Health Affairs*, Supplemental Web Exclusives W3, pp. 120–23.

Gonul, F., F. Carter and J. Wind. (2000), 'What Kind of Patients and Physicians Value Direct-to-Consumer Advertising', *Health Care Management Science*, 3(3), 215–26.

Hurwitz, M. and R. Caves (1998), 'Persuasion or information? Promotion and the shares of brand name and generic pharmaceuticals', *Journal of Law and Economics*, 31(2), 299–320.

Iizuka, T. and G. Jin (2005), 'The effects of direct-to-consumer advertising in the prescription drug markets', AEAA Conference, Philadelphia.

Jancin, B. (2001), 'N.C. Medicaid drug costs reflect national trends', *OB GYN News*, 36(13), 33.

Keith, A. (1995), 'Regulating information about aspirin and the prevention of heart attack', *American Economic Review*, 85(1), 96–9.

Kenkel, D., R. Avery, D. Lillard and A. Mathois (2005), 'Regulating advertisements: the case of smoking cessation products', presented at the American Economic Association Annual Meeting: Philadelphia.

King, C. (1996), 'Marketing, product differentiation and competition in the pharmaceutical industry', Working Paper, MIT Department of Economics.

Klein, B. and K. Leffler (1981), 'The role of market forces in assuring contractual performance', *Journal of Political Economy*, 89(3), 615–41.

Kwoka, J. (1984), 'Advertising and the price and quality of optometric services', *American Economic Review*, 74(1), 211–16.

Leffler, K. (1981), 'Persuasion or information? The economics of prescription drug advertising', *Journal of Law and Economics*, 24(1), 45–74.

Lipsky, M. and C. Taylor (1997), 'The opinions and experiences of family physicians regarding direct-to-consumer advertising', *Journal of Family Practice*, 45(6), 495–9.

Lundin, D. (2000), 'Moral hazard in physician prescription behavior', *Journal of Health Economics*, 19(15), 639–62.

Masson, A. and P. Rubin (1985), 'Matching prescription drugs and consumers: the benefits of direct advertising', *New England Journal of Medicine*, 313(8), 513–15.

Nelson, P. (1970), 'Information and consumer behavior', *Journal of Political Economy*, 78(2), 311–29.

Nelson, P. (1974) 'Advertising as information', *Journal of Political Economy*, 82(3), 729–54.

Palumbo, F. and D. Mullins (2002), 'The development of direct-to-consumer prescription drug advertising regulation', *Food and Drug Law Journal*, 57(3), 423–43.

Pines, W. (1999), 'A history and perspective on direct-to-consumer promotion', *Food and Drug Law Journal*, 54(2), 491–507.

Rizzo, J.A. (1999), 'Advertising and competition in the ethical pharmaceutical industry: the case of hypertensive drugs', *Journal of Law and Economics*, 42(1), 89–116.

Rizzo, J. and R. Zeckhauser (1990), 'Advertising and entry: the case of physician services', *Journal of Political Economy*, 98(3), 476–500.

Rosenthal, M., E.R. Berndt, J.M. Donohue, A.M. Epstein and R.G. Frank (2003), *Demand Effects of Recent Changes in Prescription Drug Promotion*, Washington DC: Kaiser Family Foundation.

Sumpradit, N., S. Fors and L. McCormick (2002), 'Consumers' attitudes and behavior toward prescription drug advertising', *American Journal of Health Behavior*, 26(1), 68–75.

Telser, L. (1975), 'The theory of supply with application to the ethical pharmaceutical industry', *Journal of Law and Economics*, 18(2), 449–78.

USGAO (2002), *Prescription Drugs: FDA Oversight of Direct-to-Consumer Advertising has Limitations*, Washington DC: Government Printing Office.

Weissman, J., D. Blumenthal, A.J. Silk, M. Newman, K. Zapart, R. Leitman and S. Feibelmann (2003), 'Consumer reports on the health effects of direct to consumer advertising', *Health Affairs*, Supplemental Web Exclusive, W4, pp. 219–33.

Zachry, W. and D. Ginsburg (2001), 'Patient autonomy and the regulation of direct-to-consumer advertising', *Clinical Therapy*, 23(12), 2024–37.

Zachry, W., J. Dalen and T. Jackson (2003), 'Clinicians' responses to direct-to-consumer advertising of prescription medications', *Archives of Internal Medicine*, 163(15), 1808–12.

Zachry, W., M.D. Shepherd, M.J. Hinich, J.P. Wilson, C.M. Brown and K.A. Lawson (2002), 'Relationship between direct-to-consumer advertising and physician diagnosing and prescribing', *American Journal of Health System Pharmacy*, 59(1), 42–9.

PART VI

ASSESSING THE PERFORMANCE OF HEALTH CARE ORGANIZATIONS

30 Concepts and challenges in measuring the performance of health care organizations
Peter C. Smith and Andrew Street

1. Introduction

In a social system of even moderate complexity it becomes necessary for an individual or organization (the principal) to delegate some activities to an agent, who is expected to carry out the wishes of the principal in return for some sort of reward. As Propper notes, the health care system – of whatever design – is replete with interlocking agency relationships (Propper, 1995). Examples include the relationships between patients and doctors, third party payers and providers, and between regulators and practitioners.

Delegated decision-making is unproblematic only if either the principal is fully informed or the objectives of principal and agent are identical. Rarely do principals enjoy perfect information. In most contexts the outcomes from agents' decisions depend both on their own actions and to a large extent on factors outside their control. Therefore a principal cannot reliably contract either on the basis of the actions of or the outcomes secured by an agent. In short, there are substantial problems with both hidden action (on the part of the agent) and hidden information (the agent's contribution to outcomes).

Imperfect information would not matter if the objectives of principal and agent coincided. This state of affairs is highly unlikely; for it to obtain, not only must the principal and agent care about the same things but they must value them similarly. In effect, they would make the same decisions when confronted with a given set of alternatives. Doctors may care about the health of their patients and patients may care about the effort of their doctors but it seems plausible to suggest that the patient's valuation of health (relative to the effort of the doctor) is greater than the doctor's.

A principal–agent problem arises whenever there is asymmetric information and non-identical objectives, and many agency relationships in health care seem to satisfy both requirements. The difference between the principal's welfare when there is full information or coincidence of objectives and when there is not, is known as the *agency cost*. The principal will seek to devise managerial, information, budgetary and payment systems to mitigate the cost of agency, taking account of the direct costs of such systems, which we can call *transaction costs*. The principal will then aim to choose a system that minimizes the sum of agency and transaction costs. Economists have examined two ways of mitigating agency costs: implementation of incentives and enhancement of information.

This chapter focuses on the latter strategy, particularly on the use of comparative information about organizational performance. We outline a rudimentary principal–agent model to provide a framework for understanding the information asymmetries that motivate organizational performance measurement, and for understanding the role of performance information. We first introduce the model. We then discuss the difficulty of specifying objectives; and the challenges for performance that arise because of the information asymmetries between principals and agents.

2.   Organizing framework

To see why performance measurement is undertaken consider a simplified model in which a principal – a regulator, health insurer, purchasing authority – contracts with an agent – a health care provider of some description (Goddard et al., 2000).

Often in health care, the principal is not completely utilitarian, but is interested in the distribution of benefits, a point that we shall return to in due course. But as a starting point, we assume that the regulator wishes to maximize a set of objectives, Y, that cannot be measured with complete accuracy. Instead there exists a vector M of *performance indicators* that is measurable and publicly available. The reported levels of M are influenced by the level of effort, e, exerted by the agent. The agent's reward (however defined) is assumed to be based on the level of measured performance M. However, environmental uncertainty means that the relationship between effort and observed performance indicator is poorly understood. For example, the costs incurred or outcomes secured by a hospital may depend on patient characteristics, the structure of the local health economy, and broader social and economic conditions, not just how much effort the hospital puts into organizing and delivering care.

Under these circumstances we can define the principal's problem as being to design a reward system $h(M)$ so as to maximize some welfare function that depends on a utility function comprising the objectives $U(Y)$, such that $\partial U/\partial Y > 0$, and on the reward R paid to the agent. In effect this reflects the usual desire to maximize achievement in relation to costs, represented algebraically as:

$$\max_{h(\cdot)} U(Y) - R$$
$$\text{subject to}$$
$$Y = f(M) + \varepsilon$$
$$M = g(e) + \delta$$
$$R = h(M)$$
$$E(U^A) = \bar{U}^0$$

where the R and e emerge from the agent's optimization problem, which we shall come to below. The function $f(.)$ indicates the relationship between desired achievement Y and measured performance M, with ε reflecting the uncertainty inherent to this imperfectly understood relationship. In effect, ε indicates the extent to which the chosen performance measures fail to capture all the intricacies of the desired achievement sought by the principal. No knowledge is assumed concerning the magnitude or distribution of the random variable ε.

The function $g(.)$ indicates the relationship between the effort of the agent and the performance indicators M. The random variable δ captures the uncertainty inherent in this relationship, and again there is no knowledge concerning its distribution. Its nature indicates the extent to which circumstances beyond the control of the agent contribute to the reported measures M.

The function $h(.)$ indicates the reward schedule, representing the various types of punishments and rewards put in place by the principal. Of course there is no reason why $h(.)$ should be set explicitly, and there may be great uncertainty on the part of both parties as to what the effective nature of the reward schedule might be. However, for the purposes of exposition, we assume that it is deterministic. The final expression in the above formulation is the usual requirement that rewards must be set so that the agent's expected level of utility $E(U^A)$ is sufficient to secure participation.

The agent is assumed to be risk averse and to wish to maximize a utility function U^A that depends on the level of effort e exerted and the level of reward R received, such that $\partial U^A / \partial R > 0$ and $\partial U^A / \partial e < 0$, as follows:

$$\max_e E(U^A(Y, R, e))$$
$$\text{subject to}$$
$$M = g(e) + \delta$$
$$R = h(M)$$

Note that the agent may to some extent share the same objectives as the principal, in which case Y may enter the agent's utility function directly. In health care, this may be explained by professional altruism or intrinsic motivation (see Chapter 31 by Propper and Wilson in this Companion). However, rarely will the agency relationship be perfect, and the principal must rely on the reward schedule to align interests. Thus Y also enters into the agent's maximization problem to the extent that it is a by-product of the effort expended on improving measured performance M.

It is important to recognize that the actions of the principal and agent will be based on their perceptions of the nature of the functions $f(.)$, $g(.)$ and $h(.)$, and that in general these will not necessarily be the same for both parties. It would therefore be more complete to use different functions for the two parties but, for the sake of simplicity, we refrain from this here.

The above framework highlights three fundamental issues that arise in applying the principal–agent model of control. First, there is the problem of *specifying* the principal's objectives. Second, the *measurement* of achievement against the objectives may be inexact. Third, design of the appropriate *reward* structure is complex, not least because knowledge of the relationship between the agent's effort and the outcome achieved may be incomplete, which we term the problem of *attribution*. We consider these issues in turn.

3. What are the principal's objectives?

As Propper and Wilson highlight in their accompanying chapter, health care agents usually face multiple objectives and often serve multiple principals. Two issues need to be addressed: what objectives, Y, ought to be pursued and what relative value, w, should be attached to each component of Y?

There is evidence to suggest that there is great variation amongst individual citizens as to what the health system ought to achieve (Charney et al., 1989; Hadorn, 1991; Nord et al., 1995). Some focus principally on health gain, while others place great weight on responsiveness, enhancing access or addressing inequalities. For the purposes of regulation, therefore, someone on behalf of society has to decide what objectives ought to be pursued. That is rarely a role for analysts or researchers – rather, it is the legitimate role of politicians. In developing a performance model, an important requirement is to seek out a clear political statement on what is valued from legitimate stakeholders. This will usually take the form of some statement of the objectives of the health system or its constituent organizations.

The objectives are unlikely to be of equal importance and, indeed, some may be correlated. The correlation may be positive, if progress against one indicator simultaneously advances another, perhaps because good management promotes all-round performance. But the correlation may be negative if trade-offs are involved, such as when resources have to be diverted from one activity in order to meet some other objective.

If an assessment of overall organizational performance is required, some means of assessing the relative value of the objectives is required. This issue is rarely afforded explicit attention. This is true, for instance, in most applications of frontier methods to assess efficiency, summarized by Burgess in his companion chapter (Chapter 32). Rather weights tend to be inferred implicitly. Non-parametric methods generate weights as a by-product of the statistical estimation process and, by default, these are specific to each organization (Cooper et al., 2000). Organization-specific weights are appropriate only if organizations have complete freedom over what objectives to pursue; in other words, when they are not in a principal–agent relationship.

A common set of weights across organizations is implicit to the other class of efficiency studies reviewed by Burgess, parametric frontier methods. When applying these methods in the context of multiple objectives, the weights simply reflect the sample average values. The implicit assumption is that the existing pattern of expenditure is a reflection of the price that society is prepared to pay (on average) for extra attainment at the margin. This is not an appealing implication, particularly given that, in undertaking the analysis, there is a pre-supposition of the presence of suboptimal performance.

If a common set of weights is required, ideally this ought to be based on societal values. These values might be elicited from studies of willingness to pay, discrete choice experiments or conjoint analysis (see the chapters by Ryan et al. (38) and Burgess et al. (39) in this Companion). An example (albeit the subject of fierce criticism) in which an attempt was made to weight objectives explicitly was the survey undertaken by the World Health Organization to infer the relative importance of health system outputs (Navarro, 2000; Williams, 2001; World Health Organization, 2000).

Applying a common set of weights will not be appropriate in contexts where organizations enjoy discretion over what emphasis to place on different objectives. For example, such an approach would be contrary to policies to decentralize decision-making or to encourage organizations to be more responsive to the concerns of the populations or client groups that they serve.

The formidable challenges associated both with determining relative values and with deciding whether organizations should be equally constrained by them caution against construction of a single index of organizational performance. Rather than subsuming the issue as part of the technical process, an alternative approach may be to employ simultaneous, multivariate techniques to analyse achievement against each objective, allowing for the possibility that objectives might be correlated with each other (Bailey and Hewson, 2004; Hauck and Street, 2004).

4. Adverse selection: what measurement instruments should be used?

If the principal–agent model is to be made operational, concrete indicators M of the objectives Y must be developed. Objectives in health care usually fall into three broad categories: health impact; responsiveness to user preferences; and equity. Economists have been very active in developing measures of health impact, using concepts such as the QALY (see chapters in Part IX). Responsiveness is a less well-developed dimension of performance, embracing concepts such as ease of access, privacy and autonomy, often loosely collected under the umbrella of patient satisfaction. A variety of surveys of patient experience are now deployed to capture aspects of responsiveness. Notions of equity, or fairness, are important to many health systems, but often poorly articulated.

Although progress is being made toward better measurement of these objectives, a major challenge is how to select from a growing set of possibilities a manageable number of performance indicators. From a regulatory perspective, the use of an extensive set of performance indicators is usually infeasible, and some way of reducing the dimensionality of the output space has to be found before an operational regulatory model can be formulated. But a selective set of indicators may be suboptimal, leading to neglect of valued but unmeasured aspects of performance. Both the need for a selective set of indicators and the difficulty of expressing these in operationally useful ways imply substantial deviation between Y and M.

Much of the information used for performance measurement is generated by the agents themselves. An important issue arises when it is in the power of the agent to manipulate the reported performance measure M in a way that improves reported behaviour without any concomitant improvement in actual behaviour. This misrepresentation of reported performance is a form of adverse selection, with the agents being selective about what they reveal to the principal (Owen and Braeutigam, 1978). Agents may control the information flow in various ways: in how they report costs allocations or make coding decisions; in the partiality of their reporting; or in how quickly they release information to the principal. Scope for such manipulation is great within health care, as the collection of data is often in the hands of health care professionals whose actions cannot readily be audited.

The reward schedule may therefore give rise to the potential for gaming on the part of the agent, in which behaviour is altered so as to obtain strategic advantage. The potential for this phenomenon arises even when such manipulation is costly to the agent. For example, suppose the agent is in a position to manipulate reported performance data from true level M to misrepresented level M^R. The optimization problem can then be amended as follows:

$$\max_{e} E(U^A(Y,R,e,p))$$
$$\text{subject to}$$
$$M = g(e) + \delta$$
$$p = p(M^R - M)$$
$$R = h(M^R)$$

where $p(.)$ represents the perceived cost to the agent of such manipulation, and $\partial U^A / \partial p < 0$. In many respects this model is analogous to the sorts of economic models developed in public finance to explain tax evasion behaviour (Adreoni et al., 1988).

Similarly, whenever multi-period systems of targets and rewards are put in place, there arises the potential for gaming in the form of the 'ratchet' effect. This phenomenon arises because rewards are often set on the basis of the agent reaching some target, the targets frequently specified in relation to improvement on past performance. Such gaming was endemic to the former Soviet Union, in which production targets were frequently based on past production levels (Nove, 1980). Although the agent may be rewarded for achieving or exceeding current targets, the penalty for securing good performance in any one year is that a high feasible level of performance has been revealed to the principal. The principal's expectations may therefore have been permanently raised, and the agent can expect to be 'rewarded' with tougher performance targets in the future: its targets have been irreversibly 'ratcheted' up.

Under these circumstances, given that performance levels are positively related to the agent's effort, the agent has a strong incentive to report persistently low levels of performance. This may result in low productivity bonuses in the current year. The reward to the agent, however, will be modest performance targets in future years, with the concomitant reduced effort requirement and increased bonuses. This can be illustrated in the context of the above model by extending the discussion to a multi-period setting.

Suppose that, as above, the agent's utility in period t is based on effort e_t and reward R_t, and is represented by the specific form $U(R_t, e_t) = -e(M_t) + \alpha(M_t - M_t^*)$, where M_t is measured performance in period t, M^* is the associated target in period t, and α is a linear piece rate. The effort function $e(.)$ gives the perceived effort required to reach performance level M_t and is such that $\partial e / \partial M > 0$. Assume, furthermore, that in a two period model, the target in period 1 is exogenously given but that the target in period 2 is dependent on measured performance in period 1: say $M_2^* = M_1$. Then, assuming separability of utility functions, two-period utility of the agent U^{TOT} is given by:

$$U^{TOT} = -e(M_1) + \alpha(M_1 - M_1^*) + \beta\{-e(M_2) + \alpha(M_2 - M_1)\}$$

where β indicates the time preference of the agent. The agent maximizes utility by solving a simple dynamic programme. In period 2, U^{TOT} is maximized by selecting M_2 such that $\partial e(M_2)/\partial M = \alpha$, in accordance with the simple static view of the incentives confronting the agent. However, for period 1, the optimal production level M_1 is such that $\partial e(M_2)/\partial M = \alpha(1 - \beta)$, a lower level of performance than that implied by the simple static analysis whenever $1 > \beta > 0$. That is, the use of the first period performance level to set the second period target results in a lower level of effort than would have been suggested by a naive one-period analysis. In a more realistic multi-period setting, this phenomenon may give rise to chronic underperformance on the part of the agents.

The importance of the ratchet effect has been acknowledged in the Soviet literature, and was widely perceived to be a crucial reason for persistently poor productivity levels (Kornai, 1992). Attempts to circumvent the ratchet effect on the part of the principal were designed, though never implemented (Weitzman, 1976). In a two-period setting, a principal who recognizes the existence of the problem can in theory design an incentive scheme which seeks to persuade the agent to reveal realistic levels of production possibilities, by offering rewards for improving future targets, as well as for achieving current targets. However, Darvish and Kahana caution that even this solution may fail in a multiperiod setting (Darvish and Kahana, 1989).

5. Moral hazard: how are rewards to be set?

As outlined by Chalkley in Chapter 22 in this Companion, it is the particular role played by effort, e, that motivates performance measurement. Whenever the agency relationship is imperfect, the principal would like the agent to exert more effort than the agent would choose. The more effort applied, the greater the level of achievement for a given level of input, so the principal would prefer the agent to maximize the effort applied. But, in general and even if intrinsically motivated to some extent, the agent's utility is decreasing in the amount of effort expended, with $\partial U^A/\partial e < 0$; the agent would prefer to minimize the amount of effort in meeting the objectives it has been set.

This would pose no problem if the principal had perfect information. But the principal is likely to be less well informed than the agent in two key respects, both of which are forms of moral hazard (Ellis and McGuire, 1990; Laffont and Tirole, 1993). First, the principal will have less information about the nature of the production function, including optimal input mix, costs, and the exogenous influences on these costs. This gives the agent latitude to incur costs above their efficient level. Second, and most especially, the principal will be unable to observe the level of effort expended by the agent, with the principal unable to distinguish accurately between hard-working and less industrious agents.

The correlation between M and e is determined by the size of the random element δ, which in a sense indicates the impact of exogenous influences on measured performance. The impact of these influences will vary for each performance indicator, implying that the extent to which health care providers can be held responsible for the observed level of achievement is highly variable. For example, Hauck et al. (2003) show that – at a strategic level – the organizational impact on public health indicators, such as population mortality rates, is very modest, whilst the impact on process measures such as waiting times is high (Hauck et al., 2003). This variation poses considerable challenges for designing reward schedules.

A common approach to reducing the principal's information deficit is by making comparisons among similar organizations. Holmström demonstrates that it is always optimal to make pay contingent upon information about common or industry variations, as it reduces the chance of wrongly rewarding poor effort and wrongly penalizing high effort (Holmström, 1979). Holmström suggests that an average of the correlated measures of similar organizations will be a sufficient summary of the relevant information for each individual contract, allowing common uncertainty shared with other organizations to be filtered out (Holmström, 1982). A similar argument informs Schleifer's proposal for 'yardstick competition' – or relative performance evaluation – of organizations that face limited competitive pressure (Schleifer, 1985). Schleifer argues that regulated prices should be based on costs observed in *all* organizations within the same industry, not just on each individual organization's costs. This information allows the regulator to infer more about the conditions within the industry and about the level of effort behind each particular organization's cost level.

A complicating feature in health care is that it may be the case that some of the objectives implicit in Y are actually the results of the joint efforts of a number of agencies. Clearly the model that we have set out assumes that agents will expend effort only on those activities that affect their own rewards. Where the variance of unattributed outcome δ is large, it becomes very difficult to design incentive schemes that encourage co-operation and progress towards improvement in joint outputs. This can lead to a form of sub-optimization: the pursuit by agents of narrow local objectives, at the expense of the objectives of the system as a whole.

We previously mentioned that health care agents often face multiple principals, and discussed the problems associated with measuring performance against multiple objectives. But principals differ in both the objectives they wish to be pursued and in the instruments available to give incentives to agents. It is often the case that rewards in the principal–agent paradigm are implicit rather than explicit. For example, the publication of surgical success rates in New York and other public reporting mechanisms are intended to motivate agents through the market mechanism. The publication of league tables of national health systems in the World Health Report 2000 was intended to motivate governments through national political processes (World Health Organization, 2000). The belief in both cases is that adverse reported performance will motivate principals (patients or voters) to make better-informed choices in the form of exit or voice, and thereby stimulate effort on the part of agents. In practice, as discussed in the chapter by Propper and Wilson in this Companion (Chapter 31), such indirect approaches to performance improvement appear to have only limited impact in health care. There is growing awareness of a need to design explicit incentives schemes to stimulate desired improvements.

6.   Conclusion

A strong rationale for regulatory interest in performance assessment of health care organizations is to reduce their information disadvantage. The information asymmetry between the regulator and the organization takes two forms: adverse selection, in which organizations exercise influence over information availability; and moral hazard, where agents can exploit their informational advantage over the principal to incur excessive costs or limit the amount of effort they employ. Whilst there is good reason to believe that reducing the level of information asymmetry will lead to major improvements in health system performance, this chapter shows that there are formidable challenges associated with making this principle a reality in health care regulation.

References

Adreoni, J., B. Erard and J. Feinstein (1988), 'Tax compliance', *Journal of Economic Literature*, **36**, 818–60.
Bailey, T.C. and P.J. Hewson (2004), 'Simultaneous modelling of multiple traffic safety performance indicators by using a multivariate generalized linear mixed model', *Journal of the Royal Statistical Society, Series A*, **163**(3), 501–17.
Charney, M.C., P.A. Lewis and S.C. Farrow (1989), 'Choosing who should not be treated in the NHS', *Social Science and Medicine*, **28**, 1331–8.
Cooper, W.W., L.M. Seiford and K. Tone (2000), *Data Envelopment Analysis: a Comprehensive Text with Models, Applications and References*, Boston: Kluwer.
Darvish, T. and N. Kahana (1989), 'The ratchet principle: a multi-period flexible incentive scheme', *European Economic Review*, **33**, 51–7.
Ellis, R.P. and T.G. McGuire (1990), 'Optimal payment systems for health services', *Journal of Health Economics*, **9**, 375–96.

Goddard, M., R. Mannion and P. Smith (2000), 'Enhancing performance in health care: A theoretical perspective on agency and the role of information', *Health Economics*, **9**(2), 95–107.

Hadorn, D.C. (1991), 'Setting health care priorities in Oregon', *Journal of the American Medical Association*, **265**, 2218–25.

Hauck, K. and A. Street (2004), *Performance Assessment in the Context of Multiple Objectives: a Multivariate Multilevel Approach*, York: Centre for Health Economics, University of York.

Hauck, K., N. Rice and P.C. Smith (2003), 'The influence of health care organizations on health system performance', *Journal of Health Services Research and Policy*, **8**(2), 68–74.

Holmström, B. (1979), 'Moral hazard and observability', *Bell Journal of Economics*, **10**(1), 74–91.

Holmström, B. (1982), 'Moral hazard in teams', *Bell Journal of Economics*, **13**(3), 324–40.

Kornai, J. (1992), *The Socialist System: the Political Economy of Communism*, Oxford: Clarendon Press.

Laffont, J.-J. and J. Tirole (1993), *A Theory of Incentives in Procurement and Regulation*, Cambridge, Massachusetts: The MIT Press.

Navarro, V. (2000), 'Assessment of the World Health Report 2000', *The Lancet*, **356**, 1598–601.

Nord, E., J. Richardson, A. Street, H. Kuhse and P. Singer (1995), 'Maximising health benefits vs egalitarianism: an Australian survey of health issues', *Social Science and Medicine*, **41**(10), 1429–37.

Nove, A. (1980), *The Soviet Economic System*, 2nd edn, London: Allen and Unwin.

Owen, B. and R. Braeutigam (1978), *The Regulation Game: Strategic Use of the Administrative Process*, Cambridge, MA: Harvard Business School Press.

Propper, C. (1995), 'Agency and incentives in the NHS internal market', *Social Science and Medicine*, **40**, 1683–90.

Schleifer, A. (1985), 'A theory of yardstick competition', *Rand Journal of Economics*, **16**(3), 319–27.

Weitzman, M.L. (1976), 'The new Soviet incentive system', *Bell Journal of Economics*, **7**, 251–57.

Williams, A. (2001), 'Science or marketing at WHO? A commentary on "World Health 2000"', *Health Economics*, **10**, 93–100.

World Health Organization (2000), *World Health Report 2000*, Geneva: WHO.

31 The use of performance measures in health care systems
Carol Propper and Deborah Wilson

1. Introduction

Performance measurement is becoming increasingly prevalent in many health care systems. The United States has the most experience of publication of data on health care performance (Marshall et al., 2000). Information is available on the comparative performance of health insurance plans, hospitals and individual doctors. Perhaps the best known reporting system is the Health Plan Employer Data Information Set (HEDIS). Other high profile systems have focused on a single aspect of care. The New York Cardiac Surgery Reporting system, for example, publishes data on hospital- and surgeon-specific risk adjusted coronary artery bypass surgery mortality. There is less release of information about quality of care in the UK (Marshall et al., 2000), but in Scotland, data that compares outcomes across both hospitals and health areas was made public from the early 1990s and since 1999 there has been a large increase in the amount of publicly released data on the performance of English health care providers.[1]

2. The special features of health care systems

The health care sector shares many features of public sector organizations. This is not surprising, given the large role of not-for-profit organizations in health care. Dixit (2002) stresses two important features of the public sector. The first is that agents often serve several masters: these may include the users of the service, payers for the service, politicians at different levels of government, professional organizations. The second, a consequence of the first, is that the organization and so the agents who work in it often have several ends to achieve. For example, they are often expected to increase both efficiency and equity in the delivery of health care. These features are termed multiple principals and multiple tasks: they mean that the goals of a health care organization may be in conflict. Consequently the performance measures used to evaluate, often complex, health care sector performance may also be in conflict. The multiple and sometimes vague goals of health care organizations mean that performance relative to these goals is difficult to measure.

A third feature of health care organizations is that their workers may exhibit 'intrinsic' motivation, which may cause them to respond in particular ways to the incentives embodied in a performance measurement system. Intrinsic motivation has been defined as occurring when an individual is 'motivated to perform an activity when [he/she] receives no apparent reward except the activity itself' (Deci 1971, p. 105, cited in Jones and Cullis 2003). Crewson (1997) distinguishes intrinsic rewards from extrinsic rewards (such as a pay rises or promotion). The distinction matters since it may affect the impact of rewards on behaviour. Extrinsic rewards may not work: they may 'crowd out' workers' intrinsic motivation and so have a negative impact on health care organization performance (Frey, 2000).

These features mean that any performance measure (PM) will at best be imperfect. A PM will at best be able to provide a partial picture of a complex process, in which there are several stakeholders, including users, who may have conflicting aims. A further consideration is that agents will respond to PMs in ways that maximize their own utility or benefit. This is not necessarily consistent with PMs improving welfare, nor is it necessarily in ways that are expected by those who design a system of performance monitoring. There are many examples of both distorted measures and altered behaviour to improve the PM at the expense of unmeasured actions (see Propper and Wilson (2003) for examples outside the health care system). All these factors mean that achieving a causal link between measurement of and improvement in health care organization performance will crucially depend on the objectives and design of the PM system.

3. Rationale for and forms of performance measure in health care

Performance measurement may be undertaken at various levels, from system-wide to the organizational level. Its purpose may differ depending on the level at which it is implemented. For example, it can be used to improve the performance of individual units (such as particular hospitals). This may or may not be linked to 'best practice' exercises, in which the best performing units provide an example for others to follow. It can be used as part of an attempt to improve the performance of the *overall* organization. In this case the focus of the exercise is to improve the performance of the parent organization as a whole, as well as possibly providing some developmental information for a single unit. It may be used as part of an attempt to generate pseudo-competition, for example, where purchasers in health care buy care from providers on the basis of measures of performance. It may also be used to improve the accountability of organizations in the health care sector. Finally, it can be used as part of a resource allocation system, for example, to enable central government to allocate funds to service providers. In the use made of performance measurement in the health care sector we can see elements of all these aims, but they are often not clearly separately identified, and the same tools may be used for different purposes.

Performance measures come in a variety of forms (Propper and Wilson, 2003). Barnow (1992) makes a distinction between gross outcomes and net outputs as performance measures. Gross outcomes are measures of the outcomes of the programme at some designated date. Health programme gross outcomes include the number of patients who do not die after emergency admission for heart attacks, or the number of individuals given hip replacements. The advantages of such measures are that they are easy to understand and easy to collect. But they do not necessarily measure the actual output of the programme itself: patients may have recovered from heart attacks without medical intervention. However, if gross outcomes are measured relative to some standard, which is set to take account of what would have happened without the programme, then the gross outcomes may be useful in assessing the impact of the programme. Gross outcomes also do not take into account the difficulty of treating a particular individual, but they can be adjusted for observed characteristics of the individual and this can partially overcome this problem. In fact, in many situations, heterogeneity across programme users means that such adjustments will be necessary. For example, performance measures for medical outcomes are frequently risk adjusted (essentially adjusted for the health of the individuals treated).[2]

Net outputs are measures of the value added of the programme. As Barnow (1992) notes, barriers to developing net output measures may be high, primarily because the output of the programme may be multi-dimensional: for example, public organizations in health care may be required to meet both efficiency and equity targets. One way of overcoming this is to calculate the value of net outputs – the health gain from treatment – so there is a common metric across outcomes, but again this is not a simple matter. More generally, measuring value added is fraught with methodological problems, a key one being the difficulty of constructing a counterfactual of what would have happened in the absence of the programme. This means that net output calculations often require evaluations that are expensive and cannot be done on a regular basis (see also section 4 below). In addition, collecting such data takes time, so net measures do not give those who run the programme information when they need it, typically at the end of the year.

We can also distinguish measures of outcome from measures of process. Smith (2002) argues that outcome measures are likely to be favoured when the nature of the outcome is relatively uncontested; when outcomes can relatively easily be captured in operational performance measures; when an indicator of the outcome can be secured reasonably soon after the intervention; when the outcome is readily attributable to clinical performance rather than external factors; and when there is a need for considerable clinical judgement as to the most appropriate intervention to offer. Outcome measures are of use in indicating good performance when the outcomes that are desired occur in the short term, when risk adjustments can be made, and when there are not too many dimensions to the output.

Process and outcome measures also might have different functions. Outcomes are often the result of factors outside the control of the health system. Measuring poor outcomes (for example, in-patient mortality) does not necessarily give guidance on what to change in order to improve. Such outcomes occur infrequently in comparison to the processes that prevent them (for example, the use of beta blockers in the treatment of patients with AMI). On the other hand, changing a process that is known to improve outcomes should lead to improvements. So measuring processes may be useful when performance measures are used internally to improve production, whereas outcome measures may be more useful when seeking to reward good outcomes (Romano and Mutter, 2004). Marshall et al. (2000) argue that there is an increasing body of evidence that process measures are more sensitive and feasible measures of quality of care than outcome measures. More generally, a theme that emerges in the discussion of performance measures in health care is the importance of the use of a range of measures.

There is also discussion of the purpose of public disclosure of information. Marshall et al. (2000) identify three models. The first is a public accountability model in which disclosure is a public responsibility, independent of the consequences. Proponents argue that the release of data, in conjunction with appropriate education and debate, will clarify important social issues. However, this model may have little impact on the quality of care, though it may (for exactly the same reasons) be perceived as least threatening by professionals. The second is a market-orientated model, in which comparative information allows informed consumers to drive quality improvements through choice. To be useful, such data need to be standardized for differences in case-mix. This model is possibly more important in health care systems in which consumers can make choices, but even in the US, the evidence suggests that individual consumers make relatively little use of perform-ance data.[3] The third model, a professional orientated model, assumes a desire on the part of professionals to improve their practice, given the appropriate environment. Providing data aids this. In this case, standardization is not the highest priority, as providers may be comparing their own performance over time using the data as an aid, rather than a measure that is linked directly to financial rewards.

4.   Evidence on the use and impact of PMs in health care

Difficulties in constructing measures
Landon et al. (2003) review the current state of physician clinical performance assessment (PCPA). PCPA is the quantitative assessment of performance based on the rates at which patients experience certain outcomes of care and/or the rates at which physicians adhere to evidence-based processes of care during their actual practice of medicine. It can be used to ensure competency of individual physicians, to support health care choices by patients or purchasers and in quality improvement within organizations or by physicians. While Landon et al. focus on the requirements for competency assessment as this is the most stringent, they note that PCPA is rarely used for this purpose.[4]

Landon et al. (2003) argue that measures used in PCPA must be feasible to collect; be evidence-based (non-controversial, from randomized control trials (RCTs) or over-whelming physician consensus); apply to a large enough population of patients to allow assessment of individual physicians; adjust for patient-level characteristics that may con-found the measure (case-mix, severity of illness, co-morbidity, factors that affect adher-ence to treatments (for example, socio-economic status)); attribute care to the individual physician; be reasonably reflective of the work performed by physicians in the field.

The obstacles to wider use include the lack of evidence in many specialties; problems in defining thresholds for acceptable care; sample size and other statistical consider-ations;[5] the issue of confounding in both process and outcome measures (risk adjustment based on administrative datasets may not be precise enough to determine physician com-petence, though it may be suitable for quality improvement) and finally, the fact that evi-dence concerning optimal processes only exists for a small faction of the routine work of most specialties. They conclude that, at present, important technical barriers fall in the way of using PCPA for evaluating the competency of individual physicians.

Lilford et al. (2004) argue that comparative outcomes data (league tables on mortality and other outcomes) should not be used by external agents to make judgements about quality of hospital care. Although they may provide a reasonable measure of quality in some high-risk surgical situations, they have little validity in acute medical settings. They are useful for monitoring trends within organizations and research purposes, but argue that sanctions and rewards should not be applied to the 'worst' 5 per cent of providers on outcomes, because these will not be the 5 per cent with the worst quality.[6] They suggest instead that central agencies should ask that organizations show that they have in place mechanisms with which to monitor trends in outcomes (deaths, changes in infec-tion rates), clinical processes (for example, speed of treatment of fractured hips) and throughput (waiting times). Romano and Mutter (2004) further warn against focusing on just one dimension of care. Quality of care has multiple dimensions, and organizations that perform well on one dimension may not perform well on others. Focusing on a single measure, or on multiple measures of a single dimension, may lead to the wrong conclusion regarding overall quality.

Potential for gaming

The potential for gaming arises from the fact that the agent has different aim(s) from the principal(s). As the principal tries to get higher effort (and so better quality health care) by implementing performance measurement, the response may be better services but also may be other less desired behaviour. Gaming can take many forms. Smith (1995) lists unintended consequences of publishing PMs in the public sector, including tunnel vision; myopia; measure fixation; sub-optimization; gaming; misrepresentation and misinterpretation.[7]

Examples in health care abound (Lilford et al., 2004). Green and Wintfeld (1995) argue that 41 per cent of New York state's reduction in risk-adjusted mortality could be accounted for by data gaming. Burack et al. (1999) surveyed 104 cardiac surgeons in New York and found that high risk coronary artery bypass grafting (CABG) patients were more likely to be denied treatment compared to similar high risk patients with aortic dissection, because the latter procedure was not subject to performance monitoring. There is also evidence from the UK of dysfunctional behaviour in response to measures of throughput (Edhouse and Wardrope, 1996). Lilford et al. (2004 p. 1151) state, 'in the UK we have seen clinical services interrupted, figures distorted, and managers falling on their swords in response to spurious process data or "bean counting"'.

Impact of information on behaviour

Marshall et al. (2000) identify possible responses to public disclosure from consumers, physicians, hospitals and provider organizations, and purchasers. One view is that while consumers claim to want such information they do not make great use of the data (Schneider and Epstein, 1998; Edgman-Levitan and Cleary, 1996; Marshall et al., 2002; Mason and Street, 2005). Farley et al. (2002) study the impact of report card information on plan choice amongst Medicaid enrollees and find that only 50 per cent of survey respondents reported receiving and using the report, and that the report card had little impact on aggregate enrolment. Evidence from focus groups suggests that most employees do not use the information when it is provided (Meyer et al., 1998).

There is some evidence that suggests the use of certain kinds of information by consumers. Scalon et al. (2002) examine the effect of health plan ratings on employee health plan choice and show that individuals do not respond to individual attributes of quality. However, they show that employees avoid plans with many below-average ratings, while they are not strongly attracted to plans with many superior ratings. Studies in laboratories and focus groups have also shown that individuals are more likely to avoid low rated plans than select high rated ones (Hibbard et al., 2000). Wedig and Tai-Seale (2002) investigate the impact of information from health insurance report cards that seek to translate complex data about plan benefits and treatments into a small number of dimensions. They conclude that 'consumers can apparently get a complete picture of most subjective dimensions of quality by focusing on just a few report card measures (two in our case)' (p. 1046) and also note that consumers find process measures of consumer satisfaction to be the most useful, largely because they can infer the meaning of measures such as overall satisfaction, time spent with the physician and so on. Measures of health outcomes (for example, mortality rates) are assigned less value by consumers.

The evidence suggests that physicians are more aware of report cards than consumers but make little use of them (Marshall et al., 2003). There are examples from the US of physicians responding by demanding that their managers' performance also be judged using report cards (Kaplan et al., 2000). In the UK some professional networks (for example, cardiothoracic surgeons) are showing some support for benchmarking on the basis of published data (Marshall et al., 2003).

Provider organizations and hospitals are the most responsive agents to these data. Marshall et al. (2000) indicate some positive responses, in that report cards induced better processes or outcomes, particularly in competitive markets (see also Marshall et al., 2003 and references therein). Other responses were less positive and included criticisms of the data, particularly among those hospitals identified as poor quality (Mason and Street, 2005). Purchasers, in contrast, are more interested in costs or gross indicators of quality (Marshall et al., 2003). A survey of the impact of HEDIS data on employer choice of health care plans suggests limited use by buyers of health care (Hibbard et al., 1997).

Impact of information on outcomes
Despite a decade or more of experience with public disclosure of performance data in the US there has been little rigorous evaluation of its impact on outcomes. Marshall et al. (2000) identify several reasons for this. Some are due to the particular nature of the sector, for example, the 'political incorrectness' of challenging a tool of informed consumerism or the power of vested business interests. However, they also note that evaluation of performance data requires a clear theoretical framework to identify the purpose of publication and an understanding of the strengths and weaknesses of the data that are being made public. The kind of academic rigour that has been applied to evaluation of performance management in the training field (Propper and Wilson, 2003) has not yet occurred in health. In part, this is due to the fact that the measurement of health care outcomes is more complex than the measurement of labour market outcomes.

The most reliable evidence comes from studies of the New York Cardiac Surgery Reporting System (Marshall et al., 2000). Hannan et al. (1994) found that mortality declined significantly following publication of data on mortality rates. Potential explanations include responses of doctors, an exodus of low volume and high mortality surgeons from the state, a marked improvement in the performance of non-low volume surgeons and improvement of surgeons new to the system. Critics of the release of data argued that its publication could have reduced access to CABG surgery by forcing sicker patients to get surgery out of the state or by surgeons refusing to operate on high-risk patients (potential 'cream-skimming' strategies). However, this behaviour was not supported by the evidence.

Dranove et al. (2003) use the same data to examine the impact of report cards on appropriate matching of patients to hospitals, on the quality and incidence of intensive cardiac treatments and on the resource use and health outcomes that determine the net consequences of report cards on social welfare. They found that report cards led to substantial selection by providers of patients, increased sorting of patients to providers on the basis of severity of their illness, and significant declines in the use of intensive cardiac procedures for sicker patients. Treated patients in the two states (New York and Pennsylvania) which had report cards were less ill than those treated in states without report cards. Patients within a hospital were more similar in terms of severity and those who were sicker were more likely to go to teaching hospitals. Report cards also altered the treatments given, such that both healthier and sicker patients received more treatment. However, while this improved outcomes for healthier patients, it worsened outcomes for sicker ones, because hospitals avoided performing intensive surgical therapies that were monitored for sicker patients and instead used less effective medical therapies. Overall, the authors concluded that these cards reduced patient welfare, though they concluded that the longer-term impacts might be more positive.[8]

Finally, Marshall et al. (2003) discuss some observational studies on the effect of performance measurement on processes related to health outcomes, such as vaccination and mammography. Bost (2001), for example, shows that US health plans which publicly reported their data showed greater relative improvement on some HEDIS measures over a three-year period compared to those plans which measured but did not publish performance data. Longo et al. (1997) find improvements in obstetrics care processes for hospitals identified as being low quality, and that this effect was stronger in more competitive markets. Improvements in processes related to patient experience (as well as reductions in within-hospital waiting times) were identified as one result of a benchmarking exercise across emergency care departments in 12 Swiss hospitals (Schwappach et al., 2003).

5.   Conclusion

The lessons from the experience in the health care sector appear to be the following. First, there are considerable technical difficulties in constructing measures of performance, and value added (net output) measures seem very far from the current agenda. There is some consensus that gross outcome PMs do not provide a sufficiently accurate picture of the relative performance of health care organizations, and that some adjustment should be made to account for the heterogeneity of the input. Such adjustment helps to (i) give a better measure of the impact of the agency and (ii) reduce the incentive for cream-skimming.

Second, several commentators argue for the need for different measures for different purposes. Health care sector organizations often have multiple stakeholders who have differing, and sometimes conflicting, goals. One PM cannot adequately address all these actors' objectives. A range of PMs should be employed, both in terms of what they measure and also in terms of their form. Some measures may be used for internal use, others for external monitoring and regulation and yet others for giving information to consumers and other user groups.

Third, the largest response to these measures is by health care providers, which suggests there is scope for PMs to lead to improvements in the quality of health care. There has been little rigorous evaluation of the impact of performance measures on health care outcomes or process, however. Such evaluation is necessary if we wish to establish whether or not performance measures actually help health care agencies achieve the goals they have been set by policy-makers.

Notes

1. The National Performance Assessment System measures performance on a range of financial, clinical and patient care indicators for hospitals, health care purchasers and primary care providers.
2. Smith (2002) discusses the need to adjust for sources of variation in more detail.
3. We discuss this point further in section 4.
4. There is some voluntary use by professional specialty societies; mandatory programmes are the hospital and physician performance programmes in New York and Pennsylvania. These programmes are limited in scope and involve only two specialties (cardiac surgery, cardiology) and a single procedure for each specialty (CABG or angioplasty).
5. Many specialists do not see enough patients, for example. This is especially problematic in primary care, but less of an issue in cardiac surgery and cardiology in which doctors perform a large number of a limited range of procedures.
6. Kane and Staiger (2002) show (in the education context) how small organizations are particularly vulnerable to fluctuations in such ranking exercises.
7. Goddard et al. (2000) show how these can be derived from a principal–agent model.
8. For example, the increased patient sorting that report cards engender might lead to more accurate and effective treatment as hospitals become more specialized in the treatment of certain types of patients.

References

Barnow, B.S. (1992), 'The effect of performance standards on state and local programs', in C. Manski and L. Garfinkel (eds), *Evaluating Welfare and Training Programs*, Cambridge MA: Harvard University Press.

Bost, J. (2001), 'Managed care organizations publicly reporting three years of HEDIS data', *Managed Care Interface*, **14**, 50–54.

Burack, J.H., P. Impellizzeri, P. Homel and J.N. Cunningham Jr (1999), 'Public reporting of surgical mortality: a survey of New York State cardiothoracic surgeons', *Annals of Thoracic Surgery*, **68**, 1195–200.

Crewson, P.E. (1997), 'Public service motivation: building empirical evidence of incidence and effect', *Journal of Public Administration Research and Theory*, **7**(4), 499–518.

Deci, E.L. (1971), 'Effects of externally mediated rewards on intrinsic motivation', *Journal of Personality and Social Psychology*, **18**(2), 105–15.

Dixit, A. (2002), 'Incentives and organizations in the public sector: an interpretive review', *Journal of Human Resources*, **37**(4), 696–727.

Dranove, D., D. Kessler, M. McClellan and M. Satterhwaite (2003), 'Is more information better? The effects of "report cards" on health care providers', *Journal of Political Economy*, **111**(3), 555–88.

Edgman-Levitan, S. and P.D. Cleary (1996), 'What information do consumers want and need?', *Health Affairs*, **15**, 42–56.

Edhouse, J.A. and J. Wardrope (1996), 'Do the national performance tables really indicate the performance of accident and emergency departments?', *Journal of Accident and Emergency Medicine*, **13**, 123–6.

Farley, D., P. Short, M.N. Elliot, D.E. Kanouse, J.A. Brown and R.D. Hays (2002), 'Effects of CAHPS health plan performance information on plan choices by New Jersey Medicaid beneficiaries', *Health Services Research*, **37**(4), 985–1007.

Frey, B. (2000), 'Motivation and human behaviour', in P. Taylor-Gooby (ed.), *Risk, Trust and Welfare*, Basingstoke: Macmillan, pp. 31–50.

Goddard, M., R. Mannion and P. Smith (2000), 'Enhancing performance in health care: a theoretical perspective on agency and the role of information', *Health Economics*, **9**, 95–107.

Green, J. and N. Wintfeld (1995), 'Report cards on cardiac surgeons: assessing New York State's approach', *New England Journal of Medicine*, **332**, 1229–32.

Hannan, E.L., H. Kilburn, M. Racz, E. Shields and M.R. Chassin (1994), 'Improving the outcomes of coronary artery bypass surgery in New York State', *Journal of the American Medical Association*, **271**, 761–6.

Hibbard J.H., J.J. Jewett, M.W. Legnini and M. Tusler (1997), 'Choosing a health plan: do large employers use the data?', *Health Affairs*, **16**, 172–80.

Hibbard, H.J., K. Harris, P. Mullin, J. Lublain and S. Garfinkel (2000), 'Increasing the impact of health plan report cards by addressing consumers' concerns', *Health Affairs*, **19**, 138–43.

Jones, P. and J. Cullis (2003), 'Key parameters in policy design: the case of intrinsic motivation', *Journal of Social Policy*, **32**(4), 527–47.

Kane, T.J. and D.O. Staiger (2002), 'The promise and pitfalls of using imprecise school accountability measures', *Journal of Economic Perspectives*, **16**(4), 91–114.

Kaplan, J. et al. (2000), 'Managed care reporting cards: evaluating those who evaluate physicians', *Managed Care Interface*, **13**, 88–94.

Landon, B.E., S.T. Normand, D. Blumenthal and J. Daley (2003), 'Physician clinical performance assessment: prospects and barriers', *Journal of the American Medical Association*, **290**(9), 1183–9.

Lilford, R., M.A. Mohammed, D. Spiegelhalter and R. Thomson (2004), 'Use and misuse of process and outcome data in managing performance of acute medical care: avoiding institutional stigma', *The Lancet*, **363**(3 April), 1147–54.

Longo, D.R., G. Land, W. Schramm, J. Fraas, B. Hoskins and V. Howell (1997), 'Consumer reports in health care: do they make a difference in patient care?', *Journal of the American Medical Association*, **278**(19), 1579–84.

Marshall, M., J. Hiscock and B. Sibbald (2002), 'Attitudes to the public release of comparative information on the quality of general practice care: a qualitative study', *British Medical Journal*, **325**(7375), 1278.

Marshall, M., P. Shekelle, R. Brook and S. Leatherman (2000), *Dying to Know: Public Release of Information about Quality of Health Care*, London: Nuffield Trust.

Marshall, M., P. Shekelle, H. Davies and P. Smith (2003), 'Public reporting on quality in the United States and the United Kingdom', *Health Affairs*, **22**(3), 134–48.

Mason, A. and A. Street (2005), *Publishing Hospital Outcomes Data in the UK*, London: Office of Health Economics.

Meyer, J.A., E.K. Wicks, L.S. Rybowski and M.J. Perry (1998), *Report on Report Cards*, Washington DC: Economic and Social Research Institute.

Propper, C. and D. Wilson (2003), 'The use and usefulness of performance measures in the public sector', *Oxford Review of Economic Policy*, **19**, 250–67.

Romano, P. and R. Mutter (2004), 'The evolving science of quality measurement for hospitals: implications for studies of competition and consolidation', *International Journal of Health Care Finance and Economics*, **4**, 131–57.

Scanlon, D., M. Chernew, C. McLaughlin and G. Solon (2002), 'The impact of health plan report cards on managed care enrolment', *Journal of Health Economics*, **21**, 19–41.

Schneider, E.C. and A.M. Epstein (1998), 'Use of public performance reports', *Journal of the American Medical Association*, **279**, 1638–42.

Schwappach, D., A. Blaudszun, D. Conen, H. Ebner, K. Eichler and M. Hochreutener (2003), ' "Emerge": benchmarking of clinical performance and patients' experiences with emergency care in Switzerland', *International Journal for Quality in Health Care*, **15**(6), 473–85.

Smith, P. (1995), 'On the unintended consequences of publishing performance data in the public sector', *International Journal of Public Administration*, **18**(2/3), 277–310.

Smith, P. (2002), 'Some principles of performance measurement and performance improvement', Report Commissioned for Commission for Health Improvement, mimeo, University of York.

Wedig, G.J. and M. Tai-Seale (2002), 'The effect of report cards on consumer choice in the health insurance market', *Journal of Health Economics*, **21**, 1031–48.

32 Productivity analysis in health care
James F. Burgess, Jr

1. Introduction

Productivity analysis of health care systems, services and providers increasingly is being conducted and applied by economists and other researchers around the world. Yet application of these results by governments, health plans and individual provider groups has been patchy and inconsistent. Much of the reason for this has been the growth of technical methods from the management science and econometrics literature that has not always paid attention to the needs and context of decision-makers.

A number of critical factors have created this difficulty. But most importantly, the fundamental nature of health care services as multi-product goods, even to the extreme conception of the treatment of each patient as a unique individual product, creates analytical complications that have been dealt with inconsistently in the literature. Nevertheless, this inconsistency could be seen as desirable for policy application, applied correctly and intelligently, since the context of the decision-maker needs to be accounted for in choosing methods and levels of aggregation of heterogeneous products and their inputs. The desirable result would be that methods chosen optimally to match research questions would differ from one-size-fits-all solutions. The potential for severe aggregation bias and other measurement error problems also exists in all types of health productivity studies.

The analytical foundations of production economics, applied to health, are the focus of this chapter, as opposed to the more general performance measures discussed in the chapters by Smith and Street (30) and Propper and Wilson (31) in this Companion. Production technology for outputs y producing inputs x is represented by input set

$$L(y) = \{x: (y, x) \text{ is feasible}\} \tag{32.1}$$

that for every y has isoquant

$$\text{Isoq. } L(y) = \{x: x \in L(y), \lambda x \notin L(y), \lambda \in [0,1)\} \tag{32.2}$$

and efficient subset

$$\text{Eff. } L(y) = \{x: x \in L(y), x' \notin L(y), x' \leq x\}$$

as in Lovell (1993). This structure can best be described in terms of distance functions, the multidimensional distance from any productive activity to the boundary of production possibilities. Then the tools of duality theory can be used to generate production, cost, revenue and profit frontiers which can be estimated in applications (Kumbhakar and Lovell, 2000).

Productivity analysis in health care builds up from specialized conceptual definitions of allocative, economic and technical efficiency from economic theory. In particular, allocative efficiency in health care tends to be assessed most often on a micro-level via economic evaluations of health care interventions and programmes that are considered in the final part of this Companion. Technical efficiency in health care at the level of country performance has been defined as catching up to what can be done under current technology while technological change or shifts in the attainable technology encompass both process innovation and product innovation (Färe *et al.*, 1997). That same conceptualization frequently is applied at other levels of health services production. Economic efficiency depends on the value or cost of inputs once technical efficiency is attained. Such analysis is complicated by the frequent lack of competitively determined input prices in health to determine local differences in economic efficiency, and thus easily generalizable results of economic evaluation and other productivity analysis are elusive. Finally, technical efficiency and economic efficiency are necessary but not sufficient conditions for allocative efficiency, which requires (a) the correct mix of outputs, given output prices, (b) the correct mix of inputs, given input prices, and (c) the correct scale, given input and output prices (Lovell and Schmidt, 1988).

The goal of this chapter is to lay out methods of general productivity analysis that have been employed or suggested for use in health care applications, to give a sense of what the most productive applications are, and to provide some suggestions of context in application based on a review of selected studies. The best studies of productivity analysis in health care get beyond a view of productivity in generating health services alone as the goal. Instead they develop some sense of the importance of generating health improvement, health maintenance, or quality of delivered health care as the key outcomes rather than the intermediate products of health services.

2.   Efficiency based methods of productivity analysis

The literature usefully separates out into methods that primarily assume that technical efficiency is attained and are based on neoclassical cost function and production function analysis, and methods that do not. This section addresses models assuming technical efficiency, yet special aspects of the health production process have created difficulties in applying these techniques in standard ways. For cost functions in health, hybrid flexible functional forms have evolved that regress total costs on output quantities, input prices, as well as other explanatory variables (Grannemann *et al.*, 1986; Vita, 1990). Major areas of research interest include measures of economies of scale and scope as well as methods for accounting for quality and unobserved heterogeneity. For production functions in health, standard methods using aggregated output quantities have encountered difficulties estimating complementarities between inputs and characterizing diverse production environments such as teaching and non-teaching providers. Some of these difficulties can be addressed using simultaneous equation methods representing the production technology as a labour requirements system (Burgess and Lehner, 1997 and Lehner and Burgess, 1995). Labour requirements methods use the labour inputs, which usually are the variables measured with the most accuracy, as dependent variables in a simultaneous equation production function system. Studies focused on nursing home and hospital productivity are separated from studies focused on physician productivity.

Use in health organizations

Most of the methodological advances have come from studying hospitals, though a substantial literature studying nursing homes also exists. The focus of this section on health organization productivity will be to highlight these methodological advances rather than formal study of each area of health organization application.

Distinguishing quality of care differences from case-mix differences and from unobserved heterogeneity is particularly vexing. Gertler and Waldman (1992) show that accounting for unobserved and endogenous quality results in an empirical nursing home model with parameter estimates that differ significantly from those in which quality is simply an unobserved factor subsumed in the error term. Carey (1997) also employs an indirect approach using panel data where individual hospital effects capture cost variation from quality or other unobservables. Carey and Burgess (1999) attempt more direct measurement of quality variables using lags of those values as instruments in a cross-sectional cost function with panel data. They conclude that perhaps an even greater problem in cost function estimation is the unmeasured case-mix or severity of illness variation in the outputs, which may well be correlated with imperfect measures of quality. Thus, attempts to measure quality could improve cost function estimation, but not measure cost/quality trade-offs.

Success in measuring economies of scale and scope using cost functions tends to depend heavily on the estimation methods employed. The hybrid flexible functional forms (for example Vita, 1990) appear to be more successful at estimating scale and scope economies since they have the ability to represent many diverse production technologies at any chosen approximation point (Schuffham *et al.*, 1996). Carey (1997) also emphasizes the impact of estimation method differences in characterizing ray scale economies, where preferred panel data estimates indicate significant scale economies while cross-sectional models on the same data illustrate diseconomies. Panel data models using non-parametric estimation (Wilson and Carey, 2004) are even more flexible and can track changes over time and across indicator variables using a discrete kernel function.

Use for physicians and physician practices

Physician productivity has been a frequently researched focus since physicians play a central actor role in health services delivery and in many countries operate independently of other health organizations. Measurement of the medical and non-medical labour inputs working with physicians is difficult because these auxiliary staff can be difficult to measure and exhibit a wide variety of complementarity and substitutability with physicians. Output specifications also vary widely as measures of physician output used have included simple measures such as billings and visits or more complex measures such as Relative Value Units (RVUs) and patient panel sizes or numbers of patients.

Walker (2000) documents that RVUs have grown increasingly common as a measure since they can relate physician effort to workload, and create equity across specialties without discriminating for payer mix. Lasker and Marquis (1999) support the RVU conceptual framework with their study of almost 20 000 visits to 339 urologist, rheumatologist, and general internist physicians, which concludes that face-to-face encounter time and a limited set of additional characteristics would reflect total work accurately. Measuring productivity on a per patient or capitated basis through primary care panel size directly has been slow to evolve; however, researchers have considered that capitation incentives may lead primary care physicians to reduce the number and length of visits with each patient in their panel. Yet Mechanic *et al.* (2001) found from 1989 to 1998 that the length of out-patient visits actually increased slightly, while the difference between prepaid and non-prepaid care diminished.

This chapter will not address physician compensation incentives in detail, nevertheless, physician productivity analysis also could benefit from more careful economic modelling. Within this limited literature, Gaynor and Gertler (1995) have studied group practices and found that physicians differ in their individual preferences regarding work effort and insulation from economic risk. Physicians were found to be more productive when individual-level financial incentives are in place. Thornton and Eakin (1997) estimate a model for solo physician practices that relates physician input, output, and labour/leisure choices with an endogenous virtual wage for the physician's own time in the practice. Their results suggest that patient-visit price increases induce small income effect reductions in physician time, but in the aggregate provide more medical care services since more support staff and medical supplies are employed to compensate.

More recently, Thurston and Libby (2002) advocate using Diewert's (1971) generalized linear production function that allows zero values for inputs and estimates of more appropriate Hicks (1970) or q-complementarity for physicians relative to other inputs. Unlike the results from other methods used in the physician productivity literature, Thurston and Libby illustrate remarkable stability in the technical relationships for patient care over the period 1965 to 1988 and find that nursing, clinical, and non-clinical support staff all are q-complements to physicians in production.

3.   Inefficiency measurement based methods of productivity analysis

In trying to measure inefficiency in hospitals and other health care organizations, the heterogeneity of health care outputs remains the most vexing of the issues raised by Newhouse (1994) concerning frontier estimation techniques. Yet attempting to measure and understand the level of waste or inefficiency by particular health care providers in the health care system remains a tempting focus for policy-makers looking for easy savings in burgeoning health budgets. Unfortunately, these two perspectives remain tantalizingly isolated from each other as researchers pursue more complex technical solutions to data and modelling difficulties without carefully considering the perspectives of decision-makers. The problems raised by Newhouse (1994) apply to one degree or another in all the research methods discussed in this chapter, specifically, unmeasured inputs, need for better case-mix controls, strong and non-testable assumptions in the estimation methodologies, omitted or improper outputs, and the fundamental problem of aggregation. This last problem is akin to a Heisenberg uncertainty principle of productivity analysis brought about by the health services process and the realities of cost accounting. If we define disaggregated health care outputs very precisely, even down to the individual patient level, then we will be uncertain about the costs and inputs required for that work. Conversely, if we define disaggregated costs or individual inputs very precisely, then we will be uncertain about the health care generated from those inputs.

Methods of measuring inefficiency

Considering the measurement of inefficiency in health is difficult in the context of a dizzying array of specialized methods that frequently have been undertaken with a weak understanding or even disregard for the underlying economic theory. The fact that Newhouse (1994) notes that many of the assumptions in some methods are untestable just adds to the shaky foundation. A crucial starting point for a journey into the literature is Hollingsworth's (2003) excellent review that provides far more detail and references than can be provided here. This discussion will be separated into a study of parametric methods, non-parametric methods, and some newer integrated methods.

Parametric frontier methods   Stochastic frontier methods have the greatest similarity to efficiency-based methods, since the form of the models is the same except for a one-sided error term (Kumbhakar and Lovell, 2000). These methods have been applied to physician practices (Gaynor and Pauly (1990) do an especially good job of building up their model from economic theory and DeFelice and Bradford (1997) also illustrate how organizational structure has a relatively small influence on the estimated inefficiency) as well as larger health care organizations. More promisingly, other studies have used stochastic frontier methods successfully on smaller units of observation (Dismuke and Sena, 1999; Bradford *et al.*, 2001) that can increase sample sizes and focus inefficiency results on more relevant dimensions that can be addressed by decision-makers. In employing these methods on cost functions, sensitivity to multicollinearity can be high, disturbing efforts to account properly for inputs, outputs and quality dimensions with a flexible functional form. Kumbhakar (1996) notes that the usual efficiency-based solution of estimating the cost function and input share equations simultaneously complicates the distributional assumptions of error terms across equations. Another complication can be the choice of distribution for the one-sided inefficiency error term. Half normal, truncated normal, and exponential distributions are commonly used, but inefficiency rankings are seldom sensitive to this choice (Kumbhakar and Lovell, 2000). Greene (2002) provides comprehensive software to estimate most specifications of these models.

Non-parametric frontier methods   Non-parametric methods using Data Envelopment Analysis (DEA), Free Disposal Hull (FDH) and other dominance measures have been commonly used and misused in health care applications since the early 1990s. Most importantly, careful attention to the Newhouse (1994) critique in a systematic way is lacking in many studies. But the heterogeneity of observations in particular samples and the need for observed better performing units to measure inefficiency, especially when trying to compare results across studies, makes comparison of average inefficiency scores generally unwise. Instead, more effective non-parametric frontier models need to hone more carefully to well-constructed research questions and conceptual frameworks to solve particular problems. As with the other methods, one important innovation is attempting to look inside health care institutions to study inefficiency, to the extent disaggregated data permit. Two noteworthy examples of this trend are Ozcan *et al.* (1998), who show the effect of physician experience on the treatment of stroke, and Harper *et al.* (2001) who identify a very small number of poorly performing general surgery units. More use of FDH measures and careful notation of dominated health care units that would provide specific advice for peers and improvements for individual units would either expose weaknesses in methodology or move these non-parametric methods over into a more useful frame of reference. Careful attention to slacks in DEA that are obtained from the linear programming methods also offers little used opportunities for identifying sparse data or recommending directional improvements. For conducting this work, Hollingsworth (2004) reviews DEA inefficiency measurement packages, including those that also estimate productivity changes using Malmquist index methods.

Integrated frontier methods   Many studies have tried to achieve a consensus of results by applying a variety of inefficiency measurement methods to the same data. This has not been especially effective in adding clarity to the implications and conclusions from results. A better method might be to define research questions clearly and connect methods to objectives directly. There have also been numerous attempts to expand and generalize inefficiency estimation methodologies. For example, Olesen and Petersen (2002) apply probabilistic assurance regions to a DRG disaggregated level hospital cost analysis which allows incorporation of output heterogeneity and new measures of inefficiency stability. Färe and Grosskopf (2004) present the directional distance function, a more general presentation of Data Envelopment Analysis that provides more flexibility in valuing outputs. And Simar and Wilson (2000) develop statistical inference methods in non-parametric inefficiency measurement, building from first principles of a data generating process for inefficiency. As each of these methodological techniques gains a foothold, though, this does not absolve the productivity analyst from careful assessment of the appropriateness of methods, formulation and specification. One of the areas of special misunderstandings follows as the last example.

Explaining inefficiency and recommending process improvement
The best advice for taking inefficiency scores and attempting to explain them by other variables and then using those second stage regressions to recommend process improvements is not to do it. The technical problems are difficult to overcome despite a seemingly obvious applicability. One approach commonly used that clearly is wrong is to address the mass of data with zero inefficiency (or efficiency of 1) and to consider it as censored data to be estimated with Tobit regression. It can be argued that the estimates are truncated, but it has not been argued that they are censored successfully. Andersen and Petersen (1993) and Burgess and Wilson (1998) have avoided boundary problems in the second stage regression with a 'leave one out' estimator, but even this estimator does not have a clear statistical interpretation and so this approach is also no longer recommended. Simar and Wilson (2003) and others have noted that the even deeper problem is that the inefficiency estimates, no matter how they are obtained, depend on each other and thus are serially correlated. Simar and Wilson (2003) have proposed a new comprehensive, but relatively tortured, bootstrapping approach to solving these problems; however, it remains to be seen how well their methods will be able to be applied in practice. Fried *et al.* (2002) have gone even further to propose a three-stage analysis that they apply to a sample of US nursing homes.

4. Concluding remarks

Productivity analysis in health care continues to be a vibrant and growing field. Nevertheless, practitioners are cautioned that methods used are complicated and not easy to understand intuitively. The Newhouse (1994) critique was directed at inefficiency-based methods of productivity analysis, but applies just as well to all forms of productivity analysis. As this area of health economics matures, it offers great promise and great danger for productive research. The challenge is to provide the right method to the right problem at the right time.

References

Andersen, N. and N.C. Petersen (1993), 'A procedure for ranking efficient units in Data Envelopment Analysis', *Management Science*, **39**, 1261–4.

Bradford, W.D., A.N. Kleit, M.A. Krousel-Wood and R.N. Re (2001), 'Stochastic frontier estimation of cost models within the hospital', *The Review of Economics and Statistics*, **83**(2), 302–9.

Burgess, J.F. and L.A. Lehner (1997), 'Testing the physicians' cooperative model: The importance of quality of care', in Stephane Jacobzone (ed.), *Institut National de la Statistique et des Etudes Economiques Methods*, Paris: INSEE (in French).

Burgess, J.F., Jr. and P.W. Wilson (1998), 'Variation in inefficiency among US hospitals', *Canadian Journal of Operational Research and Information Processing (INFOR)*, **36**, 84–102.

Carey, K. (1997), 'A panel data design for estimation of hospital cost functions', *The Review of Economics and Statistics*, **79**, 443–53.

Carey, K. and J.F. Burgess, Jr. (1999), 'On measuring the cost/quality trade-off', *Health Economics*, **8**, 509–20.

DeFelice, L.C. and W.D. Bradford (1997), 'Relative inefficiencies in production between solo and group practice physicians', *Health Economics*, **6**, 455–65.

Diewert, W.E. (1971), 'An application of the Shephard duality theorem: A generalized Leontief production function', *Journal of Political Economy*, **79**, 481–507.

Dismuke, C. and V. Sena (1999), 'Has DRG payment influenced the technical efficiency and productivity of diagnostic technologies in Portuguese public hospitals? An empirical analysis using parametric and non-parametric methods', *Health Care Management Science*, **2**, 107–16.

Färe, R. and S. Grosskopf (2004), *New Directions: Efficiency and Productivity*, Berlin/Heidelberg: Springer.

Färe, R., S. Grosskopf, B. Lindgren and J.P. Poullier (1997), 'Productivity growth in health care delivery', *Medical Care*, **35**(4), 354–66.

Fried, H.O., C.A.K. Lovell, S.S. Schmidt and S. Yaisawarng (2002), 'Accounting for environmental effects and statistical noise in Data Envelopment Analysis', *Journal of Productivity Analysis*, **17**(1/2), 157–74.

Gaynor, M. and P.J. Gertler (1995), 'Moral hazard and risk spreading in partnerships', *RAND Journal of Economics*, **26**(4), 591–613.

Gaynor, M. and M. Pauly (1990), 'Compensation and productive efficiency in partnerships: Evidence from medical group practice', *Journal of Political Economy*, **98**(3), 544–73.

Gertler, P.J. and D.M. Waldman (1992), 'Quality-adjusted cost functions and policy evaluation in the nursing home industry', *Journal of Political Economy*, **100**, 1232–56.

Grannemann, T.W., R.S. Brown and M.V. Pauly (1986), 'Estimating hospital costs: a multiple-output analysis', *Journal of Health Economics*, **5**, 105–27.

Greene, W. (2002), *LIMDEP Version 8.0: Econometric Modeling Guide Vol.2*, New York: Econometric Software.

Harper, J., K. Hauck and A. Street (2001), 'Analysis of costs and efficiency in general surgery specialties in the United Kingdom', *European Journal of Health Economics*, **2**, 150–57.

Hicks, J.R. (1970), 'Elasticities of substitution again: Substitutes and complements', *Oxford Economic Papers*, **20**, 289–96.

Hollingsworth, B. (2003), 'Non-parametric and parametric applications measuring efficiency in health care', *Health Care Management Science*, **6**(4), 203–18.

Hollingsworth, B. (2004), 'Nonparametric efficiency measurement', *The Economic Journal*, **114**(496), F307–F311.

Kumbhakar, S.C. (1996), 'Efficiency measurement with multiple outputs and multiple inputs', *Journal of Productivity Analysis*, **7**(2/3), 225–55.

Kumbhakar, S.C. and C.A.K. Lovell (2000), *Stochastic Frontier Analysis*, New York: Cambridge University Press.

Lasker, R.D. and M.S. Marquis (1999), 'The intensity of physicians' work in patient visits', *New England Journal of Medicine*, **341**(5), 337–41.

Lehner, L.A. and J.F. Burgess, Jr. (1995), 'Teaching and hospital production', *Health Economics*, **4**, 113–25.

Lovell, C.A.K. (1993), 'Production frontiers and productive efficiency', in H.O. Fried, C.A.K. Lovell and S.S. Schmidt (eds), *The Measurement of Productive Efficiency: Techniques and Applications*, Oxford: Oxford University Press.

Lovell, C.A.K. and P. Schmidt (1988), 'A comparison of alternative approaches to the measurement of productive efficiency', in A. Dogramaci and R. Färe (eds), *Studies in Productivity Analysis. Applications of Modern Production Theory Efficiency and Productivity*, Boston: Kluwer Academic Publishers.

Mechanic, D., D.D. McAlpine and M. Rosenthal (2001), 'Are patients' office visits with physicians getting shorter?', *New England Journal of Medicine*, **344**(3), 198–204.

Newhouse, J.P. (1994), 'Frontier estimation: How useful a tool for health economics?', *Journal of Health Economics*, **13**, 317–22.

Olesen, O.B. and N.C. Petersen (2002), 'The use of Data Envelopment Analysis with probabilistic assurance regions for measuring hospital efficiency', *Journal of Productivity Analysis*, **17**(1/2), 83–109.

Ozcan, Y., S.E. Watts, J.M. Harris and S.E. Wogen (1998), 'Provider experience and technical efficiency in the treatment of stroke patients: DEA approach', *Journal of the Operational Research Society*, **49**, 573–82.

Schuffham, P.A., N.J. Devlin and M. Jaforullah (1996), 'The structure of costs and production in New Zealand public hospitals: An application of the transcendental logarithmic variable cost function', *Applied Economics*, **28**, 75–85.

Simar, L. and P.W. Wilson (2000), 'Statistical inference in nonparametric frontier models: The state of the art', *Journal of Productivity Analysis*, **13**, 49–78.

Simar, L. and P.W. Wilson (2003), 'Estimation and inference in two-stage, semi-parametric models of production processes', Discussion Paper 0307, Institut de Statistique, Université Catholique de Louvain, Belgium.

Thornton, J. and B.K. Eakin (1997), 'The utility-maximizing self-employed physician', *The Journal of Human Resources*, **32**(1), 98–128.

Thurston, N.K. and A.M. Libby (2002), 'A production function for physician services revisited', *The Review of Economics and Statistics*, **84**(1), 184–91.

Vita, M.G. (1990), 'Exploring hospital production function relationships with flexible functional forms', *Journal of Health Economics*, **9**, 1–21.

Walker, D.L. (2000), 'Physician compensation: Rewarding productivity of the knowledge worker', *Journal of Ambulatory Care Management*, **23**(4), 48–59.

Wilson, P.W. and K. Carey (2004), 'Nonparametric analysis of returns to scale and product mix among US hospitals', *Journal of Applied Econometrics*, **19**, 505–24.

EVALUATION OF HEALTH CARE

PART VII

MEASURING BENEFITS

33 Conceptual foundations for health utility measurement

*Han Bleichrodt and Jose Luis Pinto**

1. Introduction

The most common approach to determine the cost-effectiveness of health care is cost–utility analysis, where costs are valued in terms of money and benefits in terms of utility. This chapter provides an overview of models that have been proposed to measure the utility of health benefits, starting with the most widely used utility measure, the quality-adjusted life-year (QALY) model. QALYs are computed by adjusting each year of life by the quality of life in which it is spent. They are intuitively appealing, that is, easy to explain to doctors and policy-makers, and are tractable for decision modelling, which explains their popularity in practical research. A disadvantage of the QALY model is that it represents individual preferences for health only under restrictive assumptions.

In this chapter, we give an overview of the assumptions that need to be imposed for QALYs to represent individual preferences for health.[1] We will distinguish two cases: first we treat the case where health quality is constant, that is where health states are chronic. This case has received most attention in the literature. Then we drop the assumption of constant health quality and consider the case where health quality can vary over time. In both cases we will start by deriving the QALY model, which we subsequently generalize. The conditions identified in the theoretical analysis are confronted with the available empirical evidence to assess how convincing these conditions are and, hence, the models that they characterize.

2. Chronic health states

Notation

We consider an individual who has to make a decision under risk. For ease of notation, throughout this chapter we will only consider situations in which there are at most two possible states of the world. The individual's decision problem is to choose between *prospects*. A prospect is a pair of chronic health states, one for each state of the world. A typical chronic health state is (q, t) denoting t years in health quality q. A prospect yielding chronic health state (q_1, t_1) with probability p and chronic health state (q_2, t_2) with probability $1 - p$ is denoted as $[p: (q_1, t_1); (q_2, t_2)]$.

A preference relation $\geq$, meaning 'at least as preferred as', is defined over the set of prospects. As usual, we denote strict preference by $>$ and indifference by $\sim$. Preferences over chronic health states are derived from $\geq$ by restricting attention to riskless prospects,

* We are grateful to Jason Doctor, Andrew Jones and an anonymous referee for helpful comments.

that is prospects in which $p = 1$. A real-valued function V *represents* the preference relation $\geq$ if for all prospects P and Q, $P \geq Q$ if and only if $V(P) \geq V(Q)$.

Characterizations under expected utility

The most commonly used theory of decision under risk is expected utility. *Expected utility* holds if preferences over prospects $[p:(q_1, t_1); (q_2, t_2)]$ can be represented by $p \cdot (U(q_1, t_1) + (1 - p) \cdot U(q_2, t_2)$, where U is a utility function over chronic health states which is unique up to unit and location, that is we can arbitrarily set the utility of two chronic health states. In most applications the scaling $U(\text{death}) = 0$ and $U(\text{full health, 1 year}) = 1$ is used.

If the QALY model holds then $U(q, t) = H(q)*t$, where H is a utility function over health quality. Pliskin et al. (1980) were the first to derive assumptions that ensure that the expected utility function U can be written as $H(q)*t$. Pliskin et al. only considered health states better than death. They started by imposing that health quality and life duration are *mutually utility independent. Utility independence of health quality from life duration* means that preferences over prospects in which life duration is kept fixed do not depend on the level at which life duration is kept fixed. That is, if $[p:(q_1, t); (q_2, t)] \geq [p: (q_3, t); (q_4, t)]$ then also $[p:(q_1, t'); (q_2, t')] \geq [p:(q_3, t'); (q_4, t')]$ for some different life duration t'. This assumption is commonly made in standard gamble measurements (see Chapter 35 by Brazier and Roberts in this Companion). *Utility independence of life duration from health quality* is defined similarly with health quality kept fixed. Mutual utility independence holds if both health quality is utility independent from life duration and life duration is utility independent from health quality.

The second assumption Pliskin et al. (1980) imposed is *constant proportional trade-offs*, which holds if the proportion of remaining life-years that one is willing to give up for an improvement in health quality from any level q_1 to any other level q_2 does not depend on the absolute number of remaining life-years involved. That is, if $(q_1, t_1) \sim (q_2, t_2)$ then $(q_1, \alpha t_1) \sim (q_2, \alpha t_2)$ for any $\alpha \geq 0$ (provided of course that αt_1 and αt_2 do not exceed some maximal possible life duration). Constant proportional trade-offs underlies time trade-off measurements (for a description of the time trade-off see Chapter 35 by Brazier and Roberts).

Finally, Pliskin et al. imposed *risk neutrality on life-years*: for any fixed level of health quality, each prospect is indifferent to its expected value. For example, risk neutrality means that the prospect giving 25 years in full health with probability 1/2 and 1 year in full health with probability 1/2 is indifferent to 13 years in full health for sure, because 13 is the expected value of the prospect.

If mutual utility independence is imposed on top of expected utility then $U(q, t)$ is either additive $U(q, t) = H(q) + L(t)$ or multiplicative $U(q, t) = H(q)*L(t)$, where L is a utility function over life duration. Constant proportional trade-offs then excludes the additive model and ensures that $L(t)$ is a power function, that is, $L(t) = t^\beta$. Risk neutrality, finally, ensures that $\beta = 1$. Hence, taken together these three conditions ensure that the QALY model represents individual preferences over chronic health states.

Bleichrodt et al. (1997) showed that Pliskin et al.'s characterization of the QALY model can be simplified by assuming the *zero condition*: all health qualities are equally valued when life duration is zero. That is, for all health qualities $q_1, q_2, (q_1, 0) \sim (q_2, 0)$. The zero condition was first introduced by Miyamoto and Eraker (1988) and is self-evident: when life duration is 0 years it obviously does not matter what the state of health is. Bleichrodt et al. (1997) showed that in the presence of the zero condition, imposing risk neutrality on life-years is already sufficient to ensure that the QALY model represents individual preferences over chronic health states. What is more, unlike Pliskin et al. (1980), their analysis also applies to health states less preferred to death (Miyamoto et al., 1998). Hence, the critical condition which needs to be examined to determine whether the QALY model holds is risk neutrality on life-years. Mutual utility independence and constant proportional trade-offs need not be imposed.

Generalizations of the QALY Model
Several studies have shown that people are not risk neutral but risk averse on life-years (McNeil et al., 1978; Stiggelbout et al., 1994; Verhoef et al., 1994; Cher et al., 1997; Oliver, 2005). Stiggelbout et al. (1994), in a sample of testicular cancer patients, found, for example, that their median respondent was indifferent between 4 years in good health for sure and a treatment giving a probability 1/2 of 10 years in good health and a probability 1/2 of death, that is 0 years in good health. Hence, the QALY model does not appear to be a good description of people's preferences for health. It seems, therefore, desirable to use a more general model. A possible candidate is the multiplicative model $U(q, t) = H(q)*L(t)$. This model is more general than the QALY model because it allows for utility curvature, but not so general that it can no longer be used in practical applications. The function $L(t)$ can generally be approximated to a reasonable degree by performing five to six preference measurements. Miyamoto et al. (1998) showed that, in the presence of the zero-condition, the multiplicative model follows from the assumption of *standard gamble invariance*. Consider an equivalence $(q, s) \sim [p:(q, t); (q, r)]$. Then we say that p is the *probability equivalent* of (q, s) with respect to (q, t) and (q, r). Standard gamble invariance holds if probability equivalents are the same in different health qualities.[2] That is, $(q, s) \sim [p:(q, t); (q, r)]$ if and only if $(q', s) \sim [p:(q', t); (q', r)]$. For example, if 15 years in full health for sure is indifferent to the prospect giving 25 years in full health with probability 1/2 and 1 year in full health with probability 1/2 then standard gamble invariance implies that 15 years with back pain for sure should also be indifferent to the prospect giving 25 years with back pain with probability 1/2 and 1 year with back pain with probability 1/2. Empirical support for standard gamble invariance can be found in Miyamoto and Eraker (1988).

Models that are in-between the QALY model and the multiplicative model impose restrictions on $L(t)$, but do not require it to be linear. For example, if we impose on the multiplicative model *constant risk posture*, $(q, s) \sim [p:(q, t); (q, r)]$ if and only if $(q, s + \varepsilon) \sim [p:(q, t + \varepsilon); (q, r + \varepsilon)]$ for any ε small enough so that the life durations involved do not exceed some maximal possible life duration, then $L(t)$ must be exponential. If we impose on the multiplicative model *constant proportional risk posture*, $(q, s) \sim [p:(q, t); (q, r)]$ if and only if $(q, \delta s) \sim [p:(q, \delta t); (q, \delta r)]$ for positive δ small enough so that the life durations involved do not exceed some maximal possible life duration, then $L(t)$ must be a power function. Miyamoto and Eraker (1989) tested constant risk posture and constant proportional risk posture but found little support for these conditions. Doctor and Miyamoto (2003) took a different approach and explored the effect of starting with the assumption of constant proportional trade-offs, a condition for which support exists in the literature (for example Stalmeier et al., 1996; Bleichrodt and Johannesson, 1997). They showed that if the zero condition, constant proportional trade-offs and constant risk posture hold but life duration is not utility independent of health status then the *expolinear QALY model* holds: $U(q, t) = \exp(H(q)^*t) - 1$. However, as has been mentioned before, empirical support exists for utility independence of life duration from health status and not for constant risk posture, which casts doubt on the validity of the expo-linear QALY model.

Characterizations under non-expected utility
Throughout the previous sub-section, it was assumed that expected utility holds. If expected utility does not hold then the aforementioned characterizations are no longer valid and hence, empirical tests of the conditions are no longer conclusive. In fact, many studies have shown that expected utility is descriptively inaccurate and that people violate expected utility in systematic ways (Starmer, 2000). Given the poor descriptive record of expected utility, the possibility cannot be excluded that the violations of risk neutrality on life-years and, hence, of the QALY model that have been observed were due to violations of expected utility. Under non-expected utility, people can both be risk averse with respect to life duration and have linear utility for duration. Suppose, for example, that an individual maximizes rank-dependent utility (Quiggin, 1981) and consider, again, the median respondent in the study by Stiggelbout et al. (1994). Under rank-dependent utility the observed indifference implies that U(good health, 4 years) $= w(1/2)^* U$(good health, 10 years) $+ (1 - w(1/2))^* U$(good health, 0 years), where w is a probability weighting function that satisfies $w(0) = 0$ and $w(1) = 1$. It is easy to verify that, under rank-dependent utility, the median indifference in the study by Stiggelbout et al. is consistent with linear utility for life duration if $w(1/2) = 0.4$.

The example illustrates that QALYs could be salvaged if they were found to hold under a descriptively accurate theory of choice under risk. Hence, there is a need of new tests of QALYs that are robust to violations of expected utility.

Bleichrodt and Quiggin (1997) were the first to derive the QALY model under nonexpected utility. They assumed a very general model of decision under uncertainty that is consistent with expected utility and with several non-expected utility theories, including the important class of rank-dependent utility models (Quiggin, 1981). Bleichrodt and Quiggin (1997) used a condition that they referred to as constant marginal utility and showed that, in the presence of the zero condition, this condition characterizes the QALY model under their general utility model. We assume for the rest of this section that all prospects are *rank-ordered*, that is it is implicit in the notation $[p: (q_1, t_1); (q_2, t_2)]$ that $(q_1, t_1) \geq (q_2, t_2)$. *Constant marginal utility* says that if $[p: (q, t); (q, s)] \sim [p: (q, w); (q, v)]$ then also $[p: (q, t + \varepsilon); (q, s)] \sim [p: (q, w + \varepsilon); (q, v)]$ and $[p: (q, t); (q, s + \varepsilon)] \sim [p: (q, w); (q, v + \varepsilon)]$ for any ε small enough so that the prospects are still rank-ordered and the life durations involved do not exceed some maximum possible life duration.[3]

Miyamoto (1999) provided another characterization of the QALY model under rankdependent utility. He showed that in the presence of the zero condition, *constant proportional coverage* implies the QALY model. Constant proportional coverage holds if whenever $(q, s) \sim [p: (q, t); (q, r)]$, $(q, s') \sim [p': (q, t'); (q, r')]$ and $(s - r)/(t - r) = (s' - r')/(t' - r')$ then $p = p'$.[4]

As noted, the characterization of Bleichrodt and Quiggin (1997) is valid under several non-expected utility theories. It is not valid, however, under prospect theory (Kahneman and Tversky, 1979; Tversky and Kahneman, 1992) when people perceive some health states as gains relative to a reference health state and others as losses. Prospect theory is today the most influential descriptive theory of decision under risk. Bleichrodt and Miyamoto (2003) characterized QALYs under prospect theory. Essentially, they adapted constant marginal utility to the case where people treat gains and losses differently. An alternative characterization of QALYs under prospect theory was provided by Doctor et al. (2004), who showed that constant proportional coverage characterizes the QALY model under prospect theory when a plausible assumption is made about the reference health state.

Miyamoto and Eraker (1988) derived the multiplicative model under a 'generic utility model' that was introduced in Miyamoto (1988) and that is consistent with several non-expected utility theories. Bleichrodt and Pinto (2005) derived the multiplicative model under the general utility model used by Bleichrodt and Quiggin (1997), which is more general than Miyamoto's (1988) model. Both Miyamoto and Eraker (1988) and Bleichrodt and Pinto (2005) showed that, in the presence of the zero condition, utility independence of duration from health quality still characterizes the multiplicative model.[5] Under rank-dependent utility, Miyamoto (1999) and Doctor and Miyamoto (2003) characterized the special cases of the multiplicative model where $L(t)$ is an exponential or a power function. Their analysis amounted to imposing constant risk posture and constant proportional risk posture for rank-ordered prospects. Bleichrodt and Miyamoto (2003) characterized these two cases, $L(t)$ power and $L(t)$ exponential, under prospect theory. In their analysis, constant risk posture and constant proportional risk posture are imposed on prospects that are not only rank-ordered, but also involve only outcomes of the same sign (that is, either all outcomes are gains or all outcomes are losses).

Empirical evidence

Because the characterizations of QALYs under non-expected utility are recent, little empirical evidence exists on the conditions that were identified. Bleichrodt and Pinto (2005) tested constant marginal utility and rejected it and, hence, the QALY model. Doctor et al. (2004), however, tested constant proportional coverage and could not reject it. Hence, their data provided support for the QALY model. Both Miyamoto and Eraker (1988) and Bleichrodt and Pinto (2005) could not reject utility independence of duration from health quality, which lends support to the use of the multiplicative model.

Two empirical phenomena have been observed in the literature, which are inconsistent with all the models discussed before regardless of whether expected utility holds or not. The first is indifference to health quality at short durations, which is illustrated in Figure 33.1. Pauker (1976) suggested that people might be unwilling to trade off life duration for improved health quality if life duration were short, but would be willing to make such trade-offs at longer life durations. Figure 33.1 displays such indifference to health quality at short durations: for the first 10 years the utility function for years in q_1 and the utility function for years in q_2 coincide and, hence, people are not willing to sacrifice life duration for an improvement in health quality from q_2 to q_1 when the remaining life duration is less than 10 years. When life duration exceeds 10 years, the utility functions diverge

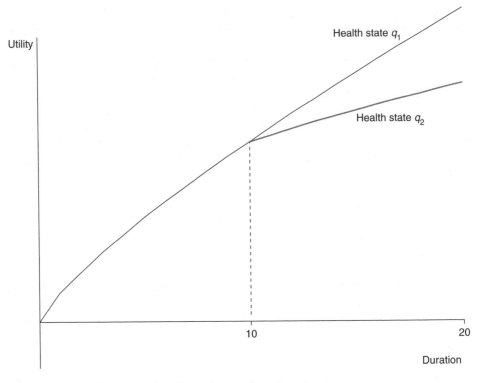

Figure 33.1   Indifference to health quality at short durations

and people are willing to forgo some life duration for a gain in health quality. McNeil et al. (1981) and Miyamoto and Eraker (1988) observed indifference to health quality at short durations in subsets of medical patients.

Another violation of the multiplicative model (and a fortiori of the other models discussed before) is the finding that there exist health states in which initially more life-years are preferred to fewer, but after some 'maximal endurable time' extra life-years decrease utility (Sutherland et al., 1982; Dolan and Stalmeier, 2003). Figure 33.2 illustrates. Health states q_1, q_3, and q_4 are health states for which no maximal endurable time exists: in health state q_1 extra life duration is always desirable, in health states q_3 and q_4 extra life duration is always undesirable. Health state q_2 is a health state for which a maximal endurable time exists: up to 10 years' extra life duration is desirable, after that extra life duration is undesirable.

3.   Non-chronic health states

Notation
We now drop the assumption that health states are chronic. Hence, the outcomes of interest are now *health profiles* $q = (q_1, \ldots, q_T)$, where q_t stands for health quality in period

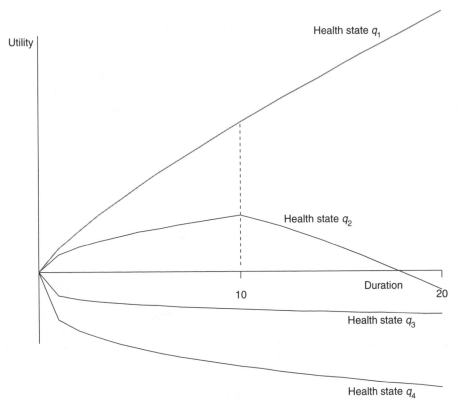

Figure 33.2   Maximal endurable time

t and T is the maximum number of periods of survival. By $\alpha_t q$ we will denote a health profile q with health quality q_t replaced by α: $(q_1, \ldots, q_{t-1}, \alpha, q_{t+1}, \ldots, q_T)$. By $\alpha_t \beta_{t+1} q$ we will denote the profile q with q_t replaced by α and q_{t+1} by β: $(q_1, \ldots, q_{t-1}, \alpha, \beta, q_{t+2}, \ldots, q_T)$. By $y_A q$ we will denote the health profile with elements equal to y_t for all t in a set $A \subset \{1, \ldots, T\}$ and equal to q_t for all t not in A.

Characterizations under expected utility
When health quality is allowed to vary over time, the QALY model is equal to $\Sigma_{t=1}^{T} H(q_t)$. Health qualities $q_1, \ldots, q_T$ are *additive independent* if preferences over prospects on $q_1, \ldots, q_T$ depend only on their marginal probability distributions and not on their joint probability distribution. To take a very simple example, suppose that there are two periods. Then by additive independence the prospect [1/2: (full health, back pain); (back pain, full health)][6] should be indifferent to the prospect [1/2: (full health, full health); (back pain, back pain)] because in each period there is a probability 1/2 of living in full health and a probability 1/2 of living with back pain. Additive independence excludes the possibility that people prefer, for example, the second prospect because that prospect gives at least a chance of living both periods in full health.

Additive independence implies that $U(q_1, \ldots, q_T) = \Sigma_{t=1}^{T} H_t(q_t)$ (Fishburn, 1965). To obtain the QALY model, the single period functions H_t must be made similar. This is achieved by imposing symmetry. A *permutation function* π is a function that specifies a rearrangement of the time periods. *Symmetry* holds if $(q_1, \ldots, q_T) \sim (q_{\pi(1)}, \ldots, q_{\pi(T)})$ for all health profiles q and for all permutation functions π. In our two-period example, symmetry says, for example, that the profile (back pain, full health) is equivalent to the profile (full health, back pain).[7] Essentially, symmetry implies that health quality is valued equally in each time period. Bleichrodt and Quiggin (1997) showed that additive independence and symmetry characterize the QALY model under expected utility.

Generalizations of the QALY model

Several authors have considered generalizations of the QALY model. One model that has often been used in cost–utility analysis is the discounted QALY model $\Sigma_{t=1}^{T} \delta^{t-1} H(q_t)$, where health quality is discounted by a constant factor δ to reflect time preference. The characterization of this model follows from replacing symmetry by *stationarity* (Koopmans, 1960; Fishburn, 1970). Stationarity says that for all constant health profiles q if $\alpha_T q \sim \alpha_T q'$ then $\alpha_1 q \sim \alpha q'$. In going from $\alpha_T q$ to $\alpha_1 q$, each q_t is updated by one period and α is shifted from the last period to the first. Stationarity says that indifferences do not change under such shifts. Stationarity is weaker than symmetry because only some indifferences are preserved and only for special permutations.

Another way to generalize the QALY model was suggested by Bleichrodt (1995). Bleichrodt suggested replacing additive independence by *utility independence*. A subset $A \subset \{1, \ldots, T\}$ is utility independent whenever $[y_A q, y'_A q] \geq [x_A q, x'_A q]$ if and only if $[y_A q', y'_A q'] \geq [x_A q', x'_A q']$. That is, if all outcomes in the prospects under comparison have common health qualities outside A then preferences do not depend on what these common health qualities are. Utility independence holds if all subsets A are utility independent. Imposing utility independence on top of symmetry implies the multiplicative model $U(q) = \Pi_{t=1}^{T} H(q_t)$.

Guerrero and Herrero (2005) relaxed utility independence further. They considered an individual who makes decisions at various points in his life and they assumed that at each point of his life, an individual's preferences over prospects involving future health quality that have a common past, do not depend on what this common past is. If $A = \{t, \ldots, T\}$ and the individual is at point t of his life then $[y_A q, y'_A q] \geq [x_A q, x'_A q]$ if and only if $[y_A q', y'_A q'] \geq [x_A q', x'_A q']$. Guerrero and Herrero's (2005) condition may, loosely speaking, be referred to as *initial utility independence*, that is they required utility independence only with respect to the first t periods of life. It does not follow from their condition that utility independence holds for all subsets A and, hence, their condition is weaker than utility independence. Guerrero and Herrero (2005) showed that if initial utility independence holds then $U(q) = \Sigma_{t=1}^{T} (H_t(q_t) \Pi_{s=1}^{t-1} c_s(q_s))$. They referred to this functional form as the *semi-separable model*. The parameters c_s reflect the weight given to the future at time point s and, hence, can be interpreted as a general type of discount factor. There are many parameters to assess in the semi-separable model. Guerrero and Herrero (2005) derived how the elicitation can be simplified by imposing additional assumptions like stationarity.

Empirical evidence

Scant empirical evidence exists on the conditions that were described above. Spencer (2003) found that violations of additive independence were common. The sample she used was, however, small and the observed violations were not systematic. Several studies have examined stationarity and found direct or indirect violations of it (Chapman, 1996; Cairns and van der Pol, 1997; Bleichrodt and Johannesson, 2001). These studies also observed discounting of the future, suggesting that symmetry does not hold. No direct evidence exists on utility independence or initial utility independence when health quality varies. Treadwell (1998) tested utility independence for prospects involving no risk,[8] that is, he tested whether $y_A q \geq x_A q$ if and only if $y_A q' \geq x_A q'$, and found a lot of support for this assumption.

There also exists indirect evidence on the QALY model and the discounted QALY model. Several studies have found that the utility of a health profile cannot be determined by adding the (discounted) single period utility functions (Dolan and Gudex, 1995; Richardson et al., 1996; Kuppermann et al., 1997; Krabbe and Bonsel, 1998). On the other hand, using similar tests, Spencer (2003) obtained mixed results on the additive utility model and Mackeigan et al. (1999) could not reject the additive model. Krabbe and Bonsel (1998) found evidence of what they called 'sequence effects', that is there were interactions between health qualities occurring at different times. In particular, people had a preference for a 'happy ending'; the perspective of recovery was important. Such sequence effects violate the (discounted) QALY model and the multiplicative model, but could be accommodated by the semi-separable model. Finally, indifference to health quality at short durations and maximal endurable time are incompatible with all models discussed.

Characterizations under non-expected utility

Additive independence can no longer be used to characterize the QALY model when violations of expected utility are allowed for. Bleichrodt and Quiggin (1997) showed that in their general utility model, a condition they referred to as *generalized marginality* serves the same purpose as additive independence under expected utility and implies an additive representation $\Sigma_{t=1}^{T} H_t(q_t)$. Generalized marginality holds whenever for all prospects and for all t, $t+i$, $(\alpha_t \mu_{t+i} q, \beta_t v_{t+i} q) \geq (\gamma_t \mu_{t+i} q, \gamma_t v_{t+i} q)$ if and only if $(\alpha_t \kappa_{t+i} q, \beta_t \lambda_{t+i} q) \geq (\gamma_t \kappa_{t+i} q, \gamma_t \lambda_{t+i} q)$. Symmetry and stationarity can also be used under non-expected utility because they involve no risk. Hence, generalized marginality and symmetry characterize the QALY model, and generalized marginality and stationarity characterize the discounted QALY model. Utility independence restricted to rank-ordered prospects and symmetry characterize the multiplicative model $U(q) = \Pi_{t=1}^{T} H(q_t)$ under Bleichrodt and Quiggin's (1997) general utility model.[9] The multiplicative model can be characterized under prospect theory by restricting utility independence to rank-ordered prospects in which either all outcomes are gains or all outcomes are losses (Zank, 2001).

The generalization of Guerrero and Herrero's (2005) semi-separable model to non-expected utility is complicated. Their model assumes that an individual makes choices at different points in time and, hence, issues of consistency of the individual's choices over time play a role in their model. Reconciling non-expected utility with dynamic consistency is not straightforward (Hammond, 1988; Machina, 1989; Sarin and Wakker, 1998).

4. Conclusion

This chapter has sought to give an overview of the rather technical literature on the conceptual basis of health utility models. While this basis seems now well established, much work needs to be done on testing the assumptions that have been identified. For chronic health states, the evidence on the QALY model that exists is mixed. The multiplicative model seems to describe preferences over chronic health states well. Given that this model is tractable, it may be a promising alternative to the QALY model for practical research. For non-chronic health states the testing of models is still at an embryonic stage. The little evidence that is available suggests that additive independence and stationarity, and, hence, the QALY model and the discounted QALY model, do not describe preferences well.

Notes

1. That is, we derive conditions under which QALYs can be interpreted as utilities. It should be mentioned here that some authors have argued that QALYs are simply an index number that need not be related to utility. This distinction between QALYs as utility and QALYs as index number relates to the issue of welfarist versus extra-welfarist interpretations of cost–utility analysis.
2. To be formally correct, this condition only holds for health qualities that are not equivalent to death. A health quality q is not equivalent to death if there is a duration t such that (q, t) is not indifferent to death.
3. Strictly speaking, we should also impose that in all cases the probability p refers to the same event.
4. Miyamoto (1999) also showed that the following condition can alternatively be used to characterize the QALY model instead of constant proportional coverage: if $(q, s) \sim [0.5:(q, t); (q, r)]$ and $(q, s') \sim [0.5:(q, t');$ $(q, r')]$ then $(s - r)/(t - r) = (s' - r')/(t' - r')$.
5. In Bleichrodt and Pinto's (2005) study utility independence of life duration from health quality only needs to be imposed for rank-ordered prospects.
6. That is, the prospect that gives probability 1/2 of living in full health in period 1 and living with back pain in period 2, and probability 1/2 of living with back pain in period 1 and living in full health in period 2.
7. Here the permutation function is $\pi(1) = 2$ and $\pi(2) = 1$.
8. In that case, utility independence is usually referred to as preferential independence.
9. This result is not available in the literature, but it follows from adding symmetry to Theorem 4 in Miyamoto and Wakker (1996).

References

Bleichrodt, H. (1995), 'QALYs and HYEs: Under what conditions are they equivalent?', _Journal of Health Economics_, **14**, 17–37.

Bleichrodt, H. and M. Johannesson (1997), 'The validity of QALYs: An empirical test of constant proportional tradeoff and utility independence', _Medical Decision Making_, **17**, 21–32.

Bleichrodt, H. and M. Johannesson (2001), 'Time preference for health: A test of stationarity versus decreasing timing aversion', _Journal of Mathematical Psychology_, **45**, 265–82.

Bleichrodt, H. and J. Miyamoto (2003), 'A characterization of quality-adjusted life-years under cumulative prospect theory', _Mathematics of Operations Research_, **28**, 181–93.

Bleichrodt, H. and J.L. Pinto (2005), 'The validity of QALYs under non-expected utility', _The Economic Journal_, **115**, 533–50.

Bleichrodt, H. and J. Quiggin (1997), 'Characterizing QALYs under a general rank dependent utility model', _Journal of Risk and Uncertainty_, **15**, 151–65.

Bleichrodt, H., P.P. Wakker and M. Johannesson (1997), 'Characterizing QALYs by risk neutrality', _Journal of Risk and Uncertainty_, **15**, 107–14.

Cairns, J.A. and M.M. van der Pol (1997), 'Saving future lives: A comparison of three discounting models', _Health Economics_, **6**, 341–50.

Chapman, G. (1996), 'Temporal discounting and utility for health and money', _Journal of Experimental Psychology: Learning Memory and Cognition_, **22**, 771–91.

Cher, D.J., J. Miyamoto and L.A. Lenert (1997), 'Incorporating risk attitude into Markov-process decision models', _Medical Decision Making_, **17**, 340–50.

Doctor, J.N. and J. Miyamoto (2003), 'Deriving quality-adjusted life-years (QALYs) from constant proportional time tradeoff and risk posture conditions', _Journal of Mathematical Psychology_, **47**, 557–67.

Doctor, J.N., H. Bleichrodt, J. Miyamoto, N.R. Temkin and S. Dikmen (2004), 'A new and more robust test of QALYs', *Journal of Health Economics*, **23**, 353–67.

Dolan, P. and C. Gudex (1995), 'Time preference, duration and health state valuations', *Health Economics*, **4**, 289–99.

Dolan, P. and P.F.M. Stalmeier (2003), 'The validity of time trade-off values in calculating QALYs: Constant proportional time trade-off versus the proportional heuristic', *Journal of Health Economics*, **22**, 445–58.

Fishburn, P. C. (1965), 'Independence in utility theory with whole product sets', *Operations Research*, **18**, 28–45.

Fishburn, P.C. (1970), *Utility Theory for Decision Making*, New York: John Wiley.

Guerrero, A.M. and C. Herrero (2005), 'A semi-separable utility function for health profiles', *Journal of Health Economics*, **24**, 33–54.

Hammond, P.J. (1988), 'Consequentialist foundations for expected utility', *Theory and Decision*, **25**, 25–78.

Kahneman, D. and A. Tversky (1979), 'Prospect theory: An analysis of decision under risk', *Econometrica*, **47**, 263–91.

Koopmans, T.C. (1960), 'Stationary ordinal utility and impatience', *Econometrica*, **28**, 287–309.

Krabbe, P.F.M. and G.J. Bonsel (1998), 'Sequence effects, health profiles, and the QALY model: In search of realistic modeling', *Medical Decision Making*, **18**, 178–86.

Kuppermann, M., S. Shiboski, D. Feeny, E.P. Elkin and A.E. Washington (1997), 'Can preference scores for discrete states be used to derive preference scores for entire paths of events?', *Medical Decision Making*, **17**, 42–55.

Machina, M.J. (1989), 'Dynamic consistency and non-expected utility models of choice under uncertainty', *Journal of Economic Literature*, **27**, 1622–68.

Mackeigan, L.D., B.J. O'Brien and P.I. Oh (1999), 'Holistic versus composite preferences for lifetime treatment sequences for type 2 diabetes', *Medical Decision Making*, **19**, 113–21.

McNeil, B.J., R. Weichselbaum and S.G. Pauker (1978), 'Fallacy of the five-year survival in lung cancer', *New England Journal of Medicine*, **299**, 1397–401.

McNeil, B.J., R. Weichselbaum and S.G. Pauker (1981), 'Tradeoffs between quality and quantity of life in laryngeal cancer', *New England Journal of Medicine*, **305**, 982–7.

Miyamoto, J. and S. Eraker (1989), 'Parametric models of the utility of survival duration: Tests of axioms in a generic utility framework', *Organizational Behavior and Human Decision Processes*, **44**, 166–202.

Miyamoto, J.M. (1988), 'Generic utility theory: Measurement foundations and applications in multiattribute utility theory', *Journal of Mathematical Psychology*, **32**, 357–404.

Miyamoto, J.M. (1999), 'Quality-adjusted life-years (QALY) utility models under expected utility and rank dependent utility assumptions', *Journal of Mathematical Psychology*, **43**, 201–37.

Miyamoto, J.M. and S.A. Eraker (1988), 'A multiplicative model of the utility of survival duration and health quality', *Journal of Experimental Psychology: General*, **117**, 3–20.

Miyamoto, J.M. and P.P. Wakker (1996), 'Multiattribute utility theory without expected utility foundations', *Operations Research*, **44**, 313–26.

Miyamoto, J.M., P.P. Wakker, H. Bleichrodt and H.J.M. Peters (1998), 'The zero-condition: A simplifying assumption in QALY measurement and multiattribute utility', *Management Science*, **44**, 839–49.

Oliver, A. (2005), 'Testing the internal consistency of the lottery equivalents method using health outcomes', *Health Economics*, **14**, 149–59.

Pauker, S.G. (1976), 'Coronary artery surgery: The use of decision analysis', *Annals of Internal Medicine*, **85**, 8–18.

Pliskin, J.S., D.S. Shepard and M.C. Weinstein (1980), 'Utility functions for life years and health status', *Operations Research*, **28**, 206–23.

Quiggin, J. (1981), 'Risk perception and risk aversion among Australian farmers', *Australian Journal of Agricultural Economics*, **25**, 160–9.

Richardson, J., J. Hall and G. Salkeld (1996), 'The measurement of utility in multiphase health states', *International Journal of Technology Assessment in Health Care*, **12**, 151–62.

Sarin, R.K. and P.P. Wakker (1998), 'Dynamic choice and nonexpected utility', *Journal of Risk and Uncertainty*, **17**, 87–119.

Spencer, A. (2003), 'A test of the QALY model when health varies over time', *Social Science and Medicine*, **57**, 1697–706.

Stalmeier, P.F.M., T.G.G. Bezembinder and I.J. Unic (1996), 'Proportional heuristics in time trade off and conjoint measurements', *Medical Decision Making*, **16**, 36–44.

Starmer, C. (2000), 'Developments in non-expected utility theory: The hunt for a descriptive theory of choice under risk', *Journal of Economic Literature*, **28**, 332–82.

Stiggelbout, A.M., G.M. Kiebert, J. Kievit, J.W.H. Leer, G. Stoter and J.C.J.M. de Haes (1994), 'Utility assessment in cancer patients: Adjustment of time tradeoff scores for the utility of life years and comparison with standard gamble scores', *Medical Decision Making*, **14**, 82–90.

Sutherland, H.U., H. Llewellyn-Thomas, N.F. Boyd and J.E. Till (1982), 'Attitudes toward quality of survival: The concept of "maximal endurable time"', *Medical Decision Making*, **2**, 299–309.
Treadwell, J.R. (1998), 'Tests of preferential independence in the QALY model', *Medical Decision Making*, **18**, 418–28.
Tversky, A. and D. Kahneman (1992), 'Advances in prospect theory: Cumulative representation of uncertainty', *Journal of Risk and Uncertainty*, **5**, 297–323.
Verhoef, L.C.G., A.F.J. de Haan and W.A.J. van Daal (1994), 'Risk attitude in gambles with years of life: Empirical support for prospect theory', *Medical Decision Making*, **14**, 194–200.
Zank, H. (2001), 'Cumulative prospect theory for parametric and multiattribute utilities', *Mathematics of Operations Research*, **26**, 67–81.

34 The multi-attribute utility approach to assessing health-related quality of life
David Feeny*

1. Introduction

The purposes of health status and health-related quality of life (HRQL) assessment include description, discrimination and evaluation (Feeny, 2005a). Discrimination refers to the ability to distinguish among groups at a point in time (cross-sectional analyses). Is the burden of morbidity higher in type 2 diabetes or arthritis? Evaluation refers to the ability to capture within-person change over time (prospective analyses). Is treatment A or treatment B more effective for treating osteoarthritis?

HRQL measures provide descriptive information on the health of subjects at a point in time. Typically physical, mental and social aspects of health are included. Patrick and Erickson (1993, p. 22) provide a prominent definition of HRQL: 'health-related quality of life is the value assigned to duration of life as modified by the impairments, functional states, perceptions and social opportunities that are influenced by disease, injury, treatment, or policy.' Preference-based or utility measures are a prominent approach to the valuation of health states.

Psychometric measures such as the Short-Form 36 (Ware and Sherbourne, 1992) are widely used to provide descriptive information on health status. Psychometric scores provide information on the 'location' of that health state in the distribution of health states experienced by patients with a particular disease and/or the distribution found in the general population. Instead the conceptual basis of scoring for utility measures is the value placed on the health state, usually as judged by patients or the general population.

The measurement of HRQL is based on a conceptual framework and a set of fundamental normative assumptions. One of the major conceptual foundations of utility measures is microeconomic theory and decision science (Feeny, 2000; Torrance, 1986; Torrance and Feeny, 1989; Feeny and Torrance, 1989; von Neumann and Morgenstern, 1944; Chapter 33 by Bleichrodt and Pinto in this Companion).

2. Two major approaches

There are two major families of utility measures: direct and multi-attribute (Drummond et al., 1997). Direct measures involve asking patients to value health states. In the multi-attribute, or indirect approach, patients complete health status questionnaires. The conventional scale for utility measures is anchored on 0.00 for dead and 1.00 for perfect health.

---

* It should be noted that David Feeny has a proprietary interest in Health Utilities Incorporated, Dundas, Ontario, Canada. HUInc. owns the copyright to and distributes HUI materials.

In the direct approach the respondent is asked to place a value on a health state (Furlong et al., 1990; Torrance et al., 2001; 2002); more detail can be found in Chapter 35 by Brazier and Roberts in this Companion. Valuations are obtained using one or more of a variety of elicitation techniques. The three most common techniques are the visual analogue scale (VAS), standard gamble (SG) and time trade-off (TTO).

Typically the direct approach to assessing preferences for health states involves the use of trained professional interviewers to administer the VAS followed by a choice-base technique such as the SG or TTO. These interviews are cognitively demanding.

An alternative approach that is frequently used is to rely instead on a multi-attribute system. In this approach the respondent completes a questionnaire, providing information on self-assessed health status. The analyst then employs a multi-attribute utility function to score that health state. That function is based on preference scores obtained using one or more of the techniques (VAS, SG, TTO) from a survey, typically a random sample of the general population (community preferences).

Functional form. There are three major functional forms for multi-attribute utility functions. The simplest form, the linear additive, makes the most restrictive assumptions. The linear additive function implies that there are no interactions in preferences among attributes. For instance, in the linear additive form, the burden (disutility) of being blind does not depend on whether or not you also have a hearing impairment.

The multiplicative form assumes mutual utility independence. It allows for one simple type of preference interaction among attributes. Attributes can be preference complements or preference substitutes.

The multi-linear form makes a weaker assumption (order-one independence). It allows different pairs of attributes (say vision and hearing) to be preference substitutes, other pairs (say emotion and cognition) to be preference complements and a lack of preference interactions for yet additional pairs (say, hearing and pain).

Conceptually, the multi-linear form is superior because it imposes fewer restrictions on the underlying structure of preferences. These advantages come, however, at a cost. The design of preference surveys to generate observations need for estimating the multi-linear form is much more complicated than the design for estimating multiplicative or linear additive functions.

The functional forms for the linear additive, multiplicative and multi-linear forms are as follows. The notation used is that $u_j(x_j) =$ the single attribute utility function for attribute j; $u(x) =$ is the utility for health state x, represented by an n-element vector; and k and k_j are model parameters. Additive utility functions take the form:

$$u(x) = \Sigma_{j=1}^{n} k_j u_j(x_j), \quad \text{where } \Sigma_{j=1}^{n} k_j = 1.$$

Multiplicative utility functions take the form:

$$u(x) = (1/k) \left[\prod_{j=1}^{n} (1 + kk_j u_j(x_j)) - 1 \right], \quad \text{where } (1 + k) = \prod_{j=1}^{n} (1 + kk_j)$$

Multi-linear utility functions take the form:

$$u(x) = k_1 u_1(x_1) + k_2 u_2(x_2) + \ldots$$
$$+ k_{12} u_1(x_1)\, u_2(x_2) + k_{13} u_1(x_1)\, u_3(x_3) + \ldots$$
$$+ k_{123} u_1(x_1)\, u_2(x_2)\, u_3(x_3) + \ldots,$$

where Σ all k's $= 1$

The three most commonly used multi-attribute measures are the EuroQol EQ-5D (Essink-Bot et al., 1993; Rabin and de Charro, 2001; Shaw et al., 2005), the Health Utilities Index (HUI) (Furlong et al., 2001; Feeny et al., 2002; Horsman et al., 2003) and the Quality of Well Being scale (QWB) (Patrick et al., 1973; Kaplan and Anderson, 1996). Recently Brazier et al. (2002) introduced the SF-6D based on the Short Form 36 (Ware and Sherbourne, 1992). Table 34.1 summarizes the characteristics of each of the systems discussed.

To date, many estimates of multi-attribute utility functions (for instance, Health Utilities Index Mark 1 (HUI1) (Torrance et al., 1982), Mark 2 (HUI2) (Torrance et al., 1996; Wang et al., 2002; McCabe et al., 2004) and Mark 3 (HUI3) (Feeny et al., 2002); the French version of HUI3 (Le Galès et al., 2002); the Spanish version of HUI3 (Ruiz et al., 2003); two disease-specific multi-attribute utility functions: Revicki et al., 1998a; 1998b; see also Torrance et al., 2002 and Salomon et al., 2003) have rejected the linear additive form. The Short-Form 6D, EuroQol EQ-5D and QWB, however, rely on the linear additive form. Interestingly, ad hoc terms in the US EQ-5D index function, D1, I3 and I3^2, could be interpreted as being consistent with preference complementarity among the attributes (Shaw et al., 2005).

In order to ensure the feasibility of estimating a multi-attribute utility function, it is necessary to limit the number of attributes of health status included in the system. Although additional attributes might be useful, adding additional attributes may generate a cognitive burden sufficient to jeopardize the estimation of a multi-attribute utility function. Evidence from psychology (Miller, 1956) indicates that people can, in general, retain seven items (plus or minus 2) in active consideration.

3.   Brief description of major multi-attribute systems

EQ-5D. The EQ-5D includes several components. First, there is a health-status classification system. Health status in the EQ-5D consists of five attributes: mobility, self-care, usual activity, pain/discomfort and anxiety/depression. There are three levels defined for each attribute: no problem, some problem, or extreme problem. The health status of an individual at a point in time can be represented as a five-element vector, one level for each dimension (Kind, 1996). A score for that categorical information on health status can be obtained by using a scoring formula. Dolan (1997) provides a scoring system based on TTO preferences obtained from a random sample of the general population in the United Kingdom and estimated using an ad hoc modified linear additive form. Because some states were considered by respondents to be worse than dead, the scale runs from -0.59 to 1.00. Shaw et al. (2005) estimate an ad hoc linear additive function based on TTO scores obtained from a random sample of the US population. The US EQ-5D index scores range from -0.11 to 1.00.

Table 34.1   Description of EQ-5D, Health Utilities Index Mark 2 (HUI2) and Mark 3 (HUI3), Quality of Well-Being (QWB), and Short-Form 6D (SF-6D) multi-attribute utility measures

Measure	Attributes and (number of levels)	Number of unique health states	Scoring function
EQ-SD	Mobility (3), Self-Care (3); Usual Activities (3); Pain/ Discomfort (3); Anxiety/ Depression (3)	243 plus unconscious, and dead	Ad hoc Modified Linear Additive Based on TTO scores from random sample of the UK population; Ad hoc Modified Linear Additive Based on TTO scores from random sample of the US population
HUI2	Sensation (4); Mobility (5); Emotion (5); Cognition (4); Self-Care (4); Pain and Discomfort (5); Fertility (3)	24 000 plus dead	Multiplicative Multi-Attribute based on SG scores from a random sample of parents in general population in Canada
HUI3	Vision (6); Hearing (6); Speech (5); Ambulation (6); Dexterity (6); Emotion (5); Cognition (5); Pain and Discomfort (5)	972 000 plus dead	Multiplicative Multi-Attribute based on SG scores from random sample of general population in Canada
QWB	Mobility (3); Physical Activity (3); Social Activity (5); Symptom/ Problem Complex (27)	1215 plus dead	Linear Additive based on VAS scores from random sample of general population in the US
SF-6D	Physical Functioning (6); Role Limitations (4); Social Functioning (5); Pain (6); Mental Health (5); Vitality (5)	18 000 plus dead	Ad hoc Modified Linear Additive Based on SG scores from a random sample of the general population in the UK

Source: Modified from Feeny (2005b).

HUI. There are three major versions of the HUI: HUI Mark 1 (Torrance et al., 1982), HUI Mark 2 (Feeny et al., 1992) and HUI Mark 3 (Feeny et al., 2002; Horsman et al., 2003). In all three cases there is a health-status classification system, a questionnaire to obtain information within which to classify subjects according to that system and a multi-attribute utility function to provide utility scores. HUI2 and HUI3 have superseded HUI1 in most applications and discussion will focus on HUI2 and HUI3.

HUI2 consists of seven attributes (dimensions or domains) of health status: sensation (vision, hearing and speech), mobility, emotion, cognition, self-care, pain and fertility. However, in most applications fertility is omitted. The scoring function for the HUI2 system is based on preference measurements using the VAS and SG obtained from a random sample of parents in the general population in Hamilton, Ontario, Canada (Torrance et al., 1996). The HUI2 scoring function employs a multiplicative functional form.

The HUI3 system was originally designed for the 1990 Ontario Health Survey. HUI3 includes eight attributes: vision, hearing, speech, ambulation, dexterity, emotion, cognition and pain. There are five or six levels per attribute. HUI3 has been widely used in population health surveys in Canada including the 1994 and ongoing National Population Health Survey and the Canadian Community Health Survey.

The HUI3 scoring system is based on VAS and SG scores obtained from a random sample of the general population in Hamilton, Ontario. The functional form is multiplicative (Feeny et al., 2002). Evidence of the out-of-sample predictive validity of the HUI3 scoring function is found in Feeny et al. (2002). Respondents were randomized to the modelling survey or the direct survey. Preference scores provided by respondents to the modelling survey were used to estimate the multiplicative function. Respondents in the direct survey provided SG scores for 73 HUI3 health states. There was a high level of agreement, an intra-class correlation of 0.88, between directly measured scores and scores generated by the multiplicative function.

QWB. The QWB is oldest of the multi-attribute systems (Patrick et al., 1973; Kaplan and Anderson, 1996). The original systems included three dimensions of health status and a problem/symptom complex: mobility (five levels), physical activity (four levels), social activity (five levels) and symptom/problem (35 items). The newer version has three levels for mobility, three for physical activity, five for social activity and 27 items in the problem/symptom complex. The scoring function is linear additive, based on VAS scores obtained from a random sample of the general population in San Diego, California. Only the worst symptom or problem is scored.

SF-6D. SF-6D includes seven of the eight dimensions of health status from the SF-36: physical functioning, role limitations, social functioning, pain, mental health and vitality (Brazier et al., 2002; Brazier and Roberts, 2004). There are four to six levels per attribute. An ad hoc modified linear additive scoring function was estimated using SG scores obtained from a random sample of the population in the United Kingdom.

A brief review of evidence on the measurement properties of the major multi-attribute measures is provided below. But first the methods for estimating multi-attribute utility functions will be described briefly.

Estimation of multi-attribute utility functions

There are two basic approaches: statistical inference (regression) and the decomposed model derived from decision science. In both approaches there is the issue of the choice of functional form (Feeny, 2002a; 2002b).

The estimation of multi-attribute utility functions for HUI has employed the decomposed approach. In each case, HUI1, HUI2 and HUI3, a multiplicative functional form was employed. Respondents in the preference survey were asked to provide preference scores for levels within each attribute ($u_j(x_j)$ in the equation given above). Respondents were also asked to value the corner states, states in which one attribute was at its lowest (most severe) level while all others were at level 1 (normal). Scores for corner states provide information on the weight of that attribute (k_j) in determining the overall score. Finally, simultaneous equations were solved to determine the value of k, the interaction term. If k is positive, the attributes are all preference complements; if k is negative the attributes are all preference substitutes; if k equals zero, the utility function is linear additive.

Empirical results from the estimation of the HUI scoring functions indicate that the attributes are preference complements. This result is corroborated by estimates for a multi-linear multi-attribute utility function for the HUI3 system. Preference complementarity implies that the loss of function in two attributes would be worse than the same losses in only one attribute but not as 'bad' as the sum of the two individual losses.

4.   Properties of multi-attribute measures and comparisons of the measures

There are a variety of important measurement properties for measures of health status and HRQL (Streiner and Norman, 1995). Among the relevant properties are reliability, construct validity, responsiveness and interpretation (Feeny et al., 1999).

One important measure of reliability is test-retest reliability: in stable subjects, do scores obtained at one time agree with scores obtained at another? Test-retest is generally measured using an intra-class correlation coefficient, a measure of agreement. In general test-retest reliability is acceptable (ICC ≥ 0.70) for EQ-5D, HUI, QWB and the SF-36 from which the SF-6D is derived (Feeny, 2005b).

Validity refers to the extent to which a measure measures what it purports to measure. In situations in which there is a gold standard measure, one can assess agreement between a measure and the gold standard (criterion validity) to assess validity. For instance, if one assumes that an x-ray is the gold standard, one could then assess the validity of physical examination by assessing agreement between physical exam and the x-ray results. In the context of HRQL there is no gold standard.

Instead one relies on assessing construct validity. Construct validity involves the specification of a series of a priori hypotheses about how a measure should behave. If it measures what it is supposed to then it should be moderately or strongly correlated with a measure of a similar attribute and uncorrelated with a measure of an unrelated attribute. For instance, one would expect mobility from the EQ-5D to be strongly correlated with ambulation on HUI3 but only weakly or negligibly correlated with speech on HUI3. Another approach is the known groups approach. We would expect lower scores for those with severe Alzheimer Disease than for those with mild disease. In general there is evidence of construct validity for the EQ-5D, HUI, QWB and SF-36 (Feeny, 2005a; Feeny, 2005b). While there is evidence of construct validity for each measure in a wide variety of applications, it cannot be assumed that a measure will work well in a new setting.

The coverage of the measures varies. The inclusion of cognition in HUI2 and HUI3 has made these measures popular in studies of stroke and Alzheimer disease. The inclusion of vitality in SF-36 has enhanced its usefulness among patients undergoing dialysis.

Responsiveness refers to the ability to detect meaningful change when it occurs. This property is particularly important in the context of using utility measures as indicators of outcome in randomized controlled clinical trials. When more than one measure has been used in the same study, one can compare responsiveness by comparing the magnitude of change observed. In making comparisons of responsiveness across studies, a variety of measures of responsiveness are typically used. Most of these measures involve a ratio of the change detected (the signal) divided by the standard deviation (noise) of the scores. Responsiveness measures vary in their choice of standard deviation. Some (standardized response mean, SRM) use the standard deviation of the change in scores; other uses the standard deviation of scores at baseline (effect size).

There is evidence that the multi-attribute measures are indeed responsive. For instance, patients who survive a stroke typically experience substantial improvements in HRQL during the first six months of their recovery. Pickard et al. (2005) provide estimates of the SRMs for the EQ-5D (UK scoring), SF-6D and HUI3 of 0.84, 0.87 and 0.78. In contrast, the change in utility score for each of the three measures during the same time period was 0.31, 0.13 and 0.25. The EQ-5D and HUI3 provided much larger estimates of the gain in HRQL. However, according to the SRM the responsiveness of the three measures was approximately equal. While the change in the SF-6D score was lower, so was the variability of change scores.

One of the threats to responsiveness is floor and ceiling effects. Floor effects occur when one can be worse than the lowest score in the range of the measure. Ceiling effects occur when one can be better than can be captured by the measure. One interpretation of the results for SF-6D in stroke is that at baseline many patients were worse than could be captured by the SF-6D and therefore the extent of recovery was underestimated.

In clinical studies HUI does not appear to be subject to important floor or ceiling effects. In contrast ceiling effects are often evident with EQ-5D (Coons et al., 2000; Macran et al., 2003; Essink-Bot et al., 1998) and floor effects are often evident with SF-6D (Hatoum et al., 2004; Hollingworth et al., 2002; Longworth and Bryan, 2003; Lee et al., 2003; Szende et al., 2004; Brazier et al., 2004; O'Brien et al., 2003; Feeny et al., 2004; Bosch et al., 2002). In population health survey applications, ceiling effects are less evident with HUI than with EQ-5D (Houle and Berthelot, 2000; Luo et al., 2005).

Interpretation refers to attaching meaning to scores. As experience with multi-attribute measures has accumulated, it has become easier to interpret scores. The availability of data from population health surveys that have included multi-attribute utility measures provides important information on population norms for the interpretation of scores.

Clinically important differences

A closely related concept is that of clinically (or policy) important difference (CID) or change in score. By how much does a mean score have to increase to conclude that an important change has occurred? With a large sample size, changes of 0.001 might well be statistically significant but are unlikely to be meaningful.

Changes or differences in overall HUI2 or HUI3 scores of 0.03 or more are regarded as clinically important (Grootendorst et al., 2000; Drummond, 2001; Horsman et al., 2003; see also Samsa et al., 1999). Smaller differences may well also be important. Walters and Brazier (2003) provide estimates of the CID for SF-6D scores that range from 0.01 to 0.05 with a weighted mean estimate of 0.033. The CID for the QWB is approximately 0.03. The developers of the EQ-5D do not provide a statement concerning differences in EQ-5D index scores that are likely to be clinically important.

Applications

Utility measures have broad applications in clinical and population health studies. Major uses include description of HRQL in cross-sectional and prospective studies, measuring outcomes in randomized controlled clinical trials (RCTs) and other prospective studies, input into economic evaluation studies such as cost-effectiveness analyses and summary measures of population health quality.

An example of a clinical application of multi-attribute measures in stroke is found in Pickard et al. (2005). The study employed EQ-5D (scored using the UK scoring function), HUI2, HUI3 and SF-36 from which SF-6D scores were derived. Questionnaires were administered to patients within two weeks of their stroke. Follow-up interviews were conducted at one, three and six months. Mean (standard deviation) scores at baseline were 0.31 (0.38) for EQ-5D, 0.51 (0.20) for HUI2, 0.19 (0.30) for HUI3 and 0.55 (0.09) for SF-6D. At baseline, deficits in mobility, self-care, usual activities and anxiety/ depression were detected by the EQ-5D. Similarly HUI2 identified problems in mobility, cognition and self-care. HUI3 identified problems in speech, ambulation, dexterity and emotion. SF-36 identified problems in physical functioning, physical role, vitality, social functioning, emotional role and mental health. All four instruments identified the kinds of problems that one would expect to observe in patients who had recently suffered a stroke – evidence of construct validity. Mean (sd) scores at the six-month follow-up were 0.62 (0.33) for EQ-5D, 0.64 (0.23) for HUI2, 0.44 (0.35) for HUI3 and 0.68 (0.15) for SF-6D. Estimates of change over the six-month period varied substantially among the multi-attribute measures: 0.32 for EQ-5D, 0.12 for HUI2, 0.25 for HUI3 and 0.13 for SF-6D. As mentioned above, floor effects associated with SF-36 may have affected the SF-6D results.

Differences in which attributes are included in each of these systems, differences in the source of scores for the scoring functions (TTO, SG) and differences in functional form for the scoring functions account for some of the differences in scores across measures. Clearly scores from different systems are not interchangeable.

A cost–utility analysis of injections of replacement synovial fluid in knees affected by osteoarthritis relied on HUI3 to assess outcomes (Torrance et al., 2002). Patients were randomized to appropriate care or appropriate care plus the injections. HRQL questionnaires were administered monthly for one year. According to all measures, patients in the appropriate care arm of the trial initially improved and then stabilized; patients in the appropriate care plus injections arm of the trial improved more dramatically and then stabilized. The incremental gain in HRQL was 0.071 quality-adjusted life years (QALYs). The incremental cost of the intervention was $CA 710, for an incremental cost–utility ratio of $CA 10 000/QALY gained, a result typically interpreted as a relative bargain.

Multi-attribute measures such as EQ-5D, HUI2, HUI3 and SF-6D have been included in population health surveys in a number of countries. Wolfson (1996) provides estimates of life expectancy and health-adjusted life expectancy for Canada based on results using HUI3, which was included in the Statistics Canada 1996–97 NPHS. Analysts at Statistics Canada used age- and gender-specific morbidity estimates derived from HUI3 scores to adjust the remaining expected years of life for the quality of those years. The adjustments matter at all ages but are more dramatic for the elderly (Table 34.2).

5.   Future directions

The health-status descriptive systems of multi-attribute measures continue to evolve. For instance, one group has added cognition to the EQ system (Krabbe et al., 1999). Similarly there have been pilot studies with HUI2 and HUI3 modifying the descriptions of the levels to enhance their relevance in particular clinical applications. In each of these cases there is the potential to enrich the descriptive system and enhance its ability to discriminate and to capture meaningful change. However, providing utility scores for such augmented

Table 34.2   Health-adjusted life expectancy based on HUI3 from the 1996–97 National Population Health Survey (Canada)

Age	Life Expectancy		Health-Adjusted Life Expectancy		HALE/LE	
Group	Male	Female	Male	Female	Male	Female
15–19	61.1	66.8	53.9	57.0	88%	85%
20–24	56.4	61.9	49.4	52.5	88%	85%
25–29	51.6	57.0	44.9	47.9	87%	84%
30–34	46.9	52.1	40.5	43.2	86%	83%
35–39	42.2	47.2	36.0	38.7	85%	82%
40–44	37.5	42.4	31.6	34.2	84%	81%
45–49	32.8	37.7	27.4	29.8	83%	79%
50–54	28.3	33.0	23.2	25.6	82%	78%
55–59	24.0	28.5	19.2	21.5	80%	76%
60–64	19.9	24.1	15.6	17.8	78%	74%
65–69	16.1	20.0	12.1	14.0	76%	70%
70–74	12.7	16.1	9.1	10.5	71%	65%
75–79	9.8	12.5	6.5	7.4	66%	59%
80–84	7.3	9.4	4.4	4.6	60%	49%
85+	3.7	4.3	1.9	1.7	51%	39%

Source: Statistics Canada

systems is problematic. Either the scoring function has to be re-estimated, or strong assumptions have to be made about the validity of interpolated scores.

There have also been pilot studies augmenting the descriptive systems to reflect 'positive health'. The capacity to engage in vigorous physical activity and emotional resilience are two areas of particular interest. Another area of recent innovation is the development of disease- or condition-specific multi-attribute utility measures. For instance, Revicki et al. (1998a; 1998b) have developed multi-attribute utility measures for asthma and rhinitis. These disease-specific multi-attribute measures have the potential to combine the focus of the specific approach with the rigour of multi-attribute utility scoring systems that provide preference-based interval-scale data. The linkage between the disease-specific scale (for example, severe asthma to free from asthma) and the conventional dead-perfect health scale is one challenge.

In summary, multi-attribute utility measures provide comprehensive descriptive information on health status. Furthermore these measures provide utility scores assessing the value of the health states so described. These measures permit broad comparisons among groups and over time. In addition, utility scores can be used to compute QALYs to support cost–utility and cost-effectiveness analyses. Similarly, utility scores can be used to construct summary measures of population health such as health-adjusted life expectancy. At the practical level, multi-attribute measures are much easier to use than direct utility measures such as the standard gamble.

Multi-attribute measures continue to evolve. There is still debate about which attributes to include in the health-status descriptive systems as well as the appropriate number of levels per attribute. In the estimation of scoring functions, there is ongoing debate about the best approach and choice of functional form. Nonetheless multi-attribute measures provide a framework for producing, analysing and interpreting policy-relevant information on the value of health states.

References

Bosch, Johanna L., Elkan F. Halpern and G. Scott Gazelle (2002), 'Comparison of preference-based utilities of the Short-Form 36 Health Survey and Health Utilities Index before and after treatment of patients with intermittent claudication', *Medical Decision Making*, **22**(5), 403–9.
Brazier, John E. and Jennifer Roberts (2004), 'The estimation of a preference-based measure of health from the SF-12', *Medical Care*, **42**(9), 851–9.
Brazier, John, Jennifer Roberts and Mark Deverill (2002), 'The estimation of a preference-based measure of health from the SF-36', *Journal of Health Economics*, **21**(2), 271–92.
Brazier, John, Jennifer Roberts, Aki Tsuchiya and Jan Busschbach (2004), 'A Comparison of the EQ-5D and SF-6D across seven patient groups', *Health Economics*, **13**(9), 873–84.
Coons, Stephen Joel, Sumati Rao, Dorothy L. Keininger and Ron D. Hays (2000), 'A comparative review of generic quality-of-life instruments', *Pharmacoeconomics*, **17**(1), 13–35.
Dolan, Paul (1997), 'Modeling valuations for EuroQol health states', *Medical Care*, **35**(11), 1095–108.
Drummond, Michael (2001), 'Introducing economic and quality of life measurements into clinical studies', *Annals of Medicine*, **33**(5), 344–9.
Drummond, Michael F., Bernie O'Brien, Greg Stoddart and George W. Torrance (1997), *Methods for the Economic Evaluation of Health Care Programmes*, second edn, Oxford: Oxford University Press.
Essink-Bot, Marie-Louise, Marlies E.A. Stouthard and Gouke J. Bonsel (1993), 'Generalizability of valuations on health states collected with the EuroQol questionnaire', *Health Economics*, **2**(3), 237–46.
Essink-Bot, Marie-Louise, Harry J. De Koning, Hubert G.T. Nijs, Wim J. Kirkels, Paul J. van der Maas and Fritz H. Schroder (1998), 'Short-term effects of population-based screening for prostate cancer on health-related quality of life', *Journal of the National Cancer Institute*, **90**(12), 925–31
Feeny, David (2000), 'A utility approach to assessing health-related quality of life', *Medical Care*, **38**(9, Supplement II), II-151–II-154.
Feeny, David (2002a), 'Health-status classification systems for summary measures of population health', in Christopher J.L. Murray, Joshua A. Salomon, Colin D. Mathers and Alan D. Lopez (eds), *Summary Measures of Population Health: Concepts, Ethics, Measurement and Applications*, Geneva: World Health Organization, pp. 329–41.
Feeny, David (2002b), 'The utility approach to assessing population health', in Christopher J.L. Murray, Joshua A. Salomon, Colin D. Mathers and Alan D. Lopez (eds), *Summary Measures of Population Health: Concepts, Ethics, Measurement and Applications*, Geneva: World Health Organization, pp. 515–28.
Feeny, David (2005a), 'The roles for preference-based measures in support of cancer research and policy', in Joseph Lipscomb, Carolyn Cook Gotay and Claire Snyder (eds), *Outcomes Assessment in Cancer: Measures, Methods, and Applications*, New York: Cambridge University Press, pp. 69–92.
Feeny, David (2005b), 'Preference-based measures: utility and quality-adjusted life years', in Peter Fayers and Ron Hays (eds), *Assessing Quality of Life in Clinical Trials*, second edn, Oxford: Oxford University Press, pp. 405–29.
Feeny, David (forthcoming), 'Comparing and contrasting utilities and willingness to pay', in William Lenderking and Dennis Revicki (eds), *Advances in Health Research Methods, Measurement, Statistical Analysis, and Clinical Applications*, Proceedings from the 2004 International Society for Quality of Life Research Symposium, 'Stating the Art: advancing outcomes research methodology and clinical applications', Boston, 27–29 June, 2004.
Feeny, David and George W. Torrance (1989), 'Incorporating utility-based quality-of-life assessments in clinical trials: two examples', *Medical Care*, **27**(3, Supplement), S190–S204.
Feeny, David, Lieling Wu and Ken Eng (2004), 'Comparing Short Form 6D, Standard Gamble, and Health Utilities Index Mark 2 and Mark 3 utility scores: results from total hip arthroplasty patients', *Quality of Life Research*, **13**(10), 1659–70.
Feeny, David, William Furlong, Raymond K. Mulhern, Ronald D. Barr and Melissa Hudson (1999), 'A framework for assessing health-related quality of life among children with cancer', *International Journal of Cancer*, Supplement 12, 2–9.
Feeny, David, William Furlong, Ronald D. Barr, George W. Torrance, Peter Rosenbaum and Sheila Weitzman (1992), 'A comprehensive multiattribute system for classifying the health status of survivors of childhood cancer', *Journal of Clinical Oncology*, **10**(6), 923–8.

Feeny, David, William Furlong, George W. Torrance, Charles H. Goldsmith, Zenglong Zhu, Sonja DePauw, Margaret Denton and Michael Boyle (2002), 'Multi-attribute and single-attribute utility functions for the health utilities index Mark 3 System', *Medical Care*, **40**(2), pp. 113–28.

Furlong, William J., David H. Feeny, George W. Torrance and Ronald D. Barr (2001), 'The Health Utilities Index (HUI) system for assessing health-related quality of life in clinical studies', *Annals of Medicine*, **33**(5), 375–84.

Furlong, William, David Feeny, George W. Torrance, Ronald Barr and John Horsman (1990), 'Guide to design and development of health-state utility instrumentation', McMaster University Centre for Health Economics and Policy Analysis Working Paper, No 90–9.

Grootendorst, Paul, David Feeny and William Furlong (2000), 'Health Utilities Index Mark 3: evidence of construct validity for stroke and arthritis in a population health survey', *Medical Care*, **38**(3), 290–9.

Hatoum, Hind T., John E. Brazier and Kasem S. Akhras (2004), 'Comparison of the HUI3 with the SF-36 Preference Based SF-6D in a clinical trial setting', *Value and Health*, **7**(5), 602–9.

Hollingworth, William, Richard A. Deyo, Sean D. Sullivan, Scott S. Emerson, Darryl T. Gray and Jeffrey G. Jarvik (2002), 'The practicality and validity of directly elicited and SF-36 derived health state preferences in patients with low back pain', *Health Economics*, **11**(1), 71–85.

Horsman, John, William Furlong, David Feeny and George Torrance (2003), 'The Health Utilities Index (HUI®): concepts, measurement properties and applications', *Health and Quality of Life Outcomes* (electronic journal), **1**(54), http://www.hqlo.com/content/1/1/54.

Houle, Christian and Jean-Marie Berthelot (2000), 'A head-to-head comparison of the Health Utilities Mark 3 and the EQ-5D for the population living in private households in Canada', *Quality of Life Newsletter*, **24**, 5–6.

Kaplan, Robert M. and John P. Anderson (1996), 'The general health policy model: an integrated approach', in Bert Spilker (ed.), *Quality of Life and Pharmacoeconomics in Clinical Trials*, second edn, Philadelphia: Lippincott-Raven Publishers, pp. 309–22.

Kind, Paul (1996), 'The EuroQol instrument: an index of health-related quality of life', in Bert Spilker (ed.), *Quality of Life and Pharmacoeconomics in Clinical Trials*, second edn, Philadelphia: Lippincott-Raven Press, pp. 191–201.

Krabbe, Paul F., M.E. Stouthard, M.L. Essink-Bot and G.J. Bonsel (1999), 'The effect of adding a cognitive dimension to the EuroQol multiattribute health-status classification system', *Journal of Clinical Epidemiology*, **52**(4), 293–301.

Le Galès, Catherine, Catherine Buron, Nathalie Costet, Sophia Rosman and Pr. Gérard Slama (2002), 'Development of a preference-weighted health status classification system in France: the Health Utilities Index', *Health Care Management Science*, **5**(1), 41–51.

Lee, Todd A., William Hollingworth and Sean D. Sullivan (2003), 'Comparison of directly elicited preferences to preferences derived from the SF-36 in adults with asthma', *Medical Decision Making*, **23**(4), 323–34.

Longworth, Louise and Stirling Bryan (2003), 'An empirical comparison of EQ-5D and SF-6D in liver transplant patients', *Health Economics*, **12**(12), 1061–7.

Luo, Nan, Jeffrey A. Johnson, James W. Shaw, David Feeny and Stephen Joel Coons (2005), 'Self-reported health status of the general adult US population as assessed by the EQ-5D and health Utilities Index', *Medical Care* **43**(11), 1078–86.

Macran, Susan, Helen Weatherly and Paul Kind (2003), 'Measuring population health: a comparison of three generic health status measures', *Medical Care*, **41**(2), 218–31.

McCabe, Christopher, Katherine Stevens and John Brazier (2004), 'Utility values for the Health Utility Index Mark 2: An empirical assessment of alternative mapping functions', Sheffield Health Economics Group Discussion Paper 04/1.

Miller, George A. (1956), 'The magical number seven, plus or minus two: some limits on our capacity for processing information', *Psychological Review*, **63**(2), 81–97.

O'Brien, Bernie J., Marian Spath, Gordon Blackhouse, J.L. Severens, Paul Dorian and John Brazier (2003), 'A view from the bridge: agreement between the SF-6D utility algorithm and the Health Utilities Index', *Health Economics*, **12**(11), 975–81.

Patrick, Donald L. and Pennifer Erickson (1993), *Health Status and Health Policy: Quality of Life in Health Care Evaluation and Resource Allocation*, New York: Oxford University Press.

Patrick, Donald L., James Bush and Milton Chen (1973), 'Methods for measuring levels of well-being for a Health Status Index', *Health Services Research*, **8**(3), 228–45.

Pickard, A. Simon, Jeffrey A. Johnson and David H. Feeny (2005), 'Responsiveness of generic health-related quality of life measures in stroke', *Quality of Life Research*, **14**(1), 207–19.

Rabin, Rosalind and Frank de Charro (2001), 'EQ-5D: A Measure of Health Status from the EuroQol Group', *Annals of Medicine*, **33**(5), 337–43.

Revicki, Dennis A., Nancy K. Leidy, F. Brennan-Deimer, C. Thompson and A. Togias (1998a), 'Development and preliminary validation of a multi-attribute rhinitis symptom utility index', *Quality of Life Research*, **7**(8), 693–702.

Revicki, Dennis A., Nancy K. Leidy, F. Brennan-Deimer, S. Sorensen and A. Togias (1998b), 'Integrating patient preferences into health outcomes assessment: the multi-attribute asthma symptom utility index', *Chest*, **114**(4), 998–1007.

Ruiz, Miguel, Javier Rejas, Javier Soto, Antonio Pardo and Irene Rebollo (2003), 'Adaptación y validación del Health Utilities Index Mark 3 al castellano y baremos de corrección en la población española', *Medicina clínica (Barcelona)*, **120**(3), 89–96.

Salomon, Joshua A., Christopher J.L. Murray, T. Bedirhan Ustun and Somnath Chatterji (2003), 'Health state valuations in summary measures of population health', in Christopher J.L. Murray and David B. Evans (eds), *Health Systems Performance Assesssment: Debates, Methods and Empiricism*, Geneva: World Health Organization, pp. 409–33.

Samsa, Greg, David Edelman, Margaret Rothman, G. Rhys Williams, Joseph Lipscomb and David Matchar (1999), 'Determining clinically important differences in health status measures: a general approach with illustration using the Health Utilities Index Mark II', *PharmacoEconomics*, **15**(2), 141–55.

Shaw, James W., Jeffrey A. Johnson and Stephen Joel Coons (2005), 'US valuation of the EQ-5D health states: development and testing of the D1 valuation model', *Medical Care*, **43**(3), 203–20.

Streiner, David L. and Geoffrey R. Norman (1995), *Health Measurement Scales. A Practical Guide to their Development and Use*, second edn, Oxford: Oxford University Press.

Szende, Agota, Klas Svensson, Elisabeth Stahl, Agnes Meszaros and Gyula Y. Berta (2004), 'Psychometric and utility-based measures of health status of asthmatic patients with different levels of disease control level', *Pharmacoeconomics*, **22**(8), 537–47.

Torrance, George W. (1986), 'Measurement of health state utilities for economic appraisal – a review', *Journal of Health Economics*, **5**(1), 1–30.

Torrance, George W. and David Feeny (1989), 'Utilities and quality-adjusted life years', *International Journal of Technology Assessment in Health Care*, **5**(4), 559–75.

Torrance, George W., Michael H. Boyle and Sargent P. Horwood (1982), 'Application of multi-attribute utility theory to measure social preferences for health states', *Operations Research*, **30**(6), 1042–69.

Torrance, George W., David Feeny and William Furlong (2001), 'Visual analog scales: do they have a role in the measurement of preferences for health states? A commentary', *Medical Decision Making*, **21**(4), 329–34.

Torrance, George W., William Furlong and David Feeny (2002), 'Health utility estimation', *Expert Reviews in Pharmacoeconomics Outcomes Research*, **2**(2), 99–108.

Torrance, George W., David H. Feeny, William J. Furlong, Ronald D. Barr, Yueming Zhang and Qinan Wang (1996), 'Multi-attribute preference functions for a comprehensive health status classification system: health utilities index Mark 2', *Medical Care*, **34**(7), 702–22.

Torrance, G.W., J.P. Raynauld, V. Walker, C.H. Goldsmith, N. Bellamy, P.A. Band, M. Schultz and P. Tugwell (2002), 'A prospective randomized, pragmatic, health outcomes trial evaluating the incorporation of Hylan G-F 20 into the treatment paradigm for patients with knee osteoarthritis (Part 2 or 2): economic results', *Osteoarthritis and Cartilage*, **10**(7), 518–27.

von Neumann, John and Oskar Morgenstern (1944), *Theory of Games and Economic Behavior*, Princeton: Princeton University Press.

Walters, Stephen J. and John E. Brazier (2003), 'What is the relationship between the minimally important difference and health statue utility values? The case of the SF-6D', *Health and Quality of Life Outcomes*, **1**(1) (electronic journal: http://www.hqlo.com/content/1/1/4).

Wang, Qinan, William Furlong, David Feeny, George Torrance and Ronald Barr (2002), 'How robust is the health utilities index Mark 2 utility function?', *Medical Decision Making*, **22**(4), 350–8.

Ware, John E. and Cathy Donald Sherbourne (1992), 'The MOS 36-item Short Form Health Survey (SF-36)', *Medical Care*, **30**(6), 473–83.

Wolfson, Michael C. (1996), 'Health-adjusted life expectancy', *Health Reports*, **6**(1), 41–6.

35 Methods for developing preference-based measures of health

John Brazier and Jennifer Roberts

1. Introduction

Preference-based measures of health are a standardized multi-dimensional health state classification. They come with pre-existing preference or utility weights and generate a single index score for each state where full health is one, and zero is equivalent to being dead (Drummond et al., 1997). The growth in recent years of the application of cost effectiveness analysis and the use of quality adjusted life years (QALYs) has resulted in an increasing demand for these preference-based measures (NICE, 2004; Ministry of Health, 1994; Commonwealth Department of Health, 1992). Whilst there are a number of existing generic preference-based measures (see Chapter 34 by Feeny in this Companion), they are unlikely to meet the varied requirements for conducting cost–utility analyses. Furthermore, they have been developed using different approaches and methods. It therefore seems appropriate to review the issues around constructing these measures and to provide a framework for future instrument development.

This chapter considers the three stages of development: the construction of the health state classification, the valuation survey and the modelling of the valuation data. Some methodological issues are positive or technical in nature and can be resolved, others are normative and thus the solution depends on the requirements of policy makers. This chapter finishes with a discussion of the implications for designing new instruments, methodological research and policy.

2. Construction of health state classifications

A key constraint in designing a descriptive system is that the set of health states must be amenable to valuation by respondents. The precise limits of respondents' processing capabilities will vary, but a rule of thumb in this field has been that people can only process between five and nine pieces of information (Miller, 1956). The more widely used measures have between 5 to 8 dimensions with 3 to 6 levels each. The extent to which a larger number of levels are possible depends on the ability of respondents to detect the differences. There is evidence from the SF-6D valuation study, for example, that respondents had difficulty distinguishing between very mild and mild pain (Brazier et al., 2002).

The definition of health

The famous WHO definition of health is a 'state of complete physical, mental and social well-being and not merely the absence of disease' (WHO, 1948); a view that has been very influential in the development of health status measures (Ware, 1987).

A criticism of this is that it is indistinguishable from the concept of utility. It has been suggested that there is something special about health and that a public system 'wishes you well, but not necessarily happy' (Evans and Wolfson, 1980). Evans and Wolfson (1980) go on to argue to: 'conceptualise health status for inclusion *within* the utility function in its narrow, negative, but more or less objectively measurable form'. On the other hand, QALYs in health care have been criticized for being too narrowly focused on health (Donaldson et al., 1988). A welfarist perspective would support the broadest possible definition. One solution to this dilemma has been to focus instruments on those aspects of quality of life which are related to health (for example, Euroqol Group, 1990).

Another way of looking at this issue is in terms of the WHO's International Classification of Impairment, Disabilities and Handicaps (or participation) (WHO, 1980). This implies a simple causal relationship between impairment, disability and participation. The HUI3 focuses on impairments (including vision, hearing and dexterity). The SF-6D and EQ-5D cover aspects of disability and participation such as physical functioning, role limitation, social functioning and usual activities. The inclusion of these quality of life domains has been criticized for incorporating people's preferences for certain activities and aspects of adaptation, things that should be left to the valuation stage (Feeny et al., 1995). However, general population respondents have little or no experience of many impairments and it may be helpful to give them a description of the resulting impact on quality of life.

Specificity
Most preference-based measures of health have a generic descriptive system (Brooks, 1996; Feeny et al., 2002; Brazier et al., 2002). However, these have been found to be inappropriate or insensitive for many medical conditions (for example, Brazier et al., 2005; Barton et al., 2004; Kobelt et al., 1999). The argument for using condition-specific descriptions is that they are likely to be more sensitive to changes in the condition than generic measures and more relevant to the concerns of patients (Guyatt, 2002; Brazier and Fitzpatrick, 2002).

On the other hand, condition-specific measures tend to focus on symptoms, which may concentrate the mind of the respondent on negative aspects of the condition. This may have a framing effect that produces lower values because the respondents are not thinking about other aspects of their lives unaffected by the condition. Another concern is that condition-specific measures fail to achieve comparability. This presupposes that different generic measures produce the same values and there is increasing evidence that this is not the case (Longworth and Bryan, 2003; Brazier et al., 2004; O'Brien et al., 2004). Differences in scores between measures (whether generic or condition-specific) result from differences in the methods of valuation as well as the descriptive system. Provided the descriptive system is valued on the same full health–dead scale using the same variant of the same valuation technique using a comparable population sample, then the valuations should be comparable. Any remaining differences in values should be a legitimate consequence of the descriptive system. However, this assumes that the value of a dimension is independent of those dimensions outside of the descriptive system and this requires empirical testing.

Item generation and selection
The aim is to provide the respondent with an accurate description of the health state being considered. This can be done *de novo*, such as the EQ-5D and HUI3, or developed from an

existing measure, such as the derivation of the SF-6D from the SF-36 (Brazier et al., 2002). Psychometrics has an important role assessing the reliability and validity of descriptive systems (Brazier and Deverill, 1999). There is no gold standard for determining descriptive validity and so the developer has, among other things, to rely on an assessment of the content and face validity of items. An empirical approach is the assessment of the severity of an item with Rasch analysis, which uses item response theory. Whilst this can be useful, it should be used with care since a rare problem may not be worse in terms of preferences. Simple valuation techniques such as ranking or rating provide a more preference-based method for determining the content of a space-constrained health state classification.

Having developed a set of items, the analyst should then consider ways to assess their construct validity in terms of the instruments' ability to reflect known or expected differences in health or changes over time. A concern that economists have with this type of work is that it does not necessarily tell us whether any expected differences in health translate into differences in preferences. This requires additional evidence on preferences. A study of people with visual impairment, for example, found strong evidence for patient preference between different visual acuity states using time trade-off; this was not reflected in the EQ-5D and SF-6D, though it was in the HUI3 (Brazier et al., 2005).

3. Valuation of health state classification

Valuation technique
Techniques used to value health states include visual analogue scaling (VAS), magnitude estimation (ME), standard gamble (SG), time trade-off (TTO) and person trade-off (PTO). More recently there has been interest in basing valuations on ordinal data from ranking and discrete choice experiments (Salomon, 2003; McCabe et al., 2005b). The selection of elicitation technique is important because the values generated are dependent on the technique. This issue has been widely reviewed elsewhere and is dealt with only briefly here (Dolan, 2000; Green et al., 2000).

There appears to be agreement in the literature that VAS and ME have no basis in economic theory for estimating strength of preference (Green et al., 2000). However, VAS has been used to estimate SG and TTO values and there are statistical models relating VAS to SG and TTO (for example, Torrance et al., 1992). While VAS data has been shown to explain a substantial portion of variance in SG and TTO, no single functional form has been dominant and no single theory explains the relationship (Brazier et al., 2003). The use of ordinal data to generate cardinal health state values drawing on random utility theory may prove to be a promising alternative to choice-based methods, particularly in more vulnerable populations.

There has been considerable theoretical debate between the choice based techniques of SG, TTO or PTO and there are advocates of all three (Dolan, 2000). None of these techniques simply reflect people's strength of preference for the health state, but include attitudes to risk in SG, time preference in TTO (Bleichrodt, 2002) and equity in PTO. While there have been attempts to remove these other factors, it has so far been incomplete (Salomon and Murray, 2004).

Differences between variants of each technique (for example, methods of administration and valuation procedure) are as important as differences between techniques (Dolan and Sutton, 1997; Brazier and Dolan, 2003). Economic theory does not provide a basis for choosing between variants. This is an important source of inconsistency and needs to be resolved to ensure comparability.

Respondents
Health state values are usually obtained from members of the general public who try to imagine quality of life in the given state, rather than by patients who are actually in that state of health. The source of values has important implications for allocating resources in health care because patients tend to give higher values than the general population (Boyd et al., 1990). The Washington Panel on Cost Effectiveness in Health and Medicine argued that the values of different patient groups are not comparable, whereas a general population sample provides a coherent set of values (Gold et al., 1996). They are sometimes described as 'social values' and so are regarded as more appropriate for resource allocation, but existing preference-based measures actually ask respondents to imagine the state for themselves and not others.

The main argument for using patient values is the fact that patients better understand the impact of a condition. They take better account of adaptations to states of ill health over time. Some adaptation may be regarded as 'laudable', such as skill enhancement and activity adjustment, whereas cognitive denial of functional health, suppressed recognition of full health and lowered expectations may be seen as less desirable (Menzel et al., 2002). Furthermore, there may be a concern that patient values are context based, reflecting their recent experiences of ill health and the health of their immediate peers.

It seems difficult to justify the exclusive use of uninformed members of the general population. Menzel and colleagues therefore suggest a 'third way', where values of the general population inform resource allocation, but the public respondents would be provided with more detailed information on what the states they are rating are like for patients experiencing them.

Selection of health states
The sampling of states depends on the proposed modelling strategy, whether using multi-attribute utility theory (MAUT) or statistical inference. Methods for sampling states using MAUT are explained by Feeny. There is little guidance on selecting samples for statistical modelling. One approach has been to select health states using an orthogonal design to select the states required to estimate an additive model (for example by applying the Orthoplan procedure of SPSS). Often this is supplemented by selecting additional states randomly, but while this does enable the estimation of more sophisticated models it also invalidates the orthogonal design. The allocation of states between respondents must be done with care in order to ensure that respondents face a balance of states between severe, moderate and mild in order to minimize the risk of anchoring. State selection issues are largely unresolved and should be a priority for future research.

Data preparation
The data from valuation surveys must be prepared for the modelling; this may include adjusting the data and considering possible exclusions. Health state valuation work with members of the general public has identified states that are worse than dead. For states

worse than dead using SG, according to expected utility theory, the appropriate value would be $-P/(1-P)$; where P is the valuation of the state. However, this results in a scale ranging from $-\infty$ to $+1$, which gives greater weight to negative values in the calculation of mean scores and presents problems for the statistical analysis. One solution has been to make the value the negative of the indifference probability of the best outcome (Patrick et al., 1994). This has the effect of bounding negative values at minus one. This has no theoretical support and is only one of a number of possible solutions.

Previous studies have 'cleaned' health state valuation data by eliminating respondents who were thought to have been confused by the valuation task (Kaplan et al., 1979; Torrance et al., 1992; Brazier et al., 1998, 2002), where confusion is generally defined as major inconsistencies in the values obtained. Excluding such cases has the advantage of improving the precision of the estimates; however, it reduces the size and the representativeness of the dataset. In addition, care must be taken when interpreting inconsistencies as evidence of confusion. Some inconsistencies may represent simple one-off mistakes and some may reflect departures from the axioms of expected utility theory (EUT) or consumer choice theory more generally (Loomes, 1993).

4.   Modelling

Most descriptive systems describe a large number of possible health states and the empirical survey can obtain valuations for only a small subset. Two main approaches have been used to estimate utility values for all states; the multi-attribute utility approach is explained by Feeny in Chapter 34 in this Companion, so our focus is on the statistical inference method.[1]

The utility associated with a health state is assumed to be a function of that state, hence by estimating a relationship between the descriptive system and the observed values we can infer values for all states. Valuation surveys generate data with a complex structure creating a number of problems for estimation. Busschbach et al. (1999) provide a good explanation of some of these, and here we expand on the issues and cover some recent developments.

Features of the data

Firstly, the distribution of observed health state values can diverge substantially from normality. Left skew and bimodality is common depending on the valuation technique employed. While non-normality is a technical problem, skewness also raises questions about the appropriate measure of central tendency, which essentially determines whose values are given greatest weight, and this is largely a normative issue (Williams, 1992). In the case of highly skewed distributions the mean gives a higher weight to extreme responses, while the median weights all responses equally.

Secondly, data can be modelled at the aggregate level (using, say, the mean value for each state) or at the individual level. This is largely a technical issue, but a view must also be taken about whether one population tariff is sufficient or whether this should vary across different groups according to characteristics like age and sex. Estimating the effect of these factors requires individual level modelling, which also maximizes degrees of freedom. Since each respondent generally values a set of states, variation is between and within respondents. Additionally, respondents generally do not value the same set of states. So the data has a multi-level structure with values clustered by respondent.

Ignoring this structure will result in underestimation of the standard errors with consequent misleading inference.

A further complexity is that the distribution of health state values is generally truncated and non-continuous. For example, SG scores are truncated at an upper limit since chance of treatment failure cannot be less than zero. Additionally the design of most surveys means that respondents can only specify values in discrete ranges. These departures from normality and continuity warrant further transformations of the data (Brazier et al., 2002; Brazier et al., 2001).

Specifying a model

A general additive individual level model for estimating health state values (U_{ij}) is:

$$U_{ij} = g(\beta' \mathbf{x}_{ij} + \theta' \mathbf{r}_{ij} + \partial' \mathbf{z}_j) + \varepsilon_{ij} \qquad (35.1)$$

where $i = 1, 2, \ldots, n$ represents individual health state values; $j = 1, 2, \ldots, m$ are respondents; g is a function specifying the appropriate form employed to account for the skewed, truncated, censored or bimodal distribution of the valuations; ε_{ij} is an error term whose properties depend on the assumptions of the underlying model; $\mathbf{x}$ is a vector of binary dummy variables ($x_{\delta\lambda}$) for each level λ of dimension δ of the descriptive system, with the best level of functioning usually representing the baseline in each case.[2] This is a relatively unrestricted model since the use of these dummies does not assume interval properties or monotonicity for the dimensions.

In a simple linear model, the intercept represents the value of the best health state, which for a generic instrument should be full health, with an expected value of one. However, this estimate has been found to be significantly lower than one in a number of empirical studies (Dolan, 1997; Brazier et al., 2002). There are strong theoretical arguments for restricting the intercept to unity, since the scaling requires a 0–1 death–full health scale.

$\mathbf{r}$ is a vector of terms to account for interactions between the levels of different attributes. Even if we limit consideration to only first order interactions, there will be a large number of possible terms, and little evidence on which are likely to be important. Therefore there is potential for considerable collinearity and the risk of finding spuriously significant interactions. Composite terms that account for the presence of the lowest level of functioning in one or more dimensions are common in the literature (Dolan, 1997; Brazier et al., 2002).[3]

$\mathbf{z}$ is a vector of personal characteristics to take account of observed individual heterogeneity. In empirical studies age, sex, education, marital status and own health have been significantly related to the values given (Dolan and Roberts, 2002; Dolan, 1996).[4]

The most appropriate specification to account for unobserved heterogeneity is the random effects (RE) model which decomposes the error term from (35.1):[5]

$$\varepsilon_{ij} = \mu_j + e_{ij} \qquad (35.2)$$

μ_j is respondent-specific variation, which is assumed to be randomly distributed across individuals and, thus, uncorrelated with $\mathbf{x}$, $\mathbf{r}$ or $\mathbf{z}$. e_{ij} is the usual error term assumed to be random across observations. In addition $\text{cov}(\mu_j, e_{ij}) = 0$, signifying that allocation of states to respondents is random.[6] Estimation of the RE model is via generalized least squares (GLS) or maximum likelihood (MLE).

Model performance

Models must be judged on how well coefficient estimates meet expectations as well as on how well the statistical and econometric assumptions underlying the estimation procedure are upheld. Violations of monotonicity are a serious shortcoming, since they suggest a worse level of functioning is associated with better health. However, in many instruments (both generic and condition-specific) the wording of some dimensions does not suggest a clear ordinal relationship; for example in the SF-6D, level 4 of physical functioning is 'your health limits you a lot in moderate activities', while level 5 is 'your health limits you a little in bathing and dressing'; both theoretically and empirically it is difficult to order these levels. One solution is to aggregate levels until monotonicity is achieved (Brazier and Roberts, 2004).

Given the overall aim of modelling, predictive ability is a central performance criterion; a portion of the observations should be reserved for checking outside sample predictions. Size, bias and systematic patterns in the prediction errors should all be assessed. The latter is often difficult to examine in practice since there is often no obvious a priori ordering of the observations. Brazier et al. (2002) order their prediction errors according to the observed mean values for each health state, but other orderings may also be considered.

While models can be shown to perform reasonably well in estimating average values for each health state, and while uncertainty around the point estimates can be quantified, this still masks the enormous amount of individual variation in preferences that underlies the results. Roberts and Dolan (2004) show that differences in individual preferences for pairs of EQ-5D states are not only cardinal, but also ordinal in that there is a substantial disagreement as to whether the move from one state to another represents an improvement or deterioration in health.

Some recent developments

Kharroubi et al. (2005) have recently used a non-parametric Bayesian method to estimate utilities for the SF-6D. This extremely flexible model includes a multiplicative random effect that can be linked to covariates and retain the feature that full health should have value equal to one. It also incorporates a covariance structure in the prior distribution that mitigates against the non-monotonicity that was found in the parametric valuation model (Brazier et al. 2002).

Salomon (2003) and McCabe et al. (2005b) have derived valuation models for the EQ-5D, HUI2 and SF-6D using rank data. Ranking was conventionally included in health valuation surveys as a warm-up exercise but largely ignored as a source of information on values. Kind (1996) identified Thurstone's (1927) model of comparative judgement as a potential theoretical basis for deriving cardinal preferences from ordinal data, and the recent models employ conditional logistic regression (McFadden, 1974) as a means of modelling the latent utility function.

To date there has been little interest in using data from discrete choice experiments to value health states,[7] although the relatively good performance of the rank data models would suggest that this may be a useful avenue to pursue.

5. Summary and conclusion

This chapter has considered the main issues in developing a preference-based measure; these issues and the basis of their resolution are summarized in Table 35.1. Issues can either be resolved by recourse to theory (for example, the choice-based techniques of valuation), empirical study (for example, the appropriateness of an item) or normative (for example, selection of respondents).

The definition of health is fundamental in the development of an instrument. It defines the scope and nature of the benefits included in an economic evaluation. For cost effectiveness analysis undertaken outside of conventional welfare economics this is ultimately an issue for policy-makers to resolve. However, it is important to bear in mind that the construction of the descriptive system has implications for value, and a view has to be reached about the extent to which the adaptation and choices of patients should be incorporated.

The construction of any measure involves a trade-off between inclusivity and simplicity. Preference-based measures need to be reasonably simple in order to be amenable to valuation. This implies a need to be selective in dimensions covered and it is going to be impossible to construct a truly generic descriptive system. Dimensions and their levels should be selected to best represent the definition of health in terms of content and performance in terms of construct validity. However, there is an empirical question about the impact of excluded dimensions on the value of health states and whether or not respondents need to be explicitly reminded about the consequences for dimensions excluded from the descriptive system.

The choice of valuation technique is partly a matter for theoretical debate, at least between the choice-based methods. The precise variant of method is partly empirical,

Table 35.1   Summary of main issues in developing a preference-based measure

Stage	Issue	Solution
Description	Scope	Normative
	Impairment – disability – participation	Normative
	Generic vs. Specific	Technical
	Item selection	Empirical
Valuation	Valuation technique	Theoretical/normative
	Variant of technique	Empirical/normative
	Respondents	Normative
	Selection of states	Technical
	Data preparation	Normative
Modelling	Statistical inference v MAUF	Normative
	Aggregate v individual modelling	Empirical/normative
	Measure of central tendency	Empirical/normative
	Model specification and functional form	Technical/empirical
	Estimation method	Technical/empirical
	Performance criteria	Technical/empirical

since it depends on their reliability, but also normative. The selection of states should be a largely technical matter, though more work is needed on how best to do it. Data preparation is partly a theoretical matter, since the valuation of states worse than dead is unresolved and the precise exclusion criteria are unclear.

The modelling stage involves a number of problems, most of which have a range of alternative technical solutions via statistical econometric techniques. The choice of appropriate solution is subject to empirical testing; however, it should also be remembered that implicit in a number of the technical solutions are normative choices that have implications for how the results might be interpreted or used.

Empirical study implies the need for further methodological research. This chapter has identified areas for further research. Theoretical disagreement and normative issues cannot be so readily resolved. Where reimbursement agencies are starting to provide guidance for economic evaluation, these issues make up a significant part of the list of recommendations (NICE, 2004). For use in economic evaluation, it is desirable to produce a reference case set of methods in order to promote comparability between studies and to best aid decision-makers.

Notes

1. A recent direct comparison of an MAUF and statistical inference valuation model for the HUI2 suggests that the latter approach has superior predictive performance (McCabe et al., 2005c).
2. A more restricted model might assume interval properties for the dimensions but this is unlikely to be valid, so is not considered here.
3. While various specifications were investigated, the use of interaction terms did not improve the performance of the UK HUI2 model (McCabe et al., 2005c).
4. While health state values have been found to vary systematically according to certain individual characteristics, most evaluation studies use a tariff based on an average of all respondents' values.
5. RE models also account for the clustering of the data by respondent.
6. While allocation of states to respondents is rarely random in valuation surveys, diagnostic tests general support the use of RE models for this data.
7. Hakim and Pathak (1999) is a notable exception.

References

Barton, G.R., J. Bankart, A.C. Davis and Q.A. Summerfield (2004), 'Comparing utility scores before and after hearing-aid provision', *Applied Health Economics and Health Policy*, 3(2), 103–5.

Bleichrodt, H. (2002), 'A new explanation for the difference between time trade-off utilities and standard gamble utilities', *Journal of Health Economics*, 11, 447–56.

Bleichrodt H., J.L. Pinto and J.M. Abellan-Perpiñan (2003), 'A consistency test of the time trade-off', *Journal of Health Economics*, 22(6), 1037–52.

Boyd, N.F., H.J. Sutherland, Z.K. Heasman and B.J. Cummings (1990), 'Whose values for decision making?', *Medical Decision Making*, 10, 58–67.

Brazier, J.E. and M. Deverill (1999), 'A checklist for judging preference-based measures of health related quality of life: learning from psychometrics', *Health Economics*, 8(1), 41–52.

Brazier, J.E. and P. Dolan (2002), 'Evidence of preference construction in a comparison of SG methods', Health Economics Study Group, University of Aberdeen.

Brazier, J.E. and R. Fitzpatrick (2002), 'Measures of health related quality of life in an imperfect world: a comment on Dowie', *Health Economics*, 11, 17–19.

Brazier, J.E. and J. Roberts (2004), 'The estimation of a preference-based measure of health from the SF-12', *Medical Care*, 42(9), 851–9.

Brazier, J., M. Deverill and C. Green (1999), 'A review of the use health status measures in economic evaluation', *Journal of Health Services Research and Policy*, 4(3), 174–84.

Brazier, J.E., N. Rice and J. Roberts (2001), 'Modelling health state valuation data', in C. Murray, J. Salomon, C. Mathers, A. Lopez and R. Lozano (eds), *Summary Measures of Population Health*, Geneva: World Health Organization, Chapter 10.3.

Brazier, J.E., J. Roberts and M. Deverill (2002), 'The estimation of a preference-based measure of health from the SF-36', *Journal of Health Economics*, **21**(2), 271–92.

Brazier, J.E., C. Green, C. McCabe and K. Stevens (2003), 'A review of VAS in Economic Evaluation', *Journal of Pharmacoeconomics and Outcomes Research*, **3**(3), 293–302.

Brazier, J.E., A. Tsuchiya, J. Roberts and J. Busschbach (2004), 'A comparison of the EQ-5D and the SF-6D across seven patient groups', *Health Economics*, **13**(90), 873–84.

Brazier, J.E., R. Harper, K. Thomas, N. Jones and T. Underwood (1998), 'Deriving a preference based single index measure from the SF-36', *Journal of Clinical Epidemiology*, **51**(11), 1115–29.

Brooks, R. and EuroQol Group (1996), 'EuroQol: the current state of play', *Health Policy*, **37**, 53–72.

Busschbach, J.J.V., J. McDonnell, M.-L. Essink-Bot and B.A. van Hout (1999), 'Estimating parametric relationships between health description and health valuation with an application to the Euroqol EQ-5D', *Journal of Health Economics*, **18**, 551–71.

Commonwealth Department of Health, Housing and Community Service (1992), '*Guidelines for the Pharmaceutical Industry on the Submission to the Pharmaceutical Benefits Advisory Committee*', Canberra: Australian Government Publishing Service.

Dolan, P. (1996), 'The effect of experience of illness on health state valuations', *Journal of Clinical Epidemiology*, **49**, 551–64.

Dolan, P. (1997), 'Modelling valuation for EuroQol health states', *Medical Care*, **35**, 351–63.

Dolan, P. (2000), 'The measurement of health related quality of life for use in resource allocation in health care', in A.J. Culyer and J.P. Newhouse (eds), *Handbook of Health Economics, volume 1*, Amsterdam: Elsevier Science.

Dolan P. and J. Roberts (2002), 'To what extent can we explain time trade-off values from other information about respondents?', *Social Science and Medicine*, **54**(6), 919–29.

Dolan, P. and M. Sutton (1997), 'Mapping VAS scores onto TTO and SG utilities', *Social Science and Medicine*, **44**, 1289–97.

Donaldson, C., A. Atkinson, J. Bond and K. Wright (1988), 'QALYS and long-term care for elderly people in the UK: scales for assessment of quality of life', *Age. Ageing*, **17**, 379–87.

Drummond, M.F., B. O'Brien, G.L. Stoddart and G.W. Torrance (1997), *Methods for the Economic Evaluation of Health Care Programmes*, 2nd edn, Oxford: Oxford Medical Publications.

Espallargues, M., C. Czoski-Murray, N. Bansback, J. Carlton, G. Lewis, L. Hughes, C. Brand and J. Brazier (forthcoming), 'The impact of age related macular degeneration on health state utility values', *Investigative Ophthalmology and Visual Science*.

EuroQol Group (1990), 'EuroQol – a new facility for the measurement of health-related quality-of-life', *Health Policy*, **16**, 199–208.

Evans, R.G. and A.D. Wolfson (1980), 'Faith, hope and charity: health care in the utility function', Department of Economics, University of British Columbia and Department of Health Administration, University of Toronto, unpublished paper.

Feeney, D., W. Furlong, M. Boyle and G.W. Torrance (1995), 'Multi-attribute health status classification systems: health utilities index', *PharmacoEconomics*, **7**, 490–502.

Feeney, D.H., W.J. Furlong, G.W. Torrance, C.H. Goldsmith, Z. Zenglong, S. Depauw, M. Denton and M. Boyle (2002), 'Multi-attribute and single-attribute utility functions for the Health Utility Index Mark 3 System', *Medical Care*, **40**(2), 113–28.

Gold, M.R., J.E. Siegel, L.B. Russell and M.C. Weinstein (1996), *Cost-Effectiveness in Health and Medicine*, Oxford: Oxford University Press.

Green, C., J. Brazier and M. Deverill (2000), 'Valuing health-related quality of life: A review of health state valuation techniques', *PharmacoEconomics*, **17**(2), 151–65.

Guyatt, G. Commentary on Jack Dowie, (2002), 'Decision validity should determine a generic of condition-specific HRQOL measure is used in health care decisions', *Health Economics*, **11**, 9–12.

Hakim, Z. and D.S. Pathak (1999), 'Modelling the EuroQol data: a comparison of discrete choice conjoint and conditional preference modelling', *Health Economics*, **8**(2), 103–16.

Kaplan, R.M., J.W. Bush and C.C. Berry (1979), 'Health status index: category rating versus magnitude estimation for measuring levels of well-being', *Medical Care*, **17**, 501–25.

Kharroubi, S., A. O'Hagan and J.E. Brazier (forthcoming), 'Estimating utilities from individual health preference data: a nonparametric Bayesian method', *Journal of Applied Statistics*.

Kind, P. (1996), 'Deriving cardinal scales from ordinal preference data: the analysis of time trade-off data using pairwise judgement models', paper presented to HESG Brunel University.

Kobelt, G., I. Kirchberger and J. Malone-Lee (1999), 'Quality of life aspects of the overactive bladder and the effect of treatment with tolterodine', *British Journal of Urology*, **83**, 583–90.

Longworth, L. and S. Bryan (2003), 'An empirical comparison of EQ-5D and SF-6D in liver transplant patients', *Health Economics*, **12**, 1061–7.

Loomes, G. (1993), 'Disparities between health state measures: is there a rational explanation?', in W. Gerrard (ed.), *The Economics of Rationality*, London: Routledge.

McCabe, C., K. Stevens, J. Brazier and J. Roberts (2005a), 'Health state values for the HUI II descriptive system: initial results from a UK survey', *Health Economics*. **14**(3), 231–44.

McCabe, C., J. Brazier, P. Gilks, A. Tsuchiya, J. Roberts, A. O'Hagan and K. Stevens (2005b), 'Estimating population cardinal health state valuation models from individual ordinal (rank) health state preference data', *Journal of Health Economics* (forthcoming).

McCabe, C., K. Stevens, J. Brazier and J. Roberts (2005c), 'MAUF vs. statistical inference models: a comparison of health state valuation', mimeo, ScHARR, University of Sheffield.

McFadden, D. (1974), 'Conditional Logit analysis of qualitative choice behaviour', in P. Zarembka (ed.), *Frontiers in Econometrics*, New York: Academic Press, pp. 105–42.

Menzel, P., O. Dolan, J. Richardson and J.A. Olsen (2002), 'The role of adaptation to disability and disease in health state valuation: a preliminary normative analysis', *Social Science and Medicine*, **55**(12), 2149–58.

Miller, G.A. (1956), 'The magical number seven, plus or minus two: some limits on our capacity for processing information', *The Psychological Review*, **63**(2), 81–97.

Ministry of Health (Ontario) (1994), *Ontario Guidelines for the Economic Evaluation of Pharmaceutical Products*, Toronto: Ministry of Health.

National Institute for Clinical Excellence (NICE) (2004), *NICE Guide to the Methods of Technology Appraisal*, London: NICE.

O'Brien, B.J., M. Spath, G. Blackhouse, J.L. Severens and J.E. Brazier (2004), 'A view from the bridge: agreement between the SF-6D utility algorithm and the Health Utilities Index', *Health Economics*, **12**(11), 975–82.

Patrick, D.L., H.E. Starks, K.C. Cain, R.F. Uhlmann and R.A. Pearlman (1994), 'Measuring preferences for health states worse than death', *Medical Decision Making*, **14**, 9–18.

Roberts, J. and P. Dolan (2004), 'To what extent do people prefer health states with higher values? A note on evidence from the EQ-5D valuation set', *Health Economics*, **13**(7), 733–37.

Salomon, J.A. (2003), 'Reconsidering the use of rankings in the valuation of health states: a model for estimating cardinal values from ordinal data', *Population Health Metrics*, **1**(12).

Salomon, J.A. and C.J.L. Murray (2004), 'A multi-method approach for measuring health state valuations', *Health Economics*, **13**, 281–90.

Thurstone, L.L. (1927), 'A law of comparative judgement', *Psychological Review*, **34**, 273–86.

Torrance, G.W., Y. Zhang, D. Feeny, W. Furlong and R. Barr (1992), 'Multi-attribute preference functions for a comprehensive health status classification system', discussion paper, Hamilton, Ontario: Centre for Health Economics and Policy Analysis McMaster University.

Ware, J.E. (1987), 'Standards for validating health measures: definition and content', *Journal of Chronic Diseases*, **40**(6), 473–80.

Williams, A. (1992), 'Measuring functioning and well-being', by Stewart and Ware, review article, *Health Economics*, **1**(4), 255–58.

World Health Organization (1948), 'Constitution of the World Health Organization', basic documents, Geneva, Switzerland: WHO.

World Health Organization (1980), 'International classification of impairments, disabilities and handicaps', Geneva: WHO.

36 The elicitation of distributional judgements in the context of economic evaluation
Paul Dolan and Aki Tsuchiya*

1. Simple QALY maximization: the assumption that a QALY is a QALY is a QALY

Standard economic evaluation estimates the efficiency of a given health care intervention. It contributes towards selecting the best set of health care interventions that will maximize health across a population subject to limited resources. The most common way in which health benefits are measured is in terms of Quality Adjusted Life Years (QALYs), which express quality of life and length of life in a single index number. One QALY is equivalent to one year of life in full health. The current practice of cost-per-QALY analysis assumes that the social value of a QALY is the same irrespective of to whom it goes, and thus applies the principle of 'a QALY is a QALY is a QALY'.

This chapter is about going beyond this principle, by exploring whether the value of a QALY might depend on to whom it goes, and why. As modern welfare economics suggests, it may be unproductive to try to derive meaningful and objective statements about how important my QALY is to me as compared to how important your QALY is to you. However, it may be possible to derive meaningful and objective statements about the relative importance of our QALYs *to society*. Therefore, the principle of 'a QALY is a QALY is a QALY' at the social level, where public policy decisions are made, can be empirically tested by examining whether or not members of the public support it.

The next section presents four different theoretical arguments that challenge the assumption that all QALYs are created equal, one based on efficiency, two based on vertical equity, and one based on horizontal equity. We then present a brief review of the rapidly growing empirical literature that examines the support for the principle of 'a QALY is a QALY is a QALY' by members of the public. This is followed by a section that presents a series of considerations involved in designing such empirical studies, and we conclude with some remarks about the best way forward; namely, to relate empirical evidence to theoretical reasons for QALY weights, and then to elicit such weights.

2. Theoretical arguments: should all QALYs be equal?

The standard approach of valuing all QALYs equally is in stark contrast to the approach underlying cost–benefit analysis, where the value of a unit of health gain will be a function of the willingness to pay of the (potential and/or actual) recipients of a given health gain. Because willingness to pay is a function of ability to pay, it is likely that a unit of

* We are grateful to comments provided by our collaborators – John Brazier, Stirling Bryan, Dick Eiser, Amy Hukin, Julie Ratcliffe, Martin Smith, Jan Abel Olsen – on a project funded by the National Co-ordinating Centre for Research Methodology and the National Institute for Clinical Excellence to look at the relative value of health gains to different beneficiaries. We would also like to thank Alan Williams for his support in developing (and sometimes criticizing) our ideas.

health gain would be valued more highly by a rich person than by a poor person. The principle of 'a QALY is a QALY is a QALY' claims that the value of a unit of health improvement is the same regardless of the characteristics of the population. In other words, it is in line with a particular egalitarian view that everybody's health should be valued equally. However, there are four main arguments against this view.

Counter-argument based on efficiency
The first one is based on efficiency. If the current distribution of income is ethically defensible, then a libertarian perspective will argue that individuals who have more to contribute to society should be rewarded more extensively than those who have less to contribute or those who are net dependants. So, if the rich are willing and able to pay more for a unit of health gain to themselves than the poor, this should be reflected in the value of that health benefit. Furthermore, it may also be acceptable that the health of those who have more to contribute should be valued more highly than others, since the fruits of human capital and productivity of such people could trickle down and contribute to a richer society overall. If so, it would be inefficient, and possibly detrimental to all, if the health of the more productive was not valued higher and thus given higher priority for health care.

If income is seen as unfairly distributed, then the 'worth' of one person's health as compared to another might be determined by a criterion other than income: for example, age. New-borns are completely dependent on others but, as they grow up and become adults, they become more productive and will contribute towards supporting younger and elderly members of the community, after which they will slowly become less productive and more dependent on others again. An important aspect of age is that its initial endowment and subsequent pathway is fair: everybody starts from zero and each of us earns one year of age each year (Tsuchiya, 1999). In order to adjust for the inefficiency implied by the 'QALY is a QALY is a QALY' approach, efficiency-based age weights have been designed for and used by the World Bank (1993).

Counter-arguments based on vertical equity
The next two counter-arguments to the principle that all QALYs are created equal are based on concerns for vertical equity. It may be regarded as egalitarian in some respects to claim that everybody's health is of equal value regardless of their willingness and ability to pay for their own health. However, given that the rich are more likely to have access to a range of health-promoting goods and services, such as a healthy lifestyle, than the poor, they are also likely to be more cost-effective to treat. So, if the rich and the poor receive the same treatment for the same medical condition, using the same value for health gains to the rich and the poor is likely to favour treatments for the rich. Standard cost-per-QALY analysis by patient income groups will then suggest, all else being equal, giving a higher priority to treating the rich than the poor. Or, similar scenarios are possible for other attributes, such as being severely ill, or being old. Poor health prospects associated with these groups predict that treating them may be less cost-effective than treating others. However, their poor health prospects call for vertical equity, which demands that a unit of health improvement to them to be weighed more than a unit of health improvement to those whose health prospects without treatment are much better (Olsen et al., 2003).

Whereas the above argument for vertical equity is based on unequal health, vertical equity can also be relevant when something other than health is unequal. For instance, if a group of patients are seen to be responsible for their own ill health, they may be held accountable, and thus their unit health improvement may be given a lower weight than the same health improvement to another group of patients with identical medical characteristics but who are not held responsible for their own ill health (Le Grand, 1987). Similar arguments may be possible, for example, for those who have had intensive use of health care resources in the past (Dolan and Olsen, 2001), or those whose ill health is caused by the medical system.

To the extent that the relevance of these vertical equity arguments can be quantified, either or both can be expressed in terms of weights that represent the degree by which a QALY to patients of different medical or non-medical characteristics is valued more or less than an average or reference QALY. However, to the best of our knowledge, there are no economic evaluations in the health care field that incorporate vertical equity-based QALY weights of either kind.

Counter-argument based on horizontal equity
Finally, there are distributional considerations that are based on horizontal equity, which deals with patients with the same characteristics, both medical and non-medical. Horizontal equity implies aversion to unequal distributions so that if there is a fixed total health benefit to be distributed across a given number of people, it will be more preferable for everybody to have a smaller share than for a select few to have a larger share (Olsen, 2000; Williams and Cookson, 2000). A variation of this is the fair innings argument (Williams, 1997), which is based on an aversion to unequal distributions of lifetime health across people. Since this will in effect translate into the size of the health benefit per person, it is conceivable to draw up an equity weight that corrects for the size of health gains. However, as above, there are currently no cost-per-QALY analyses that employ horizontal equity weights.

3.   Review of the empirical evidence: do people think all QALYs are equal?
There has been a proliferation of papers in recent years that, in various ways, have looked at whether the social value of a given health benefit might vary according to certain health and non-health characteristics of the recipient. The following summary of existing evidence is based largely on a recent systematic review of the literature for the NHS Health Technology Assessment Programme, on the principle of 'a QALY is a QALY is a QALY' (Dolan et al., 2005).

Whereas the theory of applying non-uniform weights to QALYs can be classified as in the above section, it is not always straightforward to group the empirical findings in matching categories. For example, suppose it is found that members of the public think a unit of health gain to those from the lower social classes should be given larger weight than the rest of the population. This may be because of the first vertical equity argument, due to their poorer health. But it may also be because of the second vertical equity argument, due to their socioeconomic disadvantage; or even the efficiency based argument, if it is perceived that lower social class is the result of the ill health, rather than the cause. For this reason, the evidence is presented below in relation to three categories, which only loosely correspond to the classification of arguments above: first, where the health of the patients is expected to vary depending on the characteristic in question (severity, urgency, social class, sex and age); second, where it is not expected to vary (responsibility for condition, previous use of health care, and dependants); and third, where a fixed total health benefit is distributed across different numbers of people.

Attributes across which health is expected to vary
The same size of health benefit can be valued more highly if it is given to those with a more *severe* initial quality of life than less (Nord, 1995; Dolan, 1998; Ubel, 1999; Gyrd-Hansen, 2004). However, two UK studies suggest that people may wish to give benefits to those in better health if those in poorer health are left in health states considered to be below a certain, as yet unquantified, threshold (Roberts et al., 1997; Dolan and Green, 1998). There is also a social preference for giving priority to those with more *urgent* conditions (Shmueli, 1999), although this might also be subject to some threshold effect (Dolan and Cookson, 2000). Severity and urgency both appeal to the first vertical equity argument, due to unequal health.

Some studies have also shown a willingness to target the lower *social classes* at the expense of maximizing overall health benefits (Lindholm and Rosen, 1998; Dolan et al., 1999; Emmelin et al., 1999; Dolan et al., 2002; Schwappach, 2003; Abásolo and Tsuchiya, 2004). Social class is related to the first, and possibly also to the second, vertical equity arguments. On the other hand, inequality in life expectancy across the *sexes* leads to results implying that respondents are not interested in reducing the inequality (Dolan et al., 2002). Thus, it looks as if the two vertical equity arguments cancel each other out (the first will favour men, and the second will favour women).

In relation to *age*, where both efficiency-based and equity-based arguments can be relevant, the majority of the empirical evidence is supportive of giving greater weight to younger people (for example, Nord et al., 1996; Rodriguez and Pinto, 2000; Tsuchiya, 2001; Schwappach, 2003; also see Tsuchiya, 1999 for a review). However, only one study (using a UK general population sample) has attempted to control for the size of the benefit, so it is not possible at this stage to say how a given benefit is weighted across different age groups (Tsuchiya et al., 2003).

Attributes across which health is not necessarily expected to vary
There is some evidence to support the view that people who are themselves considered to be *responsible* for the ill health should be given lower priority, (Ubel et al., 2001; Dolan and Tsuchiya, 2003), but this does not always hold (Schwappach, 2003). Evidence regarding *previous use* of health care is mixed: people were willing to give priority to second-time liver transplant patients, which may be interpreted as those patients let down by medicine on their first round (Ratcliffe, 2000). But when the previous care was described more generally, they were not given higher priority (Schwappach, 2003). Responsibility and previous use are based on vertical equity considerations. There is something of a consensus that we should discriminate in favour of those *with dependants* (Neuberger et al., 1998; Dolan et al., 1999; Browning and Thomas, 2001), although Edwards et al. (1999) is an exception. It is not always clear whether this preference for those with dependants is based on an efficiency reason (for example treating the parents will also benefit the child),

or an equity reason (for example it is unfair that some children should lose their parents prematurely).

The dispersion of fixed health benefits
This is the only category of empirical studies that corresponds fully to one of the theoretical arguments above: horizontal equity. There is evidence that people are not indifferent concerning the distribution of a given benefit (Choudhry et al., 1997; Olsen, 2000; Ubel et al., 1996; Ubel et al., 2000; Bleichrodt et al., forthcoming). Generally, they prefer to *disperse* benefits as widely as possible but, if the benefits going to any one individual are considered to be too small, they prefer to *concentrate* benefits amongst fewer people instead. However, there is evidence of a threshold effect (Rodriguez-Miguez and Pinto-Prades, 2002), although it is premature to say much about where that threshold might be. The evidence currently available suggests that simply maximizing QALY gains across the population is not the best use of limited resources according to people's preferences, but, with the exception of Bleichrodt et al. (forthcoming), it does not allow us to estimate equity weights for QALYs.

4.   Considerations for the elicitation of distributional judgements on the value of a QALY
There are many issues that any empirical study would have to consider, and below we discuss some of the most important of these. Some considerations are relevant to the design of any study involving social surveys, such as how the questions are worded, or who the respondents are, but we have concentrated on issues that are pertinent to studies designed to elicit people's preferences regarding the relative value of a QALY. There are roughly two types of study designs. One type consists of those that have an explicit numeraire. For instance, the Person Trade Off design (Nord, 1995) will ask respondents to indicate indifference between a smaller number of people with attributes that respondents want to give higher priority to (for example poor, and have severe condition) and a larger number of people with other attributes (for example rich, and have mild condition). So the number of people is the numeraire. A parallel Benefit Trade Off exercise (see for example Tsuchiya et al., 2003) is possible where respondents are asked to balance a smaller size benefit to a fixed number of people with more preferable attributes and a larger benefit to the same number of people with less preferable attributes, so the size of the benefit is the numeraire. The other type of design is where there is no explicit numeraire to elicit the point of indifference. So, with a Discrete Choice Experiment design (see the chapters in this Companion by Ryan, Gerard and Currie, Chapter 38, and by Burgess, Street, Viney and Louviere, Chapter 39), respondents can be shown pairs of patient groups, defined in terms of socioeconomic class, severity, number of people, size of health benefit if treated, and so on, and asked which should get priority. The concerns discussed here are relevant to all these different designs.

Perspective
Most of the existing studies have adopted a social perspective, in which respondents are asked to consider allocation decisions by which they personally may not be affected. Standard economic theory is concerned with the optimizing behaviour of self-interested individuals, and so many economists are rather distrustful of preferences that contain no

self-interest at all. However, although self-interest exists, it does not necessarily follow that it must – or should – be the basis for public policy decision-making. Indeed, if individuals can be said to have preferences as citizens as opposed to consumers, who are motivated by some notion of what is good for the society they are part of, then this type of preference can be used to form the basis of policy (Menzel, 1999). At a practical level, if an ethically defensible set of society-regarding preferences can be derived from forms of ethical reasoning that are clearly distinguished from self-interest, a social perspective might be a legitimate one (Dolan et al., 2003). The societal perspective can be operationalized in two ways. One is by indicating that the respondents themselves are not directly affected by the scenarios, and the other is by indicating that they are to imagine themselves making decisions for a community to which they themselves belong. The latter is sometimes called the societal inclusive perspective. In order to establish whether the social perspective is being achieved, the effect of self-interest on the results can be tested.

Context
'Context' here can encompass various aspects, but two that are most relevant to the elicitation of weights for QALYs are context as response format and context as representation. The former relates to effect of the types and categories of responses that are available to respondents and other kinds of framing such as wording. It suggests that any trade-offs are treated with caution, recognizing that they have been generated in a particular way with particular properties, which also implies a difficulty in taking any given response (out of context) as equivalent to any absolute magnitude. Context as representation means that respondents need to make the questions they are asked meaningful, and there is considerable evidence that individuals provide normatively 'rational' answers if the problems are presented in more concrete rather than abstract terms (Gigerenzer and Hoffrage, 1995). There are of course methodological concerns about whether, by making a problem more 'concrete', one is introducing additional information that could bias people's judgements in unanticipated ways. It is important, therefore, to compare responses to abstract and concrete questions, which will further serve to enhance the robustness of the data generated. Furthermore, there is the issue of decision-making context. Judgements that are appropriate and acceptable at the individual patient level may not be so at a regional or national policy level, and vice versa.

Deliberation
It is often argued that relatively 'cold' elicitation methods (such as postal surveys) provide more representative accounts of preferences, while methods that involve more deliberation result in better informed and more considered views, which may also be more stable across time; but this is associated with the danger that the elicitation process itself moves the views of the respondents away from the position of the average citizen. And what conclusions should we draw about deliberation if different deliberative methods produce different results? However, deliberative preferences may be taken more seriously by politicians than 'off the cuff' and volatile preferences. Not only are they institutionalized in the sense that they are derived from within a wider democratic legitimacy, but there is also evidence that politicians are increasingly taking account of the considered preferences of 'stakeholders' in such areas as housing and transport. More specifically, deliberation can

be encouraged in several ways. One way is to present vignettes representing conflicting positions and then encourage respondents to consider the problem from different points of view. Or, a small set of relevant philosophical theories can be presented. Another is to break down complex scenarios into simpler issues, for instance by using attitudinal questions. Implications of different alternatives can also be considered, by exploring the opportunity costs of a given choice. These can be done on an individual respondent basis, or through group discussions. Deliberation can also be used to establish the reasons for the choices respondents make. Whether or not the observed preferences are stable across time at the individual respondent level can be an indirect test of the effect of deliberation, since the extent of consideration underlying a preference is likely to be related to how firmly people hold the preferences. However, also note that individual responses may be unstable across time and yet aggregate responses may be stable, which may be satisfactory in some contexts.

Quantification
As was noted above, while the number of empirical studies on people's preferences regarding the principle of 'a QALY is a QALY is a QALY' is rapidly growing, few allow the derivation of implied efficiency and/or equity weights. Empirical studies typically report the proportion of respondents whose preferences are or are not consistent with the principle, but in order to derive the weights, strengths of these preferences need to be elicited. Also, given that there are several areas such as severity or distribution of fixed benefits where evidence of threshold effects have been found, it should not be assumed that the weight profile will be linear. A further interest is eliciting preferences for combinations of attributes. For example, which patients should be given higher priority: those who are rich and who have an urgent condition or those who are poor and have a non-urgent condition? Here, the effect of being rich or poor counteracts the effect of the urgency of the condition, and little is known on how members of the public will combine multiple considerations.

Drawing on these issues, we propose a methodological checklist for empirical studies in Table 36.1. This is not necessarily to promote a particular approach, but to illustrate the set of possible alternatives involved in the design of such a study. It can also be used as a guide when reviewing existing studies.

5.   Weighted QALY maximization

This chapter has discussed the various possibilities of moving on from the uniform weighted cost-per-QALY analysis, based on the principle that all QALYs are of equal value. There are efficiency and equity reasons to depart from this principle, and there is also empirical evidence to suggest that there are contexts in which people do not support this principle. However, there are two important steps that need to be cleared before weighted QALY maximization can become the norm in economic evaluation.

First, there needs to be an improved link between the theoretical arguments and the empirical results. The derivation of QALY weights representing health-related quality of life of different health states was carried out mostly from the consumer perspective, asking respondents to imagine themselves or somebody like them to be in the health states in question (see for example the chapters in this Companion by Bleichrodt and Pinto, 33; Feeny, 34; and Brazier and Roberts, 35). In this context, the reason why certain health

Table 36.1   *Proposed checklist on issues that are pertinent to studies designed to elicit people's preferences regarding the relative value of a QALY*

Checklist item	Possible response categories
Does it tap into societal (citizen) preferences or private (consumer) preferences, or some combination?	Social/social inclusive/private
Is there a test to see whether results are motivated by self-interest?	Yes/No
What level in the resource allocation process is the scenario aimed at?	Bedside level/local community or local facility level/national policy level
Does it test for a threshold effect regarding the size of the benefit?	Yes/No
What is the level of detail given?	Names disease: Yes/No Names intervention: Yes/No Gives names to patients: Yes/No Gives reasons behind scenario: Yes/No Indicates consequences of choices: Yes/No Indicates cost implications to different parties: Yes/No
What is the mode of administration?	Telephone/Postal/Interview/Computer/Group/Other
Does it allow opportunity for deliberation, and by what means?	Yes/No If Yes: Individual/Group Vignettes/Theories/Attitudes/Other
Does it elicit the reasons for the preferences, which are linked to theoretical arguments?	Yes/No
Is there a test of the stability of the results through time?	Individual level: Yes/No Group level: Yes/No
Is there a test for potential framing effects?	Yes/No
Would it be possible to derive quantitative relative weights from the results?	Yes/No
Does it address one attribute at a time, or multiple attributes at the same time?	Single/Multiple

states are given low values is of less importance. However, in the current context, the elicited values are about the relative value of health to different people, which comes very close to the relative value of different people, and research needs to probe into the reasons why certain attributes are given lower value than others. The line between giving the poor larger weight because of concern for their deprived condition and giving the rich smaller weight because of resentment towards their privileged lifestyle may be quite fine. It has to be acknowledged that not all preferences held by members of the public may be suitable on which to base policy decision-making.

Second, many studies have been designed from the perspective of questioning the acceptability of simple unweighted QALY maximization, but not necessarily from the perspective of eliciting the strength of the unequal value of different QALYs so that the results can be used as a basis to draw up various efficiency and/or equity weights for QALYs.

Thus, further research is required to better understand the reasons and the strengths of people's preferences, and we have provided some guidance about how this work can be taken forward. What it involves is for researchers to make deliberate and considered choices in designing empirical studies, which implies having some notion of relative weights to be attached to the relevance and importance of each item on the checklist.

References

Abásolo, I. and A. Tsuchiya (2004), 'Exploring social welfare functions and violation of monotonicity: An example from inequalities in health', *Journal of Health Economics*, **23**(2), 313–29.

Bleichrodt, H., J. Doctor and E. Stolk (forthcoming), 'A nonparametric elicitation of the equity–efficiency trade-off in cost–utility analysis', *Journal of Health Economics*.

Browning, C.J. and S.A. Thomas (2001), 'Community values and preferences in transplantation organ allocation decisions', *Social Science & Medicine*, **52**(6), 853–61.

Choudhry, N., P. Slaughter, K. Sykora and D. Naylor (1997), 'Distributional dilemmas in health policy: large benefits for a few or smaller benefits for many?', *Journal of Health Services Research and Policy*, **2**, 212–16.

Dolan, P. (1998), 'The measurement of individual utility and social welfare', *Journal of Health Economics*, **17**(1), 39–52.

Dolan, P. and R. Cookson (2000), 'A qualitative study of the extent to which health gain matters when choosing between groups of patients', *Health Policy*, **51**(1), 19–30.

Dolan, P. and C. Green (1998), 'Using the person trade-off approach to examine differences between individual and social values', *Health Economics*, **7**(4), 307–12.

Dolan, P. and J.A. Olsen (2001), 'Equity in health: the importance of different health streams', *Journal of Health Economics*, **20**(5), 823–34.

Dolan, P. and A. Tsuchiya (2003), 'The social welfare function and individual responsibility: Some theoretical issues and empirical evidence from health', Sheffield Health Economics Group, University of Sheffield, Discussion Paper Series 03/1 http://www.shef.ac.uk/~sheg/discussion/discussion.htm

Dolan, P., R. Cookson and B. Ferguson (1999), 'Effect of discussion and deliberation on the public's view of priority setting in health care: focus group study', *British Medical Journal*, **318**(7188), 916–19.

Dolan, P., J. Olsen, P. Menzel and J. Richardson (2003), 'An inquiry into the different perspectives that can be used when eliciting preferences in health', *Health Economics*, **12**, 545–51.

Dolan, P., R. Shaw, A. Tsuchiya and A. Williams (2005), 'QALY maximisation and people's preferences: A methodological review of the literature', *Health Economics*, **14**, 197–208.

Dolan, P., A. Tsuchiya, P. Smith, R. Shaw and A. Williams (2002), 'Determining the parameters in a social welfare function using stated preference data: An application to health', Sheffield Health Economics Group, University of Sheffield, Discussion Paper Series 02/2 http://www.shef.ac.uk/~sheg/discussion/discussion.htm

Edwards, R.T., A. Boland, C. Wilkinson, D. Cohen and J. Williams, (1999), 'Choosing explicit criteria for the prioritisation of elective NHS waiting lists : survey evidence of clinical and lay preferences from Wales', paper presented at the Health Economists Study Group Meeting.

Emmelin, M.A.C., L.A. Lindholm, H.C. Stenlund and L.G. Dahlgren (1999), 'Pol-ethical considerations in public health – the views of Swedish health care politicians', *European Journal of Public Health*, **9**(2), 124–30.

Gigerenzer, G. and U. Hoffrage (1995), 'How to improve Bayesian reasoning without instruction: Frequency formats,' *Psychological Review*, **102**, 684–704.

Gyrd-Hansen, D. (2004), 'Investigating the social value of health changes', *Journal of Health Economics*, **23**(6), 1101–16.

Le Grand, J. (1987), 'Equity, health and health care', *Social Justice Research*, **1**, 257–74.

Lindholm, L. and M. Rosen (1998), 'On the measurement of the nation's equity adjusted health', *Health Economics*, **7**(7), 621–8.

Menzel, P. (1999), 'How should what economists call "social values" be measured?', *The Journal of Ethics*, **3**, 249–73.

Neuberger, J., D. Adams, P. MacMaster, A. Maidment and M. Speed (1998), 'Assessing priorities for allocation of donor liver grafts: survey of public and clinicians', *British Medical Journal*, **317**(7152), 172–5.

Nord, E. (1995), 'The person-trade-off approach to valuing health-care programs', *Medical Decision Making*, **15**(3), 201–8.

Nord, E., A. Street, J. Richardson, H. Kuhse and P. Singer (1996), 'The significance of age and duration of effect in social evaluation of health care', *Health Care Analysis*, **4**(2), 103–11.

Olsen, J.A. (2000), 'A note on eliciting distributive preferences for health', *Journal of Health Economics*, **19**(4), 541–50.

Olsen, J.A., J. Richardson, P. Dolan and P. Menzel (2003), 'The moral relevance of personal characteristics in setting health care priorities', *Social Science and Medicine*, **57**, 1163–72.

Ratcliffe, J. (2000), 'Public preferences for the allocation of donor liver grafts for transplantation', *Health Economics*, **9**(2), 137–48.

Roberts, T., S. Bryan and C. Heinbotham (1997), 'Public involvement in health care priority setting: an economic perspective', *Health Expectations*, **2**, 235–44.

Rodriguez, E. and J.L. Pinto (2000), 'The social value of health programmes: Is age a relevant factor?', *Health Economics*, **9**(7), 611–21.

Rodriguez-Miguez, E. and J.L. Pinto-Prades (2002), 'Measuring the social importance of concentration or dispersion of individual health benefits', *Health Economics*, **11**, 43–53.

Schwappach, D. (2003), 'Does it matter who you are or what you gain? An experimental study of preferences for resource allocation', *Health Economics*, **12**(4), 255–62.

Shmueli, A. (1999), 'Survival vs. quality of life: a study of the Israeli public priorities in medical care', *Social Science & Medicine*, **49**(3), 297–302.

Tsuchiya, A. (1999), 'Age-related preferences and age weighting health benefits', *Social Science and Medicine*, **48**(2), 267–76.

Tsuchiya, A. (2001), 'The value of health at different ages', Centre for Health Economics, University of York, Discussion Paper 184.

Tsuchiya, A., P. Dolan and R. Shaw (2003), 'Measuring people's preferences regarding ageism in health: some methodological issues and some fresh evidence', *Social Science and Medicine*, **57**, 687–96.

Ubel, P.A. (1999), 'How stable are people's preferences for giving priority to severely ill patients?', *Social Science & Medicine*, **49**(7), 895–903.

Ubel, P.A., J. Baron, B. Nash and D.A. Asch (2000), 'Are preferences for equity over efficiency in health care allocation "all or nothing"?' *Medical Care*, **38**(4), 366–73.

Ubel, P.A., M.L Dekay, J. Baron and D.A. Asch (1996), 'Cost-effectiveness analysis in a setting of budget constraints – is it equitable?', *New England Journal of Medicine*, **334**(18), 1174–7.

Ubel, P.A., C. Jepson, J. Baron, T. Mohr, S. McMorrow and D.A. Asch (2001), 'Allocation of transplantable organs: do people want to punish patients for causing their illness?', *Liver Transplantation*, **7**(7), 600–607.

Williams, A. (1997), 'Intergenerational equity: an exploration of the "fair innings" argument', *Health Economics*, **6**, 117–32.

Williams, A. and R. Cookson (2000), 'Equity in health', in A.J. Culyer and J.P. Newhouse (eds), *Handbook of Health Economics*, Vol. 1B, Amsterdam: Elsevier Science.

World Bank (1993), *World Development Report 1993: Investing in Health*, Oxford: Oxford University Press.

37 Contingent valuation in health care
Cam Donaldson, Helen Mason and Phil Shackley

1. Introduction

> Political economy has to take as the measure of utility of an object the maximum sacrifice which
> each consumer would be willing to make in order to acquire the object . . . the only real utility
> is that which people are willing to pay for. (Dupuit, 1844, p. 262)

Despite the concept of willingness to pay (WTP) having been around for longer, it has
been used to value the benefits of publicly-provided goods only since the 1960s
(Davis, 1963). Most notable early studies involved valuing risk reductions, and thus
statistical life, in transport safety (Jones-Lee, 1974; 1976; Mooney, 1977), and WTP to
avoid heart attacks (Acton, 1973). Given that, for many publicly-funded goods, WTP
cannot be observed in a functioning market, such values are elicited hypothetically,
through a process called contingent valuation. Despite a major focus on the quality
adjusted life year (QALY) during the 1980s, contingent valuation has increased in
popularity in the health arena since 1990 (Diener et al., 1998; Klose, 1999; Olsen and
Smith, 2001).

Nevertheless, contingent valuation remains controversial.[1] Therefore, the aims of this
chapter are, first to outline what WTP[2] is and why it is important, and, second, to discuss
some important criticisms of contingent-valuation-based WTP. The latter aim is achieved
through structuring the chapter along the lines of three levels of decision-making at
which WTP information could prove useful; namely clinical, health authority and
national.

2. What is WTP and why measure it?

What is WTP?
WTP measures 'strength of preference' for, or value of, a commodity. In health care, where
conventional markets do not exist, decisions still have to be made about how best to allocate limited resources. This requires valuation of resource costs of interventions and their
benefits (that is, health/well-being). The latter can be elicited through surveys using hypothetical WTP questions; that is, contingent valuation. In principle, with this type of information, the combination of interventions can be chosen which maximizes the value of
benefits to the community.

It is important to distinguish WTP, as a measure of benefit, from cost of a good. Many
people would be willing to pay more than the market-clearing price of a good. For any
individual, the difference between benefit, as represented by his/her maximum WTP for
the good, and the price paid by him/her for the good, represents a gain in well-being from

having the good provided. This is why it is important to measure *maximum* WTP, as emphasized by Dupuit (1844).

Why measure WTP?

In addition to the above, Shackley and Ryan (1995) outlined other reasons why WTP may have advantages over other methods of eliciting community values, whilst Johannesson and Jonsson (1991) and Gafni (1997) have argued more specifically that WTP has advantages over other valuation methods, such as QALYs. These arguments centre around three main areas:

- First, many exercises asking members of the public to rank alternatives as general as 'long-stay care' and 'preventive services' are unlikely to relate to any specific changes a decision-maker is thinking of making and do not indicate strength of preference for alternatives.
- Secondly, there are health care attributes which may not be (adequately) captured by QALYs, such as non-health-enhancing aspects of the process of care and other consumption benefits like provision of information (Gerard and Mooney, 1993; Mooney, 1994; Ryan and Shackley, 1995).
- Going beyond QALYs and using a more holistic measure like WTP could also avoid the separability assumption used in construction of QALYs whereby health-related quality of life is valued independently of life years before the two are combined, which is thought by some to be theoretically unsound (Bleichrodt, 1995).

Despite these favourable aspects, WTP has some remaining (perceived) problems, these being the hypothetical nature of survey questions, different payment vehicles giving different WTP values, how to use the values in decision-making, the fact that the method is rarely used in policy, and the association of WTP with ability to pay, which may be inconsistent with resource allocation on the basis of 'need'.

The first two of these are worth addressing at this point. Most WTP studies of health care are hypothetical. Although it might be argued that in any decision-making context it is relative values for options that are important, the extent to which values derived in such surveys reflect 'real-world' behaviour is an issue, influencing perceived credibility of the method. Studies from non-health areas, especially the environment, have been mixed in their reporting of the extent to which hypothetical WTP responses are out of line with values distilled from real behaviour (Hanemann, 1993) and have even shown revealed preference methods to give higher estimates than contingent valuations (Carson et al., 1996). Results from health care are also mixed, showing similar valuations from revealed and hypothetical approaches (Kennedy, 2002) and higher values from hypothetical (Clarke, 1997); although, through using secondary datasets (and thus modelling) to derive revealed preference estimates, it is not clear that these represent the 'correct' values. Blumenschein et al. (2001), having established a field experiment to compare real and hypothetical behaviour, claim it may still be possible to correct for any overestimation.

Related to this, another important test of such studies is response to scope: are respondents faced with greater amounts of the good being valued, willing to pay more? Carson

(1997) shows that most studies (31 of 35 reviewed) are scope sensitive. Despite such positive results, doubts remain about hypothetical WTP values. Again, in health care, results have been mixed (Olsen et al., 2004; Smith, 2001), although the latter study showed that WTP is more sensitive to changes in health than the time trade-off procedure on which many QALY valuations are based.

On the issue of payment vehicles, different vehicles have been promoted on the basis that they represent 'real world' behaviour. Originally, open-ended questions were common, whereby a scenario was presented to respondents and they would be asked for their maximum WTP for it, with no other guidance provided. These types of question have largely been discredited, although evidence supporting their validity exists (Bateman et al., 1994). Payment scales and bidding games have been argued to represent the phenomenon of shopping around and have been shown to be more valid in terms of demonstrating a relationship between WTP and ability to pay (Donaldson et al., 1998b; O'Brien et al., 1995). These methods also tend to reveal higher WTP values than open-ended questions, leading one to think they may draw people closer to their maximum WTP (Donaldson et al., 1995; Frew et al., 2003). In less-developed countries, a variant of these approaches shown to have some validity is based on the notion of haggling (Onwujekwe, 2004). A popular method, largely due to its having been recommended by the National Oceanic and Atmospheric Administration (NOAA) Panel (Arrow et al., 1993), is the closed-ended, or referendum/dichotomous choice, approach. Recently, this method has been compared with the payment scale approach; the former leading to significantly higher values, likely due to the encouragement of 'yea-saying', refuting the claim of the NOAA Panel that the closed-ended approach would lead to 'conservative values' (Whynes et al., 2003; Ryan et al., 2004). Examples of the main approaches are shown in the Appendix.

Other criticisms of WTP are dealt with in the remaining sections of this chapter. Extending the theoretical arguments of Shackley and Donaldson (2000), the layout of the next three sections is based on how results can be used, at clinical, health authority and national levels. Within each of these, reference will be made to the important distributional issue, although it should be noted that criticisms of WTP with respect to associations with ability to pay have also been shown to extend to other common valuation methods, like QALYs (Donaldson et al., 2002).

3.   Decision-maker's dilemma I: clinical

Many economic evaluations address the question of which type of care to provide for a given group. These are the types of question addressed in randomized trials. Despite the potential usefulness of WTP in such situations, the first problem faced is that WTP questions can be asked in at least three ways.

The first is to ask patients in a trial for their maximum WTP for the treatment they receive. Those having treatment A would give a WTP for A, $V(A)$. Those having treatment B would provide a value $V(B)$. The problem with this method is that, because respondents are unaware of the fact that there is an alternative on offer, they tend to provide a value for the care they have had relative to 'no treatment'; thus patients in each arm of the trial are valuing essentially the same thing, treatment versus no treatment. Not surprisingly, therefore, WTP studies which have used this method have struggled to discriminate between treatments evaluated (Donaldson et al., 1995; Johannesson and Fagerberg, 1992;

Ryan et al., 1997). A WTP approach which focuses the respondent on differences between alternatives may be more discriminating, suggesting elicitation of either:

1.   a value for each alternative from each respondent ('*WTP for each*'); or
2.   a value for one's preferred over one's less-preferred option (the '*marginal*' approach).

Each of these involves making respondents aware of the choice between a good and a close substitute and, thus, in a sense, recognizes the importance of 'reference points' used in prospect theory (Kahneman and Tversky, 1979; Schoemaker, 1982). Furthermore, data on respondents' preferences can be collected. A person's WTP for his/her preferred option can then be compared with that for his/her less-preferred option, making it easier to test (within individual respondents) the validity of the approach.

WTP for each involves each respondent estimating $V(A)$ and $V(B)$. However, it has been shown to result in significant preference reversals, that is, lack of congruence between simple preferences and the magnitudes of WTP responses, most likely because respondents compare the cost of alternatives on offer and base their WTP on that rather than on strength of preference for each (Donaldson et al., 1997b).

With the marginal approach, a value, $V(A - B)$, can be elicited directly. Respondents are asked to choose between the status quo (current care) and an alternative (experimental care), and are then asked for their maximum WTP to have their preferred option instead of that which is less preferred. The aim is to clarify to respondents that it is their additional valuation of their preferred option that is required, regardless of whether the preferred option is more or less costly than their less-preferred option. The method also fits more closely with Kaldor–Hicks theory (Hicks, 1939; Kaldor, 1939). The simple rule provided by this theory is that a change should be made if the expressed value to gainers (that is, those who prefer experimental care) is greater than the value of losses associated with those who lose out from the change (that is, those who prefer current care), assuming costs are not under consideration.

Studies using the marginal approach have resulted in WTP values which discriminate between options on offer, and, by including losers as well as gainers from a given policy change (or retention of the status quo), have shown that net benefits would have been overestimated if respondents had been asked to value the experimental treatment only (Donaldson et al., 1997a; Donaldson et al., 1998a; Gibb et al., 1998). Furthermore, in two of the three cases referred to, the (apparently) less costly alternative received a higher mean WTP than the alternative option, and in none of the studies did respondents indicate cost as a reason underlying their stated WTP value. Thus, it seems that the marginal approach is promising and further studies of its validity are ongoing.

The marginal approach provides a useful illustration of why distributional issues may not be as problematic as one might first think when using WTP. First, knowing people's preferences, the researcher can investigate whether people in a higher income group tend to choose one option more frequently than those in lower income groups. Second, the researcher can also examine whether WTP values from those in higher income groups distort the overall value given for one or other option. A scheme along these lines for at least diagnosing whether ability to pay is a problem was outlined by Donaldson (1999a) who also showed how sensitivity tests can be used to estimate a break-even distributional weight at which the final decision on which option to choose would alter. In line with Harberger (1978), the work showed that, to alter initial results, such weights have to be set at a draconian level, such that the preference of higher-income groups would hardly count at all.

Of course, it is not necessary for studies of patients' values always to be tied to a randomized trial. One alternative is to ask patients for a value of the health care good of concern, whilst another is to ask only for a valuation of a characteristic of the good (such as the health gain it might provide, or information if it is a diagnostic tool), with this value being fed into a broader cost–benefit analysis (Currie et al., 2002).

Finally, it is important to note that there are limitations to the use of such values elicited from patients in an *ex post* situation. If a WTP study indicates that significant benefits would be gained by implementing a new option, but the new option would also lead to increased costs, then in most health care systems which operate with a fixed budget, the opportunity cost of implementation will manifest itself as benefits forgone by some other group of patients. There is an argument that values between such competing options are better elicited in an *ex ante* situation where members of the community consider alternatives based on some idea of risk to themselves and/or other members of the community needing such care. Examples of this *ex ante* approach are provided in the following two sections.

4.   Decision maker's dilemma II: health authority

In priority setting at the broader level, it would be useful to know if members of the population at large can compare disparate alternatives and express their strength of preference for each in terms of WTP. This is a good example of using WTP to activate attributes in respondents' utility functions which go beyond health (for example preferences for equity in access). An opportunity to test the feasibility of such a notion arose in an evaluation of a new helicopter ambulance service in Northern Norway (Olsen and Donaldson, 1998).

Initially the aim was to obtain a monetary valuation from the population at large for the helicopter ambulance for use in a cost–benefit analysis (CBA). However, if such a service were to use resources from a fixed public sector pot, an opportunity cost would arise through not having the resources available for other services. Therefore, each respondent was asked to rank the ambulance service against providing 80 more elective heart operations and 250 more elective hip operations, each described in terms of who would get treated (for example men aged 50–60 years) and expected outcomes in the presence and absence of the intervention. The respondents were told that these options were competing for funding. After ranking them, respondents were asked for their WTP in extra taxation per annum for each option.

The most obvious fault of this study was that, if hips were always asked about last, then it is possible respondents reached some kind of budget constraint (despite being told the options were competing with one another) which deflated their WTP for hips. Thus, it is important to test for ordering effects in the future. Other problems were that rankings implied by WTP often did not match initial rankings given by respondents (Olsen, 1997). Also, respondents were asked to express their WTP through taxation payments. However, at around the same time, suggestions had been made for taking an 'insurance-based' approach to WTP questioning, whereby respondents would get information on their own (or their families') probabilities of needing care (Gafni, 1991; O'Brien and Gafni, 1996). This contrasted with the 'community-based' approach in Northern Norway where enhancements in programmes were described as being for the community (rather than using individual probabilities explicitly) and payments were through taxation, under which substantial numbers of people mentioned altruistic reasons for being willing to pay. However, another study, in the field of safety improvements, has shown, surprisingly, that valuations for private safety improvement were higher than for public safety improvements (Johannesson et al., 1996).

These problems and issues led to a project which gathered together a wider network of researchers around Europe who were interested in improving the method of WTP in the context of eliciting community values for priority setting. 'EuroWill', a project funded by the European Commission, involved surveys in six European countries (Donaldson, 1999b). As well as addressing the issues listed above, the project addressed several other issues which had arisen in the WTP literature during the 1980s and 1990s. These are listed in Table 37.1, along with other details of the surveys in each country.

Amongst other things, the work has shown: the importance the population puts on community *vis-à-vis* acute services; the existence of ordering effects, reasons for them and potential solutions; the potential for improving consistency between explicit and implied rankings by using a marginal approach, whereby respondents are asked for their WTP for their least preferred programme and then how much more than that for their more preferred programmes; the difficulty of detecting scope effects (with respect to different sizes of health gain or different numbers of people benefiting); that the closed-ended approach yields significantly higher WTP values than the payment scale; that different values are obtained by providing respondents with different amounts of information about the same option; and that improved econometric techniques are feasible for estimating factors associated with WTP where multiple alternatives are valued by each respondent (O'Shea et al., 2002; Stewart et al., 2002; Shackley and Donaldson, 2002; Olsen et al., 2004; Ryan et al., 2004; Protière et al., 2004; Luchini et al., 2003).

A variation of the marginal approach has also been applied to explore choice dilemmas in public health (Shackley and Dixon, 2000). Distributional problems can be handled here much as outlined above. With multiple alternatives, as in EuroWill, the main issue is whether distributions of WTP by income group for each option follow the same pattern.

In other countries, where the issue might be whether an intervention should be added to the 'menu' of items covered, at an extra cost to payers, WTP questions could be asked about that single intervention. This has been done in health maintenance organizations in the US (O'Brien et al., 1998) and is similar to the issue addressed in the following section.

5. Decision maker's dilemma III: national

At a national level, each decision made by a health technology assessment agency, such as the National Institute for Health and Clinical Excellence (NICE) in England, is a one-off decision about whether or not to fund a specific intervention rather than how to allocate resources across projects.

Given that many such agencies use cost per QALY as the basis for such one-off decisions, questions have been raised about what value (price) to place on a QALY. Society's

Table 37.1   *EuroWill: issues addressed and numbers of responses in each country*

Country (dates of survey)	Areas of care	Issues addressed	Numbers receiving different versions of the questionnaire		Total in each country
Norway (March 1997)	More heart operations	Insurance versus community-based questions	Community-based	= 80	
	More cancer treatments		Insurance-based	= 83	
	Helicopter ambulance	Size of effects	Community-based (2 cancer progs)	= 79	323
			Community-based (all progs for less people)	= 81	
Portugal (Oct–Nov 1997)	More heart operations	Numbers treated	Cancer, hearts, ambulance	= 104	
	More cancer treatments		Cancer, hearts, improved hearts	= 103	
	Improved car ambulance		Cancer, improved hearts, ambulance	= 103	310
Denmark (April 1998)	More heart operations	Insurance-based versus community-based questions	Insurance	= 168	
	More hip operations		Community	= 168	
	More cataract operations	Test–retest	Test–retest	= 50	386
UK (May–June 1998)	More heart operations	Payment scale versus closed-ended	Payment scale	= 236	
	More cancer treatments		Closed-ended	= 342	
	Helicopter ambulance				578
France (Oct–Nov 1998)	More heart operations	Process utility	No process	= 100	
	More cancer treatments		Neutral process	= 104	
	Helicopter ambulance	Cognitive capacity	Positive process	= 99	
	Reduction in pollution		Pollution/no process	= 154	
		Test–retest	Pollution/process	= 149	353
			Test–retest	= 50	
Ireland (April 1999)	More heart operations	Marginal approach	Basic approach	= 113	
	More cancer treatments		Marginal approach	= 121	335
	More community care	Ordering effects	Different ordering	= 101	
Grand total					**2285**

WTP for a QALY can indicate what this 'threshold' value should be. Thus, a WTP-based value of a QALY has the potential to become an important aid to decision-making at the national level. In the UK, and other countries, this would mirror the use of a value of a prevented fatality (VPF) which is used in transport safety policy.

A WTP-based value of a QALY can be estimated in two ways; by inference from the VPF, or through a direct survey of the public. The former would provide a quicker result, if a VPF exists, and a small number of studies have attempted such a conversion. A number of different methods have been used to do this, each falling into one of two groups. The simplest method combines a VPF, an estimated age of fatality, the expected life years otherwise lived and a profile of the quality of these extra life years to produce a discounted value of a QALY. Studies using this method have reported values of a QALY of US\$90 000 (Johannesson and Meltzer, 1998), US\$161 305 (Hirth et al., 2000) and Aus\$108 000 (Abelson, 2003). These values are not directly comparable with each other due to differences in base year and currency.

Currently, work in the UK is being undertaken based on this method but also using the recent concept of the 'value of living per se' (Loomes, 2002), whereby the value of a QALY incorporates the notion that an individual's WTP to reduce the risk of premature death may depend on other factors besides the remaining number of life years, such as a desire to see their family grow up or the pain caused to others if they die.

A more direct way to estimate a WTP based value of a QALY is through surveying the public. Using a discrete choice experiment on members of the public in Denmark, Gyrd-Hansen (2003) estimated a WTP-based value of QALY of DK80 000 (\$10 000). This value is based on an individual *ex post* valuation and not a societal *ex ante* valuation, which would be preferred for decision-making at the national level. A social valuation obtained in the form of a public health insurance question would be more useful as it would include the utility derived from both option value, any altruistic motives of the individual and incorporate decision-making under uncertainty where the individual would not know *ex ante* whether they would move to a better health state as a result of some intervention. Again, within the UK, and based on parallel work which has taken place in the area of transport safety policy to update the UK VPF (Carthy et al., 1999), work is being undertaken to determine the feasibility of estimating a monetary value of a QALY from a societal perspective (Baker et al., 2003; Bateman et al., 2003).

Finally, in such national-level studies, distributional issues are easier to deal with as the WTP value that is estimated should be based on a representative sample of the community. With each income group being represented in the elicitation process, and with each individual being asked about their strength of preference for the same thing, the resulting value would in a sense be based on society's overall budget constraint.

6. Conclusions

WTP is now an established method in health care evaluation. Recent research, much of it original, has addressed important issues such as feasibility of deriving values, how to elicit values that make sense and how to approach difficult problems such as the association of willingness and ability to pay. Important issues, some unique to health, remain to be researched. Our hope is that these have been clearly outlined and that, once resolved, we will be nearer to knowing the value of health care in various contexts.

Notes

1. Other ways of eliciting WTP, of course might be through discrete choice experiments (see the chapters by Ryan et al., 38, and Burgess et al., 39, in this volume).
2. While the focus here is WTP, it should be noted that contingent valuation can also incorporate willingness to accept (WTA) measures. See Donaldson and Shackley (2003) for an explanation as to why we focus here on WTP.

References

Abelson, P. (2003), 'The value of life and health for public policy', *The Economic Record*, **79**, S2–S13.
Acton, J.P. (1973), *Evaluating Public Programs to Save Lives: the Case of Heart Attacks*, RAND Corporation, Santa Monica, Report No R950RC.
Arrow, K., R. Solow, P.R. Portney, E.E. Leamer, R. Radner and H. Schuman (1993), 'Report of the National Oceanic and Atmospheric Administration Panel of Contingent Valuation', *Federal Register*, **58**(10), 4601–14.
Baker, R., S. Chilton, C. Donaldson, M. Jones-Lee, H. Metcalf, P. Shackley and M. Ryan (2003), *Determining the Societal Value of a QALY by Surveying the Public in England and Wales: a Research Protocol*, Birmingham, NCCRM Publications.
Bateman, I., K. Willis and G. Garrod (1994), 'Consistency between contingent valuation estimates: a comparison of two studies of UK national parks', *Regional Studies*, **28**, 457–74.
Bateman, I., G. Loomes, M. Mugford, A. Robinson, R. Smith, K. Sproston and R. Sugden (2003), *What is the value to Society of a QALY? Issues raised and Recommendations for how to Address Them*, Birmingham: NCCRM Publications.
Bleichrodt, H. (1995), QALYs and HYEs: under what conditions are they equivalent?, *Journal of Health Economics*, **14**, 17–37.
Blumenschein, K., M. Johannesson, K.K. Yokoyama and P.R. Freeman (2001), Hypothetical versus real willingness to pay in the health sector: results from a field experiment, *Journal of Health Economics*, **20**, 441–57.
Carson, R.T. (1997), 'Contingent valuation surveys and tests of insensitivity to scope', in R.J. Kopp, W. Pemmerhene and N. Schwartz (eds), *Determining the Value of Non-Marketed Goods: Economic, Psychological and Policy Relevant Aspects of Contingent Valuation Methods*, Boston: Kluwer.
Carson, R.T., N.E. Flores, K.M. Martin and J.L. Wright (1996), 'Contingent valuation and revealed preference methodologies: comparing the estimates for quasi-public goods', *Land Economics*, **72**, 80–99.
Carthy, T., S. Chilton, J. Covey, L. Hopkins, M. Jones-Lee, G. Loomes, N. Pidgeon and A. Spencer, (1999), 'On the contingent valuation of safety and the safety of contingent valuation: part 2 – the CV/SG "chained" approach', *Journal of Risk and Uncertainty*, **17**, 187–213.
Clarke, P.M. (1997), 'Valuing the benefits of health care in monetary terms with particular reference to mammographic screening', Ph.D. Thesis, Australian National University, Canberra.
Currie, G., C. Donaldson, B. O'Brien, G.L. Stoddart, G.W. Torrance and M.F. Drummond (2002), 'Willingness to pay for what? A note on alternative definitions of health care programme benefits for contingent valuation studies', *Medical Decision Making*, **22**, 493–7.
Davis, R.K. (1963), 'Recreation planning as an economic problem', *Natural Resources Journal*, **3**, 239–49.
Diener, A., B. O'Brien and A. Gafni (1998), 'Health care contingent valuation studies: a review and classification of the literature', *Health Economics*, **7**, 313–26.
Donaldson, C. (1999a), 'Valuing the benefits of publicly-provided health care: does "ability to pay" preclude the use of "willingness to pay"?', *Social Science and Medicine*, **49**, 551–63.
Donaldson, C. (1999b), 'Developing the method of "willingness to pay" for assessment of community preferences for health care', final report to Biomed 2 Programme (PL950832) of the European Commission, Health Economics Research Unit, University of Aberdeen and Departments of Economics and Community Health Sciences, University of Calgary.
Donaldson, C. and P. Shackley (2003), 'Willingness to pay for health care', in A. Scott, A. Maynard and R. Elliott (eds), *Advances in Health Economics*, Chichester: John Wiley, pp. 1–24.
Donaldson, C., S. Birch and A. Gafni (2002), 'The pervasiveness of the "distribution problem" in economic evaluation in health care', *Health Economics*, **11**, 55–70.
Donaldson, C., V. Hundley and T. Mapp (1998a), 'Willingness to pay: a method for measuring preferences for maternity care?', *Birth*, **25**, 33–40.
Donaldson, C., P. Shackley and M. Abdalla (1997b), 'Using willingness to pay to value close substitutes: carrier screening for cystic fibrosis revisited', *Health Economics*, **6**, 145–59.
Donaldson, C., R. Thomas and D.J. Torgerson (1998b), 'Validity of open-ended and payment scale approaches to eliciting willingness to pay', *Applied Economics*, **29**, 79–84.

Donaldson, C., P. Shackley, M. Abdalla and Z. Miedzybrodzka (1995), 'Willingness to pay for antenatal carrier screening for cystic fibrosis', *Health Economics*, **4**, 439–52.

Donaldson, C., T. Mapp, S. Farrar, A. Walker and S. Macphee (1997a), 'Assessing community values in health care: is the "willingness to pay" method feasible?', *Health Care Analysis*, **5**, 7–29.

Dupuit, J. (1844), 'On the measurement of utility of public works', translated by R.H. Barback in *International Economic Papers 2* (1952), pp. 83–110 from 'De la Mesure de l'Utilité des Travaux Publics', *Annales des Ponts et Chausees*, 2nd Series Vol. 8, (another English version in J.J. Arrow and T. Scitovsky (eds), *Readings in Welfare Economics*, London: George Allen and Unwin, 1969).

Frew, E., D. Whynes and J. Wolstenholme (2003), 'Eliciting willingness to pay: comparing closed-ended with open-ended and payment scale formats', *Medical Decision Making*, **23**, 150–59.

Gafni, A. (1991), 'Willingness to pay as a measure of benefits: relevant questions in the context of public decision making about health care programmes', *Medical Care*, **29**, 1246–52.

Gafni, A. (1997), 'Willingness to pay in the context of an economic evaluation of healthcare programs: theory and practice', *American Journal of Managed Care*, **3**(supp), S21–S32.

Gerard, K. and G. Mooney (1993), 'QALY league tables: handle with care', *Health Economics*, **2**(1), 59–64.

Gibb, S., C. Donaldson and R. Henshaw (1998), 'Assessing strength of preference for abortion method using willingness to pay', *Journal of Advanced Nursing*, **27**, 30–36.

Gyrd-Hansen, D. (2003), 'Willingness to pay for a QALY', *Health Economics*, **12**, 1049–60.

Hanemann, W.M. (1993), 'Valuing the environment through contingent valuation', *Journal of Economic Perspectives*, **8**(4), 19–43.

Harberger, A.C. (1978), 'On the use of distributional weights in social cost–benefit analysis', *Journal of Political Economy*, **86**, S87–S120.

Hicks, J.R. (1939), 'The foundations of welfare economics', *Economic Journal*, **49**, 696–710.

Hirth, R.A., M.E. Chernew, E. Miller, M.F. Fendrick and W.G. Weissert, (2000), 'Willingness to pay for a quality-adjusted life year: in search of a standard, *Medical Decision Making*, **20**, 332–42.

Johannesson, M. and B. Fagerberg (1992), 'A health economic comparison of diet and drug treatment in obese men with mild hypertension', *Journal of Hypertension*, **10**, 1063–70.

Johannesson, M. and B. Jonsson (1991), 'Economic evaluation in health care: is there a role for cost–benefit analysis?', *Health Policy*, **17**, 1–23.

Johannesson, M. and D. Meltzer (1998), 'Some reflections on cost effectiveness analysis', *Health Economics*, **7**, 1–7.

Johannesson, M., P.O. Johansson and R.M. O'Conner (1996), 'The value of private safety versus the value of public safety', *Journal of Risk and Uncertainty*, **13**, 263–75.

Johannesson, M., B. Jonsson and L. Borgquist (1991), 'Willingness to pay for anti-hypertensive therapy – results of a Swedish pilot study', *Journal of Health Economics*, **10**, 461–74.

Jones-Lee, M.W. (1974), 'The value of changes in the probability of death or injury', *Journal of Political Economy*, **82**, 835–49.

Jones-Lee, M.W. (1976), *The Value of Life: an Economic Analysis*, London: Martin Robertson.

Kahneman, D. and A. Tversky (1979), 'Prospect theory: an analysis of decision under risk', *Econometrica*, **47**, 263–91.

Kaldor, N. (1939), 'Welfare propositions and interpersonal comparisons of utility', *Economic Journal*, **49**, 542–9.

Kennedy, C. (2002), 'Revealed preference compared to contingent valuation: radon-induced lung cancer prevention', *Health Economics*, **11**, 586–98.

Klose, T. (1999), 'The contingent valuation method in health care', *Health Policy*, **47**, 97–123.

Loomes, G. (2002), 'Valuing life years and QALYs: transferability and convertibility of values across the UK public sector', in A. Towse, C. Pritchard and N. Devlin (eds), *Cost Effectiveness Thresholds: Economic and Ethical Issues,* London: Kings Fund and Office of Health Economics.

Luchini, S. C. Protière. and J.P. Moatti (2003), 'Evaluating several willingness to pay in a single contingent evaluation: application to health care', *Health Economics*, **12**, 51–64.

Mooney, G. (1977), *The Valuation of Human Life*, London: Macmillan.

Mooney, G. (1994), *Key Issues in Health Economics*, London: Harvester Wheatsheaf.

O'Brien, B. and A. Gafni (1996), 'When do the "dollars" make sense? Toward a conceptual framework for contingent valuation studies in health care', *Medical Decision Making*, **16**, 288–99.

O'Brien, B.J., S. Novosel, G. Torrance and D. Streiner (1995), 'Assessing the economic value of a new antidepressant: a willingness-to-pay approach', *Pharmacoeconomics*, **8**(1), 34–45.

O'Brien, B.J., R. Goeree, A. Gafni, G.W. Torrance, M.V. Pauly, H. Erder, J. Rusthoven, J. Weeks, M. Cahill and B. Lamont (1998), 'Assessing the value of a new pharmaceutical: a feasibility study of contingent valuation in managed care', *Medical Care*, **36**(3), 370–84.

Olsen, J.A. (1997), 'Aiding priority setting in health care: is there a role for the contingent valuation method?', *Health Economics*, **6**, 603–12.

Olsen, J.A. and C. Donaldson (1998), 'Helicopters, hearts and hips: using willingness to pay to set priorities for public sector health care programmes', *Social Science and Medicine*, **46**, 1–12.

Olsen, J.A. and R.D. Smith (2001), 'Theory versus practice: a review of "willingness-to-pay" in health and health care', *Health Economics*, **10**, 39–52.

Olsen, J.A., C. Donaldson and J. Periera (2004), 'The insensitivity of "willingness to pay" to the size of the good: new evidence for health care', *Journal of Economic Psychology*, **25**, 445–60.

Olsen, J.A., K. Kidholm, C. Donaldson and P. Shackley (2004), 'Willingness to pay for public health care: a comparison of two approaches', *Health Policy*, **70**, 217–28.

O'Shea, E., J. Stewart, C. Donaldson and P. Shackley (2002), 'Eliciting preferences for resource allocation for health care', *Economic and Social Review*, **32**, 217–38.

Onwujekwe, O. (2004), 'Criterion and content validity of a novel structured haggling contingent valuation question format versus the bidding game and binary with follow-up format', *Social Science & Medicine*, **58**, 525–37.

Protière, C., C. Donaldson, Stéphane Luchini, J.P. Moatti and P. Shackley (2004), 'The impact of information on non-health attributes on willingness to pay for multiple health care programmes', *Social Science and Medicine*, **58**, 1257–69.

Ryan, M. and P. Shackley (1995), 'Assessing the benefits of health care: how far should we go?', *Quality in Health Care*, **4**(3), 207–13.

Ryan, M., J. Ratcliffe and J. Tucker (1997), 'Using willingness to pay to value alternative models of antenatal care', *Social Science and Medicine*, **44**, 371–80.

Ryan, M., D. Scott and C. Donaldson (2004), 'Valuing health care using willingness to pay: a comparison of the payment card and dichotomous choice methods', *Journal of Health Economics*, **23**, 237–58.

Schoemaker, P.J.H. (1982), 'The expected utility model: its variants, purposes, evidence and limitations', *Journal of Economic Literature*, **20**, 529–63.

Shackley, P. and S. Dixon (2000), 'Using contingent valuation to elicit public preferences for water fluoridation', *Applied Economics*, **32**(6), 777–87.

Shackley, P. and C. Donaldson (2000), 'Willingness to pay for publicly-financed health care: how should we use the numbers?', *Applied Economics*, **32**(15), 2015–21.

Shackley, P. and C. Donaldson (2002), 'Should we use willingness to pay to elicit community preferences for health care? New evidence from using a "marginal" approach', *Journal of Health Economics*, **21**, 971–91.

Shackley, P. and M. Ryan (1995), 'Involving consumers in health care decision-making', *Health Care Analysis*, **3**, 196–204.

Smith, R.D. (2001), 'The relative sensitivity of willingness-to-pay and time-trade-off to changes in health status: An empirical investigation', *Health Economics*, **10**, 487–97.

Stewart, J., E. O'Shea, C. Donaldson and P. Shackley (2002), 'Do ordering effects matter in willingness to pay studies of health care?', *Journal of Health Economics*, **21**, 585–99.

Whynes, D.K., E.J. Frew and J.L. Wolstenholme, (2003), 'A comparison of two methods for eliciting contingent valuations of colorectal cancer screening', *Journal of Health Economics*, **22**, 555–74.

Appendix

Close-ended WTP question

ANTI-HYPERTENSION TREATMENT

This question concerns how you personally value your treatment against high blood pressure. Since the treatment against high blood pressure claims a lot of health care resources a possible development is that patients in the future will have to pay a larger proportion of the treatment cost, in the form of higher user fees. Assume that this will be the case and that user fees are raised. At present a patient treated for high blood pressure pays on average SEK 350 a year in user fees for drugs and physician visits. Would you choose to continue your current treatment against high blood pressure, if the user fees for the treatment were raised to SEK 2000* per year?

☐ Yes

☐ No

* The amount was varied between SEK 100 and SEK 10 000 in 15 sub-samples

Source: Johannesson et al. (1991)

Open-ended and payment scale questions

CYSTIC FIBROSIS SCREENING STUDY

For the purposes of the questionnaire we would like you to imagine that you live in a country like the USA where people do have to pay for tests. Because of the way the health service is run in the UK, there is **no question** of you being asked to actually pay any money.

We are interested in the value you place on having the cystic fibrosis carrier test. One way of doing this is to ask you how much you would theoretically be willing to pay for the test.

Open-ended
1.   What is the maximum amount of money you would be prepared to pay for the test? *(Please write in the space below).*

£_____

Payment scheme in which respondent gets a scale from which to choose a value
1.   What is the maximum amount of money you would be prepared to pay for the test?

	£0
Put a ✓ next to the amounts that you are sure you **would** pay.	£1
	£2
	£4
	£6
	£8
Put a **X** next to the amounts that you are sure you **would not** pay	£10
	£12
	£16
	£20
	£30
Put a circle around the **maximum amount** you would be prepared to pay	£50
	£75
	£100
	£100+

Source: Donaldson et al. (1995)

38 Using discrete choice experiments in health economics
Mandy Ryan, Karen Gerard and Gillian Currie

1. Introduction

A key challenge in health economics is that of identification and valuation of the benefits from health and health care interventions. The notion of value used, based on economic theory, implies sacrifice or trade-offs. That is, the value of a particular choice is revealed by what we are prepared to give up in order to make that choice. In the health context, there are very limited opportunities to observe individuals' valuations through the purchase decisions they make in the market. Therefore we rely on techniques designed to elicit these valuations outside actual market-based choice settings – that is, stated preference methods as opposed to revealed preference methods.

The initial focus of research measuring benefits in the evaluation of health care was on the valuation of health outcomes, most commonly in the context of the quality adjusted life years (QALY) model, and there is on-going application and methodological innovation in this regard (see the chapters in this Companion by Bleichrodt and Pinto (33); Feeny (34); and Brazier and Roberts (35)). Methods for valuing health states, such as standard gamble and time trade-off, which underlie QALYs, have been substantially developed. However, in the early 1990s recognition that preferences for health interventions may go beyond health gains, and interest in priority setting at a broader programme level context, gave the impetus for a different research direction for valuing benefits. This direction involved new methods, and moving beyond the QALY model, to incorporate so-called 'non-health' and 'process' aspects. Non-health outcomes refer to sources of benefit such as the provision of information, reassurance, autonomy, distributional concerns and dignity in the provision of care. Process attributes include such aspects of care as waiting time, location of treatment, continuity of care and staff attitudes. This led to the application and development of contingent valuation (CV), which is the topic of the chapter by Donaldson, Mason and Shackley in this Companion (Chapter 37), and discrete choice experiments (DCEs) which are also the subject of the Chapter by Burgess et al. in this Companion (Chapter 39).

The remainder of this chapter is organized as follows. First, the concept of the DCE will be described, followed by an outline of the key stages involved in conducting a DCE. Consideration is also given here to issues raised at each of the stages. Attention then turns to how the DCE method can be used. Here we show the breadth of applications to date, and discuss potential applications in future research. Finally, consideration is given to current evidence on the validity of DCEs. For more on DCEs in health economics see Ryan and Gerard (2003) or Viney et al. (2002), and generally see Bateman et al. (2002) and Louviere et al. (2000).

2. The concept

DCEs are an *attribute based* stated preference valuation technique that enables consideration of the contribution to overall value of each of the defined characteristics or attributes. This distinguishes it from CV that values health programmes or interventions as a whole. The DCE approach comes from a family of stated preference methods broadly consistent with the axioms of welfare economic theory. McFadden (1973; 1974) initially developed the DCE model making it consistent with economic theory, and others have since added to it (for example Louviere and Hensher, 1982 and Louviere and Woodworth, 1983). Like other stated preference methods – including standard gambles, time trade-off exercises or CV – a DCE is a means of quantifying preferences by analysing the responses that research participants provide in surveys about how they would behave in hypothetical choice situations. In a DCE, participants choose their preferred alternative from a choice set, and this is repeated for a series of hypothetical choice sets where each alternative is uniquely described as a 'bundle' of attributes. One of the strengths of the approach is that it mirrors 'real life' choices. In this sense, it has the capacity to elicit valid responses from the respondent.

3. Stages of a discrete choice experiment

Step 1: Identifying the attributes

Each option in a choice set is uniquely described by a combination of attribute levels. Thus the first stage of a DCE is to define the relevant decision-making context and identify the relevant factors affecting the choice over the intervention being valued. These factors form the basis for identifying key attributes. Attributes may be determined in a number of ways. Often, the attributes may be pre-defined by a particular policy question. For example, decision-makers may be interested in how patients trade between waiting time and location of treatment (Ryan et al., 2000). In other cases, significant preliminary work will be required to determine what characteristics are relevant. This preliminary work may take the form of a review of the relevant literature, focus group discussions, or one-on-one interviews with individuals from the relevant group from which the participants for the DCE will be drawn (for example, patients, health care providers, or the general public).

In many applications, a price attribute is included. This allows the indirect estimate of willingness to pay (WTP) for specific configurations of attributes that represent an existing or potential health intervention or programme (see more on this below).

An important question is what effect the number of attributes has on a respondent's ability to complete the choice task. Louviere et al. (1997) argue that increasing the number of attributes will not significantly affect results although there is a consensus of opinion that DCEs should not be too 'complex' (Hensher et al., 2001). As noted in the chapter by Burgess et al. (Chapter 39), factors that increase error variability, such as task complexity may lead to more variability and potentially biased parameter estimates. As it stands, more research is needed to clarify what is a manageable number of attributes; particularly as applications in health economics to date have included anywhere between 2 and 24, with a mode of 6 (Ryan and Gerard, 2003).

Step 2: Assigning levels to attributes

Once attributes have been determined, two or more levels must be assigned to them in order to introduce necessary variability for parameter estimation. These levels may be numerical units (cardinal), such as cost, time, distance, or number of visits. When levels are described qualitatively it is important to minimize the ambiguity with which the levels are perceived, for example, 'severe pain' should be described in such a way that it will have similar meaning for all respondents.

An important question when including price as an attribute is the appropriate payment vehicle to use in collectively funded health care systems. Most studies in health economics have used payment at the point of consumption. Other alternatives include; willingness to accept (WTA) compensation, travel costs and taxation (Ryan and Gerard, 2003). Better understanding of the appropriateness of these alternative payment vehicles is needed for applications of DCEs to collectively funded health care interventions.

A number of studies in health care have included time as an attribute, defining it in a number of different contexts such as; waiting time, travel time, time to return to normal activities, duration of illness and preference for present or future time (time preference). Whilst most studies use a price proxy when estimating the overall value of health care, Ryan et al. (2001) and Gerard et al. (2004) estimated value in terms of time. Given individuals are used to trading time in a publicly provided health care system and it is measured on an interval scale, its potential use within the framework of an economic evaluation should be explored further. In the former study, a monetary measure of the value of time was estimated using the value of waiting time for public transport (Department of Environment, Transport and Region Highways, 1997). This method assumes that the value of time when waiting for public transport is the same as waiting time in a health care setting. Such an assumption should be tested empirically, and consideration should also be given to the relative value of the different types of time included in DCEs.

Another important question when defining attribute levels is the sensitivity of the parameter estimates to the number and range of levels. Ryan and Wordsworth (2000) conducted an experiment to look at the sensitivity of the coefficients to the level of attributes. They found that whilst estimated coefficients were not significantly different across five of the six attributes included in the experiment, mean WTP estimates were significantly different for four of the five welfare estimates. Within the marketing literature, Ohler et al. (2000) found that whilst attribute range influences main effects to a small degree, substantial effects were found on attribute interactions and model goodness of fit. Ratcliffe and Longworth (2002) varied the number of attribute levels within a DCE and found that the relative importance of the attributes whose levels were varied increased as the number of levels increased, whilst remaining stable for those attributes whose levels did not vary. Future work should investigate this issue in more detail.

Step 3: Constructing choice sets

Once the attributes and levels have been defined, the respondent is presented with a number of alternative scenarios that describe the commodity being valued in terms of different combinations of attribute levels. A number of different preference elicitation formats may be used – rating, ranking and choice-based exercises – but not all are consistent with an economic framework (as noted by Burgess et al. in this Companion). In this chapter we focus on choice-based exercises.[1]

The choice-based approach requires respondents to choose their preferred scenarios from a series of choices, and the question can be posed in a variety of ways. The single binary choice approach involves presenting individuals with a number of scenarios described in terms of the alternative attribute levels and for each scenario asking if they would take it up, with possible responses being 'yes' or 'no'. Alternatively subjects may be presented with multiple options and asked to choose between them. Individuals may be forced to choose between two or more options (would you choose A, B, . . ., N), or they may be given an opt-out (the opportunity to say they would choose none of the options on offer or defer their decision). Alternatively they may be given the option to state their strength of preference for the alternatives posed (on a scale ranging from strongly prefer B to strongly prefer A).

A central part of DCEs is deciding what scenarios to present to respondents. The number of possible scenarios increases factorially with the number of attributes and levels. Rarely can all the scenarios generated be included in the set of choices presented to respondents. Experimental designs are purposeful samples of scenarios from the full factorial number and are used to reduce scenarios presented in the questionnaire to a manageable number. The sample of scenarios is sufficient to estimate a utility model of a given form (usually additive linear, see below). Catalogues, computer software or experts may be used to identify optimal designs. The topic of optimal experimental design and development of statistically efficient DCEs is the focus of the chapter by Burgess et al. in this Companion (Chapter 39).

Step 4: Survey design
In addition to the construction of efficient choice sets, a crucial element in the design of a DCE instrument relates to more general survey design principles. Because of the nature of stated preference exercises, respondents are often relatively unfamiliar with the choices they will be faced with. Thus, careful attention to setting the context in a way that is understandable and realistic to respondents is important. The usual principles of good survey design apply (Dillman, 2000). This includes paying attention to the nature of the supporting information included in the questionnaire. San Miguel et al. (2005) emphasized just how important it is to provide respondents with sufficient information about the commodity being valued and the context of the choice, to allow respondents to be in the position where they have all the relevant information to make rational choices.

Step 5: Data analysis and interpretation
The standard tool for analysing responses to DCEs is McFadden's (1973) discrete choice model based on the random utility hypothesis. The idea behind random utility models (RUM) is that researchers cannot observe all factors affecting preferences (represented by utilities). Therefore, the latent utility U_{in} that an individual n associates with alternative i is considered decomposable in two additively separable parts, namely a systematic (or explainable) component, V_{in}, and a random (or unexplainable) component ε_{in} representing unmeasured variation in preferences:

$$U_{in} = V_{in} + \varepsilon_{in} \tag{38.1}$$

Where:

$$V_{in} = \beta_0 + \Sigma \beta_j X_{inj} + \lambda P_{in} \qquad (38.2)$$

Here β_0, β_j, and λ are the parameters of the model to be estimated, X_j's represent the levels of the j attributes of the commodity being valued ($j = 1, 2, \ldots, k$), $\Sigma \beta_j X_j$'s represents the summation of all the model effect coefficients; P the price level (or some proxy for price). β_0 reflects the subject's preferences for one commodity over another when all attributes in the model are the same (referred to in the literature as the alternative specific constant (ASC) most likely to be important in 'labelled' DCEs). The β parameters are equal to the marginal utilities of the given attributes (that is, $\partial V / \partial X_k = \beta_k$), and the ratio of any two parameters shows the marginal rates of substitution between attributes (that is how much of one attribute an individual is willing to give up to have more of another attribute, holding utility constant). Following on from this, the ratio of any given attribute to the parameter on the price attribute shows how much money an individual is willing to pay for a unit change in that attribute (that is, β_k / λ). Finally, given a particular assumption about the distribution of the random component, which will be elaborated on shortly, WTP for a change in the overall way health care is provided can be estimated as:

$$-\frac{1}{\lambda} \left[\ln \sum_{j=1}^{J} e^{V_j^0} - \ln \sum_{j=1}^{J} e^{V_j^1} \right] \qquad (38.3)$$

where V_j^0 is the value for the systematic component of utility for an initial state and V_j^1 is the value for a new state of the world, for example, following a policy change. Equation (38.3) reduces to:

$$-1/\lambda (V^0 - V^1) \qquad (38.4)$$

for state of the world models (where we know with certainty that individuals will take up the health care intervention) (Lanscar and Savage, 2004; Ryan, 2004).

Given the random component is inherently stochastic, the probability that individual n chooses alternative i from any other alternative in the choice set k of J alternatives can be estimated. Assuming utility maximizing behaviour, this can be expressed as:

$$P(i|k) = \Pr\left[(V_{in} + \varepsilon_{in}) > (V_{Jn} + \varepsilon_{Jn})\right] \qquad (38.5)$$

Solutions to equation (38.5) depend on assumptions about the form of systematic utilities V_{in} and distributional and statistical properties of ε_{in}. For a traditional linear-index model as outlined above (that is, restated in vector notation, $V_{in} = \beta' X_k$) and assuming independent and identically distributed Extreme Value I disturbances, the familiar multinomial logit (MNL) model is derived (Ben-Akiva and Lerman, 1985).

$$P(i \backslash K) = \exp(\mu \beta' X_{ik}) \Big/ \sum_{j=1}^{J} \exp(\mu \beta' X_{ik}) \qquad (38.6)$$

where X_{jk} is a vector of attribute levels corresponding to alternative j, β is the vector of indirect marginal utilities, and μ is a scale factor inversely related to the variance σ^2 of ε ($\mu = \pi/\sqrt{6}\sigma$). In any one dataset, μ cannot be uniquely identified; hence, means and variances are perfectly confounded and only the combined effect of μ and β can be estimated. However, the assumption of identically distributed disturbances allows the utility function to be scaled by an arbitrary factor without affecting the choice probabilities. Thus the scale parameter, μ, typically is set by the analyst to a value that provides a convenient estimate of the standard deviation of disturbances σ, usually one (Ben-Akiva and Lerman, 1985).

4. Using DCEs in health economics

Whilst DCEs were introduced into health economics to go beyond the QALY paradigm, over the last 10 years they have been used to address a range of questions. From a policy and planning point of view the DCE approach is extremely versatile. It allows identification of which attributes are significant determinants of the values individuals place on non-market commodities; the value of changing more than one attribute simultaneously; and the total economic value of a commodity (Bateman et al., 2002). Furthermore, by giving the attributes different values, it becomes possible to determine their relative importance (size of coefficient estimate), marginal rate of substitution between attributes (ratio of the estimates of any two attribute coefficients) and estimate the total explained utility (benefit) and probabilities for uptake for different combinations of attributes, thereby being able to determine the combination respondents prefer (Ryan and Gerard, 2003). Using the results in this way is appealing because it provides benefit estimates that are consistent with economic theory. It also has the advantage that it can include benefit estimates for new feasible options that are not yet available.

For a recent review of the application of DCEs in health economics see Ryan and Gerard (2003). Initial studies applied DCEs to go beyond health outcomes, and look at the value of process and non-health outcomes in the delivery of health care. Some of these studies did consider the trade-off between health outcomes (however defined), non-health outcomes and process attributes. For example, Ryan (1999) looked at the trade-offs between health outcome (chance of leaving the service with a child), non-health outcomes (provision of follow-up support to help to come to terms with infertility) and process attributes (time on waiting list, continuity of care, attitudes of staff, and cost) in the provision of infertility services. Many applications throughout the 1990s applied the DCE approach to look at trade-offs between such attributes, and indirectly estimated willingness to pay by including a price proxy (Ryan and Hughes, 1997; Bryan et al., 1998; van der Pol and Cairns, 1998; Ratcliffe and Buxton, 1999; Ryan et al., 2000; Jan et al., 2000; San Miguel et al., 2000). More recent applications have applied DCEs to value health outcomes (Johnson et al., 2000; Sculpher et al., 2004), estimate utility weights within the QALY framework (Netten et al., 2002), estimate the importance of different criteria within a priority setting context (Farrar et al., 2000; Bryan et al., 2002), model doctors' behaviour when choosing jobs (Godsen et al., 2000; Ubach et al., 2003), and look at take-up rates for screening programmes (Hall et al., 2002; Gerard et al., 2003).

Given the role of the UK's National Institute for Health and Clinical Excellence (NICE) in recommendations concerning optimal treatments and its wider sphere of influence outside the UK, an interesting question concerns the potential use of DCEs by

NICE. As noted above, to date the dominant evaluation framework within health economics has been the cost per QALY approach. Using this approach poses empirical challenges involving judgements about whether the QALYs gained are worthwhile (Towse et al., 2002). Two main challenges are to determine:

- how the weights attached to QALY health gains differ with respect to different types of health care beneficiary (patient); and
- how much it is reasonable to spend to achieve these gains in length and quality of life: that is, what monetary value should be placed upon a QALY.

Work is currently underway assessing the feasibility of the DCE methodology in addressing these questions (Baker et al., 2003; Donaldson et al., 2004).[2]

Further, NICE is under increasing pressure to take account of patient preferences. To date consideration of such preferences has been limited. Patients may have preferences over aspects of care that go beyond the attributes of QALY models. NICE plan to have a 'patient-centred' evaluation of technologies, in addition to the current assessments of clinical and cost-effectiveness. Adopting the DCE approach will allow the integration of patient values on all aspects of care within one measure. Valuation of process and health outcomes from the patient's perspective may lead to conclusions that conflict with the recommendations of the cost per QALY approach. This is more likely to be the case when comparing technologies that differ with respect to outcomes beyond those measured in a QALY, as well as process attributes. Recent examples include the reviews commissioned by NICE on the effectiveness and cost-effectiveness of both metal on metal hip resurfacing arthroplasty for treatment of hip disease where treatment options differed with respect to process (surgical versus conservative management) (Vale et al., 2002) and of home versus hospital or satellite unit haemodialysis for people with end stage renal failure (Mowatt et al., 2002).

5.   Validity of DCEs

DCEs, as with CV and the methods used to elicit health state valuations to calculate QALYs (standard gamble and time trade-off), rely on individual responses to hypothetical questions. Thus the problem of attempting to demonstrate that the values obtained actually do reflect individuals' true preferences is common to all stated preference measures. It is therefore important to include tests of validity, that is to test the extent to which individuals behave in real settings as they state they would. Given that many of the applications of DCEs have taken place in countries with a publicly provided health care system, where individuals have very limited choice, a number of alternative validity tests have been applied. The most common test is theoretical (internal) validity. This involves checking that model coefficients have the signs expected, given theory or previous evidence. The evidence on the theoretical validity of DCEs is encouraging (Ryan and Gerard, 2003). More recently assessments of validity have tested the underlying axioms of DCEs. The application of DCEs, as with any method of preference elicitation, assumes that individuals have complete (individuals are able to form and express a complete order of preferences), rational (an individual should prefer more of a good thing rather than less) and continuous (individuals trade between all attributes that are important to them, adopting compensatory decision-making) preferences. Evidence suggests that completeness and rationality are satisfied (Ryan and Gerard, 2003). However, there is some evidence that continuity may be violated in some contexts, and consideration is now being given to this in both the design and analysis of DCEs (Ryan and Gerard, 2003; Swait, 2001).

The preferred test of validity is whether individuals behave in the real world as they state in the DCE. To date there have been two studies testing the external validity of DCEs. Watson et al. (2003) asked patients at a family planning clinic to complete a DCE concerned with preferences for alternative chlamydia screening programmes. The questionnaire, presented before their consultation, included 16 screening options and, for each, subjects were asked if they would be prepared to go through with screening. Possible responses were 'yes' or 'no'. Included amongst these options was the 'actual choice' which, unknown to them at the time of completion of the DCE, they were offered in their consultation. Eighty-one per cent responded to the real choice as they had stated they would in the hypothetical context. Mark and Swait (2004) compared DCE responses with revealed preferences in the context of physicians' perceptions of existing alcoholism medication attributes and their prescribing rates of those medications. They concluded that the preference functions retrieved from the two sources were similar, suggesting that respondents can manage hypothetical questions about prescribing decisions.

6. Conclusions

This chapter discussed the role of the DCE technique in health economics. DCEs can be used to address a wide range of questions, ranging from use within an economic evaluation framework through to priority setting and understanding labour market decisions and individual behaviour more generally. As long as the policy question can be broken down into attributes, DCEs are potentially useful. However, it is important that DCEs are carried out in a rigorous manner, with due consideration given to identifying and defining attributes and levels, defining the choice set to present to respondents, and the external validity of responses.

Notes

1. Discrete choice experiments have also been referred to in the literature as 'conjoint analysis'. However, conjoint analysis is an umbrella term which refers to ranking, rating and choice based exercises concerned with the contribution of individuals attributes to the overall value of a good or service. It is important to stress that only DCEs (and contingent ranking) have demonstrably close links with economic theory, which allows results to be interpreted as marginal (or total) values for use in Cost Benefit Analysis or other contexts (Louviere et al., 2000; Viney et al., 2002).
2. Dolan and Tsuchiya (Chapter 36 in this Companion) discuss the issue of weights for different beneficiaries of QALYs.

References

Baker, R., S. Chilton, C. Donaldson, M. Jones-Lee, H. Metcalf, P. Shackley and M. Ryan (2003), *Determining the Societal Value of a QALY by Surveying the Public in England and Wales: a Research Protocol*, Birmingham: NCCRM Publications.
Bateman, I., R. Carson, B. Day, M. Hanemann, N. Hanley, T. Hert, M. Jones-Lee, G. Loomes, S. Mourato, E. Ozdemiroglu, D. Pearce, R. Sugden and J. Swanson (2002), *Economic Valuation with Stated Preference Techniques: a Manual*, Cheltenham, UK and Northampton, MA, USA: Edward Elgar.
Ben-Akiva, M. and S.R. Lerman (1985), *Discrete Choice Analysis*, Cambridge: MIT Press.
Bryan, S., M. Buxton, R. Sheldon and A. Grant (1998), 'Magnetic resonance imaging for the investigation of knee injuries: an investigation of preferences', *Health Economics*, 7, 595–603.

Bryan, S., T. Roberts, C. Heginbotham and A. McCallum (2002), 'QALY-maximisation and public preferences: results from a general population survey', *Health Economics*, **11**(8), 679–93.

Department of the Environment, Transport and the Regions Highways (1997), 'Economics Note 2, November 1997', *Design Manuals for Roads and Bridges*, **13**, London: TSO.

Dillman, D. (2000), 'Mail and internet surveys: the tailored design method', 2nd edn, John Wiley.

Donaldson, C., G. Loomes, A. Robinson, R. Smith, M. Ryan and the Social Value of a QALY (SVQ) Team (2004), 'A nice solution to a nice problem: A proposed method to assess the societal value of a QALY', paper presented at the Health Economic Study Group Meeting, Glasgow.

Farrar, S., M. Ryan, D. Ross and A. Ludbrook (2000), 'Using discrete choice modelling in priority setting: An application to clinical service departments', *Social Science and Medicine*, **50**, 63–75.

Gerard, K., V. Lattimer, J. Turnbull, H. Smith, S. George and S. Brailsford (2004), 'Reviewing emergency care systems II: measuring patient preferences using a discrete choice experiment', *Emergency Medicine Journal*, **21**, 692–7.

Godsen, T., I. Bowler and M. Sutton (2000), 'How do general practitioners choose their practice? Preferences for practice and job characteristics', *Journal of Health Services Research and Policy*, **5**(4), 208–13.

Hall, J., P. Kenny, M. King, J. Louviere, R. Viney and A. Yeoh (2002), 'Using stated preference discrete choice modelling to evaluate the introduction of varicella vaccination', *Health Economics*, **11**, 457–65.

Hensher, D., P. Stopher and J. Louviere (2001), 'An exploratory analysis of the effect of numbers of choice sets in designed choice experiments: an airline choice application', *Journal of Air Transport Management*, **7**(6), 373–9.

Jan, S., G. Mooney, M. Ryan, K. Bruggeman and K. Alexander (2000), 'The use of conjoint analysis to elicit community preferences in public health research: a case study of hospital services in Australia', *Australian and New Zealand Journal of Public Health*, **24**(1), 64–70.

Johnson, R., M. Banzhaf and W. Desvousges (2000), 'Willingness to pay for improved respiratory and cardiovascular health: a multiple-format, stated preference approach', *Health Economics*, **9**, 295–317.

Lanscar, E. and E. Savage (2004), 'Deriving welfare estimates from discrete choice experiments: inconsistency between current methods and random utility and welfare theory', *Health Economics*, **13**(9), 901–7.

Louviere, J. and D. Hensher (1982), 'Design and analysis of simulated choice or allocation experiments in travel choice modelling', *Transportation Research Record*, **890**, 11–17.

Louviere, J. and G. Woodworth (1983), 'Design and analysis of simulated choice or allocation experiments: an approach based on aggregation data', *Journal of Marketing Research*, **20**, 350–67.

Louviere, J., D. Hensher and J. Swait (2000), *Stated Choice Methods. Analysis and Application*, Cambridge: Cambridge University Press.

Louviere, J., H. Oppewal, H. Timmermans and T. Thomas (1997), 'Handling large numbers of attributes in conjoint applications: who says existing techniques can't be applied? But if you want an alternative, how about hierarchical choice experiments?', mimeograph.

Mark, T. and J. Swait (2004), 'Using stated preference and revealed preference modeling to evaluate prescribing decisions', *Health Economics*, **13**(6), 563–73.

McFadden, D. (1973), 'Conditional logit analysis in analysis of qualitative choice behaviour', in P. Zarembka (ed.), *Frontiers in Econometrics*, New York: Academic Press.

McFadden, D. (1974), 'The measurement of urban travel demand', *Journal of Public Economics*, **3**, 303–28.

Mowatt, G., L. Vale, L. Wyness, J.G. Gonzalez-Perez and S.C. Stearns (2002), *Systematic Review of the Effectiveness and Cost-effectiveness of Home versus Hospital or Satellite Unit Haemodialysis for People with End Stage Renal Failure*, London: National Institute for Clinical Excellence.

Netten, A., M. Ryan, P. Smith, D. Skatun, A. Healey, M. Knapp and T. Wykes (2002), 'The development of a measure of social care outcome for older people', PSSRU Discussion Paper 1690/02.

Ohler, T., A. Le, J. Louviere and J. Swait (2000), 'Attribute range effects in binary response tasks', *Marketing Letters*, **11**, 249–60.

Ratcliffe, J. and M. Buxton (1999), 'Patients' preferences regarding the process and outcomes of life-saving technology', *International Journal of Health Technology Assessment in Health Care*, **15**(2), 340–51.

Ratcliffe, J. and L. Longworth (2002), 'Investigating structural reliability within health technology assessment: a discrete choice experiment', *International Journal of Technology Assessment*, **18**(1), 139–44.

Ryan, M. (1999), 'Using conjoint analysis to take account of patient preferences and go beyond health outcomes; an application to in vitro fertilisation', *Social Science and Medicine*, **48**, 535–46.

Ryan, M. (2004), 'Deriving welfare measures in discrete choice experiments: A comment to Lanscar and Savage', *Health Economic Letters*, **8**, 10–13.

Ryan, M. and K. Gerard (2003), 'Using discrete choice experiments to value health care: current practice and future prospects', *Applied Health Economics and Policy Analysis*, **2**, 55–64.

Ryan, M. and J. Hughes (1997), 'Using conjoint analysis to assess women's preferences for miscarriage management', *Health Economics*, **6**(3), 261–73.

Ryan, M. and S. Wordsworth (2000), 'Sensitivity of willingness to pay estimates to the level of attributes in discrete choice experiments', *Scottish Journal of Political Economy*, **47**(5), 504–24.

Ryan, M., A. Bate, C. Eastmond and A. Ludbrook (2001), 'Using discrete choice experiments to elicit preferences', *Quality in Health Care*, **10**, 155–60.

Ryan, M., E. McIntosh, T. Dean and P. Old (2000), 'Trade-offs between location and waiting times in the provision of health care: the case of elective surgery on the Isle of Wight', *Journal of Public Health Medicine*, **22**, 202–10.

San Miguel, F., M. Ryan and M. Amaya-Amaya (2005), ' "Irrational" stated preferences: a quantitative and qualitative investigation', *Health Economics*, **14**(3), 307–22.

San Miguel, F., M. Ryan and E. McIntosh (2000), 'Demonstrating the use of conjoint analysis in economic evaluations: an application to menorrhagia', *Applied Economics*, **32**, 822–33.

Sculpher, M., S. Bryan, Frt P. de Winter, P. H. Pasyne and M. Emberton (2004), Patient preferences for the management of non-metastatic prostate cancer: a discrete choice experiment. BMJ, **328**; 382–4.

Swait, J. (2001), 'A non-compensatory choice model incorporating attribute cut-offs', *Transportation Research*, **35**, 903–28.

Towse, A., C. Prichard and N. Devlin (eds) (2002), *Cost-effectiveness Thresholds: Economic and Ethical Issues*, London: King's Fund and Office of Health Economics.

Ubach, C., A. Scott, F. French, M. Awramenko and G. Needham (2003), 'What do hospital consultants value about their jobs? A discrete choice experiment', *British Medical Journal*, **326**, 1432–42.

Vale, L., L. Wyness, K. McCormack, L. McKenzie, M. Brazzelli and S.C. Stearns (2002), *Systematic Review of the Effectiveness and Cost-effectiveness of Metal on Metal Hip Resurfacing Arthroplasty for Treatment of Hip Disease*, London: National Institute for Clinical Excellence.

van der Pol, M. and J. Cairns (1998), 'Establishing patient preferences for blood transfusion support: an application of conjoint analysis', *Journal of Health Services Research and Policy*, **3**(2), 70–76.

Viney, R., E. Lancsar and J. Louviere (2002), 'Discrete choice experiments to measure preferences for health and health care', *Expert Review Pharmacoeconomics Outcomes Research*, **2**, 319–26.

Watson, V., M. Ryan and E. Watson (2003), 'Testing the validity of discrete choice experiments: evidence from a chlamydia screening study', paper presented at the Scottish Economic Society Conference, Glasgow University.

39 Design of choice experiments in health economics

Leonie Burgess, Deborah J. Street, Rosalie Viney and Jordan Louviere

1. Introduction

In many areas of applied economics, economists use observations of actual choices, or revealed preference (RP) data, to model behaviour. Individuals are assumed to make utility maximizing choices, and utility functions are estimated by analysing observed choices. A need for stated preference (SP) data arises when there are limited or no RP data available, because the good or service is new, not provided in a market context, or there is insufficient variability in choice attributes to obtain reliable estimates of their effects. Such situations often arise in the health and health care sectors. Discrete choice experiments (DCEs) are an SP method of increasing interest in health economics because they allow analysis of preferences for complex, multi-attribute goods like health care. DCEs were developed in marketing and transport research and are applied elsewhere (for example, environmental economics and telecommunications) (Louviere et al., 2000). Since the first application of DCEs in health (Propper, 1990) there has been rapid growth in their use (Viney et al., 2002; Ryan and Gerard, 2003).

DCEs ask individuals to state preferences in surveys designed to simulate market choices. Respondents evaluate a series of choice sets that each have m options, and choose their preferred option in each choice set. Options in each choice set are described by attributes (which may be quantitative or qualitative) that are varied over a plausible and policy-relevant range, generally expressed as a set of discrete levels. Responses are discrete observations (one option in the choice set is chosen, or 'yes/no' if only one option is in each choice set), and discrete choice methods are used to estimate preferences from the choices. By varying the attribute levels of options across choice sets, one can generate data to estimate the impact of attributes on utility. Inclusion of respondents' personal characteristics allows estimation of these effects as well.

As numbers of attributes and levels in experiments increase, numbers of options and numbers of possible ways of combining them to form choice sets grow large. Typically, it is infeasible to present respondents with all possible choice sets; hence, experimental design principles are used to select samples from the set of all the possible choice sets to allow efficient estimation of attribute main effects and interactions.

DCEs share some common features with conjoint methods commonly used in marketing, and DCEs in health have sometimes been described as 'conjoint analysis' (Ryan and Hughes, 1997; Ratcliffe and Buxton, 1999). Both methods describe goods/services in terms of underlying attributes, use experimental designs to develop sets of descriptions for preference elicitation, and use statistical models to estimate the effects of each attribute on preferences (Louviere, 2001a). However, in DCEs respondents are asked to choose one option from those presented, rather than ranking or rating all options, and the analysis uses the random utility model (RUM) as a behavioural theory. Thus, DCEs are consistent with economic theory (Hanley and Mourato, 2001), and can be designed to simulate real market situations (Ryan and Farrar, 2000), particularly if the options presented in choice sets include 'do not choose' when not choosing is feasible (Louviere, 2001a).

Economic analysis based on DCEs differs from most empirical research in economics because the data are derived from experiments designed by the researchers to answer specific questions, rather than from administrative data or statistical collections. DCE researchers decide what data are to be collected, and design the data collection instruments, including deciding the combinations of options to present to respondents. This requires the researcher to consider in advance of data collection what models and forms of utility function are to be estimated, and, particularly, any interactions among attributes. As data collection is costly, one should design experiments to maximize the information that can be obtained, ensuring all relevant attributes are included with an appropriate range of levels. However, DCEs can be complex cognitive tasks, so it is also important to consider how complexity might impact on respondent choices, and in turn on model estimates. This chapter focuses on identifying issues relevant to the design and development of highly efficient DCEs. The chapter provides a guide to the principles of efficient experimental design, and directs readers to key sources for more information.

2.   Understanding choice behaviour in designing choice experiments

Conceptually, individuals' choices are based on an underlying choice process, which is assumed to be utility maximization. Potentially unknown factors can affect consumer choices so some factors relevant to choices will be unobserved or unobservable, and individuals' choice processes and preferences are likely to differ. One cannot measure and include all relevant factors in any choice experiment, which has two important implications: 1) the data collected limit the models that can be estimated; and 2) which options are presented (and how) and which responses are obtained, and how they are measured, can affect response variability, which impacts on the quality of inferences. The goal of data collection and modelling is to minimize the unexplained variability in the observed choices by including as many factors as possible that systematically affect choices and by minimizing random variability (noise) in choices.

Factors not explicitly measured or included in models contribute to random error variance, and there is error in the measurement of responses in choice experiments (like all measurement instruments). There is also inherent variability in individuals' responses to survey questions, which can increase if tasks are difficult or surveys do not provide complete information about factors relevant to decisions. In designing DCEs one must consider how all aspects of data collection affect response variability and how to ensure that DCEs provide the maximum information at each stage.

Conceptualizing the choice process involves understanding individuals' decision-making contexts, options likely to be available, how options are presented, and factors that are likely to drive choices. The policy context must be considered, as well as how respondents are likely to interpret choice sets that they evaluate. Accurate conceptualization of choice processes involves literature reviews, qualitative research, and (iterative) pilot studies. Design and framing of DCE tasks should consider whether choices are once-off or repeated, the importance of the outcome of the choice (is it a life-or-death decision, for instance), and how familiar individuals are with the decision-making context. In many DCE contexts like transport mode choice, choices are familiar. However in health care, decisions may be made under stress, options may be less familiar, and there may be serious consequences. Decisions like choice of health insurance may be familiar to all individuals, but other health decisions, such as choices about medical interventions, may require provision of detailed information about the choice context and the attributes of options.

One must also consider whether combinations of attributes and levels presented in choice sets are not feasible or credible, in which case adjustments must be made to the design and presentation. As previously noted, because parameters of choice models cannot be estimated independently of random error variances, factors that increase error variability like task complexity or unrealistic attribute options may lead to more variability and possibly biased parameter estimates; see Louviere et al. (2002) and (2003). There is often confusion about the idea of feasibility in DCEs. What researchers or policy-makers know to be 'feasible' is irrelevant in DCEs. Concerns about feasiblity should arise only if respondents regard particular combinations of attributes as nonsensical, resulting in credibility issues. Feasibility issues can be addressed by framing an appropriate explanation in the instructions for what might seem unlikely. Eliminating 'infeasible' options/sets can result in loss of efficiency and orthogonality, which can cause serious bias, particularly in small designs. Thus, efforts should be made prior to fieldwork to determine whether feasibility is a real issue for respondents.

3. Discrete choice experiments, random utility theory and choice models

A DCE consists of a set of N choice sets, each with m options. Respondents evaluate each choice set and choose one option (or possibly 'none of these'). Each option in a choice set is described by k attributes, where the qth attribute has l_q levels, $q = 1, \ldots, k$. The attributes may be generic (common across options) or option-specific (belonging only to a particular option). The options may be labelled, to allow utilities specific to a product or brand (for example, medical intervention, surgical intervention), or they may be unlabelled (intervention A, intervention B).

Analysis of DCEs is based on Lancaster's theory of value, which assumes that utility is derived from the underlying characteristics or attributes of goods/services (Lancaster, 1966), and on the Random Utility Model (RUM) (McFadden, 1973; Manski, 1977). Utility is not directly observable but can be estimated from observed choices.

Consider a choice experiment in which there are N choice sets, each consisting of m options, $T_{i_1}, T_{i_2}, \ldots, T_{i_m}$. Given these m options, we assume that if the individual chooses option T_{i_j}, the utility of choice T_{i_j}, U_{i_j}, is the maximum among the m utilities. Under the RUM, the individual's indirect utility function for a particular option is assumed to have a systematic component, V_{i_j}, and a random component, ε_{i_j}, so $U_{i_j} = V_{i_j} + \varepsilon_{i_j} = X'_{i_j}\beta + \varepsilon_{i_j}$, where X_{i_j} is a vector of variables representing observed attributes of option T_{i_j}, and β is the vector of coefficients to be estimated. The random component may be due to unobserved or unobservable attributes of the choice, unobserved taste variation or measurement error (McFadden, 1973; Ben-Akiva and Lerman, 1985).

The estimated model depends on assumptions made about the distribution of the random component and the nature of the choice being modelled. It is commonly assumed that the ε_{i_j} are independently and identically distributed with a Gumbel distribution, leading to a multinomial logit (McFadden, 1973), where the probability that an individual chooses T_{i_1} is given by:

$$P(T_{i_1} > T_{i_2}, \ldots, T_{i_m}) = P(U_{i_1} > U_{i_n}, \forall n \neq 1) = P(V_{i_1} - V_{i_n} > \varepsilon_{i_n} - \varepsilon_{i_1}) = \frac{\exp(\mu(X'_{i_1}\beta))}{\sum_j \exp(\mu(X'_{i_j}\beta))}.$$

The parameter μ is a positive scale parameter that is inversely proportional to the variance of the random component. It is not possible to estimate the model coefficients separately from the scale parameter, and it is commonly assumed that $\mu = 1$. When responses from a series of choice sets are observed for one individual there may be correlation among the ε_{i_j} for that individual, which needs to be taken into account in the analysis. For example, one can include individual fixed effects in the systematic utility components, or estimate random parameter models such as the mixed logit model.

To discuss the design of discrete choice experiments, it is useful to follow Burgess and Street (2003) and define π_{i_j} by $\ln(\pi_{i_j}) = U_{i_j}$. Then

$$\Pr(T_{i_1} > T_{i_2}, \ldots, T_{i_m}) = \frac{\pi_{i_1}}{\sum_{j=1}^{m} \pi_{i_j}}$$

for $i_j = 1, 2, \ldots, t$ treatments, where no two treatments are the same. Maximum likelihood methods are used to estimate the π_{i_j}.

More information can be obtained from a DCE by using appropriate groupings of options. DCE designs can be compared by using the generalized variance of the parameter estimates, called the *D-optimal* value of the design. The variance–covariance matrix of the parameter estimates is the inverse of the Fisher information matrix; D-optimal designs will have the maximum determinant of the information matrix which is equivalent to the minimum value of the determinant of the variance–covariance matrix. Thus a D-optimal design is the natural extension of univariate minimum variance estimators. In El-Helbawy and Bradley (1978) the information matrix is defined to be $C = B\Lambda B'$, where B is the matrix with rows comprising the contrasts[1] for the effects to be estimated (that is, main effects or main effects plus two-factor interactions), and Λ is the matrix of second derivatives of the likelihood function.

To define Λ we first define $\lambda_{i_1, i_2, \ldots, i_m} = n_{i_1, i_2, \ldots, i_m}/N$, where $n_{i_1, i_2, \ldots, i_m} = 1$ if $(T_{i_1}, T_{i_2}, \ldots, T_{i_m})$ is a choice set and is 0 otherwise. Then the entries of Λ are given by

$$\Lambda_{i_1, i_1} = \pi_{i_1} \sum_{i_2 < i_3 < \ldots < i_m}' \frac{\lambda_{i_1, i_2, \ldots, i_m} \sum_{j=2}^{m} \pi_{i_j}}{(\sum_{j=1}^{m} \pi_{i_j})^2} = \frac{(m-1)}{m^2} \sum_{i_2 < i_3 < \ldots < i_m}' \lambda_{i_1, i_2, \ldots, i_m} \text{ if all } \pi_{i_j} = 1$$

and

$$\Lambda_{i_1,i_2} = -\pi_{i_1}\pi_{i_2}\sum_{i_3<i_4<\ldots<i_m}\!\!\!{}' \frac{\lambda_{i_1,i_2,\ldots,i_m}}{(\sum_{j=1}^{m}\pi_{i_j})^2} = -\frac{(m-1)}{m^2}\sum_{i_3<i_4<\ldots<i_m}\!\!\!{}' \lambda_{i_1,i_2,\ldots,i_m} \quad \text{if all } \pi_{i_j}=1$$

where the summations are over all choice sets that contain item T_{i_1} (for the diagonal elements) and are over all choice sets that contain items T_{i_1} and T_{i_2} (for the off-diagonal elements). Under the null hypothesis of no differences between the effects of the levels of each attribute (that is, all $\pi_{i_j}=1$), Λ contains the proportions of choice sets in which pairs of treatments appear together; see Burgess and Street (2003) and Street et al. (forthcoming) for more details.

Since optimal designs maximize the determinant of the information matrix, we denote the largest determinant by $\det(C_{opt})$. For any design d with information matrix C, the *D-efficiency* of d is given by $(\det(C)/\det(C_{opt}))^{1/p}$ where p is the number of parameters to be estimated.

Example 1 Suppose that there are two attributes, so $k=2$, and that $l_1=2$ and $l_2=4$. Suppose that the levels are 0 and 1 for the first attribute and 0, 1, 2 and 3 for the second attribute. Then there are $2\times4=8$ possible options that can be described: 00, 01, 02, 03, 10, 11, 12 and 13. Suppose that the choice sets are of size $m=3$. Then there are 56 distinct choice sets of this size: (00, 01, 02), (00, 01, 03), (00, 01, 10) and so on to (11, 12, 13). Suppose that we use (00, 01, 12) and (02, 13, 10) to be the choice experiment. Under the null hypothesis the matrices for these two choice sets are B, Λ_1 and C_1 in Table 39.1. These two choice sets are 86.6 per cent efficient. A diagonal C matrix requires at least eight choice sets; for example, (00, 01, 12), (01, 02, 13), (02, 03, 10), (03, 00, 11), (10, 11, 02), (11, 12, 03), (12, 13, 00) and (13, 10, 01) have a diagonal C matrix and are optimal for the estimation of main effects. Under the null hypothesis the matrices for these eight choice sets are B, Λ_2 and C_2 in Table 39.1.

4. Design of choice experiments

Binary response experiments
In binary response experiments respondents are shown treatment combinations one-at-a-time, and are asked whether they would choose/use each or not. If one wants to estimate the main effects of attributes independently of each other, the optimal set of treatment combinations to present to respondents are those from an orthogonal main effects plan (OMEP) (often called a resolution 3 design)[2] in which all levels of all attributes are equally replicated. If the goal of the experiment is to estimate both main effects and two-factor interactions independently of each other, the optimal set of treatment combinations to show to respondents form what is known as a fractional factorial design of resolution 5.[3] Some OMEPs and designs of resolution 5, together with definitions, may be found in Sloane (2005).

Generic forced choice experiments for main effects only
Burgess and Street (2005) provide an upper bound for $\det(C)$ for estimating main effects only. It applies for any choice set size for any number of attributes with any number of levels. All attributes can have the same number of levels, or attributes can have different numbers of levels. Recall that B is a matrix of contrasts for the effects of interest. If the

Table 39.1 Matrices for choice sets in Example 1 ($k=2$, $l_1=2$, $l_2=4$)

$$B = \begin{bmatrix}
-\frac{1}{2\sqrt{2}} & -\frac{1}{2\sqrt{2}} & -\frac{1}{2\sqrt{2}} & -\frac{1}{2\sqrt{2}} & \frac{1}{2\sqrt{2}} & \frac{1}{2\sqrt{2}} & \frac{1}{2\sqrt{2}} & \frac{1}{2\sqrt{2}} \\
-\frac{3}{2\sqrt{10}} & -\frac{1}{2\sqrt{10}} & \frac{1}{2\sqrt{10}} & \frac{3}{2\sqrt{10}} & \frac{3}{2\sqrt{10}} & -\frac{1}{2\sqrt{10}} & -\frac{1}{2\sqrt{10}} & \frac{3}{2\sqrt{10}} \\
\frac{1}{2\sqrt{2}} & -\frac{1}{2\sqrt{2}} & -\frac{1}{2\sqrt{2}} & \frac{1}{2\sqrt{2}} & \frac{1}{2\sqrt{2}} & -\frac{1}{2\sqrt{2}} & -\frac{1}{2\sqrt{2}} & \frac{1}{2\sqrt{2}} \\
-\frac{1}{2\sqrt{10}} & \frac{3}{2\sqrt{10}} & -\frac{3}{2\sqrt{10}} & \frac{1}{2\sqrt{10}} & -\frac{1}{2\sqrt{10}} & -\frac{3}{2\sqrt{10}} & \frac{3}{2\sqrt{10}} & \frac{1}{2\sqrt{10}}
\end{bmatrix}$$

$$\Lambda_1 = \frac{1}{18}\begin{bmatrix}
2 & -1 & 0 & 0 & 0 & 0 & -1 & 0 \\
-1 & 2 & 0 & 0 & 0 & 0 & 0 & -1 \\
0 & 0 & 2 & 0 & -1 & 0 & 0 & 0 \\
0 & 0 & 0 & 2 & 0 & -1 & 0 & 0 \\
0 & 0 & -1 & 0 & 2 & 0 & 0 & 0 \\
0 & 0 & 0 & -1 & 0 & 2 & 0 & 0 \\
-1 & 0 & 0 & 0 & 0 & 0 & 2 & 0 \\
0 & -1 & 0 & 0 & 0 & 0 & 0 & 2
\end{bmatrix}$$

$$\Lambda_2 = \frac{1}{72}\begin{bmatrix}
6 & -1 & -1 & 0 & -1 & 0 & -2 & -1 \\
-1 & 6 & 0 & -1 & 0 & -1 & -1 & -2 \\
-1 & 0 & 6 & -1 & -2 & -1 & 0 & -1 \\
0 & -1 & -1 & 6 & -1 & -2 & -1 & 0 \\
-1 & 0 & -2 & -1 & 6 & -1 & 0 & -1 \\
0 & -1 & -1 & -2 & -1 & 6 & -1 & 0 \\
-2 & -1 & 0 & -1 & 0 & -1 & 6 & -1 \\
-1 & -2 & -1 & 0 & -1 & 0 & -1 & 6
\end{bmatrix}$$

$$C_1 = B\Lambda_1 B' = \begin{bmatrix}
\frac{1}{9} & \frac{1}{18\sqrt{5}} & \frac{1}{18\sqrt{5}} & -\frac{1}{36\sqrt{5}} \\
\frac{1}{18\sqrt{5}} & \frac{1}{36} & \frac{1}{9} & \frac{1}{36} \\
\frac{1}{36} & -\frac{1}{9\sqrt{5}} & \frac{1}{9} & 0 \\
-\frac{1}{36\sqrt{5}} & 0 & \frac{1}{18\sqrt{5}} & \frac{1}{9}
\end{bmatrix}$$

$$C_2 = B\Lambda_2 B' = \begin{bmatrix}
\frac{1}{9} & 0 & 0 & 0 \\
0 & \frac{1}{9} & 0 & 0 \\
0 & 0 & \frac{1}{9} & 0 \\
0 & 0 & 0 & \frac{1}{9}
\end{bmatrix}$$

main effect of attribute q, which has l_q levels, is of interest then B will contain $l_q - 1$ rows that correspond to $l_q - 1$ independent contrasts (one for each degree of freedom) associated with that attribute. Any set of $l_q - 1$ independent contrasts results in the same information matrix and hence the same variance–covariance matrix of the parameter estimates. For each attribute one finds an appropriate set of contrasts and these are used as the rows of the matrix B to calculate the information matrix $C = B\Lambda B'$.

Once the C matrix for a DCE is calculated, the statistical efficiency of the design can be calculated. The *D-efficiency* is given by $[\det(C) / \det(C_{opt})]^{1/p}$, where p is the number of parameters to be estimated in the model. For designs that estimate main effects only, $p = \Sigma_i(l_i - 1)$. The maximum possible value of the determinant of C is

$$\det(C_{opt}) = \prod_{q=1}^{k} \left(\frac{2S_q}{m^2(l_q - 1) \prod_{i=1, i \neq q}^{k} l_i} \right)^{l_q - 1}$$

where

$$S_q = \begin{cases} (m^2 - 1)/4 & l_q = 2, m \text{ odd}, \\ m^2/4 & l_q = 2, m \text{ even}, \\ (m^2 - (l_q x^2 + 2xy + y))/2 & 2 < l_q < m, \\ m(m - 1)/2 & l_q \geq m \end{cases}$$

and positive integers x and y satisfy the equation $m = l_q x + y$ for $0 \leq y < l_q$. S_q is the maximum number of differences in the levels of attribute q in each choice set. Hence, an optimal design is one where the maximum number of level differences is attained for each attribute.

To construct designs that are optimal or near-optimal, an OMEP is required. The OMEP is used to represent the treatments in the first option of each choice set. Systematic level changes are made so that there are as many pairs of options as possible with different levels for each attribute in each choice set. For attributes with two levels this gives the foldover pairs advocated in Louviere, Hensher and Swait (2000), for example. These systematic changes are equivalent to adding generators, using modular arithmetic, to the OMEP to create the rest of the options in the choice sets. In most situations these generators are not unique and different generators can give rise to equally good designs; see Street et al. (forthcoming) for instance.

Example 2 Suppose that there are $k = 4$ attributes and that $l_1 = l_2 = 2$ and $l_3 = l_4 = 4$. There is an OMEP with 16 treatment combinations available; each level of the 2-level attributes is replicated 8 times and each level of the 4-level attributes is replicated 4 times. The 16 treatment combinations in the OMEP are used as the first option in the 16 choice sets. The other options in each choice set are obtained by adding a generator. For instance, use the generator 1111 (or 1112 or 1131 or 1133) to get choice sets of size $m = 2$. The addition is done modulo 2 in the first two positions (so $0 + 0 \equiv 1 + 1 \equiv 0$ and $0 + 1 \equiv 1 + 0 \equiv 1$) and is done modulo 4 in the third and fourth positions (so $1 + 3 \equiv 2 + 2 \equiv 0$ and $2 + 3 \equiv 1$, for example). Thus the first choice set is $(0000, 0000 + 1111)$ which is $(0000, 1111)$, for

Table 39.2   Main effects only: two attributes with two levels, two attributes with four levels

m	generators	# sets	Eff	Choice sets
2	1111	16	96%	(0000,1111), (0011,1122), (0122,1033), (0133,1000), (0012,1123), (0003,1110), (0130,1001), (0121,1032), (1023,0130), (1032,0103), (1101,0012), (1110,0021), (1031,0102), (1020,0131), (1113,0020), (1102,0013)
3	1111, 1122	16	100%	(0000,1111,1122), (0011,1122,1133), (0122,1033,1000),(0133,1000,1011), (0012,1123,1130), (0003,1110,1121), (0130,1001,1012), (0121,1032,1003), (1023,0130,0101),(1032,0103,0110), (1101,0012,0023), (1110,0021,0032), (1031,0102,0113), (1020,0131,0102), (1113,0020,0031), (1102,0013,0020)
4	0111, 1022, 1133	16	100%	(0000,0111,1022,1133), (0011,0122,1033,1100), (0122,0033,1100,1011), (0133,0000,1111,1022), (0012,0123,1030,1101), (0003,0110,1021,1132), (0130,0001,1112,1023), (0121,0032,1103,1010), (1023,1130,0001,0112), (1032,1103,0010,0121), (1101,1012,0123,0030), (1110,1021,0132,0003), (1031,1102,0013,0120), (1020,1131,0002,0113), (1113,1020,0131,0002), (1102,1013,0120,0031)

instance. The 16 choice sets that result are given in Table 39.2. Examples with $m = 3$ and $m = 4$ are also given in the table. See Burgess and Street (2005) or Street et al. (forthcoming) for more on choosing generators.

Generic choice experiments for main effects plus two-factor interactions
If all attributes have two levels, the optimal design consists of all choice sets in which the number of attributes that differ between any pair of profiles in the choice set is $(k + 1)/2$, if k is odd, or $k/2$ or $k/2 + 1$ if k is even (Burgess and Street, 2003). Furthermore, the maximum possible determinant of C for any choice set size has been determined and is given by

$$\det(C_{opt}) = \begin{cases} \left(\dfrac{(m-1)(k+2)}{m(k+1)2^k} \right)^{k+k(k-1)/2} & k \text{ even} \\ \left(\dfrac{(m-1)(k+1)}{mk2^k} \right)^{k+k(k-1)/2} & k \text{ odd.} \end{cases}$$

The *D-efficiency* of any design is given by $[\det(C) / \det(C_{opt})]^{1/p}$, where p is given by $p = k + k(k-1)/2$ when all the attributes are binary. In general $p = \Sigma_i (l_i - 1) + \Sigma_i \Sigma_{j, i<j} (l_i - 1)(l_j - 1)$.

Table 39.3   Main effects and two factor interactions: four attributes with two levels

m	Generators	# sets	Eff	Choice sets
2	1110, 1011, 0111	24	94%	(0000,1110), (0001,1111), (0010,1100), (0011,1101), (0100,1010), (0101,1011), (0110,1000), (0111,1001), (0000,1011), (0001,1010), (0010,1001), (0011,1000), (0100,1111), (0101,1110), (0110,1101), (0111,1100), (0000,0111), (0001,0110), (0010,0101), (0011,0100), (1000,1111), (1001,1110), (1010,1101), (1011,1100)
3	1100, 0110 and 1100, 0111	32	97%	(0000,1100,0110), (0001,1101,0111), (0010,1110,0100), (0011,1111,0101), (0100,1000,0010), (0101,1001,0011), (0110,1010,0000), (0111,1011,0001), (1000,0100,1110), (1001,0101,1111), (1010,0110,1100), (1011,0111,1101), (1100,0000,1010), (1101,0001,1011), (1110,0010,1000), (1111,0011,1001), (0000,1100,0111), (0001,1101,0110), (0010,1110,0101), (0011,1111,0100), (0100,1000,0011), (0101,1001,0010), (0110,1010,0001), (0111,1011,0000), (1000,0100,1111), (1001,0101,1110), (1010,0110,1101), (1011,0111,1100), (1100,0000,1011), (1101,0001,1010), (1110,0010,1001), (1111,0011,1000)
4	1100, 0110, 1011	16	99%	(0000,1100,0110,1011), (0001,1101,0111,1010), (0010,1110,0100,1001), (0011,1111,0101,1000), (0100,1000,0010,1111), (0101,1001,0011,1110), (0110,1010,0000,1101), (0111,1011,0001,1100), (1000,0100,1110,0011), (1001,0101,1111,0010), (1010,0110,1100,0001), (1011,0111,1101,0000), (1100,0000,1010,0111), (1101,0001,1011,0110), (1110,0010,1000,0101), (1111,0011,1001,0100)

Example 3   Suppose there are $k = 4$ binary attributes. Then the only resolution 5 design consists of all 16 treatment combinations. Table 39.3 shows some good designs for choice sets of size 2, 3 and 4.

When attributes can have any number of levels, and choice sets can be of any size, an explicit expression for det(C) in terms of the differences between the levels of each attribute in the choice sets is provided by Burgess and Street (2005). No general constructions are known, but Burgess and Street (2005) give optimal designs for some specific values of k and m. A method similar to that given for main effects only can be used to construct choice sets and the det(C) values compared to choose the best design.

Choice experiments with constant options

In this section we consider two types of choice experiments with constant options, the 'none of these' option and a common base option (for example, the status quo). Street and Burgess (2004) consider both types, and show that the designs that are optimal for the generic forced choice setting also are optimal when a 'none of these' option is included in each choice set, but designs with a 'none of these' option are not as efficient at estimating main effects as a forced choice design of the same size. Including a 'none of these' option may be more realistic and certainly means that interaction effects can be estimated, although inefficiently and not necessarily independently; see Street and Burgess (2004).

Sometimes each treatment combination needs to be compared to a common base option. In this situation the optimal design is one in which all the treatment combinations, including the common base option, form an OMEP. This can always be accomplished by a suitable renaming of the attribute levels.

Street and Burgess (2004) give an expression for det(C) for this situation. Assume that all levels of all attributes are equally replicated and let $p = \Sigma_{q=1}^{k}(l_q - 1)$ (total degrees of freedom for main effects), $L = \Pi_{q=1}^{k}l_q$ and assume that the OMEP has t treatments. Then

$$\det(C) = \frac{1+p}{(4(t-1))^p}\left(\frac{t}{L}\right)^p$$

Thus we can also evaluate the efficiency of the DCEs with a common base relative to generic forced choice designs as well as observing that the smallest OMEP is the most efficient if a common base must be used.

5.　Unresolved issues in choice experiments

Results exist for the design of optimal choice experiments when only some attributes are presented to respondents in each choice set and all attributes are binary (Grasshoff et al., 2003), and for the general case (Burgess and Street, 2005). However, it is unclear how respondents deal with unpresented attributes, as noted by Bradlow et al. (2004) and Islam et al. (2004).

There appear to be no results on the design of optimal choice experiments when certain combinations of attribute levels cannot appear together, nor if one wants to avoid having choice sets in which one option dominates all others on all attribute levels.

Sandor and Wedel (2001) discuss Bayesian design of choice experiments. Kanninen (2002) constructs optimal designs when attributes are assumed to be continuous. More work is needed on both of these problems.

This chapter has focused on models in the MNL family and there appear to be no results on the design of optimal choice experiments for any model more complicated than this. Much recent work in economics, transport and marketing has focused on new classes of discrete choice models that relax various aspects of the assumptions that underlie MNL models. For example, mixed logit models (for example, McFadden and Train, 2000) allow one to capture forms of preference heterogeneity, while retaining IID Extreme Value Type I errors; and variants of heteroscedastic error models (for example, Swait and Adamowicz, 2001) allow one to capture and parameterize non-constant error variances. Unfortunately, at this time we do not know whether designs developed for MNL models can be used to estimate such other models. That is, there are identification issues associated with these more complex models, and there has been no work that maps the model properties and constraints into design specifications.

Those who wish to apply more complex choice models should note that a number of serious questions have been raised recently about them. For example, Louviere (2001b, 2004a, 2004b), Louviere and Islam (2004), Louviere et al. (2004), Train and Weeks (2004) and Sonnier et al. (2004) have raised concerns about likely failure of real choice data to satisfy constant variance assumptions. If the errors associated with choices do not exhibit constant variances, there are serious confounding issues that can lead to incorrect and biased estimation of model parameters and associated variances, with evidence now revealing that estimates of willingness-to-pay not only can be highly unrealistic, but also can differ by large orders of magnitude. More recent work on what they call a 'Scale Decomposition Model' (for example, Islam et al., 2004) demonstrates that the errors do not have constant variance, but can be parameterized by specifying them as a function of certain design factors and/or individual characteristics. While promising, it is unclear at this time how to construct designs that are consistent with these models, or how to construct designs that will maximize the statistical efficiency of the resulting model estimates. Thus, more research on these issues would be welcome as theoretical and methodological advances are outpacing advances in design research.

Notes

1. For example for a 2-level attribute a contrast is the difference between the sum of the π_i with the high and low levels of the attribute. Polynomial contrasts are defined for attributes with more than two levels.
2. In a resolution 3 design any combination of levels from any pair of attributes appears together in the same number of treatment combinations in the stated choice experiment.
3. In a resolution 5 design any combination of levels from any four attributes appears together in the same number of treatment combinations in the stated choice experiment.

References

Ben-Akiva, M. and S.R. Lerman (1985), *Discrete Choice Analysis: Theory and Application to Travel Demand*, Cambridge, US: MIT Press.

Bradlow, E.T., Y. Hu and T.H. Ho (2004), 'A learning-based model for imputing missing levels in partial conjoint profiles', *Journal of Marketing Research*, **41**, 369–81.

Burgess, L. and D. Street (2003), 'Optimal designs for 2^k choice experiments', *Communications in Statistics – Theory & Methods*, **32**, 2185–206.

Burgess, L. and D.J. Street (2005), 'Optimal designs for choice experiments with asymmetric attributes', *Journal of Statistical Planning and Inference*, **134**, 288–301.

El-Helbawy, A.T. and R.A. Bradley (1978), 'Treatment contrasts in paired comparisons: large-sample results, applications and some optimal designs', *Journal of the American Statistical Association*, **73**, 831–9.

Grasshoff, U., H. Grossmann, H. Holling and R. Schwabe (2003), 'Optimal paired comparison designs for first order interactions', *Statistics: A Journal of Theoretical and Applied Statistics*, **37**, 373–86.

Hanley, N. and S. Mourato (2001), 'Choice modelling approaches: a superior option for environmental valuation?', *Journal of Economic Surveys*, **15**, 435–62.

Islam, T., J. Louviere and P. Burke (2004), 'Modeling the effects of including/excluding attributes in choice experiments on systematic and random components', unpublished working paper, School of Marketing, Faculty of Business, University of Technology, Sydney (December).

Kanninen, B.J. (2002), 'Optimal design for multinomial choice experiments', *Journal of Marketing Research*, **39**, 214–27.

Lancaster, K. (1966), 'A new approach to consumer theory', *Journal of Political Economy*, **74**, 132–57.

Louviere, J. (2001a), 'Choice experiments: an overview of concepts and issues', in J. Bennett and R. Blamey (eds), *The Choice Modelling Approach to Environmental Valuation*, Cheltenham, UK and Northampton, MA, USA: Edward Elgar, pp. 13–36.

Louviere, J. (2001b), 'What if consumer experiments impact variances as well as means? Response variability as a behavioral phenomenon', *Journal of Consumer Research*, **28**, 506–11.

Louviere, J. (2004a), 'Random utility theory-based stated preference elicitation methods: applications in health economics with special reference to combining sources of preference data', CenSoC Working Paper No. 04-001, Centre for the Study of Choice, Faculty of Business, University of Technology, Sydney.

Louviere, J. (2004b), 'Complex statistical choice models: Are the assumptions true, and if not, what are the consequences?', CenSoC Working Paper No. 04-002, Centre for the Study of Choice, Faculty of Business, University of Technology, Sydney.

Louviere, J. and T. Islam (2004), 'A comparison of importance weights/measures derived from choice-based conjoint, constant sum scales and best-worst scaling', CenSoC Working Paper No. 04-004, Centre for the Study of Choice, Faculty of Business, University of Technology, Sydney.

Louviere, J.J., D.A. Hensher and J.D. Swait (2000), *Stated Choice Methods: Analysis and Applications*, Cambridge, UK and New York, US: Cambridge University Press.

Louviere, J., D. Street and L. Burgess (2003), 'A 20+ years retrospective on choice experiments', in Y. Wind and P.E. Green (eds), *Marketing Research and Modeling: Progress and Prospects*, New York: Kluwer, pp. 201–14.

Louviere, J., D. Street, R. Carson, A. Ainslie, J.R. Deshazo, T. Cameron, D. Hensher, R. Kohn and T. Marley (2002), 'Dissecting the random component of utility', *Marketing Letters*, **13**, 175–91.

Louviere, J., K. Train, M. Ben-Akiva, C. Bhat, D. Brownstone, T. Cameron, R. Carson, J. DeShazo, D. Fiebig, W. Greene, D. Hensher and D. Waldman (2004), 'Recent progress on endogeneity in choice modeling', Workshop Report, University of Colorado 6th Invitational Choice Symposium, September.

Manski, C. (1977), 'The structure of random utility models', *Theory and Decision*, **8**, 229–54.

McFadden, D. (1973), 'Conditional logit analysis of qualitative choice behavior', in Zarembka, P. (ed.), *Frontiers of Econometrics*, New York, US: Academic Press, pp. 105–42.

McFadden, D. and K. Train (2000), 'Mixed MNL models for discrete response', *Journal of Applied Econometrics*, **15**, 447–70.

Propper, C. (1990), 'Contingent valuation of time spent on NHS waiting lists', *The Economic Journal*, **100**, 193–9.

Ratcliffe, J. and M. Buxton (1999), 'Patients' preferences regarding the process and outcomes of life-saving technology. An application of conjoint analysis to liver transplantation', *International Journal of Technology Assessment in Health Care*, **15**, 340–51.

Ryan, M. and S. Farrar (2000), 'Using conjoint analysis to elicit preferences for health care', *British Medical Journal*, **320**, 1530–3.

Ryan, M. and K. Gerard (2003), 'Using discrete choice experiments to value health care programmes: current practice and future research reflections', *Applied Health Economics and Health Policy*, **2**, 55–64.

Ryan, M. and J. Hughes (1997), 'Using conjoint analysis to assess women's preferences for miscarriage management', *Health Economics*, **6**, 261–73.

Sandor, Zsolt and Michel Wedel (2001), 'Designing conjoint choice experiments using managers prior beliefs', *Journal of Marketing Research*, **38**, 430–44.

Sloane, N.J.A. (2005), 'A library of orthogonal arrays', available at http://www.research.att.com/~njas/oadir/.

Sonnier, G., A. Ainsle and T. Otter (2004), 'The effect of parameterization on heterogeneous choice models', working paper, Anderson School of Management, UCLA.

Street, D.J. and L. Burgess (2004), 'Optimal stated preference choice experiments when all choice sets contain a specific option', *Statistical Methodology*, **1**, 37–45.

Street, D.J., L. Burgess and J.J. Louviere (forthcoming), 'Quick and easy choice sets: Constructing optimal and nearly optimal stated choice experiments', *International Journal of Market Research*, **22**.

Swait, J. and W. Adamowicz (2001), 'Incorporating the effect of choice environment and complexity into random utility models', *Organizational Behavior and Human Decision Performance*, **86**, 141–67.

Train, K. and M. Weeks (2004), 'Discrete choice models in preference space and willingness-to-pay spaces', working paper, University of California, Berkeley.

Viney, R., E. Lancsar and J. Louviere (2002), 'Discrete choice experiments to measure consumer preferences for health and healthcare', Expert reviews in *Pharmacoeconomics and Outcomes Research*, **2**, 319–26.

PART VIII

MEASURING COSTS
AND STATISTICAL ISSUES

40 Estimating costs for economic evaluation
Maria Raikou and Alistair McGuire

1. Introduction

The analysis of cost data has received limited attention compared to the discussion of effectiveness data, even though the estimation of treatment costs is a fundamental element in the calculation of the incremental cost-effectiveness ratio. A small number of reviews cover specific aspects relating to the concepts underlying cost measurement and cost collection and statistical estimation (Brouwer et al., 2001; Dranove, 1996; Gold et al., 1996; Johnston et al., 1999; Sculpher, 2001).

Dranove (1996) argues that identification of the relevant cost components to be included in a given study and their measurement will be determined by the perspective adopted for the analysis. In the majority of economic evaluations the cost elements are confined to those directly related to the treatment. For a societal based analysis all cost elements must be identified. Olsen (1994) highlights the importance of the inclusion of productivity losses as a cost even when a social welfare function is constrained to the consideration of health maximization alone. The importance of these considerations notwithstanding, this chapter is concerned with specific issues surrounding the measurement and statistical analysis of direct treatment costs.

2. Cost collection

Direct treatment costs are normally estimated by quantifying resource use attributable to the intervention under study and attaching unit cost information to these resources. Commonly data restrictions lead to limited capture of economic variables alongside clinical studies. Unit costs are usually deemed of secondary importance and are normally obtained from alternative sources on the basis that any variation in total cost is due to variation in resource volumes across treatment centres reflecting variation in clinical practice, while unit costs are not expected to vary substantially across centres (Spiegelhalter et al., 1996). This appears to represent an extreme view as charges are known to vary across treatment centres, thus providing evidence to the contrary. Economic theory suggests that there should be some defined predictable relationship between the mix of resources used in producing treatments and the relative costs of these resources. If operating efficiently, each treatment centre would define technical efficiency with regard to a production function which related factor mix to maximum output. Moreover if the treatment centre were operating as a cost minimizing firm, it would choose the least cost input combination to produce the desired level of output. Therefore given a change in the relative input prices, there should be a substitution away from the relatively more expensive input which would result in a change in the mix of resources. Glick et al. (2001) and Raikou et al. (2000) illustrate the differences in the cost estimates resulting from the use of an average of unit costs compared to use of individual centre-specific unit costs, and recommend using the latter approach as the former will result in biased estimates as it ignores the relationship between resource volumes and unit costs. In contrast, Coyle and Drummond (1996) and the Australian guidelines on economic evaluation of pharmaceuticals (Commonwealth of Australia, 1995) recommend that a single set of unit cost data, applied to centre-specific resource volumes, may suffice, although no evidence is provided to support their stance. Within a related literature addressing similar concerns in the context of multi-centre clinical trials opinions on the appropriate methodology to be adopted diverge (Drummond et al., 1992; Coyle, 1996; O'Brien, 1996; Jonsson and Weinstein, 1997; Schulman et al., 1998; Wilke et al., 1998; Drummond and Pang, 2001).

In theory, cost ought to represent the true opportunity cost of the resource reflecting the minimum price required to keep the resource in its current use rather than some alternative use. Such prices are not available in the health care sector and a number of proxies are used. Dranove (1996) and Johannesson (1996) provide useful discussion of the problems of using such proxies. In identifying which costs ought to be included in an economic evaluation, Johnston et al. (1999) suggest that it is enough to identify the major components of total cost by studying the expected frequency of occurrence of different cost generating events and identifying resources associated with high unit costs. Whynes and Walker (1995) and Knapp and Beecham (1993) suggest that while aggregation of cost elements into categories is possible with direct implications for the collection of cost data, it would be difficult to identify the important cost categories at the outset of a study, due to the variation in the distribution of costs across individual patients and the variation in the distribution of costs across disease areas. On the same issue, Gold et al. (1996) argue that ease of measurement is not a justifiable criterion, while Glick et al. (2001, p. 121) note that in practice 'there are no *a priori* guidelines about how much data are enough, nor are there data on the incremental value of specific items' to be included in the cost elements.

3.   Cost analysis

Cost analysis raises a number of statistical problems, some of which require treatment by specific statistical methods while others stem from more general concerns. One important issue relates to the representativeness of a typical study population and is addressed in the chapter by Polsky and Basu in this Companion (Chapter 43). A related issue is concerned with the bias imparted in the estimates by omitted variables. Viewed within a linear regression setting, Mullahy and Manning (1995) argue that within a clinical trial setting the randomization process must appropriately account for confounding variables. In other words, randomization must ensure orthogonality between the covariates measured in the study and the unobservables for the bias due to omitted variables to be avoided.

Statistical estimation of treatment costs can be undertaken using a number of alternative approaches: both parametric and non-parametric. The former may be preferred when there is interest in assessing covariate effects on cost or in the extrapolation of costs beyond the end of the study period or to different patient populations. On the other hand, a parametric approach imposes a particular distributional form on costs which may not be justified. Additional concerns which influence the choice of the analytical methodology relate to the pattern of the observed cost data and include positive skewness in the cost observations, a substantial proportion of zero costs, missing data, censoring, and lack of independence in the cost observations in situations where each individual in the sample contributes multiple data points over time. Each of these problems is considered in turn below with the exception of the issue of skewness and zero cost observations which are addressed in the chapter by Manning in this Companion (Chapter 41). Similar topics are discussed in Heyse et al. (2001) and Lipscomb et al. (1998). In what follows the main interest lies in deriving estimates of mean cost over the duration of the study.

Missing data

Rubin (1976) considered various mechanisms that may cause missing data and identified the weakest conditions under which it is appropriate to ignore the process that causes missing data. In situations where the process cannot be ignored, modelling is required. If statistical inference means sampling distribution inference, then the process causing missing data can be ignored if the data are missing at random and the observed data are observed at random (Rubin, 1976, p. 582).

Methods for handling missing data are related to the mechanism that causes the missing values. In most cases missing data are analysed based on the assumption that the missing data are missing at random, in the sense of Rubin (1976), or on the stronger assumption that the missing data are missing completely at random, that is the process that causes the missing data does not depend on the values of the variables of interest in the data. A test statistic for testing whether the data are missing completely at random has been proposed by Little (1988). Under either of the above assumptions the mechanism causing the missing data can be ignored. If this is the case, which implies that the missing data mechanism need not be modelled, the main approaches to analysing such data are briefly presented below.

Assuming the classic linear regression model given by:

$$E(Y|X) = \beta_0 + \beta'X, \quad \text{where } \text{var}(Y|X) = \sigma^2$$

the problem is to derive estimates of the parameters and their associated variance when some of the data are missing. Although missing data could be present both in the outcome variable Y as well as the regressors X, the methods discussed below concentrate on the case of missing X's but this does not restrict the outcome variable which could have some missing values as well.

The complete case analysis is a least squares method that results from minimizing the sum of squared residuals with respect both to the parameters and the missing values. This is performed by assigning a zero residual to any incomplete case with missing values which effectively results in the removal of that case from the estimation of the regression parameters. Completely discarding the cases with missing values in this manner leads to loss of information, which could be a substantial problem if the proportion of cases with missing values is high. On this basis the approach has been deemed useful only for providing a baseline method for comparisons. Another method is first to impute the missing X values and then to perform the regression of Y on X using the imputed X values either by ordinary least squares or by a weighted least squares regression that attaches lower weights to the incomplete cases. A simple approach for imputing the missing X values is to replace the missing X's by their unconditional sample means. This method will result in poor estimates if there is substantial correlation in the data. An improvement is to use information on the observed X's in a case to impute the missing X's. Another method is to impute the missing X by using both Y and the observed X's for imputation. A further approach is to assume a joint distribution for Y and X, a typical choice being a multivariate normal distribution, and to estimate the parameters of this distribution by maximum likelihood (Beale and Little, 1975). The estimates of the parameters are then substituted into the regression model yielding maximum likelihood estimates of the regression parameters.

The imputation methods described above could result in low standard error estimates because errors in the imputations are not taken into account. A solution to this problem was proposed by Rubin (1978a, 1978b) and is referred to as multiple imputation. According to this approach instead of imputing a single mean for each missing value, $N \geq 2$ values are drawn from the predictive distribution of the missing values given the remaining covariates and Y, and then complete data analysis is repeated N times, once with each imputation substituted. The final estimate of the parameter is then the sum of the parameter values obtained for each imputation divided by the number of imputations. Multiple imputation has the advantage that once the imputations are constructed, analysis proceeds by complete-data methods. Multiple imputations could be predictions based on an explicit model or they could be based on an implicit model for the missing values. An example of the latter is hot-deck imputation, which matches incomplete cases to complete cases using information on covariates and then imputes values from the complete cases.

Robins et al. (1994) proposed a class of estimators to account for a subset of regressors having missing values either by design or happenstance. Their estimating equations make use of the inverse of the probability of non-missingness and the estimators for the regression parameters of the conditional mean model are consistent under the following conditions: the data are missing at random, in the sense of Rubin (1976), the probabilities of missingness are bounded away from zero and the probabilities of missingness are known or can be estimated parametrically. Comparisons between estimators belonging to their general class and established estimators showed asymptotic equivalence between the estimators being compared, but the weighted estimators were always more efficient. Efficiency was improved by retrieving information lost due to missingness from subjects with incomplete data, an approach also adopted by Dagenais (1973), Gourieroux and Montfort (1981), Beale and Little (1975), Pepe and Fleming (1991), and Carroll and Wand (1991). Compared with the latter set of estimators, the estimators proposed by Robins et al. (1994) are again more efficient.

Censoring
Censoring occurs whenever some individuals' behaviour with respect to the variable under study is not observed for the full time up to the event of interest, which results in information being incomplete for these patients. Patients who are lost to follow-up, who drop out of the study or who are observed until the end of the study period without having reached the event of interest are right censored. Estimators of statistics of interest are biased if no account is taken of censoring, with the bias increasing as the degree of censoring increases.

Until recently the problem of censored cost data had not received much attention and the analysis was based on the following two 'naive' estimators. The first, referred to as the uncensored cases estimator, only uses the uncensored cases in the estimation of mean cost while the second, referred to as the full-sample estimator, uses all cases but does not differentiate between censored and uncensored observations. Both these estimators will always be biased. The full-sample estimator is always biased downward because the costs incurred after censoring times are not accounted for, whereas the uncensored-cases estimator is biased toward the costs of the patients with shorter survival times, because larger survival times are more likely to be censored (Lin et al., 1997).

Given the existence of consistent estimators of failure time statistics in the presence of censoring, initial attempts to adjust estimates of cost statistics for censoring were based on application of traditional survival analysis techniques to cost data (for example, Fenn et al., 1995; 1996). The assumption underlying the validity of these approaches is the one of independence between the variable of interest and its censoring variable. This implies independence between time to event and time to censoring when failure time data are considered and independence between cost at event and cost at censoring when cost data are analysed. Under random censoring, as is generally the case in medical studies, the assumption is valid with respect to time to event data but it is normally violated with respect to cost to event data. The violation is due to the lack of a common rate of cost accrual over time among individuals, as patients who are in poorer health states generate higher costs per unit of time and consequently are expected to generate higher cumulative costs at both the failure time and the censoring time (Lin et al., 1997; Etzioni et al., 1999). This positive correlation implies that removal of certain observations from the sample, due to censoring, affects the joint distribution of cost for the remaining observations, in the sense that, at any point in time, future cost expectation is statistically altered by censoring. As a result, any analysis that does not model this dependency will lead to erroneous inferences. Consequently cost estimators based on traditional survival analysis approaches are normally inappropriate in the analysis of censored cost data. Recently a number of alternative methods have been introduced: both non-parametric and parametric.

Lin et al. (1997) proposed two non-parametric estimators of average cost under conditions of censoring. Under both methods the study period is partitioned into a number of sub-intervals, an estimate of average cost in the interval is derived and the estimator of cost for the whole duration of analysis is obtained by summing over the sub-intervals the interval cost estimates weighted by interval-specific Kaplan–Meier probability estimates of time to event (Kaplan and Meier, 1958). The difference between the two alternatives is that the first only uses information on the total costs of uncensored individuals incurred up to the point of the individual's event in the estimating process, while the second uses information on intermediate individual cost history from all individuals. Both estimators are shown to be consistent under the assumption of independent censoring, an extension of this assumption to require that the censoring mechanism is unrelated to cost levels, continuous distribution of failure time and a discrete pattern for the censoring distribution.

An alternative approach, proposed by Bang and Tsiatis (2000), allows arbitrary censoring distribution patterns and attempts to improve efficiency of the proposed estimators by recovering information lost due to censoring, adding functionals of the cost history process in the estimating equations. The idea underlying all estimators in this class is the use of the inverse of the probability of an individual not being censored in the estimating equations. The first estimator uses cost information from the uncensored individuals alone, while the second estimator also incorporates information on intermediate cost history from censored individuals. Under the first approach, the estimate of mean cost is derived as the average of the complete individual costs weighted by the inverse of the Kaplan–Meier probability of an individual not being censored evaluated at the point of the individual's death. Under the second approach, the duration of analysis is partitioned into a number of sub-intervals, the first estimator is used to derive the estimated cost incurred in each of these sub-intervals and the final estimate of mean cost is derived by summing over these intervals. The advantage of the latter estimator is an increase in efficiency, by allowing use of additional cost information. Each of these estimators is accompanied by an improved variant that attempts to increase efficiency in the estimates through use of some functional of the cost history process that allows recovery of information lost due to censoring. Under independent censoring, all four estimators are shown to be consistent.

Turning to the parametric approaches, the first method, introduced by Carides et al. (2000), assumes a relationship between cost and failure time and involves two stages in deriving estimates of mean cost. In the first stage of the estimation process the expected cost at any given point in time is estimated as a function of failure time and in the second stage the estimated expected costs at given points in time are weighted by the Kaplan–Meier probability of death at these points in time. The estimate of mean total cost over the duration of interest is then derived as the sum over time of these weighted individual cost estimates. A regression approach is used to derive the expected costs where only uncensored individuals contribute cost information in order to avoid the bias in the regression parameter estimates imparted by censoring. Alternative parametric assumptions can be made regarding the relationship between cost and survival time depending on the data under consideration. Due to the consistency of the Kaplan–Meier estimator, consistency of the proposed estimator is ensured if the regression model specifying the relationship between cost and failure time is consistently estimated.

The second parametric alternative was introduced by Lin (2000) and assumes a linear regression model in which cost is related to a set of individual covariates. The method derives estimates of the regression parameters accounting for the presence of censoring and is not restricted by the censoring pattern. Two estimators result from this approach. The first uses the individual total accumulated costs at the individual's point of death or censoring while the second makes use of multiple cost observations on each subject obtained at various points in time over the study period. The advantage of the latter estimator is an increase in efficiency by allowing use of cost information that is not used by the preceding estimator. In both cases the estimates of the regression parameters are adjusted for censoring by incorporating the inverse of the probability of an individual not being censored evaluated at the point of the individual observed cost in the estimating equations. Both approaches derive consistent estimates for the regression parameters.

Raikou and McGuire (2004) attempted to assess the non-parametric estimators' performance empirically under heavy censoring. They identify two estimators that perform well under all conditions considered; namely the estimator by Lin et al. (1997), using intermediate individual cost history information, and the estimator by Bang and Tsiatis (2000), also using intermediate individual cost history information. A similar study of the parametric estimators' performance, under the same censoring conditions and using the same data, found that the regression methodology proposed by Lin (2000) that uses intermediate cost history information performs well under heavy censoring, resulting in cost estimates that are very close to the ones derived from application of the best performing non-parametric estimators mentioned above. Use of the inverse of the probability of an individual not being censored in the estimating equations is instrumental in deriving unbiased estimates of medical care costs under conditions of censoring. Nevertheless the success of the approach is also dependent on the amount of available information on the cost history process with the value of this information increasing as the degree of censoring increases.

Given that censoring is a missing data process, the statistical theory for analysing missing data can also be applied to the problem of censoring. There are obviously circumstances in which the problem of missing data on some of the covariates can arise alongside the problem of censoring of the dependent variable. For example, Lin and Ying (1993b) have considered this issue within the context of the Cox proportional hazards regression model where time to failure is subject to censoring. Under conditions where some of the regressors have missing values, and although the model adjusts for censoring of the dependent variable, the authors state that not accounting for the missing covariate values appropriately will result in biased and inefficient parameter estimates.

Dependency among multiple measurements on the same subject
An issue inherent in data consisting of repeated measurements of the variables of interest is the dependency among the repeated measurements for any subject. In such circumstances ordinary least squares regression is not an appropriate estimation procedure as the assumptions concerning the error terms are no longer valid.[1] The general procedure to analysing such data in the econometric and statistical literature is to adopt a generalized linear regression model which accommodates more general patterns for the distribution of the disturbances.

A class of generalized estimating equations for the regression parameters has been proposed by Liang and Zeger (1986) which result in consistent estimates of the regression parameters and their variances without requiring specification of the joint distribution of a subject's observations. This approach has wide application if interest is in modelling the dependence of the outcome variable on the covariates and not in the pattern of change of the outcome variable over time. If this is the case, the approach models the marginal expectation of the outcome variable as a function of the covariates at each point in time, whilst accounting for the correlation among the repeated measurements for a given subject by treating the time dependence among repeated measurements for an individual as a nuisance. When the time dependence is of primary importance, then, as stated by the authors, models for the conditional distribution of the outcome variable given its past values would be more appropriate. The authors argue that if observations gained from different subjects are independent, the estimates of the regression parameters will be consistent even if the correlation structure is misspecified, provided that the model for the marginal means of the outcome variable at each point in time is correctly specified.

In addition, this approach can also be adopted in the event of some observations being missing, in which case the same results hold provided that data are missing completely at random in the sense of Rubin (1976). Within this framework of generalized linear regression, Lin (2000) derived estimators for the regression parameters when repeated measurements on the outcome variable were obtained within the context of censored cost analysis.

4.   Concluding remarks

The emphasis in this overview of the literature has been on the concepts underlying the definition of cost in economic evaluation and the estimation problems most commonly encountered in the collection and analysis of cost data. The specific issues arising in a given analysis will be determined by the general nature of cost data and the cost pattern observed in the particular application considered.

Note

1.   Partly in an attempt to resolve the problem of dependency among the multiple observations for each subject, Lipscomb et al. (1998) used the stratified variant of the Cox proportional hazards model with time being the stratification variable in deriving estimates of patient cost within each stratum. They argue that a great advantage of this model is that it does not make any assumptions about the distributional form of the error terms, and as such it is likely to be amongst the best alternatives when interest lies in modelling complex distributions such as distributions of cost. In addition, they suggest that this model overcomes the problem of dependency between multiple observations on the same individual, as it assumes different baseline hazards for cost across different strata. Given, however, the criticism of this approach (for example, Etzioni et al., 1999), it seems unlikely that such a methodology would be useful.

References

Bang, H. and A.A. Tsiatis (2000), 'Estimating medical costs with censored data', *Biometrika*, **87**, 329–43.
Beale, E.M.L. and R.J.A. Little (1975), 'Missing values in multivariate analysis', *Journal of the Royal Statistical Society*, B 37, pp. 129–45.
Brouwer, W., F. Rutten and M. Koopmanschap (2001), 'Costing in economic evaluation' in M. Drummond and A. McGuire (eds), *Economic Evaluation in Health Care: Merging Theory with Practice*, Oxford: Oxford University Press, pp. 68–93.
Carides, G.W., J.F. Heyse and B. Iglewicz (2000), 'A regression-based method for estimating mean treatment cost in the presence of right-censoring', *Biostatistics*, **1**, 299–313.
Carroll, R.J. and M.P. Wand (1991), 'Semiparametric estimation in logistic measurement error models', *Journal of the Royal Statistical Society*, B 53, pp. 573–87.
Commonwealth of Australia (1995), *Guidelines for the Pharmaceutical Industry on Preparation of Submissions to the Pharmaceutical Advisory Committee*, Australian Government Print Office, Canberra.
Coyle, D. (1996), 'Statistical analysis in pharmacoeconomic studies', *Pharmacoeconomics*, **9**, 506–16.
Coyle, D. and M. Drummond (1996), 'Analysing differences in costs of treatment across centres within economic evaluations', paper presented to iHEA, Vancouver.
Dagenais, M.G. (1973), 'The use of incomplete observations and multiple regression analysis: A generalised least squares approach', *Journal of Econometrics*, **1**, 317–28.
Dranove, D. (1996), 'Measuring costs', in F.A. Sloan (ed.), *Valuing Health Care*, Cambridge University Press, pp. 61–75.
Drummond, M. and F. Pang (2001), 'Transferability of economic evaluation results', in M. Drummond and A. McGuire (eds), *Economic Evaluation in Health Care: Merging Theory with Practice*, Oxford: Oxford University Press, pp. 256–76.
Drummond, M., B. Bloom, G. Carrin et al. (1992), 'Issues in the cross-national assessment of health care technology', *International Journal of Health Technology Assessment*, **8**, 671–82.
Duan, N., W.G. Manning and C.N. Morris (1983), 'A comparison of alternative models for the demand for medical care', *Journal of Business and Economic Statistics*, **1**, 115–26.
Etzioni, R., E. Feuer, S. Sullivan, D. Lin, C. Hu and S.D. Ramsey (1999), 'On the use of survival analysis techniques to estimate medical care costs', *Journal of Health Economics*, **18**, 365–80.
Fenn, P., A. McGuire, M. Backhouse and D. Jones (1996), 'Modelling programme costs in economic evaluation', *Journal of Health Economics*, **15**, 115–25.
Fenn, P., A. McGuire, V. Phillips, M. Backhouse and D. Jones (1995), 'The analysis of censored treatment cost data in economic evaluation', *Medical Care*, **33**, 851–63.
Glick, H., D. Polsky and K. Sculman (2001), 'Trial-based economic evaluations: an overview of design and analysis', in M. Drummond and A. McGuire (eds), *Economic Evaluation in Health Care: Merging Theory with Practice*, Oxford: Oxford University Press, pp. 113–40.

Gold, M., J.E. Seigal, L.B. Russell and M.C. Weinstein (1996), *Cost-Effectiveness in Health and Medicine*, New York: Oxford University Press.

Gourieroux, C. and A. Montfort (1981), 'On the problem of missing data in linear models', *Review of Econometric Study*, **xlviii**, 579–86.

Heyse, J.F., J.R. Cook and C.W. Carides (2001), 'Statistical considerations in analyzing health care resource utilisation and cost data', in M. Drummond and A. McGuire (eds), *Economic Evaluation in Health Care: Merging Theory with Practice*, Oxford: Oxford University Press, pp. 215–35.

Horvitz, D.G. and D.J. Thompson (1952), 'A generalisation of sampling without replacement from a finite universe', *Journal of the American Statistical Association*, **47**, 663–85.

Johannesson, M. (1996), *Theory and Methods of Economic Evaluation of Health Care*, Amsterdam: Kluwer.

Johnston, K., M. Buxton, D.R. Jones and R. Fitzpatrick (1999), 'Assessing the costs of healthcare technologies in clinical trials', *Health Technology Assessment Review*, **3**(6).

Jonsson, B. and M.C. Weinstein (1997), 'Economic evaluation alongside clinical trials: study considerations for GUSTOIIb', *International Journal of Health Technology Assessment*, **13**, 49–58.

Kaplan, E.L. and P. Meier (1958), 'Nonparametric estimation from incomplete observations', *Journal of the American Statistical Association*, **53**, 457–81.

Knapp, M. and J. Beecham (1993), 'Costing mental health services', *Psychological Medicine*, **20**, 892–908.

Koul, H., V. Susarla and J. van Ryzin (1981), 'Regression analysis with randomly right-censored data', *The Annals of Statistics*, **9**, 1276–88.

Liang, K.-Y. and S.L. Zeger (1986), 'Longitudinal data analysis using generalised linear models', *Biometrika*, **73**, 13–22.

Lin, D.Y. (2000), 'Linear regression analysis of censored medical costs', *Biostatistics*, **1**, 35–47.

Lin, D.Y. and Z. Ying (1993a), 'A simple nonparametric estimator of the bivariate survival function under univariate censoring', *Biometrika*, **80**, 573–81.

Lin, D.Y. and Z. Ying (1993b), 'Cox regression with incomplete covariate measurements', *Journal of the American Statistical Association*, **88**, 1341–9.

Lin, D.Y., E.J. Feuer, R. Etzioni and Y. Wax (1997), 'Estimating medical costs from incomplete follow-up data', *Biometrics*, **53**, 113–28.

Lipscomb, J., M. Ancukiewicz, G. Parmigiani, V. Hasselblad, G. Samsa and D. Matchar (1998), 'Predicting the cost of illness: A comparison of alternative models applied to stroke', *Medical Decision Making*, **18** Supplement, S39–S56.

Little, R.J.A. (1988), 'A test of missing completely at random for multivariate data with missing values', *Journal of the American Statistical Association*, **83**, 1198–202.

Mullahy, J. and W.G. Manning (1995), 'Statistical issues in cost effectiveness analysis', in F.A. Sloan (ed.), *Valuing Health Care*, Cambridge: Cambridge University Press.

O'Brien, B. (1996), 'Economic evaluation of pharmaceuticals: Frankenstein's monster or vampire of trials', *Medical Care*, **34**, DS99–DS108.

Olsen, J.A. (1994), 'Production gains should they count in health care evaluations?', *Scottish Journal of Political Economy*, **79**, 687–705.

Pepe, M.S. and T.R. Fleming (1991), 'A nonparametric method for dealing with mismeasured covariate data', *Journal of the American Statistical Association*, **86**, 108–13.

Raikou, M. and A. McGuire (2004), 'Estimating medical care costs under conditions of censoring', *Journal of Health Economics*, **23**, 443–70.

Raikou, M., A. Briggs, A. Gray and A. McGuire (2000), 'Centre-specific or average unit costs in multi-centre studies? Some theory and simulation', *Health Economics*, **9**, 191–8.

Robins, J.M. and A. Rotnitzky (1992), 'Recovery of information and adjustment for dependent censoring using surrogate markers', in J. Jewell, K. Dietz and V. Farewell (eds), *AIDS Epidemiology–Methodological Issues*, Birkhäuser, Boston, pp. 297–331.

Robins, J.M., A. Rotnitzky and L.P. Zhao (1994), 'Estimation of regression coefficients when some regressors are not always observed', *Journal of the American Statistical Association*, **89**, 846–66.

Robins, J.M., A. Rotnitzky and L.P. Zhao (1995), 'Analysis of semiparametric regression models for repeated outcomes in the presence of missing data', *Journal of the American Statistical Association*, **90**, 106–21.

Rotnitzky, A. and J.M. Robins (1995), 'Semiparametric regression estimation in the presence of dependent censoring', *Biometrika*, **82**, 805–20.

Rubin, D.B. (1976), 'Inference and missing data', *Biometrika*, **63**, 581–92.

Rubin, D.B. (1978a), 'Multiple imputations in sample surveys – A phenomenological Bayesian approach', in *Proceedings of the Survey Research Methods Section, American Statistical Association*, pp. 20–34.

Rubin, D.B. (1978b), *Multiple Imputation for Nonresponse in Surveys*, New York: John Wiley.

Schulman, K., J. Burke, M. Drummond et al. (1998), 'Resource costing for multinational neurologic clinical trials: methods and results', *Health Economics*, **7**, 629–38.

Sculpher, M. (2001), 'The role and estimation of productivity costs in economic evaluation', in M. Drummond, A. McGuire (eds), *Economic Evaluation in Health Care: Merging Theory with Practice*, Oxford: Oxford University Press, pp. 94–112.

Spiegelhalter, F.A., D.R. Jones, M.K.B. Parmar et al. (1996), 'Being economical with the costs', Department of Epidemiology and Public Health Technical Paper 96-06, University of Leicester, Leicester.

Whynes, D. and A.R. Walker (1995), 'On approximations in treatment costing', *Health Economics*, **4**, 31–40.

Willke, R., H. Glick, D. Polsky and K. Schulman (1998), 'Estimating country-specific cost-effectiveness from multinational clinical trials', *Health Economics*, **7**, 481-94.

Zhao, H. and A.A. Tsiatis (1997), 'A consistent estimator for the distribution of quality adjusted survival time', *Biometrika*, **84**, 339–48.

41 Dealing with skewed data on costs and expenditures
*Willard Manning**

1. Introduction

The distribution of costs and expenditures for health care shares a number of character-istics that make their use in economic analysis difficult. These include: a substantial frac-tion of the population with no health care costs or use during the period of observation; and the costs and utilization for those with any care is typically quite skewed to the right.[1] As a result of these two together, the top one per cent of distribution of health care costs will often account for a quarter of the grand mean for a general population. Some types of costs are even more skewed, with the top tenth of the distribution accounting for half of all costs.

Under these circumstances, analysts have often found that use of standard least squares estimators often leads to analytical problems from highly influential outliers – catastrophic cases with unusual or rare characteristics. But it is also often the case, that removing or trimming such an extreme case only makes the results sensitive to a nearly as extreme, catastrophic case. Analysts often find that results are not replicable across alternative subsets of the data. Least squares estimation under these circumstances is inefficient and in some cases biased, especially if zeros are prevalent. Even when the estimates are unbi-ased, the inferences are biased because of the underlying heteroscedasticity implicit in a model with a strictly non-negative dependent variable. The inefficiency in the estimates and bias in the inference statistics for OLS results arises from the property that the vari-ability in costs is often an increasing function of the mean or of some function of the covariates x.

The sensitivity to extreme cases is a natural byproduct of the skewness in the data. If we were to analyse expenditures, y, by a standard OLS model $y = x\beta + \varepsilon$ where y is cost or expenditure on the raw scale (dollars, euros, or pounds), x is a row vector of observed characteristics, and β is a column vector of coefficients to be estimated, then we can char-acterize the effect of an individual observation i on the estimate of β by Cook's distance: $D_i = r_i^2 h_{ii}/(k(1 - h_{ii}))$ where r_i is the studentized residual, and h_{ii} is the ith diagonal element of $X'(X'X)^{-1} X$, where X is the data matrix for the covariates. With data on a general population, it is not uncommon for cases in the top one per cent of the distribu-tion to have values that are nine times the sample mean, have studentized residuals that are over 4, and maybe in double digits for the far right tail of the distribution. The extreme cases have tremendous influence if the characteristics x for that case are far from sample mean ($\bar{x}$). Since the data are skewed right, there are no countervailing large residuals in the left tail. The consequence is that in small and moderate sized samples, a single case

*   I would like to thank Anirban Basu for his suggestions on an earlier draft of this chapter.

can have tremendous influence on an estimate. In the Health Insurance Experiment (HIE), one single observation accounted for about 17 per cent of the mean for that insurance plan. Note that as N increases, the hat matrix element h_{ii} goes to zero. Thus the issue of influence is not an issue for very large datasets, such as those used in estimating risk adjusters for the US Medicare programme.

The replicability of the results over datasets raises a potential problem for forecasting. To the extent that the extreme cases have overly influenced the estimates, the corresponding estimates ($\hat{\beta}$) may differ from the population parameter. The result is that the forecast to a new dataset (drawn from the same population) will tend to underpredict for high x's and overpredict for low x's, more than would occur if the error term was symmetric.

2.   Alternative estimation approaches

There are several approaches to dealing with such data: do nothing; Box–Cox transformations of the dependent variable; generalized linear models (GLM); and the use of discrete approximations to the underlying distribution. The most prevalent is to ignore the risks and apply ordinary least squares to raw cost or expenditure data. As noted above, the problem with this approach is that the results are sensitive to the skewness in the dependent variable, especially if the dataset is small or moderate in size, and some of the characteristics are rare.

Box–Cox models

A second alternative is to transform the dependent variable by the natural logarithm or a power transformation to eliminate the skewness in the error.[2] Both of these transformations are special cases of the Box–Cox (1964) transformation; see Sakia (1992) for a review of this literature. Specifically, the Box–Cox models consider transformed equations $f(y)$ of the form:

$$f(y) = (y^{\lambda} - 1)/\lambda = x\beta + \varepsilon \quad \text{if } \lambda \neq 0 \tag{41.1a}$$
$$f(y) = \log(y) = x\beta + \varepsilon \quad \text{if } \lambda = 0 \tag{41.1b}$$

It is also often assumed that ε is either symmetric or normally distributed. The model can be estimated by either MLE or by use of least squares for suitable values of λ; see Foster et al. (2001) for a semi-parametric method that does not rely on normality.

The advantage of the power transformation, especially if $\lambda < 1$, is that it pulls in the right tail of the distribution faster than it does the middle or the left tail. As λ decreases toward zero, the error term in the estimated equation should become more symmetric, reducing the influence of the extreme cases in the tails of the distribution. However, very low values of λ may lead to overcorrection in the sense that it converts a right skewed distribution into a left skewed one after the transformation.

The problem with the Box–Cox approach is that we are often not interested in the transformed scale per se – the government does not spend log dollars or log euros. We are actually interested in the raw scale of y and predictions in dollars or euros. This leads to concerns about the retransformation of the results from the scale of estimation (for example, the log or the λth power) to the scale of actual interest (for example, raw dollars or euros). Because of the non-linear nature of the Box–Cox transformation, we cannot simply invert the transformation to obtain unbiased estimates of the $E(y|x)$ because $E(f(y|x)) \neq f(E(y|x))$. This is the retransformation problem discussed by Duan (1983), Duan et al. (1983), Zhou et al. (1997), Manning (1998), Mullahy (1998) and Blough et al. (1999).

The difference between the two is easy to see in the case of OLS on log(y). OLS generates unbiased estimates of $E(\ln(y)) = x\beta$ if $E(X'\varepsilon) = 0$. But, the term $E(e^{x\beta})$ yields an estimate of the geometric mean, not the arithmetic mean of the response function. The arithmetic mean is $E(y|x) = \exp(x\beta + 0.5\sigma^2)$ if ε is i.i.d. and normally distributed, and $\exp(x\beta + 0.5\sigma^2(x))$ if normally distributed and heteroscedastic in x (Manning, 1998). If the error is not normally distributed, then the estimates of $x\beta$ may be consistent, but one must apply Duan's smearing factor in the homoscedastic case, or its analogue in the heteroscedastic case.

The goal of most analyses is some statement about how the mean or some function of the mean of y on the raw scale changes with x. In general, the expectation of y depends on the variance and heteroscedasticity on the log scale.[3] If the variable of interest x_i is not discrete, then the slope of the expected value is given by:

$$\frac{\partial E(y|x)}{\partial x_i} = E(y|x)\left[\beta_i + 0.5\frac{\partial \sigma_\varepsilon^2}{\partial x_i}\right] \tag{41.2}$$

It is this derivative which should be used in the calculation of the elasticity of the mean response, rather than β_i alone.

In the non-normal case or for values of λ other than zero, the derivative will depend on the nature of the distribution as well as the form of the heteroscedasticity:

$$\frac{\partial E(y|x)}{\partial x_i} = \beta_i \int (\lambda(x\beta + \varepsilon) + 1)^{(1-\lambda)/\lambda} dF(\varepsilon) \tag{41.3}$$

where $F(\varepsilon)$ is the cdf for the error term (Abrevaya, 2002).

There are a number of technical issues that arise with Box–Cox models. One of these is how to deal with observations where $y = 0$.[4] Second, the estimates of the power transform are sensitive to extreme outliers in ε; see Carroll (1980) for robust alternatives, and Cook and Wang (1983) for diagnostics for influential outliers. In practice, it may be difficult to tell the effect of an influential outlier from skewness in the dependent measure that is not associated with the covariates. Third, there is some debate about whether one takes the power transform λ as fixed or as estimated in calculating the variance of the estimates of β or of any function of β and λ, such as equations (41.2) and (41.3) above. For the debate on this issue, see the articles by Bickel and Doksum (1981) and the paper (and associated exchange) by Hinkley and Runger (1984).

Generalized Linear Models (GLM)
A third alternative is to deal with the problem of skewness in the data by addressing the property that the variance function is an increasing function of the mean. This can be done by using some iteratively reweighted least squares alternative or the generalized linear models (such as gamma regression) estimated with quasi-maximum likelihood methods. In the GLM case, the analyst specifies: a link function between the linear model

$x'\beta$ and the mean, so that $g(E(y|x)) = x'\beta$; and a variance function $v(y|x)$ that character-izes the nature of the relationship between the mean and the variance on the raw scale. The $v(y|x)$ function is assumed to be a function of the mean, not of individual covariates in x directly. The correct specification of the variance function results in efficient estima-tors (Crowder, 1987) and may correspond to an underlying distribution of the outcome measure.[5] If the distribution is from the exponential family, then the estimation can be done by quasi-maximum likelihood methods.[6]

Much of the work to date on health care expenditures has used a log link: $\log(E(y|x)) = x\beta$. But some cases have also used power transformations, such as the square root. If the link function is misspecified, then the estimates will provide a biased estimate of the response.

Following the work of Blough et al. (1999), the most commonly used distribution for GLM models applied to positive health care cost or expenditure data has been the gamma. This is an appealing working assumption for the distribution function because the standard deviation under the gamma is proportional to the mean, a property often exhibited by health care cost data. But this is only one of several cases where the standard deviation or the variance is a power of the mean function. But if the variance is not a func-tion of the mean, then a Gaussian assumption may be used; this is Mullahy's non-linear model (1998); see also Wooldridge (1991). If the variance is proportional to the mean, then the Poisson may be more appropriate. If the standard deviation is proportional to the cube of the mean, then the inverse Gaussian is an alternative. If the distribution is misspecified, then there is a loss of efficiency, and the inference statistics need to be cor-rected using the appropriate variant of the Huber–White correction. Thus, unlike some maximum likelihood approaches (such as the Tobit), the estimates of the mean function are quite robust to misspecification of the distribution function; for example, see the sim-ulation results from Manning and Mullahy (2001).

Note the difference in the role of the log or the power in Box–Cox models and in the GLM alternatives. In both cases, the mean function depends on $\exp(x'\beta)$, but in the OLS on $\log(y)$ case, this may be only part of the mean response to the covariates x. In the Box–Cox variants one picks the power transform to achieve symmetry in the error term on the scale of estimation. In the GLM models, the power merely helps one go from a linear function $x\beta$ to the response on raw scale. If the response is linear in the x's on the raw scale, then the correct link is the identity link. If the responses are proportional on the raw-scale, then the choice should be the log link. In the GLM, the degree of skewness is dealt with by the appropriate choice of a variance function.

A related alternative   There is a hybrid of the Box–Cox type of model and the GLM. Basu and Rathouz (2005) describe an algorithm that allows one to use the data to esti-mate both the link function from the power family and the power family relationship between the mean and the variance function. This approach is more general than the two preceding alternatives. Given the sensitivity of Box–Cox methods to extreme cases, one of the unexplored issues is how robust is the procedure of Basu and Rathouz.

Manning and Mullahy (2001) propose a method for choosing among the exponential conditional mean models – the GLM with log link and OLS on log link. In a second paper, Manning et al. (forthcoming) propose using an exponential conditional mean regression based on the three parameter generalized gamma distribution that would be estimated by maximum likelihood. The generalized gamma model includes the gamma, Weibull, and exponential models with log link, as well as models for $\log(y)$ with normal errors. This approach also provides a robust alternative to either the GLM or the OLS on $\log(y)$ when those two alternatives do not apply, assuming that the mean is an exponential function of $x\beta$. However, the generalized gamma is susceptible to bias in the presence of certain forms of heteroscedasticity on the log scale. Manning et al. propose a modification of the model that corrects for this.

Conditional density estimation
Gilleskie and Mroz (2004) have suggested that one can use a series of conditional models to address the skewed nature of health care expenditures. Building on the work by Efron (1988) and Donald et al. (2000), they suggest breaking up the dependent variable into different segments, modelling the probability p of being in a specific segment as a function of the covariates x's, and then using least squares of the y in those segments as a polynomial function f of the covariates x. The basic approach takes advantage of the way conditional distributions work. Namely, the $E(y) = E(y|z)\,E(z)$. In this case, the expected value of y, given the observed characteristics of the population is:

$$E(y|x) = \Sigma p_i(y \text{ in range } i)(E(y|y \text{ in range } i)) \tag{41.4}$$

The overall response $E(y|x)$ is given by

$$E(y|x) = \Sigma p_i(x\alpha_i)(x\beta_i) \tag{41.5}$$

where i is an index for segments, and x's are polynomials in the underlying independent variables. They propose a very specific form for the probability functions $p_i(x'\alpha_i)$, but one can use a more general approach than they used. By breaking the dependent variables into bounded values (except for the last segment), they avoid some of the issues with skewness in y because the values of y in a specified range are not as long-tailed as the whole distribution of y. By using a polynomial in the underlying covariates, they allow for a non-linear response to the individual characteristics.

The model can be thought of as a generalization of the two and four-part models in the literature, without the use of either transformed dependent variables or of alternative links (other than that for the p's) in the conditional equation. Given the complexity of the results, the effects of covariates are assessed using a marginal effects approach.

They find that the model performs well in a range of simulated conditions. Also, they are able to obtain well-behaved results with data drawn from the Health Insurance Experiment.

3.   Comments on relative strengths and weaknesses
There have been a substantial number of papers of econometric and statistical models for modelling health care costs and expenditures as a function of patient characteristics of interest. Many of these deal with the whole distribution, especially the substantial fraction of the cases that have zero expenditure. For an overview of some of this literature,

see Jones (2000). Many of these papers involve comparisons for alternative models with the evaluation largely limited to how well specific models do for a specific dataset. One of the concerns about such studies is their generalizability to other populations or to other types of health care expenditures. A second concern is that the performance in a specific application may reflect overfitting of badly skewed data, because many of the papers use within-estimation sample methods to evaluate the relative performance of the alternatives. Split sample, out-of-sample tests, and methods such as the Copas' tests would provide more confidence in the results.

Manning and Mullahy (2001) report the results of simulation comparisons of several exponential conditional mean models under a range of different data-generating mechanisms. These include the use of OLS on log(y), various types of generalized linear models with log links (Gaussian, Poisson and Gamma). In each case, the true response was exponential conditional mean $E(y|x) = \exp(x\beta)$. They examined a number of data-generating mechanisms that lead to varying degrees of skewness, heteroscedasticity on the log scale, and even heavy-tailed distributions for log(y). In the absence of heteroscedasticity on the log scale, they found that both the OLS on log(y) and GLM with log link models provided consistent estimates of the $E(y|x)$. But if the true model was linear on the log scale with an additive error term that was heteroscedastic in x, the log OLS provided biased estimates of $E(y|x)$ without suitable retransformation. Although the GLM models were always consistent, the choice of variance function assumption had substantial impact on the efficiency of the estimation, especially when compared with the results based on OLS on log(y). Further, the loss of efficiency relative to OLS on log(y) increased as the data became more skewed or became heavy-tailed on the log scale.

Because of the potential for bias from OLS on log(y) and of efficiency losses from the GLM with log link models when the log scale variances are large or the log scale error is heavy-tailed, they propose an approach for determining which estimation approach is better for a specific dataset.

Basu and Rathouz (2005) also simulate the behaviour of various GLM models versus their proposed extension. They find evidence of bias and inefficiency when the incorrect power transformations are used for either or both of the link and the variance functions. But they do not examine the traditional Box–Cox estimator.

4.   Conclusions

Because of the very skewed nature of health care costs and expenditures, analysis based on simple regressions of cost and expenditures are not robust in datasets with the number of observations encountered by most analysts. The literature offers a number of alternative estimation strategies, including Box–Cox transformations (especially the log) of the dependent variable, and generalized linear models (for example, the gamma regression model with log link). More recently a less restrictive version of the GLM-type approach for alternative power transforms for the link and the variance functions, a discrete approximation, has been suggested as alternative estimators, as well as a broader class of distributional assumptions (the generalized gamma). At this point, it does not appear that either the Box–Cox or GLM approach dominates the others. The other alternatives discussed here have promise but need more study.

Notes

1. A further complication is that the shape of the distribution and the size of the right tail of distribution may respond differently to covariates than the heart of the distribution. For example, the response of in-patient expenditures may differ from that of out-patient care. In the Health Insurance Experiment, the in-patient expenses were less responsive to cost sharing than out-patient care.
2. Transformations may also be used to achieve a model that is linear in the parameters (as in the Cobb–Douglas production function) or to stabilize the variance of the equation estimated (as in the square root transformation for count data or the inverse sine root transform for proportions).
3. And how higher order terms depend on the covariates.
4. In principle, the Box–Cox can only be applied to strictly positive data if the log is included as one of the options, because the log of zero is undefined. There is an extension of the model, a two-parameter transformation of y, that can address this issue. A constant can be added to y before the power is taken. Both the constant and the power can be estimated by maximum likelihood methods.

    Duan et al. (1983) find that such a model does not deal well with modelling a population with a substantial fraction of zeros. The dataset was from the early years of the Health Insurance Experiment. They find evidence of systematic bias in the predictions once the estimates are retransformed back to the raw scale.

    A number of analysts have dealt with the zero mass problem by using variants of two-part models; these models decompose the overall response into the probability of any cost, and the level of cost or expense (given any). See Duan et al. (1983), Blough et al. (1999), and Jones (2000) for further discussion of these alternatives.
5. Although one can perform a MLE using the specific distributions, the conventional GLM is more robust in the sense that it does not assume the distribution beyond the first and second moments. So, for the gamma GLM, only the gamma variance is assumed and not the full gamma distribution.
6. Other members of the GLM family include logit and probit regression for binary outcomes, least squares for continuous outcomes with normal error terms, and Poisson and negative binomial models for count data.

References

Abrevaya, J. (2002), 'Computing marginal effects in the Box–Cox model', *Econometric Reviews*, **21**(3), 383–93.

Basu, A. and P.J. Rathouz (2005), 'Estimating marginal and incremental effects on health outcomes using flexible link and variance models', *Biostatistics*, **6**, 93–109.

Bickel, P. and K. Doksum (1981), 'An analysis of transformation revisited', *Journal of the American Statistical Association*, **76**, 296–311.

Blough, D.K., C.W. Madden and M.C. Hornbrook (1999), 'Modeling risk using generalized linear models', *Journal of Health Economics*, **18**, 153–71.

Box, G.E.P. and D.R. Cox (1964), 'An analysis of transformations (with discussion)', *Journal of the Royal Statistical Society, Series B*, **26**, 211–46.

Carroll, R. (1980), 'A robust method for testing transformations to achieve approximate normality', *Journal of the Royal Statistical Society, Series B*, **42**, 71–8.

Cook, R.D. and P.C. Wang (1983), 'Transformations and influential cases in regression', *Technometrics*, **25**, 337–44.

Crowder, M. (1987), 'On linear and quadratic estimating functions', *Biometrika*, **74**(3), 591–7.

Donald, S.G., D.A. Green and H.J. Paarsch (2000), 'Differences in wage distributions between Canada and the United States: An application of a flexible estimator of distribution functions in the presence of covariates', *The Review of Economic Studies*, **67**, 609–33.

Duan, N. (1983), 'Smearing estimate: a nonparametric retransformation method', *Journal of the American Statistical Association*, **78**, 605–10.

Duan, N., W.G. Manning, et al. (1983), 'A comparison of alternative models for the demand for medical care', *Journal of Business and Economics Statistics*, **1**, 115–26.

Efron, B. (1988), 'Logistic regression, survival analysis and the Kaplan–Meier curve', *Journal of the American Statistical Association*, **83**, 414–25.

Foster, A.M., L. Tian and L.J. Wei (2001), 'Estimation for the Box–Cox transformation model without assuming parametric error distribution', *Journal of the American Statistical Association*, **96**(455), 1097–101.

Gilleskie, D.B. and T.A. Mroz (2004), 'A flexible approach for estimating the effects of covariates on health expenditures', *Journal of Health Economics*, **23**: 391–418.

Hinkley, D.V. and G. Runger (1984), 'The analysis of transformed data (with discussion)', *Journal of the American Statistical Association*, **79**, 302–19.

Jones, A.M. (2000), 'Health econometrics', in A. Culyer and J. Newhouse (eds), *Handbook of Health Economics*, Amsterdam: Elsevier.

McCullagh, P. and J.A. Nelder (1989), *Generalized Linear Models*, 2nd edn, London: Chapman and Hall.
Manning, W.G. (1998), 'The logged dependent variable, heteroscedasticity, and the retransformation problem', *Journal of Health Economics*, **17**, 283–95.
Manning, W.G. and J. Mullahy (2001), 'Estimating log models: To transform or not to transform?', *Journal of Health Economics*, **20**(4), 461–94.
Manning, W.G., A. Basu and J. Mullahy (2005), 'Generalized modeling approaches to risk adjustment of skewed outcomes data', NBER Technical Report T0293. Also, *Journal of Health Economics*, **24**, 465–88.
Manning, W.G., N. Duan and W.H. Rogers (1987a), 'Monte Carlo evidence on the choice between sample selection and two-part models', *Journal of Econometrics*, **35**, 59–82.
Manning, W.G., J.P. Newhouse et al. (1987b), 'Health insurance and the demand for medical care: Evidence from a randomized experiment', *American Economic Review*, **77**(3), 251–77.
Mullahy, J. (1998), 'Much ado about two: Reconsidering retransformation and the two-part model in health econometrics', *Journal of Health Economics*, **17**, 247–81.
Newhouse, J.P. et al. (1993), *Free-for-all: Health Insurance, Medical Costs, and Health Outcomes: the Results of the Health Insurance Experiment*, Cambridge: Harvard University Press.
Sakia, R.M. (1992), 'The Box–Cox transformation technique – a review', *The Statistician*, **41**(2), 169–78.
Wooldridge, J.M. (1991), 'On the application of robust, regression-based diagnostics to models of conditional means and conditional variances', *Journal of Econometrics*, **47**, 5–46.
Zhou, X.H., S. Gao and S.L. Hui (1997), 'Methods for comparing the means of two independent log-normal samples', *Biometrics*, **53**(3), 1129–35.

42 Future costs in medical cost-effectiveness analysis
David Meltzer

1. Introduction

Medical cost-effectiveness analyses may be conducted from numerous perspectives, almost all of which naturally involve consequences that extend into the future. The most widely accepted perspective adopted in medical cost-effectiveness analysis is the societal perspective, which aims to account for all costs and benefits of a medical intervention, regardless of to whom they accrue (Gold et al., 1996). In a societal perspective, quality-adjusted life years (QALY) are the most commonly used framework to account for future benefits in length and quality of life. Accounting for future costs has been more controversial. While there has always been broad agreement that cost-effectiveness analysis performed from a societal perspective should account for future medical costs for related illnesses, there have been theoretical differences in the literature about how to account for future medical costs for unrelated illnesses and for non-medical costs associated with the extension of life. There has also been relatively little empirical work on how to estimate such future costs.

2. Theoretical basis of cost-effectiveness analysis and implications for future costs

Historical background

Early theoretical treatments of cost-effectiveness analysis (for example, Weinstein and Zeckhauser, 1973) provided no explicit treatment of the intertemporal nature of costs or benefits associated with medical interventions. Beginning with the earliest empirical cost-effectiveness studies (for example, Stason and Weinstein, 1977), quality-adjusted life years have been commonly used to measure the benefits in length and quality of life associated with medical interventions, and future costs have generally been included to the extent they are considered related to the medical intervention. For example, future reductions in the cost of treating heart disease due to the treatment of hypertension might be modelled as a reduction in future costs.

Over time, a number of researchers have discussed the possibility that cost-effectiveness should consider other effects on future costs. Some textbooks (for example, Weinstein et al., 1980) have argued that all changes in future medical costs should be included, regardless of the specific conditions that they treat. For example, if the treatment of hypertension causes an individual to live to an age at which they develop cancer, the cost of treating that cancer should also be included. Weinstein (1986) even considered the possibility that cost-effectiveness analysis should include future consumption costs net of earnings. Despite these theoretical speculations, until recently almost all cost-effectiveness studies have excluded such future costs, arguing they are 'unrelated' to the intervention in question. The sole exception was a 1981 OTA study of influenza vaccination that considered all effects on future medical costs.

Lifetime decision-making models and implications for future costs

One reason for the continuing disagreements over the treatment of future costs in cost-effectiveness analysis over the years has been the lack of a formal theoretical model of future costs on which to base cost-effectiveness analysis. Papers by Garber and Phelps (1997) and Meltzer (1997) addressed this with the suggestion that appropriate methods to account for future costs in cost-effectiveness analysis could be derived from the conditions under which lifetime utility is maximized in a lifetime utility maximization model. Surprisingly, these two papers came to different conclusions. Garber and Phelps suggested that only future costs for related illnesses had to be included, while future costs for unrelated illnesses and future non-medical costs could be either included or excluded without changing the relative ranking of medical interventions, as long as they were done so consistently across all interventions. Meltzer, on the other hand, suggested that it was necessary to include all future net resource, including both medical costs for related and unrelated illnesses and non-medical costs net of any earnings. This future net resource use in added years of life is sometimes called 'future costs', 'survivor costs', or 'costs in added years of life' in the literature. The reason for the discrepancy in the findings between these papers relates to the fact that the Garber and Phelps paper implicitly assumed that future net resource use was zero by applying a condition derived from a model with zero future net resource use in developing conclusions in a model where future net resource use was not supposed to be zero. Thus the Garber and Phelps result implicitly excluded future costs by making an assumption that implied net future resource use was zero in each year.

To better understand the intuition behind the inclusion of all future costs, consider a simple example in which two interventions A and B, costing \$10 000 each, can each produce one additional QALY. However, assume that intervention A produces 1 QALY by increasing life expectancy by 1 year at a quality of life of 1 while intervention B produces 1 QALY by increasing life expectancy by 2 years at a quality of life of 0.5. Assume also that the cost of being alive for each additional year of life in terms of unrelated medical costs plus non-medical costs net of earnings is \$20 000. In this example, interventions A and B produce an equal number of QALYs at equal current cost, so standard methods that exclude future costs would view them as equivalent in both health benefits and costs. However, if one considers future medical costs for 'unrelated' conditions and/or non-medical costs, it becomes clear that intervention A is preferred since it requires supporting only one year of such costs at a cost of \$20 000 while intervention B requires supporting two years at a cost of \$40 000. Thus the cost-effectiveness of A and B compared to doing nothing is \$10 000 per QALY if one ignores future costs and one is indifferent between them. In contrast, if future costs are included, the cost-effectiveness ratios of A and B are \$30 000 per QALY and \$50 000 per QALY, respectively, and it is clear that A is preferred to B. In addition to providing a simple example of the finding that inclusion of future costs can change the relative cost-effectiveness of interventions, this example also illustrates another key finding: that correctly including positive future costs tends to improve the cost-effectiveness of interventions that produce greater improvements in quality of life (for example, A) compared to interventions that produce greater increases in the length of life (for example, B).

Meltzer (1997) derived this result from a lifetime expected utility maximization model. In this model, at any age t, utility ($U_t(c_t, h_t)$) depends on consumption (c_t) and health (h_t).

Medical care affects utility by increasing survival and health so that the probability of survival to age t (S_t) and health at age t (h_t) depend on the whole history of medical interventions up to that time ($\overrightarrow{m}_t$). This implies that lifetime expected utility is:

$$\sum_{t=0}^{T} \beta^t S_t(\overrightarrow{m}_t) u(c_t, h_t(\overrightarrow{m}_t)) \tag{42.1}$$

where β is a rate of time preference ($0<\beta<1$). If we also define the interest rate (r), and income at age t (i_t), we can write down the lifetime budget constraint:

$$\sum_{t=0}^{T} \frac{1}{(1+r)^t} S_t(\overrightarrow{m}_t)(c_t + m_t) = \sum_{t=0}^{T} \frac{1}{(1+r)^t} S_t(\overrightarrow{m}_t)(i_t) \tag{42.2}$$

To derive the conditions for optimal allocation of spending on medical care, the analysis maximizes lifetime utility subject to the lifetime budget constraint to yield the finding that the optimal cost-effectiveness ratio is given by:

$$\frac{\dfrac{1}{(1+r)^t} S_t(\overrightarrow{m}_t) + \sum_{\tau=t}^{T} \dfrac{1}{(1+r)^\tau} \dfrac{\partial S_\tau(\overrightarrow{m}_t)}{\partial m_t}(c_\tau + m_\tau - i_\tau)}{\sum_{t=\tau}^{T} \left[\beta^\tau \dfrac{\partial s_\tau(\overrightarrow{m}_t)}{\partial m_t} u(c_\tau, h_\tau(\overrightarrow{m}_\tau)) + s_\tau(\overrightarrow{m}_t) \dfrac{\partial u(c_\tau, h_\tau(\overrightarrow{m}_\tau))}{\partial m_t} \right]} \tag{42.3}$$

Equation (42.3) shows the criterion for the optimal medical spending at age t. The denominator shows the health benefits of the medical intervention, reflecting the sum of a first term that includes the effects of the medical intervention on survival (length of life), and a second term that reflects effects on quality of life. The numerator also has two terms. The first is the discounted direct current cost of the medical intervention. The second is the effects on future costs, which are shown to include consumption plus medical care less earnings. Note that there is no intrinsic distinction between these types of costs; the findings suggest that all must be included. Meltzer (1997) also includes a more notationally complex version of the same results that indexes specific medical interventions more finely so that there are multiple interventions in a period. Likewise, one could divide consequences of an intervention into those operating through their effect on a single set of consequences one could label as 'related' and the remainder that one could consider 'unrelated'. Whichever way such divisions were done, however, both would be appropriately included in cost-effectiveness analysis.

3.   Empirical studies of future costs

Methods for estimating costs
The effects of including future costs on the cost-effectiveness of a specific intervention are most precisely determined by incorporating a model describing those costs directly into the decision analysis. The relevant cost components are consumption, medical care and earnings. With respect to medical costs and other consequences of treatment that are

modelled (such as employment), some of these components may already be partially modelled as 'related' costs following the approach of traditional cost-effectiveness analyses. Because all benefits and costs should be counted once and only once, it is important to consider whether these other measures of costs, and even measures of benefits, used in the analysis may already reflect some of these components (Johannesson and Meltzer, 1998; Blomqvist, 2002). For example, national surveys can be used to obtain estimates of average consumption, medical care, and earnings by age (see Meltzer, 1997 for an illustration). In this context, the double counting question arises to the extent that some of the costs in added years of life related to the disease in question may already be modelled as part of the original model of related costs. This effect is likely to be largest when the disease being examined is common and expensive to treat across the population, such as diabetes or coronary heart disease. Practically, this issue may be difficult to disentangle perfectly since it may be difficult to fully separate out average population costs into parts related and unrelated to a specific illness. This is especially true since diseases often interact in complex ways, for example when the presence of diabetes changes the prevalence and optimal treatment of hypercholesterolemia. As a reasonable approximation, however, an analyst may attempt to remove average population expenditures related to illness from estimates of unrelated future cost that are added into a model.

More research is needed to understand these challenges in avoiding double counting of costs but the magnitude of the different components of costs provides some solace for the pragmatic analyst seeking a reasonable approximation of the effects of accounting for future costs. For example, Meltzer's (1997) estimates of average annual consumption in the US by age hover around $10 000 per person, while annual earnings are about $20 000 per person from age 20 to 65, and average medical expenditures are less than a few thousand dollars, accelerating rapidly at older ages to a maximum of about $10 000 for persons in their 80s. Since the future costs of extending life that are omitted in standard cost-effectiveness analyses are consumption ($10 000) + (unrelated) medical expenditures (a few thousand dollars annually until old age) – earnings ($20 000 annually during working years), errors in double counting future related medical costs are likely to be modest in magnitude relative to the cost of the consumption and earnings components of future costs, except perhaps for interventions targeted primarily at the most common diseases in the oldest patients.

Concerns such as these may be daunting to an analyst who is considering incorporating future costs into a cost-effectiveness analysis. However, despite these theoretical concerns about double counting, there is to date no evidence of serious bias from estimating 'unrelated' future costs by simply using population estimates of average annual net resource use by age as measured by average consumption plus medical expenditure minus earnings by age.

The parallel concern about double counting costs already reflected in effectiveness measures is also worthy of consideration but does not have clear implications for how to account for future costs. The uncertainty about this issue stems from ambiguity about what is reflected in effectiveness measures. For example, when people report quality of life measures in some health state, it is unknown the extent to which they incorporate the loss in welfare that might come from lost earnings in that health state. Indeed a number of papers have focused on this concern (Johannesson and Meltzer, 1998; Meltzer et al., 1999;

Brouwer and Rutten, 2003). At this point all that can be said with certainty is that there is uncertainty and likely substantial variability in the extent to which such factors may be incorporated in existing quality of life measures. This work does suggest that persons lower their quality of life ratings of health states when explicitly told to consider effects on earnings, so it seems highly unlikely that current measures of quality of life fully incorporate such effects. Until more work is done to clarify these double counting issues, estimating cost-effectiveness both with and without a population level estimate of unrelated future net resource use is a way to assess likely bounds on the effects of future costs.

A related argument has been used by Nyman (2004) to argue that future unrelated costs for consumption should not be included in cost-effectiveness analysis since they are not explicitly accounted for in quality of life measures. Nevertheless, it is clear that the benefits of such consumption must be implicitly assumed for these quality of life measures to apply since consumption is required in order for these years of life to occur. Thus such costs must also enter cost-effectiveness calculations through the cost side, unless somehow also implicitly netted out in the benefit side. As in the above discussion of double counting, it is unlikely that that is the case.

Methods to estimate the effects of future costs
The most direct way in which to include the effects of future costs in a cost-effectiveness analysis is to include the full costs and benefits in all years of life in the analysis by assigning consumption, medical expenditures and earnings to every health state in all years lived. As discussed below, this has now been done in analyses for a substantial number of health interventions. Because many papers in the literature have not included estimates of future unrelated costs, it is also useful to have an approach to approximate the magnitude of those costs. Meltzer (1997) suggests that the cost-effectiveness ratio in equation (42.3) can be approximated as:

$$CE\,Ratio = \frac{\Delta Cost}{\Delta QALY} = \frac{\Delta Present\,Cost + \Delta Future\,Cost}{\Delta QALY}$$

$$= \frac{\Delta Present\,Cost}{\Delta QALY} + \frac{\Delta Future\,Cost}{\Delta QALY}$$

$$= \frac{\Delta Present\,Cost}{\Delta QALY} + C\frac{\Delta LY}{\Delta QALY} \qquad (42.4)$$

In this equation, $\Delta QALY$ is the change in QALYs, ΔLY is the change in life years lived, and C is the average annual value of net future resources use from the age in question to the maximum age at death. In Meltzer's 1997 estimates, C ranged from about $-\$10\,000$ per year for young adults with their high-earnings years ahead of them to a maximum of $\$20\,000$ per year for adults in their 80s and above. The first term on the right-hand side of equation (42.4) represents the part of cost-effectiveness analysis based on present costs per QALY that is included in standard analyses, the second term represents the future cost per QALY that has traditionally been omitted, and is estimated by assuming that future costs are C per life year times the number of life years. When there is no increase in life expectancy, $\Delta LY=0$ and there is no bias from omitting future costs. When ΔLY is positive and annual net future resource is positive, as it tends to be in older persons, future costs are positive, and omitting them biases the cost-effectiveness ratio downwards. This provides the basic intuition for why omitting future costs tends to favour interventions that extend life over interventions that improve quality of life, especially among the elderly. The opposite may be true in interventions that extend life among young persons.

Empirical estimates of the effects of including future costs
Approximately 25 original published papers have included future costs in the calculation of cost-effectiveness ratios, either in the base case or in a sensitivity analysis. Interventions have been studied relating to diabetes, hypertension, exercise and diet to prevent coronary artery disease, acute coronary syndromes, congestive heart failure, osteoporosis and hip fracture prevention, haemodialysis for end-stage renal disease, highly active antiretroviral therapy for HIV, hormone replacement therapy, and pneumonia and influenza vaccination. Not all of these papers calculate cost-effectiveness ratios with and without future costs, but, where they do, the effects of including future costs vary following predictable patterns. For example, studies of interventions among older persons often show increases in the range of $20 000/QALY or more while studies of interventions among younger persons (for example, HAART) may show improvements in the cost-effectiveness ratio of up to $10 000. Changes tend to be smaller for interventions targeted at middle-aged persons whose future life years combine working and non-working years that together produce little net future resources use, and for interventions that produce little or no effect on survival, such as hip replacement. Even the largest changes in cost-effectiveness ratios that have come about including future costs are modest relative to the $50 000 or $100 000 figures often used as thresholds for cost-effectiveness, but the differences are enough to change the relative rankings of interventions in some cases. Moreover, some interventions that seem highly cost-effective when future costs are excluded (for example, cost-effectiveness ratios of <$10 000) are no longer highly cost-effective by this standard once future costs are considered. Such observations are to some extent addressed by recommendations by several authors that different (higher) thresholds be applied for cost-effectiveness analyses that include future costs than for analyses that exclude them (for example, Kanis et al., 2002). Regardless, there is agreement that cost-effectiveness ratios that include future costs should not be directly compared to those that exclude them.

As equation (42.4) suggests, the effects of including future costs may be largest when an intervention extends length of life more than quality of life, and especially among the elderly. Meltzer (1997) uses equation (42.4) to estimate the effect of including future costs for several interventions and suggests that some treatments for cancer that have large negative effects on current quality of life may have major decrements in their cost-effectiveness once future costs are accounted for, with increases in the cost-effectiveness ratio of more than $100 000 per QALY. However, there are not yet studies that directly examine the effects of including future costs for such interventions that have very large effects on length of life relative to quality of life for older persons. Other studies have been done, however, that use equation (42.4) to approximate the effects of including future costs in a cost-effectiveness analysis, and have generally found at least reasonable correspondence (Meltzer et al., 2000; Manns et al., 2003). Because equation (42.4) implicitly assumes that net resource use and quality of life are constant in all future years, it should not be assumed that the equation can reliably be used in all cases to identify the effects of including future costs. Nevertheless, it may be a useful guide for approximating the effects of future costs in advance of direct calculations and inferring when direct calculations of future costs are likely to have the greatest effects on the analysis.

4.   Ethical and policy concerns

Including future costs may be criticized on the grounds that it may disadvantage older persons (whose net future resource tends to be positive) compared to younger persons. As in all matters of resource allocation, this argument could be made in the opposite manner to suggest that analyses that exclude future costs are biased to disadvantage younger people (whose future net resource use will tend to be negative) compared to older people. It is also worth pointing out that to the extent that older people are more likely to experience problems that affect quality of life, the tendency of including future costs to place greater emphasis on interventions that extend life over interventions that improve quality of life, may also benefit older persons. There may also be concerns about application of cost-effectiveness to groups or diseases that have low earnings, especially if analysts chose to incorporate differences in earnings across groups into their analysis. Ultimately, whether including future costs is desirable will depend on the goals of social resource allocation, which may rely on principles of welfare economics, as implicit in the justification of future costs, or extra-welfarist considerations.

From a policy perspective, the future costs argument may also raise important issues, since it suggests that some of the costs of medical interventions that extend life may be borne by social insurance programmes that provide income support to older persons after retirement. Assessing the budgetary impact of such programmes may be important. In the United States, for example, from 1970 to 2002, the life table probability of surviving from birth to age 65 rose from 72 per cent to 83 per cent, while life expectancy at age 65 rose from 15 years to 18 years (Vital Statistics of the United States, 1970; National Center for Health Statistics, 2004). This implies, from a life table perspective, a 40 per cent increase, from about 11 to about 15, in the number of years expected at birth to be lived after age 65, when social security benefits might typically be received. To the extent that medical care plays an important role in this change, this clearly suggests the potential for medical interventions to have important budgetary impact related to non-medical expenditures.

5.   Conclusions and future directions

Medical interventions have effects on future medical costs, consumption and earnings that theoretical models of life-cycle decision-making suggest should be considered in medical cost-effectiveness analyses. While there are questions as to whether some of these effects may be captured by some quality of life measures, there is no empirical evidence that this is the case, suggesting that future costs are not likely to be adequately accounted for in traditional cost-effectiveness analysis. Empirically, explicitly including future costs can change the cost-effectiveness ratio of interventions that vary in the age of patients treated, and the effects of the intervention on length and quality of life. Including sensitivity analysis of future costs routinely in cost-effectiveness analyses can help address this issue, and lay the foundation for future decisions about whether future costs should be included routinely in the base case of all cost-effectiveness analyses. Simultaneously, development of improved methods to estimate futures costs can help to improve the measurement of this often-neglected aspect of the costs of medical interventions.

References

Blomqvist, A. (2002), 'QALYs, standard gambles, and the expected budget constraint', *Journal of Health Economics*, **21**, 181–95.
Brouwer, W.B.F. and F.F.H. Rutten (2003), 'The missing link: on the line between C and E', *Health Economics*, **12**, 629–36.
Garber, A.M. and C.E. Phelps (1997), 'Economic foundations of cost-effectiveness analysis', *Journal of Health Economics*, **16**, 1–31.
Gold, M.R., J.E. Siegel, L.B. Russell and M.C. Weinstein (1996), *Cost-effectiveness in Health and Medicine*, New York: Oxford University Press.
Johannesson, M. and D. Meltzer (1998), 'Some reflections on cost-effectiveness analysis', *Health Economics*, **7**, 1–7.
Kanis, J.A., O. Johnell, A. Oden, C. De Laet, A. Oglesby and B. Jonsson (2002), 'Intervention thresholds for osteoporosis', *Bone*, **31**(1), 26–31.
Manns, B., D. Meltzer, K. Taub and C. Donaldson (2003), 'Illustrating the impact of including future costs in economic evaluations: an application to end-stage renal disease care', *Health Economics*, **12**(11), 949–58.
Meltzer, D. (1997), 'Accounting for future costs in medical cost-effectiveness analysis', *Journal of Health Economics*, **16**, 33–64.
Meltzer, D., C. Weckerle and L. Chang (1999), 'Do people consider financial effects in answering quality of life questions?', *Medical Decision Making*, **19**(4), 717.
Meltzer, D., B. Egleston, D. Stoffel and E. Dasbach (2000), 'The effect of future costs on the cost-effectiveness of medical interventions among young adults: the example of intensive therapy for type-1 diabetes', *Medical Care*, **38**(6), 679–85.
National Center for Health Statistics, *Vital Statistics of the United States 1970*, **2**(5).
National Center for Health Statistics (2004), *National Vital Statistics Reports*, **53**(6), Rockville, Maryland, Public Health Service.
Nyman, J., (2004), 'Should the consumption of survivors be included as a cost in cost–utility analysis?', *Health Economics*, **13**, 417–27.
Office of Technology Assessment (1981), *Cost-effectiveness of Influenza Vaccination*, Washington, DC: Office of Technology Assessment, US Congress.
Stason, W.B. and M. Weinstein (1977), 'Allocation of resources to manage hypertension', *New England Journal of Medicine*, **296**, 732–9.
Weinstein, M. (1986), 'Challenges for cost-effectiveness research', *Medical Decision Making*, **6**, 194–8.
Weinstein, M. and R. Zeckhauser (1973), 'Critical ratios and efficient allocation', *Journal of Public Economics*, **2**(2), 147–57.
Weinstein, M., H. Fineberg, A. Elstein, H. Frazier, D. Newhauser, R. Neutra and B. McNeil (1980), *Clinical Decision Analysis*, Philadelphia: Saunders.

43 Selection bias in observational data
*Daniel Polsky and Anirban Basu**

1. Introduction

Economic evaluation of medical interventions aims to aid decision-makers to achieve the goal of efficient use of health care resources at a community level by quantifying the trade-offs between resources for medical care and the resulting health outcomes. Ideally, these evaluations would lead to the adoption of treatment options that provide value for money and the elimination of those that do not. Unless these evaluations express the causal relationship between the economic endpoint and the treatment, interventions that do not provide sufficient value may be adopted and treatments that do may be eliminated. Hence, it is essential that estimates of differences between treatments reflect the causal effect of treatment on outcomes.

When observational data rather than data from randomized clinical trials are used for the estimates of economic endpoints, there is always a possibility that selection bias may limit an investigator's ability to generate an unbiased estimate of the causal relationship between treatment and the economic outcome. The treatment option delivered in a clinical setting is typically the result of decisions made by patients and physicians. Selection bias arises when factors that can influence the treatment choice such as patient health and provider skills also influence outcomes. Adequately accounting for these factors is necessary if observational data are to be used in economic evaluations.

The primary objective of this chapter is to describe how observational data can be used to estimate the causal relationship between treatment and outcomes. To achieve this objective it is necessary to define the parameters of interest for economic evaluations, describe observational study designs, explain selection bias and the mechanism that generates selection of treatment, and then review and compare the various methods introduced in the literature that attempt to address selection bias in observational studies. We will compare the methods using an example study evaluating surgical treatments for breast cancer.

2. An illustrative example

While clinical trials have shown that breast conservation surgery with radiation treatment (BCSRT) and mastectomy have equivalent survival, the objective of this observational example study was to compare the cost-effectiveness of BCSRT relative to mastectomy. The initial sample, drawn from CMS Medicare claims 1992–1994, required a reported diagnosis of breast cancer and surgical procedures indicating breast conservation surgery or mastectomy and a physician confirmation of diagnosis and determination of disease stage. Quality of life was obtained through patient surveys in 1997 and cost data were

* We are grateful to Andrew Jones, Willard G. Manning, Edward C. Norton and Paul J. Rosenbaum for very helpful comments and suggestions on earlier versions of this chapter. All errors are ours. This work was supported in part by the National Institute of Alcohol Abuse and Alcoholism (NIAAA) Grant 1RO1 AA12664.

obtained from CMS Medicare claims 1991–1997. The sample included women aged 67 and older with stage I or stage II breast cancer and relevant surgery procedure codes. The QALY outcome for the 5-year post-diagnosis period is the discounted annual survival adjusted for quality of life using a visual analogue scale. Costs are defined as the total Medicare reimbursement amount over the 5-year post diagnosis period.

A comparison of baseline characteristics showed the BCSRT group to be generally healthier because they are younger, have more stage I's, have fewer comorbidities, and fewer pre-surgery costs. The QALYs were 3.54 for the BCSRT group and 3.22 for the mastectomy group; a difference of 0.32 (95 per cent CI: 0.26, 0.38). The costs were $48 604 for BCSRT and $40 125 for mastectomy; a difference of $8479 (95 per cent CI: $4852, $12 105). The incremental cost-effectiveness ratio was $26 496 per QALY (95 per cent CI: 16 600, 39 600).

Given that younger patients, those with stage I disease, and those with fewer comorbidities typically have higher QALYs and lower treatment costs regardless of the type of surgery, and that this risk group is more likely to select (or be selected into) BCSRT treatment, the estimates of QALYs, costs, and cost-effectiveness above are biased estimates of the causal relationship between treatment and the economic outcome. This bias, called selection bias, makes it unclear whether observed outcomes are caused by BCSRT or whether they are caused by the factors that lead to the treatment decision. At the end of the chapter we will return to this example.

3.   Evaluation and selection bias

The evaluation problem
We start with a model of potential outcomes to signify the relationship between the characteristics of a patient, presumed to undergo a treatment, and the outcomes (costs or effects) that the current treatment has the potential to produce (Rubin, 1974; 1978; Holland, 1986). For simplicity, we will restrict our discussion to two treatments $j = T, S$ and their corresponding potential outcomes, Y_T and Y_S, where T denotes the new intervention being evaluated and S denotes the standard therapy. Again for simplicity, let the potential outcomes be represented by a linear function of observable characteristics (X) and unobservables (U_j).

$$Y_T = X\beta_T + U_T$$
$$Y_S = X\beta_S + U_S \qquad (43.1)$$

Throughout this chapter, we will refer to observed and unobserved components from the perspective of the analyst and not from the perspective of the patient. The individual level treatment effect (Δ) can be represented as the difference in potential outcome if the patient were treated by the new therapy rather than standard treatment:

$$\Delta = Y_T - Y_S \qquad (43.2)$$

In most situations, each patient can only be observed in state T or state S, but never both, at any point in time. If T is not received, the patient receives S. Therefore, the observed outcome (Y) (Neyman et al., 1990; Rubin, 1974) becomes:

$$Y = DY_T + (1 - D)Y_S \qquad (43.3)$$

where D is an indicator $= 1$ if T was received and $= 0$ if S was received. Obtaining a consistent estimate of the treatment effect, Δ, using observed rather than potential outcomes represents the problem confronted by those attempting to evaluate alternative medical therapies. The first step towards identifying and understanding the cause of this problem is to understand why certain subjects are observed with T while others are observed with S. Therefore, we start with an explicit model of treatment choice.

Model of treatment choice

A behavioural model of treatment choice can be derived from the classical microeconomic theory of choice where a subject chooses treatment based on expected utility maximization. If the expected net utility, which is the difference in expected utilities from being treated with T as compared to being treated with S, is positive, then the patient will choose to undergo treatment T. Thus the model of treatment choice can be denoted as follows:

$$V = Z\gamma + U_V \quad E(U_V) = 0 \quad D = 1(V > 0), \qquad (43.4)$$

where V is the net utility and $1(.)$ is an indicator function that represents that $D = 1$ if the patient chooses treatment T and $D = 0$ otherwise. Z and U_V are observed and unobserved factors determining choice of treatment.

It is important to note that this choice model is specific to the choice between treatments after the subject has already made a decision to seek and receive therapy. While not the focus of this chapter, the choice to seek and receive care and how this choice interacts with the outcomes of the alternative therapy options should not be ignored when generalizing treatment comparisons to broader settings.

Parameter of interest in economic evaluation

One can obtain the full model for observed outcome by substituting the potential outcomes equations (43.1) in equation (43.3) (Quandt, 1972; 1988; Roy, 1951; Heckman and Sedlacek, 1985):

$$Y = X\beta_S + D[(X\beta_T - X\beta_S) + (U_T - U_S)] + U_S \qquad (43.5)$$

Note that equation (43.5) can be visualized as a simple ordinary-least-squares regression model, where the coefficient on the treatment variable D contains two components: $(X\beta_T - X\beta_S)$, the average gain for a person with characteristics X; and $(U_T - U_S)$, the idiosyncratic gain for a particular person undergoing treatment. The idiosyncratic gain allows the treatment effect to vary across individuals with identical X.

The outcome of interest in most conventional economic evaluations in medicine and health is the expected gain from undergoing treatment T vs. S for a randomly chosen patient. This is the Average Treatment Effect (ATE):

$$\text{ATE}(X) = E(\Delta|X) = X(\beta_T - \beta_S) + E(U_T - U_S|X) = X(\beta_T - \beta_S) \qquad (43.6)$$

It estimates the average gain if everyone undergoes treatment T as compared to treatment S, which informs whether a new treatment should completely replace the standard treatment. ATE is the focus of this chapter.

Defining selection bias
When the estimated ATE does not represent the expected gain from the treatment alternative it may be the result of selection bias. Selection bias occurs when there is an imbalance in the characteristics that independently influence Y between those who receive T and S. This type of bias is common when estimating ATE because outcomes can be observed only in the *state* that corresponds to the chosen treatment. Consequently, the potential outcome in the state that does not correspond to the chosen treatment is never observed. It is constructed by balancing the characteristics of those who receive T and S.

Overt selection bias exists if the levels of observed factors (X) influencing outcomes are different for treated and the untreated group or if observed factors (Z) influencing treatment choice are correlated with the unobserved characteristics U_S and U_T affecting outcomes and the levels of Z are different for treated and the untreated group. Hidden bias exists when the estimated ATE reflects imbalance in unobserved characteristics between treatment groups. In order to understand hidden bias, let us rewrite the observed outcome, following (43.5), as:

$$Y = X\beta_S + DE(\Delta|X) + (U_S + D(U_T - U_S)). \tag{43.7}$$

A regression of Y on D following (43.7) will generally yield a biased estimator for $E(\Delta|X)$ when D is non-orthogonal to either U_S or $(U_T - U_S)$. This happens if there are common unobserved factors that influence both outcomes (that is they belong in U_S and U_T) and treatment selection (that is they belong in U_V). The resulting bias, called the hidden bias, is given by:

$$[E(U_T|X, D=1) - E(U_S|X, D=0)] \neq 0 \tag{43.8}$$

4.   Addressing selection bias

Study designs
Both overt and hidden biases can be eliminated or at least reduced through study design. This requires designs that can generate comparison groups that are arguably similar on both observed and unobserved characteristics. Randomized design accomplishes this by generating comparison groups through a random process rather than through a selection process that may be related to outcomes. This design prevents both overt and hidden biases by balancing, on average, both the observed and unobserved differences between groups.

Because treatment groups are formed naturally rather than through an artificial random process in observational studies, the design cannot eliminate the potential for selection bias. There are, however, certain observational study designs that may minimize selection bias. A common feature of these designs is the use of some form of comparison to construct the required counterfactual. The most common design is a cross-sectional design that addresses selection bias entirely based on characteristics observed by the analyst, X and Z, and offers no advantages in minimizing the possibility of hidden biases that may arise from the mechanism of treatment choice. Studies that use before–after designs or difference-in-difference designs may offer opportunities to address both overt and certain forms of hidden biases. A before–after design uses observations on the same subject 'before' (on old treatment S) and 'after' (on new treatment T). This method addresses selection bias to the extent that important characteristics are not time trended. A difference-in-difference design is similar to the before–after, but has the added advantage of controlling for time invariant effects that may interfere with treatment choice. However, if the switch from one therapy to another is driven by characteristics of the patient that influence outcomes, these designs will not necessarily reduce or eliminate selection bias.

Methods for addressing overt biases

The primary method of addressing overt biases in observational studies is to adjust for observed information that affects either outcomes or treatment choices. These methods can be jointly referred to as the methods of matching since they try to match or balance the levels of observed covariates between the treated and the untreated groups. As conventionally formulated, these methods do not make a distinction between X and Z. They are discussed in detail below.

Model-based covariate adjustment   This is the most traditional method of addressing imbalances in observed covariates between treatment groups. Here a regression framework is used to estimate the coefficient on the treatment indicator variable after adjusting for all observed covariates. This procedure gives an unbiased estimate of ATE under the assumptions that there are no common unobserved factors in U_V, U_T and U_S that may give rise to hidden bias. The independence assumption is written as:

$$(Y_T, Y_S) \perp D | X \qquad (43.9)$$

where $\perp$ denotes independence given the conditioning variables after |. The assumption says that independence between outcomes and treatment selection can be achieved by conditioning on all observed factors (Heckman and Robb, 1985; 1986).

Propensity score matching   Rosenbaum and Rubin (1983) showed that under the assumptions in (43.9), independence between outcomes and treatment selection can be achieved by conditioning on the most discrete grouping X, the propensity score $P(X)$. that is,

$$(Y_T, Y_S) \perp D | P(X) \qquad (43.10)$$

In other words, the covariates X may strongly predict who will receive treatment, $D = 1$, and who will remain untreated, $D = 0$, but (43.10) asserts that among subjects with the same value of the propensity score, $P(X)$, the covariates X no longer predict treatment assignment D. When this independence is achieved conditioning on a scalar propensity score, the dimensionality of the matching problem is reduced (Lu and Rosenbaum, 2004).

Typically, the propensity score $P(X)$ is estimated from a model, such as a logit model, $\log[P(X)/\{1 - P(X)\}] = X\theta$, and then one matches on the estimated propensity score or on $X\hat{\theta}$.

Combination – propensity score matching + covariate adjustments   Using simulations, Rubin (1973) found that if the model used for model-based covariate adjustment is correct, then model-based adjustments may be more efficient than propensity score matching. On the other hand, if the model is substantially incorrect, model-based adjustments may not only fail to remove overt biases, they may even increase them, whereas propensity score matching methods are fairly consistent in reducing overt biases. Rubin concluded that the combined use of propensity score matching along with model-based covariate adjustment is the superior strategy to implement in practice, being both robust and efficient.

Other methods: matched sampling/stratification   Various other methods of balancing levels of observed covariates between treatment groups exist. Matched sampling selects controls that appear comparable to treated subjects and is most common when a small treated group is available together with a large reservoir of potential controls. An alternative to matching is stratification, in which subjects are grouped into strata based on levels of a few observed covariates, so that, within each stratum, treated and untreated subjects have similar distribution of all observed covariates.

A summary of methods used to address overt biases is given in Table 43.1.

Method for addressing hidden biases
In the previous section we discussed methods to address overt biases in observational studies. The key assumption required to assert that addressing overt bias is sufficient for obtaining a consistent estimate of ATE is that conditional on X, the outcome

Table 43.1   Summary of estimators addressing selection bias in observational studies

Estimator	Assumptions
Address overt bias	
Covariate adjustment	$(Y_T, Y_S) \perp D \mid X$ **and** $0 < \Pr(D = 1 \mid X) = P(X) < 1$
Propensity scoring	$(Y_T, Y_S) \perp D \mid P(X)$ **and** $0 < \Pr(D = 1 \mid X) = P(X) < 1$
Combination	$(Y_T, Y_S) \perp D \mid P(X)$ **and** $0 < \Pr(D = 1 \mid X) = P(X) < 1$
Matched sampling/stratification	$(Y_T, Y_S) \perp D \mid S(X)^*$ **and** $0 < \Pr(D = 1 \mid X) = P(X) < 1$
Address hidden bias	
Conventional IV	$E(U_S + D(U_T - U_S) \mid Z, X) = 0$ **and** $E(D \mid X, Z) = \Pr(D = 1 \mid X, Z)$
Local IV	$(U_S, U_T, U_V) \perp Z \mid X$. $\Pr(D = 1 \mid Z, X)$ is a nontrivial function of Z for each X. (Heckman and Navarro-Lozano, 2004)
Control functions	$E(U_S \mid Z, X, D = 0)$ and $E(U_T \mid Z, X, D = 1)$ can be varied independently of $E(Y_S \mid X)$ and $E(Y_T \mid X)$ respectively. (Heckman and Navarro-Lozano, 2004)

Note: * $S(X)$ represents the stratification based on X.

unobservables (U_T, U_S) are random with respect to D (that is, $U_V \perp (U_T, U_S)$). That is, unobserved factors influencing treatment choice do not affect treatment outcomes. However, this assumption is often violated, giving rise to hidden biases. These biases may be quite important for the application of comparing therapies in observational study. First, measurement of risk (that is, variables for X) may be quite limited. Often X is represented by demographic risk factors and comorbidities only. This may not be sufficient. Second, even if risk is measured well, there may be important factors that are difficult for the analyst to quantify, such as physician skill and patient motivation. Third, there may be measurement error associated with observed covariates that can lead to violation of the independence assumption.

The most common method used to assess the impact of hidden biases on the results is sensitivity analysis. A sensitivity analysis is a specific statement about the magnitude of hidden bias that would need to be present to explain the associations actually observed. Weak associations in small studies can be explained away by very small biases, but only a very large bias can explain a strong association in a large study. A detailed description of sensitivity analyses can be found in Rosenbaum (1991, 2002). However, sensitivity analyses only indicate the magnitude of hidden biases that would alter a study's conclusions but do not address how to overcome these biases. Therefore, in order to draw conclusions about treatment effects that are insensitive to hidden biases, other strategies must be employed, one of which is the instrumental variable analysis.

The method of instrumental variable (IV) is a commonly used econometric method that tries to address hidden biases in observational studies. It tries to model the dependence on unobserved characteristics that influence both treatment choice and outcomes using factors (Z, say) that influence treatment choice but are not contained in X. There are two basic assumptions that instrumental variables need to satisfy in order to consistently estimate ATE:

$$\text{Assumption (1) } E(U_S + D(U_T - U_S)|Z, X) = 0$$
$$\text{Assumption (2) } P(D = 1|X, Z) \text{ is a non-trivial function of } Z \text{ given } X. \quad (43.11)$$

The first assumption indicates that the instrumental variables must be mean-independent of the error term in (43.7). The second assumption is that Z can be varied, independently of X, to change the probability of receipt of treatment. In particular, it is required that for each X, there be two values of Z, $z \neq z'$, which produce different values of the probability. These two assumptions respectively represents the traditional requirements for instrumental variables that they should be uncorrelated with the error term and correlated with the endogenous treatment variable. Under both these assumptions, the population instrumental variable equation for $E(\Delta|X)$ is given by:

$$\operatorname*{Lim}_{z \to z'} E(\Delta|X) = \frac{\partial E(Y|X, Z = z')}{\partial Z} \bigg/ \frac{\partial \Pr(D = 1|X, Z = z')}{\partial Z} \quad (43.12)$$

The parameter is the ratio of the change in the conditional expectations with respect to Z to the change in the probability of receiving treatment with respect to Z, and does not depend on Z.

It is worth noting here that in general, such instrumental variables are difficult to find. Most conventional IV applications assume dependence of outcome unobservable (U_T, U_S) on treatment choice unobservables U_V but independence of $(U_T - U_S)$ and U_V conditional on X and Z. This implies that the individual idiosyncratic gain from treatment does not determine who selects into treatment even though treatment choice is correlated with the outcome unobservables (U_S). This assumption is met under two conditions: firstly, when there are no unobservable components of gain $(U_T = U_S)$, implying that everyone with the same X responds to treatment in the same way. This model is call the 'Dummy endogenous regression' model or the common coefficient model (Heckman, 1978; LaLonde, 1986). Secondly, when $U_T \neq U_S$ but $(U_T - U_S) \perp D|Z, X$, implying that though people with the same X respond differently to treatment, their expectation of $(U_T - U_S)$ prior to making the treatment choice is typical of that of the entire population. In other words, people do not make treatment choices on the basis of unobserved gains. This model is analogous to the random coefficients model in traditional economics (Heckman and Robb, 1985). Note that under either condition, assumption 1 in (43.10), required for IV to work, reduces to $E(U_S|Z, X) = 0$, and one can use the conventional textbook instrumental variable methods to identify the ATE parameter.

However, in many health care applications, the assumption of independence of $(U_T - U_S)$ and U_V conditional on X and Z turns out to be restrictive because the choice of medical treatment is often guided by individual idiosyncratic gains from alternative treatment (that is, the probability of treatment choice is dependent on $(U_T - U_S)$) as determined by their preferences. This issue has received relatively little attention or no attention in the health economics and health services literature. Methods such as the Local Instrumental Variable (LIV) method (Heckman and Vytlacil, 1999; 2000; 2004; Heckman, 2001; Vytlacil, 2002) and control functions (Heckman, 1976; 1978; 1980; Heckman and Robb, 1985; 1986; Heckman and Navarro-Lozano, 2004) may be used to address the hidden biases in situations where the conventional IV method fails. However, discussing these methods is beyond the scope of this chapter and the interested readers are pointed towards the relevant references. A summary of methods used to address hidden biases is given in Table 43.1.

The Heckman selection model (Heckman, 1976; 1979) deserves a special mention in this context. This method is a special case of the control function methods and is often used to address a different form of selection bias. Conventionally, it is applied when the outcomes data within a certain subgroup of patients is unobserved and that subgroup status is correlated with treatment choice, however, the interest lies in estimating a treatment effect that encompasses that subgroup. Some researchers (Dusheiko et al., 2004) have used this method to model the exogenous variation in treatment selection as a first step and have used these selection probabilities in the second step to control for endogeneity of treatment status, even though there is no unobserved data in either treatment arm. Note that in this situation, the coefficient on the treatment indicator variable in no longer an estimate of the ATE (a common misconception in the health economics literature). Here, one has to follow the general methods of control functions or use the selection probabilities as an instrumental variable in order to compute the ATE.

Example: back to breast cancer example

We now demonstrate an application of model-based covariates, propensity scores, and instrumental variables to the illustrative example of the evaluation of ATE between BCSRT (i.e., T) and mastectomy (i.e., S). The independent covariates used for all three methods are age, race, Charlson comorbidity index score, pre-surgery costs, breast cancer stage and income, education, and poverty level of the zip-code of patient residence. In this illustrative example, both QALYs and costs are estimated using linear regression. Alternatively, we could have used the net-benefit regression framework discussed in the chapter by Briggs in this Companion (Chapter 47).

The propensity score was estimated using logistic regression and the sample was stratified into four equal-size propensity groups based on the propensity score. The difference in outcomes and costs between mastectomy and BCSRT was estimated for each propensity group in a multivariate least-squares regression which included the covariates. The propensity score treatment effect is the average of these propensity group estimates. A more detailed description of methods is available in Polsky et al. (2003).

The exogenous identifying variables used as instrumental variables include the distance between residence of patient and nearest hospital with a radiation therapy facility (as a proxy for travel and inconvenience costs to receive radiation therapy), a regional dummy variable to represent regional variations in practice patterns, and the Medicare physician fee differential between mastectomy and breast conserving surgery. The details and justification for these instruments are available in Hadley et al. (2003).

These results, displayed in Table 43.2, suggest that there is considerable selection bias in the observational data that diminishes as the selection correction methods are applied. The direction of the bias appears to favour BCSRT in terms of outcomes, but favour mastectomy in terms of costs. As risk is adjusted, first using covariates in a linear regression and then using propensity score, the selection bias diminishes. For example, the difference in QALYs is 0.32 with no risk adjustment, 0.12 with risk adjustment, 0.08 with propensity scores, and −0.29 with instrumental variables. The results between risk adjustment and propensity scores are similar, but when the instrumental variable method is used, large differences appear. This may suggest that hidden bias plays a large role in the observed differences. It may also be a result of the weak instruments used in the instrumental variables method because the confidence intervals for the instrumental variable estimates are much larger than for the other estimates.

5. Conclusions

We have presented the theoretical motivations for addressing selection bias in observational studies using structural models for treatment choice and potential outcomes. We have also discussed various methods available in the literature that attempt to overcome these biases. Although overt biases are easier to address, addressing hidden biases are tricky and often require some behavioural assumption about how persons make their decisions (regarding treatment choice). The burden of proof to defend these assumptions falls on the analyst. Based on the empirical example, we saw that hidden biases can be substantial in observational studies and addressing them should not only be a priority but also essential in the economic evaluation of medical care. We hope that this chapter will be helpful to researchers from all fields intending to account for these biases appropriately.

Table 43.2   Illustrative example.

	BCSRT [A]	Mastectomy [B]	Difference [A] – [B] (95% CI)
5-year quality adjusted life years			
No risk-adjustment	3.54	3.22	0.32 (0.26, 0.38)
Covariate adjustment	3.40	3.28	0.12 (0.05, 0.19)
Propensity matching	3.35	3.27	0.08 (−0.01, 0.17)
IV – adjust for hidden bias	3.11	3.40	−0.29 (−0.095, 0.38)
5-year medical costs			
No risk-adjustment	$48 604	$40 125	$8479 (4852, 12 105)
Covariate adjustment	$52 724	$38 525	$14 199 (10 279, 18 118)
Propensity matching	$54 423	$38 616	$15 807 (11 146, 17 252)
IV – adjust for hidden bias	$79 229	$28 233	$50 997 (12 879, 89 114)
Incremental costs per QALY			
No risk-adjustment			$26 495 (16 600, 39 600)
Covariate adjustment			$1 18 325 (70 040, 2 50 000)
Propensity matching			$1 97 587 (1 05 000, Dominated)
IV – adjust for hidden bias			Dominated (1 50 200, Dominated)

References

Dusheiko, M., H. Gravelle and R. Jacobs (2004), 'The effects of practice budgets on patient waiting times: allowing for selection bias', *Health Economics*, **13**(10), 941–58.

Hadley, J., D. Polsky, J.S. Mandelblatt, J.M. Mitchell, J.C. Weeks, Q. Wang and Y. Hwang (2003), 'An instrumental variable analysis of the outcomes of localized breast cancer treatments in a medicare population', *Health Economics*, **12**, 171–86.

Heckman, J.J. (1976), 'The common structure of statistical models of truncation, sample selection, and limited dependent variables and a simple estimator for such models', *Annals of Economic and Social Measurement*, **5**, 475–92.

Heckman, J.J. (1978), 'Dummy endogenous variables in a simultaneous equations system', *Econometrica*, **46**(4), 931–59.

Heckman, J.J. (1979), 'Sample selection bias as a specification error', *Econometrica*, **47**, 153–61.

Heckman, J.J. (1980), 'Addendum to sample selection bias as a specification error', in Ernst Stromsdorger and George Farkas (eds), *Evaluation Studies Review Annual*, vol. V, Beverly Hills: Sage Publications.

Heckman J.J. (2001), 'Micro data, heterogeneity, and the evaluation of public policy: Nobel Lecture', *Journal of Political Economics*, **109**(4), 673–748.

Heckman, J.J. and S. Navarro-Lozano (2004), 'Using matching, instrumental variables, and control functions to estimate economic choice models', *Review of Economic Statistics*, **86**(1), 30–57.

Heckman, J.J. and R. Robb (1985), 'Alternative methods for evaluating the impact of interventions', in James Heckman and Burton Singer (eds), *Longitudinal Analysis of Labor Market Data*, New York: Wiley, pp. 156–245.

Heckman, J.J. and R. Robb (1986), 'Alternative models for solving the problem of selection bias in evaluating the impact of treatment on outcomes', in H. Wainer (ed.), *Drawing Inferences from Self-Selected Samples*, Berlin: Springer Verlag, pp. 63–107.

Heckman, J.J. and G. Sedlacek (1985), 'Heterogeneity, aggregation and market wage functions: An empirical model of self selection in the labor market', *Journal of Political Economics*, **93**(6), 1077–25.

Heckman, J.J. and E. Vytlacil (1999), 'Local instrumental variables and latent variable models for identifying and bounding treatment effects', *Proceedings of the National Academy of Sciences*, **96**, 4730–4.

Heckman, J.J. and E. Vytlacil (2000), 'The relationship between treatment parameters within a latent variable framework', *Economic Letters*, **66**(1), 33–9.

Heckman, J.J. and E. Vytlacil (2004), 'Econometric evaluation of social programs', in *Handbook of Econometrics*, vol. V, Amsterdam: Elsevier.

Holland, P. (1986), 'Statistics and causal inference', *Journal of the American Statistical Association*, **81**, 945–70.

LaLonde, R. (1986), 'Evaluating the econometric evaluations of training programs with experimental data', *American Economic Review*, **76**(4), 604–20.

Lu, B. and P.R. Rosenbaum (2004), 'Optimal pair matching with two control groups', *Journal of Computational and Graphical Statistics*, **13**, 422–34.

Neyman, J., D.M. Dabrowska and T.P. Speed (1990), 'On the application of probability theory to agricultural experiments. Essay on Principles. Section 9', *Statistical Science*, **5**, 465–80.

Polsky, D., J.S. Mandelblatt, J.C. Weeks, L. Venditti, Y. Hwang, H.A. Glick, J. Hadley and K.A. Schulman (2003), 'An economic evaluation of breast cancer treatment: considering the value of patient choice', *Journal of Clinical Oncology*, **21**(6), 1139–46.

Quandt, R.E. (1972), 'A new approach to estimating switching regressions', *Journal of the American Statistical Association*, **67**, 306–10.

Quandt, R.E. (1988), *The Econometrics of Disequilibrium*, Oxford: Blackwell.

Rosenbaum, P.R. (1991), 'Discussing hidden bias in observational studies', *Annals of Internal Medicine*, **115**, 901–5.

Rosenbaum, P.R. (2002), *Observational Studies: Chapter 4 – Sensitivity Analysis*, New York: Springer.

Rosenbaum, P.R. and D. Rubin (1983), 'The central role of the propensity score in observational studies for causal effects', *Biometrika*, **70**(1), 41–55.

Roy, A.D. (1951), 'Some thoughts on the distribution of earnings', *Oxford Economic Papers*, **3**, 135–46.

Rubin, D. (1973), 'The use of matched sampling and regression adjustment to remove bias in observational studies', *Biometrics*, **29**, 185–203.

Rubin, D. (1974), 'Estimating causal effects of treatment in randomized and non-randomized studies', *Journal of Educational Psychology*, **66**, 688–701.

Rubin, D. (1978), 'Bayesian inference for causal effects: The role of randomization', *Annals of Statistics*, **6**, 34–58.

Vytlacil, E. (2002), 'Independence, monotonicity, and latent index models: An equivalence result', *Econometrica*, **70**(1), 331–41.

PART IX

ECONOMIC EVALUATION AND DECISION MAKING

44 Decision rules for incremental cost-effectiveness analysis

Milton C. Weinstein

1. Introduction

Consider the following choices faced by health care decision-makers:

For HIV:

- Which antiretroviral drug regimen should be offered to persons with HIV infection?
- What criterion should be used for starting antiretroviral therapy?
- What test(s) (CD4 counts, viral loads) should be used to monitor patients prior to initiation of treatment, and to monitor response to treatment?
- Should a second line of treatment be provided to patients who fail to respond to the initial treatment?

For cervical cancer:

- What technique should be used to screen women for cervical cancer – visual inspection, human papillomavirus DNA testing, or cytologic testing with a Pap smear?
- How often should women be screened?

For cardiovascular disease:

- What combination of drugs (aspirin, beta-blockers, angiotensin-converting enzyme inhibitors, statins) should be provided for cardiovascular prevention?
- Should these drugs be targeted to individuals based on individual risk factors (such as hypertension or hyperlipidemia), or based on overall cardiovascular risk, or should they be offered universally?

The element common to each of these choices is that they involve competing, mutually exclusive, options to address a single health problem. For example, the choice is between initiating antiretroviral therapy based on the occurrence of an opportunistic infection, *or* based on a measured CD4 cell count of ≤ 200 cells/ml, *or* based on the presence of either one of these indicators. In these *competing-choice* situations, decisions in resource-constrained settings should be guided by *incremental cost-effectiveness ratios* – the ratio of the additional resource cost to the additional health benefit when comparing competing options. This chapter concerns the proper use and interpretation of incremental cost-effectiveness ratios in economic evaluations of health care programmes (see also Hunink et al., 2001.)

2. A simple example

To illustrate the principles of incremental cost-effectiveness analysis, a simple stylized example will take us a long way. Suppose that a health ministry has to decide which of four HIV treatment programmes, M_1–M_4, to implement. These programmes may each involve a different drug regimen or sequence of regimens, different monitoring policies, different criteria for starting or stopping treatment, and so forth. For example, the low-cost option, M_1, might involve starting treatment only after three distinct serious opportunistic infections have been diagnosed, using a single low-cost drug regimen with no second-line treatment, and stopping at the first occurrence of an opportunistic infection. In contrast, the high-cost option, M_4, might involve monitoring CD4 cell counts every six months, starting treatment based on a CD4 count of ≤ 350, switching to a second line of treatment after two consecutive declines in CD4 counts on therapy, and never stopping the second line of treatment. Intermediate between these are options that blend these programme characteristics in various combinations. We assume that the resource costs of all options have been measured in international dollars ($) and that the health effects have been valued in terms of quality-adjusted life years (QALYs) gained (Table 44.1). Both costs and effects have been measured against a comparator of no treatment. Assume that these costs and QALY gains apply to full implementation of each programme in the target population (so that it is impossible to scale up the programmes to gain proportionally more QALYs at proportionally higher costs). However, for now we assume that it is possible to implement a mixture of programmes in the target population with proportional costs and QALYs; for example, M_1 and M_2 could each be implemented in half the population, with a gain of 25 $(= (0.5)(20) + (0.5)(30))$ QALYs, and at a cost of $50 000.

To muddy the waters a bit before clearing things up, consider the following possible (mostly spurious) interpretations of this evidence:

- 'Programme M_1 should be chosen. It is the most cost-effective alternative. Its cost-effectiveness ratio is $1250 $(=\$25 000/20)$ per QALY gained, which is lower than the ratio for M_2 $(\$2500 = \$75 000/30)$, M_3 $(\$5625 = \$225 000/40)$, or M_4 $(\$4688 = \$375 000/80)$.'
- 'Programme M_4 should be chosen. In our country, our budget permits us to pay up to $5500 per QALY, and M_4 comes in under that threshold. Therefore, option M_4 represents a cost-effective use of resources compared to other programmes we are considering with our limited budget.'
- 'Programme M_2 should be chosen. While it is true that M_1 is cost-effective, the additional cost of M_2, $50 000, is worth paying for the additional gain of 10 QALYs.

Table 44.1   Competing choice example

Programme	QALYs gained	Cost ($)
M_1	20	25 000
M_2	30	75 000
M_3	40	225 000
M_4	80	375 000

We are willing to pay up to $5500 per QALY, and the incremental cost-effectiveness ratio of M_2 is $5000 per QALY. On the other hand, programme M_3 is not worth the additional cost compared to M_2, and neither is M_4.'

All of these arguments may have some appeal at first, *but only the last is correct*. The rest of this chapter develops a systematic framework for deriving decision rules for the competing choice problem, and explains the correct calculation and interpretation of incremental cost-effectiveness ratios. It also describes how decision rules based on incremental cost-effectiveness ratios must be modified when key assumptions made in the basic framework do not hold. But it begins with the situation in which choices are limited only by a budget constraint.

3.   Maximizing health improvement subject to a budget constraint: the 'shopping spree' problem

Suppose the health ministry has a budget of $6 million to spend on interventions against different diseases. It seeks to allocate the funds in the way that gains the greatest number of quality-adjusted life years. The ministry has developed a list of programmes that could be implemented and has estimated their expected health benefits and resource costs in comparison to the alternative of no programme (Table 44.2).

For now we assume that the benefits and costs of each programme are independent of which other programmes are implemented. Moreover, each programme is divisible into any fraction, with constant returns to scale. For example, programme E could be delivered to 25 per cent of the population at a cost of $100 000, yielding a benefit of

$$\frac{\$100\ 000}{\$400\ 000} \times 800\ \text{QALYs} = 200\ \text{QALYs}.$$

Both of these assumptions – independence between programmes and constant returns to scale – will be relaxed later in this chapter; also see the discussion of their importance in the chapter by Birch and Gafni in this Companion (chapter 46).

Table 44.2   The 'shopping spree'

Programme	Benefft (QALYs gained)	Cost ($*1000)
A	1000	1000
B	400	600
C	100	400
D	200	900
E	800	400
F	200	600
G	200	5000
H	300	2250
I	500	1000
J	200	2500
K	200	1100

The health ministry would maximize the number of QALYs saved within its budget by (1) computing the cost-effectiveness ratios for all the programmes, (2) ranking them from most cost-effective (smallest ratios) to least cost-effective (largest ratios), and (3) selecting them in increasing order of the ratios until the budget is exhausted (Table 44.3).

Observe that the cost-effectiveness ratio of the last programme funded, programme K, is $5500/QALY. This means that every $5500 removed from the budget would result in a loss of 1 QALY, and every $1 removed from the budget would result in the loss of 1/5500 QALY. This ratio is significant because it represents the maximum amount the QALY-maximizing health minister would be willing to pay per QALY if a new programme option were introduced. It represents the health minister's *cost-effectiveness threshold*. For example, if a new programme Y, had a C/E ratio of $3500/QALY, it would be worth implementing, because its cost could come out of programme K, which is currently buying QALYs at a higher price than the new programme Y. The net effect of substituting Y for part of all of K would be a gain in total QALYs. Conversely, if a new programme Z had a C/E ratio of $6500/QALY, it would not be worth implementing, because it buys QALYs at a higher price than programme K (or any of the programmes above it on the rank list). The net effect of substituting Z for part or all of K would be a loss in total QALYs.

Please note that all of the cost-effectiveness ratios in this *shopping spree* problem are *incremental*, because they reflect an incremental comparison between each programme and its absence. The solution to the shopping spree problem is a ranking of incremental cost-effectiveness ratios. *However, the ratios reflect increments between each programme and its absence (for example, A vs. not A), not increments between different programmes on the menu of options (for example, B vs. A). The latter is appropriate when the options are mutually exclusive alternatives – the 'competing choice' problem to which we now turn.*

Table 44.3   Ranking of 'shopping-spree' programmes by cost-effectiveness ratio

Programme	C/E Ratio ($/QALY)	Cost of programme ($000)	QALYs gained by programme	Total costs ($000)	Total QALYs
E	500	400	800	400	800
A	1000	1000	1000	1400	1800
B	1500	600	400	2000	2200
I	2000	1000	500	3000	2700
F	3000	600	200	3600	2900
C	4000	400	100	4000	3000
D	4500	900	200	4900	3200
K	**5500**	**1100**	**200**	**6000**	**3400**
H	7500	2250	300	8250	3700
J	12 500	2500	200	10 750	3900
G	25 000	5000	200	15 750	4100

4. Choosing among programme alternatives: The 'competing-choice' problem

We return now to the competing-choice example presented earlier in this chapter – the choice among alternative programmes M_1–M_4 (Table 44.1). These alternatives are mutually exclusive; unlike the choice of programmes A, B, C, D, E, F, I, and K in the shopping spree, it is possible only to fund at most one among M_1–M_4, if any at all. Higher levels of programme M offer more benefit than lower levels, but they are more expensive as well. Resources for whatever version of programme M is chosen must come out of the overall budget. The correct way to analyse this problem is to calculate the rate at which additional costs can purchase additional benefits as each competing alternative is compared to the next less costly alternative. The price at which additional (incremental) costs are used in order to produce additional (incremental) QALYs – the *incremental cost-effectiveness ratio* – is then compared to the cost-effectiveness threshold ($5500/QALY in our example) to determine whether more QALYs are gained than lost by diverting resources from their next best use. This is the essence of incremental cost-effectiveness analysis.

To solve this competing-choice problem, we would start with the least expensive alternative, M_1, which is compared to doing nothing. Here the incremental cost-effectiveness ratio is determined by dividing the total costs of M_1 by the total number of QALYs gained: $25\,000/20$ QALYs $= \$1250/$QALY. (Note that the costs and QALYs gained with M_1 have already been calculated relative to a null alternative.) We can conclude that it is worth adopting *at least* M_1, because its incremental cost-effectiveness ratio is better than that of a programme like K, which costs $5500/QALY. Diverting $25\,000 from K to M_1 will yield a net gain in QALYs. From M_1 we would gain 20 QALYs, and from K we would lose

$$\frac{\$25\,000}{\$1\,100\,000} \times 200 \text{ QALYs} = 4.5 \text{ QALYs},$$

for a net gain of 15.5 QALYs. Next, having tentatively decided on M_1, we consider whether it is worth spending the additional resources to 'upgrade' from M_1 to M_2. The *additional* cost of M_2 is $50\,000$ ($= \$75\,000$–$\$25\,000$), and the net benefit is 10 QALYs ($= 30 - 20$). The incremental cost-effectiveness ratio of M_2, compared to M_1, is therefore $5000/QALY ($= \$50\,000/10$ QALY). This 'upgrade' is worth doing because it is still below the threshold of $5500/QALY. We continue along these lines, looking first at M_3 versus M_2, then M_4 versus M_3. Table 44.4 shows the results:

Table 44.4 Incremental cost-effectiveness ratios of programmes M_1–M_4

Level	Cost of programme ($000)	QALYs gained by programme	Incremental costs ($000)	Incremental QALYs	Incremental C/E ratio ($/QALY)
M_1	25	20	25	20	1250
M_2	75	30	50	10	5000
M_3	225	40	150	10	15000
M_4	375	80	150	40	3750

Table 44.5 *Revised incremental cost-effectiveness ratios after eliminating programmes ruled out by extended dominance*

Level	Cost of programme ($000)	QALYs gained by programme	Incremental costs ($000)	Incremental QALYs	Incremental C/E ratio ($/QALY)
M_1	25	20	25	20	1250
M_2	75	30	50	10	5000
M_4	375	80	300	50	6000

We observe in Table 44.4 that the incremental cost-effectiveness ratio (that is, the ratio of *additional* costs per *additional* life-year saved) of M_3 compared to M_2 is higher than that of M_4 compared to M_3. This means that if you are willing to pay the incremental cost per QALY of 'upgrading' from M_2 to M_3 (at least $15000/QALY), then *a fortiori* you would be willing to pay the additional $3750/QALY to further upgrade to M_4. No matter what the cost-effectiveness threshold, M_3 would never be selected. We say that M_3 is ruled out by *extended dominance*, also known as *weak dominance*. So we remove it from the list. But now we have to recalculate the incremental cost-effectiveness of M_4 because it must now be compared to M_2. The final result is shown in Table 44.5.

These incremental ratios are in increasing order, so we have no more extended dominance. If the incremental ratio for M_4 versus M_2 had been, say $4000 per QALY instead of $6000/QALY, then we would have eliminated M_2 by extended dominance, because its incremental ratio of $5000 would have exceeded that of a more expensive competing alternative, namely M_4. But that is not the case in this example, so Table 44.5 is a complete description of the incremental cost-effectiveness analysis.

We interpret the results in Table 44.5 as follows. If we are unwilling to pay as much as $1250 per QALY, the cost-effective option is not to adopt any of the competing options among M_1–M_4. If we are willing to pay at least $1250/QALY but not more than $5000/QALY, then M_1 would be cost-effective. If we are willing to pay at least $5000/QALY but not more than $6000/QALY, then M_2 would be cost-effective. If we are willing to pay at least $6000/QALY, then M_4 would be cost-effective. Note that M_3 is never cost-effective, even if we are willing to pay $15000/QALY. In that case, we would opt for M_4, which would yield more QALYs at a price we are willing to pay.

We can think of the incremental 'upgrades' from no M to M_1, thence to M_2, and thence to M_4, as independent programmes that comprise items on the menu in the budget-constrained 'shopping spree' represented in Table 44.3. As we spend our budget, starting with the most cost-effective programme E, then A, and so on, we pause to consider whether some resources ought to be diverted to buy QALYs through one of the options for programme M. We can represent this expanded shopping spree as shown in Table 44.6.

Notice that the competing alternatives M_1–M_4 are represented as incremental steps, or 'upgrades': from no programme M to M_1, from M_1 to M_2, and from M_2 to M_4. The costs and QALY gains for each of these incremental programmes are their incremental costs and incremental QALY gains (from Table 44.5). Programme M_3 does not appear because it is weakly dominated. This incremental representation of the options for programme

Table 44.6   Expanded 'shopping-spree' incorporating competing choices

Programme	C/E ratio ($/QALY)	Cost of programme ($000)	QALYs gained by programme	Total costs ($000)	Total QALYs
E	$500	$400	800	$400	800
A	$1000	$1000	1000	$1400	1800
No M → M$_1$	$1250	$25	20	$1425	1820
B	$1500	$600	400	$2025	2220
I	$2000	$1000	500	$3025	2720
F	$3000	$600	200	$3625	2920
C	$4000	$400	100	$4025	3020
D	$4500	$900	200	$4925	3220
M$_1$ → M$_2$	$5000	$50	10	$4975	3230
K	$5500	$1100	200	$6075	3430
M$_2$ → M$_4$	$6000	300	50	$6375	3480
H	$7500	$2250	300	$8625	3780
J	$12 500	$2500	200	$11 125	3980
G	$25 000	$5000	200	$16 125	4180

M is entirely consistent with the way the other programmes are represented in Table 44.6, since each programme (A–K) reflects a comparison between the absence of the programme and the adoption of the programme. Thus, E really means the upgrade from no E → E, A means no A → A, and so forth.

In reality, virtually all programmes share the characteristic of programme M, in that they are available in many possible varieties. For example, programme A may represent an antiretroviral treatment programme for HIV, with different possible criteria for starting treatment (for example, based on different CD4 cell count levels and/or disease histories), different possible drug regimens or sequences of drug regimens (lines of treatment), different monitoring strategies (for example, frequency of CD4 cell count measurement, or even whether or not CD4 counts are measured at all), and so on. In other words, the 'shopping spree' paradigm should really be thought of as having embedded within it sets of competing choices for each programme in the choice set. The representation of the 'competing choice' framework in Table 44.6 can be generalized so that *every* programme has several competing alternatives, analogous to programme M (Murray et al., 2000). The competing choice model encompasses a wide variety of situations in which mutually exclusive alternative options exist for a single condition. Examples include:

- criterion for initiating treatment (for example, based on disease progression, risk factors, or test results)
- criterion for discontinuing treatment
- choice of screening interval
- choice of drug regimen or dosage
- choice of diagnostic or monitoring test, or of sequence of tests
- combinations of the above.

5.   Extensions of the cost-effectiveness framework

Interdependence between programmes: costs and effects

The assumption that the health effects and costs of programmes do not depend on which other programmes are adopted is not very realistic. Owing to shared resource requirements of programmes, costs of implementing combinations of programmes may be less than the sum of the costs of implementing them individually. Likewise, combinations of interventions may result in greater or lesser health benefits than the sum of the individual interventions. Greater total benefits might result, for example, if two treatments were both necessary to achieve a positive effect, as in the case of combination antiretroviral therapy for HIV infection. A situation in which the combination of interventions may result in a smaller overall effect than the sum of the separate effects is illustrated by prevention and treatment. In the absence of effective, inexpensive treatment, a prevention programme may be very cost-effective, but in the presence of a widely implemented and inexpensive treatment programme for the condition, prevention may be much less beneficial and cost-effective. Other situations in which the benefits of a combined programme would be less than the sum of the components would arise if there were adverse drug interactions, or problems with adherence to multiple behavioural interventions. Naive application of the shopping spree and competing choice paradigms would lead to wrong conclusions in those circumstances. Fortunately the restriction of independence among programmes can be bypassed by expanding the set of competing choices to encompass *combinations* of individual programmes. For example, suppose that competing options A_1 and A_2 are available for condition A, and that competing options B_1 and B_2 are available for condition B. The competing choice paradigm says that we should perform an incremental analysis of no A versus A_1 versus A_2, and a separate competing choice analysis of no B versus B_1 versus B_2. However, if the costs and benefits of the A programmes depended on which version, if any, of programme B is adopted, and vice versa, we would need to construct composite programmes consisting of all nine possible combinations of A and B (three options each): neither A nor B, A_1 only, A_2 only, B_1 only, A_1 and B_1, A_2 and B_1, B_2 only, A_1 and B_2, or A_2 and B_2. These nine competing choices would be considered as a single cluster, along with other clusters of combined programmes for other conditions, in a composite incremental analysis. In the extreme situation where no programmes can be reasonably regarded as independent of any other programmes, all possible combinations of programme options would have to be considered in a single competing choice analysis. Undoubtedly, many combinations would be ruled out by strong or weak dominance, but in principle they would all have to be considered jointly if we wish to avoid the independence assumptions.

Indivisibilities

Another assumption in the basic shopping spree and competing choice paradigms is that programmes can be partially implemented, for example, in a fraction of the target population, with proportional aggregate health effects and costs. This is the assumption of programme *divisibility*. In the competing choice setting, the divisibility assumption means that it is possible to implement one programme alternative (for example, M_1) in a fraction of the target population and another alternative (for example, M_2) in the remaining fraction. One may object to this assumption on ethical grounds, that it is unfair to offer a better programme to some people than to others. Another objection to the divisibility assumption is that it may not be technically possible, as would be the case for a public health or environmental programme that of necessity affects the entire population (what economists would call a 'public good').

One response to the ethical objection to the divisibility assumption is that it may be possible to separate the target population into subgroups who would receive differential benefits from a programme and/or incur differential costs. It is rarely the case that the target population is completely homogeneous. For example, most public health authorities give priority for vaccination programmes according to age or comorbid conditions. Similarly, programmes to treat hypertension or HIV are routinely stratified according to blood pressure or overall cardiovascular risk, in the case of hypertension, or by CD4 cell count or prior history of opportunistic infections, in the case of HIV. By defining programmes within population subgroups, the problem can be recast as a 'shopping spree' in which each programme–subgroup pair is viewed as an independent entity. If, in addition, there are interactions between subgroups (as in the case of herd immunity for communicable diseases), then each combination of subgroups can be entered into a competing choice analysis for the programme.

If, after taking account of subgroups, there are still ethical objections to offering a programme to only a fraction of the population, or if there are technical obstacles to partial implementation of programmes, then a generalized optimization framework would be necessary (see Chapter 46 by Birch and Gafni in this Companion). The problem with the standard shopping spree and competing choice paradigms under those circumstances is that it may turn out that it is not possible to spend the very last dollar of the budget if programmes are ranked in order of their cost-effectiveness ratios. Suppose, for example, that programme K in Table 44.6 were actually 10 times as effective *and* expensive, with a cost of \$11 000 000 and a benefit of 2000 QALYs. Suppose further that it were impossible to implement programme K only in part. In that situation, programme K would not be affordable, and the last programme in Table 44.3 to be implemented within the budget would be M_2. This would leave \$1 025 000 (\$6 000 000–\$4 975 000) unspent! We could gain more QALYs by skipping over the indivisible programme K, and moving down the list to programme M_4 (actually substituting M_4 for M_2). This would cost only an additional \$300 000 and keep us within the budget, and it would also produce 50 more QALYs than we would achieve by truncating the selection after programme M_2. If there were programmes even farther down the list (with even higher C/E ratios) that could 'use up' the slack resources in the budget, we might be able to gain even more QALYs. A formal method for exploring which combinations of indivisible programmes would yield the most benefit within a fixed budget is called binary integer programming, and computer programs exist to solve these optimization problems rapidly, even though a manual solution could require tedious trial-and-error. In using binary integer programming one would have to take care that the 'upgrades' among competing choices (such as from no $M \to M_1 \to M_2 \to M_4$) were adopted in a proper order (such that $M_2 \to M_4$ is never selected before $M_1 \to M_2$). Available software allows one to introduce constraints such that certain combinations of programmes are disallowed.

Multiple resource constraints

A further extension of the optimization framework would allow for multiple constraints on resources. For example, there might be constraints on budgets in each fiscal year, not on the present value of streams of resource flows over time. While the use of a present-value budget constraint can be justified if there are unlimited opportunities for the government or payer to borrow and lend at fixed interest rates, this stylized rationale may not have much appeal in reality. In addition to period-specific budgets, there may also be constraints on real resources, such as physicians, other health-care workers, and hospital beds – constraints that it may not be possible to overcome in the short or medium run even with adequate funds. More complex mathematical programming models, such as linear or integer programming with multiple constraints, may be suitable in this situation, but these methods are beyond the scope of this chapter.

6.   Summary

This chapter has introduced the proper use and interpretation of cost-effectiveness ratios when programmes compete for limited resources (the 'shopping spree') and when mutually exclusive alternative programmes for a given condition compete with each other in the context of limited resources ('competing choices'). In both situations, cost-effectiveness ratios are always incremental, even if the comparator is the absence of a programme, as in the basic shopping spree. In the competing choice situation, the incremental comparisons are between pairs of increasingly effective and expensive competing approaches to intervention. Programmes that are more costly and less effective than competing alternatives are said to be dominated and are ruled out. Programmes that are incrementally less cost-effective than more effective (and costly) alternatives are said to be weakly dominated and are likewise ruled out. Assumptions that underlie the conventional interpretation of incremental cost-effectiveness ratios, such as independence between programmes and divisibility with proportional returns to scale, can often be relaxed without abandoning the simple, basic paradigm, by redefining the programme options as combinations of programmes or as different levels of individual programmes.

References

Hunink, M.G.M., P.P. Glasziou, J.E. Siegel, J.C. Weeks, J.S. Pliskin, A.S. Elstein and M.C. Weinstein (2001), *Decision Making in Health and Medicine: Integrating Evidence and Values*, Chapter 9, Cambridge: Cambridge University Press.

Murray, C.J.L., D.B. Evans, A. Acharya and R.M.P.M. Baltussen (2000), 'Development of WHO guidelines on generalized cost-effectiveness analysis', *Health Economics*, **9**, 235–51.

45 Generalized cost-effectiveness analysis: principles and practice

David B. Evans, Dan Chisholm and
*Tessa Tan-Torres Edejer**

1. Introduction: the challenge of sectoral cost-effectiveness analysis

Cost-effectiveness analysis (CEA), a subset of efficiency analysis, is concerned with how to make the best use of scarce health resources. It does this by assessing the gains in health associated with any investment decision. The large and growing literature on the topic is dominated by the comparison of interventions aimed at a particular disease, risk factor or health problem. This can range from a simple comparison of two pharmacological agents to the broader evaluation of alternative ways of reducing the disease burden associated with malaria or with HIV/AIDS (Goodman et al., 1999; Creese et al., 2002). This type of analysis provides important information to programme managers or practitioners with a specific disease mandate.

In practice, however, different types of policy-makers and practitioners have different demands. Managers of hospital drug formularies must decide which of a vast array of pharmaceuticals they should stock, taking into account the available budget. Countries where health is funded predominantly from the public purse make decisions on what type of pharmaceuticals or technologies can be publicly funded or subsidized, while all types of health insurance – social, community or private – must select a package of services that will be provided (Drummond et al., 1997; Taylor et al., 2004). These types of decisions require a broader set of information, involving comparison of different types of interventions across the entire health sector – whether they are aimed at treating tuberculosis, reducing the risk of stroke, or providing kidney transplants. This type of analysis we call 'sectoral cost-effectiveness analysis'.

Although the number of published cost-effectiveness studies is now huge, there are a series of practical problems in using them for sectoral decision-making (Leidl, 1994; Hutubessy et al., 2003). The first is that most published studies take an incremental approach, addressing questions such as how best small changes (almost always increases) in resources should be allocated, or whether a new technology is more cost-effective than the existing one it would replace. Traditional analysis has not been used to address whether existing health resources are allocated efficiently, despite evidence that in many settings current resources do not in fact achieve as much as they could (Tengs et al., 1995; Jamison et al., 1993). Elsewhere we have called this standard form of CEA 'intervention-mix constrained cost-effectiveness analysis' (IMC-CEA) because it does not question the mix of interventions currently available (Murray et al., 2000; Tan Torres et al., 2003).

---

* Disclaimer: The named authors alone are responsible for the views expressed in this chapter.

The second problem is that most studies are very context-specific. The efficiency of additional investment in an intervention aimed at a given disease depends partially on the level and quality of the existing health infrastructure (including human resources). This varies substantially across settings and is related to a third problem – individual interventions are almost always evaluated in isolation despite the fact that the effectiveness and costs of most will vary according to whether other related interventions are currently undertaken or are likely to be introduced in the future.

Two final concerns relate to uncertainty and scale effects. Although there is now increasing attention given to uncertainty in the theoretical CEA literature (see Chapter 48 by Claxton, Fenwick and Sculpher in this Companion), full and appropriate handling of uncertainty in published economic evaluations is still not reported in a majority of studies (Briggs and Gray, 1999). This makes it unclear how certain policy-makers can be that one intervention is more efficient than another. Uncertainty when interventions are interrelated in terms of costs and effects is an even more complex issue. Similarly, analysts rarely estimate costs and effects at different levels of coverage or scale, so do not provide policy-makers with important information about how far they should expand (or contract) an intervention.

2.   Principles of generalized cost-effectiveness analysis (GCEA)

GCEA was designed to allow policy-makers to evaluate the efficiency of the mix of health interventions currently available and to maximize the generalizability of results across settings. At the same time, it has sought to rectify some of the other problems of traditional CEA by incorporating interactions between interventions in terms of costs and effects as well as by evaluating interventions, and combinations of interventions, at different levels of coverage. It has also made some progress in considering uncertainty, although more remains to be done in this area (as it does with traditional CEA). It can be used for sectoral analysis, or for the more common disease-specific analysis.

GCEA allows for an assessment of the efficiency of the current mix of interventions by analysing all interventions and combinations incremental on doing nothing, sometimes called the null (Murray et al., 2000; Tan Torres et al., 2003). This does not mean assuming that no interventions were ever undertaken, something that is not feasible or necessary. Operationally, the counterfactual that has been adopted in applied studies is defined in terms of what would happen to population health if all interventions being provided now were stopped (see, for example, Baltussen et al., 2004a; Chisholm et al., 2004a; Murray et al., 2003; Shibuya et al., 2003).

Consider Figure 45.1, in which two sets of interventions are depicted, one for reducing exposure to hazardous alcohol use, the other for reducing exposure to tobacco use, for a region consisting of Latin American and Caribbean countries with low levels of child and adult mortality – designated here as AmrB (Chisholm et al., 2004b; Shibuya et al., 2003; Table 45.1 reports intervention definitions and the summary cost-effectiveness results). The vertical axis is the yearly cost of the intervention in a standardized population of a million people, in international dollars, while the horizontal axis measures health improvements in terms of disability adjusted life years (DALYs) averted. The analysis could be undertaken in terms of any outcome indicator, such as QALYs or years of life saved.

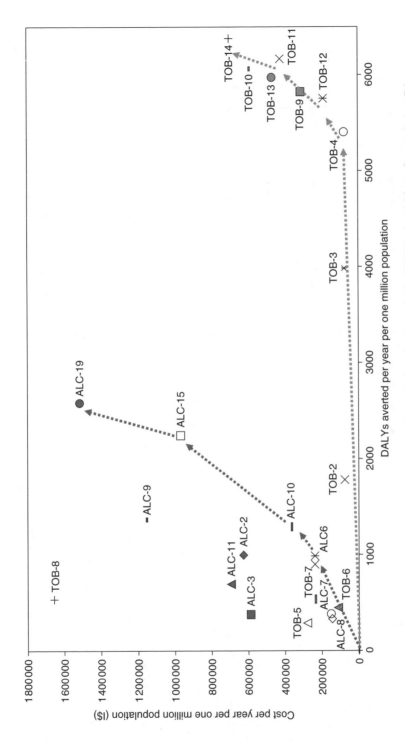

Figure 45.1   Costs and effects of interventions for reducing alcohol and tobacco use (WHO American subregion Amr B)

Table 45.1   Costs, effects and cost-effectiveness of interventions for reducing exposure to selected risk factors in a region of the Americas

WHO Subregion AmrB (Total population: 431 million)	Total cost per year (I$)	Cost per 1m per year (I$)	Total DALYs per year	DALYs per 1m per year	Avg Cost per DALY	Incrl Cost per DALY
HAZARDOUS ALCOHOL USE						
ALC-2: Brief PHC advice	269 976 373	626 541	429 430	997	629	
ALC-3: Random Breath Testing	252 870 675	586 843	162 718	378	1554	
ALC-4: Taxation (current)	102 353 789	237 535	347 229	806	295	
ALC-5: Taxation (current + 20%)	102 353 789	237 535	387 238	899	264	
ALC-6: Taxation (current + 50%)	102 353 789	237 535	425 137	987	241	241
ALC-7: Reduced access (sales)	64 767 895	150 308	165 177	383	392	
ALC-8: Advertising ban	61 930 657	143 724	142 654	331	434	
ALC-9: Combination (ALC2 + ALC3)	496 704 696	1 152 715	580 305	1347	856	
ALC-10: Combination (ALC6 + ALC8)	156 070 224	362 196	556 436	1291	280	409
ALC-11: Combination (ALC3 + ALC8)	299 061 266	694 039	299 265	695	999	
ALC-15: Combination (ALC2 + ALC6 + ALC8)	416 890 387	967 488	967 305	2245	431	635
ALC-19: Combination (ALC2 + ALC3 + ALC6 + ALC8)	652 774 920	1 514 910	1 113 542	2584	586	1613
TOBACCO USE						
TOB-2: Global average tax rate (44%)	32 115 750	74 532	766 905	1780	42	
TOB-3: Highest regional tax rate (75%)	32 115 750	74 532	1 715 827	3982	19	
TOB-4: Doubling highest tax	32 115 750	74 532	2 328 421	5404	14	14
TOB-5: Clean indoor air law enforcement	120 294 883	279 171	123 783	287	972	
TOB-6: Comprehensive advertise banning	47 987 184	111 365	193 283	449	248	
TOB-7: Information dissemination	100 827 013	233 992	231 517	537	436	
TOB-8: Nicotine replacement therapy	713 816 387	1 656 571	231 517	537	3083	
TOB-9: Combination (TOB4 + TOB7)	132 942 764	308 523	2 509 213	5823	53	
TOB-10: Combination (TOB4 + TOB5 + TOB7)	253 237 647	587 695	2 603 344	6042	97	
TOB-11: Combination (TOB4 + TOB6 + TOB7)	180 929 948	419 888	2 656 811	6166	68	568
TOB-12: Combination (TOB4 + TOB6)	80 102 935	185 897	2 479 361	5754	32	318
TOB-13: Combination (TOB4 + TOB5 + TOB6)	200 397 818	465 068	2 573 853	5973	78	

TOB-14: Combination (TOB4 + TOB5 + TOB6 + TOB7)	301 224 831	699 060	2 749 157	6380	110	1303
TOB-15: Combination (ALL)	1 015 041 219	2 355 631	2 920 572	6778	348	4164

CARDIOVASCULAR DISEASE RISK FACTORS

CVD-2: Salt reduction in food (voluntary)	82 034 499	190 379	336 235	780	244	
CVD-3: Salt reduction in food (enforced)	82 120 383	190 579	648 129	1504	127	127
CVD-4: Mass media / health education	81 202 708	188 449	597 621	1387	136	
CVD-5: Hypertensive drug & education (BP > 160)	3 121 573 030	7 244 310	3 846 873	8928	811	
CVD-6: Hypertensive drug & education (BP > 140)	8 805 994 633	20 436 284	4 727 107	10 970	1863	
CVD-7: Statins & education (cholesterol > 240)	2 425 956 389	5 629 975	2 804 358	6508	865	
CVD-8: Statins & education (cholesterol > 220)	4 397 095 615	10 204 446	3 317 088	7698	1326	
CVD-9: Triple drug therapy (absolute CVD risk > 35%)	1 334 706 282	3 097 485	5 146 051	11 943	259	
CVD-10: Triple drug therapy (absolute CVD risk > 25%)	2 058 820 457	4 777 954	5 622 719	13 049	366	
CVD-11: Triple drug therapy (absolute CVD risk > 15%)	3 351 703 504	7 778 379	6 184 627	14 353	542	
CVD-12: Triple drug therapy (absolute CVD risk > 5%)	6 456 478 634	14 983 705	6 937 418	16 100	931	
CVD-13: Combination (CVD2 + CVD3)	163 323 091	379 028	1 209 159	2806	135	145
CVD-14: Combination (CVD6 + CVD7)	11 231 951 022	26 066 259	6 130 377	14 227	1832	
CVD-15: Combination (CVD2 + CVD3 + CVD9)	1 364 640 638	3 166 954	5 409 820	12 555	252	286
CVD-16: Combination (CVD2 + CVD3 + CVD10)	2 056 192 256	4 771 855	5 842 475	13 559	352	
CVD-17: Combination (CVD2 + CVD3 + CVD11)	3 332 480 081	7 733 767	6 376 102	14 797	523	
CVD-18: Combination (CVD2 + CVD3 + CVD12)	6 394 137 461	14 839 029	7 084 868	16 442	903	

IRON DEFICIENCY

IRD-2: Iron supplementation (50%)	63 385 379	147 100	130 202	302	487	
IRD-3: Iron supplementation (80%)	116 771 583	270 995	208 323	483	561	
IRD-4: Iron supplementation (95%)	165 492 669	384 063	247 383	574	669	1349
IRD-5: Iron fortification (50%)	15 594 183	36 190	72 874	169	214	
IRD-6: Iron fortification (80%)	16 510 432	38 316	116 599	271	142	
IRD-7: Iron fortification (95%)	18 565 556	43 086	138 461	321	134	134

The slope of a ray from the origin to any point shows the cost-effectiveness of introducing the intervention compared to the null while the slope of a line between two intervention points is the cost-effectiveness of moving from one intervention to the other – an incremental ratio. If a country could select its interventions from scratch and if efficiency were the only objective, it would choose the ray with the lowest slope first, the lowest cost per unit of health effect. TOB4 (a significant increase in the rate of taxation on tobacco products) would be chosen on those grounds. As resources increase, it would move to TOB12, since the slope of the line TOB4 to TOB12 is lower than that from the origin to ALC6. Should more resources become available, it would also purchase ALC6, the most cost-effective intervention for reducing hazardous alcohol use, and this process continues.

If we assume, however, that a country had decided for various reasons not to tax alcohol products, relying instead on the enforcement of drink-driving laws via random breath-testing of drivers (ALC3). Traditional incremental analysis would suggest that if new resources became available for reducing the burden of hazardous alcohol use, it would be most efficient to move from ALC3 to ALC2 (brief physician advice for heavy drinkers), and then to the combination of these (ALC9). Such an analysis would simply not identify that ALC3 was an inefficient use of resources compared to other single or combined interventions, thereby providing decision-makers with incomplete and potentially misleading information. By identifying the health benefits and the costs of current and new interventions incremental on doing nothing, GCEA allows decision-makers to consider if some current interventions should be scaled down or even stopped in favour of more efficient alternatives. This is analogous to the 'shopping spree' problem described by Weinstein in Chapter 44 in this Companion.

Many interventions interact in terms of either costs or effects at the population level, and interacting interventions are undertaken in different combinations in different settings. The health impacts of undertaking two interventions together are not necessarily additive, nor are the costs of their joint production. To understand whether they are efficient uses of resources independently or in combination requires assessing their costs and health effects independently and in combination, something which is routine in GCEA but which should also be done in traditional analysis. Only then is it possible to account for non-linearities in costs and effects.

For example, the health effects of population screening and treatment for high cholesterol will depend on whether there is already screening and treatment for high blood pressure in the same population. Provision of both together would have synergies in costs. This means that three interventions should be evaluated – screening and treatment for elevated blood pressure, for high cholesterol, and for both combined. By evaluating such interrelated interventions in a single cluster, interactions can be captured and much more useful information can be provided to decision-makers than if the interventions were only evaluated by themselves. Table 45.1 and Figure 45.2 include a comparison for AmrB of the use of a drug to reduce blood pressure plus education for people with a systolic blood pressure greater than 140 mmHg (CVD6), use of cholesterol-lowering drugs (statins) plus lifestyle modification for people with cholesterol levels above 240 mg/dl (CVD7), plus a combination of these two (CVD14).

Non-linearities also exist when it comes to scaling up the coverage of an intervention but results rarely are reported for different levels of coverage (see Chapter 46 by Birch and

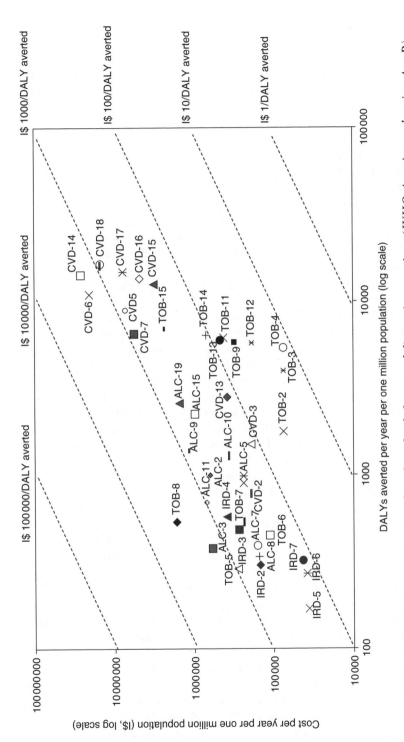

Figure 45.2   Cost-effectiveness isoquants for selected risk factor and disease interventions (WHO American subregion AmrB)

485

Gafni in this Companion). It is unlikely to be possible to obtain information that would allow a cost-effectiveness curve of all possible levels of coverage to be obtained given data limitations, but the WHO-CHOICE (Choosing Interventions that are Cost-Effective) project that is implementing GCEA routinely reports costs and effects at 50 per cent, 80 per cent and 95 per cent coverage (Tan Torres et al., 2003). Again, this is illustrated in Table 45.1 and Figure 45.2, this time with reference to iron deficiency: for iron supplementation to pregnant women (IRD2–4), cost-effectiveness worsens as coverage is extended, whereas the reverse is true for population-wide iron fortification (IRD5–7).

The final important feature of GCEA is that it seeks to maximize generalizability across settings. Most cost-effectiveness studies have been undertaken in developed countries, but not even the richest have been able to evaluate the full set of interventions required to undertake a sectoral analysis specific to their own country. The shortage of timely information on costs and health effects is particularly acute in low and middle-income countries where the majority of the world's poor live. All countries need to borrow results of cost or effectiveness studies from other settings, but the fact that most published studies are very specific to a particular setting makes this difficult. The proliferation of multiple national or sub-national guidelines for CEA practice, all using slightly different methods, adds to the problems.

Prior to the WHO-CHOICE project, only a few applications of sectoral CEA could be found. Examples include the work of the Oregon Health Services Commission, the World Bank Health Sector Priorities Review and the Harvard Life Saving Project (Dixon and Welch, 1991; Jamison et al., 1993; World Bank, 1993; Tengs et al., 1995). Only the World Bank attempted to undertake a global analysis and inform decision-making across a range of countries. It was in many ways a pioneering effort, collating the available information on a wide range of interventions and diseases (Jamison et al., 1993). However, it attempted to draw policy conclusions from studies undertaken in very different epidemiological and cost settings, many of which used different methods so that the resulting cost-effectiveness ratios were simply not comparable. Nor was it clear to which part of the world each reported cost-effectiveness ratio applied, which limited the policy relevance of the results.

As a compromise between a global analysis, which is not applicable to any country, and analysis for every country, which would require many more resources than is feasible for the foreseeable future, WHO-CHOICE has chosen to report results for 14 regions of the world. They have been selected to ensure maximum comparability between countries in terms of health systems and epidemiological profiles (WHO, 2002). By evaluating interventions compared to the starting point of doing none of the current set, the constraint that the current intervention mix must be continued is removed, eliminating differences in starting points which makes the results of incremental analysis difficult to transfer across settings. Only one constraint remains, the budget, allowing simple decision rules to be developed based on the calculated cost-effectiveness ratios.

3.   The practice of generalized cost-effectiveness analysis

GCEA has now been applied to a wide range of specific diseases (including malaria, tuberculosis, cancers and mental disorders) as well as risk factors (for example, child under-nutrition, unsafe sex, unsafe water, hygiene and sanitation, hypertension and smoking) (Baltussen et al., 2004a, 2004b; Chisholm et al., 2004a, 2004b; Dziekan et al.,

2003; Mehta and Shahpar, 2004; Murray et al., 2003; Shibuya et al., 2003; WHO, 2002). The application of Generalized CEA in a systematic and standardized manner involves a number of key analytical steps:

Step 1: Construct an epidemiological profile. Because estimates are required of population health with and without interventions over time, it is important to have a set of empirically-based but internally consistent data on the incidence, prevalence, remission and case-fatality for the conditions being considered.

Step 2: Construct the null scenario. For some conditions such as psychiatric disorders, natural history models can be used to establish what would happen in the absence of an intervention. In other cases, a process of back-adjustment from existing effective coverage of interventions in the population is required.

Step 3: Calculate population-level intervention effectiveness. Intervention effectiveness has been determined via a state transition population model, which traces the development of a regional population taking into account births, deaths and the disease in question (Lauer et al., 2003). Key transition rates, each expressed in terms of number of events per year at risk, include the incidence of the disorder in the population, case-fatality and remission. In addition, a disability weight is specified (on a 0–1 scale) for time spent in different states of (ill-)health. Utility weights could be substituted for people wishing to use QALYs rather than DALYs. Two epidemiological situations are modelled over a lifetime analytic horizon, to give the total number of healthy years lived by the population: 1) a counterfactual epidemiological situation representing the scenario of no interventions in place; and 2) the epidemiological situation reflecting the population-level impact of each specified intervention (such as reduced incidence of ischaemic heart disease following an increase in tobacco taxation). The WHO-CHOICE project has chosen to run the intervention for a period of 10 years but this can be modified as required. The difference between these two simulations represents the population-level health gain (measured in DALYs averted) due to the implementation of the intervention, relative to the situation of doing nothing. Combinations of interventions are evaluated in the same way.

Step 4: Construct resource utilization and cost profile(s) for each intervention and combination. An 'ingredients' approach to the costing of health interventions has been used, which requires separate identification and valuation of the quantity of resource inputs needed (such as numbers of health personnel) and the price or unit cost of those resource inputs (such as the salary of a health professional). Unit costs have been calculated for the 14 regions to help standardization, and can also be used at country-level (for example Adam et al., 2003). In addition, programme costs have been computed, which are resources that are used in the production of an intervention at a level above that of the patient or health facility. This includes resources required for planning, policy and administration functions, as well as those devoted to training health providers or enforcing legislation (Johns et al., 2003). All costs for the 10-year implementation period are discounted at 3 per cent and expressed in international dollars (I\$), which adjusts for differences in the relative price and purchasing power of countries and better facilitates comparison across regions than US dollars at official exchange rates.

Step 5: Cost-effectiveness analysis (including uncertainty). The components described in steps 1 to 4 provide the building blocks for analysis of the costs and effects of an intervention. Summary results for population-level costs, effectiveness and cost-effectiveness can be generated, expressed as average and incremental cost-effectiveness ratios (CERs), here shown as I$ per DALY averted (see Table 45.1 for an example). In common with any robust economic evaluation, however, it is important to provide an indication of the uncertainty around point estimates of cost, effect or CER. For this, WHO-CHOICE builds upon recent work reported in the literature concerning probabilistic sensitivity analysis, Monte Carlo simulation and acceptability curves (Briggs and Gray, 1999; Fenwick et al., 2001; see also Chapter 48 by Claxton, Fenwick and Sculpher in this Companion). Specifically, because GCEA considers combinations of interventions as well as single interventions, the requirements for uncertainty analysis are more complex, requiring information on the covariance of different components of costs and effectiveness across the range of interrelated interventions. Stochastic league tables have been developed as an approach to inform decision-makers about the probability that a specific intervention would be included in the optimal mix of interventions for various levels of resource availability, taking into account the uncertainty around cost and effectiveness of different interventions simultaneously (Baltussen et al., 2002; Hutubessy et al., 2001; Tan Torres et al., 2003). Work in this area is still ongoing, however, since these stochastic league tables do not as yet capture the full complexity of interacting interventions.

A number of other technical issues remain with the use and practice of GCEA. One of these issues relates to questions of what outcome indicator to use (applications of GCEA to date have used DALYs, a measure of population health rather than a utility-based outcome measure); whether to weight these summary outcome measures according to the age, sex or socioeconomic standing of the person who benefits; what discount rate should be used and whether it should differ for costs and health benefits; and whether unrelated health costs and productivity gains should be included (Tan Torres et al., 2003; see also Chapter 42 by Meltzer in this Companion). Because these are common to all forms of CEA, they are not discussed further here.

4. Illustrative results for four selected risk factors

Table 45.1 provides summary baseline results for the estimated costs, effects and cost-effectiveness of 50 single and combined interventions aimed at reducing exposure to four risk factors: hazardous alcohol use (Chisholm et al., 2004b); tobacco use (Shibuya et al., 2003); cardiovascular disease risk (Murray et al., 2003); and iron deficiency (Baltussen et al., 2004a). Cost and effectiveness results in Table 45.1 relate to a total population of 431 million people living in the AmrB region as described earlier, but are expressed in Figures 45.1 and 45.2 for a standardized population of one million.

As discussed already, Figure 45.1 depicts the set of interventions analysed for reducing exposure to alcohol and tobacco use, and shows the so-called 'expansion path' that would be pursued if a country could select its interventions from scratch and if efficiency were the only objective. As progressively fewer cost-effective interventions are introduced or selected, so the incremental cost-effectiveness ratio (ICER) rises. Point estimates for the

ICER are also reported in Table 45.1. It is clear that this type of analysis could be used by people interested only in tobacco control, only in reducing risks of alcohol abuse, or by more general policy-makers interested in the best way of reducing risks to health.

Finally, Figure 45.2 also plots these interventions for reducing addictive substances, along with those for two other risk factors (CVD and iron deficiency), but this time on a logarithmic scale in order to provide a 'bird's eye' view of the comparative cost-effectiveness of these widely diverging strategies. Each diagonal isoquant represents one order of magnitude difference in cost-effectiveness terms, ranging from I$1–I$100 000 per DALY averted. Although total costs and total effects per one million population vary substantially (for example, cost per capita ranges from less than I$0.05 to more than I$20), all of the interventions considered here have an average CER of between I$10–I$10 000, with the majority clustered between I$100–I$1000.

Comparing across the different sets of risk factors, the most cost-effective ways to reduce these risks to health relate to tax-based tobacco control strategies (each averted DALY costs less than I$100), followed by interventions such as salt reduction in processed foods and iron fortification in staple foods (CVD3, IRD7). Compared to doing nothing, each DALY can be averted by these interventions at a cost less than I$150.

5. Policy uses of Generalized CEA

Problems with data availability, particularly where interventions interact, mean that the uncertainty around most point estimates of cost-effectiveness will be relatively large. Because of this we argue that results of GCEA, or indeed any CEA, should not be used formulaically. It is not, in general, possible to be certain that an intervention that costs $10 per DALY is better than one where the point estimate of CE is $20 per DALY, or even perhaps $50 per DALY. It is usually possible to be sure that one costing $1000 per DALY averted is less efficient than one costing $10 per DALY. Accordingly for policy purposes, we have divided interventions into those that are very cost-effective, those that are cost-effective, and those that are not cost-effective in each setting.

Although there is continuing debate about how to determine acceptability cut points for cost-effectiveness, one useful and universally available metric for determining the threshold values for these categories – and one which matches quite closely existing thresholds in industrialized nations – is gross national income per capita. We have used the convention that any intervention that costs less than average yearly income per capita to produce each unit of health benefit is deemed very cost-effective. At the other extreme, interventions exceeding three times GDP per capita are considered not cost-effective. Policy debate should focus on why interventions that are in the latter group are being undertaken, when some in the first group are not implemented, rather than trying to apply decision rules formulaically.

The development of a database on the costs and effects of a wide range of interventions, and combinations, in 14 regions of the world is a compromise between a global analysis and the idea of a separate analysis for all countries, as explained earlier. The analysis has already proved useful in policy debate about the appropriate mix of health interventions in different settings, but there is still a tendency for country policy-makers to distrust analysis that was not undertaken specifically for their setting. Accordingly, tools for country contextualization of the regional results have been developed. Country analysts can modify the subregional analysis to their own settings using the priors incorporated in the subregional analysis, allowing a much more rapid and complete analysis than if the work had started from scratch (Hutubessy et al., 2003).

Like all CEA, GCEA focuses on only one outcome, population health. There are many other possible outcomes people care about – inequalities in health, responsiveness and fairness of financing for example (Murray and Evans, 2003). The results of GCEA cannot be used to set priorities by themselves but should be introduced into the policy debate to be considered along with the impact of different policy and intervention mixes on other outcomes. To help in this process, we are moving towards trying to formalize how to assess these impacts at the same time as assessing impact on population health.

References

Adam, T., D.B. Evans and C.J.L. Murray (2003), 'Econometric estimation of country-specific hospital costs', *Cost Effectiveness and Resource Allocation*, **1**(3), (available at http://www.resource-allocation.com/content/1/1/3).

Baltussen, R., C. Knai and M. Sharan (2004a), 'Iron fortification and iron supplementation are cost-effective interventions to reduce iron deficiency in four subregions of the world', *Journal of Nutrition*, **134**, 2678–84.

Baltussen, R., M. Sylla and S.-P. Mariotti (2004b), 'Cost-effectiveness analysis of cataract surgery: a global and regional analysis', *Bulletin of the World Health Organization*, **82**(5), 338–45.

Baltussen, R., R. Hutubessy, D. Evans and C. Murray (2002), 'Uncertainty in cost-effectiveness analysis: probalistic uncertainty analysis and stochastic league tables', *International Journal of Technology Assessment in Health Care*, **18**(1), 112–19.

Briggs, A.H. and A.M. Gray (1999), 'Handling uncertainty when performing economic evaluation of healthcare interventions', *Health Technology Assessment*, **3**(1), 1–134.

Chisholm, D., K. Sanderson, J.-L. Ayuso-Mateos and S. Saxena (2004a), 'Reducing the global burden of depression: population-level analysis of intervention cost-effectiveness in 14 world regions', *British Journal of Psychiatry*, **184**, 393–403.

Chisholm, D., J. Rehm, M. van Ommeren and M. Monteiro (2004b), 'Reducing the global burden of hazardous alcohol use: a comparative cost-effectiveness analysis', *Journal of Studies on Alcohol*, **65**, 782–93.

Creese, A., K. Floyd, A. Alban and L. Guinness (2002), 'Cost-effectiveness of HIV/AIDS interventions in Africa: a systematic review of the evidence', *The Lancet*, **359**, 1635–43.

Dixon, J. and H.G. Welch (1991), 'Priority setting: lessons from Oregon' [see comments], *The Lancet*, **337**, 891–4.

Drummond, M., B. Jonsson and F. Rutten (1997), 'The role of economic evaluation in the pricing and reimbursement of medicines', *Health Policy*, **40**, 199–215.

Dziekan, G., D. Chisholm, B. Johns et al. (2003), 'The cost-effectiveness of policies for the safe and appropriate use of injection in health care settings', *Bulletin of the World Health Organization*, **81**, 277–85.

Fenwick, E., K. Claxton and M. Sculpher (2001), 'Representing uncertainty: the role of cost-effectiveness acceptability curves', *Health Economics*, **10**, 779–87.

Goodman, C.A., P.G. Coleman and A.J. Mills (1999), 'Cost-effectiveness of malaria control in sub-Saharan Africa', *The Lancet*, **354**, 378–85.

Hutubessy, R., D. Chisholm and T. Tan Torres (2003), 'Generalized cost-effectiveness analysis for national-level priority-setting in the health sector', *Cost Effectiveness and Resource Allocation*, **1**(8), (available at http://www.resource-allocation.com/content/1/1/8).

Hutubessy, R.C., R.M. Baltussen, D.B. Evans et al. (2001), 'Stochastic league tables: communicating cost-effectiveness results to decision-makers', *Health Economics*, **10**, 473–7.

Jamison, D.T., W.H. Mosley, A.R. Measham and J.L. Bobadilla (1993), *Disease Control Priorities in Developing Countries*, New York: Oxford University Press.

Johns, B., R. Baltussen, T. Adam and R. Hutubessy (2003), 'Programme costs in the economic evaluation of health interventions', *Cost Effectiveness and Resource Allocation*, **1**(1), (http://www.resource-allocation.com/content/1/1/1).

Lauer, J.A., C.J.L. Murray, K. Roehrich and H. Wirth (2003), 'PopMod: a longitudinal model with two interacting disease states', *Cost Effectiveness and Resource Allocation*, **1**(6), (http://www.resource-allocation.com/content/1/1/6).

Leidl, R.M. (1994), 'Some factors to consider when using the results of economic evaluation studies at the population level', *International Journal of Technology Assessment in Health Care*, **10**, 467–78.

Mehta, S. and C. Shahpar (2004), 'The health benefits to interventions to reduce indoor air pollution from solid fuel use: a cost-effectiveness analysis', *Energy for Sustainable Development*, **VIII**(3), 53–9 (available at http://ieiglobal.org/ESDVol8No3/cost-effectiveness.pdf).

Murray, C.J.L. and D.B. Evans (2003), 'Health systems performance assessment: goals, framework and overview', in C.J.L. Murray and D.B. Evans (eds), *Health System Performance Assessment: Debates, Methods and Empiricism*, Geneva: World Health Organization, pp. 3–18.

Murray, C.J.L., D. Evans, A. Acharya and R. Baltussen (2000), 'Development of WHO guidelines on generalized cost-effectiveness analysis', *Health Economics*, **9**, 235–51.

Murray, C.J.L., J.A. Lauer, R.C.W. Hutubessy et al. (2003), 'Effectiveness and costs of interventions to lower systolic blood pressure and cholesterol: a global and regional analysis on reduction of cardiovascular disease', *The Lancet*, **361**, 717–25.

Shibuya, K., C. Ciecierski, E. Guindon et al. (2003), 'WHO Framework Convention on Tobacco Control: development of an evidence based global public health treaty', *British Medical Journal*, **327**, 154–7.

Tan Torres, T., R.M. Baltussen, T. Adam et al. (2003), 'Making choices in health: WHO guide to cost-effectiveness analysis', Geneva: World Health Organization.

Taylor, R.S., M.F. Drummond, G. Salkeld and S.D. Sullivan (2004), 'Inclusion of cost-effectiveness in licensing requirements of new drugs: the fourth hurdle', *British Medical Journal*, **329**(7472), 972–5.

Tengs, T.O., M.E. Adams, J.S. Pliskin et al. (1995), 'Five-hundred life-saving interventions and their cost-effectiveness' [see comments], *Risk Analysis*, **15**, 369–90.

World Bank (1993), *World Development Report 1993: Investing in Health*, New York: Oxford University Press.

World Health Organization (2002), 'Some strategies to reduce risk', *World Health Report 2002: Reducing Risks, Promoting Health Life*, Chapter 5, pp. 101–44, Geneva, Switzerland: WHO.

46 Decision rules in economic evaluation
Stephen Birch and Amiram Gafni

1. Introduction

Decision-makers struggle to satisfy the increasing demands for health care services associated with ageing populations, increasing health care technologies and changing population expectations using the resources available to the health care system. Economics has been identified as providing a relevant 'toolbox' for addressing these challenges aimed at 'ensuring that the value of what is gained from an activity outweighs the value of what has to be sacrificed' (Williams, 1983).

More recently movements to promote more systematic and standardized approaches to using economics as an input to health care decision-making have emerged. In this chapter we identify the problems facing health care decision-makers, the objectives of a systematic approach and the 'decision-rules' derived from the proposed approaches. We show that the needs of decision-makers are not met by the decision rules. The consequences of adopting these rules are shown to confirm theoretical predictions. We present an alternative approach that is consistent with both economic theory and the problems facing decision-makers. Finally, we identify implications for health economics research aimed at providing an evidence-base for health care decision-making.

2. The economic basis of decision-makers' problems

Economic evaluation of health care interventions combines outcome measurement with the measurement of opportunity cost. Hence economic evaluation is consistent with the fundamental principles of economics that (1) resources are scarce, (2) choices are made between alternative uses of resources and (3) a particular deployment of resources involves forgoing the benefits generated from alternative deployments of the same resources. Should these principles not apply, that is, where additional resources are available with no other possible use, the only choice is between providing an intervention or leaving resources unused. Hence the only relevant consideration would be whether the intervention does more good than harm. To the best of our knowledge, such situations do not exist in health care. Whatever resources are available are insufficient to support all effective interventions for all potential clients. The problem context may differ; the decision-maker could be faced with an increase in the number of possible interventions but the same budget, or a change in the resources available to support existing interventions, or a combination of changes in both the budget and the range of possible interventions. Each context involves decisions pertaining to changes in the range of interventions and/or the resources available. The decision-maker is concerned with whether a particular programme represents an efficient use of resources. Hence the problem involves constrained maximization of an objective function, irrespective of the particular context.

Cost-Effectiveness Analysis (CEA) is the most common methodology of economic evaluation in health care, aimed at informing decision-makers faced with this problem of

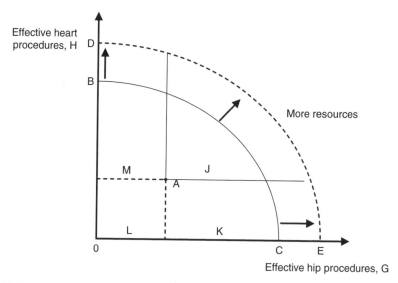

Figure 46.1   Improvements in technical efficiency versus increases in the resource use

scarce resources. For a particular level of health care resources, which need not be the current level, the goal is to choose from among all possible health care programmes the combination of programmes that maximizes total health benefits produced (for example, Weinstein and Stason, 1977; Gold et al., 1996; Williams, 2004). Suppose resources can be used to produce effective hip treatment, G, or effective heart treatment, H. The production possibilities frontier (PPF) BC in Figure 46.1 shows the maximum production of G for any level of production of H, given a resource constraint. With a combination of G and H inside the PPF (for example, point A), technical efficiency is increased by reallocating resources to shift the combination of interventions produced either north and/or east (for example, within area J).

More hips could be treated without treating fewer hearts by redirecting resources from elsewhere in the economy but this neither reflects the problem facing the decision-maker nor provides a solution to that problem. Instead it means more of either activity can now be produced (that is, an outward shift in the PPF to DE). But the most productive use of such additional resources remains to be determined by a careful evaluation of alternative resource deployments. The design of the economic evaluation must reflect the context of the decision-maker's problem (that is, what are . . . the objectives? . . . the choices under consideration? . . . the constraints?).

Weinstein and Zeckhauser (1973) (WZ) provide the theoretical basis for CEA based on a government agency, working with a fixed budget, choosing between many projects based on a comparison of the difference in effects between a programme under consideration and the current way of serving the same patient population (incremental effects), and the difference in costs between the two programmes (incremental costs). Figure 46.2 presents the possible combinations of incremental effects and incremental costs (Birch and Gafni, 1992). Where these have different signs, the solution is trivial (Birch and Gafni, 1994), for example, the new programme costs more (that is, reduces resources available for other

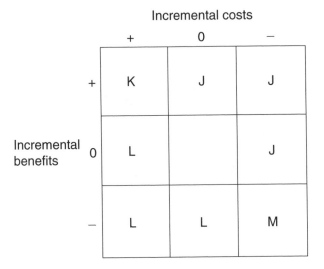

Figure 46.2   Incremental costs and benefits of a new programme

unrelated programmes) and produces fewer effects. An economist is not needed to conclude it is not worthwhile. It lies in the bottom left cell in Figure 46.2 and represents a movement into area L in Figure 46.1. Similarly with negative incremental costs and positive incremental effects, a 'win–win'[1]. (top right cell in Figure 46.2 and a movement into area J in Figure 46.1) no substantial reflection is required. In most cases, however, a new intervention involves incremental effects and incremental costs with the same sign, for example, the intervention is more effective but costs more than the existing intervention (top left cell in Figure 46.2 and a movement into area K in Figure 46.1). To provide the greater effects of the new hip treatments, the number of heart treatments must be reduced because the resources used by current hip treatments are insufficient to support the new hip treatment. Here the decision-maker looks to the economist for 'inputs' to the decision-making process. The economist offers guidelines to economic evaluation that incorporate decision rules for CEA to provide these inputs.

3.   The decision rules of cost-effectiveness analysis

The traditional analytical tool of CEA is the incremental cost-effectiveness ratio (ICER), which represents the incremental cost of the new programme divided by the incremental effects of the new programme. Based on assumptions of perfect divisibility and constant returns to scale in all programmes, the following decision rules have been presented (Weinstein and Zeckhauser, 1973 and Chapter 44 by Weinstein in this Companion), both of which produce maximum health gain from available resources:

The league table rule: Select programmes in ascending order of ICER (that is, project with lowest ICER first) until available resources are exhausted.

The threshold ICER rule: Select programmes with ICER less than or equal to λ, the shadow price of the budget.

Because ICERs are not available for all programmes, comprehensive league tables are not available and the league table rule is not feasible (Devlin, 2002; Gafni and Birch, 2003a). Hence, the threshold approach has provided the basis for economic evaluation guidelines in, for example, Australia (Commonwealth of Australia, 1995), Ontario, Canada (Ontario Ministry of Health, 1994), and UK (National Institute for Clinical Excellence, 2001). In each case the use of cost-effectiveness approaches is linked to the problem of maximizing the production of health improvements from available resources.

4.   Decision rules and the needs of decision-makers

Although the constrained maximization problem considered by WZ reflects the problem faced by the decision-maker, the WZ assumptions of perfect divisibilities and constant returns to scale in all programmes do not. Decision-makers are usually faced with choices between programmes of different sizes. The resource requirements to support new programmes, and hence the opportunity costs of those programmes, depend crucially on programme size. Hence the opportunity costs of programmes competing for available resources are not comparable. The ICER is the *average cost per QALY* or the inverse of the average rate of return on additional investments required by a programme. Comparisons of ICERs across programmes ignore problems introduced by the different sizes of programmes. Moreover, decision-makers cannot purchase individual units of QALYs. Each programme produces a 'package' of QALYs and the average price per QALY may differ by programme size.

Because the WZ assumptions do not hold for the problems faced by decision-makers (Birch and Gafni, 1992; 1993; Johannesson, 1995), the ICER threshold decision rule is not sufficient to maximize health effects from available resources. Hence, as Doubilet et al. (1986) noted 'there is no theoretical justification for asserting that the strategy with the lowest cost-effectiveness ratio . . . is the most desirable one'.

To adopt the threshold ICER approach in the absence of the WZ assumptions requires an unspecified supply of resources with constant marginal opportunity cost. Anything further from the reality of decision-making is hard to imagine. Even under the assumptions of the WZ model, the problem of how to determine λ remains. Under the model, λ is given by the opportunity cost of the marginal programme funded from available resources (Weinstein and Zeckhauser, 1973). This is determined either by solving the constrained optimization exercise, or by constructing the ICER league table. Without information on the incremental costs and effects of *all* possible programmes, neither approach can be used. Hence the λ value required for the maximization of health gains from available resources cannot be determined. So, regardless of whether the theoretical assumptions of the WZ model hold or not, λ cannot be determined endogenously (Gold et al., 1996; Devlin, 2002; Gafni and Birch, 2003a; Ubel et al., 2003).

The failure of the threshold ICER decision rule to determine whether a new programme represents an efficient use of resources is illustrated using the cost-effectiveness plane in Figure 46.3 based on Sendi et al. (2002). The slope of $0Y_1$ describes the inverse of the average rate of return on the additional resources required for new Y at Y_1. Perfect divisibility means that this programme can be bought in infinitely small increments. Constant returns to scale imply that the ICER is independent of the size of the programme, that is, the line $0Y_1$, including its continuation beyond Y_1, represents the expansion path for Y.

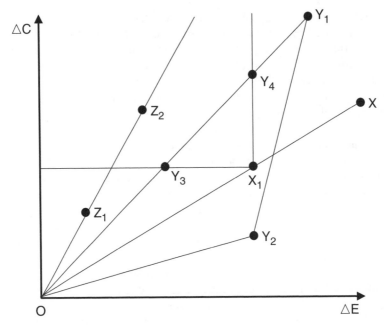

Figure 46.3   Indivisibilities and non-constant returns to scale

Without constant returns to scale, Y might be described by expansion path $0Y_2Y_1$. Here the ICER for Y depends on the size of Y being considered. In addition, a programme could be indivisible, because of either technical constraints (for example, high capital costs), or policy considerations (for example, a requirement of equitable access to services even though the ICER differs among identifiable groups in the population). Hence, only certain points on the expansion path represent real options for the decision-maker.

Consider new programme X at X_1. Because X_1 requires more resources than the current programme it is intended to replace (that is, incremental cost >0) the additional resource requirements of X_1 must be found from other programmes. Any point North West of X_1 satisfies the condition for increased efficiency, that is, sufficient resources released to support the additional resource requirements of X_1 and incremental effects to be forgone are not greater than the incremental effects of X_1. Suppose Y is considered for cancellation to release the additional resources required by X_1. Note Y_1 does not satisfy the efficiency condition. It lies North East of X_1, indicating that cancelling Y_1 involves incremental losses that exceed the incremental effects of X_1, even though enough resources are released to support X_1. A smaller version of Y lying between Y_3 and Y_4, is North West of X_1 and hence meets the conditions for increased efficiency. But this only applies if Y is perfectly divisible with constant returns to scale. Suppose these conditions do not hold and the expansion path for Y is $0Y_2Y_1$. There is no size of Y falling North West of X_1. Although the ICER for Y_1 is greater than the ICER for X_1, using resources currently allocated to Y_1 to support X_1 leads to a reduction in total health improvements.

Consider existing programme Z, expansion path $0Z_2$ and its continuation beyond Z_2. For each size of Z, the ICER is higher than for X_1. Reallocating resources currently used

Table 46.1 Choosing between programmes to maximize additional health gains

Programme	ICER $000s/QALY	Cost $M	Effects QALYs
A	49 120	14	285
B	52 080	10	192
C	59 700	8	134
D	117 650	4	34

for Z to support investment in X_1 appears to increase efficiency. But suppose Z is given by Z_1 to the South West of X_1. The effects forgone by cancelling Z_1 are less than the incremental effects of X_1, but there are insufficient resources released by Z_1 to support X_1. Again, information about the ICER is insufficient to address the efficiency of resource allocation because it does not include information on programme sizes. Important information about the sizes of programmes is lost when ICERs are calculated. Moreover, use of the ICER as a basis for decision-making can lead to the wrong decision being made. For example, based on the ICER values, the decision-maker would implement X_1 and cancel Z_1. However, only by cancelling Y_3 are the conditions for increased efficiency satisfied. In order to maximize health improvements from available resources the programme with the lower ICER should be cancelled – precisely the opposite result of the WZ model.

In the absence of endogenously determining λ, attention has focused on what value to use to make recommendations about the efficiency of allocating available resources to programmes (for example, Laupacis et al., 1992; Devlin, 2002; Ubel et al., 2003; Williams, 2004, and Donaldson et al.'s Chapter 37 in this Companion). Potential problems of choosing a threshold λ are illustrated in Table 46.1. Suppose the decision-maker has $18 million for new programmes and must decide which of programmes A, B, C and D to fund. If the ICER threshold has been set arbitrarily at $50 000 per QALY, the threshold rule funds A since this is the only programme that produces additional QALYs at an average cost per QALY below the ICER threshold (or decision-maker's willingness to pay). But consider the data on incremental costs and effects of each programme in columns 3 and 4. Programme A generates 285 additional QALYs but leaves $4 million unused. Investing these resources in programme D generates an additional 34 QALYs, even though D does not satisfy the ICER threshold. However, this does not maximize health gains from the additional budget. Instead, investing resources in B and C, both falling above the ICER threshold, generates 326 QALYs. So, although the ICER threshold indicates that A is the only programme to be implemented, this is precisely what should not be done if resources are used to maximize health gains. The ICER values do not provide sufficient information to enable the decision-maker to maximize health gains.

While the use of the same threshold across settings might appear to provide some notion of consistency, this fails to consider the determinants of the λ value required to satisfy the constrained maximization problem. Following WZ, the shadow price of the budget is a function of, *inter alia*, the size of the budget (Birch and Gafni, 1993). Hence, two communities with identical populations and faced with the same range of programmes but different budgets will have different λ values against which to judge programmes (Birch and Gafni, 2003). Similarly, a change in health care expenditures means that the possible mixes of programmes that can be funded changes, and hence λ, given by the ICER of the last programme funded, will change *ceteris paribus*. Where populations are not identical, or the range of programmes, together with the costs and effects of those programmes, are not identical across settings, the efficient allocation of resources also requires different threshold values (Birch and Gafni, 2003). Although a new programme might have the same incremental costs and benefits (and hence the same ICER value) in two different settings, its implemetation may be an efficient use of resources in one setting but not in the other. The ICER value does not inform the decision-maker about the efficiency of using resources to support the new programme (Birch et al., 1996).

The WZ model was developed for situations where the costs and effects of all programmes are deterministic. The solution for the decision-maker's constrained optimization problem under uncertainty have yet to be developed. However, the WZ model has been extended to accommodate situations where programme costs and effects are stochastic (for example, O'Brien and Sculpher, 2000). But uncertainty is not restricted to the programme under evaluation; the opportunity cost of the last programme funded and hence the λ value to support an efficient allocation of resources from available resources is also stochastic (Sendi et al., 2002). Moreover, as new programmes are funded and others replaced, the portfolio of programmes is dynamic. Hence the identification of the last programme funded and hence the λ distribution changes (Sendi et al., 2002).

5.   Consequences of adopting *ICER* decision rules

We have shown that using ICERs in economic evaluations is not useful to decision-makers concerned with the efficient use of health care resources. In this section we support these claims using examples from jurisdictions that have adopted the CEA approach in their guidelines for economic evaluation. Australia uses CEA for determining changes to the pharmaceutical benefits programme as a means of controlling cost escalation and promoting efficient use of programme resources. Costs of the programme were observed to increase by over 14 per cent per annum over the first ten years of using the approach (Zinn, 2002). However, no evidence has been provided that this has led to a net increase in health gains.

Guidelines based on the ICER threshold approach were developed for decision-making about new technologies in Canada (Ontario Ministry of Health, 1994). Faced with escalating costs and a desire to use available resources to achieve maximum health gain, the approach was implemented by the committee that recommends which drugs to include on the provincial formulary covered by public funding for senior citizens and those on social assistance. At that time it was argued that use of these guidelines was a prescription for uncontrolled growth of programme expenditures (Gafni and Birch, 1993). According to the chair of the Committee responsible for recommending changes to the formulary, programme expenditures increased by 10 per cent per annum over the period 1997–2000 and by 15 per cent in 2001 (Laupacis, 2002). As with the Australian programme, no evidence has been provided to indicate that net health gains among beneficiaries of the programme have increased. In response, questions have been raised about the affordability and sustainability of such programmes (Laupacis, 2002).

Cost escalations have been observed in the NHS following the introduction of new interventions evaluated using the NICE cost-effectiveness guidelines. The first ten drugs recommended for adoption by NICE required additional funding for the NHS of £250 million (Taylor, 2002). NICE was unable to provide an estimate of the actual increased expenditures generated by these recommendations because of 'methodological difficulties'. However, other evidence reported that NHS expenditure on these drugs was around £150 million (House of Commons' Select Committee, 2002). The discrepancy is apparently explained by the failure of some authorities to implement the NICE recommendations (Taylor, 2002). More recent estimates suggest the additional resources absorbed by NICE recommendations (and hence the additional revenues of companies producing those technologies) exceeded £575m in the first 2.5 years of NICE (Mayor, 2002).

6. An alternative approach: economic evaluation in context

For an intervention to represent an efficient use of resources the additional effects it generates must exceed the effects forgone from the most productive alternative use of the same resources. Hence efficiency cannot be established only by reference to the resources required and QALYs produced by a particular intervention. Information on alternative uses of those resources is needed. As shown elsewhere (Birch and Gafni, 2003), efficiency is context-specific. Even where incremental costs and effects of an intervention are identical in different contexts, it does not mean the efficiency of that intervention is the same in all contexts.

If economics is to inform decision-makers about the efficiency of investments, we must look beyond traditional approaches to CEA and the use of ICERs. Elsewhere we argue that existing approaches to constrained maximization such as integer programming (IP), solve the decision-maker's problem (Birch and Donaldson, 1987; Birch and Gafni, 1992). The identification of the efficient mix of programmes presented in Table 46.1 involved integer programming at its simplest level. Other authors have suggested flexible programming versions of the general IP approach where applicable (Stinnett and Paltiel, 1996). The key requirement of the IP approach is that the specification of the problem (that is, objective function and constraints) must accurately reflect the decision-maker's problem setting.

The substantial data requirements of the IP approach, specifically the incremental costs and effects of all programmes together with the resources available for investment, may be difficult to satisfy. However, these requirements reflect the complex nature of the decision-maker's problem. Moreover the league table approach derived from the WZ model also has substantial data requirements, but the IP approach does not also require the additional assumptions needed to support the WZ model.

An alternative practical approach is available (Birch and Gafni, 1992; Gafni and Birch, 1993) which satisfies a modified objective of an unambiguous increase in health improvements from available resources. This requires that the health improvements of the proposed programme be compared with the health improvements produced by that combination of programmes that have to be given up to generate sufficient funds for the proposed programme. Only where the health improvements of the proposed programme exceed the health improvements of the combination of programmes to be given up does the new technology represent an improvement in the efficiency of resource utilization. The approach has been extended to deal with the uncertain nature of costs and outcomes providing a simple graphical presentation denoted as the decision-making plane (Sendi et al., 2002). The approach does not rely on an arbitrarily determined threshold value to ascertain the efficiency of the programme, nor is it dependent on unrealistic assumptions about perfect divisibility and constant returns to scale. Instead, the source of additional resource requirements is identified and the implications of cancelling programmes to generate these resources form part of the analysis.

7. Discussion

> To improve efficiency, decision makers need information on . . . opportunity costs . . . In absence of any information about opportunity cost, however, they cannot attempt to achieve the efficient use of resources (Cookson et al., 2001)

We have shown that the inverse of the average rate of return on investment of resources provided by the ICER is insufficient to determine whether investing in a particular programme represents efficient use of resources. Drummond (1980) noted that 'the only universal approach to ranking under a constraint is through the use of mathematical programming techniques'. These techniques require additional information on the resources available for investment and the sizes of programmes and outcomes produced. Where this information is available, ICERs still serve no purpose since they provide no additional information relevant to the problem.

Concern with maximizing health improvements from available resources may be just one of several objectives that decision-makers face. For example, decision-makers may be constrained by political considerations associated with providing equal access to services and providing greater priority to health improvements of specific population groups (National Institute for Clinical Excellence, 2001). Equity considerations have been used to 'support' the adoption of multiple, ad hoc, ICER thresholds without any justification of how the use of these thresholds helps achieve any of the objectives (Rawlins and Culyer, 2004). However, as Williams and Cookson (2000) note

> [I]f . . . equity principles are to be clarified in a policy-relevant way, it is necessary to quantify what might otherwise merely remain vaguely appealing but ambiguous slogans. Only with some quantification will it be possible to convert them into criteria that can be applied in a consistent manner, and with a reasonable chance of checking on performance (that is, holding people accountable)

The presence of multiple objectives and constraints does not reduce the importance of adopting a constrained maximization model as the basis for analysis. The explicit identification of each objective and constraint enables the full range of policy concerns to be incorporated systematically into the analysis. Hence, the complex objectives faced by decision-makers, far from limiting the role of economic analysis, represent precisely the challenges that the economic model of constrained maximization is intended to accommodate.

Notes

1. Incremental effects or incremental costs equal to zero represent boundary conditions for these trivial problems, that is, more (same) effects with same (fewer) costs. The central cell in Figure 46.2 is the status quo represented by A in Figure 46.1.

References

Birch, S. and C. Donaldson (1987), 'Applications of cost–benefit analysis to health care: Departures from welfare economic theory', *Journal of Health Economics*, **6**, 61–72.

Birch, S. and A. Gafni (1992), 'Cost effectiveness/utility analyses: do current decision rules lead us to where we want to be?', *Journal of Health Economics*, **11**, 279–96.

Birch, S. and A. Gafini (1993), 'Changing the problem to fit the solution: Johannesson and Weinstein's (mis)-application of economics to real world problems', *Journal of Health Economics*, **12**, 469–76.

Birch, S. and A. Gafni (1994), 'Cost-effectiveness ratios: In a league of their own', *Health Policy*, **28**, 133–44.

Birch, S. and A. Gafni (2003), 'Economics and the evaluation of health care programmes: Generalizability of methods and implications for generalizability of results', *Health Policy*, **64**, 207–19.

Birch, S., J. Leake and D. Lewis (1996), 'Economic issues in the development and use of practice guidelines: an application to resource allocation in dentistry', *Community Dental Health*, **13**, 70–5.

Commonwealth of Australia (1995), *Guidelines for the Pharmaceutical Industry on Preparation of Submissions to the Pharmaceutical Benefits Advisory Committee: Including Major Submissions involving Economic Analyses*, Canberra, Australia: Australian Government Publishing Service.

Cookson, R., D. McDaid and A. Maynard (2001), 'Wrong SIGN, NICE mess: is national guidance distorting allocation of resources?', *British Medical Journal*, **323**, 743–5.

Devlin, N. (2002), 'An introduction to the use of cost-effectiveness thresholds in decision-making: what are the issues?' in A. Towse, C. Pritchard and N. Devlin (eds), *Cost Effectiveness Thresholds: Economics and Ethical Issues*, London, UK: Kings Fund and Office of Health Economics, pp. 16–22.

Doubilet, P., M. Weinstein and B. McNeil (1986), 'Use and misuse of the term "cost effective" in medicine', *New England Journal of Medicine*, **314**, 253–6.

Drummond, M. (1980), '*Principles of Economic Appraisal in Health Care*', Oxford: Oxford University Press.

Gafni, A. and S. Birch (2003a), 'NICE methodological guidelines and decision making in the National Health Service in England and Wales', *Pharmacoeconomics*, **21**, 149–57.

Gafni, A. and S. Birch (2003b), 'Inclusions of drugs in provincial drug benefit programs: Should "reasonable decisions" lead to uncontrolled growth in expenditures?', *Canadian Medical Association Journal*, **168**, 849–51.

Gold, M., J. Siegel, L. Russel and M. Weinstein (1996), *Cost-effectiveness in Health and Medicine*, New York: Oxford University Press.

House of Commons' Select Committee (2002), *Health: National Institute for Clinical Excellence*, London, UK: Her Majesty's Stationery Office.

Johannesson, M. (1995), 'The relationship between cost-effectiveness analysis and cost–benefit analysis', *Social Science and Medicine*, **41**, 483–9.

Laupacis, A. (2002), 'Inclusion of drugs in provincial drug benefit programs: who is making these decisions, and are they the right ones?', *Canadian Medical Association Journal*, **166**, 44–7.

Laupacis, A., D. Feeny, A. Detsky and P. Tugwell (1992), 'How attractive does a new technology have to be to warrant adoption and utilization?: Tentative guidelines for using clinical and economic evaluations', *Canadian Medical Association Journal*, **146**, 473–81.

Mayor, S. (2002), 'News extra: NICE estimates that its recommendations have cost the NHS £575m', *British Medical Journal*, **325**, 924.

National Institute for Clinical Excellence (2001), 'Technical guidance for manufacturers and sponsors on making a submission to a technology appraisal', National Institute for Clinical Excellence: London.

O'Brien, B. and M. Sculpher (2000), 'Building uncertainty into cost-effectiveness rankings. Portfolio risk-return tradeoffs and implications for decision rules', *Medical Care*, **38**, 460–68.

Ontario Ministry of Health (1994), *Ontario Guidelines for Economic Analysis of Pharmaceutical Products*, Toronto: Ministry of Health of Ontario.

Rawlins M. and A. Culyer (2004), 'National Institute for Clinical Excellence and its value judgements', *British Medical Journal*, **329**, 224–7.

Sendi, P. and A. Briggs (2001), 'Affordability and cost effectiveness: decision making on the cost effectiveness plane', *Health Economics*, **10**, 675–80.

Sendi, P., A. Gafni and S. Birch (2002), 'Opportunity costs and uncertainty in the economic evaluation of health care interventions', *Health Economics*, **11**, 23–31.

Stinnett, A. and D. Paltiel (1996), 'Mathematical programming for the efficient allocation of health care resources', *Journal of Health Economics*, **15**, 641–53.

Taylor, R. (2002), 'Generating national guidelines – a NICE model?', paper presented at the 5th International Conference on Strategic Issues in Health Care Management Policy, Finance and Performance in Health Care, St. Andrews, UK, 11–13 April.

Ubel, P., R. Hirth, M. Chernew and A. Fendrick (2003), 'What is the price of life and why doesn't it increase at the rate of inflation?', *Archive of Internal Medicine*, **163**, 1637–41.

Weinstein, M. and W. Stason (1977), 'Foundation of cost effectiveness analysis for health and medical practices', *New England Journal of Medicine*, **296**, 716–21.

Weinstein, M. and R. Zeckhauser (1973), 'Critical ratios and efficient allocation', *Journal of Public Economics*, **2**, 147–57.

Williams, A. (1983), 'The economic role of health indicators', in G. Teeling Smith (ed.), *Measuring the Social Benefit of Medicine*, London: Office of Health Economics, pp. 63–7.

Williams, A. (2004), *What could be Nicer than NICE?*, London: Office of Health Economics.

Williams, A. and R. Cookson (2000), 'Equity in health', in A. Culyer and J. Newhouse (eds), *Handbook on Health Economics*, Vol. 1B, Amsterdam: North Holland, pp. 1862–910.

Zinn, C. (2002), 'Plan to cut drug spending attacked by doctors', *British Medical Journal*, **324**, 937.

47 Statistical methods for cost-effectiveness analysis alongside clinical trials

Andrew Briggs

1. Introduction

It has become increasingly common for clinical trials to incorporate an economic appraisal in order to inform an assessment of not only a new intervention's clinical effect, but also its value for money. This has led to many more health economic appraisals where patient-level data are available, and this in turn has led to developments in the statistical methods used to estimate cost-effectiveness.

This chapter outlines a general framework for evaluating cost-effectiveness where patient-level data are available on cost and effect from a randomized controlled trial (RCT). What has now become the 'standard' approach to estimating cost-effectiveness from trial information will be used as the starting point, with a focus on the use of net-benefits and acceptability curves to overcome some of the problems of presenting uncertainty that arise with interval estimates for the cost-effectiveness ratio. The standard approach will then be extended to consider issues associated with covariate adjustment and subgroup analysis in economic evaluation studies, within a net-benefit regression framework. A more general framework of statistical modelling will then be proposed, based on modelling the separate components of cost and effect. A recent example of the application of such an approach in the area of cholesterol lowering therapy will be presented. Finally, consideration will be given to the issues of chance subgroup effects, the importance of model uncertainty for the results of analyses, and the role of evidence synthesis of external information to model the policy decision directly.

2. Standard approach to stochastic CEA

In the most common case, an economic analysis involves an evaluation of an intervention treatment (T) compared to a standard care treatment (S). Denoting the true (but unobserved) values of cost and effect for treatment as C_T and E_T, compared to C_S and E_S for standard, the incremental cost-effectiveness ratio, which provides a summary measure of value for money of the new intervention relative to the current standard, is defined as:

$$ICER = \frac{C_T - C_S}{E_T - E_S} = \frac{\Delta C}{\Delta E}$$

with the implication that the intervention offers good value for money if the ICER falls below some maximum willingness to pay for health gain (call this λ). That is, a decision should be made to implement the more costly but more effective treatment intervention if:

$$\frac{\Delta C}{\Delta E} < \lambda. \tag{47.1}$$

The ICER statistic
Of course, it is never possible to know the true incremental costs and true incremental effects of an intervention, since it is impossible to simultaneously observe the costs and effects of two different treatments in the same population of patients (Mullahy and Manning, 1995). Instead, the average experience of patients randomized between the treatments to be compared is employed. Using sample data for economic information collected in a clinical trial setting it is possible to define an estimator for the ICER by

$$\widehat{ICER} = \frac{\overline{C}_T - \overline{C}_S}{\overline{E}_T - \overline{E}_S} = \frac{\Delta \overline{C}}{\Delta \overline{E}},$$ (47.2)

using the sample mean costs and effects in each of the treatment arms.

It is this statistic that is estimated in the majority of economic appraisals conducted as part of clinical trials (Gray et al., 2000; Raikou et al., 1998; Sculpher et al., 2000). However, the use of the ICER as the statistic of interest in cost-effectiveness studies can pose substantial statistical challenges. For example, the variance of a ratio statistic is not defined, and confidence interval estimation can be problematic, particularly when the denominator of the ratio has non-negligible probability of having a zero value leading to a discontinuity in the sampling distribution (Heitjan et al., 1999). Many research papers have addressed the issue of accurate confidence interval estimation of the ICER statistic of equation (47.2) (Briggs et al., 1997; Chaudhary and Stearns 1996; Heitjan, 2000; O'Brien et al., 1994; van Hout et al. 1994), with consensus falling on the parametric method of Fieller's theorem and the non-parametric bootstrap as the most appropriate approaches (Briggs et al., 1999; Polsky et al., 1997).

Where there is considerable uncertainty relating to the ICER, an interval estimate may include all of the real line. In such situations, Fieller's theorem will fail to provide a solution, and care must be taken when interpreting any non-parametric bootstrap confidence interval estimate of the interval. The issue is that, where uncertainty covers several quadrants of the cost-effectiveness plane, the use of the ICER results in loss of information. For example, two ICERs can have the same absolute value, but if one were generated from a negative effect difference and the other from a positive effect difference, the decision-making implications of the two ICERs are exactly opposite. Without knowledge of the sign of the denominator of the ratio, this information is lost. An alternative approach to presenting uncertainty for such cases is the cost-effectiveness acceptability curve (van Hout et al., 1994), which shows the proportion of the joint density of incremental cost and effect that favours the intervention, as a function of the decision threshold, λ, from equation (47.1). This approach correctly distinguishes the parts of the joint density falling into different quadrants of the cost-effectiveness plane.

The net-benefit statistic
More recently, the use of net-benefit statistics has emerged in preference to the ICER, chiefly due to the statistical properties of the net-benefit estimator, and the fact that the use of the net-benefit statistic does not result in the same loss of information as the ICER when uncertainty is high. Two alternative formulations of net-benefit have been suggested (Stinnett and Mullahy, 1998; Tambour et al., 1998) based on a simple rearrangement of

the decision rule in equation (47.2), such that the new treatment should be implemented over the existing standard if net monetary benefit (NMB) is positive

$$\text{NMB} = \lambda \cdot \Delta E - \Delta C > 0 \qquad (47.3)$$

or, entirely equivalently, for positive net health benefit (NHB)

$$\text{NHB} = \Delta E - \Delta C / \lambda > 0.$$

The same sample analogues are employed to estimate the mean effect and cost differences in order to give the estimated net-benefit statistics

$$\widehat{NMB} = \lambda \cdot \Delta \bar{E} - \Delta \bar{C}$$
$$\widehat{NHB} = \Delta \bar{E} - \Delta \bar{C} / \lambda$$

However, in contrast to the ICER, where the variance is not defined, the variance of net-benefits estimated from sample mean cost and effects in the trial arms is simply a linear combination of two asymptotically normal variables and can therefore be defined as:

$$\text{var}(\widehat{NMB}) = \lambda^2 \text{var}(\Delta \bar{E}) + \text{var}(\Delta \bar{C}) - 2\lambda \text{cov}(\Delta \bar{E}, \Delta \bar{C})$$

in terms of the monetary net-benefit measure, or:

$$\text{var}(\widehat{NMB}) = \text{var}(\Delta \bar{E}) + \frac{1}{\lambda^2} \text{var}(\Delta \bar{C}) - \frac{2}{\lambda} \text{cov}(\Delta \bar{E}, \Delta \bar{C})$$

for the net health benefit measure. Therefore, the advantage of the net-benefits approach is that the $(1 - \alpha)\%$ confidence interval for net-benefits can be easily determined in the standard fashion, as $\widehat{NB} \pm z_{\alpha/2} \sqrt{\sigma_{NB}^2}$ where $\widehat{NB}$ is the estimated net-benefit measure, with variance σ_{NB}^2, and $z_{\alpha/2}$ is the critical value from the standard normal distribution.

Of course, the net-benefit statistics make use of the threshold decision rule, λ, from equation (47.1), which is itself unknown. Although some commentators prefer to plot the net-benefit statistic itself as a function of λ (Stinnett and Mullahy, 1998; Willan and Lin, 2001), the net-benefit statistic can be employed to provide a simple way to estimate the acceptability curve, and it is this curve which answers the fundamental question of how likely it is that treatment is cost-effective.

Average cost-effectiveness ratios and average net-benefits
Introductory textbooks emphasize the importance of taking an incremental approach (Drummond et al., 1997; Weinstein and Fineberg, 1980) rather than comparing average cost-effectiveness ratios, since the difference between two average ratios does not equal the incremental cost-effectiveness ratio

$$\frac{\bar{C}_T}{\bar{E}_T} - \frac{\bar{C}_S}{\bar{E}_S} \neq \frac{\bar{C}_T - \bar{C}_S}{\bar{E}_T - \bar{E}_S}.$$

By contrast, the difference in the mean net-benefit between arms will give the overall incremental net-benefit statistic of equation (47.3). This is straightforward to see algebraically through simple manipulation of the net-benefit expressions

$$
\begin{aligned}
N\overline{M}B_1 - N\overline{M}B_0 &= (\lambda\cdot\overline{E}_T - \Delta\overline{C}_T) - (\lambda\cdot\Delta\overline{E}_S - \Delta\overline{C}_S) \\
&= \lambda(\overline{E}_T - \overline{E}_S) - (\overline{C}_T - \overline{C}_S) \\
&= \lambda\cdot\Delta\overline{E} - \Delta\overline{C} \\
&= \Delta N\overline{M}B.
\end{aligned}
$$

Therefore the usefulness of average net-benefit is not directly in terms of the average figures themselves, but in the simple linear relationship between average and incremental net-benefit.

3.   Net-benefit regression framework

The net-benefit framework can be employed to directly estimate cost-effectiveness within a regression framework (Hoch et al., 2002) by formulating a net-benefit value for each individual patient i as

$$
NMB_i = \lambda\cdot E_i - C_i
$$

where E_i and C_i are the observed effects and costs for each patient. At the simplest level, the following linear model

$$
NMB_i = \alpha + \Delta t_i + \varepsilon_i \tag{Model 1}
$$

can be employed where α is an intercept term, t a treatment dummy taking the values zero for the standard treatment and one for the new treatment, and a random error term ε. The coefficient Δ on the treatment dummy gives the estimated incremental net-benefit of treatment and will coincide with the usual estimate of incremental net-benefit obtained by aggregating across the treatment arms in a standard cost-effectiveness analysis. Similarly, the standard error of the coefficient is the same as that calculated from the standard approach.

Covariate adjusted CEA

The power of the net-benefit regression framework is that it is straightforward to add additional explanatory variables in order to examine their impact on cost-effectiveness directly. For example, where baseline characteristics of patients have been measured prior to randomization, these can be employed to make allowance for prognostic information in the treatment comparison using a multiple regression framework as given below

$$
NMB_i = \alpha + \sum_{j=1}^{p}\beta_j x_{ij} + \Delta t_i + \varepsilon_i \tag{Model 2}
$$

where there are p prognostic covariates x. That is, in this model the coefficient Δ on the treatment dummy gives the incremental net-benefit, and therefore the cost-effectiveness, of implementing the new treatment controlling for the known covariates.

In the context of an experimental design like a randomized controlled trial, the randomization process is expected to ensure a balance of both observed and unobserved potentially confounding factors across the treatment arms. In this case, the use of prognostic covariates will not materially affect the magnitude of the estimated cost-effectiveness, but may improve the precision of the estimate and lead to a corresponding narrowing of the estimated confidence intervals (Altman, 1985; Pocock, 1984).

Where an experimental study has, by chance, resulted in an imbalance of prognostic factors between arms, then allowing for that imbalance through a multiple regression model such as that presented in Model 2 will affect both the magnitude and precision of the estimate. Of course, in a well-designed study, patients should be stratified with respect to important prognostic factors. Covariate adjustment is likely to be particularly important in non-randomized clinical trials or observational studies, and the appropriate methods are discussed in the chapter by Polsky and Basu in this Companion (Chapter 43). The importance of the net-benefit regression approach comes from the ability to employ standard regression techniques directly to an estimate of cost-effectiveness. Nevertheless, in going beyond the simple randomization of Model 1 it will be important to use standard approaches to assess model fit to see if the linear approximation holds.

Cost-effectiveness subgroups

Although regression methods can be used to correct for unbalanced allocation in observed covariates which has arisen by chance in clinical evaluation, the main advantage of adopting a regression-based approach to cost-effectiveness analysis relates to the ability to explore potential subgroup effects. Since economics is concerned fundamentally with the margin, the impact of covariates such as age, sex and disease severity on the cost-effectiveness of treatment interventions is of fundamental interest. All too often in RCT-based cost-effectiveness analyses, the results are simply aggregated across the two arms to provide the overall ICER without any consideration of how the ICER varies at the margin.

In order to answer the question of whether cost-effectiveness varies by patient characteristics it is natural to consider extending the additive model presented in Model 2 above to test interactions between treatment and baseline covariates (the potential role of multiplicative models in the absence of interaction for the estimation of subgroups is explored in section 4 below). Consider the model

$$NMB_i = \alpha + \sum_{j=1}^{p} \beta_j x_{ij} + \Delta t_i + t_i \sum_{j=1}^{p} \gamma_j x_{ij} + \varepsilon_i \qquad \text{(Model 3)}$$

where the final term is the interaction between the treatment dummy and the prognostic covariates. The significance of the coefficients γ_j on the interaction between the covariates of the model and the treatment dummy represent the appropriate test for subgroup effects (Altman and Matthews, 1996) – although this does not protect against spurious subgroup effects being detected by chance. Where treatment effect modification is detected, the fact that cost-effectiveness varies for different types of patient may have important consequences for decision-making.

4.   Extensions and applications

The key advantage of the net-benefit regression framework is the ability to use standard regression techniques for model selection and diagnostics to choose an appropriate model for cost-effectiveness, instead of the usual approach of aggregating cost and effect differences across arms of the trial. For example, Manca and colleagues have used a net-benefit regression framework to adjust for the multi-level nature of cost and effect data in a multi-centre study (Manca et al., 2005).

Nevertheless there are some problems associated with the net-benefit regression approach. Firstly, by combining cost and effect into a single net-benefit, the ability to allow for different covariates to influence cost and effect is lost. Second, the assumption is that the scale of measurement for modelling cost and effect is the same. In a follow-up paper to that where they outlined the net-benefit regression approach, Willan and colleagues argued that modelling cost and effect in a bivariate regression, using 'seemingly unrelated regression' (or SURE) could have potential benefits (Willan et al., 2004). By using generalized least squares, more efficient estimation is possible if different covariates are explanatory in the cost and effect equations (Greene, 1993), although if the same covariates appear, the SURE approach will be equivalent to standard fitting by ordinary least squares which will be equivalent to the net-benefit regression approach described above. Data generated from randomized clinical trials are often subject to administrative censoring and in a further paper, Willan and colleagues go on to describe an adaptation of the SURE procedure to handle data that are censored (Willan et al., 2005).

The other potential advantage of the bivariate SURE regression approach is that by separating costs and effects, the appropriate form of the model could in principle be different for both the cost and effect equations. For example, as Manning discusses in Chapter 41 in this Companion, the skewed nature of cost data often results in the use of a log transformation of the data. Such a multiplicative model for cost could be combined with an additive model for effects using the SURE framework, although the same issues surrounding the back transformation of results to the original cost scale outlined by Manning would apply.

A framework for the statistical modelling of cost-effectiveness

The increased flexibility of the SURE approach can be further extended by modelling components of cost and effect separately. In a seminal article, Weinstein and Stason introduced cost-effectiveness analysis to a medical audience (Weinstein and Stason, 1977). In doing so, they emphasized an incremental approach to estimating additional costs and health gains (in terms of QALYs) and went on to describe net health care costs of consisting of several components

$$\Delta C = \Delta C_{Rx} + \Delta C_{SE} - \Delta C_{Morb} + \Delta C_{\Delta LE}$$

including differences in the health care costs of treatment (ΔC_{Rx}), differences in the health care costs related to adverse side-effects associated with treatment (ΔC_{SE}), differences in the costs associated with treating the adverse consequences of the disease (ΔC_{Morb}), and a final component representing the increased costs associated with differential life expectancy ($\Delta C_{\Delta LE}$).

Similarly, they described the net health effectiveness in terms of QALYs as also being comprised of a number of components

$$\Delta E = \Delta E_{LE} + \Delta E_{Morb} - \Delta E_{SE}$$

relating to differences in life-expectancy due to treatment (ΔE_{LE}), differences in quality of life due to treatment (ΔE_{Morb}), and quality of life effects related to side-effects (ΔE_{SE}).

The importance of separating out the components of the incremental cost and incremental effect estimates of cost-effectiveness comes from the ability to model the components differently. For example, the vast majority of health outcomes from clinical trials are relative measures, such as relative risk reductions, odds and hazard ratios. By contrast, treatment side-effects are likely to be additive in that all patients may be at risk. A recent paper by Sutton and colleagues (Sutton et al., 2005), building on an earlier paper by Glasziou and colleagues (Glasziou and Irwig, 1995), demonstrates the statistical estimation of health outcome in the presence of a relative treatment effect and an additive side-effect profile.

The same argument can be applied to the estimation of incremental cost. Differences in the health care costs of treatment are likely to be additive, as are the costs of managing any side-effects of treatment. By contrast, the reduction in costs from morbidity and the additional costs associated with increased life expectancy may best be modelled as a relative reduction, especially when these correspond to a reduction in serious adverse disease events, the risk of which may be reduced proportionally by treatment.

This distinction between additive and relative components is of crucial importance when considering subgroup analysis. In the additive model of net-benefit outlined in Model 3 above, cost-effectiveness subgroups where identified by testing treatment interactions with covariates. By contrast, in a multiplicative model with covariates, the absence of treatment interactions on the relative scale implies important subgroup effects as a constant relative treatment effect is applied to different baselines.

An example of statistical modelling of cost-effectiveness of statin treatment
The Heart Protection Study was a large simple trial which examined the effectiveness of cholesterol reduction by randomizing over 20 000 patients to 40 mg simvastatin daily versus matching placebo. The original clinical trial report showed that allocation to simvastatin was associated with a 25 per cent reduction in major vascular events (MVEs) and that this relative treatment effect was constant across a number of univariate subgroup analyses (Collins et al., 2002). Although the trial monitored potential side-effects, no differences between the allocation groups was found suggesting that 40 mg simvastatin was well tolerated.

In a subsequent economic analysis (Mihaylova et al., 2005), five risk subgroups were defined from the quintiles of predicted multivariate five-year risk of an MVE, and absolute reductions in MVEs were estimated for each group by applying the relative risk reduction from the whole trial to the placebo event rates in each of the risk groups. To estimate costs, the assumption was that treatment costs of simvastatin were additive, but that the reduction in vascular event costs was multiplicative (to correspond with the main clinical outcome). Cost-effectiveness was estimated by combining the incremental cost and incremental effect estimates for each of the multivariate risk subgroups to form an

Table 47.1   Cost-effectiveness of 40 mg simvastatin daily

Risk group (5-year MVE risk)	Incremental cost* (£) (SE)	MVE avoided per 1000 persons (SE)	Cost (£) per MVE avoided (95% CI)
1 (12%)	1164 (45)	37 (5)	31 100 (22 900–42 500)
2 (18%)	1062 (61)	58 (7)	18 300 (13 500–25 800)
3 (23%)	987 (71)	80 (9)	12 300 (8900–17 600)
4 (28%)	893 (83)	93 (11)	9600 (6700–13 900)
5 (42%)	630 (126)	141 (16)	4500 (2300–7400)
Overall	947 (72)	82 (9)	11 600 (8500–16 300)

Source: Adapted from webtable1 of Mihaylova et al. (2005)

ICER. The reported results of the analysis are reproduced in Table 47.1. Note that non-parametric bootstrapping was employed to calculate the confidence intervals (using the simple percentile method) such that the correlation between the estimates of the different components of the ICER was maintained. These results show an almost eight-fold difference in estimated cost-effectiveness between the lower and upper risk quintiles – a result that would be lost had the focus been on the overall trial estimate of the ICER.

5.   Discussion

In this chapter, the standard approach to the statistical estimation of cost-effectiveness based on data collected alongside clinical trials has been outlined. The predominant approach in the literature is to estimate a single ICER for the trial as a whole, and much of the research activity over the past decade has focused on the appropriate way to characterize statistical uncertainty in the estimated cost-effectiveness. By contrast, little effort has been aimed at understanding how cost-effectiveness varies by patient characteristics. Through the development of the net-benefit framework the ability to estimate cost-effectiveness directly within a regression framework was outlined. Nevertheless, net-benefit regression may still be quite restrictive since covariates cannot vary between cost and effect, and the same functional form must be employed. Furthermore, at a practical level, a number of regressions must be run when varying λ in the net-benefit expression. Therefore, separate modelling of costs and effects is likely to be more convenient and potentially more efficient compared to direct regression modelling of net-benefit. An even more flexible framework, based on modelling the individual components of cost and effect was proposed and illustrated using the example of an economic appraisal conducted alongside a large trial of cholesterol-lowering therapy. This example illustrates the potential importance of modelling the inherent heterogeneity in cost-effectiveness results. The overall trial cost-effectiveness was estimated quite precisely as £11 600 (8500–16 300) per MVE avoided. However, as the estimated cost-effectiveness by risk subgroup showed, this overall figure masks considerable variation in cost-effectiveness from an estimated £4500 (2300–7400) per MVE avoided in the highest risk group to £31 100 (22 900–42 500) per MVE avoided in the highest risk group.

Of course the dangers of spurious subgroup effects arising by chance are well known, and it is commonly advised that subgroup analysis should be avoided unless the analyses are pre-specified and appropriately powered (Oxman and Guyatt, 1992). The concern is one of making inappropriate inference about differences that do not exist, but which have simply arisen by chance when splitting the data. The dangers of trawling the data for *ad hoc* subgroup effects is exemplified in the classic example from Collins and colleagues who showed that, in an RCT of thrombolytic therapy, Scorpios had a four-fold increase in benefit from treatment compared to patients born under all other star-signs combined (Collins et al., 1987).

However, it is important to recognize the importance of the scale of measurement when discussing subgroup effects. The testing of interaction terms in the additive net-benefit regression of Model 3 is based on splitting the data and provides no protection against spurious subgroup effects if potential interactions were not pre-specified. By contrast, the multiplicative assumption in the absence of treatment interactions is not based on splitting the data, and therefore subgroup effects are based on the full dataset, arising from the assumed relative nature of the treatment effect. This was illustrated in the example of cholesterol-lowering therapy, where cost-effectiveness estimates for subgroups were based on relative effects estimated from the whole trial applied to baseline event rate and costs estimates.

From the point of view of estimation, cost-effectiveness subgroup estimates based on the application of trial-wide relative effects to baseline event rates and costs, can be considered to be more robust than estimates based on splitting the data. This is particularly so in a large trial like the Heart Protection Study, where the constancy of the relative treatment effect was rigorously tested. Nevertheless, it is the case that the robustness of this approach stems from the additional assumptions placed on the analysis. The general framework of modelling the components of cost and effect outlined in this chapter and exemplified in the cholesterol-lowering example places a large degree of structure in the analysis compared to the standard approach. As a result, the estimates made are conditional on the model assumptions holding. This introduces model uncertainty into the analysis in that a different set of modelling assumptions may have produced a different result. Draper argues that without considering model uncertainty, results that are conditional on a specific model structure may be too precise (Draper, 1995). While it is undoubtedly important to bear in mind the potential impact of model uncertainty, the importance of providing estimates of how cost-effectiveness may vary by patient characteristics is likely to lead to the increasing use of statistical modelling of clinical trial data, compared to the standard approach of estimating a single cost-effectiveness ratio for an economic appraisal alongside a clinical trial.

Finally, it is worth noting that while this chapter has outlined statistical approaches to cost-effectiveness analysis alongside clinical trials, it is increasingly recognized that a single clinical trial cannot in and of itself answer policy questions relating to cost-effectiveness, (Claxton et al., 2002). While clinical trials are likely to remain an important source of information for cost-effectiveness, a full analysis is likely to include external data, perhaps involving synthesis of evidence across a number of trials, and is likely to involve extrapolating over time. While techniques such as decision analysis have often been used for this purpose, the traditional distinction between 'trial-based' evaluation on the one hand and 'decision models' on the other is increasingly blurred as trial-based analyses include more explicit modelling of the data (as described above) and as decision models incorporate more explicitly statistical approaches to evidence synthesis and representation of statistical uncertainty (Cooper et al., 2004).

References

Altman, D.G. (1985), 'Comparability of randomised groups', *Statistician*, **34**, pp. 125–36.

Altman, D.G. and J.N. Matthews (1996), 'Statistics notes. Interaction 1: Heterogeneity of effects', *British Medical Journal*, **313**(7055), p. 486.

Briggs, A.H., C.Z. Mooney and D.E. Wonderling (1999), 'Constructing confidence intervals for cost-effectiveness ratios: an evaluation of parametric and non-parametric techniques using Monte Carlo simulation', *Statistics in Medicine*, **18**(23), 3245–62.

Briggs, A.H., D.E. Wonderling and C.Z. Mooney (1997), 'Pulling cost-effectiveness analysis up by its bootstraps: a non-parametric approach to confidence interval estimation', *Health Economics*, **6**(4), 327–40.

Chaudhary, M.A. and S.C. Stearns (1996), 'Estimating confidence intervals for cost-effectiveness ratios: An example from a randomized trial', *Statistics in Medicine*, **15**, pp. 1447–58.

Claxton, K., M.J. Sculpher and M. Drummond (2002), 'A rational framework for decision making by the National Institute For Clinical Excellence (NICE)', *The Lancet*, **360**, pp. 711–15.

Collins, R., R. Gray, J. Godwin and R. Peto (1987), 'Avoidance of large biases and large random errors in the assessment of moderate treatment effects: the need for systematic overviews', *Statistics in Medicine*, **6**(3), 245–54.

Collins, R., S. Parish, J. Armitage, P. Sleight and R. Peto for the Heart Protection Study Collaborative Group (2002), 'MRC/BHF Heart Protection Study of cholesterol lowering with simvastatin in 20,536 high-risk individuals: a randomised placebo-controlled trial', *The Lancet*, **360**(9326), 7–22.

Cooper, N.J., A.J. Sutton, K.R. Abrams, D. Turner and A. Wailoo (2004), 'A comprehensive decision analytic modelling in economic evaluation: A Bayesian approach', *Health Economics*, **13**(3), 203–26.

Draper, D. (1995), 'Assessment and propagation of model uncertainty', *Journal of the Royal Statistical Society, Series B*, **57**(1), 45–97.

Drummond, M.F., B. O'Brien, G.L. Stoddart and G.W. Torrance (1997), *Methods for the Economic Evaluation of Health Care Programmes*, 2nd edn, Oxford: Oxford University Press.

Glasziou, P.P. and L.M. Irwig (1995), 'An evidence based approach to individualising treatment', *British Medical Journal*, **311**(7016), 1356–9.

Gray, A., M. Raikou, A. McGuire, P. Fenn, R. Stevens, C. Cull, I. Stratton, A. Adler, R. Holman and R. Turner (2000), 'Cost effectiveness of an intensive blood glucose control policy in patients with type 2 diabetes: economic analysis alongside randomised controlled trial (UKPDS 41). United Kingdom Prospective Diabetes Study Group', *British Medical Journal*, **320**(7246), 1373–8.

Greene, W.H. (1993), *Econometric Analysis*, 2nd edn, New York: Macmillan.

Heitjan, D.F. (2000), 'Fieller's method and net health benefits', *Health Economics*, **9**(4), 327–35.

Heitjan, D.F., A.J. Moskowitz and W. Whang (1999), 'Problems with interval estimates of the incremental cost-effectiveness ratio', *Medical Decision Making*, **19**(1), 9–15.

Hoch, J.S., A.H. Briggs and A. Willan (2002), 'Something old, something new, something borrowed, something BLUE: a framework for the marriage of health econometrics and cost-effectiveness analysis', *Health Economics*, **11**, 415–30.

Manca, A., M. Sculpher, N. Rice and A. Briggs (2005), 'Assessing generalisability by location in trial-based cost-effectiveness analysis: the use of multilevel models', *Health Economics*, **14**, 487–96.

Mihaylova, B., A. Briggs, A. Gray, J. Armitage, S. Parish and R. Collins for the Heart Protection Study Collaborative Group (2005), 'Cost-effectiveness of simvastatin in people at different levels of vascular disease risk: a randomised trial in 20 536 individuals', *The Lancet*, **365**, 1779–86.

Mullahy, J. and W.G. Manning (1995), 'Statistical issues in cost-effectiveness analyses', in F.A. Sloan (ed.), *Valuing Health Care*, Cambridge: Cambridge University Press, pp. 149–84.

O'Brien, B.J., M.F. Drummond, R.J. Labelle and A. Willan (1994), 'In search of power and significance: issues in the design and analysis of stochastic cost-effectiveness studies in health care', *Medical Care*, **32**(2), 150–63.

Oxman, A.D. and G.H. Guyatt (1992), 'A consumer's guide to subgroup analyses', *Annals of Internal Medicine*, **116**, 78–84.

Pocock, S.J. (1984), *Clinical Trials: a Practical Approach*, Chichester: John Wiley.

Polsky, D., H.A. Glick, R. Willke and K. Schulman (1997), 'Confidence intervals for cost-effectiveness ratios: a comparison of four methods', *Health Economics*, **6**, 243–52.

Raikou, M., A. Gray, A. Briggs, R. Stevens, C. Cull, A. McGuire, P. Fenn, I. Stratton, R. Holman and R. Turner (1998), 'Cost effectiveness analysis of improved blood pressure control in hypertensive patients with type 2 diabetic patients (HDS7): UKPDS 40', *British Medical Journal*, **317**, 720–26.

Sculpher, M.J., L. Poole, J. Cleland, M. Drummond, P.W. Armstrong, J.D. Horowitz, B.M. Massie, P.A. Poole-Wilson and L. Ryden (2000), 'Low doses vs. high doses of the angiotensin converting-enzyme inhibitor lisinopril in chronic heart failure: a cost-effectiveness analysis based on the Assessment of Treatment with Lisinopril and Survival (ATLAS) study. The ATLAS Study Group', *European Journal of Heart Failure*, **2**(4), 447–54.

Stinnett, A.A. and J. Mullahy (1998), 'Net health benefits: a new framework for the analysis of uncertainty in cost-effectiveness analysis', *Medical Decision Making*, **18**(2)Suppl, S68–S80.

Sutton, A.J., N.J. Cooper, K.R. Abrams, P.C. Lambert and D.R. Jones (2005), 'A Bayesian approach to evaluating net clinical benefit allowed for parameter uncertainty', *Journal of Clinical Epidemiology*, **58**, 26–40.

Tambour, M., N. Zethraeus and M. Johannesson (1998), 'A note on confidence intervals in cost-effectiveness analysis', *International Journal of Technology Assessment in Health Care*, **14**(3), 467–71.

van Hout, B., M.J. Al, G.S. Gordon and F.F. Rutten (1994), 'Costs, effects and C/E-ratios alongside a clinical trial', *Health Economics*, **3**(5), 309–19.

Weinstein, M.C. and H.V. Fineberg (1980), *Clinical Decision Analysis*, Philadelphia (PA): WB Saunders Company.

Weinstein, M.C. and W.B. Stason (1977), 'Foundations of cost-effectiveness analysis for health and medical practices', *New England Journal of Medicine*, **296**, pp. 716–21.

Willan, A.R. and D.Y. Lin (2001), 'Incremental net benefit in randomized clinical trials', *Statistics in Medicine*, **20**(11), 1563–74.

Willan, A.R., A.H. Briggs and J.S. Hoch (2004), 'Regression methods for covariate adjustment and subgroup analysis for non-censored cost-effectiveness data', *Health Economics*, **13**(5), 461–75.

Willan, A., D. Lin and A. Manca (2005), 'Regression methods for cost-effectiveness analysis with censored data', *Statistics in Medicine*, **24**(1), 131–45.

48 Decision-making with uncertainty: the value of information

Karl Claxton, Elisabeth Fenwick and Mark J. Sculpher

1. Introduction

There are two conceptually distinct but simultaneous decisions that must be made within any health care system. Firstly, should a technology be adopted or reimbursed given the existing evidence and the current uncertainty surrounding outcomes and resource use? In particular, which of the range of possible strategies should be adopted for particular patient groups? Secondly, is additional evidence required to support the adoption or reimbursement decision and, if more evidence is required, what is the appropriate design of the future research?

By clearly distinguishing these two separate decisions, it is possible to identify analytic methods that can inform the adoption decision, the decision to acquire more evidence and inform research design in a way that is consistent with the objectives and constraints on health care provision. This chapter addresses each of these questions in turn. It draws on recent developments in methods for the evaluation of health care technologies, and the experience of the UK National Institute for Health and Clinical Excellence (NICE) in using these methods in order to address decisions about the adoption of health care technologies and the requirements for future research in an explicit and transparent way.

2. Requirements of decision-making

These two policy decisions lead to a number of requirements that an analytic framework should meet. These include a means of structuring the decision problem; a characterization of the uncertainty surrounding the decision; and a process of interpreting the results of the analysis so that decisions about adoption and additional evidence can be made in a way that is consistent with both the objectives and constraints on health care provision.

Policy decisions should benefit from an analytic framework that can provide estimates of the expected costs and health outcomes for each of the possible strategies that could be adopted. This includes the full range of comparators and possible strategies, which may use the technology in different ways, many of which may not have been directly compared in clinical trial evidence; and for a range of patient groups over an appropriate time horizon, where outcomes and costs differ. This suggests an analytic framework that can structure the decision problem so that evidence can be combined from a variety of sources, that facilitates extrapolation over time and between surrogate endpoints and health outcomes, and that can generalize to different clinical, population and system settings. In addition, it should allow the uncertainty surrounding the decision problem to be characterized. The different forms of uncertainty that arise in the context of economic evaluations are discussed further by Vanness and Mullahy in Chapter 49 in this Companion.

Characterizing the uncertainty surrounding the decision problem as a whole, rather than simply the uncertainty surrounding measures of efficacy, means that all the relevant evidence surrounding the parameters for the decision problem should be identified and synthesized. This entails a broad view of evidence, which sees evidence as informing a range of parameters, not just clinical effectiveness, and regards relevant evidence as a network of direct and indirect evidence. The task of synthesizing this broad range of evidence also suggests that a formal framework for learning is needed to update estimates of parameters as evidence accumulates. Bayesian analysis is, in essence, a formal framework of learning from accumulating evidence, whether that evidence is accumulating over time or from a network of related evidence. Therefore, the type of synthesis of evidence and characterization of uncertainty which is required suggests the use of Bayesian methods (Sutton and Abrams, 2001; Ades, 2003; Spiegelhalter et al., 2004).

3. The decision to adopt a technology

Bayesian decision theory and value of information analysis provides such an analytic framework. These methods have firm foundations in statistical decision theory (Raiffa and Schlaifer, 1959; Pratt et al., 1995), and have been successfully used in other areas of research such as engineering and environmental risk analysis (Thompson and Evans, 1997). More recently, these methods have been extended to the evaluation of health care technologies (Claxton and Posnett, 1996; Claxton et al., 2001; Claxton et al., 2004). The application of these methods requires three tasks to be completed: (i) the construction of a decision analytic model to represent the decision problem; (ii) a probabilistic analysis of this model to characterize the current decision uncertainty; and (iii) establishing the value of additional information. The first two tasks have been described elsewhere (Hunink et al., 2001; Briggs et al., 2002a). Here we address how decision-makers should interpret the results of probabilistic modelling and how to address the question of whether more evidence is required.

The uncertainty surrounding the decision problem can be characterized by 'propagating' the distributions assigned to parameters through the model using Monte Carlo simulation methods (Doubilet et al., 1985; Critchfield et al., 1986; Briggs et al., 2002a). The output of these simulations provides the joint distribution of expected costs and outcomes for each strategy being compared. The uncertainty surrounding the cost-effectiveness of a strategy can be represented as a cost-effectiveness acceptability curve (CEAC) (Van Hout et al., 1994; Fenwick et al., 2001; Fenwick et al., 2004). This plots the probability that each of the strategies is cost-effective (has the highest expected net benefit (Stinnett and Mullahy, 1998)) for a range of cost-effectiveness thresholds. The decision uncertainty can be represented by a cost-effectiveness acceptability frontier. The frontier indicates the probability that the alternative with the highest expected net benefit will be cost-effective (Fenwick et al., 2001). The decision uncertainty or the error probability is then one minus the value of the frontier. In contrast, although the cost-effectiveness plane has been used to illustrate the uncertainty in cost and effect when comparing two alternatives (Black, 1990; Briggs et al., 2002a), this becomes impossible to interpret appropriately for more than two alternatives and cannot provide a summary measure of decision uncertainty.

Figure 48.1 illustrates an example of a CEAC for a simple model of zanamivir for the treatment of influenza. This is based on a probabilistic re-analysis of a simple model

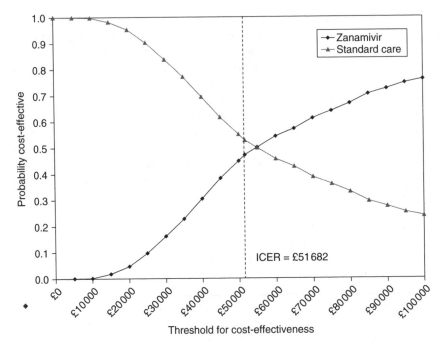

Figure 48.1   Cost-effectiveness acceptability curve

contained in the independent Technology Assessment Report, which was submitted as part of the NICE appraisal of zanamivir in 2000 (Burls et al., 2000a; 2000b). In this example the probability that the intervention is cost-effective increases with the threshold for cost-effectiveness. The vertical line reflects the point at which the value of the threshold equals the incremental cost-effectiveness ratio for Zanamivir (£51 682 per QALY) and the point at which the cost-effectiveness acceptability frontier switches between treatments. If the threshold for cost-effectiveness is just greater than £51 682, then the intervention should be regarded as cost-effective although the probability that it is cost-effective is less than 0.5 (the probability that zanamivir is cost-effective when threshold equals ICER = 0.472). This is because the distribution of the additional net benefits is positively skewed, with a mean greater than its median value (Fenwick et al., 2001).

A key question is how should this be interpreted by decision-makers and how should a decision be made under uncertainty? For example, if society is willing to pay £60 000 per QALY gained, then the probability that zanamivir is cost-effective is only 0.543. There is substantial decision uncertainty with an error probability of 0.457. In these circumstances what decision should be made about zanamivir?

The irrelevance of inference
If we base decisions on the traditional rules of inference (either Frequentist or Bayesian), then we would conclude that the apparent cost-effectiveness of zanamivir is not statistically significant, neither does it fall within a Bayesian range of equivalence, we cannot

reject the null hypothesis and the result is indeterminate. In practice this would lead to the rejection of zanamivir despite the fact that it is the alternative with the highest expected net-benefit on the basis of the information currently available. If we fail to adopt an intervention simply because the differences in net-benefit are not regarded as 'statistically significant' or the error probability is 'too high', then we will impose opportunity costs on patients who could benefit from it. These opportunity costs are the forgone expected net benefits. For an individual patient, these forgone expected net-benefits are £3 and, for the UK population of current and future patients, they could be valued at £2.7m, or 45 QALYs.

If the objective underlying health technology assessment is to make decisions that are consistent with maximizing health gains from available resources then, in the absence of substantial irreversibilities (Palmer and Smith, 2000), decisions should be based on expected cost-effectiveness (expected net-benefit) given the existing information, irrespective of whether any differences are regarded as statistically significant. The traditional rules of inference impose unnecessary costs on individual patients and on the population of current and future patients, and are irrelevant to the decision to adopt or reimburse a technology.

4. The decision to acquire more evidence

Although decisions should be based on expected cost-effectiveness given the existing information, this does not mean that adoption decisions should simply be based on little – or poor quality – evidence, as long as the decision to conduct further research to support adoption (or rejection) is made simultaneously.

Expected value of perfect information

Decisions based on existing information will be uncertain, and there will always be a chance that the wrong decision will be made (the error probability). The expected cost of uncertainty will be determined jointly by the error probability and the consequences of decision error (net-benefit forgone). The expected costs of uncertainty can be interpreted as the expected value of perfect information (EVPI), which is also the maximum that the health care system should be willing to pay for additional evidence to inform this decision in the future, and it places an upper bound on the value of conducting further research.

With current information, a decision must be made before it is known how the uncertainties will resolve based on the expected net benefits of each of the alternatives. However, with perfect information, decisions can be made when it is known how the uncertainties in the model will resolve, so different decisions can be made for different resolutions of net benefit. The EVPI is simply the difference between the payoff (expected net-benefit) with perfect and current information.

For example, if there are alternative interventions (j), with uncertain parameters θ, the optimal decision with current information is to choose the intervention that generates the maximum expected net-benefit (NB):

$$\max_j E_\theta NB(j, \theta)$$

Table 48.1   Calculating EVPI

	Treatment A	Treatment B	Treatment C	Optimal choice	Maximum net-benefit	Opportunity loss
Iteration 1	11	12	13	C	13	1
Iteration 2	12	10	9	A	12	2
Iteration 3	13	18	15	B	18	0
Iteration 4	14	16	17	C	17	1
Iteration 5	15	14	11	A	15	1
Expectation	13	14	13		15	1

With perfect information, the decision-maker would know how the uncertainties would resolve and could select the intervention that maximizes the net-benefit for a particular value of θ:

$$\max_j NB(j, \theta)$$

However, the true values of θ are unknown, so the expected value of a decision taken with perfect information is that found by averaging the maximum net-benefit over the joint distribution of θ:

$$E_\theta \max_j NB(j, \theta),$$

The expected value of perfect information for an individual patient is simply the difference between the expected value of the decision made with perfect information about the uncertain parameters θ, and the decision made on the basis of existing evidence:

$$\text{EVPI} = E_\theta \max_j NB(j, \theta) - \max_j E_\theta NB(j, \theta)$$

This approach is illustrated in Table 48.1 for three alternative treatments A, B and C. The table represents simulated output from five iterations (of, for example, a Monte Carlo simulation) generating a net-benefit for each of the treatments. With current information the alternative with the highest expected net-benefit ($\max_j E_\theta NB(j, \theta)$) is treatment B with expected net-benefits of 14. With perfect information, the decision-maker could choose the alternative with the maximum net-benefit (column 4) for each resolution of uncertainty ($\max_j NB(j, \theta)$), that is, choose C for iteration 1; A for iteration 2 and B for iteration 3 and so on. However, it is not known in advance which of these possibilities will turn out to be true, so the expected net-benefit with perfect information is simply the expectation of the maximum net-benefits. The EVPI is then simply the difference between the expected maximum net-benefit and the maximum expected net-benefit ($15 - 14 = 1$). It should be noted that this is entirely equivalent to taking the expectation of the opportunity losses in column 5, demonstrating that EVPI is also the expected opportunity loss or the expected costs of the uncertainty surrounding the decision.

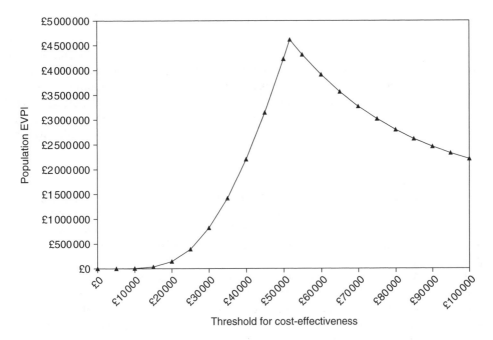

Figure 48.2   Population EVPI

This approach provides the EVPI surrounding the decision as a whole each time this decision is made (for an individual patient or individual episode). However, information has public good characteristics (that is, it is non-rival). Therefore, the EVPI for the population can be calculated based on some assessment of the effective lifetime of the technology (T), estimates of incidence over this period (I_t) and a discount rate (r):

$$\text{EVPI for the population} = \text{EVPI}.\Sigma_{t=1,\dots,T}\, I_t/(1+r)^t$$

Figure 48.2 illustrates the population EVPI for zanamivir. When the threshold for cost-effectiveness is low, the technology is not expected to be cost-effective and additional information is unlikely to change that decision. That is, EVPI is low and, assuming that the cost of research is higher than the EVPI, current evidence can be regarded as sufficient to support the decision to reject the technology. Conversely, when the threshold is higher than the ICER, the intervention is expected to be cost-effective and this decision is less likely to be changed by further research as the threshold is increased. In this particular case, the population EVPI reaches a maximum when the threshold is equal to the expected incremental cost-effectiveness ratio of this technology (the error probability reaches a maximum). However, most decision problems involve more than two alternatives. The principles of calculating EVPI remain the same (as illustrated in Table 48.1) but the EVPI curve can take a variety of shapes.

The EVPI provides an upper bound to the value of additional research and provides a necessary condition for deciding to acquire more information, that is, the EVPI must exceed the cost of further investigation. It should be clear from this discussion of EVPI that the value of information will depend on both the uncertainty surrounding estimates of cost and effect, but also on how cost-effective or cost-ineffective a technology is expected to be, given existing evidence, and the size of the patient population that could benefit from additional research. The value of information and the amount of evidence required to support a decision to adopt a technology will differ across different technologies, applied to different patient populations, and for the same technology in different circumstances (different indications, patient populations and different cost-effectiveness thresholds).

EVPI for parameters

The EVPI surrounding the decision problem can indicate whether further research is potentially worthwhile. However, it would be useful to have an indication of what type of additional evidence would be most valuable. The value of reducing the uncertainty surrounding particular parameters in the decision model can be established using a similar approach (Ades et al., 2003).

The value of perfect information about a parameter or a subset (ϕ) of all the uncertain parameters θ (partial EVPI or EVPPI) is simply the difference between the expected net-benefit with perfect information about ϕ and the expected value with current information. With perfect information the value of ϕ is known and the expected net-benefits are calculated over the remaining uncertainties (Ψ).

$$\max_j E_{\Psi|\phi} NB(j, \phi, \Psi)$$

However, the true values of ϕ are unknown and the expected value of a decision taken with perfect information is found by averaging these maximum expected net-benefits over the distribution of ϕ:

$$E_\phi \max_j E_{\Psi|\phi} NB(j, \phi, \Psi)$$

The expected value with current information is the same as before, so the EVPPI for the parameter or group of parameters ϕ is simply the difference between the expected value of a decision made with perfect information and the expected value with current information:

$$\text{EVPPI}_\phi = E_\phi \max_j E_{\Psi|\phi} NB(j, \phi, \Psi) - \max_j E_\theta NB(j, \theta)$$

This provides a general solution for non-linear models. However, it is computationally intensive because it requires an inner and outer loop of simulation (Ades et al., 2003). The computational requirements can be somewhat simplified if the model has either a linear or multi-linear relationship between the parameters and net-benefit. If the model is multi-linear in Ψ, the parameters in Ψ are uncorrelated with each other and ϕ and Ψ are independent then:

$$E_{\Psi|\phi} NB(j, \phi, \Psi) = NB(j, \phi, E(\Psi))$$

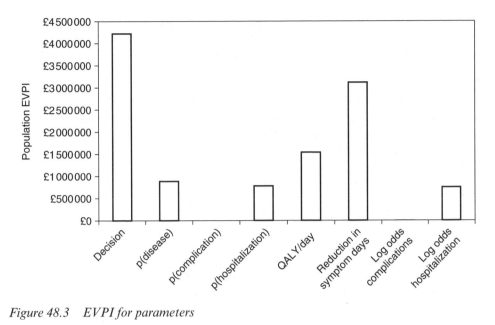

Figure 48.3   EVPI for parameters

The expected net-benefit for a particular value of φ can be calculated based on the means of the other parameters ψ and the inner loop of simulation is unnecessary.

This type of analysis can be used to focus research on the type of evidence that will be most important by identifying those parameters for which more precise estimates would be most valuable. In some circumstances, this will indicate which endpoints should be included in further experimental research. In other circumstances, it may focus research on getting more precise estimates of particular parameters that may not necessarily require experimental design and that can be provided relatively quickly.

For example, Figure 48.3 illustrates the EVPPIs associated with the decision EVPI in Figure 48.2 at a threshold of £50 000 per QALY. In this example, the EVPPI associated with reduction in symptom days on zanamivir is relatively high. A more precise estimate of the reduction in symptom days will require experimental design to avoid selection bias and suggests that a further randomized trial may be worthwhile. However, other parameters with lower EVPPI such as the quality of life associated with influenza symptoms, the probability of hospitalization with standard care and the probability that a patient presenting with influenza-like symptoms does actually have influenza, may not require experimental research and may be important if the costs of further investigation (resources and delay) are low. Other parameters have negligible EVPPI and are relatively unimportant. It is clear in Figure 48.3 that the EVPPIs will not necessarily sum to the overall decision EVPI due to the interactions within the model structure.

Efficient research designs
The EVPI and EVPPI place an upper bound on the returns to further research. This provides a *necessary* condition for conducting further research: additional research about

the decision problem as a whole or about particular parameters may be worthwhile if the EVPI or EVPPI exceeds the cost of conducting further research. However, to establish a *sufficient* condition, to decide if further research will be worthwhile and identify efficient research design, estimates of the expected benefits and the cost of sample information are required.

The same value of information analysis framework can be extended to establish the expected value of sample information for particular research designs (Ades et al., 2003). For example, a sample of n on θ will provide a sample result D. If the sample result was known, then a decision-maker would choose the alternative with the maximum expected net-benefit when those expected net-benefits are averaged over the posterior distribution of the net-benefit of each treatment j given the sample result D:

$$\max_j E_{\theta|D} NB(j, \theta)$$

However, the results of the sample are unknown, so the expected value of a decision taken with the sample information is that found by averaging these maximum expected net-benefits over the distribution of possible values of D, that is, the expectation over the predictive distribution of the sample results D conditional on θ, averaged over the prior distribution (possible values) of θ:

$$E_D \max_j E_{\theta|D} NB(j, \theta)$$

The EVSI is simply the difference between the expected value of a decision made with sample information and the expected value with current information:

$$\text{EVSI} = E_D \max_j E_{\theta|D} NB(j, \theta) - \max_j E_\theta NB(j, \theta)$$

The EVSI calculations require the likelihood for the data to be conjugate with the prior so there is an analytic solution to combining the prior (θ) with the predicted sample result (D) from the predicted posterior ($\theta|D$). If the prior and likelihood are not conjugate, the computational burden of using numerical methods to form predicted posteriors is considerable. Even with conjugacy, EVSI still requires intensive computation (Ades et al., 2003).

The EVSI calculation described above is for a single study design and only one sample size. To establish the optimal sample size for a particular type of study these calculations need to be repeated for a range of sample sizes. The difference between the EVSI and the costs of acquiring the sample information (Cs) is the expected net benefit of sample information (ENBS) or the societal payoff to research. The optimal sample size is simply the value of n that generates the maximum ENBS.

The EVSI and ENBS are illustrated in Figure 48.4 when all the parameters in the zanamivir model are updated together (at a cost-effectiveness threshold of £50 000 per QALY). The ENBS reaches a maximum of £2.26m at an optimal sample size of 1100. This suggests that an additional clinical trial which collected evidence on all parameters within the model will be worthwhile. However, this may not be the most efficient design as there are a range of possible study designs, which would generate information about different

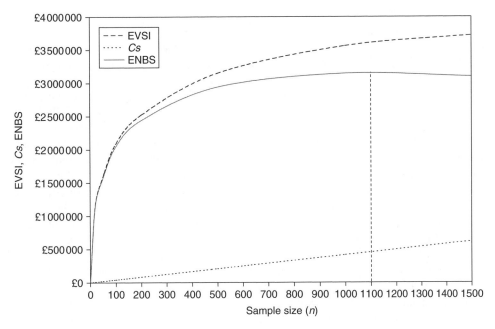

Figure 48.4 EVSI, ENBS and optimal sample size

groups of parameters, or studies with different follow-up periods or different allocations of the sample between the arms of the study. An EVSI and ENBS calculation would be needed for each possible design and for a range of sample sizes. The efficient research design will be the one that provides the maximum ENBS. Indeed this framework can be used to identify a portfolio of different types of studies that may be required.

It should be recognized that EVSI, just like EVPI, depends on the cost-effectiveness threshold, and there will be different ENBS and different optimal sample sizes for different cost-effectiveness thresholds. The implication is that economic arguments are central to fundamental research design issues. The application of value of information analysis makes it possible to answer a range of design questions such as: is an additional clinical trial required? If so, should an economic evaluation be conducted alongside the new trial? What is the optimal follow-up, sample size and allocation of entrants between the arms of the proposed trial? When should a sequential trial be stopped?

5. Discussion

Analytic methods are available that can inform the decisions to adopt or reimburse a technology based on current evidence, whether to acquire more evidence and identify efficient research design in a way that is consistent with the objectives of and constraints on health care provision. This is not possible using more traditional approaches based on hypothesis testing and power calculations, which fail to provide an adequate guide. What seems clear is that the questions of whether to adopt a technology, whether more evidence is required and how further research should be designed cannot be addressed independently and all depend on economic considerations.

In many countries, decisions to adopt, reimburse or issue guidance on health technologies are increasingly based on explicit cost-effectiveness analysis using a decision analytic framework (Hjelmgren et al., 2001). A prime example is the National Institute for Health and Clinical Excellence (NICE) in the UK, where recent guidance on the methods of technology appraisal reflect the importance of representing decision problems explicitly, synthesizing evidence from a range of sources and characterizing decision uncertainty through probabilistic analysis (National Institute for Clinical Excellence (NICE) 2004). In addition, value of information analysis is also recommended. Almost all the Technology Assessment Reports commissioned by NICE already include decision analysis and synthesis of evidence. A number have also included probabilistic analysis and value of information analysis, and more recently NICE commissioned a pilot study of value-of-information analysis to support the Institute's research recommendations made as part of its Guidance to the NHS in England and Wales (Claxton et al., 2004).

Of course, there are a number of methodological and computational challenges associated with this type of analysis (Sculpher et al., 2005). Many of these challenges are associated with the interpretation of evidence, methods of synthesis and reflecting potential bias and exchangeability. These have always been present in any informal and partial review of evidence but, until quite recently, they could be conveniently ignored by policymakers, clinicians and analysts while decision-making was opaque and based on implicit criteria and unspecified 'weighing' of the evidence. These challenges must be faced as more explicit and transparent approaches to decision-making are being used. Indeed, one of the many advantages of taking more analytic, transparent and explicit approaches to decision-making is that it exposes many important methodological issues which have previously been ignored or avoided by partial analyses that do not directly address the decisions which must be made in any health care system.

References

Ades, A.E. (2003), 'A chain of evidence with mixed comparisons: models for multi-parameter evidence synthesis and consistency of evidence', *Statistics in Medicine*, **22**, 2995–3016.

Ades, A.E., G. Lu and K. Claxton (2003), 'Expected value of sample information in medical decision modelling', *Medical Decision Making*, **24**, 207–27.

Black, W.C. (1990), 'The CE plane: a graphic representation of cost-effectiveness', *Medical Decision Making*, **10**, 212–14.

Briggs, A.H., B.J. O'Brien and G. Blackhouse (2002a), 'Thinking outside the box: Recent advances in the analysis and presentation of uncertainty in cost-effectiveness studies', *Annual Review of Public Health*, **23**, 377–401.

Briggs, A.H., R. Goeree, G. Blackhouse and B.J. O'Brien (2002b), 'Probabilistic analysis of cost-effectiveness models: choosing between treatment strategies for gastroesophageal reflux disease', *Medical Decision Making*, **22**, 290–308.

Burls, A., W. Clark, C. Preton, S. Bryan, A. Stewart, T. Jefferson et al. (2000a), *Is Zanamivir Effective for the Treatment of Influenza in Adults*, www.nice.org, London: National Institute for Clinical Excellence.

Burls, A., W. Clark, C. Preton, S. Bryan, A. Stewart, T. Jefferson et al. (2000b), *Zanamivir for the Treatment of Influenza in Adults: Supplement to the Assessment Report*, www.nice.org, London: National Institute for Clinical Excellence.

Claxton, K. and J. Posnett (1996), 'An economic approach to clinical trial design and research priority-setting', *Health Economics*, **5**, 513–24.

Claxton, K., P.J. Neuman, S.S. Araki and M.C. Weinstein (2001), 'The value of information: an application to a policy model of Alzheimer's disease', *International Journal of Technology Assessment in Health Care*, **17**, 38–55.

Claxton, K., L. Ginnelly, M. Sculpher, Z. Philips and S. Palmer (2004), 'A pilot study on the use of decision theory and value of information analysis as part of the National Health Service Health Technology Assessment Programme', *Health Technology Assessment*, **8**(31).

Claxton, K., S. Eggington, L. Ginnelly, S. Griffin, C. McCabe, Z. Philips et al. (2004), *Pilot Study of Value of Information Analysis to Support Research Recommendations for the National Institute for Clinical Excellence*, www.nice.org.uk, London: National Institute for Clinical Excellence.

Critchfield, G.C., K.E. Willard and D.P. Connelly (1986), 'Probabilistic analysis of decision trees using Monte Carlo simulation', *Medical Decision Making*, **6**, 85–92.

Doubilet, P., C.B. Begg, M.C. Weinstein, P. Braun and B.J. McNeill (1985), 'Probabilistic sensitivity analysis using Monte Carlo simulation: a practical approach', *Medical Decision Making*, **5**, 157–77.

Fenwick, E., K. Claxton and M. Sculpher (2001), 'Representing uncertainty: the role of cost-effectiveness acceptability curves', *Health Economics*, **10**, 779–89.

Fenwick, E., B.J. O'Brien and A. Briggs (2004), 'Cost-effectiveness acceptability curves – facts, fallacies and frequently asked questions', *Health Economics*, **13**, 405–15.

Hjelmgren, J., F. Berggren and F. Andersson (2001), 'Health economic guidelines – similarities, differences and some implications', *Value in Health*, **4**, 225–50.

Hunink, M., P. Glaziou, J. Siegel, J. Weeks, J. Pliskin, A. Elstein et al. (2001), *Decision Making in Health and Medicine. Integrating Evidence and Values*, Cambridge: Cambridge University Press.

National Institute for Clinical Excellence (NICE) (2004), *Guide to the Methods of Technology Appraisal*, London: NICE.

Palmer, S. and P.C. Smith (2000), 'Incorporating option values into the economic evaluation of health care technologies', *Journal of Health Economics*, **19**, 755–66.

Pratt, J., H. Raiffa and R. Schlaifer (1995), *Statistical Decision Theory*, Cambridge: MIT Press.

Raiffa, H. and R. Schlaifer (1959), *Probability and Statistics for Business Decisions*, New York: McGraw-Hill.

Sculpher, M., K. Claxton and R. Akehurst (2005), 'It's just evaluation for decision making: recent developments in, and challenges for, cost-effectiveness research', in P.C. Smith, L. Ginnelly and M. Sculpher. *Health Policy and Economics. Opportunities and Challenges*, Maidenhead: Open University Press.

Spiegelhalter, D.J., K.R. Abrams and J.P. Myles (2004), *Bayesian Approaches to Clinical Trials and Health-care Evaluation*, Chichester: John Wiley.

Stinnett, A. and J. Mullahy (1998), 'Net health benefits: a new framework for the analysis of uncertainty in cost-effectiveness analyses', *Medical Decision Making*, **18**, S68–S80.

Sutton, A.J. and K.R. Abrams (2001), 'Bayesian methods in meta-analysis and evidence synthesis', *Statistical Methods in Medical Research*, **10**, 277–303.

Thompson, K.M. and J.S. Evans (1997), 'The value of improved national exposure information for per-chloroethylene (perc): a case study for dry cleaners', *Risk Analysis*, **17**, 253–71.

Van Hout, B.A., M.J. Al, G.S. Gordon and F.F.H. Rutten (1994), 'Costs, effects and c/e-ratios alongside a clinical trial', *Health Economics*, **3**, 309–19.

49 Perspectives on mean-based evaluation of health care

David J. Vanness and John Mullahy*

1. Introduction

The fundamental statistical problem in health care evaluations involves determining the value of alternative treatments based on data indicating how their costs (c) and health outcomes (y) are distributed in a target population. Even though net benefit to an individual (i) assigned to a specific treatment (T_j), $NB_{j,i} = M_i(y_i(T_j)) - c_i(T_j)$ (where M_i is a possibly heterogeneous money-metric utility function), is likely to vary across the target population, evaluation methods typically produce a single treatment recommendation for the entire target population based on estimated mean costs and outcomes (with consideration of the sampling variation of such estimates).

This chapter examines some theoretical underpinnings behind this 'mean-based' approach, suggests alternative perspectives in light of these underpinnings, and explores statistical characteristics of tools commonly used in health care evaluations.

2. Mean-based evaluation in health care

The mean-based approach boasts two central features, one economic, the other statistical. First, it is consistent with the Kaldor–Hicks (potential Pareto improvement) criterion, which holds that so long as individuals with higher net-benefit can potentially compensate those with lower (or negative) net-benefit, policy recommendations should depend only on the sign of total, or mean, incremental net-benefit. Second, given exogenous treatment assignment, *mean incremental* net-benefit between two treatments, $E_i[NB_{1,i} - NB_{0,i}]$, equals *incremental mean* net-benefit $E_i[NB_{1,i}] - E_i[NB_{0,i}]$. This is of tantamount importance since the former relies on the *joint* distribution, $F(NB_0, NB_1)$, while the latter relies only on the respective *marginals*, $F_0(.)$ and $F_1(.)$. Knowledge about the joint distribution requires that we observe both $NB_{0,i}$ and $NB_{1,i}$ for each individual, one of which is purely counterfactual.

The subtle yet significant power of the expectation operator's linearity has obscured fundamental issues in evaluation that necessitate looking beyond means (see Bitler et al., 2003). Recent literature (see Heckman, 2001, and Heckman et al., 1997, for discussion) has emphasized that net benefits for any individual under competing interventions may be correlated, albeit not perfectly so, and that familiar cost–benefit postulates regarding anonymity or exchangeability may not reflect how real-world decision-makers evaluate interventions. In other words, the mean may not be the only statistic that matters to

* Mullahy and Vanness acknowledge NIAAA Grant R01-AA012664 and NIA/NIAMS Grant R01-AG12262, respectively, for partial financial support. The authors thank Anirban Basu, Will Manning and Ritesh Banerjee for helpful comments.

medical decision-makers – variance (or other moments) may matter as well (Zivin, 2001; O'Brien and Sculpher, 2000).

Examples of such decision-making contexts in the United States include: HMO procedure coverage for uncommon illnesses; Medicaid policies reducing benefits for current beneficiaries to extend coverage to uninsured individuals; FDA policy providing special considerations for 'orphan drug' treatments; and interventions in ICUs to save lives when the odds are weighted strongly against recovery. The notion that comparison of population-expected benefits with population-expected costs drives the underlying evaluation of these interventions is tenuous at best (see Horwitz et al., 1996, and Kravitz et al., 2004).

Our reaction to such decision-making orientations differs from that of many health policy analysts. Instead of changing the environment to encourage concordance with the Kaldor–Hicks criterion, we suggest that preferences of real-world decision-makers deserve more respect. Because clinicians and administrators make choices that impact non-exchangeable, non-anonymous individuals, they may care about features of the distributions of costs and health outcomes beyond the mean. Clinicians never really treat the 'average patient' and may be reluctant to base decisions for unique individuals on guidelines developed not to maximize each individual patient's benefit but rather to maximize population benefit (Granata and Hillman, 1998).

While 'potential compensation' may be reasonable for allocations involving wealth alone, it may be more difficult for decision-makers to accept the concept of compensating transfers of health (Mishan, 1971). With a population of $N = 3$ individuals, for instance, a social decision-maker may value differently the net-benefit distributions $NB_0 = [5, 5, 20]$ and $NB_1 = [10, 10, 10]$ induced by interventions T_0 and T_1, even though the population means are the same and even though at the individual level a Kaldor–Hicks approach suggests that individual 3 might value her gain sufficiently to compensate individuals 1 and 2 to accept T_0 over T_1.

3. Risk, heterogeneity and uncertainty from the decision-maker's perspective

If only we knew, *ex ante*, $NB_{j,i}$ for each individual under every alternative treatment, there would be no need for statistics. Such god-like perception equates to knowing the exact state of the world and the precise way in which each treatment translates that state into costs and health outcomes. However, human decision-makers lack omniscience in three fundamental ways. First, biological complexity implies that some relevant aspect of the true state of the world always remains unknowable (Sonnenberg, 2001). Such 'first-order' uncertainty gives rise to what has been termed 'risk' in the decision theory literature (Knight, 1921).

Second, many relevant aspects of the true state of the world, while potentially knowable, remain unobserved. Thus, two apparently identical states may yield different outcomes because of unobserved (or ignored) heterogeneity. This limit to knowledge presents challenges for extrapolation or prediction, since it violates the assumption that the hypothetical realization is exchangeable with the realizations that generated the data.

Third, we are unlikely to know the exact functional relationship between the state of the world and outcomes. This 'second-order' uncertainty (simply 'uncertainty' in the decision theory literature) is often called 'parametric' because we assume that the data generating process can be parameterized and that our limited knowledge can be expressed as a probability distribution over those unknown parameters (Spiegelhalter and Best, 2003; Briggs and Gray, 1999).

Preliminaries
We proceed by formalizing these three knowledge limitations and their relation to health care evaluation using a decision-theoretic framework, following Savage (1954). We first define a set Ω of possible states of the world comprising all combinations of observed individual characteristics $x \in X$, unobserved individual characteristics $u_i \in U$, sets of parameters (including functional form) $\theta \in \Theta$, and pure chance events $v \in V$. We define an outcome space, Z, to be the Cartesian product of total costs C and health outcomes Y. We assume a standard preference relationship on Z such that a utility function (increasing in Y and decreasing in C) represents those preferences. We also define a set of treatments T that map the state space Ω into the outcomes space such that $(c_{j,i}, y_{j,i}) = T_j(x_i, u_i, v_i; \theta)$. We note that there need not be a temporal dimension to the relationship between Ω and Z. This implies that treatment need not be exogenous because x_i could contain information on which treatment individual (i) selects. The analyst's goal is to rank-order treatments consistent with the decision-maker's preferences over costs and health outcomes, given limited knowledge about Ω.

Scenario I: Evaluation under perfect knowledge
In this idealized scenario, we know all relevant individual characteristics (x_i), there are no unobservable characteristics ($u_i = \emptyset$), we know the 'true' set of parameters ($\theta = \theta^*$), and there is no effect of pure chance ($v_i = \emptyset$). We can directly observe the point-to-point mappings from state to outcomes, $(c_{j,i}, y_{j,i}) = T_j(x_i, u_i = \emptyset, v = \emptyset; \theta = \theta^*)$ (depicted as points and solid arrows in Figure 49.1), and choose the optimal treatment for each individual (i) as $\text{Max}_j(NB_{j,i})$. For example, following a net health/monetary benefit framework in which there is a constant conversion rate λ between cost and health outcomes (Stinnett and Mullahy, 1998), we can pick any treatment as the comparator and rank each alternative as preferred if and only if it lies below a line through the comparator's outcomes with slope equal to λ.

Scenario II: Evaluation under risk
Pure chance (or risk) in outcomes for individual (i) derives from imperfect knowledge of their true v_i. We assume that V is measurable such that a probability can be assigned for all $v \in V$ and that V is orthogonal to all other components of Ω (that is, the disturbance term is 'white noise' that carries no information about X, U or θ). Through the mapping of T, the probability distribution $p(v)$ in the state space induces a bivariate distribution of costs and outcomes for individual (i). Abusing notation slightly, let $\phi^*_{j,i}(c, y|x_i, u_i, \theta^*) = T_j(x_i, u_i = \emptyset, p(v); \theta^*) = T_j(x_i, u_i = \emptyset, v_i = \emptyset; \theta^*) + \xi_{j,i}(\varepsilon_c, \varepsilon_y|x_i, u_i = \emptyset, \theta^*)$ (depicted as dashed lines and contour plots in Figure 49.1), where ξ is a functional mapping v into a joint disturbance term $(\varepsilon_c, \varepsilon_y)$ with an expected value of zero, but with possible correlation between the marginal distributions of ε_c and ε_y.

Rank ordering treatments is now more challenging because v is unknown and we can no longer compare the location of point mappings in the outcomes space. Some form of inference is required. Holding x_i and u_i constant, repeated experiments yield 'clouds' of

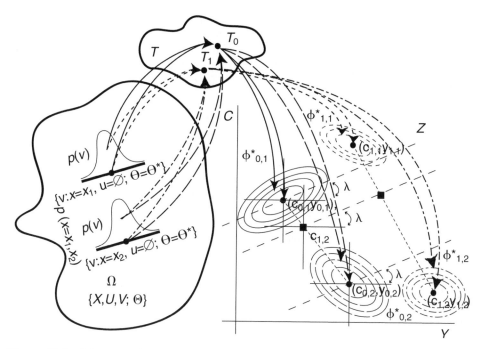

Figure 49.1 Mappings from states to outcomes

individual observations distributed according to $\phi^*_{j,i}$, the joint density of costs and outcomes induced by $p(v)$.

The analyst's goal is to represent decision-maker preferences over distributions $\phi^*_{0,i}$ and $\phi^*_{1,i}$ rather than over single points. Because parameters are known with certainty and there is no heterogeneity (observed or unobserved), the law of large numbers reveals the mean of the joint distribution of cost and effectiveness under each treatment, and inference may be based on the location of our estimated means and the precision of their estimates. Since each individual we observe is fundamentally identical, the only differences in outcomes are due to pure chance. If we adopt the Kaldor–Hicks criterion, we must imagine that those lucky enough to do 'better than expected' could potentially compensate those who do worse. Hence, maximizing total utility (or net benefit) would be all that matters, since we could attain any equitable distribution of outcomes by making simple *post hoc* transfers.

Scenario III: Evaluation under observable heterogeneity with and without risk
But what if individuals are not identical? Suppose there is more than one value of x in the target population. We assume that x captures all relevant individual characteristics and that x and v are orthogonal. Figure 49.1 demonstrates discrete heterogeneity with two types of individuals differing in observable characteristics $(x = x_1, x_2)$. When there is no risk, optimal decisions for individuals $(i = 1$ and $2)$ differ, with T_0 preferred for $(i = 1)$ and T_1 preferred for $(i = 2)$ (that is, $NB_{0,1} > NB_{1,1}$ and $NB_{0,2} < NB_{1,2}$ when there is a constant conversion rate λ between cost and health outcomes).

Since all heterogeneity is perfectly observed, separate treatment recommendations could be made for each type of individual. Unfortunately, this is not true in the case of unobserved heterogeneity, as we discuss in detail in Scenario V. For now, we can glimpse the effect of unobserved heterogeneity by considering the case where a decision-maker chooses (or is forced) to ignore observed heterogeneity. The Kaldor–Hicks criterion could be invoked, and a single treatment recommendation for this population could be made on the basis of mean (over x) incremental net benefit: $p(x = x_1)\Sigma(NB_{1,1} - NB_{0,1}) + p(x = x_2) \cdot (NB_{1,2} - NB_{0,2})$. In Figure 49.1, we have assumed $p(x = x_1) = 2/3$. Mean cost and clinical outcomes under each treatment are represented by squares lying on the line segment connecting $(c_{j,1}, y_{j,1})$ and $(c_{j,2}, y_{j,2})$. In this example, the expected incremental net benefit of T_1 is positive, implying that T_1 would be recommended. Note, however, that 2/3 of all individuals in this population would receive suboptimal treatment, since T_0 is preferred when conditioning on $x = x_1$. If the group recommendation were made on the basis of the median voter's preferences, T_0 would be recommended instead.

Under risk (that is, limited knowledge of v), the same inferential problem applies as in scenario II. Again, the law of large numbers and the Kaldor–Hicks criterion can be applied to base decisions on differences in mean net benefit, but in this case, subgroup analysis would be performed on $\phi^*_{j,1}$ and $\phi^*_{j,2}$ yielding different recommendations for type 1 and 2 individuals. The same concerns about the applicability of potential Pareto compensation within groups and decision-maker interest in moments of ϕ other than the mean still apply.

Scenario IV: Evaluation under risk, uncertainty and observable heterogeneity
Healthcare evaluations conducted alongside clinical trials commonly compare mean effectiveness and cost between groups of individuals assigned to alternative treatments without adjustment or modelling (Hoch et al., 2002). In essence, analysts rely on randomization (possibly with stratification on key characteristics) to guarantee homogeneity of groups. Such evaluations seek to identify the treatment with the best average outcome in the target (sub-)population from which the trial group is a representative sample. Specific mechanisms (that is, θ) relating individual characteristics to outcomes are irrelevant to this goal.

However, difficulties arise when the target population differs from the trial population. The most extreme instance of this deviation is also perhaps the most common (and most critical) – when data from a heterogeneous trial *population* are incorporated into guidelines applied to *individual* treatment decisions. Knowledge of the mechanism by which heterogeneity affects the distribution of individual outcomes then becomes valuable since it allows extrapolation of recommendations beyond the trial population. Hence, observed heterogeneity in x and uncertainty about θ (the relationship between x and outcomes) both demand further attention.

In addition to only knowing $p(v)$ rather than v_i itself, we now must contend with 'second-order' uncertainty about θ. The observed joint distribution of costs and clinical outcomes under risk and uncertainty for individual (i) on treatment (j) may be defined as: $\phi_{j,i}(c, y) = T_j(x_i, u_i = \emptyset, p(v); p(\theta)) = T_j(x_i, u_i = \emptyset, v_i = \emptyset; \theta^*) + p(\theta) \cdot \xi_{j,i}(\varepsilon_c, \varepsilon_y | x_i, u_i = \emptyset, \theta)$. Figure 49.2 demonstrates how both first and second order uncertainty affect the resulting joint distribution of costs and effects under treatments T_0 and T_1. Note that from the decision-maker's point of view, first and second-order uncertainty are difficult to distinguish from one another. One cannot tell whether any individual's outcome deviated from its expected value because the relationship between x and (c, y) was not as expected (uncertainty about θ) or because of pure chance (risk associated with v).

Under the Kaldor–Hicks criterion, one treats v and θ as nuisance parameters and relies on repeated observations to identify the functional relationship $E_\theta E_v[T(x, v; \theta)]$, consequently basing the decision on expected (over both first- and second-order uncertainty) costs and outcomes (Claxton, 1999). Under a parametric approach, estimation of the functional T, and therefore of $\phi_{j,i}(c, y)$, requires specification of a functional form (for example, $f(x'\theta) + v$) and estimation of either θ^* and the asymptotic distribution of θ through extremum methods or of the posterior distribution $p(\theta|\text{Data})$ using Bayes's Rule or of the prior $p(\theta)$ under standard elicitation procedures (Vanness and Kim, 2002). Whichever way, if the model is correctly specified, additional observations increase our information about θ, resulting in sharper predictions of the distribution of cost and outcomes. Bayesian characterizations of uncertainty allow direct statements about the probability that one treatment is preferred to another given existing second-order uncertainty and willingness to pay for improved health outcomes. As we discuss below, this premise underlies 'cost-effectiveness acceptability curves' (Fenwick et al., 2001; Fenwick et al., 2004).

However, decision-makers who care about variation in outcomes as well as their expected value may wish to identify the effect of v rather than simply 'integrating it out.' From the decision-maker's point of view, risk and uncertainty are interrelated since they jointly contribute to $\phi_{j,i}(c, y)$ through the term $p(\theta) \cdot \xi_{j,i}(\varepsilon_c, \varepsilon_y | x_i, u_i = \emptyset, \theta)$. One may be relatively certain about θ for a 'high-risk' treatment in which pure chance (v) greatly affects outcomes, and yet be relatively uncertain about θ for a low-risk treatment. For clinicians making decisions about identifiable, non-exchangeable individuals (as opposed to performing a hypothetically infinitely-repeated experiment), whether the variation is primarily first- or second-order may be irrelevant. All that matters is that one is essentially choosing among various joint distributions of costs and health outcomes.

The value of accounting for heterogeneity may also be seen in Figure 49.2. A population with two sets of observable characteristics, (x_1) and (x_2), whose frequency is determined by $p(x)$ might generate two joint distributions of costs and outcomes (solid and dashed) under different treatments. Since x is observed, we can condition on it and estimate each joint distribution separately. Treatment T_1 appears more likely to be preferred by x_2-type individuals than by x_1-types. As in scenario IV, if we did not condition on x, the joint distribution used for inference would be an amalgamation of distributions (solid and dashed): $\phi_j(c, y) = T_j(p(x), u_i = \emptyset, p(v); p(\theta)) = p(x) \cdot T_j(x, u = \emptyset, v = \emptyset; \theta^*) + p(x) \cdot p(\theta) \cdot \xi_{j,i}(\varepsilon_c, \varepsilon_y | x, u = \emptyset, \theta)$. In this example, inference yields different treatment recommendations at the population and individual levels.

Scenario V: Evaluation under risk, uncertainty and unobservable heterogeneity
We now allow unobservable characteristics (u) to affect outcomes – the scenario that we probably encounter most often in actual practice. Although pure chance (v) remains orthogonal to observable and unobservable characteristics, (x) and (u), respectively, from the analyst's point of view, u and v cannot be distinguished from one another and their effects are typically lumped together as a single 'residual'. Correlation between x and u

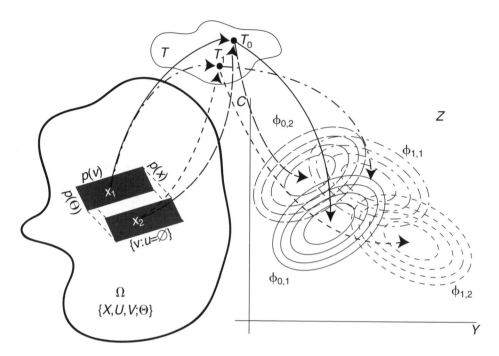

Figure 49.2   First and second order uncertainty and the joint distribution of costs and effects

then implies correlation between the residual and x, violating the orthogonality condition for consistent estimation of θ.

The effects of non-ignorable unobservables can be visualized in Figure 49.3. Observed joint distributions of costs and outcomes under alternative treatments are distorted by the non-orthogonality of x and u: $\phi'_j(c, y) = T_j(p(x, u), p(v); p(\theta)) = p(x, u) \cdot T_j(x, u, v = \varnothing; \theta^*) + p(x, u) \cdot p(\theta) \cdot \xi_{j,i}(\varepsilon_c, \varepsilon_y | x, u, \theta)$. Estimation becomes challenging and inference becomes problematic since there is no obvious way to deal with $p(x, u)$ when u is unobserved.

Endogeneity bias, for example, arises when variation in outcomes causes variation in observable characteristics. Suppose individuals with higher-than-average treatment costs (due to unobservable heterogeneity) are also more likely to purchase generous private health insurance (an observable x) and that individuals with generous coverage have systematically different outcomes (c, y) under treatment T than those with less generous coverage, perhaps due to different specialty care access. Estimates of θ with respect to the effect of insurance on outcomes are likely to be biased due to correlation in the joint distribution $p(x, u)$, with potential ramifications for inference on treatment optimality.

In observational studies or pragmatic clinical trials, analysts should consider the potential for endogenous treatment selection. Selection bias is a special case of endogeneity if, for example, individuals more likely to have success with a given treatment (due to unobservable heterogeneity) are also more likely to select that treatment when offered a choice. Since actual treatment selected is an observable (x), which is now correlated with

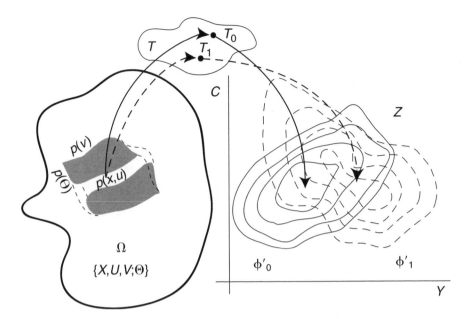

Figure 49.3   Effects of non-ignorable unobservables

u, estimates of the treatment effect parameter (θ) are likely to be biased. Available estimation methods include instrumental variables, data augmentation and Heckman-type two-stage selection correction models (see Angrist, 2001; Tanner, 1996; Heckman, 2001). However, in the absence of knowledge about u, no method is guaranteed to yield estimates of $p(\theta)$ that are closer to the true distribution in any given application.

4.   Implications of current health care evaluation criteria

This discussion provides a backdrop for better understanding the tools used commonly in economic evaluations of health care. Three such tools – (incremental) cost-effectiveness ratios (CERs), (incremental) net health/monetary benefit measures (NHBs, NMBs), and cost-effectiveness acceptability curves (CEACs) – are particularly prominent in the literature. The sampling properties of these methods have been discussed extensively elsewhere and need no further discussion here (see Chapter 47 by Briggs in this Companion; Mullahy and Manning, 1995; Stinnett and Mullahy, 1998; Briggs et al., 2002; and Fenwick et al., 2001).

Considerations for inference

A few recent findings bear note, however. Glick et al., 2004, show that inferences conducted about any of the 'holy trinity' – CER, NHB/NMB, or CEAC – should lead to the same technology adoption decision as would inference about any other(s), assuming that the respective population parameters actually exist (for example, if the treatment is ineffective, then $\mu_y = 0$, and the (incremental) CER does not exist as a population parameter while the NHB/NMB does). Furthermore, the data on costs and outcomes (c_i, y_i) are jointly distributed in populations but often not jointly observed (except in a simulation). Inference about the *population* parameters of CER, NHB/NMB, or CEAC will thus often be based on incomplete information about how the element parameter estimates may themselves vary jointly owing to the joint distribution of the underlying data on which they are based; recalling $\mathrm{Var}(R-S) = \mathrm{Var}(R) + \mathrm{Var}(S) - 2\mathrm{Cov}(R, S)$ for arbitrary random variables (R, S) (for example, statistics of data) is often useful for assessing the extent to which ignoring covariation may influence inferences.

Mean vs. Mean-variance welfare assessment
Of even greater relevance is that, as typically deployed, these methods are defined by and, therefore, at least implicitly concerned with statements about relationships involving population means of (incremental) costs and outcomes. While such a focus is fitting in the context of Kaldor–Hicks welfare considerations, it may provide an incomplete sense of the population welfare implications of interventions in light of the framework set forth above. A leading example of this is the literature that uses cost-effectiveness acceptability curves (CEACs) to summarize data on the cost-effectiveness of interventions (for example National Emphysema Treatment Trial Research Group, 2003). In such applications, the primary concern is usually with the probability that a particular intervention is cost-effective along a continuum of non-negative threshold values (λ) for the cost-effectiveness ratio, that is $\mathrm{Pr}(c/y < \lambda)$ (which may not correspond to $\mathrm{Pr}(\lambda y - c > 0)$) due to problems associated with negative CERs: see Stinnett and Mullahy, 1998). However, concern with $\mathrm{Pr}(c/y < \lambda)$ typically does *not* entail consideration of the fraction of the underlying population of individuals for which $\lambda y - c > 0$ (that is, for which $\mathrm{NHB}(\lambda) > 0$) – a first-order concern that would require reference to the joint *population* distribution $\phi(c, y)$ – but involves rather the *sampling* distribution of some statistic $s(\hat{\mu}_c, \hat{\mu}_y)$, specifically the fraction of the joint sampling distribution of $(\hat{\mu}_c, \hat{\mu}_y)$ sitting below the line $c = \lambda y$ in the (y, c)-plane.

Yet the more general evaluative framework sketched above would allow the decision-maker to proceed with a social welfare *function* (an approximation to the welfare *functional* $V[\phi(c, y)]$) defined on the parameters θ which itself might be expressed explicitly in terms of the moments implied by θ, that is $W = W(\mu, \Sigma, \dots)$, wherein μ is a vector of population means, Σ is a matrix of population variances and covariances, and so on. Such a set-up is immediately familiar to students of introductory finance who learn early on about linear mean-variance utility functions $W = \alpha'\mu + \beta'\Sigma\beta$ defined on means and variances of returns across portfolios of financial instruments, but it is unfamiliar to health policy analysts concerned with a portfolio (or population) of individuals and their returns (or health outcomes) (see O'Brien and Sculpher, 2000, for a related idea). The mean-based evaluation literature in health care can be taken as one that takes $\alpha > 0$ and $\beta = 0$, but in imposing such zero restrictions analysts should be aware of what is being ignored.

Quantile treatment effects
To close this section, it should be noted that there is a growing evaluation literature that focuses on median and other quantile treatment effects, typically defined as $\mathrm{med}(z_1) - \mathrm{med}(z_0)$, for some outcome of interest z measured in two samples (see Abadie et al., 2002; Koenker and Bilias, 2001). Outside the economics literature, such differences in medians

are often at the core of evaluations in the clinical literature, appearing, for example, as differences in median survival time in two arms of a clinical trial (LD50 or ED50); indeed, such measures as derived from clinical trials are often at the centrepiece of regulatory decisions like FDA NDAs in the US.

Of course, $\text{med}(z_1) - \text{med}(z_0)$ does not generally equal $\text{med}(z_1 - z_0)$, which would more often be the evaluative quantity of interest when anonymity or exchangeability are not assumed (see Heckman, 1997 and 2001, and Lee, 2000, who establishes some conditions when $\text{med}(z_1) - \text{med}(z_0)$ is informative about $\text{med}(z_1 - z_0)$). Nonetheless, we suggest that focus on features of outcome distributions apart from just their means is likely to be a productive approach for the evaluative field and anticipate significant future prospects along these lines.

5. Conclusion

The literature dealing with evaluation outside of the traditional mean-based methods is growing, a trend we view as highly desirable. Ultimately the goal in health care evaluations is to understand whether an intervention is or is not 'worthwhile', and evaluation methods and data collection strategies that better speak to decision-makers' sense of 'worth' are to be lauded and encouraged.

References

Abadie, A. et al. (2002), 'Instrumental variables estimates of the effect of subsidized training on the quantiles of trainee earnings', *Econometrica*, **70**, 91–117.

Angrist J.D. and A.B. Krueger (2001), 'Instrumental variables and the search for identification: from supply and demand to natural experiments', *Journal of Economic Perspectives*, **15**(4), 69–85.

Bitler, M., J. Gelbach and H. Hoynes (2003), 'What mean impacts miss: distributional effects of welfare reform experiments', NBER working paper number 10121.

Briggs A.H. and A.M. Gray (1999), 'Methods in health service research – handling uncertainty in economic evaluations of healthcare interventions', *British Medical Journal*, **319**, 635–8.

Briggs, A.H. et al. (2002), 'Thinking outside the box: recent advances in the analysis and presentation of uncertainty in cost-effectiveness studies', *Annual Review of Public Health*, **23**, 377–401.

Claxton, K. (1999), 'The irrelevance of inference: a decision-making approach to the stochastic evaluation of health care technologies', *Journal of Health Economics*, **18**, 341–64.

Fenwick, E., K. Claxton and M. Sculpher (2001), 'Representing uncertainty: the role of cost-effectiveness acceptability curves', *Health Economics*, **10**, 779–87.

Fenwick, E., B.J. O'Brien and A.H. Briggs (2004), 'Cost-effectiveness acceptability curves – facts, fallacies and frequently asked questions', *Health Economics*, **13**, 405–15.

Glick, H.A. et al. (2004), 'Equivalence of confidence intervals for cost-effectiveness ratios, net monetary benefit, and acceptability curves', mimeo, University of Pennsylvania.

Granata, A.V. and A.L. Hillman (1998), 'Competing practice guidelines: using cost-effectiveness analysis to make optimal decisions', *Annals of Internal Medicine*, **128**(1), 56–63.

Heckman, J.J. (2001), 'Accounting for heterogeneity, diversity and general equilibrium in evaluating social programmes', *Economic Journal*, **111**, F654–F699.

Heckman, J.J. et al. (1997), 'Making the most out of programme evaluations and social experiments: accounting for heterogeneity in programme impacts', *Review of Economic Studies*, **64**, 487–535.

Hoch J.S., A.H. Briggs and A.R. Willan (2002), 'Something old, something new, something borrowed, something BLUE: a framework for the marriage of health econometrics and cost-effectiveness analysis', *Health Economics*, **11**(5), 415–30.

Horwitz, R.I. et al. (1996), 'Can treatment that is helpful on average be harmful to some patients? A study of the conflicting information needs of clinical inquiry and drug regulation', *Journal of Clinical Epidemiology*, **49**, 395–400.

Knight, F.H. (1921), *Risk, Uncertainty and Profit*, Chicago: University of Chicago Press.

Koenker, R. and Y. Bilias (2001), 'Quantile regression for duration data: a reappraisal of the Pennsylvania reemployment bonus experiments', *Empirical Economics*, **26**, 199–220.

Kravitz, R.L., N. Duan and J. Braslow (2004), 'Evidence-based medicine, heterogeneity of treatment effects, and the trouble with averages', *The Milbank Quarterly*, **82**, 661–87.

Lee, M.J. (2000), 'Median treatment effects in randomized trials', *Journal of the Royal Statistical Society-Series B*, **62**, 595–604.

Mishan, E.J. (1971), 'Evaluation of life and limb: a theoretical approach', *Journal of Political Economy*, **79**(4), 687–705.

Mullahy, J. and W.G. Manning (1995), 'Statistical issues in cost-effectiveness analyses', in F. Sloan (ed.), *Valuing Health Care: Costs, Benefits, and Effectiveness of Pharmaceuticals and Other Medical Technologies*, Cambridge: Cambridge University Press.

National Emphysema Treatment Trial Research Group (2003), 'Cost effectiveness of lung-volume-reduction surgery for patients with severe emphysema', *New England Journal of Medicine*, **348**, 2092–102.

O'Brien, B.J. and M.J. Sculpher (2000), 'Building uncertainty into cost-effectiveness rankings: portfolio risk-return tradeoffs and implications for decision rules', *Medical Care*, **38**, 460–68.

Savage, L.J. (1954), *The Foundations of Statistics*, New York: John Wiley.

Siegel, C. et al. (1996), 'Statistical methods for cost-effectiveness analyses', *Controlled Clinical Trials*, **17**, 387–406.

Sonnenberg, A. (2001), 'A medical uncertainty principle', *American Journal of Gastroenterology*, **96**(12), 3247–50.

Spiegelhalter, D.J. and N.G. Best (2003), 'Bayesian approaches to multiple sources of evidence and uncertainty in complex cost-effectiveness modelling', *Statistics in Medicine*, **22**, 3687–709.

Stinnett, A. and J. Mullahy (1998), 'Net health benefits: a new framework for the analysis of uncertainty in cost-effectiveness analysis', *Medical Decision Making*, **18**, S68–S80.

Tanner, M.A. (1996), *Tools for Statistical Inference*, New York: Springer.

Vanness, D.J. and W.R. Kim (2002), 'Bayesian estimation, simulation and uncertainty analysis: the cost-effectiveness of ganciclovir prophylaxis in liver transplantation', *Health Economics*, **11**, 551–66.

Zivin, J.G. (2001), 'Cost-effectiveness analysis with risk aversion', *Health Economics*, **10**, 499–508.

50 Economic evaluation and decision-makers
Michael Drummond

1. Introduction

The implicit or explicit objective of economic evaluation is to improve decisions about the allocation of health care resources. The problems and prospects for using economic evaluation have been widely debated in recent years, following the attempts to use it in priority setting in the State of Oregon's plan to revise its Medicaid programme (Eddy, 1991), the inclusion of a formal requirement for economic analysis in the process for reimbursement of pharmaceuticals in Australia (Commonwealth of Australia, 1995) and several provinces of Canada (Ontario Ministry of Health, 1994; Anis and Gagnon, 2000), and the use of economic modelling in technology appraisals undertaken by the National Institute for Health and Clinical Excellence (NICE) in England and Wales (NICE, 2004).

2. Evidence of the use of economic evaluation in health care decision-making

A distinction is made here between two decision-making contexts: (i) the *central level*, where a single agency or organization makes decisions for the whole health care system; and (ii) the *local level*, where a range of decisions are made by various actors within the health care system itself. Some commentators also consider the *meso level* (that is regional health agencies). However, for the purposes of the discussion to follow, the local and meso levels are combined.

Use at the central level

At the central level there is usually a public agency or organization making decisions for the whole health care system. This could be a branch of the Ministry of Health, an advisory committee, or an ad hoc group charged with tackling a particular health care issue. Normally the terms of reference of the decision-making agency will be clear, and the agency may also specify its requirements for economic data, either through guidelines for submissions or through the research it commissions.

In most jurisdictions these requirements apply only to pharmaceuticals, as with submissions to the Pharmaceutical Benefits Advisory Committee (PBAC) in Australia and the Ministry of Health's Drug Quality and Therapeutics Committee (DQTC) in Ontario (Ontario Ministry of Health, 1994). However, in some jurisdictions, including Australia, through the Medical Services Advisory Committee (MSAC), and the United Kingdom, through the National Institute for Health and Clinical Excellence (NICE), similar economic data are also required for devices and/or procedures.

Since 1999, the National Institute for Health and Clinical Excellence (NICE) in the United Kingdom has conducted more than 100 appraisals of health technologies, including drugs, devices and procedures. An important feature of the process adopted by NICE is the commissioning of a technology assessment report (TAR) from an academic review team. The TARs contain a substantial review of the available economic, as well as clinical, evidence, including submissions from manufacturers. (Detailed guidelines on how to prepare submissions, including the economic evaluation component, have been issued by NICE (NICE, 2004).)

Although NICE has been widely criticized from a number of perspectives (Drummond, 2002), the review conducted by the House of Commons, Health Committee welcomed 'the support we have seen for the establishment of NICE, and we recognise that this represents an improvement on the previous situation'. In respect of the use of economic data, the Committee concluded that

> whether or not quality-adjusted life-years are used, we recommend that NICE should consider the wider societal costs and advantages of particular treatments and in particular the wider costs and benefits to the public purse of reduced benefit dependency and improved ability to work both for patients and their carers (House of Commons, Health Committee, 2002).

Use at the local level

Several surveys of the use of economic evaluation have already been conducted in a number of countries (Drummond et al., 2003). These identify some positive impacts of economic evaluation. However, there are very few documented examples of the direct use of studies in making particular decisions. In one survey in the United Kingdom (Drummond et al., 1997), prescribing advisors claimed that, on occasions, cost-effectiveness studies had influenced the advice they gave to family physicians. But in the same survey, two fictitious studies (invented by the authors) achieved a rate (of influencing advice) of around 15 per cent.

In another study, using focus groups in two health authorities in the United Kingdom (Hoffmann et al., 2002), decision-makers were asked about resource allocation issues they were currently considering, and a literature search was then conducted to identify relevant economic evaluations. Although several of the 237 studies identified by the search were found to be generally useful, only one 'direct hit' was obtained. This was a cost-effectiveness study on assertive community treatment for people with severe mental illnesses; this proved useful in one of the authorities as it was contemplating developing services in this field (Nixon et al., 2002).

On the other hand, the vast majority of the evidence points to very limited use of economic evaluation at the local level. The reasons for this are many and varied. Duthie et al. (1999) point to decision-makers' lack of understanding of the methodology of economic evaluation and economists' jargon. Thirty-four decision-makers were presented with 44 statements of results likely to be generated by health services research studies. Of the three statements that were 'not understood', two related to economics terminology, such as 'quality adjusted life years'. Of the two statements where the 'premise was not accepted', one related to trade-offs between health states and the other to willingness-to-pay for health benefits, two concepts which are central to economic evaluation.

In addition, several surveys (Hoffmann et al., 2000; Drummond et al., 1997) suggest that barriers exist owing to decision-makers' uncertainties about the quality of the studies and to rigidities in the health care system itself (for example the lack of ability to vire from one budget to another). Another practical difficulty relates to the potential lack of transferability of economic study results from one setting to another, owing to factors such as differences in practice patterns, the availability of health care resources and relative prices

(Drummond and Pang, 2001). This makes decision-makers doubtful about whether the findings of a cost-effectiveness study undertaken elsewhere will apply in their own setting (Hoffmann et al., 2002).

Finally, a number of surveys make it clear that efficiency is only one of a number of objectives pursued by local decision-makers. Others include preserving their own interests, or those of their parent institution, equity in health care provision and meeting targets imposed by central government (Duthie et al., 1999; Weatherly et al., 2002). This issue has been raised by Hutton and Brown (2002), who, in a commentary on the focus group results of Hoffmann et al. (2002), suggested that, if decision-makers are rejecting economic evaluation as a basis for their decisions, they owe it to us to be more explicit about their decision-making criteria. Certainly, explicitness is one attribute of economic evaluation that is not very apparent in most health care decision-making contexts.

3. Methodological issues arising in the use of economic evaluation

Developing methodological guidelines
As mentioned above, formal requirements for economic evaluation are usually accompanied by a set of methodological guidelines to be used by those submitting data. The guidelines all cover the main methodological features of studies, such as the viewpoint (or perspective) for the analysis, the comparators to be assessed, the form of economic evaluation, the choice of discount rate and the characterization of uncertainty.

In a review of 25 published guidelines for economic evaluation, Hjelmgren et al. (2001) found that the guidelines were in agreement for about 75 per cent of methodological aspects. The main areas of disagreement were in the choice of perspective, the range of costs and benefits to be included and their monetary valuation. They note that such differences are to be expected, given differences in countries' health systems and the different purposes of guidelines. In particular, those guidelines that have been developed in conjunction with formal requirements for the use of economic data in reimbursement decisions for health technologies are, by their very nature, more prescriptive.

Making indirect clinical comparisons
One problem is that, at the time of a reimbursement decision, it is highly unlikely that there will be head-to-head clinical trials of the therapies concerned. In part this may be because such trials are costly and time consuming to undertake. In part it may be because it is not possible to undertake a trial comparing two investigational therapies. Whatever the reason for the lack of head-to-head studies, an economic evaluation seeking to provide relevant information to a reimbursement agency will have to incorporate an estimate of treatment effect which is based on indirect comparisons.

It has long been argued that indirect comparisons are potentially subject to methodological flaws, mainly because, outside the confines of a single randomized controlled clinical trial, one cannot be sure that the patients enrolled in the various trials are equivalent in terms of baseline risk, that the settings for the trials are comparable and that endpoints are measured in the same way. Therefore an apparent superiority for one therapy over another, in an indirect comparison may be as much due to differences in the trials as to differences between the therapies themselves.

The use of estimates of treatment effect based on indirect comparisons when there is a common comparator has recently been shown on many occasions to agree with the results of head-to-head clinical trials (Song et al., 2003). Clearly a more challenging situation exists where there is not a common parameter. This was the case in a recent study of the relative cost-effectiveness of newer drugs for treatment of epilepsy (Wilby et al., 2005). In this case Bayesian Markov Chain Monte Carlo models for multi-parameter synthesis were used (Ades, 2003). Whilst the use of such models cannot guarantee the absence of bias (neither can head-to-head trials!), they may give decision-makers the best available estimate of relative effectiveness (and cost-effectiveness) within the constraints of data availability.

Extrapolating beyond the period observed in clinical studies
The issue of extrapolation is probably the most debated point in economic submissions to reimbursement agencies, because only in a minority of cases (for example studies of antibiotic drugs) are the full benefits (and harms) of therapy observed during the period of the clinical trial. In some cases the need for extrapolation is self-apparent, such as in diseases like diabetes, where the major consequences occur in the long term. Here, the validity of extrapolation rests on the quality of the epidemiological data, linking risk factors that can be modified by therapy to the long-term outcomes. Clearly it would not be possible to wait 20 or 30 years for the definitive clinical trial demonstrating that modification of the risk factor led to a superior outcome.

The problems inherent in predicting future clinical benefits are well illustrated by the study by Schulman et al. (1991) on the cost-effectiveness of early zidovudine therapy for patients with HIV. The study used clinical data from the 019 trial, which was stopped on ethical grounds after one year, when it was observed that the patients randomized to zidovudine therapy had a slower progression to AIDS, as measured by CD4 counts. Schulman et al., estimated the cost-effectiveness of zidovudine, compared with no therapy, based on two assumptions: (i) that the total benefit was only that observed during the first year, this one-year difference in the survival curves being projected into the future; and (ii) that there was a continuous benefit of therapy; namely the benefit observed in the first year was repeated in subsequent years (that is, divergent survival curves). In the absence of any other data, one might argue that the first assumption was reasonable (and probably conservative). However, longer-term studies showed that there was a 'catch-up' effect, such that after three years there was no difference in life expectancy irrespective of whether the patient received zidovudine or not.

Clearly there are many different approaches to the projection of benefit beyond the trial. The most conservative would be the so-called 'stop and drop' approach, where no benefit is assumed beyond that observed. This may be appropriate in some diseases, such as chronic renal failure, where cessation of therapy is likely to result in death, but is probably inappropriate for most chronic diseases. Here the most likely possibility is a gradual decline in effect over time. In some cases there may also be a 'catch-up' effect when the patient discontinues therapy.

Another study by Caro et al. (1997) illustrates the difficulties of even defining the within-trial period. Their study was an economic evaluation of primary prevention with pravastatin for people with elevated cholesterol. Although the trial lasted for a considerable period of time (with an average follow-up of about five years), only 10 per cent of the benefit (in life-years gained) used in the cost-effectiveness estimates was actually observed during the period of the trial. The vast majority of the benefit was extrapolated from events that occurred during the trial period (for example unstable angina), but whose consequences would mainly manifest themselves in the future. The approach taken by Caro et al. was in some respects, a within-trial analysis, since it considered only the costs and events occurring during the period of the trial. However, the benefits attributable to some of these events were projected into the future.

In short, there are few obvious rights or wrongs when deciding on the most appropriate method of extrapolation. In part, this is why the payers for health care have a growing interest in risk-sharing deals with manufacturers. It is also one of the main reasons why agencies such as NICE determine a future point in time when their guidance will be reviewed and also specify the additional research they would like to see during the intervening period. From a methodological standpoint, it is important for analysts not to present just one set of cost-effectiveness estimates using a single method of extrapolation. Rather, a series of scenarios should be presented based on different extrapolation techniques. This will provide an indication of how robust the cost-effectiveness results are to the extrapolation approach. When results are sensitive to the choice of method, the onus is on decision-makers to identify which methods they consider to be the most reasonable.

Incorporating equity considerations
Economic evaluation, as normally practised, also embodies equity assumptions, in that a life-year or QALY is considered to be of equal value no matter who receives it. Whilst on the face of it, this may appear to be egalitarian, there are equally plausible equity propositions. For example, as a society we may prefer to give a QALY to someone who is in very poor health compared with someone who is close to full health. Alternatively, we may prefer to give a QALY to someone who has not experienced much good health during their lifetime, compared with someone who has experienced a 'fair innings' (Williams, 1997).

This being the case, some analysts have proposed incorporating equity weights in QALY calculations, in order to allow for societal concerns about the severity of health conditions and the realization of potential in health (that is the notion that we would not want to discriminate against the permanently disabled in that life years provided to them bring fewer QALYs) (Nord et al., 1999). See Johannesson (2001), Nord (2001) and Williams (2001) for a lively debate on this issue, which is discussed by Dolan and Tsuchiya in Chapter 36 in this Companion.

4. Practical issues arising in the use of economic evaluation

Setting priorities for economic evaluation
Since there are not the resources available to evaluate all health technologies, priorities need to be set. As mentioned above, some jurisdictions limit requirements to pharmaceuticals only. There is no logic to this, beyond administrative convenience. Within the pharmaceutical field, some jurisdictions, such as Australia and Canada, evaluate every new

drug individually. In The Netherlands, the decision whether or not to evaluate a given drug depends on whether the manufacturer wants a premium price, over and above drugs in the same reference group or 'cluster'.

In the United Kingdom, the Department of Health asks NICE to evaluate health technologies that have a major impact on the NHS. Although not formally based on efficiency considerations, this approach is more consistent with obtaining the best value for money from the use of resources on economic evaluation. More recently, methods involving the estimation of the expected value of perfect information have been used in a pilot study to inform research priorities in the UK (Claxton et al., 2004, and Chapter 48 by Claxton, Fenwick and Sculpher in this Companion).

Adapting economic data from one setting to another
In interpreting economic evaluation results, decision-makers need to form a view on whether the results apply in their own setting. Some scientific data are clearly transferable. For example, the clinical effect of a patient taking a given medicine is likely to be similar in the USA and Canada. However, the same may not be true of the same operation performed by different surgeons. Also, in some cases the clinical endpoints may not be totally independent of the health care setting. For example, the EPIC trial of a new drug in cardiology (EPIC Investigators, 1994) used a combined endpoint of death, non-fatal myocardial infarction, unplanned surgical revascularization, unplanned repeat PTCA (angioplasty), unplanned insertion of an intra-aortic balloon pump for refractory ischaemia, and unplanned implantation of a coronary stent. Because of these issues, the applicability of economic evaluation results from one setting to another has been widely debated and is an issue both within countries and between countries (Drummond and Pang, 2001; Sculpher et al., 2004).

With the growing international literature on economic evaluation and the rapid international spread of new health technologies, there is a need to undertake, or at least interpret, economic evaluations on the international level. For example, health care decision-makers, especially in those countries having limited resources for health technology assessment, may wish to reinterpret in their own setting the results of an economic evaluation that was done elsewhere. Also, controlled clinical trials are often mounted on an international basis in order to recruit sufficient numbers of patients or to satisfy the needs of different national medical and regulatory agencies which like to see evidence of efficacy in their own patient population. Increasingly, these trials may incorporate the gathering of economic data.

There are a number of reasons to suppose that economic data may not be easily transferable. These include differences in the availability of alternative treatments, in clinical practice patterns, in relative prices, and in the incentives to health care professionals and institutions. The next section discusses in more depth the differences, between countries or locations, that are likely to affect cost-effectiveness.

An analyst seeking to adapt economic evaluation results from one setting to another could be faced with one of three situations. First, only clinical data may have been collected in the clinical trials and there is a need to produce economic evaluations for more than one country or setting. Here the appropriate option is likely to be to undertake a modelling study, where the clinical data are combined with cost (and possibly quality of life) data from a number of sources (for example routinely available statistics, free-standing cost studies, and so on).

Secondly, economic data (for example quantities of resource use) may have been collected alongside a clinical trial undertaken in one country, but economic evaluations are required for other settings. Here, a modelling study using only the clinical data could be undertaken, as above. Alternatively, the resource use data could be adapted in some way in order to make them relevant to another setting.

Thirdly, economic data may have been collected alongside a multinational clinical trial and economic evaluations are required for all the countries enrolling patients in the trial. Here the analyst has a number of options for analysing the resource use data. Either they could be pooled, as is common for the clinical data, and priced separately for each country; another option is that the resource use data for patients from each country could be allowed to vary in the analysis and then priced for each country as above. In this case the analysts would also have the option of calculating cost-effectiveness ratios for each country using the pooled clinical results or using the individual clinical results for each country. Another option would be to estimate cost-effectiveness for each country but for this to be based on a combination of data from the country of interest and those from other countries. This approach has recently been pursued through the use of multilevel modelling (Willan et al., forthcoming).

Applying cost-effectiveness thresholds
One of the main topics of interest, in studies of NICE and other public decision-making bodies, is whether they apply a threshold cost-effectiveness ratio in their decision-making and, if so, what the ratio is. In a study of the decisions made by the PBAC in Australia, George et al. (2001) concluded that the committee 'appears to be unlikely to recommend a drug for listing if the additional cost per life-year exceeded $AU76 000 (1998/99 values) and unlikely to reject a drug for which the additional cost per life-year was less than $AU42 000. However, the cost-effectiveness ratio was not the only factor determining the reimbursement decision. Other factors include the scientific rigour and relevance of the evidence for comparative safety, efficacy and cost-effectiveness, the lack, or inadequacy of alternative treatments currently in use, the perceived need in the community, whether the drug is likely only to be used in a hospital setting and the seriousness of the intended indication (health condition).

In an econometric analysis of decisions made by NICE, Devlin and Parkin (2004) also found that their results supported the broad notion of a threshold, where the probability of rejection of the technology increases as the cost per QALY increases. However, cost-effectiveness, together with uncertainty and the burden of disease, explained NICE decisions better than cost-effectiveness alone. They also pointed out that there could be different notions of what a cost-effectiveness threshold might be.

The objections to the specification of a cost-effectiveness threshold are numerous. First, the outcome measure used (that is the QALY) may not capture all the relevant benefits of health care programmes. Secondly, most of the comparisons include studies from a range of settings and economic data may not be transferable from one setting to another. Thirdly, the adoption of a threshold implies a 'shadow price' for a QALY. Whereas it might be argued that the shadow price represents society's willingness to pay for a QALY,

Gafni and Birch (1993) argue that it is unlikely that the shadow price would be independent of the size of the health programme being considered (see Chapter 46 by Birch and Gafni in this Companion). That is, the programme's true opportunity cost can only be assessed by examining what is forgone in terms of other health care programmes (given a fixed health care budget), or in other sectors (for example education) if the health care budget were increased. Thus, a single cost per QALY threshold is meaningless and may be a recipe for unconstrained growth of health care expenditures. Therefore, several authors (Donaldson et al., 2002; Birch and Gafni, 2002) have argued that there should be less focus on cost-effectiveness ratios and more on the true opportunity cost of adopting the programme concerned.

The guide to the methods of technology appraisal issued by the National Institute for Health and Clinical Excellence (NICE) also acknowledges that 'given the fixed budget of the NHS, the appropriate threshold is that of the opportunity cost of programmes displaced by new, more costly, technologies'. However, it goes on to argue that, in the absence of the information required to calculate this threshold,

> comparisons of the most plausible incremental cost-effectiveness ratio (ICER) of a particular technology compared with other programmes that are currently funded are possible and are a legitimate reference (for the Committee). Such comparisons are helpful when the technology has an ICER that is lower than programmes that are widely regarded as cost-effective, substantially higher than other currently funded programmes, or higher than programmes previously rejected as not cost effective (by the Committee) (NICE 2004; p. 33).

There is now growing evidence of the use of economic evaluation by decision-makers, particularly at the central level. Several methodological and practical issues have emerged, many of which are already being addressed by economic analysts.

References

Ades, A. (2003), 'A chain of evidence with mixed comparisons: models for multi-parameter evidence synthesis and consistency of evidence', *Statistics in Medicine*, **22**, 2995–3016.

Anis, A.H. and Y. Gagnon (2000), 'Using economic evaluations to make formulary coverage decisions: so much for guidelines', *PharmacoEconomics*, **18**, 55–62.

Birch, S. and A. Gafni (2002), 'On being NICE in the UK: guidelines for technology appraisal for the NHS in England and Wales', *Health Economics*, **11**, 185–91.

Caro, J., W. Klittich, A. McGuire and I. Ford (1997), 'The West of Scotland coronary prevention study: economic benefit analysis of primary prevention with pravastatin', *British Medical Journal*, **315**, 1577–82.

Claxton, K., L. Ginnelly, M. Sculpher et al. (2004), 'A pilot study on the use of decision theory and value of information analysis as past of the National Health Service Technology Assessment Programme', *Health Technology Assessment*, **8**(31), (whole issue).

Commonwealth of Australia (1995), *Guidelines for the Pharmaceutical Industry on Preparation of Submissions to the Pharmaceutical Benefits Advisory Committee: Including Economic Analyses*, Canberra: Department of Health and Community Services.

Devlin, N. and D. Parkin (2004), 'Does NICE have a cost-effectiveness threshold and what other factors influence its decisions? A binary choice analysis', *Health Economics*, **13**, 437–52.

Donaldson, C., G. Currie and C. Mitton (2002), 'Cost-effectiveness analysis in health care: contraindications', *British Medical Journal*, **325**, 891–4.

Drummond, M.F. (2002), 'Nasty or NICE? The formal requirements for economic evaluation of pharmaceuticals in England and Wales', *Pharmaceutical News*, **9**, 57–62.

Drummond, M.F. and F. Pang (2001), 'Transferability of economic evaluation results', in M.F. Drummond and A. McGuire (eds), *Economic Evaluation in Health Care: Merging Theory with Practice*, Oxford: Oxford University Press.

Drummond, M.F., J. Cooke and T. Walley (1997), 'Economic evaluation under managed competition: evidence from the UK', *Social Science and Medicine*, **45**, 583–95.

Drummond, M.F., R. Brown, A.M. Fendrick et al. (2003), 'Use of pharmacoeconomics information – Report of the ISPOR Task Force on Use of Pharmacoeconomic/Health Economic Information in Health-Care Decision Making', *Value in Health*, **6**(4), 407–16.

Duthie, T., P. Trueman, J. Chancellor and L. Diez (1999), 'Research into the use of health technologies in decision making in the United Kingdom – phase II', *Health Policy*, **46**, 143–57.

Eddy, D. (1991), 'Oregon's methods: did cost-effectiveness analysis fail?', *Journal of the American Medical Association*, **266**(15), 2135–41.

EPIC Investigators (1994), 'Use of monoclonal antibody directed against the platelet glycoprotein lib/111a receptor in high-risk coronary angioplasty', *New England Journal of Medicine*, **330**, 956–61.

Gafni, A. and S. Birch (1993), 'Guidelines for the adoption of new technologies: a prescription for uncontrolled growth in expenditures and how to avoid the problem', *Canadian Medical Association Journal*, **148**(6), 913–17.

George, B., A. Harris and A. Mitchell (2001), 'Cost-effectiveness analysis and the consistency of decision-making: evidence from Pharmaceutical Reimbursement in Australia (1991 to 1996)', *PharmacoEconomics*, **19**(11), 1103–09.

Hjelmgren, K., F. Berggren and F. Andersson (2001), 'Health economics guidelines – Similarities, differences and some implications', *Value in Health*, **4**, 225–50.

Hoffmann, C. and J.M. Graf von der Schulenburg on behalf of the EUROMET group (2000), 'The influence of economic evaluation studies on decision making: a European survey', *Health Policy*, **52**, 179–92.

Hoffmann, C., B.A. Stoykova, J. Nixon et al. (2002), 'Do healthcare decision makers find economic evaluations useful? The findings of focus group research in UK health authorities', *Value in Health*, **5**, 71–8.

House of Commons, Health Committee (2002), 'National Institute for Clinical Excellence', second report of session 2001–2, HC515-1, London: The Stationery Office.

Hutton, J. and R.E. Brown (2002), 'Use of economic evaluation in decision making: what needs to change?', *Value in Health*, **5**, 65–66.

Johannesson, M. (2001), 'Should we aggregate relative or absolute changes in QALYs?', *Health Economics*, **10**, 573–7.

National Institute for Clinical Excellence (2004), *Guide to the Methods of Technology Appraisal*, London: NICE.

Nixon, J., K. Phipps, J. Glanville et al. (2002), 'Using economic evidence to support decision making: a case study of assertive community treatment within the UK National Service Framework for Mental Health', *Applied Health Economics and Health Policy*, **1**(4), 179–90.

Nord, E. (2001), 'The desirability of a condition versus the well being and worth of a person', *Health Economics*, **10**, 579–81.

Nord, E., J.L. Pinto, J. Richardson, P. Menzel and P. Ubel (1999), 'Incorporating societal concerns for fairness in numerical valuations of health programmes', *Health Economics*, **8**, 25–39.

Ontario Ministry of Health (1994), *Ontario Guidelines for Economic Analysis of Pharmaceutical Products*, Toronto: Ministry of Health.

Schulman, K.K.A., L.A. Lynn, H.A. Glick and J.M. Eisenberg (1991), 'Cost effectiveness of low-dose zidovudine therapy for asymptomatic patients with human immunodeficiency virus (HIV) infection', *Annals of Internal Medicine*, **114**(9), 798–802.

Sculpher, M.J., F.S. Pang, A. Manca, M.F. Drummond, S. Golder, H. Urdahl, L.M. Davies and A. Eastwood (2004), 'Generalisability in economic evaluation studies in health care: a review and case studies', *Health Technology Assessment*, **8**(49), (whole issue).

Song, F., D.G. Altman, A.-M. Glenny and J. Deeks (2003), 'Validity of indirect comparison for estimating efficacy of competing interventions: empirical evidence from published meta-analyses', *British Medical Journal*, **326**, 472.

Weatherly, H., M.F. Drummond and D. Smith (2002), 'Using evidence in the development of local health policies: Some evidence from the United Kingdom', *International Journal of Technology Assessment in Health Care*, **18**, 771–81.

Wilby, J., A. Kainth, N. Hawkins, D. Epstein, C. McDaid et al. (2005), 'A rapid and systematic review of the Clinical effectiveness, tolerability and cost-effectiveness of newer drugs for epilepsy in adults: a systematic review and economic evaluation' *Health Technology Assessment*, **9**(15), 1–172.

Willan, A.R., E.M. Pinto B.J. O'Brien et al. (2005), 'Country specific cost comparisons from multinational clinical trials using empirical Bayesian shrinkage estimation: the Canadian ASSENT-3 economic analysis', *Health Economics*, **14**(4), 327–38

Williams, A.H. (1997), 'Intergenerational equity: an exploration of the "fair innings" argument', *Health Economics*, **6**, 117–32.

Williams, A.H. (2001), 'The "fair innings" argument deserves a fairer hearing! Comments by Alan Williams on Nord and Johannesson', *Health Economics*, **10**, 583–5.

Index

accidents 7, 32
  see also traffic deaths
ACE inhibitors 290
Adam, Taghreed 46–61
addiction 62
  see also drug use
adolescence *see* young people
adult day care 298
advertising, direct to consumer 306–14
  and agency relationships 309–10
  care-seeking effect 309
  and chronic illness 310
  consumer reaction 310–11
  historical background to 306–8
  impact of 311–12
  literature on 308–9, 310–12
  and Medicaid spending 312–13
  and Medicare 313
  moral hazard 309
  prescribing patterns 312
  price elasticity 310
Afghanistan
  contracting-out 252, 256
  public health intervention 55
Africa
  internet access 167
  public health intervention 55, 58
ageing 19, 20, 33
  disability rate 297
  and distributional judgements 383–4, 385
  and health subsidies 115–16
  mortality rate 297–8
  and risk adjustment 279, 280, 282
  see also retirement
AIDS 55, 251, 252, 479, 540
  see also HIV
air quality 47
Albania
  GATS commitments 168
  unofficial health care economy 156
alcohol use 5, 11, 36
  by young people 62, 64, 65, 66, 67, 68–9
  cost-effective analysis 480–86, 488–9
  legal drinking age 84
  and traffic deaths 10
  Zero Tolerance laws 68–9
Alzheimer Disease 364

ambulance services, and EuroWill project
    396–7, 398
amphetamines 85
anthropometric records 48
antibiotics 173, 540
Antigua and Barbuda, GATS commitments
    168
antimicrobials 53
antiretrovirals 54, 58
Argentina
  child mortality 50
  unofficial health care economy 159
Armenia, GATS commitments 168
Arrow, K.J. 46, 97–8, 104, 131, 270, 394
arthritis 114, 115, 118
Asia, equity in health and health care systems
    205–18
  benefit incidence analysis 209–11
  empirical analysis of 205–6
  empirical evidence 206–14
  Equitap study 206, 208, 209, 210, 211, 212
  ETEN (equal treatment for equal need) 207
  Europe, comparisons with 213–14
  financing, vertical equity in 211–12, 214
  future agenda 215–16
  high income countries 207, 209
  low- and middle-income countries 206–7,
    208, 209, 211, 214, 215–16
  poverty impact of health care expenditure
    212–13, 216
  private financing 214
  rent-seeking 215
  social security systems 214
  tax systems, predominant 214–15
  transition economies 215
  see also individual countries
Asian Development Bank 254
assisted living 298
asthma 77, 120, 367
Auld, M. Christopher 36–45, 68, 152, 154
Australia
  child mortality 50
  cost-effective analysis 495, 498
  drug insurance scheme, national 120
  drug-related crime 83, 85
  drugs price bargaining 237
  GATS commitments 168